Governing Globalization

Also in this series...

Global Transformations
Politics, Economics and Culture

'...*a must have for any student of globalisation is* Global Transformations. *This 515 page survey, packed with facts and theories, provides a comprehensive account of the widespread impact of globalisation.*' **Mark Perryman, New Statesman**

246 x 171 mm 550 pages March 1999
0-7456-1498-1 hb £60.00 / 0-7456-1499-X £16.99

The Global Transformations Reader
An Introduction to the Globalization Debate

'*Everything you wanted to know about globalization, but were afraid to ask.*'
Stuart Hall, The Open University

246 x 171 mm 496 pages May 2000
0-7456-2199-6 hb £60.00 / 0-7456-2200-3 pb £16.99

web resource

Why not visit the *Global Transformations* website at **www.polity.co.uk/global**

- With around 1,000 links to sites concerned with UK politics, international affairs, economics, statistics, law, political parties and much more, this is the only site you will ever need to locate the best sources of web information

- The site supports *Global Transformations*, *The Global Transformations Reader* and *Governing Globalization*

- You will be able to view sample pages of the featured books on the website

- Browse new articles and read interviews with the authors

Governing Globalization

Power, Authority and Global Governance

Edited by

David Held and Anthony McGrew

polity

First published in 2002 by Polity Press in association with Blackwell Publishing Ltd.

Reprinted 2003

Editorial office:
Polity Press
65 Bridge Street
Cambridge CB2 1UR, UK

Marketing and production:
Blackwell Publishing Ltd
108 Cowley Road
Oxford OX4 1JF, UK

Published in the USA by
Blackwell Publishing Inc.
350 Main Street
Malden, MA 02148, USA

ISBN 0-7456-2733-1
ISBN 0-7456-2734-X (pbk)

A catalogue record for this book is available from the British Library and has been applied for from the Library of Congress.

Typeset in 10 on 12pt Times Ten
by Graphicraft Limited, Hong Kong
Printed in Great Britain by TJ International, Padstow, Cornwall

This book is printed on acid-free paper.

Contents

Part I   The Global Governance Complex

Part II   Governing Global Problems

Contents

Figures and Tables

Figures

Tables

Contributors

Gregory Baudin-O'Hayon is a doctoral candidate at the University of Pittsburgh. He is currently working on his doctoral dissertation, which principally explores the role of transnational organized crime in the disaggregation and reconfiguration of states and societies. With William A. Cook, Gregory Baudin-O'Hayon created a proprietary database of contract killings (successful and attempted) linked to organized criminal groups from the former Soviet Union operating there and abroad. His other research interests include the wider confrontation between hierarchical and network-based organizations, as well as religiously motivated terrorism, specifically millenarian groups.

Alex Callinicos is Professor of Politics at the University of York, where he has taught since 1981. His books include *Althusser's Marxism* (1976), *Is There a Future for Marxism?* (1982), *The Revolutionary Ideas of Karl Marx* (1983), *Making History* (1987), *Against Postmodernism* (1989), *The Revenge of History* (1991), *Race and Class* (1993), *Theories and Narratives* (1995), *Social Theory* (1999), *Equality* (2000), and *Against the Third Way* (2001). He is currently working on *An Anti-Capitalist Manifesto*.

Robert Gilpin is the Eisenhower Professor of Public and International Affairs Emeritus at Princeton University. He is the author of many books, including most recently *Global Political Economy* (2001) and *The Challenge of Global Capitalism* (2000).

David Held is Graham Wallas Professor of Political Science at the London School of Economics. He is the author of many works including *Democracy and the Global Order: From the Modern State to Cosmopolitan Governance* (1995), *Models of Democracy* (2nd edition, 1996) and, as co-author, *Global Transformations: Politics, Economics and Culture* (1999). He is currently working on *Cosmopolitanism: Globalization Tamed* (forthcoming).

Mark F. Imber is Senior Lecturer in International Relations at the University of St Andrews. He has published widely on the United Nations system, with particular reference to the specialized agencies and to environmental issues. He is author of *The USA, ILO, UNESCO and IAEA: Politicization and Withdrawal in the Specialized Agencies* (1989) and *Environment, Security and UN Reform* (1994).

Robert O. Keohane is James B. Duke Professor of Political Science, Duke University. He is interested in the role played by governance in world politics, and in particular in how international institutions and transnational networks operate. His many books include *After Hegemony: Cooperation and Discord in the World Political Economy*

(1984), for which he was awarded the second annual Grawemeyer Award in 1989 for Ideas Improving World Order. Between 1974 and 1980 he was editor of the journal *International Organization*. He was president of the International Studies Association, 1998–9, and the American Political Science Association, 1999–2000. He is a fellow of the American Academy of Arts and Sciences and has been the recipient of a Guggenheim fellowship.

Mathias Koenig-Archibugi is a Marie Curie postdoctoral fellow in the Government Department of the London School of Economics. He holds a Ph.D. in political science from the University of Florence, and is author of articles on international relations theory, the international dimensions of democratization, transnational civil society, and European integration in foreign and security policy.

Anthony McGrew is Professor of International Relations at Southampton University. He is co-author of *Global Transformations: Politics, Economics and Culture* (1999) and co-editor of *The Global Transformations Reader* (2000), both with David Held.

Perri 6 is Director of the Policy Programme at the Institute for Applied Health and Social Policy at King's College London and formerly Senior Research Fellow in the Department of Government at the University of Strathclyde. He has published (as author, co-author, editor or co-editor) more than twenty books, including *Towards Holistic Governance: The New Reform Agenda, Divided by Information, Governing in the Round, The Future of Privacy* and *The Contract Culture in Public Services*. He is currently working on a book on public policy and personal social networks, and conducting research on how policy-makers use decision support tools to cultivate political judgement.

Nana K. Poku is Senior Lecturer in Politics at Southampton University. He also serves as a special adviser to the government of Ghana on the politics of health. He has recently edited special issues of *Third World Quarterly* (April 2002) and the *Journal of International Relations* (December 2001) on global health issues and the politics of governance.

Michael Pugh is Director of the Plymouth International Studies Centre, University of Plymouth, and editor of the quarterly journal *International Peacekeeping* (London). He has published articles on peacekeeping and humanitarianism. His latest edited book is *Regeneration of War-Torn Societies* (2000).

James N. Rosenau is University Professor of International Affairs at George Washington University. A former president of the International Studies Association, his authored or edited books include *Turbulence in World Politics: A Theory of Change and Continuity* (1990), *Governance without Government: Order and Change in World Politics* (1992), and *Along the Domestic-Foreign Frontier: Exploring Governance in a Turbulent World* (1997). His latest book, *Distant Proximities: Dynamics beyond Globalization*, will be published in 2003.

Jan Aart Scholte is Professor in the Department of Politics and International Studies and Associate of the Centre for the Study of Globalisation and Regionalisation at the

University of Warwick. He is author of *Globalization: A Critical Introduction* (2000), co-author of *Contesting Global Governance* (2000), and editor of *Civil Society and Global Finance* (2002).

Susan K. Sell is Associate Professor of Political Science and International Affairs at George Washington University. She is the author of *Power and Ideas: North-South Politics of Intellectual Property and Antitrust* (1998) and *Private Power, Public Law: The Globalization of Intellectual Property Rights* (forthcoming). Her work has also been published in such journals as *International Organization, Review of International Political Economy* and *Global Governance*.

Jill Steans is Lecturer in International Relations Theory at the University of Birmingham. Her main research interests are in the fields of gender and international relations theory and international political economy. She is the author of *Gender and International Relations* (1998), co-editor (with Neil Renwick) of *Identities in International Relations* (1996) and co-author (with Lloyd Pettiford) of *International Relations: Perspectives and Themes* (2001). Her next books will be *Globalization and Women's Human Rights* and *Globalization and Gender*.

Phil Williams is Professor of International Security in the Graduate School of Public and International Affairs at the University of Pittsburgh. From 1992 until April 2001, he was the Director of the University's Matthew B. Ridgway Center for International Security Studies. Phil Williams has published extensively in the field of international security, and during the last eight years his research has focused primarily on transnational organized crime, with articles appearing in *Survival, Washington Quarterly, The Bulletin on Narcotics, Temps Stratégique, Scientific American, Criminal Organizations*, and *Cross Border Control*. In addition, he is editor of the journal *Transnational Organized Crime*. He has been a consultant to both the United Nations and United States government agencies on organized crime and has also given congressional testimony on the subject. In 2001–2 he is on Sabbatical from the University of Pittsburgh and is a Visiting Scientist at CERT/CC (a centre for internet security expertise) Carnegie Mellon University, where he is working on computer crime and organized crime. His latest book is *Transnational Organized Crime* (2002).

Ngaire Woods is Fellow in Politics and International Relations at University College, Oxford and a Senior Research Associate of Oxford International Development Centre, Queen Elizabeth House. She is presently completing a book on the politics of the IMF and the World Bank, having recently published *The Political Economy of Globalization* (2000), *Inequality, Globalization and World Politics* (with Andrew Hurrell) (1999), and numerous articles on international institutions, globalization, and governance.

Preface

Globalization has been accompanied, some would say driven, by a thickening web of multilateral agreements, global and regional institutions and regimes, transgovernmental policy networks and summits. This evolving global governance complex regulates and intervenes in virtually all aspects of global affairs. It is far from being a nascent world government, but it is much more than a system of limited intergovernmental cooperation. While, in relation to the scale of global problems, the achievements of global governance appear decidedly thin, few would dismiss the fact that international institutions have become crucial sites of political struggle over globalization and the nature of world order. The essays in this volume offer a comprehensive assessment and critique of this emerging global governance complex, paying particular attention to its implications for globalization.

This is the third volume in the Global Transformations series, the product of a continuing and intellectually rewarding collaboration between the co-editors which began longer ago than we now care to remember. The volume would not have been possible, however, without the professionalism and dedication of its many contributors. Edited volumes can present many problems of coordination, integration and scheduling. In this case, such problems proved insignificant primarily because of the willingness of the authors to write to an agreed framework and to meet a demanding schedule. We are indebted to them and record our thanks here for a series of excellent essays which will advance the subject in many significant ways.

There are also many others whose effort is less visible but nonetheless critical to the successful completion of a project like this. Jane Parker produced the final manuscript with great accuracy and under great duress; Sue Pope ensured a swift transition to production; Gill Motley, Sandra Byatt, Ali Wyke and Jenny Liddiard provided every professional support at all the key stages of production and marketing; and, finally, Ann Bone whose editing skills and professionalism can only be described as extraordinary – in the most literal sense of that word!

DH and AM

Acronyms and Abbreviations

Figure 2.3 on p. 64 has its own abbreviations key

ACC	American Chemistry Council
ACTN	Advisory Committee for Trade Negotiations (US)
AIDS	Acquired Immune Deficiency Syndrome
APEC	Asia-Pacific Economic Cooperation
ARF	ASEAN Regional Forum
ASEAN	Association of South East Asian Nations
BCBS	Basel Committee on Banking Supervision
BIS	Bank for International Settlements
BWS	Bretton Woods System
CBD	Convention on Biological Diversity
CFCs	chlorofluorocarbons
CPT	Consumer Project on Technology
CSW	casual sex workers
DHA	Department of Humanitarian Affairs (UN)
DNS	domain name system
DPG	Derivatives Policy Group
DPKO	Department of Peacekeeping Operations (UN)
DWSR	Dollar–Wall Street Regime
EMU	European Monetary Union
EPZ	export production zone
EU	European Union
FAO	Food and Agriculture Organization
FATF	Financial Action Task Force
FCCC	Framework Convention on Climate Change
FfD	Financing for Development (UN initiative)
FSF	Financial Stability Forum
FTAA	Free Trade Area of the Americas
FTZ	free trade zone
FYROM	Former Yugoslavian Republic of Macedonia
G7	Group of Seven (leading industrial nations): Canada, France, Germany, Italy, Japan, UK, USA
G8	Group of Eight: G7 plus Russia
G10	Group of Ten: G7 plus Belgium, the Netherlands, Sweden, Switzerland (actually eleven)
G20	Group of Twenty: G7 plus countries regarded as 'emerging markets'

GATS	General Agreement on Trade in Services
GATT	General Agreement on Tariffs and Trade
GDP	gross domestic product
GPA	Global Programme on AIDS
GSP	Generalized System of Preferences
HAI	Health Action International
HIV	Human Immunodeficiency Virus
HRW	Human Rights Watch
IAEA	International Atomic Energy Agency
IAIS	International Association of Insurance Supervisors
IASC	International Accounting Standards Committee (now Board)
ICANN	Internet Corporation for Assigned Names and Numbers
ICAO	International Civil Aviation Organization
ICC	International Chamber of Commerce
ICRC	International Committee of the Red Cross
IETF	Internet Engineering Task Force
IFIAC	International Financial Institutions Advisory Commission
IGO	intergovernmental organization / international governmental organization
IIPA	International Intellectual Property Alliance
ILO	International Labour Organization
IMF	International Monetary Fund
IMO	International Maritime Organization
INGO	international non-governmental organization
INSTRAW	International Research and Training Institute for the Advancement of Women
IOSCO	International Organization of Securities Commissions
IPC	Intellectual Property Committee
ISMA	International Securities Market Association
ISO	International Organization for Standardization
ITU	International Telecommunication Union / International Telegraph Union
MDB	multilateral development bank
MERCOSUR	Southern Cone Common Market (Latin America)
MNC	multinational corporation
MSF	Médecins Sans Frontières
NAFTA	North American Free Trade Agreement
NASDAQ	National Association of Securities Dealers Automated Quotations System (US)
NATO	North Atlantic Treaty Organization
NGO	non-governmental organization
NIE	newly industrializing economy
NPT	Nuclear Non-Proliferation Treaty
OAS	Organization of American States
OCHA	Office for the Coordination of Humanitarian Affairs (UN)
OECD	Organization for Economic Cooperation and Development
OHCHR	Office of the High Commissioner for Human Rights

OSCE	Organization for Security and Cooperation in Europe
PhRMA	Pharmaceutical Research and Manufacturers of America
PMA	Pharmaceutical Manufacturers Association
PSO	peace support operation
RAFI	Rural Advancement Foundation International
SOA	sphere of authority
SRI	socially responsible investment
STD	sexually transmitted disease
SWIFT	Society for Worldwide Interbank Financial Telecommunication
TNC	transnational corporation
TRIPS	Agreement on Trade-Related Aspects of Intellectual Property Rights
TVA	Tennessee Valley Authority
UD	Universal Declaration of Human Rights
UN	United Nations
UNAIDS	Joint UN Programme on HIV/AIDS
UNCITRAL	UN Commission on International Trade Law
UNCTAD	UN Conference on Trade and Development
UNDP	UN Development Programme
UNEP	UN Environment Programme
UNESCO	UN Educational, Scientific and Cultural Organization
UNFPA	UN Population Fund
UNHCR	UN High Commissioner for Refugees
UNICE	Union of Industrial and Employers' Confederations of Europe
UNICEF	UN Children's Fund
UPOV	Union for the Protection of New Varieties of Plants
UPU	Universal Postal Union
USTR	US Trade Representative
WEU	Western European Union
WHO	World Health Organization
WID	Women in Development
WIPO	World Intellectual Property Organization
WTO	World Trade Organization

Introduction

David Held and Anthony McGrew

In his report to the special Millennium Summit, UN Secretary-General Kofi Annan sought to define a new role for the United Nations at the centre of 'global governance' (UN Secretary-General, 2000). Since the UN's creation in 1945 a vast nexus of global and regional institutions has evolved, surrounded by a proliferation of non-governmental agencies and advocacy networks seeking to influence the agenda and direction of international public policy. As Kofi Annan's remarks acknowledged, though world government remains a fanciful idea, there does exist an evolving global governance complex – embracing states, international institutions, transnational networks and agencies (both public and private) – which functions, with variable effect, to promote, regulate or intervene in the common affairs of humanity. Over the last five decades, its scope and impact have expanded dramatically such that its activities have become significantly politicized, as global protests against the World Trade Organization attest. Few architects of the UN system could have envisaged that postwar multilateralism would be transformed into the 'complex multilateralism' of the twenty-first century (O'Brien et al., 2000). Whether the rhetoric of global governance conceals an underlying historical continuity in the geopolitical management of world affairs remains, however, the focus of intense theoretical and political controversy.

This volume provides a critical and comprehensive assessment of this professed shift in the way world affairs are governed. It brings together contributions from theorists and analysts of global public policy to explore the relevance of the concept of global governance to an understanding of how global issues and key areas of global activity are currently regulated. It combines an elucidation of substantive theories of global governance with a systematic analysis of its structures and processes in key issue areas from humanitarian intervention to the regulation of global finance. In doing so, it maps the intellectual and empirical contours of the debate about the changing nature and form of global governance. Responding to those of a more sceptical persuasion who consider that global governance is little more than 'a theme in search of a focus', the essays provide a comprehensive assessment of the sources of and limits to the shift from national government to multilayered global governance (Groom and Powell, 1994).

Globalization and the New Political Circumstances of World Order

Any discussion of global governance must start with an understanding of the changing fabric of international society. Woven into this are the complex processes known as globalization. Globalization refers to a historical process which transforms the spatial organization of social relations and transactions, generating transcontinental or inter-regional networks of interaction and the exercise of power (Held et al., 1999). Different historical forms of globalization can be identified, including the epoch of world discovery in the early modern period, the era of European empires and the present era shaped by the neoliberal global economic project. These different historical forms of globalization are characterized by distinctive spatio-temporal and organizational attributes; that is, particular patterns of extensity, intensity, velocity and impact in global relations, flows and networks, alongside different degrees of institutionalization, modes of stratification and reproduction. Although contemporary globalization has elements in common with its past phases, it is distinguished by unique spatio-temporal and organizational features, creating a world in which the extensive reach of global relations and networks is matched by their relative high intensity, high velocity and high impact propensity across many facets of social life, from the economic to the environmental.

To understand the implications of globalization for the governance of world affairs it is necessary to specify some of the key domains of activity and interaction in and through which global processes are evolving. The focus here is on the economic, the environmental and the political. The focus is on the economic because it is clearly a principal driving force of contemporary globalization, and no account of the nature and form of globalization can be pursued without reference to it. The focus is on the environment because it illustrates most acutely the changing scale of market failure and the new global risks faced not just by individual political communities but also by humankind as a whole. And the focus is on politics, law and security in order to highlight the changing form and context of state power, and the pressing agenda of global public issues that require more extensive and intensive forms of global regulation.

Economic globalization

Today, all countries are engaged in international trade, and in nearly all the value of trade accounts for significant proportions of their national income. The historical evidence shows that international trade has grown to unprecedented levels, both absolutely and relatively in relation to national income. Among the OECD (Organization for Economic Cooperation and Development) states, trade levels today (measured as a share of GDP) are much greater than they were in the late nineteenth century, the belle époque of world trade growth. World trade (merchandise and services) in 1999 was valued at over $6.8 trillion, with exports having grown, as a percentage of world output, from 7.9 per cent in 1913 to 17.2 per cent in 1998 (Maddison, 2001; WTO, 2001).

As barriers to trade have fallen across the world, markets have become global for many goods and, increasingly, services. No economy can any longer be insulated from global competition. While national economies taken together can gain overall from increased trade, the gains are highly uneven. There are clear winners and losers, both between and within countries. An increased proportion of trade between developed and developing countries, for example, can hurt low-skilled workers in developed countries while simultaneously increasing the income of higher skilled workers. National governments may protect and compensate those who are vulnerable as a result of structural change, but increased demands on and costs of the welfare state tend to be resisted by employers in the trading industries vulnerable to global competition (Garrett, 1998; Rodrik, 1997). The politics of trade creates complex and sometimes unstable political coalitions.

While global exports and trading relations are more important than ever in the world economy, transnational production is even more significant. Foreign direct investment reached three times as many countries in 2000 as it did in 1985 (UNCTAD, 2001, p. 4). Today, 60,000 multinational corporations (MNCs), with nearly 820,000 foreign subsidiaries, sell goods and services worth $15,680 billion across the globe each year, and employ twice as many people today compared with 1990 (UNCTAD, 2001). Multinational corporations have taken economic interconnectedness to new levels. They account for about 25 per cent of world production and 70 per cent of world trade, while their sales are equivalent to almost half of world GDP (Held et al., 1999; UNCTAD, 2001). A quarter to a third of world trade is intrafirm trade between branches of multinationals.

The bulk of the assets of multinationals are typically found in OECD countries and in a relatively small number of developing ones (see Held and McGrew, 2000, pp. 25–7). Of total world foreign direct investment in 2000, 95 per cent went to 30 countries (UNCTAD, 2001, p. 5). Nevertheless, over the last few decades developing economies' shares of foreign investment flows (inwards and outwards) and of world exports have increased considerably (Castells, 1998; UNCTAD, 2001; UNDP, 1998). The newly industrializing economies (NIEs) of East Asia and Latin America have become an increasingly important destination for OECD investment and an increasingly significant source of OECD imports: São Paulo, it is sometimes said, is Germany's largest industrial city (Dicken, 1998). By the late 1990s almost 50 per cent of the world's total of manufacturing jobs were located in developing economies, while over 60 per cent of the exports of developing countries to the industrialized world were manufactured goods, a twelvefold increase in less than four decades (UNDP, 1998). Contemporary economic globalization, albeit highly unevenly spread, is not just an OECD phenomenon, but embraces all continents and regions.

Alongside transnational production networks, the power of global finance has become central to economic globalization. World financial flows have grown exponentially, especially since the 1970s. Daily turnover on the foreign exchange markets exceeds $1.2 trillion, and billions of dollars of financial assets are traded globally, particularly through derivative products (BIS, 2001). Few countries today are insulated from the fluctuations of global financial markets, although their relationship to these markets differs markedly between North and South.

The 1997 East Asian crisis forcibly illustrated the impact of global financial markets. The financial disruption triggered by the collapse of the Thai baht demonstrated new levels of economic connectedness. The Asian 'tiger' economies had benefited from the rapid increase of financial flows to developing countries in the 1990s and were widely held to be positive examples to the rest of the world. But the heavy flows of short-term capital, often channelled into speculative activity, could be quickly reversed, causing currencies to fall dramatically and far in excess of any real economic imbalances. The inability of the prevailing international financial regime (the International Monetary Fund, Bank for International Settlements, etc.) to manage the turmoil created a wide-ranging debate on its future institutional architecture.

A further important structural change is arising from recurrent exchange rate crises, which have become, since the 1990s, a dominant feature of the current system. Fixed exchange rates are ceasing to be a viable policy option in the face of global capital flows of the current scale and intensity. Between 1990 and 1999 the percentage of countries operating floating exchange rate regimes increased from 21 per cent to 41 per cent (*Financial Times*, 8 Jan. 2002, p. 10). The choice faced by countries is increasingly between floating rates and monetary union – shown by the launch of the euro and discussion of dollarization in Latin America.

It is easy to misrepresent the political significance of the globalization of economic activity. National and international economic management remains feasible (Held et al., 1999; Hirst and Thompson, 1999). Many states continue to be immensely powerful and to enjoy access to a formidable range of resources, infrastructural capacity and technologies of coordination and control. The continuing lobbying of states and intergovernmental organizations (for example, the World Trade Organization (WTO)) by MNCs confirms the enduring importance of states to the mediation and regulation of global economic activity. Yet economic globalization has significant and discernible impacts which alter the balance of resources, economic and political, within and across borders, requiring more sophisticated and developed systems of global and regional regulation (see the discussion below, pp. 5–7).

Global environmental change

Economic globalization has had a substantial impact on the environment, although it is by no means the sole cause of global environmental problems. From the outset, it is important to distinguish a number of different forms of global environmental change. They include:

- encounters between previously separated ecological systems of different parts of the world;
- the overspill of the effects of environmental degradation from one state to another (involving the creation, for example, of environmental refugees);
- transboundary pollution and risks (such as acid rain and nuclear power);
- transportation and diffusion of wastes and polluting products across the globe (toxic waste trade, global relocation of dirty industries);
- pollution and degradation of the global commons (the oceans and the atmosphere);
- and, finally, the formation of global institutions, regimes, networks and treaties that seek to regulate all these forms of environmental degradation.

It needs to be stressed that until the early to mid twentieth century most forms of environmental damage – at least those that could be detected – were concentrated in particular regions and locales. Since then, the globalization of environmental degradation has accelerated as a result of a number of critical factors: fifty years of resource-intensive, high-pollution growth in the countries of the OECD; the industrialization of Russia and other states of the former Soviet Union and of Eastern Europe; the rapid industrialization of many parts of the South; and a massive rise in the global population. In addition, it is now possible to understand risk and environmental change more deeply and with much greater accuracy: for instance, the consequences of the steady build-up of damaging gases in the earth's atmosphere (carbon dioxide, methane, nitrous and sulphur oxides, CFCs).

In response to the intensification of, and publicity surrounding, environmental issues, there has been an interlinked process of cultural and political globalization. This can be exemplified by the emergence of new scientific and epistemic communities; new environmental movements organized transnationally and with transnational concerns; and new international institutions, regimes and conventions such as those agreed in 1992 at the Earth Summit in Brazil and in subsequent follow-up meetings. Unfortunately, none of the latter have as yet been able to acquire sufficient political influence, domestic support or international authority to do more than (at best) limit the worst excesses of some of the global environmental threats.

Not all environmental problems are global, of course; such a view would be highly misleading. Nonetheless, there has been a striking shift in the physical and environmental conditions – that is, in the extent, intensity and rapid transmission of environmental problems – affecting human affairs in general. These processes have moved politics dramatically away from an activity which crystallizes first and foremost around state and interstate concerns. It is clearer than ever that the fortunes of political communities and peoples can no longer be simply understood in exclusively national or territorial terms. In the context of intense global and regional interconnectedness, the very idea of political community as an exclusive, territorially delimited unit is at best unconvincing and at worst anachronistic. In a world in which global warming connects the long-term fate of many Pacific islands to the actions of tens of millions of private motorists across the globe, the conventional territorial conception of political community appears profoundly inadequate. Globalization weaves together, in highly complex and abstract systems, the fates of households, communities and peoples in distant regions of the globe (McGrew, 1997, p. 237). While it would be a mistake to conclude that political communities are without distinctive degrees of division or cleavage at their borders, they are clearly shaped by multiple cross-border interaction networks and power systems. Thus questions are raised both about the fate of the idea of political community, and about the appropriate level for the effective regulation of human affairs: the national, the regional or the global. The proper locus of politics and the articulation of the public interest becomes a puzzling matter.

Political globalization

Economic and environmental globalization has not occurred in a political vacuum; there has been a shift in the nature and form of political organization as well. The distinctive form this has taken in the contemporary period is the emergence of 'global politics' – the increasingly extensive form of political networks and activity. Political decisions and actions in one part of the world can rapidly acquire worldwide ramifications. Sites of political action and/or decision-making can become linked through rapid communications into complex networks of political interaction. Associated with this 'stretching' of politics is a frequent intensification or deepening of global processes such that 'action at a distance' permeates the social conditions and cognitive worlds of specific places or policy communities (Giddens, 1990). Consequently, developments at the global level – whether economic, social or environmental – can have almost instantaneous local consequences and vice versa.

The idea of global politics challenges the traditional distinctions between the domestic and the international, the territorial and the non-territorial, and the inside and the outside, as embedded in conventional conceptions of 'the political' (see Held et al., 1999, chs 1, 2 and 8). It also highlights the richness and complexity of the interconnections that transcend states and societies in the global order. Global politics today, moreover, is anchored not just in traditional geopolitical concerns but also in a large diversity of economic, social and ecological questions. Pollution, drugs, human rights and terrorism are among an increasing number of transnational policy issues which cut across territorial jurisdictions and existing political alignments, and which require international cooperation for their effective resolution.

Nations, peoples and organizations are linked, in addition, by many new forms of communication, which range across borders. The revolution in microelectronics, in information technology and in computers has established virtually instantaneous worldwide links which, when combined with the technologies of the telephone, television, cables, satellites and jet transportation, have dramatically altered the nature of political communication. The intimate connection between 'physical setting', 'social situation' and politics, which distinguished most political associations from premodern to modern times, has been ruptured; the new communication systems create new experiences, new modes of understanding and new frames of political reference independently of direct contact with particular peoples, issues or events. The speed with which the events of 11 September 2001 ramified across the world and made mass terrorism a global issue is one poignant example.

The development of new communication systems generates a world in which the particularities of place and individuality are constantly represented and reinterpreted through regional and global communication networks. But the relevance of these systems goes far beyond this, for they are fundamental to the possibility of organizing political action and exercising political power across vast distances (Deibert, 1997). For example, the expansion of international and transnational organizations, the extension of international rules and legal mechanisms – their construction and monitoring – have all received an impetus from the new communication systems, and organizations of all sorts depend on them as a means to further their aims.

In mapping these developments, it is important to explore the way in which the sovereign state now lies at the intersection of a vast array of international regimes and organizations that have been established to manage whole areas of transnational activity (trade, financial flows, crime and so on) and collective policy problems. The rapid growth of transnational issues and problems has involved a spread of layers of political regulation both within and across political boundaries. It has been marked by the transformation of aspects of territorially based political decision-making, the development of regional and global organizations and institutions, and the emergence of regional and global law.

This can be illustrated by a number of developments, including, most obviously, the rapid emergence of multilateral cooperation and international organizations. New forms of multilateral and transnational politics have evolved, involving governments, intergovernmental organizations (IGOs) and a wide variety of transnational pressure groups and international non-governmental organizations (INGOs). At the beginning of the twentieth century there were just 37 IGOs and 176 INGOs, whereas in 1996 there were 1,830 IGOs and 38,243 INGOs (UIA, 1997). In addition, there has been a very substantial development in the number of international treaties in force, as well as in the number of international regimes, altering the situational context of states (Held et al., 1999, chs 1–2).

To this pattern of extensive political interconnectedness can be added the dense web of activity of the key international policy-making forums, including the summits of the UN, the G7 (Group of seven leading industrial nations), the IMF, WTO, EU, APEC (Asia-Pacific Economic Cooperation), ARF (the regional forum of ASEAN, the Association of South East Asian Nations) and MERCOSUR (Southern Cone Common Market – in Latin America), as well as many other official and unofficial meetings. In the middle of the nineteenth century, there were two or three interstate conferences or congresses a year; today the number totals over 4,000. National government is increasingly locked into an array of global, regional and multilayered systems of governance – and can barely monitor it all, let alone stay in command.

Political communities can no longer be thought of, if they ever could with any validity, simply as discrete worlds or as self-enclosed political spaces; they are enmeshed in complex structures of overlapping forces, relations and networks. Clearly, these are structured by inequality and hierarchy. However, even the most powerful among them – including the most powerful states – do not remain unaffected by the changing conditions and processes of regional and global enmeshment. In particular, the idea of a political community of fate – of a self-determining collectivity – can no longer be located meaningfully only within the boundaries of a single nation-state. Some of the most fundamental forces and processes which determine the nature of life chances within and across political communities are now beyond the reach of individual nation-states.

The political world at the start of the twenty-first century is marked by a significant series of new types of political externality or 'boundary problem'. In the past, of course, nation-states principally resolved their differences over boundary matters by pursuing reasons of state backed by diplomatic initiatives and, ultimately, by coercive means. But this geopolitical logic appears singularly inadequate and inappropriate to resolve the many complex issues, from economic regulation to resource depletion and environmental degradation, which engender – at seemingly ever greater speeds – an intermeshing of 'national fortunes'. In all major areas of government policy, the enmeshment of national political communities in regional and global processes involves them in intensive issues of transboundary coordination and control. Political space for the development and pursuit of effective government and the accountability of political power is no longer coterminous with a delimited national territory. National communities themselves by no means make and determine decisions and policies exclusively for themselves when they decide on such issues as the regulation of health, conserving the environment and combating terrorism; and national governments by no means simply determine what is right or appropriate exclusively for their own citizens.

These new political circumstances present a unique challenge to a world order designed in accordance with the Westphalian principle of exclusive sovereign rule over a bounded territory and its associated geopolitical mechanisms for governing world affairs.

From Geopolitics to Global Governance?

Globalization poses, with renewed immediacy, the question of how world affairs are, and should be, governed (Smouts, 2001). At issue is whether the thickening institutional density, expanding jurisdiction, intensifying transnational politics and deepening impact of suprastate regulation denotes a qualitative – structural – shift in how global affairs and transboundary problems are governed. For Rosenau, and many others, these developments represent the evolving infrastructure of a fragile system of global governance – a new complex multilateralism (Rosenau, 1999). Just how far this system embodies a radical break with traditional geopolitical modes of regulating world order (hegemony and the balance of power), or whether indeed it is displacing or supplementing them, remains the source of continuing disagreement (Cox, 1997; Gill, 2000; Keohane and Nye, 2000; Rosenau, 1999, 2000a; Ruggie, 1998). Sceptics, such as Gilpin, doubt that there is any substance to these claims, arguing that global governance is at best pure rhetoric, at worst a utopian aspiration (Gilpin, 2001).

Several factors have encouraged this burgeoning discourse on global governance. First, the end of the Cold War brought to a close the era of stalemate politics within the UN and associated agencies. This created the prospect of a more active and effective international governance. It also enabled a more inclusive form of multilateralism than had been feasible in a politically and economically divided world. Moreover, it contributed to the dwindling legitimacy accorded to hierarchical or hegemonic modes of regulating world order. These modes are contested by a diverse range of transnational pressure groups, social movements and protest movements. Second, as already noted, the intensification of globalization has increased the demand for multilateral cooperation and the provision of global public goods, including financial stability, the setting of common standards in ever more areas, and environmental protection. A new infrastructure of global regulation has evolved, reaching ever more deeply into the domestic affairs of states and societies, and it remains central to the promotion and management of globalization. Third, during the last three decades there has been a significant reconfiguration of state power and authority. Governing has become a more complex and volatile process. Realizing cherished domestic political goals, delivering core policy programmes and resolving domestic crises increasingly involve the state in a negotiated order between diverse agencies, both public and private, within and beyond the state (Bergesen and Lunde, 1999). Governance, as a concept of analysis, refers to this process of social coordination with a public purpose – a process in which the state plays a strategic but not necessarily the dominant role (Pierre and Peters, 2000).

Given the absence of a world government, the concept of global governance provides a language for describing the nexus of systems of rule-making, political coordination and problem-solving which transcend states and societies (Rosenau, 2000a, 2000b). It is particularly relevant to describing the structures and processes of governing beyond the state where there exists no supreme or singular political authority. Theoretically, it is much more than simply a descriptive term: it constitutes a broad analytical approach to addressing the central questions of political life under conditions of globalization, namely: who rules, in whose interests, by what mechanisms and for what purposes?

Global Governance: Towards a New World Order?

As an analytical approach, global governance rejects the conventional state-centric conception of world politics and world order. The principal unit of analysis is taken to be global, regional or transnational systems of authoritative rule-making and implementation. As Rosenau comments,

> By locating rule systems at the heart of our theoretical formulations, we can trace and assess the processes of governance wherever they may occur. That is, through focusing on rule systems we will not be confined to the world of states and will be empowered to explore issues and processes in terms of the way in which authority is created, dispersed, consolidated or otherwise employed to exercise control with respect to the numerous issues and processes that states are unable or unwilling to address. (2000a, p. 188)

At the analytical core of the global governance approach is a concern with understanding and explaining the political significance of global, regional and transnational authority structures (Boli, 1999; Smouts, 2001).

Accordingly, the focus is on the evolving system of (formal and informal) political coordination – across multiple levels from the local to the global – among public authorities (states and IGOs) and private agencies seeking to realize common purposes or resolve collective problems. Although this system transcends the classic postwar form of multilateralism, it is far from a 'unified global system underpinned by global law enforcement' (Cable, 1999, p. 54). It differs dramatically from the concept of world government in that it does not presuppose the idea of a central global public authority, which legislates for the common affairs of humanity. On the contrary, it is defined by diverse sources of rule-making, political authority and power.

Several observations are made in the literature concerning the institutional architecture of global governance:

1 It is *multilayered* in the sense that it is constituted by and through the structural enmeshment of several principal infrastructures of governance: the suprastate (such as the UN system), the regional (EU, MERCOSUR, ASEAN, etc.), the transnational (civil society, business networks and so on), and the substate (community associations, and city governments) (Scholte, 2000). Sandwiched between these layers is national government.

2 It is often described as polyarchic or *pluralistic* since there is no single locus of authority. This is not to imply any equality of power between the participants but simply to acknowledge that political authority is decidedly fragmented.

3 It has a *variable geometry* in so far as the relative political significance and regulatory capacities of these infrastructures vary considerably around the globe and from issue to issue.

4 The system is *structurally complex*, being composed of diverse agencies and networks with overlapping (functional and/or spatial) jurisdictions, not to mention differential power resources and competencies.

5 Far from national governments being sidelined in this system, they become increasingly crucial as *strategic sites* for suturing together these various infrastructures of governance and legitimizing regulation beyond the state.

A central characteristic of global governance, emphasized particularly in the existing literature, is the reconfiguration of authority between the various layers or infrastructures of governance. This is evident in the expanding jurisdiction and competencies of both suprastate (for instance, the World Intellectual Property Organization (WIPO)) and substate institutions (such as devolved governments and autonomous regions). Although there is considerable variance from sector to sector – compare for instance the global impact of the IMF and the International Labour Organization (ILO) – for the most part the activities of suprastate bodies reach ever more deeply into the internal life of states, from food standards to banking regulation. Indeed, the most recent and comprehensive study of global regulation concluded that 'today most citizens greatly underestimate the extent to which most nations' shipping laws are written at the IMO [International Maritime Organization] in London, air safety laws at the ICAO [International Civil Aviation Organization] in Montreal, food standards at the FAO [Food and Agriculture Organization] in Rome, intellectual property rights in Geneva at the WTO/WIPO . . . motor vehicles standards by the ECE [Economic Commission for Europe] in Geneva', to mention but a few sectors (Braithwaite and Drahos, 1999, p. 488).

This relocation and delegation of political authority between the various layers of governance has created what some refer to as a 'new medievalism' since it resembles the complexity of competing jurisdictions, porous administrative boundaries and multiple levels of political authority which characterized medieval Europe. Global governance embodies a complex patchwork of overlapping jurisdictions, generating ambiguities about the principal location of authority and political responsibility. This is particularly evident where conflicts of legal or regulatory principles occur – should global, regional, national or local rules take precedence and how is this to be decided? In the context of the European Union, with a developed supranational legal infrastructure, such conflicts are resolved through juridical mechanisms. At the global level, such mechanisms are largely absent, but where they exist in some form (as with the WTO dispute machinery or WIPO machinery on patents) they provoke concerns about democratic accountability, legitimacy and subsidiarity.

Such concerns are reinforced by what in the study of global governance is sometimes referred to as the privatization of global regulation, that is, a redrawing of the boundaries between public authority and private power. From technical standards to the disbursement of humanitarian assistance and official aid through non-governmental organizations (NGOs), private agencies have become increasingly influential in the formulation and implementation of global public policy. The International Accounting Standards Committee establishes global accounting rules, while the major bond rating agencies make critical judgements about the credit status of governments and public and private organizations around the globe. Much of this privatized governance occurs in the shadow of global public authorities, but to the extent to which corporate and private interests have captured the agendas of such bodies, like those of the WTO, the International Organization of Securities Commissions (IOSCO) and others, there is a fusion of public and private power. The current salience of public–private partnerships, such as the Global AIDS Fund and the Global Compact, articulates the expanding influence of private interests in the formulation as well as the delivery of global policies. Contemporary global governance involves a relocation of authority from public to quasi-public, and to private, agencies.

Associated with this relocation of authority is a shift in the principal modalities of global rule-making and implementation. Although much of the formal business of global governance is conducted within and through established international organizations, a growing literature indicates that significant aspects of the formulation and implementation of global public policy occur within an expanding array of political networks: transgovernmental (such as the Basel Committee on Banking Supervision (BCBS) and the Financial Action Task Force (FATF)), trisectoral (public, corporate, and NGOs), and transnational (such as Médecins Sans Frontières). These networks – which can be ad hoc or institutionalized – have become increasingly important in coordinating the work of experts and functionaries within governments, international organizations, and the corporate and the NGO sectors (further examples are the Global Water Partnership, the World Commission on Dams, the Global Alliance for Vaccines and Immunization). They function to set policy agendas, disseminate information, formulate rules, establish and implement policy programmes – from measures against money laundering taken by the FATF to global initiatives to counter AIDS. Many of these networks are of a purely bureaucratic nature, but they have also become mechanisms through which civil society and corporate interests are effectively embedded in the global policy process. In part, the growth of these networks is a response to the overload and politicization of multilateral bodies, but it is also an outcome of the growing technical complexity of global policy issues and the communications revolution.

To the extent that a global communications infrastructure has facilitated the evolution of global policy networks, so too it has underwritten the effective worldwide mobilization of protest against the agencies of global governance. This contestation takes many political forms other than direct action, from advocacy (as with the Campaign to Ban Landmines, Jubilee 2000), through surveillance of corporate activities in order to police voluntary codes of conduct (CorpWatch), to resisting the terms of economic globalization (campaigns to outlaw child labour or sweatshop practices). Transnational civil society is integral to the politics of global governance.

For the advocates of the global governance perspective, geopolitical management of global affairs is becoming less plausible (and legitimate) as the sole governing principle of world order. In a highly interconnected world of diverse nation-states, in which non-state actors also wield enormous influence, hierarchical forms of managing global affairs are losing their efficacy and legitimacy.

Global Governance: Two Concepts in Search of a Theory?

Those who are sceptical of the utility of focusing on global governance do not contest the assertion that there has been a significant expansion of international regulation or that it involves a complex politics between states, civil society and international organizations. On the contrary, as Robert Gilpin contends, 'the rapid globalization of the world economy has elevated the governance issue to the top of the international economic agenda . . . the battleground has become the entire globe, and the types as well as the number of participants have greatly expanded to include states, international organizations, and nongovernmental organizations' (2001, pp. 378, 402). What the sceptics contest is the interpretation that global governance transcends geopolitics or that global institutions, or transnational civil society, are autonomous sites of power in world politics.

Since the publication of Keohane and Nye's seminal study, *Power and Interdependence*, which stimulated an avalanche of literature on international regimes, the question as to why, and under what circumstances, states engage in international cooperation and institution building has been at the core of much international theory. In general terms, there are three principal explanatory accounts – with some variants[1] – of global governance: liberal institutionalist, realist and neo-Gramscian (Cox, 1993; Gill, 1992; Keohane, 1984, 1988; Krasner, 1982; Stein, 1990). Although each has an interest in explaining patterns of governance beyond the state, there are considerable differences in their analytical and epistemological frameworks. These differences reflect underlying commitments to rationalist, historicist or reflectivist interpretations of the social world, as well as to different ontological assumptions about the constituent elements of world politics: states, social forces, or ideas.

Liberal institutionalism argues that governance beyond the state is endemic since it arises from the functional benefits which, in an interdependent world, states can realize through the strategic coordination of their policies and activities. International institutions matter because they deliver important benefits to states, and their absence would undermine the achievement of domestic objectives. Accordingly, they 'empower governments rather than shackle them' (Keohane, 1984, p. 13). Crucially, they also moderate the effects of power politics and support distinctive forms of multilateral, transgovernmental and transnational politics that constrain the powerful (Ikenberry, 2001). They matter because they function as relatively autonomous mechanisms mediating between the hierarchy of state power and global public policy outcomes.

For realism, geopolitics remains essential to understanding the conduct and dynamics of global governance. Governance beyond the state is largely contingent on the policies and interests of the most powerful states (Krasner, 1982). International institutions are principally devoid of autonomous power and function largely as instruments for the advancement of the interests of the most dominant states or coalitions of states. Moreover, no convincing account of global governance can ignore, even in a globalizing era, the centrality of the inequalities of power between states. The hierarchy of power moulds the architecture as well as the substantive purposes and priorities of global governance. The present liberal world order – of free trade and unhindered capital flows – is primarily a product of US global hegemony, although it relies on the consent of other leading industrial powers. The structural power of the US is expressed in the very existence of global institutions and the liberal constitution of world order. Of course, this is not to argue that global governance is simply a transmission belt for US policy, or Western interests, since these same institutions are also arenas through which their dominance is contested. Nevertheless, in the account given by realism, geopolitics retains a disproportionate role in shaping the structures, patterns and outcomes of global governance.

Marxist and neo-Gramscian theories share with realism an emphasis on geopolitics and US hegemony in explaining the pattern and significance of global governance. However, they consider that both these factors have to be understood in the context of the structural imperatives of globalizing capitalism (Cox, 1993; 1997). As the hegemonic capitalist state, the US has a critical interest in expanding the reach and rule of globalizing capitalism. Global institutions are an instrument for sustaining and expanding the predominance of global corporate capitalism. In this respect, the conduct and project of global governance is shaped by an unwritten constitution that structurally privileges the interests and agenda of global capital, often at the expense of the welfare of nations, communities and the natural environment (Gill, 2000; Gill and Law, 1993). However, the institutions of global governance serve more than a regulatory or managerial function, for they also provide arenas within which this unwritten global constitution is legitimized and contested. In this respect, they are sites of struggle with the potential for transforming world order.

Both realism and Marxism are highly critical of the unreflective nature of much of the existing literature on global governance. This scepticism arises from three principal considerations: that the existing literature exaggerates the autonomous power and efficacy of global institutions and civil society organizations; that as an approach to understanding how world order is managed, this literature is theoretically flawed in so far as it elides global governance with the effective sources of international order; and that in adopting a form of pluralist analysis, conventional studies of global governance fail to penetrate beyond the dynamics of global politics to the underlying structures of power. For these reasons, the sceptics conclude, the global governance perspective may be descriptively accurate but it is largely devoid of explanatory power: it is, for the most part, little more than two concepts in search of a theory.

From Distorted to Genuine Global Governance: the Normative Argument

If the explanatory value of global governance is the subject of considerable debate, so too is its normative status. There is widespread agreement in the literature that the existing system of global governance is severely deficient in many fundamental respects. In the view of many critics, the present system is a form of 'distorted',[2] as opposed to 'genuine', global governance (Hurrell, 2001; Murphy, 2000). However, there is little consensus as to whether more genuine global governance is either desirable, or plausible, nor agreement on what normative principles should inform its institutional design (Beitz, 1999; Cox and Sinclair, 1996; Falk, 1995; Held, 1995; Jones, 1999; Keohane, 1998; O'Neill, 2000, 2001; Pogge, 1997; Zurn, 1998).

In the normative literature, global governance is said to be distorted in so far as it promotes the interests of the most powerful states and global social forces, and restricts the realization of greater global social justice and human security. Distorted global governance is understood as a product of the mutually reinforcing dynamics of the inequalities of power between states; the structural privileging of the interests and agenda of global capital; and the technocratic nature of the global policy process (Cerny, 1999; Cutler, Haufler and Porter, 1999; Gill, 2000; Hurrell, 2001; Murphy, 2000; Woods, 1999). These factors reinforce a number of significant deficits in the governance capacity of the existing system, most especially in respect of its role in welfare, human security and poverty reduction (Bergesen and Lunde, 1999; Thomas, 2000).

Although human security and development have been (at least nominally) among the principal goals of global governance for almost five decades, the widening of both global inequalities and social exclusion articulates a growing gap between rhetoric and performance. By contrast, the considerable success of public and private agencies in promoting economic globalization suggests that the structural constraints on global governance apply more strongly to its redistributive than its promotional functions. This problem highlights a growing disjuncture or deficit in respect of the market-enhancing and market-correcting functions of global governance. This is compounded by a growing democratic deficit. In seeking to promote or regulate the forces of globalization, states have created new suprastate layers of political authority which have weak democratic credentials and stand in an ambiguous relationship to existing systems of national accountability. Many of the participants in the global policy process, especially the leading agencies of global civil society, are also highly unrepresentative of the world's states and peoples. Under these conditions the legitimacy and account-ability of global governance are decidedly problematic. Accordingly, redressing this democratic deficit and promoting global social justice are the principal ethical con-siderations which dominate the normative literature on global governance.

This literature embodies two distinct (and largely discrete) discourses: one con-cerned with the democratization of global governance, and the other with problems of global justice (Caney, 2001; Held, 1995; Jones, 1999; Pogge, 1997). The first seeks to specify the principles and institutional arrangements for making accountable those global sites and forms of power which presently operate beyond the scope of national democratic control. Several different normative conceptions of democracy beyond borders have been elaborated, including cosmopolitan democracy, radical democracy and transnational deliberative democracy (McGrew, 2002). By contrast, the discourse of global social justice is concerned primarily with the elaboration of justificatory arguments and normative principles. In particular, the emphasis is on elaborating the moral reasoning behind the pursuit of global distributive justice (Caney, 2001; Pogge, 2001). Again, there are distinctive normative perspectives in addressing this ethical challenge, including liberal cosmopolitanism, critical theory, and social cosmopolitanism (Beitz, 1999).

Both the discourse of global democracy and that of global justice inform the wider academic and political debate concerning the necessary conditions for genuine global governance. Indeed the official rhetoric of institutional reform, as well as the global politics of protest against distorted global governance, draws heavily on both these discourses (O'Brien et al., 2000; Summers, 2000; Woods, 1999; UN Secretary-General, 2000). To the extent to which global governance is becoming a significant site 'in which struggles over wealth, power and knowledge are taking place', the issue of its ultimate ethical purposes and proper institutional design is a matter both of great academic and of great political import (Murphy, 2000, p. 799). Indeed, the normative debate about transnational democracy and global social justice is increasingly central to the politics of contemporary global governance.

Governing Globalization

Together, the essays which follow explore and develop the themes elaborated in this introduction. The volume seeks to map the nature and form of contemporary global governance, to evaluate the effectiveness and legitimacy of existing global structures for dealing with the most pressing global issues, and to assess the principal descriptive and normative theories of global governance. It is divided into three parts. Part I examines the broad implications of globalization for the institutional development and politics of global governance. Part II explores some of the most urgent issues of global public policy, assessing the limits and possibilities for effective global governance. Part III develops a series of critical reflections on the main descriptive and normative approaches to the study of global governance.

Part I opens with an essay by Ngaire Woods which seeks to analyse 'the actors and challenges in a globalizing world which new forms of "global governance" are attempting to address'. The essay examines the institutional and organizational challenges to global governance posed by economic globalization. It discusses the politics of contemporary global governance with particular emphasis on the possibilities for reform in the context of a system in which global public policy-making is being undertaken not just by intergovernmental organizations but by a variety of networks, coalitions and informal arrangements.

This web of arrangements is analysed further in the essay by Mathias Koenig-Archibugi, which provides a novel mapping of 'the complex structure of contemporary global governance'. In exploring the demand and supply of global governance, Mathias Koenig-Archibugi deploys a typology of the institutional structures and mechanisms which define contemporary global governance. While he concludes that 'the heterogeneous and at times contradictory character of global governance presents a challenge to any attempt to understand its operation and evolution in theoretical terms', the essay presents a systematic conceptual framework for making sense of this complexity.

This complexity is the principal theme in the chapter by James Rosenau, who argues that 'world affairs can be conceptualized as governed through a bifurcated system – what can be called the two worlds of world politics – one an interstate system of states and their national governments that has long dominated the course of events, and the other a multicentric system of diverse types of other collectivities . . . who collectively form a highly complex system of global governance.' Developing the concept of 'spheres of authority', Rosenau explains how governance comes about in a world that is rapidly both integrating and fragmenting – what he names 'fragmegration' – under the pressures of globalization. Though this 'fragmegration will be with us for a long time and surely many of its tensions will intensify . . . the collective will to preserve and use the new, horizontal forms of authority is not lacking', such that global governance, he concludes, is now central to the effective management of human affairs.

In the final contribution to part I, Jill Steans develops a feminist perspective on global governance. Since women often bear the principal 'burdens' of global public policy, the perspective developed in this essay offers distinctive insights into the important questions of power and purpose in the conduct of global governance. Steans elucidates 'the gender politics at work in global governance, notably the way that women's groups have attempted to both shape agendas and contest the dominant rules and norms'. In conclusion, Steans examines the importance of gender politics for 'constructing an effective system of global governance, as a counterweight to the globalization of the world economic system'.

In part II the contributions illuminate further the politics of global governance, as well as its effectiveness and limits. This is achieved through an analysis of the global public policy process with respect to several of the most critical contemporary global problems. Nana Poku's chapter discusses the global governance of AIDS, 'the single greatest threat to continual global development'. Following an examination of the institutional structures and the global politics of AIDS programmes, Poku discusses the limits and possibilities of public–private partnerships, such as the new Global AIDS Fund, concluding with the assessment that, in key respects, it is 'still far from axiomatic that the existing institutional frameworks will be empowered to deal with the multiplicity of challenges posed by the pandemic'.

The limits of global governance are also a significant theme developed in the chapter by Phil Williams and Gregory Baudin-O'Hayon. Globalization, they argue, has contributed to a disorderly world, especially evident in the phenomenal growth in transnational organized crime. By contrast, attempts to establish order through international regimes and mechanisms designed to combat these developments confront the problems of jurisdictional disputes and of limited powers and enforcement mechanisms. Despite some significant developments (especially in the aftermath of 11 September) in the legal and institutional machinery to deter and detect transnational criminal activity – from money laundering to people trafficking – the governance capacity of the system remains constrained by jurisdictional and political disputes. However, the limits of global governance might reflect the broader consideration that 'the forces of disorder might be impossible for governments to control.'

Similar constraints, as Perri 6's essay demonstrates, are evident in the transnational regulation of the internet, itself a significant vehicle for the conduct of transnational organized crime. In arguing 'that there is more transnationalization of regulation than first meets the eye', the essay develops a framework for assessing just 'how effective this regulation really is'. Arguing that horizontal regulation – governance through transnational networks of public and private agencies – is an increasingly significant feature of the governance of cyberspace, Perri 6 concludes that what 'is now required is an institutional framework for an open transnational debate about the accountability to citizens of the new clubs through which the regulation of information systems is now conducted'.

This effectively privatized form of network global governance is analysed further in the chapter by Susan Sell. In a searching examination of the global property rights regime, Sell argues that 'the 1994 Agreement on Trade-Related Aspects of Intellectual Property Rights (TRIPS . . .) introduced a brand new era that extends the global reach of intellectual property regulation . . . TRIPS is a significant instance of global rule-making by a small handful of well-connected corporate players and their governments.' In many key respects, TRIPS is evidence not just of the growing significance of global governance, but also its effectiveness in terms of its capacity to shape domestic policies around the world. Moreover, it has also become a focal point for contesting globalization, particularly in respect of drugs patents and biopiracy in the South. This contest, Sell concludes, is centrally about 'redressing the imbalance between private and public interests in the context of intellectual property'. But it has a wider political resonance since it expresses the growing politicization of global governance even in its most technical and legalistic policy domains.

In the context of international finance, the balance between public and private power is a critical variable in determining the effectiveness of global governance arrangements. As Jan Aart Scholte's essay suggests, 'taming transworld financial flows has ranked as one of the top priorities of governance in an emergent global polity.' Yet, as he explains, despite the vital importance of this task to the stability of the world economy, and human security across the globe, 'the effectiveness of present regulatory arrangements is found to be seriously wanting.' The regulation of global finance, Scholte argues, illustrates the growing shift towards a new form of post-statist governance involving 'complex networks of state, suprastate, substate, and private sector actors' in which political authority 'is both multilayered and dispersed'.

If taming global finance is central to ensuring global economic stability, the final chapter in part II by Michael Pugh explains both why and how the maintenance of international security has 'moved in from the periphery of world politics' to become a priority on the global governance agenda. Despite the dramatic failures of humanitarian intervention in Rwanda and Bosnia, the essay concludes that by the twenty-first century the 'instruments for maintaining peace and security, order and justice had not only been institutionalized but were integral to the structure of global governance'. Irrespective of their failures or limitations, Pugh argues that peacekeeping and humanitarian missions are now crucial to the global policing and management of world order and disorder.

Explaining the sources of world order and global governance is the principal task of part III. These six chapters present a critical overview of the dominant traditions or theories of global governance: from realism to cosmopolitanism. Each chapter offers an exposition, and a reflective advocacy, of a particular theoretical tradition.

Accordingly, Robert Gilpin delivers a powerful realist critique of the concept of global governance. He contends that the institutions of global governance do not have the 'capacity to enforce decisions. The nation-state continues to be the only institution in the contemporary world that has this capacity.' Similarly, Alex Callinicos cuts through the rhetoric of global governance to reveal the workings of the structural power of capital and US (liberal capitalist) hegemony. Though Marxism acknowledges that global governance constitutes 'unprecedentedly developed forms of institutionalized policy-coordination and cooperation among the main states . . . these forms represent, not the abolition, but the continuation of the economic and political conflicts that have driven global capitalism since its inception.' In this respect, global governance is far from genuinely global: it is simply another form of political domination.

Taking issue with the more strident aspects of the realist and Marxist analyses, Anthony McGrew explores the continuing relevance of liberal internationalist theories to explaining the pattern of contemporary global governance. He argues that, despite what its many critics suggest, liberal internationalism is undergoing a theoretical renaissance. The much exaggerated crisis of liberal internationalism, evident in the growing separation between its normative aspirations and attempts to construct explanatory theory, is contributing to its rejuvenation. Far from losing its radical normative edge, the liberal literature on global distributive justice represents a fundamental critique of the existing form of global governance and world order. Having noted this, McGrew argues that there is little dialogue between the normative and the explanatory dimensions of contemporary liberal internationalism. In this respect, there is no coherent liberal internationalist theory of global governance but instead a clash of liberal internationalisms.

Just as liberal internationalism invites renewed scrutiny, so, Mark Imber argues, 'Functionalism deserves re-examination.' Functionalism, as this essay reminds us, is 'the unwritten constitution of international order'. Associated with the liberal internationalism of the interwar period, but also drawing on Fabian socialist and New Deal thinking, functionalism provided the rationale for the postwar multilateral order. As a theory of global governance it remains highly relevant, since, as Imber concludes, the UN functional agencies and programmes are after five decades still 'binding together those interests which are common, where they are common, to the extent that they are common'. Functionalism therefore remains 'our best chance for advancing environmental, medical and developmental welfare into the twenty-first century'.

In the concluding two essays, the emphasis shifts to the possible future trajectory of global governance. David Held's essay advocates a cosmopolitan approach to global governance, not just because it assists our understanding, but because 'it ought also to be embraced further in thinking about the proper form of globalization and global governance.' The chapter demonstrates that cosmopolitan principles are not utopian but on the contrary 'are at the centre of significant post-Second World War legal and political developments'. In arguing for 'greater accountability, democracy and social justice in global politics', the essay advocates a form of cosmopolitan global governance. In doing so, it also identifies in current political developments the conditions of possibility for its effective institutionalization.

In the final chapter, Robert Keohane develops this theme of institutional design by exploring, in the context of global governance, the question of 'What normative standards should institutions meet, and what categories should we use to evaluate institutions according to those standards?' Central to this normative enquiry is an attempt to address the problem of how to 'design institutions for a partially globalized world that perform valuable functions while respecting democratic values'. Drawing together the lessons from empirical political theory, Keohane presents a valuable corrective to those who argue that global governance cannot, in any meaningful sense, be democratized or made more effective in the performance of its core tasks. However, the essay concludes by cautioning that 'if global institutions are designed well, they will promote human welfare. But if we bungle the job, the results could be disastrous. Effective and humane global governance arrangements are not inevitable. They will depend on human effort and on deep thinking about politics.'

Taken together, the essays in this volume are a significant contribution to such 'deep thinking' about the current predicament and the proper form of global governance. Arguably, among the greatest ethical and political challenges of the new century is the realization of a more 'genuine' and effective system of global governance as an institutional bridge to a democratic and just world order.

Notes

1   For simplicity, the discussion focuses on the three principal traditions. As understood here, these embrace variants such as functionalism and constructivism. Whereas the former is normally associated with liberal theory, there is some debate as to whether the latter is a discrete school in itself (Keohane, 1988). Constructivism acknowledges that international institutions matter. Their importance lies in the development and promotion of international

norms which act not only to shape state behaviour but also to redefine states' understanding of their own national interests. International institutions are significant in two ways: they socialize states into international cooperative norms; and their cumulative impact is to reinforce a culture of cooperation in international society which moderates geopolitical modes of governing the common affairs of humanity (Finnemore, 1996; Haas, 1999; Ruggie, 1998). Milder versions of constructivism are compatible with liberal institutionalism and neo-Gramscian theory, but more radical versions challenge the rationalist and materialist assumptions of both (see Wendt, 1999).

2   The concept of distorted global governance borrows from Nordlinger's study of the American state which he describes as distorted because of its bias towards powerful organized interests and the corporate world. See Nordlinger, 1981.

References

Beitz, C. R. (1999) 'Social and cosmopolitan liberalism', *International Affairs*, 75, pp. 347–77.

Bergesen, H. and Lunde, L. (1999) *Dinosaurs or Dynamos? The United Nations and the World Bank at the Turn of the Century*, London: Earthscan.

BIS (2001) *Quarterly Report, December*, Geneva: Bank For International Settlements.

Boli, J. (1999) 'Conclusion: world authority structures and legitimations', in J. Boli and G. M. Thomas (eds), *Constructing World Culture: International Nongovernmental Organizations since 1875*, Stanford: Stanford University Press.

Braithwaite, J. and Drahos, P. (1999) *Global Business Regulation*, Cambridge: Cambridge University Press.

Cable, V. (1999) *Globalization and Global Governance*, London: Royal Institute of International Affairs.

Caney, S. (2001) 'International distributive justice', *Political Studies*, 49, pp. 974–97.

Castells, M. (1998) *End of the Millennium*, Oxford: Blackwell.

Cerny, P. (1999) 'Globalization, governance and complexity', in A. Prakash and J. A. Hart (eds), *Globalization and Governance*, London: Routledge.

Cox, R. (1993) 'Gramsci, hegemony and international relations', in S. Gill (ed.), *Gramsci, Historical Materialism and International Relations*, Cambridge: Cambridge University Press.

Cox, R. W. (ed.) (1997) *The New Realism: Perspectives on Multilateralism and World Order*, London: Macmillan.

Cox, R. W. and Sinclair, T. J. (eds) (1996) *Approaches to World Order*, Cambridge: Cambridge University Press.

Cutler, A. C., Haufler, V. and Porter, T. (1999) *Private Authority and International Affairs*, Albany: State University of New York Press.

Deibert, R. (1997) *Parchment, Printing and Hypermedia*, New York: Cornell University Press.

Dicken, P. (1998) *Global Shift*, London: Paul Chapman.

Falk, R. (1995) *On Humane Global Governance*, Cambridge: Polity.

Finnemore, M. (1996) 'Norms, culture, and world politics: insights from sociology's institutionalism', *International Organization*, 50, pp. 325–47.

Garrett, G. (1998) *Partisan Politics in the Global Economy*, Cambridge: Cambridge University Press.

Giddens, A. (1990) *The Consequences of Modernity*, Cambridge: Polity.

Gill, S. (1992) 'Economic globalization and the internationalization of authority: limits and contradictions', *GeoForum*, 23, pp. 269–83.

Gill, S. (2000) 'New constitutionalism, democratization and global political economy', *Peace Research Abstracts*, 37.

Gill, S. and Law, D. (1993) 'Global hegemony and the structural power of capital', in S. Gill (ed.), *Gramsci, Historical Materialism and International Relations*, Cambridge: Cambridge University Press.

Gilpin, R. (2001) *Global Political Economy*, Princeton: Princeton University Press.

Groom, A. J. R. and Powell, D. (1994) 'From world politics to global governance: a theme in need of a focus', in A. J. R. Groom and M. Light (eds), *Contemporary International Relations*, London: Pinter.

Haas, P. M. (1999) 'Social constructivism and the evolution of multilateral environmental governance', in A. Prakash and J. Hart (eds), *Globalization and Governance*, London: Routledge.

Held, D. (1995) *Democracy and Global Order*, Cambridge: Polity.

Held, D. and McGrew, A. (eds) (2000) *The Global Transformations Reader*, Cambridge: Polity.

Held, D., McGrew, A., Goldblatt, D. and Perraton, J. (1999) *Global Transformations: Politics, Economics and Culture*, Cambridge: Polity.

Hirst, P. and Thompson, G. (1999) *Globalization in Question*, Cambridge: Polity.

Hurrell, A. (2001) 'Global inequality and international institutions', in Pogge 2001.

Ikenberry, G. J. (2001) 'America's liberal grand strategy: democracy and national security in the postwar era', in M. Cox, G. J. Ikenberry and T. Inoguchi (eds), *American Democracy Promotion*, Oxford: Oxford University Press.

Jones, C. (1999) *Global Justice: Defending Cosmopolitanism*, Oxford: Oxford University Press.

Keohane, R. O. (1984) *After Hegemony*, Princeton: Princeton University Press.

Keohane, R. O. (1988) 'International institutions: two approaches', *International Studies Quarterly*, 32, pp. 379–96.

Keohane, R. O. (1998) 'International institutions: can interdependence work?', *Foreign Policy*, pp. 82–96.

Keohane, R. and Nye, J. (1977) *Power and Interdependence*, Boston: Little, Brown.

Keohane, R. and Nye, J. (2000) 'Introduction', in J. Nye and J. Donahue (eds), *Governance in a Globalizing World*, Washington DC: Brookings Institution.

Krasner, S. D. (1982) 'Structural causes and regime consequences: regimes as intervening variables', *International Organization*, 36, pp. 185–205.

McGrew, A. (1997) 'Democracy beyond borders? Globalization and the reconstruction of democratic theory and practice', in A. G. McGrew (ed.), *The Transformation of Democracy? Globalization and Territorial Democracy*, Cambridge: Polity.

McGrew, A. (2002) 'Transnational democracy: theories and prospects', in A. Carter and G. Stokes (eds), *Democratic Theory Today*, Cambridge: Polity.

Maddison, A. (2001) *The World Economy: A Millennial Perspective*, Paris: OECD.

Murphy, C. N. (2000) 'Global governance: poorly done and poorly understood', *International Affairs*, 76, pp. 789–804.

Newman, J. (2001) *Modernizing Governance*, London: Sage.

Nordlinger, E. A. (1981) *On the Autonomy of the Democratic State*, Boston: Harvard University Press.

O'Brien, R., Goetz, A. M., Scholte, J. A. and Williams, M. (2000) *Contesting Global Governance: Multilateral Economic Institutions and Global Social Movements*, Cambridge: Cambridge University Press.

O'Neill, O. (2000) 'Bounded and cosmopolitan justice', *Review of International Studies*, 26, pp. 45–61.

O'Neill, O. (2001) 'Agents of justice', in Pogge 2001.

Pierre, J. and Peters, B. G. (2000) *Governance, Politics and the State*, London: Palgrave.

Pogge, T. (1997) 'Creating supranational institutions democratically', *Journal of Political Philosophy*, 5, pp. 163–82.

Pogge, T. W. (ed.) (2001) *Global Justice*, Oxford: Blackwell.

Rodrik, D. (1997) *Has Globalization Gone Too Far?* Washington DC: Institute for International Economics.

Rosenau, J. N. (1999) 'Toward an ontology for global governance', in M. Hewson and T. J. Sinclair (eds), *Approaches to Global Governance Theory*, Albany: State University of New York Press.

Rosenau, J. N. (2000a) 'Change, complexity, and governance in globalizing space', in J. Pierre (ed.), *Debating Governance: Authority, Steering, and Democracy*, Oxford: Oxford University Press.

Rosenau, J. (2000b) 'Governance in a globalizing world', in Held and McGrew 2000.

Ruggie, J. (1998) *Constructing the World Polity*, London: Routledge.

Scholte, J. A. (2000) *Globalization: A Critical Introduction*, London: Macmillan.

Smouts, M.-C. (2001) 'International cooperation: from coexistence to world governance', in M.-C. Smouts (ed.), *The New International Relations*, London: Hurst.

Stein, A. (1990) *Why Nations Co-operate*, New York: Cornell University Press.

Summers, L. (2000) Statement to the International Monetary and Financial Committee, IMF, Washington DC, 16 April.

Thomas, C. (2000) *Global Governance, Development and Human Security*, London: Pluto Press.

UIA (1997) *Yearbook of International Organizations*, Brussels: Union of International Associations.

UN Secretary-General (2000) *Renewing the United Nations*, New York: United Nations (www.un.org).

UNCTAD (2001) *World Investment Report*, Geneva: UNCTAD.

UNDP (1998) *Globalization and Liberalization*, New York: UNDP.

Wendt, A. (1999) *Social Theory of International Politics*, Cambridge: Cambridge University Press.

Woods, N. (1999) 'Good governance in international organizations', *Global Governance*, 5, pp. 39–61.

WTO (2001) *World Trade Report*, Geneva: World Trade Organization.

Zurn, M. (1998) *Democratic Governance beyond the Nation State?* Bremen: Institut für Interkulturelle und Internationale Studien, Universität Bremen.

Part I

The Global Governance Complex

1

Global Governance and the Role of Institutions

Ngaire Woods

Introduction

Globalization poses exciting new opportunities and deep new risks for policy-makers. As trillions of dollars worth of investments, capital flows, goods and services make their way around the world economy, so too at almost equal speed, people, ideas, consumer fashions, and rebellion against globalization move across borders. There are powerful reasons for policy-makers to worry about how they might manage globalization and its impact.

What is globalization? It is a combination of internationalization, political and economic liberalization, and a technological revolution. Internationalization has been occurring over a long period of time as states forge more links with one another, as well as with more international institutions, to pursue mutual goals. Economic liberalization has accelerated since the 1980s as more governments adopt policies which integrate their economies more closely into the world economy, often under intense pressure from bilateral donors and international institutions. Hot on the heels of economic liberalization since the end of the Cold War, political liberalization and democratization have also spread, along with a new international attention to human rights and the prosecution of humanitarian intervention.

The ever closer linking of economies and political and social communities has been fuelled by a revolution in technology and communications. This makes it easier for market actors, companies, refugees, religious groups, non-governmental organizations and the like – not to mention criminal gangs – to operate transnationally. The product is an international system in which policy-makers and their constituencies are less sure of what can be managed and how.

Policy-makers worry that they are losing yet more of their control over their own economies, and policy choices as key policy instruments seem to dangle just out of reach. They are turning increasingly to regional or international institutions in the hope that coordinated solutions will provide some respite. On the streets, however, demonstrators argue that governments should not turn to international organizations. In so doing they remove key decisions from the people and make them in a secretive and undemocratic way.

Critics accuse international organizations like the WTO, the IMF and the World Bank of accelerating globalization primarily (if not purely) in the interests of big business. And this is but one part of the highly contested terrain of global governance. Many developing countries are increasingly concerned that growing intervention in the realms of politics, human rights and security is a strictly one-way affair which carries overtones of a new imperialism. The contemporary debates underline profound disagreements on two core issues: (1) who should govern at the international level and how; and (2) what they should govern.

The emerging pattern of global governance comprises a rich mixture of actors and processes. Vying for influence and control are powerful and less powerful states, experts, transnational corporations, non-governmental organizations, international institutions, and other actors. Each has a view of what should (or should not) be subject to international regulation, discussion or engagement.

This chapter will begin by analysing the actors and challenges in a globalizing world which new forms of 'global governance' are attempting to address. The second section will examine the present state of multilateralism and the limits of traditional inter-governmental governance. The third section will discuss the rise of private and public–private networks and their increasing contribution to global governance. The fourth section will probe the benefits and problems posed by the trend towards network governance. The fifth section will address the role of the US and the implications of its unilateral or bilateral as opposed to multilateral strategies for global govern-ance. The conclusion will offer a comment on the prospects for democratizing global governance.

New Actors and Challenges in a Globalizing World

The new challenges created by globalization are compellingly illustrated by the inter-national financial system. Liberalization and integration into global capital markets has dramatically increased the vulnerability of countries to volatile movements of capital across borders. This was highlighted in 1997 when a financial crisis in Thailand sparked what the IMF called a 'currency meltdown' across East Asia, catalysing a collapse of the rouble in Russia in 1998. Russia's crisis in turn brought down a US hedge fund called Long Term Capital Management, the collapse of which would have put at risk the largest banks in the USA. Economic policy-makers call the phenomenon 'contagion'. It has its parallels in other areas. The spread of HIV/AIDS in the 1980s and antibiotic-resistant tuberculosis in the 1990s, the cross-border passage of weapons and dangerous biochemicals, not to mention the uptake of anti-Western ideologies and the fate of scores of innocent refugees in the 1990s, have all underlined the new challenges of a 'shrinking world'.

Globalization has also affected domestic politics and thereby the capacity of govern-ments to manage these new forces. Economic liberalization and integration has led to greater income inequality within countries without strong welfare states as the incomes of increasingly demanded skilled workers rise while those of unskilled labour drop (Berry and Stewart, 1999; A. Wood, 1994; Berger and Dore, 1996; Keohane and Milner, 1996). Even within wealthy states with good infrastructure, as recently summed up by a US Commission on National Security, the future holds out 'serious and unexpected downturns, major disparities of wealth, volatile capital flows, increasing vulnerabilities in global electronic infrastructures, labor and social disruptions...' (USCNS, 1999, p. 4). In many developing countries the prospects are yet grimmer. Having integrated into the world economy, many have found that they are now yet more vulnerable to the caprices of trade policies in industrialized countries, volatile capital markets, and an unstable international financial system (Rodrik, 1997; Fitzgerald, 2000).

The twenty-first century began with a wide set of reflections on the need for more effective international cooperation and coordination. Policy-makers the world over have begun to ask what kinds of institutions are needed to manage the challenges associated with globalization. A host of answers have been provided by a new industry of expert, high-level groups. To give just three examples, the 'Zedillo Panel' reported to the Secretary-General of the United Nations in June 2001 (UN, 2001), the 'Meltzer Commission' reported to the US Congress in 2000 (IFIAC, 2000), an Emerging Markets Eminent Persons Group completed a study for the Ford Foundation in 2001 (Ford Foundation, 2001). Each has propounded new institutions, reforms to existing institutions, and a continuing attention and evolution of global governance. This process is not one in which only policy-makers and academic experts are participating.

The financial crises of the 1990s demonstrated the capacity of private sector actors such as banks, investment houses, security brokerages, hedge funds and asset managers to create turmoil. As these actors create profit centres out of currency derivatives, and emerging market security trading departments, and take large positions in leveraged instruments on proprietary accounts, their frenetic trading activities create what one analyst has described as a 'global whirlpool' (Mistry, 1998). Crucially, these actors are also powerful political lobbyists and participants in the debate about how to govern (or leave to the markets) the global financial system. Similarly, large energy corporations are powerful lobbyists in global environmental negotiations, and pharmaceutical companies in the global HIV/AIDS strategy. Global governance creates an international arena for lobbying and the representation of vested interests. The risk is that powerful private interests begin to gain a 'double' voice whereby their interests are represented by their own governments with whom they lobby very effectively, and also directly in international negotiations by their own private representatives.

A further set of actors which have become particularly prominent in the new arena of global governance are non-governmental organizations, often referred to as 'global civil society'. At least two kinds of groups might be included under this title. The most visible and vocal are large transnational non-governmental organizations based in industrialized countries, lobbying for particular principles or issues such as debt relief, environmental protection and human rights, such as Amnesty International, Worldwide Fund for Nature and Oxfam. These groups do not claim to represent countries or geographical groups, nor do they represent particular commercial interests (although they are accountable to their donors and members, and many are also in the business of delivering aid or similar goods). Their stake in the arena of global governance is more of a deliberative one. They bring principles and values to the attention of policy-makers and firms. They also play a role in monitoring global governance, analysing and reporting on issues as diverse as the Chemical Weapons Treaty, negotiations on global climate change, world trade, and the actions of the IMF and World Bank. In so doing, these transnational NGOs open up information, debate and criticism which can play an important role in holding both private and governmental sectors to account: although critics would ask 'accountable to whom', emphasizing that these NGOs are formally accountable at most to their fee-paying members.

A rather different community of NGOs is now also becoming increasingly involved in the debate and implementation of global governance. More 'locally based' NGOs, predominantly in developing countries, are being drawn into the fray. These groups claim to represent local constituencies. Many operate to plug gaps in their own country's government. Some try to make up for the fact that their government fails to represent a certain section of the population. Others attempt to make up for a government's lack of capacity to deliver assistance or services. Some are opposed and repressed by their government. Others work closely with their government.

Increasingly these groups are being included in discussions with international aid donors, international organizations and in other arenas of global governance. Their entry has been catalysed by a number of shifts in thinking about both aid and governance. Already in the 1980s non-governmental organizations, private charities and voluntary services were applauded by new conservatives, especially in the Thatcher and Reagan governments in the UK and USA, as alternatives to government involvement in welfare, aid and social policy. This thinking spilled over into aid policies which sought to channel aid through non-governmental groups in both the industrialized and developing countries. That trend changed in the 1990s with the rise of international support for democratization and a wave of development thinking focused on strengthening and modernizing the state. It is now recognized that good policies and outcomes require good politics. That means effective government, not effective NGOs competing with a weak government.

Another logic now drives the inclusion of locally based NGOs in international forums. Aid institutions and donor governments have recognized that wider participation and 'ownership' on the ground is necessary for development policies to be successfully implemented. This has been reiterated in numerous World Bank and IMF publications (World Bank, 1989, 1992, 1994, 1996, 1999; IMF, 1997, 2000). Getting wider ownership and participation is difficult, especially in countries where governments have few networks for consultation or representation and where wide gaps exist in who they represent and how. For these reasons, agencies such as the UN, the IMF, the World Bank and the United Nations Development Programme (UNDP) are encouraging both their own local representatives and government officials to develop consultative links and closer relations with local NGOs. This brings new tensions and problems to both local and international politics.

A key issue raised by the emergence of NGOs in global governance is who chooses which NGOs to include or consult in national or international negotiations. At the national level, if the government plays a key role, critics allege that genuine consultation is not taking place. Where outsiders play a role, governments argue that their sovereignty and their own processes of democracy are being subverted. Where the local representatives of international organizations are involved, they risk becoming powerful gate-keepers who use their power to favour some groups over others to cement and further their own position. At the international level all these problems are replicated. For these reasons, the new involvement of NGOs poses important new challenges to the legitimacy and accountability of international institutions.

Global governance is a contested terrain at best. Some would say that the very term obscures more than it describes, proposing or assuming a 'global community' which does not really exist and a form of management or government that is not really about governing (Streeten, 2001). What is clear is that globalization creates problems which require some degree of coordination, cooperation or regulation beyond the nation-state. Furthermore, a range of actors are demanding to be included in that process, with varying degrees of success. It is worth now turning to examine the various modes of governance that have emerged and to which actors they give most voice and on what grounds.

Multilateralism and its Limits

One way in which governments have responded to globalization has been through intergovernmental cooperation. States have sought to strengthen and institutionalize cooperation among governments at the international level. We see this in the new emphasis being put on institutions such as the United Nations, NATO, the IMF, the Bank for International Settlements (BIS), the World Bank and the WTO. The hope is that multilateral negotiations and a sharing of technical expertise will provide solutions to the new vulnerabilities created by globalization, and that international agencies will then be able to implement these solutions. Many new international institutions have recently been proposed, such as a Global Environment Organization (UN, 2001), a global bankruptcy mechanism (Ford Foundation, 2000; Raffer, 1993), a global financial regulator (Eatwell, 2000), an International Tax Organization (UN, 2001), an Economic and Social Security Council (Daws and Stewart, 2000) or Economic Security Council (UN, 2001), to deal with the new challenges of globalization.

One strand of belief in multilateralism proceeds from a rational-functional or 'institutionalist' approach to international relations and institutions. This theory assumes that cooperation among states permits governments to achieve goals which reflect everyone's interests. Multilateralism emerges because governments see it as a way to share and pool resources, reducing transactions costs and enabling a concentration of the expertise and capacity necessary to achieve particular kinds of international policy. In other words, governments create international institutions to promulgate their national interests in a cooperative way. They do this by delegating some power to international agencies of their own making (Keohane, 1984; Krasner, 1983). The result is multilateral agencies which ensure mutual benefits are gained from globalization and that losses are compensated. Agencies such as the IMF, the World Bank and the WTO smooth over the gaps and failures in the operation of markets, ensuring a more robust and stable global economy for all.

To some extent, multilateralism is a form of global governance which is both representative and accountable. Interstate institutions are representative because their governing bodies represent (even if not equally) all member governments. They are accountable because these same bodies enable governments to control budgets, mandates and operations.

Multilateralism, however, faces two problems in the contemporary world. In the first place, not all governments accept that their interests are best pursued through interstate agencies such as the IMF, the World Bank or the UN Security Council. The most powerful states in the world enjoy the luxury of being able to 'shop around' for the arena in which they can best achieve their ends. Sometimes this means turning their back on multilateralism and pursuing their goals through private–public alliances, regional, unilateral or minilateral means (see further discussion on this below). So too, developing and emerging countries argue that they are underrepresented and often ill-served by these organizations, which too often act like 'rich men's clubs' (Woods, 1999).

Equally importantly, large sections of the public do not buy the idea that they are represented in institutions such as the IMF, the World Bank, the UN Security Council, or the WTO. They are not altogether wrong. In reality, representation and accountability have always been weak in these multilateral institutions. Now, however, the weaknesses are glaring because the institutions are being called on by their powerful members to intrude much more deeply into areas which were previously the preserve of national governments.

The new intrusiveness of international institutions is evident in the work of the IMF and the World Bank, now seeking to ensure 'forceful, far-reaching structural reforms' in the economies of their members (IMF, 1998). Likewise, in trade, the WTO works on many issue-related domestic policy matters, and it is now considering involvement in competition policy, government procurement and the environment. In the security realm, the UN Security Council has become involved in mandating or undertaking interventions within the borders of sovereign states as in Somalia, Kosovo and Bosnia-Herzogovina aimed *inter alia* at protecting the rights or lives of sections of the population – although this new interventionism is neither universal nor uniform (Chesterman, 2001).

In both G7 and developing countries, people are beginning to ask: by what right are these international institutions stepping into domestic policy? And when they do so, to whom are they accountable? The UN Security Council was structured by the victors of the Second World War to reflect the balance of power at that time. Five of the fifteen seats on the Council are held by what were then the Great Powers (USA, UK, France, People's Republic of China and Russia) and each has the power to veto an action or resolution undertaken by the Council. All other states are represented in constituency groups and only modest steps have been taken to improve the transparency and accountability of the Council to all of its members (Wood, 1996).

The structures of the IMF and World Bank reflect their origins as essentially technical agencies dealing with issues of international coordination. The institutions are supposedly accountable to their member governments through representatives on the executive boards. Yet there are deep flaws in this structure. Only eight countries are directly represented (the US, UK, Germany, France, Japan, China, Russia and Saudi Arabia). As argued elsewhere (Woods, 2001), if their accountability is to come closer to matching their functions, the institutions need at least to have properly representative executive boards which actively control and monitor and are accountable for the work of the institutions, as well as open and legitimate processes for the appointment of the heads and staffs of the institutions. The new 'opening up' of the institutions to the public by publishing their work and consulting more with non-governmental organizations and 'civil society' is a recognition that the old-style multilateralism has to find new ways to legitimate itself.

The World Trade Organization is ostensibly the most equal of the agencies discussed so far. All member states enjoy an equal vote in the organization. Furthermore, unlike the more technical economic agencies, decision-making at all levels is member-driven rather than undertaken by expert staff. Voting power, however, means much less than it seems in the WTO for decisions are adopted by consensus and that consensus tends to be thrashed out in informal negotiations meetings (often called the 'Green Room' process) which are dominated by the United States, the European Union, Japan and Canada ('the Quad'). The bottom line in these negotiations on trade is that states with large market shares enjoy significant input and influence over decisions, indeed one might describe them as decision-makers, while states with smaller market shares are effectively decision-takers (Woods and Narlikar, 2001). Furthermore, private sector actors play a vital behind-the-scenes role in the delegations from the Quad countries (Dobson and Jacquet, 1999). NGOs enjoy a much lesser role (WTO, 1996), but are now accredited for ministerial conferences and can present amicus briefs in the dispute settlement processes (Robertson, 2000).

Multilateral institutions ideally provide opportunities for genuinely international debate and cooperation. In this they are a vital aspect of governance in the world economy. However, increasingly they are being accused of being insufficiently democratic, insufficiently expert, and/or insufficiently effective. For these reasons we see all actors involved in global governance turning to other forums.

The Rise of Private and Public–Private Networks

A tier of global governance increasing in size occurs in parallel to states and their multilateral organizations. In essence this is a form of private-sector or mixed public and private governance. In part it reflects the needs of companies who have become more global in their operations, production networks and commodity chains (Gereffi and Korzeniewicz, 1994). Where possible, such transnational corporations avoid state or interstate regulation. Instead they create their own tier of private sector 'governance', 'standard setting', 'codes of best practice' or self-regulation. For example, from 1973 onwards the International Accounting Standards Committee (IASC) successfully edged out intergovernmental efforts to promulgate regulation and the setting of accountancy standards, taking up a central role recognized since 1998 by the G7, the IMF and the World Bank (Martinez, 2001). This kind of regime leaves major private sector actors (based in the world's largest economies) in the driving seat, yet it is not evidence of the death of the nation-state. Far from it. On the whole, private sector governance emerges where powerful states choose not to regulate, or indeed where states actively support private sector actors in generating their own regime and then cooperate closely with that regime. This is worth illustrating.

One of the longer standing private networks is the International Chamber of Commerce, which was founded in 1919 and represents private sector companies and associations from over 130 countries. The ICC has no qualms about its role in governance, describing itself as having 'unrivalled authority in making rules that govern the conduct of business across borders. Although these rules are voluntary, they are observed in countless thousands of transactions every day and have become part of the fabric of international trade' (ICC, 2001). Along with its private rule-setting function, the ICC provides the International Court of Arbitration, the world's leading arbitral institution. Like other private sector organizations, the ICC has close links to governments and multilateral organizations. Indeed, within a year of the creation of the United Nations, the ICC was granted consultative status at the highest level with the UN and its specialized agencies.

Private sector governance and standard-setting emanates almost without exception from the most powerful industrialized countries. For example, in the international chemistry industry it is the American Chemistry Council (ACC), representing all major US chemical companies, which launched a 'Responsible Care' code in 1988 in response to public concerns about the manufacture and use of chemicals. The code requires members continually to improve their health, safety and environmental performance; to listen and respond to public concerns; to assist each other to achieve optimum performance; and to report their goals and progress to the public. The code is now being adopted in some forty-six countries, representing over 85 per cent of the world's chemical production (ACC, 2001). Likewise based in the United States are the Institute for International Finance, lobbying and proposing self-regulation for financial sector actors; major private credit-rating agencies such as Moody's and Standard & Poor's; cyberspace companies crafting codes on privacy, property rights and copyright laws (Lessig, 1999); and large corporations such as Nike and Mattel who have created codes of conduct governing their subcontractors in less developed countries. In large part these governance bodies have been created to obviate the need for government or intergovernmental regulation, and in the latter case as a response to growing NGO and media pressure.

In some instances, governments have played an active role in promulgating these private sector organizations. For example, the United States government helped to create the Internet Corporation for Assigned Names and Numbers (ICANN), a non-profit corporation formed to assume responsibility for the governance of various aspects of the internet such as the internet provider address space allocation, protocol parameter assignment, domain name system management, and root server system management functions previously performed under US government contract by IANA (Internet Assigned Numbers Authority) and other entities (ICANN, 2001). In this instance, the US turned to a non-governmental form of governance because it feared that a formal intergovernmental organization would be too slow and cumbersome in dealing with rapidly developing issues (Keohane and Nye, 2000, p. 24).

In other instances, private sector actors have joined with government and non-governmental organizations in order to create a new mixed form of governance, monitoring both private-sector and official policy and actions. The World Commission on Dams which began work in 1998 is an example, comprising four commissioners from governments, four from private industry, and four from NGOs. It was set up to review the development effectiveness of large dams and to develop internationally acceptable criteria, guidelines and standards for the planning, design, appraisal, construction, operation, monitoring and decommissioning of dams (World Commission on Dams, 2000). This network highlights a growing sensitivity of private corporations and governments to criticism and monitoring by transnational NGOs, whom they are now including within networks of governance.

A yet more ambitious example of global cooperation among private companies, governments, multilateral organizations, and NGOs is the UN's recently launched Global Compact initiative. The objective of the Compact is to bring together governments, companies, workers, civil society organizations and the United Nations organization itself to advocate and promulgate nine core principles drawn from the Universal Declaration of Human Rights, the ILO's Fundamental Principles on Rights at Work and the Rio Principles on Environment and Development. In signing up to the Compact, companies are asked to commit themselves to act on these principles in their own corporate domains. Since the formal launch of the Compact on 26 July 2000, the Compact has grown to encompass several hundred participating companies, as well as international labour groups and more than a dozen international civil society organizations.

The Global Compact is clearly not a regulatory regime nor even a code of conduct. The UN describes it as 'a value-based platform designed to promote institutional learning. It utilizes the power of transparency and dialogue to identify and disseminate good practices based on universal principles' (UN Global Compact, 2001). Nevertheless, the Compact reflects the degree to which international organizations and large multinational private actors today perceive a need to respond not just to global markets but to global social and political pressures: 'as markets have gone global, so, too, must the idea of corporate citizenship and the practice of corporate social responsibility. In this new global economy, it makes good business sense for firms to internalize these principles as integral elements of corporate strategies and practices' (UN Global Compact, 2001).

Globalization has forced a new openness on multinational companies wary of the power of consumers in their largest markets to boycott or respond negatively to bad press. For example, large oil companies such as BP and Royal Dutch/Shell have been publicly accused of colluding in human rights violations in countries such as Colombia and Chad-Cameroon. Both companies have adopted human rights policies strongly endorsing the UN Universal Declaration of Human Rights. Both are also offering to work more closely and openly with NGOs (British Petroleum, 2001; Shell, 2001). On a sceptical view, these companies are simply investing more in their public relations. Nevertheless, the potential power of corporations to effect change in this area is recognized even by their critics. As Human Rights Watch notes,

> a well-implemented policy [by BP] could have far-reaching effects, since BP merged with the US oil major, Amoco, to form the third-largest oil company in the world (behind Shell and Exxon), with operations in countries with poor human rights records such as Algeria and Colombia, and operating in alliance with Statoil – which also has a human rights policy – in Angola and Azerbaijan. (Human Rights Watch, 1999)

In a similar vein, diamond companies such as De Beers have attracted bad publicity about their role in mining 'blood' and 'conflict' diamonds in countries where the industry funds and perpetuates brutal civil wars, such as Sierra Leone. In their annual report for 2000, De Beers writes of the 'threat to the entire legitimate diamond industry' posed by the 'effect of conflict diamonds on consumer confidence' (De Beers, 2000). To ward off this threat, the diamond industry has created a World Diamond Council based in New York to develop, implement and oversee a tracking system for the export and import of rough diamonds to 'prevent the exploitation of diamonds for illicit purposes such as war and inhumane acts' (World Diamond Council, 2001). As with the oil companies above, the extent to which diamond companies implement effective policies in this area will depend not on governments or intergovernmental institutions but on NGOs who monitor and publicize infractions and thereby create the link between consumers in the North and corporate operations in the South.

Private sector initiatives to improve the environment, human rights, workers' rights and such-like reflect a response to the growing capacity of consumers and shareholders to hold companies to account. They also reflect companies' fears that not only consumers but also employees (both present and future) may turn away from companies branded pariahs by transnational NGOs. Equally companies fear that governments might intervene and regulate at the behest of voters. The result is a web of private-sector generated and monitored 'standards', 'principles' and policies, sometimes in cooperation with governments or intergovernmental institutions, which form an important element of global governance. These are areas in which the world is relying on transnational NGOs as agencies of accountability without which many global corporate activities would remain almost entirely unmonitored.

A New, More Technocratic 'Network' Governance?

A new trend has recently begun to emerge in intergovernmental attempts to manage and regulate globalization. Technical issues and areas are being identified, and expert networks are being fostered as a flexible and efficient way to manage them. The approach eschews old-fashioned representative institutions in which power differences among states are obvious. To cite two prominent scholars: 'any emerging pattern of governance will have to be networked rather than hierarchical and must have minimal rather than highly ambitious objectives' (Keohane and Nye, 2000, p. 37). In other words, state-based institutions of governance which exercise authority over all other actors should be replaced by 'network minimalism' which seeks 'to preserve national democratic processes and embedded liberal compromises while allowing the benefits of economic integration' (ibid.).

We see in these arguments clear institutionalist and functionalist assumptions which focus on cooperation rather than power, and on 'getting the job done' rather than on the justice or legitimacy of the process. Networks comprise participants with special technical expertise and material stakes in an issue, such as the chemicals, accountancy and financial stability networks mentioned above. Because they are selective, these networks are cohesive, technically sophisticated and efficient. Their legitimacy in large part depends on the quality of the outcomes they produce, that is, if they do their job well or not. Results not process matter most, or to express it in the language of some political scientists, the quality of the outputs matters more than the democratic inputs.

For example the Financial Stability Forum (FSF) was convened at the behest of the G7 in April 1999, to promote international financial stability through information exchange and international cooperation in financial supervision and surveillance. The new network was self-consciously selective, bringing together experts from the most important players in the international financial system, including national authorities responsible for financial stability in significant international financial centres, international financial institutions, sector-specific international groupings of regulators and supervisors, and committees of central bank experts. The FSF does not represent all countries or regions of the world. Rather its goal is to coordinate the efforts of various bodies in order to promote international financial stability, improve the functioning of markets and reduce systemic risk (FSF, 2001). The legitimacy of the FSF rests on its efficiency in achieving its stated goals. That said, however, interestingly the G7 has found it necessary to expand its membership to include representatives from Hong Kong, Singapore, Australia and the Netherlands (FSF, 2001).

The 'efficiency' or output rationale for governance seems to be exercising a growing appeal. Indeed, we find it being applied to a number of other intergovernmental bodies. Three examples come to mind: the IMF, the European Union, and the WTO. In each case arguments have been made for more independent and expert-oriented governance so as to avoid the problems, vested interests and contradictions which arise from domestically rooted intergovernmentalism. Part of the argument has been elegantly expressed by Ernst-Ulrich Petersmann in the following terms: 'governments risk to become prisoners of the sirene-like pressures of organized interest groups unless they follow the wisdom of Ulysses (when his boat approached the island of the Sirenes) and tie their hands to the mast of international guarantees' (Petersmann, 1995). Away from the hurly-burly of domestic politics, policy-makers can come to more rational and selfless conclusions, or so we are led to believe.

In respect of the IMF it has been argued that the IMF 'should be made truly independent and accountable' so as 'to permit it to focus more efficiently on surveillance and conditionality' (De Gregorio et al., 1999). Like a central bank, we are told the IMF must be permitted to work in a more technocratic, independent way with its accountability ensured through transparency and a different kind of oversight by member governments. Just as independent central banks have proved better at fighting inflation, so too, we are led to believe, an independent world authority would better protect international financial stability. Of course, there are real problems in comparing the diverse tasks taken on by the IMF to that of a central bank. More deeply, the presumption underpinning the argument is that intergovernmental organizations can improve their legitimacy by bolstering their efficiency. 'Democratizing' the organization or attempting to link it more directly to a wider range of constituencies would, by contrast, derail the institution and delegitimize it further, or so the argument suggests.

In the European Union the output-oriented rationale for governance is that: 'At the end of the day, what interests them [people living in the EU] is not *who* solves these problems, but the fact that they are being tackled' (Prodi, 1999). This output-oriented rationale has underpinned the push for European Monetary Union (EMU) in spite of popular ambivalence about it. 'Efficiency' arguments have been used to suppress concerns about democratic representation and accountability. The institution at the heart of the EMU, the European Central Bank, is an independent and relatively politically unaccountable body (compared to its counterparts in the UK and USA). Its claim to legitimacy rests on its technical and expert nature rather than its potential representativeness or democratic accountability. Such efficiency arguments are now being made for yet wider and more political initiatives such as institutional reform and enlargement. Questions of legitimacy and democracy, it has been argued by one scholar, are increasingly being left to be dealt with as issues for public relations not institutional reform (Kohler-Koch, 1999).

The World Trade Organization is a final example of an organization we are told should be more independent. In order to minimize the rent-seeking producer interests that have so much power at the national level, it has been argued that the global trading system should be 'constitutionalized', where a written constitution is under-stood as 'a contractual means by which citizens secured their freedom through long-term basic rules of a higher legal rank' (Petersmann, 1995). Similar arguments are made by quite a wide range of scholars pressing for the WTO to become a vehicle for enforcing core values in human rights, environmental protection and labour standards.

In constitutionalizing the WTO, it is assumed that the 'long-term basic rules' on the basis of which trade should proceed are uncontested or uncontestable. These higher laws or values should not be shipwrecked on the ragged shores of national politics. Yet many would argue that trade rules which encroach into issues of welfare, the environment, labour rights, and intellectual property protection belong in the national realm. They reflect not some higher legal truth but deeply political priorities and choices over which citizens should have some say. This is not just a crude contest between economists and NGOs, liberalization versus the protection of human rights and values. It involves subtle adjudications over priorities, means and ends. Should one form of environmental protection be privileged over another? Should one species of dolphin be protected more than another? Who should decide?

One response to the political problems of constitutionalizing the WTO has been to argue that the institution should be more 'inclusive' (Howse and Nicolaidis, 2000). NGOs and other interested or expert parties, for example, should be included in deliberations on trade issues. To quote one enthusiast: 'the right way to defeat bad ideas is with better ideas. Just as national democracy entails participation and debate at the domestic level, so too does democratic global governance entail participation by transnational NGOs' (Charnovitz, 2000). There are a couple of problems embedded in this argument.

In the first place, the inclusion of NGOs will not necessarily redress the failure of the WTO adequately to represent some countries and groups while overrepresenting others. Indeed, inclusion might exacerbate rather than redress the lack of voice and influence suffered by developing countries. Note for instance that of the 738 NGOs accredited to the Ministerial Conference of the WTO in Seattle, 87 per cent were based in industrialized countries. Enthusiasts of inclusion need to consider more carefully how NGOs might be included without further distorting the underrepresentation of developing countries and peoples in the WTO.

A second problem arises with the broader argument that we might consider the WTO as a deliberative space within which the best ideas win. In this argument for 'network governance', the focus shifts from procedures and 'inputs' (such as elections and representative government) to the quality of debate and the 'outputs' of the system. The inclusion of NGOs and experts supposedly ensures high-quality delibera-tion which, the argument suggests, improves outputs. This is because the process of deliberation is (ideally) one in which the best ideas can be aired and genuinely expert participants can partake (without the limitations of a representative system). Through the process of deliberation, participants 'learn' and change their minds, coming to understand alternatives better and to modify their own starting positions.

The missing element in the deliberative network model is politics. The kinds of vested interests which 'distort' trade policy at the national level are assumed to disappear at the international level. Yet even a cursory examination of private sector participation in existing WTO negotiations reveals their powerful influence. Groups such as the US Coalition of Services Industries (CSI, 2001) and International Financial Services, London (IFSL, 2001) were deeply involved in negotiations on the General Agreement on Trade in Services, and the WTO Basic Telecommunications and Financial Services Agreements. The Financial Leaders Group, a private sector group of North American, European, Japanese, Canadian and Hong Kong financial leaders, publicizes its role as 'a key player in securing the 1997 Financial Services Agreement' and 'continues its work in the current WTO services negotiations' (FLG, 2001). Naturally representatives of private sector organizations bring a high level of expertise and ideas to the negotiating table. However, they represent, indeed they have a duty to represent, the narrow sectoral and material interests of their members. It distorts reality to propose that they are participants in a deliberation in which the best or better ideas will win because rationality triumphs over interests. The *raison d'être* of participating private sector groups is to represent the interests of their members.

The debate about deliberative networks highlights the need to pay attention in global governance to the issue of who defines the rules and outcomes of deliberation. Those who focus on 'outputs' pay too little attention to inputs and to questions such as: Who determines who can participate in the exercise? Who sets the agenda? Who sets the parameters within which acceptable outcomes must fall? As a result, the network governance enthusiasts overlook deep problems of legitimacy and account-ability arising from these processes.

The significance of the question of who controls networks lies in the content and impact of the work being undertaken at the global level. In the FSF example, three issues are on the agenda: capital flows, offshore financial centres, and highly leveraged institutions (FSF, 2001). All three have a direct impact on developing countries, which are vulnerable to the systemic risks and issues involved, and some of which will be directly affected by regulation in this area because it could reduce offshore financial activities on which they rely. Governance in these areas – be it regulation or standards – will benefit some countries and cause significant costs to others. What will justify these choices? For output-oriented governance specialists the answer is the quality of the results and their contribution to international financial stability. Critics, on the other hand, will point out that there are many competing models of international financial stability. Some focus on regulation, others on liberalization. Some put the emphasis on capital controls, others on universal openness of capital accounts. The vigorous debate about which measures best achieve international financial stability reflects why the process of goal-setting and policy-making is so important.

Network governance has an important contribution to offer in managing the world economy, bringing as it does considerable and varied expertise to increasingly complex issues. However, even in seemingly technical areas such as financial stability, trade rules, monetary union, or accounting standards, the choice of goals and outcomes reflects the interests of those who control the process. For this reason, there are real dangers in substituting democratic accountability for expertise and independence.

The Role and Alternative Diplomacies of the United States

At the core of all the above models of global governance lies the role of the most powerful state in the system, the United States. For some the US is a constructive leader in world affairs, providing the necessary public goods for global cooperation and stability. To quote the 1999 US Commission on National Security, 'in the world we see emerging, American leadership will be of paramount importance . . . It is a rare moment and a special opportunity in history when the acknowledged dominant global power seeks neither territory nor political empire' (USCNS, 1999). For others, US leadership is better described as self-interested hegemony. In reality there are both internationalist and unilateralist tendencies in US foreign policy and in the different arms of the US government. This is evident in US attitudes both towards multilateral institutions and to the promulgation of alternative, smaller regimes where we find evidence of unilateralism and bilateralism.

A unilateralist impulse has characterized many US postures in international organizations. Much has been written in this respect about US policy towards the United Nations (Rivlin, 1996; Ruggie, 1996). A similar impulse also emerges in respect of international economic institutions. In the wake of the financial crises of the 1990s mentioned above, the US appealed to the IMF to engage in each crisis, yet at the same time a strongly unilateralist response emerged from the US Congress. In the Congressional debate on allocating the IMF more resources so as to deal with the crises in 1997–8, Congress made its approval conditional on the creation of an International Financial Institutions Advisory Commission (IFIAC).

IFIAC considered the future roles and structures of the IMF, the World Bank and other institutions and reported back to the US Congress in the so-called 'Meltzer Commission Report' of 2000 (IFIAC, 2000). The approach of the Commission was notable in that it undertook no consultation with other countries, not even those most affected by the work of the international financial institutions. Rather, the report presents a purely US-centred vision of how the institutions should be reformed, framed within the presumption (comparable to US positions on other UN agencies) that if the US is not 'tough' with multilateral institutions, then foreigners will take US taxpayers for a ride. The approach was not isolationist (as some would describe it) for it did not reflect a desire to disengage from the rest of the world. Rather, the approach was solidly unilateralist, reflecting a desire to engage with the rest of the world on US terms. In reality, however, few of the Commission's recommendations have found their way into policy. Nevertheless, they succeeded in bringing direct pressure to bear on both the World Bank and the IMF. Indeed, one of the first acts of the new managing director of the IMF, Horst Kohler, in 2000 was to meet with Allan Meltzer to discuss the report.

The US has disproportionate power in every international organization to which it belongs. I use the term disproportionate to mean power greater than its formal voting rights or stake in the organization. This means that unilateralist positions taken within the US cannot fail to influence international organizations and induce some submission on their part to the US agenda. Nevertheless, it is equally true that US administrations almost always stop short of adopting the unilateralist positions expressed by their colleagues in the US Congress. As will be discussed below, this is because the US needs multilateral organizations and cooperation from other governments in order to fulfil many of its core objectives.

A different form of unilateralism is apparent in other aspects of US foreign policy. The US engagement with other countries on trade issues offers an important illustration. Although the US has pushed for a new trade round within the framework of the

World Trade Organization, it is clear that this is not the only means by which the US pursues its international trade policy preferences. Trade policy within the WTO requires the US and other states to compromise in order to achieve the consensus necessary for measures to go through. Indeed, this is the essence of multilateralism. However, where the WTO rules do not match US preferences, the US has two other alternatives. It can disregard the application of WTO rulings. It can also seek to forge agreements – with countries individually or in groups – which better reflect the US desiderata.

In bilateral negotiations, the US has shown its capacity to achieve its own goals with very little compromise. One example is the US–Jordan Free Trade Agreement which was signed on 24 October 2000, eliminating duties and commercial barriers to bilateral trade in goods and services originating in the United States and Jordan (USTR, 2000). The agreement includes requirements which go well beyond what the US has managed to insert into the WTO agreements. The US–Jordan Free Trade Agreement includes provisions on intellectual property right protection, trade and the environment, labour, and electronic commerce, and side letters concerning marketing approval for pharmaceutical products, and trade in services. In essence, the US–Jordan Free Trade Agreement sets an example of how the US can achieve its trade goals without recourse to multilateral institutions. However, that is only if such agreements become more widespread.

The Free Trade Area of the Americas (FTAA) offers another example of a US initiative. The proposed agreement covers thirty-four countries in the Western hemisphere and extends across nine issues: market access; agriculture; services; investment; intellectual property; government procurement; subsidies, antidumping, countervailing duties; competition policy; and dispute settlement. Like the US–Jordan Trade Agreement, the FTAA includes a number of issues which the US has been unable to insert into WTO agreements. For example, on intellectual property protection, the US proposal 'complements and adds to the obligations that the US and most FTAA have undertaken through the WTO Agreement on Trade-Related Aspects of Intellectual Property Rights' (USTR, 2001).

The issue for all other countries in the Americas is whether they will choose to submit to the FTAA, essentially riding the coat-tails or 'bandwagoning' with the United States, or whether they might attempt to counterbalance US power by reinforcing their capacity to negotiate collectively in groupings such as MERCOSUR (Tussie and Woods, 2000). The present disarray among MERCOSUR countries, due in large part to the divergent economic policies of Argentina and Brazil, make the prospects of the latter option rather dim.

What does all this mean for global governance? Bilateralism and regional arrangements offer all states an alternative to purely multilateral regimes. However, the states which benefit most from such arrangements are those with the largest market access to offer, the largest security umbrella to share, and the greatest capacity to threaten negative consequences from non-compliance or exclusion. The United States has the largest single trade market and defence capacity. This means that in negotiations with any one state or small combination of states, negotiations are asymmetrically weighted towards US preferences and policies. For this reason smaller and less powerful states have long endorsed the need to undertake negotiations in universal, multilateral institutions, even as they 'cover their bets' by participating in bilateral or regional arrangements with the United States (Krasner, 1985).

The consequences for multilateralism are not absolutely obvious. There is a long-standing debate in the political economy of international trade as to whether regional blocs assist or hinder moves to a more multilateral free trade regime. From the US perspective, its bilateral and regional measures are intended as building blocks of an international regime. The US would be only too happy for the standards embodied in the US–Jordan Free Trade Agreement or the FTAA to be applied internationally. For some this is evidence of enlightened leadership and of the US forging rules and institutions to create a system from which everyone will benefit.

Seen from other countries, the fine print of the agreements reveals specific priorities which reflect powerful US economic interests such as in the financial and technology sectors. Agreements to 'free trade' in these areas and to create standards in others (such as labour and the environment) will create winners within the US (and in other countries) but at others' expense. The US is not pushing free trade across-the-board but is pushing for liberalization in those sectors in which its interests lie. For these reasons, countries other than the US worry that the longer term impact of bilateral and regional arrangements will be to create a preferential area within which the US calls all the shots and other countries have little choice but to belong. Global governance built in this way casts most countries as rule-takers rather than rule-makers, bolstering a view of the US as an imperial hegemon.

All that said, there are powerful limits on how far the US can turn its back on multilateralism and the genuine participation of other countries in the forging of international institutions. In the security realm, this is due both to the nature of security threats and to the emergence of new actors. Long prior to the terrorist attacks on the United States of 11 September 2001, it was clear to the US Commission on National Security that the military superiority of the US would not protect it from the emerging threats to US security. Not only did the Commission note with extraordinary foresight that terrorists and other disaffected groups would cause Americans to die, possibly in large numbers, on American soil, but in the Commission's words, 'the most serious threat to our security may consist of unannounced attacks on American cities by sub-national groups using genetically engineered pathogens' (USCNS, 1999, p. 8). Countering these kinds of threats requires not just different domestic institutions but a new form of diplomacy, international intelligence collection, security provision, and the building of international coalitions. This has been dramatically demonstrated since 11 September 2001 whereby even the most unilateralist of American policy-makers have had to dive deeply back into international engagement and diplomacy.

Similarly in the economic realm, financial crises in several different parts of the world have underlined US dependence on international institutions such as the Bank for International Settlements, the IMF, the World Bank and new arrangements such as the Financial Stability Forum discussed above. For all these reasons, participation in multilateral institutions is essential to the US, as is its engagement in less formal coalitions and networks of states. Other states must work with US preponderance in informal intergovernmental and private sector arrangements and a dominant but not always preponderant US participation in multilateral institutions.

Conclusions: Is a More Democratic Global Governance Possible?

Global governance stands accused of being unaccountable and deaf to the world's diversity of peoples and issues. The accusation is not altogether unfounded. This chapter has described a web of governance comprising multilateral institutions, private sector networks, interstate networks and coalitions, and bilateral and regional arrangements. It portrays a system in which the underlying power and hierarchy of states and the most powerful transnational corporations are unavoidable, even (or even especially) in the so-called technocratic, expert arrangements to which policy-makers seem increasingly attracted.

The alternative as some see it is to consider democratizing global governance. Political theorists have long argued that globalization or growing interdependence presents an opportunity – if not the need – to establish a more global democracy, or at the very least to enshrine human rights and some form of global redistribution as a corner-stone of global governance (Beitz, 1979; Doyle, 1997). In recent debates we see this in arguments for 'mainstreaming human rights' and for implementing a universal set of moral values – a 'law of peoples' – and a clear set of principles regarding the nature and composition of international institutions (Held, 2001).

The practical problem for advocates of global democracy lies in how such values might be implemented. Should they advocate using existing institutions such as the IMF, the World Bank and the WTO, however unfairly or unaccountably constituted, to push a further agenda of conditionality in the area of human rights? Critics argue that the institutions are not adequately legitimate. Developing countries have too little voice within them and the institutions are too unaccountable and too unrepresentative to impose further conditionality.

Morally, it has already been argued in this chapter that the case for global conditionality on human rights, environmental protection or the like casts profound questions about whose ends are being sought. To this we must add that actions to this end might produce unintended consequences which may cancel out the 'good' ends.

Practically, extending the kinds of conditionalities applied by international organizations on individual states will not work without the commitment of governments and peoples on the receiving end. This has already been learnt in the realm of economic policy. It applies even more strongly in the political and social realms.

A more modest approach to democratizing global governance starts by recognizing the limits of democracy at the international level. As elegantly argued by Robert Dahl, we should be 'wary of ceding the legitimacy of democracy to non-democratic systems' (Dahl, 1999, p. 33). The point here is that domestic political systems have a *potential* to be democratically accountable even if they are not yet so, in a way that international organizations cannot. Rather than reinforcing the power and scope of existing institutions, the more pressing question is how to make these institutions (including the informal networks) more representative of the wide range of people and values in the world and more accountable to those they most affect. There may well be some top-down steps which would assist in this.

One oft-recurring proposal for reforming global governance is to create an Economic and Social Security Council (Daws and Stewart, 2000) or 'Economic Security Council'

(UN, 2001). This proposal has had many proponents over the years (Bertrand, 1985; UNDP, 1994; Commission on Global Governance, 1995; Ul Haq, 1995; Stewart and Daws, 1996). Most recently it was reinvigorated by the Zedillo Panel which reported to the Secretary-General of the United Nations in 2001. The Panel described an Economic Security Council as a body which 'would have the same standing on international economic matters that the Security Council has with regard to peace and security'. A small, powerful Council could comprise representatives from each region as well as smaller states, using the existing five UN regional economic commissions to elect representatives (UN, 2001). This proposal would not cure the ailments of global governance discussed in this chapter. However, its recent shift into mainstream high-level discussions of global governance underscores the current preoccupations of many policy-makers and academics.

The global governance debate is focused heavily on the reform and creation of international institutions and the need for these agencies to consult and to include non-governmental organizations and 'global civil society'. Yet global governance is increasingly being undertaken in a variety of networks, coalitions and informal arrangements which lie a little further beyond the public gaze and the direct control of governments. It is these forms of governance that need sustained and focused attention, to bring to light whose interests they further and to whom they are accountable.

References

ACC (American Chemistry Council) (2001) 'Responsible care', at www.cmahq.com.

Beitz, Charles R. (1979) *Political Theory and International Relations*, Princeton: Princeton University Press.

Berger, Suzanne and Dore, Ronald P. (1996) *National Diversity and Global Capitalism*, Ithaca: Cornell University Press.

Berry, Al and Stewart, Frances (1999) 'Liberalization and globalization', in Andrew Hurrell and Ngaire Woods (eds), *Inequality, Globalization and World Politics*, Oxford: Oxford University Press.

Bertrand, Maurice (1985) 'Some reflections on reform of the United Nations', JIU/REP/85/9, Geneva: United Nations.

British Petroleum (2001) 'Human rights policy', at www.bp.org.

Charnovitz, Steve (2000) 'On constitutionalizing the WTO: a comment on Howse and Nicolaidis', at www.ksg.harvard.edu/cbg/trade/charnovitz.htm.

Chesterman, Simon (2001) *Just War or Just Peace? Humanitarian Intervention and International Law*, Oxford: Oxford University Press.

Commission on Global Governance (1995) *Our Global Neighbourhood*, Oxford: Oxford University Press.

CSI (US Coalition of Services Industries) (2001) Documentation at www.uscsi.org.

Dahl, Robert A. (1999) 'Can international organizations be democratic?', in Ian Shapiro and Casiano Hacker-Cordon (eds), *Democracy's Edges*, Cambridge: Cambridge University Press.

Daws, Sam and Stewart, Frances (2000) *Global Challenges: An Economic and Social Security Council at the United Nations*, London: Christian Aid.

De Beers (2000) *De Beers Annual Report 2000*, London: De Beers.

De Gregorio, Jose, Eichengreen, Barry, Takatoshi Ito and Wyplosz, Charles (1999) *An Independent and Accountable IMF*, International Center for Monetary and Banking Studies (Geneva) and the Centre for Economic Policy Research (London), Oxford: UK Information Press.

Dobson, Wendy and Jacquet, Pierre (1998) *Financial Services Liberalization in the WTO*, Washington DC: Institute for International Economics.

Doyle, Michael (1997) *New Thinking in International Relations Theory*, Boulder: Westview Press.

Eatwell, John (2000) *Global Finance at Risk: The Case for International Regulation*, New York: New Press.

Fitzgerald, E. V. K. (2000) 'International capital market failure and the least developed countries', background paper for the UNCTAD *Least Developed Countries Report 2000*.

FLG (Financial Leaders Group) (2001) Documentation, membership and description at www.uscsi.org/groups/finLeader.htm.

Ford Foundation (2001) Emerging Markets Eminent Persons Group Report on International Financial Architecture, Ford Foundation, Seoul and Oxford.

FSF (Financial Stability Forum) (2001) Documentation at www.fsforum.org.

Gereffi, Gary and Korzeniewicz, Miguel (eds) (1994) *Commodity Chains and Global Capitalism*, Westport, Conn.: Greenwood Press.

Held, David (2001) 'The law of peoples', MS, London School of Economics, London.

Howse, Robert and Nicolaidis, Kalypso (2000) 'Legitimacy and global governance: why constitutionalizing the WTO is a step too far', in Roger Porter et al. (eds), *Efficiency, Equity and Legitimacy: The Multilateral Trading System at the Millennium*, Washington DC: Brookings Institution Press.

Human Rights Watch (1999) *Human Rights Watch World Report 1999*, at www.hrw.org.

ICANN (Internet Corporation for Assigned Names and Numbers) (2001) At www.icann.org.

ICC (International Chamber of Commerce) (2001) Description and documentation at www.iccwbo.org/home/intro_icc/introducing_icc.asp.

IFIAC (International Financial Institutions Advisory Commission) (2000) Final Report and transcripts of meetings and hearings, Washington DC, 2000: http: //phantom-x.gsia.cmu.edu/IFIAC.

IFSL (International Financial Services, London) (2001) Documentation at www.bi.org.uk.

IMF (1997) *Good Governance: The IMF's Role*, Washington DC: International Monetary Fund.

IMF (1998) 'External evaluation of the ESAF', Report by a Group of Independent Experts, Washington DC: International Monetary Fund.

IMF (2000) *A Guide to Progress in Strengthening the Architecture of the International Financial System*, Washington DC: International Monetary Fund.

Keohane, Robert O. (1984) *After Hegemony: Cooperation and Discord in the World Political Economy*, Princeton: Princeton University Press.

Keohane, Robert O. and Milner, Helen V. (1996) *Internationalization and Domestic Politics*, Cambridge: Cambridge University Press.

Keohane, Robert O. and Nye, Joseph S. (2000) 'Introduction', in Joseph S. Nye and John D. Donahue (eds), *Governance in a Globalizing World*, Washington DC: Brookings Institution.

Kohler-Koch, Beate (1999) 'Europe in search of legitimate governance', *ARENA Working Papers WP 99/27* (www.arena.uio.no/publications).

Krasner, Stephen (ed.) (1983) *International Regimes*, Ithaca: Cornell University Press.

Krasner, Stephen (1985) *Structural Conflict: The Third World against Global Liberalism*, Berkeley: University of California Press.

Lessig, Lawrence (1999) *Code and Other Laws of Cyberspace*, New York: Basic Books.

Martinez, Leonardo (2001) 'Setting the rules for global business: the political economy of accounting standards', M.Phil. thesis, University of Oxford.

Mistry, Percy (1998) 'The challenges of financial globalisation', in Jan Joost Teunissen (ed.), *The Policy Challenges of Global Financial Integration*, The Hague: Forum on Debt and Development.

Petersmann, Ernst-Ulrich (1995) 'The transformation of the world trading system through the 1994 agreement establishing the World Trade Organization', *European Journal of International Law*, 6, no. 2, pp. 161–221.

Prodi, Romano (1999) Speech to the European Parliament as President-Designate of the European Commission, 21 July.

Raffer, Kunibert (1993) 'What's good for the United States must be good for the world: advocating an international Chapter 9 Insolvency', in Bruno Kreisky (ed.), *From Cancún to Vienna: International Development in a New World*, Vienna: Forum for International Dialogue.

Rivlin, Benjamin (1996) 'UN reform from the standpoint of the United States', UN University Lectures Series no. 11, United Nations University, Tokyo.

Robertson D. (2000) 'Civil society and the WTO', *World Economy*, 23, no. 9, pp. 1119–35.

Rodrik, Dani (1997) *Has Globalization Gone Too Far?* Washington DC: Institute for International Economics.

Ruggie, John Gerard (1996) *Winning the Peace: America and World Order in the New Era*, New York; Columbia University Press.

Shell (Royal Dutch/Shell) (2001) 'Human rights policy', at www.shell.org.

Stewart, Frances and Daws, Sam (1996) *Global Challenges: The Case for a United Nations Economic and Social Security Council*, London: Christian Aid.

Streeten, Paul (2001) *Globalisation: Threat or Opportunity?* Copenhagen: Copenhagen Business School Press.

Tussie, Diana and Woods, Ngaire (2000) 'Trade, regionalism and the threat to multilateralism', in Ngaire Woods (ed.), *The Political Economy of Globalization*, Basingstoke: Macmillan.

Ul Haq, Mahbub (1995) *The UN and the Bretton Woods Institutions: New Challenges for the Twenty-First Century*, London: Macmillan.

UN (2001) 'Technical report of the high-level panel on Financing for Development', United Nations, 28 June.

UN Global Compact (2001) 'Updates', at www.unglobalcompact.org.

UNDP (1994) *Human Development Report 1994*, New York: United Nations Development Programme.

USCNS (US Commission on National Security in the Twenty-First Century) (1999) 'New world coming: major themes and implications', Phase 1 Report on the Emerging Global Security Environment for the First Quarter of the Twenty-First Century, 15 Sept.

USTR (United States Trade Representative) (2000) The US–Jordan Free Trade Agreement, Washington DC, 24 Oct. 2000 and at www.ustr.gov/regions/eu-med/middleeast/US-JordanFTA.shtml.

USTR (United States Trade Representative) (2001) The FTAA and FTAA Negotiating Group in Intellectual Property: Public Summary of US Position, Washington DC, 17 Jan., and at www.ustr.gov.

Wood, Adrian (1994) *North–South Trade, Employment and Inequality*, Oxford: Clarendon Press.

Wood, Michael (1996) 'Security Council: procedural developments', *International and Comparative Law Quarterly,* 45, pp. 150–61.

Woods, Ngaire (1999) 'Good governance in international organizations', *Global Governance*, 5, pp. 39–61.

Woods, Ngaire (2001) 'Making the IMF and the World Bank more accountable', *International Affairs*, 77, no. 1, pp. 83–100.

Woods, Ngaire and Narlikar, Amrita (2001) 'Governance and the limits of accountability: the WTO, the IMF and the World Bank', *International Social Science Journal*, 170, pp. 569–83.

World Bank (1989) *Sub-Saharan Africa: From Crisis to Sustainable Growth*, Washington DC: World Bank.

World Bank (1992) *Governance and Development*, Washington DC: World Bank.

World Bank (1994) *Governance: The World Bank's Experience*,Washington DC: World Bank.

World Bank (1996) *The World Bank Participation Source Book*, Washington DC: World Bank.

World Bank (1999) *Annual Review of Development Effectiveness*, Washington DC: World Bank.

World Commission on Dams (2000) *Dams and Development: A New Framework for Decision-Making*, World Commission on Dams, 16 Nov., www.dams.org.

World Diamond Council (2001) 'About WDC', at www.worlddiamondcouncil.com.

WTO (1996) 'Guidelines for Arrangements with Non-governmental decisions', adopted by the General Council on 18 July, WT/L/162, World Trade Organization, Geneva.

2
Mapping Global Governance
Mathias Koenig-Archibugi

This chapter represents an attempt to grasp the complex structure of contemporary global governance. The first section focuses on the demand for governance at the global level and suggests a framework for looking at its sources. The second section deals with the supply side and suggests a taxonomy of global governance arrangements. The third section looks at the interplay between these arrangements in the global arena.

While the chapter aims to offer an overall picture of its subject-matter, its scope is limited in at least two ways. First, attention is restricted to structures and processes that are 'global' (transcontinental) in scale. Second, the historical dimension of global governance is largely neglected. In other words, no attempt is made to show how its objects have changed in response to changing circumstances and how they evolved or proliferated in the context of wider 'global transformations'.[1]

The Demand for Global Governance

The best starting point for examining the demand side of global governance is still the state. The state, as an institutional form, emerged as the winner of a long competition between different ways to organize political authority (Spruyt, 1994; Philpott, 1999). First in Europe and later in most of the world, the sovereign state prevailed over institutional alternatives such as feudalism, theocracy, empire, city-states and tribes. It succeeded in securing a near monopoly of the legitimate use of violence and expanded its activity into most social spheres, such as education and income support. In short, states became and still are the main providers of governance services to societies.

The expansion of state activities has been accompanied by the development of expectations: in the contemporary world, states are expected to perform a range of functions for the benefit of their populations and their legitimacy can be questioned if they do not. Some of these tasks are considered mandatory regardless of contingent factors such as cultural tradition and level of economic development.

Broadly speaking, the core state functions include the containment of physical violence among citizens, defence against external military threats, relief from and protection against natural and impersonal threats (such as epidemics, earthquakes and floods), provision of mass education, poverty relief, and the promotion of economic prosperity by building infrastructures, securing property rights and other measures.[2] More fundamentally, states are required to respect basic human rights while carrying out their activities.[3]

The core tasks of states are codified in international declarations and conventions and/or derive from universalistic cultural models that constitute the 'script of modernity': 'such models are quite pervasive at the world level, with a considerable amount of consensus on the nature and value of such matters as citizen and human rights, the natural world and its scientific investigation, socioeconomic development, and education' (Meyer et al., 1997, p. 148).

Whatever the expectations laid on them, governments often fail to perform those functions. It is possible to distinguish three general reasons for this failure. The first reason is the presence of external effects: governments cannot perform certain tasks adequately because of the interference of factors originating outside their jurisdiction. Since in many cases external effects are reciprocal (if not symmetrical), it is appropriate to speak of interdependence. The second reason is resource deficiency: governments fail because their material, organizational or epistemic resources are not sufficient to perform adequately particular functions. The third reason is unwillingness: governments have no interest in carrying out specific functions for their populations or significant sectors of them, or do not perceive the existence of a problem. Interdependence and resource deficiency are problems of capacity, while unwillingness is a problem of motivation. Of course, particular instances of state failure can stem from a combination of causes.

Table 2.1 delineates different situations characterized by the presence or absence of interdependence, resource deficiency and unwillingness, shows the main governance problems arising from these different combinations, and indicates the tasks that governance arrangements beyond the state are called to perform.

In the first situation shown in table 2.1, governments are both able and willing to perform certain functions and therefore no need for global governance arises. For instance, most governments in the world are able to prevent street crime from escalating into chaos.

In the second case, interdependence – more precisely, the perception of interdependence – creates incentives for governments and other actors to coordinate their policies, which they have the ability to implement in their respective spheres of authority. Uncoordinated action might bring about or prolong a situation that is detrimental to the interests of all actors involved. Whenever a range of solutions is possible, though, coordination can be hindered by the need to select one of them (Snidal, 1985). Crucially, actors interested in coordination often disagree on which policy option should be chosen, and this might generate a serious bargaining problem. This often occurs, for instance, in the domain of technical standardization: uniform standards would be beneficial to all, but each participant in the standard-setting process prefers that everybody else adopt its own standards. In such situations, the task of global governance arrangements is to facilitate coordination by providing institutional settings where parties can exchange information and negotiate, as well as by presenting focal points to negotiators (Fearon, 1998; Martin, 1993).

In the third situation indicated in table 2.1, interdependence makes international collaboration desirable, but collaboration is unstable because the participants are tempted to cheat or exploit the efforts of others, or suspect that the other parties are prepared to cheat or exploit them. The provision of global public goods, such as reducing the emission of greenhouse gases in the atmosphere or making military personnel available to UN peacekeeping missions, is beset by free-rider problems

Table 2.1 Potential sources of state failure and the resulting demand for global governance

Interdependence	Resources	Willingness	Problem	Global governance task
absent	present	present	none	none
present	present	present	multiple equilibria	coordination, mediation
present	present	conditional	free riding	monitoring, sanctioning
absent	absent	present	resource deficiency	assistance, substitution
present	absent	present	resource deficiency with spillover effects	assistance, substitution
absent	present	absent	dysfunctional goals	persuasion, compulsion, substitution
present	present	absent	dysfunctional goals with spillover effects	persuasion, compulsion, substitution

(Kaul, Grunberg and Stern, 1999). Similarly, the conclusion and implementation of certain mutually beneficial international agreements, on issues such as arms control and trade liberalization, is problematic because of the risk of unilateral defection and the uncertainty about the other parties' true intentions (Keohane, 1984). In such situations, the principal task of global governance is to deter free riding and cheating by monitoring compliance and organizing moral and material sanctions against defectors (Martin, 1993).

In the fourth and fifth scenarios of table 2.1, the central problem is that some governments lack the resources necessary to carry out functions they would be willing to perform. In some cases, such as bringing relief to victims of famines, floods and earthquakes, other countries might not be directly affected by the problems at hand. In other cases, such as the eradication of infectious diseases and the suppression of terrorism, other countries might have a stake in the resolution of the problem, in so far as this can spill over beyond state borders. Whether interdependence is present or not, structures of global governance can contribute to problem-solving in two ways. The first is to strengthen the capacities of the underperforming government by transferring material resources and technical knowledge to it. This is generally the option preferred by other governments, which might provide aid such as capital, food, medicine, technical advice, training and police assistance. The second method is to take the place of the government and perform directly the functions it is unable to carry out adequately. This option is sometimes chosen by non-governmental organizations, which side-step governments and supply goods such as food, medical assistance and education directly to the people who need them. International public agencies tend to practise both methods, generally collaborating with governments and NGOs. In rare cases, the 'international community' takes charge of a broad range of tasks normally performed by states, as it did in Cambodia, Bosnia-Herzegovina, East Timor and Kosovo in the 1990s.

In the sixth and seventh scenarios of table 2.1, governments are unwilling to perform some or all core functions. An extreme case is that of genocidal governments, willing to eliminate physically part of their population. Less extreme examples include repressive governments that systematically violate human rights within their jurisdictions. Again, in some cases (such as human rights violations that do not generate refugee flows) people living in other countries are not directly affected, while in other cases (as with aggressive international behaviour of governments) the impact is wider. External actors tackle such situations in various ways: governments and intergovernmental organizations generally try to put pressure on the unwilling government and use deterrence, persuasion or coercion to induce it to fulfil what they consider are its responsibilities; private actors, on the other hand, often try to set up parallel mechanisms for delivering the goods that the government is unwilling to provide.[4]

State failure stemming from unwillingness is certainly the most difficult and controversial situation from the point of view of global governance. It involves a genuine disagreement about the duties of states, both towards their own population and towards other states and societies, or a serious difference in problem perception. Since no world government exists, it is not clear who is entitled to resolve the conflicts arising from such disagreements. On the one hand, in fact, the United Nations provides a forum in which an embryonic global will-formation process can take place, and several declarations and conventions adopted in that context define how governments are expected to behave in a number of important areas. On the other hand, the principle of sovereignty and its corollary, the prohibition of intervention in the domestic affairs of other states, represent substantial hurdles in the way of imposing the respect of externally determined behavioural standards on recalcitrant governments.

During the last decade of the twentieth century, however, 'sovereignty increasingly came to be seen as conferring on states the obligation of being accountable to the international community' (Taylor, 1999, p. 564). This trend was evident especially with regard to humanitarian crises. The provisions of the United Nations Charter are now widely interpreted as permitting the possibility of legitimate humanitarian intervention – which can be defined as 'military intervention in a State, without the approval of the authorities, and with the purpose of preventing widespread suffering or death among the inhabitants' (Roberts, 1999, p. 35). An emerging consensus suggests that external intervention can be legitimate, provided it is conducted according to generally accepted international norms and is based on humanitarian concerns or the desire to prevent massive cross-border refugee flows (Dowty and Loescher, 1999; Wheeler, 2000). In addition, the creation of international tribunals for war crimes and crimes against humanity reflects, among other motives, the determination to deter future governments from violating the internationally recognized rights of the individuals within their reach (Ratner and Abrams, 2001). However, so far the 'international community' has been willing to enforce its standards on 'failing' states only in particular circumstances.

The Structures of Global Governance

The various forms of state failure discussed in the previous section generate a demand for governance, but there is no reason to expect that alternative structures will automatically arise to meet this demand. Governance above the level of individual states is often inadequate and in some domains it is virtually non-existent. What causes interstate governance arrangements to arise and endure is the topic of a large portion of the international relations literature; why some arrangements are more effective than others in solving the problems that led to their creation is also a topic of extensive research (Hasenclever, Mayer and Rittberger, 1997; Martin and Simmons, 1998; Young, 1999). Moreover, the causes and consequences of transnational governance and authority are attracting the attention of an increasing number of researchers (Cutler, Haufler and Porter, 1999; Higgott, Underhill and Bieler, 2000; Josselin and Wallace, 2001; Rosenau, 1997).[5] Other chapters in this volume illustrate the diversity of perspectives from which these questions have been considered. This section aims rather at providing a conceptual framework that might be useful to grasp the variety of governance structures to be found in the global system.

The term 'governance arrangement' is used here to describe how the interaction between various actors pursuing common goals is structured. Thus governance arrangements represent the link between the demand and the supply of global governance. Among the features of the contemporary system of global governance there is not only the coexistence and interaction of many governance arrangements, but also the fact that they come in a variety of institutional forms.

The attempt to classify governance arrangements involves the selection of certain core dimensions of institutional variation. This is a difficult task, since governance arrangements differ on many dimensions. These include, for instance, the use of hard or soft law, the role of technical expertise, the availability of financial resources and enforcement mechanisms, and many other details of institutional design. Which attributes are more relevant depends on the specific question asked. However, if the aim is to gain an overall vision of the forms of contemporary global governance, then three dimensions of institutional variation seem especially important. They can be called publicness, delegation and inclusiveness.

The first dimension, *publicness*, refers to the nature of the active participants in the governance arrangement. To be an active participant means to contribute to the definition of a rule or a policy, or, in other words, to be a governance-giver rather than a governance-taker. The publicness dimension involves two aspects. The first is whether the participants are governments or private actors such as firms and NGOs. Intermediate cases are public agencies that possess a degree of autonomy from national executives, such as central banks, regulatory authorities, and members of the judiciary. While traditionally executives have maintained a monopoly over the external relations of states, the growth of transgovernmental networks represents a remarkable addition to global governance. Some would argue that private actors differ too in their degree of publicness: NGOs promoting the general interest, or rather their conception of it, are not the same as profit-seeking companies.

The second aspect of the publicness dimension is the nature of the interaction: to what extent do actors with different degrees of 'publicness' collaborate within the same arrangement? While some arrangements have a homogeneous membership, others are hybrid, bringing together public and private actors. From this point of view, all governance arrangements can be located on a continuum that includes state-centred arrangements with no access for private actors, state-centred arrangements with private actor access (such as a consultative role for NGOs and business), private–public

Legislative delegation

	Low		High
Diplomacy	*Plenary organ* *unanimity ÷ majority*	*Non-plenary organ* *unanimity ÷ majority*	*Independent agencies*

Executive delegation

	Low		High
Governments		*Non-plenary organ*	*Independent agencies*

Judicial delegation

	Low		High
Diplomacy	*Mediation commissions*	*Arbitration tribunals*	*Independent courts*

Figure 2.1 Possible levels of delegation of legislative, executive and judicial powers in public governance arrangements

partnerships, private governance with public supervision, and purely private regimes without public oversight.

The second dimension, *delegation*, refers to the fact that in both public and private governance arrangements a number of functions can be performed by organizations created ad hoc.[6] However, many arrangements operate without the assistance of any organization (Young, 1994, p. 174). This dimension involves two aspects as well. The first aspect is scope: which functions are delegated to organizations? In general, three groups of functions can be delegated: rule- and policy-making (legislative delegation), policy implementation (executive delegation) and dispute resolution (judicial delegation). The second aspect is independence: within its assigned sphere of competence, how much autonomy and discretion does the agent have vis-à-vis its principals? Figure 2.1 shows several possible sites of authority in public governance arrangements and ranks the level of delegation corresponding to each.[7] Concerning legislative delegation, rule-making by a body in which not every member state is represented, such as the UN Security Council or the IMF Executive Board, means a higher level of delegation than rule-making emerging from diplomatic bargaining or plenary assemblies – but less than rule-making by independent agencies, such as the European Commission. Majority voting rules imply higher levels of delegation than unanimity.[8] When the implementation of policies is left to national administrations, delegation is lower than when this task is performed by independent agencies, such as the UN World Food Programme. In dispute resolution, delegation is very high when independent courts are able to take decisions that are binding for the parties, as provided for instance in the 1998 Treaty of Rome establishing the International Criminal Court.[9]

On the delegation dimension, the continuum extends from regimes where all policies are decided through negotiation and implemented by the participating actors themselves (as with the 1987 Montreal protocol on the protection of stratospheric ozone) to arrangements where significant legislative, executive and judicial functions are performed by autonomous supranational agencies (such as the European Union).

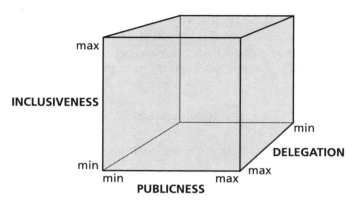

Figure 2.2 An attribute space of governance arrangements

The third dimension is *inclusiveness*. In some areas of global governance, decisional power might be shared by all or most actors affected by the resulting policies and rules, while in others it might be concentrated in very few hands. Again, this dimension has two aspects. The first is access. What share of the actors bounded by a rule or directly affected by a policy participates actively in determining its content? The second aspect is weight. How equally is influence distributed among the active participants? In the UN General Assembly, for instance, nearly all states of the world are represented and entitled to participate in drafting and voting resolutions. Voting power, moreover, is equally distributed among member states. Most countries of the world are members of the World Bank, too, but here a weighted voting system gives more power to the largest financial contributors, that is, the developed countries. In the field of banking regulation, finally, standards are set by a dozen central bankers from developed countries.

Inclusiveness is properly seen as a continuum, but regarding this dimension it might be useful to distinguish decision-making in unilateral, minilateral or multilateral contexts (Kahler, 1993).

The three dimensions of publicness, delegation and inclusiveness form an attribute space (Lazarsfeld and Barton, 1951), in which all actual or hypothetical governance arrangements can be located. Figure 2.2 represents visually this three-dimensional space. The position of any particular arrangement along the three dimensions is a matter of degree. The corners of the attribute space correspond to eight ideal-typical governance arrangements. The properties of these (empirically implausible but heuristically useful) ideal types are summarized in table 2.2.

The first two ideal types denote governance arrangements in which all governments of the world have a significant role. In global supranationalism, moreover, governments delegate to autonomous bodies substantial legislative, executive and judicial powers. If the governance of many issue areas were ever organized according to this modality, we would witness 'global government'. No such thing is in sight, however, and the governance arrangement closest to this ideal type can be found at the regional level: the European Union.

Hegemony means that governance is 'supplied' by one single public actor.[10] The hegemon might choose to delegate the management of these rules to an independent

Table 2.2   Ideal-typical governance arrangements

Governance type	Publicness	Delegation	Inclusiveness
global intergovernmentalism	max	min	max
global supranationalism	max	max	max
direct hegemony	max	min	min
indirect hegemony	max	max	min
direct global transnationalism	min	min	max
delegated global transnationalism	min	max	max
direct monopoly	min	min	min
indirect monopoly	min	max	min

agency, for instance in order to make them more acceptable to the passive participants of the regime.

Similarly, monopoly means that governance is 'supplied' by one single private actor. The monopolist might choose to administer the system through independent agencies. In the case of global transnationalism, on the other hand, all private actors affected by the regulation of a certain policy area are able to participate in decision-making, from which public agencies are excluded.

In order to illustrate the institutional variety of contemporary global governance, in the following pages I present a number of examples drawn from different regions (not corners) of the three-dimensional attribute space identified above.

Example 1: high publicness, low delegation, high inclusiveness

The international postal regime is a venerable example of an intergovernmental governance arrangement. Established in 1874, the Universal Postal Union (UPU) is the second oldest international organization after the International Telecommunications Union. Its task is to facilitate the cross-border flow of mail, which currently amounts to around 10 billion items each year, and make sure that the world remains 'one single postal territory'. For this purpose, the UPU members have agreed on a body of norms regulating the rights and duties of transit states, the protection of both mail and mail handlers, the compensation for lost or damaged items, the use of uniform technical standards, and the allocation of market shares and revenues among national postal administrations. Replacing the previous network of bilateral agreements with a multilateral regulatory regime has allowed a significant reduction of international postal rates and an increase in speed and reliability (Codding, 1964; Zacher and Sutton, 1996).

The members of the UPU are states, currently 189. They have one vote each, although generally decisions are taken by consensus. The level of delegation is low:

decisions are taken by the member states themselves in the Congress, which meets every five years. Since the 1980s, however, more regulatory power has been delegated to the Council of Administration and the Postal Operation Council, which are composed of forty elected member states. The competences of the secretariat of the Union are limited: it provides logistical support to the other organs; collects and disseminates information on postal rates, transport routes, custom regulations, and related matters; provides technical assistance to member states; maintains accounts on what member states owe each other because of transit fees and unbalanced mail flows; and mediates disputes over the interpretation of UPU regulations. No enforcement mechanisms exist within the Union, but there are not many incentives to defect from its regulations.

Example 2: high publicness, high delegation, low inclusiveness

A core governance arrangement for the management of international monetary relations is the International Monetary Fund. Before the breakdown of the Bretton Woods system in the early 1970s, the Fund's main task was to manage the regime of fixed exchange rates and provide short-term loans to countries with balance of payment difficulties. Since the 1980s, the activities of the IMF have included the close surveillance of the economic policies of the member states, the design of structural adjustment packages that combine longer-term loans and economic conditionality, the coordination of emergency rescue operations of countries hit by financial crises, and the provision of technical assistance and training to member state officials. The IMF's overall goal is to stabilize the global monetary and financial system and indirectly to promote international trade.

The members of the IMF are states and, so far, the organization has remained largely impermeable to non-state actors (O'Brien et al., 2000). While 183 states are members of the IMF and affected by its policies, the Fund is less inclusive than other international organizations (in the sense defined earlier), since the power to create and modify rules is very unequally distributed among its members. This is partly the result of formal operational rules: the voting power of each country depends on its financial contribution to the organization and therefore on its economic strength. The US and the EU member states, which between them account for approximately a tenth of the world population, together control more than half of the votes in the Fund's Executive Board. Moreover, special majority requirements on certain policy matters increase further the influence of the big contributors. During the first two decades of the IMF's life, the US held a position of clear predominance within the organization, bringing it close to the 'hegemonic' ideal type. Afterwards, the US had to share its power with the stronger European economies and Japan, but maintained a preponderant position (Kahler, 1990, pp. 94–7). Most notably, 'in the several financial crises that have afflicted the international economy, including the 1994–1995 Mexican crisis and the post-1997 East Asian crisis, the United States in effect dictated IMF responses' (Gilpin, 2001, p. 385).

In the IMF there are two major steps of delegation. First, the Board of Governors, which is composed of representatives of all member states, delegates almost all its powers to the Executive Board, which is composed of representatives of the most important contributors as well as states elected by geographic constituencies. Second, while the Executive Board is the main permanent decision-making organ of the IMF, the policies of the organization are strongly influenced by the preferences of its staff, to which important functions are delegated. The Executive Board chooses a Managing Director, who has considerable freedom to appoint the rest of the staff. The staff has wide-ranging agenda-setting power, since the Executive Board takes its decisions on the basis of recommendations presented by the staff and is unlikely to amend them. In addition, the staff can use the possession of confidential information not available to the Executive Board to influence the latter's decisions (Kafka, 1996; Southard, 1979).

Example 3: high publicness, high delegation, high inclusiveness

In 1995 the contracting parties to the General Agreement on Tariffs and Trade (GATT) created the World Trade Organization, which is now the main forum for negotiating the basic rules of global trade. The WTO bolsters the gradual liberalization of world trade by promoting the principles of non-discrimination, reciprocity, and preferential access for less developed countries.

The members of the WTO are states.[11] Each of the 142 members is entitled to an equal vote, but decisions are taken by consensus rather than by voting. While the major economic powers unquestionably have a disproportionate influence on the decisions taken within the organization, they lack the formal privileges they enjoy in the IMF and other international economic organizations. Less powerful countries, by building coalitions, can use their voting power to block decisions harmful to their interest, as became especially evident during the 1999 WTO meeting in Seattle. 'The less developed countries discovered at Seattle that they could influence the rules governing the international economy and at least prevent adoption of new rules contrary to their interests' (Gilpin, 2001, p. 386). Inclusiveness is thus relatively high.

Contrary to what happens in the IMF, none of the powers of the plenary organs (the ministerial conference and the general council) is delegated to a smaller group of member states, and the secretariat lacks both agenda-setting and enforcement powers. Nevertheless, delegation is quite high in the WTO because of its compulsory dispute settlement system. Once a member state files a complaint against another for violation of a WTO agreement, the case is examined by a panel consisting of experts chosen by the parties and, on appeal, by an appellate body composed of seven independent experts, three of whom sit on each case in rotation (Garrett and McCall Smith, 1999; Hudec, 1999). Since panel reports and appellate body decisions are adopted unless all member states agree to reject them – a very unlikely scenario – 'it will be virtually automatic that the parties are by treaty law obligated to carry out the recommendation' (Jackson, 1998, p. 167). While not realizing full judicial delegation, the system is closer to adjudication than to diplomatic bargaining (Stone Sweet, 1999). Concerning enforcement, the WTO cannot directly punish a country that has violated its rules, but it can authorize and legitimate bilateral trade sanctions.

Example 4: high publicness, low delegation, low inclusiveness

The G7 is a governance arrangement centred on the annual meetings of the political leaders of the US, Japan, Germany, France, the United Kingdom, Italy, Canada, and the European Community. Since 1998, the G7 has been complemented but not replaced by the G8 meetings, which include Russia as a full member. The summit participants generally include the chief executives (presidents or prime ministers), the finance ministers and the foreign ministers of each country, representatives of the European Community, and occasionally representatives of other states or institutions. In addition to summit meetings, today the wider G7/G8 system includes regular or ad hoc meetings among ministers (responsible for finance, trade, environment, employment, etc.), central bankers, the leaders' personal representatives, and a number of task forces, working groups and expert groups.

Through their meetings, leaders establish personal contact (side-stepping bureaucracies), exchange information and opinions, coordinate national policies, send signals to domestic constituencies, enhance the credibility of their commitments, and agree on collective action, sometimes to be implemented through other international organizations. Over the years, the G7/G8 system has dealt with a broad range of issues: macroeconomic policy coordination, international trade, energy supply, unemployment, development, debt relief, arms control, terrorism, environment, nuclear safety, human rights, AIDS, narcotic drugs, transnational crime, money laundering, post-communist transitions, nuclear non-proliferation, financial market stability, the global information society, and the reform of various international organizations, notably the United Nations, the IMF and the World Bank (Bayne, 2000; Hajnal, 1999; Putnam and Bayne, 1987).

According to some observers, 'the G7/8 is emerging as the effective centre of global governance for the new era' (Kirton, 1999, p. 65). While many of the decisions taken or instigated by the G7/G8 affect a large portion of the world population, the arrangement is intentionally designed as a club with exclusive membership rules. Delegation is non-existent: the G7/G8 has no secretariat, and governments are responsible both for setting the agenda and for fulfilling the commitments made at the meetings.

Example 5: low publicness, high delegation, high inclusiveness

Transnational commercial arbitration consists of an extensive web of institutions that allows companies to resolve business disputes without having to resort to national courts. In this system of private governance, companies entering a contractual relationship with one another agree to delegate to private judges, the arbitrators, the power to adjudicate on their claims should a dispute arise. Created in 1919, the International Chamber of Commerce, through its International Court of Arbitration, is still the main provider of arbitration services to international business. Since the late 1970s, however, the number of arbitrators has grown considerably, as arbitration itself has become a lucrative business. Today over 120 arbitration centres in various parts of the world offer services in competition with each other (Dezalay and Garth, 1996).

Many arbitrators resolve disputes by applying, among other sources, a body of customary law known as *lex mercatoria*, or law merchant. Originally, the *lex mercatoria* was developed in the Middle Ages by the transnational merchant community on the basis of their trading practices and usages. Adjudication and enforcement occurred within the merchant community itself, independently from the coercive powers of territorial lords. In the new *lex mercatoria* developed in the twentieth century, commercial practices are complemented by legal doctrines and a substantial number of standard contract clauses, codes of practice, collections of transnational commercial customs, conventions, and model laws drafted by international agencies.

Compliance is not a serious problem. About 90 per cent of ICC arbitration awards, for instance, are complied with voluntarily. Arbitral decisions can be enforced through a variety of private mechanisms: publication of a party's non-compliance, exclusion from future arbitration procedures, exclusion from the industry's professional association, and other measures that can seriously damage a company's reputation. Moreover, a convention signed in 1958 and ratified by many states makes foreign arbitral awards enforceable by national courts, and a growing number of them are prepared to accept awards referring to the *lex mercatoria* only (Medwig, 1993).

Example 6: low publicness, low delegation, low inclusiveness

For over a century, the world market for diamond gemstones has been dominated and regulated very effectively by a strictly disciplined diamond cartel. The cartel controls most of the world's diamond mines, sets production quotas, defines standards, handles all sorting of the gemstones, and determines who can buy which stones at what price (Spar, 1994). Within the cartel, one actor has overwhelming power: the De Beers Corporation. Although less than a tenth of the world's diamonds come from its South African mines, De Beers sets the rules of the diamond industry and has been able to enforce cooperation among the cartel members and suppress centrifugal inclinations. The company has contractual links with most diamond producers, which ensure its position as sole purchaser, price setter, and distributor. It controls the Central Selling Organization (also known as the Syndicate), through which over 80 per cent of the world's rough diamonds are sold. De Beers is able to impose its rules on both producers and buyers through a careful use of rewards and sanctions.

It is remarkable that not only the relations between De Beers and the selected buyers of its rough stones, but also the relations among the members of the broader community of diamond dealers (organized in the World Federation of Diamond Bourses) are governed by a complex system of rules designed to avoid the interference of state law. As Bernstein (1992) has shown in her study on the New York diamond bourse, deals are made through extralegal contracts, and disputes are settled cooperatively or, in exceptional cases, by arbitrators. Arbitration proceedings and awards are based on internal regulations and customary norms, and are kept secret unless a party fails to comply. Enforcement depends mainly on social ostracism and reputational damage, and is very effective: an arbitrator can put a dealer 'out of business almost instantaneously by hanging his picture in the clubroom of every [diamond] bourse in the world with a notice that he failed to pay his debt' (Bernstein, 1992, p. 149).

Example 7: low publicness, low delegation, high inclusiveness

The growth of economic globalization in recent decades – notably of international trade, foreign exchange transactions, foreign investment, and financial derivatives (options, futures and swaps) – has produced a dramatic increase in the number of cross-border payment transactions handled by banks. This expansion is also due to the massive increase in the personal use of credit cards and cash dispensers in foreign countries. The banks have created a global network of institutions that allow them to organize their interactions and resolve disputes without recurring to national legislation and adjudication (Frick, 1998). In particular, since the mid-1970s transnational bank transfers and some other financial transactions have been increasingly handled through the Society for Worldwide Interbank Financial Telecommunication (SWIFT). SWIFT is a private-law corporation owned by over 2,500 banks through the world, which transmits financial messages between its affiliated banks and financial institutions (approximately 7,000 in 193 countries) by means of a worldwide computerized communications network. Currently the network carries 1.2 billion messages a year. The average value of payment messages is about $5 trillion a day.

Through SWIFT and other networks, banks have developed their own technical standards and coding systems independently from national and intergovernmental regulation. The banks try to avoid intervention by governments or bodies such as the European Commission whenever possible. Participants in the SWIFT network have to comply with a number of rules, which *inter alia* aim to prevent disputes from being decided by state courts. 'Judicial contests between banks participating in the cross-border business are still an absolute exception'; moreover, 'even arbitration tribunals are turned to only in exceptional cases; in this respect as well, the banks, with their policy of sectoral-internal conflict resolution, occupy a special position among the actors in cross-border legal transactions' (Frick, 1998, pp. 96–7). Agreement based on business practices, professional standards and shared understandings is preferred to litigation and arbitration.

Example 8: low publicness, high delegation, low inclusiveness

The internet relies on a centralized domain name system (DNS) to control the routing for the vast majority of global internet traffic. Control over the DNS confers substantial power over the users and providers of internet services worldwide, for instance in relation to intellectual property issues. Since 1998, this crucial aspect of the internet is managed by the Internet Corporation for Assigned Names and Numbers (ICANN). When the US government decided that the governance of the internet's infrastructure should be privatized and left to 'industry self-regulation', ICANN took over the management of the DNS and root server system and the allocation of internet protocol numbers from US government contractors (Mueller, 1999). ICANN, a private non-profit organization, has already taken several controversial policy decisions, notably the award of new top-level domains, and created a compulsory dispute resolution mechanism to protect trademark owners.

The exercise by a private body of what are essentially public policy functions with global implications has raised serious concerns about the representativeness and accountability of its decision-making procedures (Froomkin, 2000). At the time of writing, the majority of the members of ICANN's legislating body are nominated by three 'supporting organizations', which represent mainly technical and business interests. However, the corporation's bylaws contain a formal commitment to make the decisional process more inclusive, and in 2000 the global 'At-Large' community of individual internet users was allowed to elect a limited number of ICANN directors by means of electronic voting. Currently, an intense debate is underway between those who think that ICANN's decision-making rules should privilege the most direct 'stakeholders', and those advocating the inclusion of the At-Large community of users as members in the organization (NAIS, 2001).

Intermediate cases

The preceding examples have been selected to show that there is substantial variation in contemporary global governance regarding institutional forms. However, it should be noted that some of the most interesting governance arrangements in the global system take on intermediate values on one or more dimensions of institutional variation. Authors such as Reinicke and his associates (2000), for instance, have stressed the contribution to global governance made by 'global policy networks', which combine trisectoral membership (public actors, business actors, and NGOs) and low formality.

As noted above, an arrangement displays an intermediate degree of publicness in two situations (which are not mutually exclusive): both public and private actors participate in the arrangement, or the participants are neither governments nor private actors, but public independent agencies (transgovernmental arrangement). A prominent example of the first situation is the International Labour Organization, with its distinctive tripartite structure. In the ILO each country has four votes: two are cast by its government, one by the accredited workers organization of the country, and one by the accredited employers association. Inclusiveness is high and significant powers are delegated to the International Labour Office (Bartolomei de la Cruz, von Potobsky and Swepston, 1996; Haas, 1964). Another case of hybrid membership is the International Organization for Standardization (ISO), which has developed highly influential technical and environmental standards that have been accepted by firms, governments and international organizations worldwide. Its members are the standards-setting bodies of 117 countries, of which around half are government departments, a third are mixed private–public bodies themselves, and the remaining are strictly private organizations (Clapp, 1998).

An important example of the second situation (collaboration between national public agencies other than governments) is the Basel Committee on Banking Supervision. Created in 1974, it consists of representatives of twelve central banks that oversee the activities of the world's most important financial markets. The Basel Committee has no formal constitution and no staff or facilities of its own: delegation is therefore non-existent. It is an exclusive club, which agrees on rules for the banking industry that are also adopted in many countries not represented in the committee, and that affect worldwide financial stability. Another, more inclusive, example is the International Organization of Securities Commissions (IOSCO), which consists of representatives of over a hundred security regulators from around the world, covering 85 per cent of the world's capital markets (Zaring, 1998).

Many governance arrangements can also be found at intermediate locations on the delegation continuum. An example of moderate delegation is the Chemical Weapons Convention, which was signed by 130 states and became operative in 1997. Contrary to most arms control agreements, CWC provides for a relatively strong supervisory body, the Organization for the Prohibition of Chemical Weapons, which consists of a plenary congress of member states, an executive council, and a technical secretariat with around 200 inspectors (Bothe, Ronzitti and Rosas, 1998).

Complex Architectures of Governance

In the previous section, for the sake of clarity, various types of governance arrangements have been examined in isolation from each other. This method is useful to shed light on the institutional diversity of contemporary global governance, but ignores its intertwined pattern. In reality, governance arrangements rarely operate in a vacuum; more often they interact with other arrangements in complex ways. Oran R. Young (1999, pp. 163–88) has presented a framework for studying the interplay among international regimes that is useful for understanding global governance in general. According to Young, institutional linkages can take four forms: embedded regimes, nested regimes, clustered regimes, and overlapping regimes. Young does not consider his list necessarily exhaustive, and in fact a fifth type of interplay is suggested here: institutional competition.

Embedded arrangements   The creation and operation of many arrangements depends on the existence of a broader set of constitutive principles and norms that predetermine who the potential members are and the basic rules of their interaction. Most intergovernmental regimes are 'predicated on an understanding of international society as made up of territorial states possessing exclusive authority over their own domestic affairs, enjoying sovereign equality in their dealing with one another, and refusing to be bound by rules of the game to which they have not consented explicitly' (Young, 1999, pp. 165–6). In the Middle Ages, the *lex mercatoria* was embedded in the transnational community of merchants. In the future, individual private governance arrangements might be seen as components of a global civil society based on distinctive rules and practices (Anheier, Glasius and Kaldor, 2001; Wapner, 1997).

Nested arrangements   Frequently, specific governance arrangements are created within, or subsequently brought under, more comprehensive arrangements that deal with the same set of issues at a more general level. A very visible example of nesting is the relationship between the United Nations – essentially an all-purpose political framework – and the large number of organs and programmes operating under that umbrella, such as the UN Development Programme, the UN High Commissioner for Refugees, the UN Environmental Programme and UNICEF. In addition, a number of organizations are formally nested in the UN system as 'specialized agencies' (but in reality they are largely autonomous from the central UN organs): UNESCO, the World Health Organization, the Food and Agriculture Organization, the Universal Postal Union, the International Labour Organization, the IMF, the World Bank, and others. A different example of 'nesting' is the hierarchical relationship between the WTO and the Asia-Pacific Economic Cooperation grouping (APEC), where the former sets the boundaries of permissible liberalization among the members of the latter (Aggarwal, 1998, p. 6).

Clustered arrangements   It often occurs that several governance arrangements are linked in a non-hierarchical fashion to increase their problem-solving capacity. For instance, in global finance a growing number of conglomerates is involved in various kinds of financial services (bank lending, securities, derivatives, insurance) and these new developments have induced the Basel Committee on Banking Supervision, IOSCO and the International Association of Insurance Supervisors to form the Joint Forum on Financial Conglomerates, with the aim of developing a comprehensive approach to the regulation of those entities (Slaughter, 2000, p. 187). Meanwhile, IOSCO is working with the private International Accounting Standards Committee on the formulation of common accounting standards for securities firms (Braithwaite and Drahos, 2000, p. 155).

An example of clustering in the public health field is the fight against malaria, a disease that kills 1 million people each year. In 1998, the World Health Organization, UNICEF, the World Bank and the UN Development Programme decided to unite their efforts and launched the Roll Back Malaria initiative (RBM). In turn, the members of RBM have joined other public and private actors – such as the International Federation of Pharmaceutical Manufacturers Associations, the Global Forum for Health Research, the Rockefeller Foundation, and the governments of the Netherlands, Switzerland and the UK – in a non-profit business venture (Medicines for Malaria) aimed at the development of new and affordable drugs (Reinicke et al. 2000). These initiatives are instances of a proliferation of 'networks of networks' (Slaughter, 2000, p. 186) at the global level.

Overlapping arrangements   Sometimes a governance arrangement has a significant impact on the functioning of another arrangement, although they were formed for different purposes and their intersection was not intended by their creators (Young, 1999, p. 170). For instance, several multilateral environmental agreements (such as the Basel Convention on hazardous waste, the Convention on International Trade in Endangered Species, and the Montreal Protocol on ozone-depleting substances) include the possibility of trade restrictions, because the trade itself damages the environment and/or because trade sanctions can be useful as enforcement mechanisms. Yet these trade restrictions are in tension with the WTO rules, which do not provide for discrimination based on participation in or compliance with environmental accords (Brack, 1999). Another example of overlapping is the intersection between the international whales regime, which is functionally very specific but whose geographical scope is encompassing, and the regime created by the Convention on the Conservation of Antarctic Marine Living Resources, which is functionally broader but delimited to a particular portion of the world's oceans (Young, 1999, pp. 171–2; Vogler, 2000).

Competing arrangements   Institutional competition could be added to Young's list as a distinct form of institutional interplay. For instance, considering that the GATT was too biased in favour of the developed countries, the G77 developing countries established the UN Conference on Trade and Development (UNCTAD) as a competing forum in which their concerns would receive more attention (Braithwaite and Drahos, 2000, pp. 194–5). Another example is the conflict in the mid-1970s between the supporters of the IMF and those of the OECD over the question of which organization should be responsible for providing financial assistance to Western countries with balance-of-payment difficulties after the first oil shock (Cohen, 1998).

Many cases of institutional competition occur between private and public arrangements. The main function of transnational commercial arbitration, considered above, is the avoidance of national legal systems and courts. Frequently, business actors engage in transnational self-regulation in order to avoid regulation by intergovernmental agreements (Braithwaite and Drahos, 2000). An instance of what might be called 'preventive self-regulation' is the Code on Pharmaceutical Marketing Practices, which was launched by the International Federation of Pharmaceutical Manufacturers Associations to prevent the adoption of stricter regulation of drug promotion by the World Health Organization and other international bodies (Ronit and Schneider, 1999, pp. 251–5).

Conclusion

This chapter has shown that contemporary global governance is characterized by a high degree of diversity and complexity. Governance arrangements can take public, private, or hybrid forms. They can involve substantial delegation of functions or reflect the desire not to create and empower independent bodies. They can involve many of the stakeholders in the decision-making process or convey the overwhelming power of a few. Furthermore, the interplay among distinct governance arrangements is also remarkably diverse, as the modalities of interaction range widely, from symbiosis to rivalry. The heterogeneous and at times contradictory character of global governance presents a challenge to any attempt to understand its operation and evolution in theoretical terms.

Many scholars of global governance are concerned with the possibilities and conditions of its improvement. Some focus on the capacity of governance arrangements to solve the problems that led to their creation, and ask which institutional designs are more conducive to effectiveness (Miles et al., 2001). Others stress the need to strengthen the mechanisms for participation and accountability in global policy-making, and explore ways to increase the 'congruence' between the input and the output sides of global governance, that is, those who are entitled to participate in decision-making and those who are affected by the decisions taken (Held, 1995; Archibugi, Held and Köhler, 1998). Grasping the multidimensional and intertwined nature of existing arrangements, and in particular the elusive role of private authority, is an important step towards the conception and construction of institutions capable of simultaneously attaining these crucial goals: improving the performance of global governance and increasing its public accountability.

Appendix

Figure 2.3 overleaf maps the organizational infrastructure of global governance. It includes a number of formal intergovernmental and transnational organizations operating at the global level (not included are corporations and regimes not supported by organizations).

Of course, the drawing of a map, in this as in other domains, is never a neutral process. A first contentious decision concerns what to put at the centre of the map. This problem is solved here by adopting a consciously UN-centred perspective. A second major problem is to select which specific organizations should be included. This task is far from easy, considering that the Union of International Associations has collected information on 5,244 intergovernmental and 25,504 international non-governmental organizations, of which many have a global reach (UIA, 2001). Thus the following graph reflects a rather personal assessment of the importance or exemplary character of the organizations, especially with regard to the outer zone of the map.

Notes

I wish to thank David Held, Tony McGrew and Daniele Archibugi for their helpful comments.

1   On these aspects see Held et al., 1999, and Murphy, 1994.
2   To be sure, more functions can be added to this list, but they are likely to be more controversial, both within and between different regions of the world. For instance, the African Charter on Human and Peoples' Rights (Article 17.3) states that 'The promotion and protection of morals and traditional values recognized by the community shall be the duty of the State.'
3   While the discussion in this chapter focuses on the services that governments are expected to provide to their own citizens, it is widely held that governments also have obligations towards the citizens of other countries. The prescribed conduct can be omissive (e.g. the prohibition to wage a war of aggression) or, more controversially, commissive (e.g. the obligation to help populations hit by famines and natural disasters).
4   For simplicity, table 2.1 does not depict all possible situations, since a government might be unable *and* unwilling to perform a certain task (and in turn this might or might not affect other countries). In those cases, global governance would require a mixture of persuasion/compulsion and assistance/substitution.
5   'Transnational' refers to relations and arrangements between private actors that cross state borders and for which governments do not act as intermediaries or gatekeepers (Keohane and Nye, 1972; Risse-Kappen, 1995). 'Transgovernmental' refers to cross-border contacts between governmental agencies other than cabinets and foreign ministries (Keohane and Nye, 1974; Slaughter, 2000).
6   Abbott and Snidal (1998) have identified several reasons why states create international organizations and delegate functions to them. First, states can benefit from centralization: international organizations facilitate bargaining between states and can manage operational activities more efficiently as a result of economies of scale. Other benefits stem from the

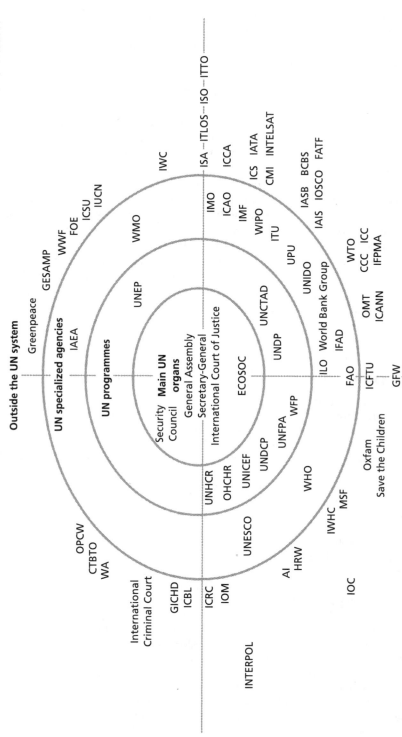

SECURITY

ENVIRONMENT

ECONOMY

HUMAN WELFARE

Outside the UN system

UN specialized agencies

UN programmes

Main UN organs

Security Council
General Assembly
Secretary-General
International Court of Justice
ECOSOC

IWC

ISA — ITLOS — ISO — ITTO

ICCA
ICS   IATA
CMI INTELSAT

IMO
ICAO
IMF
WIPO
ITU
UPU
UNIDO
World Bank Group
IFAD
ICFTU
GFW

IASB BCBS
IAIS IOSCO FATF

WTO
CCC ICC
IFPMA

OMT
ICANN

ILO

FAO

UNCTAD

UNDP

UNEP

WMO

Greenpeace
GESAMP
WWF
FOE
ICSU
IUCN
IAEA

OPCW
CTBTO
WA
International
Criminal Court
GICHD
ICBL
ICRC
IOM

INTERPOL

UNESCO

AI
HRW
IWHC
MSF

IOC

WHO

UNHCR
OHCHR
UNICEF
UNDCP
UNFPA
WFP

Oxfam
Save the Children

Key to abbreviations

AI	Amnesty International
BCBS	Basel Committee on Banking Supervision
CCC	Customs Cooperation Council
CMI	Comité Maritime International
CTBTO	Comprehensive Nuclear-Test-Ban Treaty Organization (not yet operational)
ECOSOC	UN Economic and Social Council
FAO	Food and Agriculture Organization
FATF	Financial Action Task Force
FOE	Friends of the Earth
GESAMP	Joint Group of Experts on the Scientific Aspects of Marine Environmental Protection
GFW	Global Fund for Women
GICHD	Geneva International Centre for Humanitarian Demining
HRW	Human Rights Watch
IAEA	International Atomic Energy Agency
IAIS	International Association of Insurance Supervisors
IASB	International Accounting Standards Board
IATA	International Association of Transport Airlines
ICANN	Internet Corporation for Assigned Names and Numbers
ICAO	International Civil Aviation Organization
ICBL	International Campaign to Ban Landmines
ICC	International Chamber of Commerce
ICCA	International Council of Chemical Associations
ICFTU	International Confederation of Free Trade Unions
ICRC	International Committee of the Red Cross
ICS	International Chamber of Shipping
ICSU	International Council for Science
IFAD	International Fund for Agricultural Development
IFPMA	International Federation of Pharmaceutical Manufacturers Associations
ILO	International Labour Organization
IMF	International Monetary Fund
IMO	International Maritime Organization
INTELSAT	International Telecommunications Satellites Organization
INTERPOL	International Criminal Police Organization
IOC	International Olympic Committee
IOM	International Organization for Migration
IOSCO	International Organization of Securities Commissions
ISA	International Seabed Authority
ISO	International Organization for Standardization
ITLOS	International Tribunal for the Law of the Sea
ITO	International Tropical Timber Organization
ITU	International Telecommunication Union
IUCN	World Conservation Union
IWC	International Whaling Commission
IWHC	International Women's Health Coalition
MSF	Médecins Sans Frontières
OHCHR	Office of the High Commissioner for Human Rights
OMT	World Tourism Organization
OPCW	Organization for the Prohibition of Chemical Weapons
UNCTAD	UN Conference on Trade and Development
UNDCP	UN Drug Control Programme
UNDP	UN Development Programme
UNEP	UN Environment Programme
UNESCO	UN Educational, Scientific and Cultural Organization
UNFPA	UN Population Fund
UNHCR	UN High Commissioner for Refugees
UNICEF	UN Children's Fund
UNIDO	UN Industrial Development Organization
UPU	Universal Postal Union
WA	Wassenaar Arrangement on Export Controls for Conventional Arms and Dual-Use Goods and Technologies
WFP	World Food Programme
WHO	World Health Organization
WIPO	World Intellectual Property Organization
WMO	World Meteorological Organization
WTO	World Trade Organization
WWF	Worldwide Fund for Nature

Figure 2.3 The organizational infrastructure of global governance: a UN-centric view

independence of international organizations: these can identify problems and possible solutions, monitor the behaviour of states, legitimize international policies, provide impartial information, act as trustees, distribute scarce resources in a 'technical' way, arbitrate between competing claims, and promote the values and norms of the 'international community'. This list is not exhaustive. For instance, national executives might be willing to delegate functions in order to increase their policy influence vis-à-vis other domestic actors (Moravcsik, 1994) or to make it more difficult for future governments to reverse policy decisions made by the present government (Moravcsik, 1998b).

7   On the conceptualization of delegation see also Abbott et al. (2000, pp. 415–18).

8   Strictly speaking, majority voting is a manifestation of sovereignty pooling rather than sovereignty delegation (Moravcsik, 1998a, p. 67), but here delegation is understood broadly and includes both situations.

9   Keohane, Moravcsik and Slaughter (2000) discuss various forms of international and transnational dispute resolution mechanisms.

10   This use of the word hegemony is close to that of Keohane and Nye (2001, p. 38), defining hegemony as a situation in which 'one state is powerful enough to maintain the essential rules governing interstate relations, and willing to do so. In addition to its role in maintaining a regime, such a state can abrogate existing rules, prevent the adoption of rules that it opposes, or play the dominant role in constructing new rules.'

11   However, it can be argued that the WTO has a lesser degree of publicness than the IMF, because, 'although states retain formal gatekeeping authority in the GATT/WTO system, they often have incentives to open the gates, letting actors in civil society set much of the agenda' (Keohane et al., 2000, p. 486).

References

Abbott, Kenneth W. and Snidal, Duncan (1998) 'Why states act through formal international organizations', *Journal of Conflict Resolution*, 42, pp. 3–32.

Abbott, Kenneth W., Keohane, Robert O., Moravcsik, Andrew, Slaughter, Anne-Marie and Snidal, Duncan (2000) 'The concept of legalization', *International Organization*, 54, pp. 401–19.

Aggarwal, Vinod K. (1998) 'Reconciling multiple institutions: bargaining, linkages, and nesting', in Vinod K. Aggarwal (ed.), *Institutional Designs for a Complex World: Bargaining, Linkages, and Nesting*, Ithaca: Cornell University Press.

Anheier, Helmut, Glasius, Marlies and Kaldor, Mary (eds) (2001) *Global Civil Society Yearbook 2001*, Oxford: Oxford University Press.

Archibugi, Daniele, Held, David and Köhler, Martin (eds) (1998) *Re-imagining Political Community: Studies in Cosmopolitan Democracy*, Cambridge: Polity.

Bartolomei de la Cruz, Héctor, von Potobsky, Geraldo and Swepston, Lee (1996) *The International Labor Organization: The International Standards System and Basic Human Rights*, Boulder: Westview Press.

Bayne, Nicholas (2000) *Hanging In There: The G7 and G8 Summit in Maturity and Renewal*, Aldershot: Ashgate.

Bernstein, Lisa (1992) 'Opting out of the legal system: extralegal contractual relations in the diamond industry', *Journal of Legal Studies*, 21, pp. 115–57.

Bothe, Michael, Ronzitti, Natalino and Rosas, Allan (eds) (1998) *The New Chemical Weapons Convention: Implementation and Prospects*, The Hague: Kluwer Law International.

Brack, Duncan (1999) 'International trade and the environment', in Brian Hocking and Steven McGuire (eds), *Trade Politics: International, Domestic and Regional Perspectives*, London and New York: Routledge.

Braithwaite, John and Drahos, Peter (2000) *Global Business Regulation*, Cambridge: Cambridge University Press.

Clapp, Jennifer (1998) 'The privatization of global environmental governance: ISO 14000 and the developing world', *Global Governance*, 4, pp. 295–316.

Codding, George A. Jr (1964) *The Universal Postal Union: Coordinator of the International Mails*, New York: New York University Press.

Cohen, Benjamin J. (1998) 'When giants clash: the OECD Financial Support Fund and the IMF', in Vinod K. Aggarwal (ed.), *Institutional Designs for a Complex World: Bargaining, Linkages, and Nesting*, Ithaca: Cornell University Press.

Cutler, A. Claire, Haufler, Virginia and Porter, Tony (eds) (1999) *Private Authority and International Affairs*, Albany: State University of New York Press.

Dezalay, Yves and Garth, Bryant G. (1996) *Dealing in Virtue: International Commercial Arbitration and the Construction of a Transnational Legal Order*, Chicago: University of Chicago Press.

Dowty, Alan and Loescher, Gil (1999) 'Changing norms in international responses to domestic disorder', in Raimo Väyrynen (ed.), *Globalization and Global Governance*, Lanham: Rowman and Littlefield.

Fearon, James D. (1998) 'Bargaining, enforcement, and international cooperation', *International Organization*, 52, pp. 269–305.

Frick, Klaus (1998) 'Third cultures versus regulators: cross-border legal relations of banks', in Volkmar Gessner and Ali Cem Budak (eds), *Emerging Legal Certainty: Empirical Studies on the Globalization of Law*, Aldershot: Ashgate.

Froomkin, A. Michael (2000) 'Wrong turn in cyberspace: using ICANN to route around the APA and the constitution', *Duke Law Journal*, 50, pp. 17–184.

Garrett, Geoffrey and McCall Smith, James (1999) 'The politics of WTO dispute settlement', Leitner Working Paper 1999–05, Yale University, New Haven.

Gilpin, Robert (2001) *Global Political Economy: Understanding the International Economic Order*, Princeton: Princeton University Press.

Haas, Ernst B. (1964) *Beyond the Nation-State: Functionalism and International Organization*, Stanford: Stanford University Press.

Hajnal, Peter I. (1999) *The G7/G8 System: Evolution, Role and Documentation*, Aldershot: Ashgate.

Hasenclever, Andreas, Mayer, Peter and Rittberger, Volker (1997) *Theories of International Regimes*, Cambridge: Cambridge University Press.

Held, David (1995) *Democracy and the Global Order: From the Modern State to Cosmopolitan Governance*, Cambridge: Polity.

Held, David, McGrew, Anthony, Goldblatt, David and Perraton, Jonathan (1999) *Global Transformations: Politics, Economics and Culture*, Cambridge: Polity.

Higgott, Richard A., Underhill, Geoffrey R. D. and Bieler, Andreas (eds) (2000) *Non-state Actors and Authority in the Global System*, London and New York: Routledge.

Hudec, Robert E. (1999) 'The new WTO dispute settlement procedure', *Minnesota Journal of Global Trade*, 8, pp. 1–53.

Jackson, John H. (1998) 'Designing and implementing effective dispute settlement procedures: WTO dispute settlement, appraisal and prospects', in Anne O. Krueger (ed.), *The WTO as an International Organization*, Chicago: University of Chicago Press.

Josselin, Daphné and Wallace, William (eds) (2001) *Non-State Actors in World Politics*, Basingstoke: Palgrave.

Kafka, Alexandre (1996) 'Governance of the Fund', in G. K. Helleiner (ed.), *The International Monetary and Financial System: Developing-Country Perspectives*, Basingstoke: Macmillan.

Kahler, Miles (1990) 'The United States and the International Monetary Fund: declining influence or declining interest?', in Margaret Karns and Karen A. Mingst (eds), *The United States and Multilateral Institutions: Patterns of Changing Instrumentality and Influence*, London and New York: Routledge.

Kahler, Miles (1993) 'Multilateralism with small and large numbers', in John Gerard Ruggie (ed.), *Multilateralism Matters: The Theory and Praxis of an Institutional Form*, New York: Columbia University Press.

Kaul, Inge, Grunberg, Isabelle and Stern, Marc A. (eds) (1999) *Global Public Goods: International Cooperation in the 21st Century*, Oxford: Oxford University Press.

Keohane, Robert O. (1984) *After Hegemony: Cooperation and Discord in the World Political Economy*, Princeton: Princeton University Press.

Keohane, Robert O. and Nye, Joseph S. Jr (eds) (1972) *Transnational Relations and World Politics*, Cambridge, Mass.: Harvard University Press.

Keohane, Robert O. and Nye, Joseph S. Jr (1974) 'Transgovernmental relations and international organizations', *World Politics*, 27, pp. 39–62.

Keohane, Robert O. and Nye, Joseph S. Jr (2001) *Power and Interdependence*, 3rd edn, New York: Longman.

Keohane, Robert O., Moravcsik, Andrew and Slaughter, Anne-Marie (2000) 'Legalized dispute resolution: interstate and transnational', *International Organization*, 54, pp. 457–88.

Kirton, John J. (1999) 'Explaining G8 effectiveness', in Michael R. Hodges, John J. Kirton and Joseph P. Daniels (eds), *The G8's Role in the New Millennium*, Aldershot: Ashgate.

Lazarsfeld, Paul F. and Barton, Allen H. (1951) 'Qualitative measurement in the social sciences: classification, typologies, and indices', in Daniel Lerner and Harold D. Lasswell (eds), *The Policy Sciences*, Stanford: Stanford University Press.

Martin, Lisa L. (1993) 'The rational state choice of multilateralism', in John Gerard Ruggie (ed.), *Multilateralism Matters: The Theory and Praxis of an Institutional Form*, New York: Columbia University Press.

Martin, Lisa L. and Simmons, Beth A. (1998) 'Theories and empirical studies of international institutions', *International Organization*, 52, pp. 729–57.

Medwig, Michael T. (1993) 'The new law merchant: legal rhetoric and commercial reality', *Law and Policy in International Business*, 24.

Meyer, John W., Boli, John, Thomas, George M. and Ramirez, Francisco (1997) 'World society and the nation-state', *American Journal of Sociology*, 103, pp. 144–81.

Miles, Edward L., Underdal, Arild, Andresen, Steinar, Wettestad, Jorgen, Skjaerseth, Jon Birger and Carlin, Elaine M. (2001) *Environmental Regime Effectiveness: Confronting Theory with Evidence*, Cambridge, Mass.: MIT Press.

Moravcsik, Andrew (1994) 'Why the European Community strengthens the state: domestic politics and international cooperation', Center for European Studies Working Paper no. 52, Harvard University, Cambridge, Mass.

Moravcsik, Andrew (1998a) *The Choice for Europe: Social Purpose and State Power from Messina to Maastricht*, Ithaca: Cornell University Press.

Moravcsik, Andrew (1998b) 'The origin of human rights regimes: democratic delegation in postwar Europe', *International Organization*, 54, pp. 217–52.

Mueller, Milton (1999) 'ICANN and internet governance', *Info*, 1, pp. 497–520.

Murphy, Craig N. (1994) *International Organization and Industrial Change: Global Governance since 1850*, Cambridge: Polity.

NAIS (2001) *ICANN, Legitimacy, and the Public Voice: Making Global Participation and Representation Work*, Report of the NGO and Academic ICANN Study (NAIS), available at www.naisproject.org.

O'Brien, Robert, Goetz, Anne Marie, Scholte, Jan Aart and Williams, Marc (2000) *Contesting Global Governance: Multilateral Economic Institutions and Global Social Movements*, Cambridge: Cambridge University Press.

Philpott, Daniel (1999) 'Westphalia, authority, and international society', *Political Studies*, 47, pp. 566–89.

Putnam, Robert D. and Bayne, Nicholas (1987) *Hanging Together: Cooperation and Conflict in the Seven-Power Summits*, Cambridge, Mass.: Harvard University Press.

Ratner, Steven R. and Abrams, Jason S. (2001) *Accountability for Human Rights Atrocities in International Law: Beyond the Nuremberg Legacy*, Oxford: Oxford University Press.

Reinicke, Wolfgang H. et al. (2000) *Critical Choices: The United Nations, Networks, and the Future of Global Governance*, Ottawa: International Development Research Centre.

Risse-Kappen, Thomas (ed.) (1995) *Bringing Transnational Relations Back In: Non-State Actors, Domestic Structures, and International Institutions*, Cambridge: Cambridge University Press.

Roberts, Adam (1999) 'The role of humanitarian issues in international politics in the 1990s', *International Review of the Red Cross*, 81, pp. 19–43.

Ronit, Karsten and Schneider, Volker (1999) 'Global governance through private organizations', *Governance*, 12, pp. 243–66.

Rosenau, James N. (1997) *Along the Domestic-Foreign Frontier: Exploring Governance in a Turbulent World*, Cambridge: Cambridge University Press.

Slaughter, Anne-Marie (2000) 'Governing the global economy through government networks', in Michael Byers (ed.), *The Role of Law in International Politics*, Oxford: Oxford University Press.

Snidal, Duncan (1985) 'Coordination versus prisoners' dilemma: implications for international cooperation and regimes', *American Political Science Review*, 79, pp. 923–42.

Southard, Frank A. Jr (1979) *The Evolution of the International Monetary Fund*, Princeton: International Finance Section, Department of Economics, Princeton University.

Spar, Debora L. (1994) *The Cooperative Edge: The Internal Politics of International Cartels*, Ithaca: Cornell University Press.

Spruyt, Hendrik (1994) *The Sovereign State and its Competitors: An Analysis of Systems Change*, Princeton: Princeton University Press.

Stone Sweet, Alec (1999) 'Judicialization and the construction of governance', *Comparative Political Studies*, 32, pp. 147–84.

Taylor, Paul (1999) 'The United Nations in the 1990s: proactive cosmopolitanism and the issue of sovereignty', *Political Studies*, 47, pp. 538–65.

UIA (Union of International Associations) (2001) *Yearbook of International Organizations 2001/2002*, 5 vols, Munich: K. G. Saur Verlag.

Vogler, John (2000) *The Global Commons: Environmental and Technological Governance*, Chichester: Wiley.

Wapner, Paul (1997) 'Governance in global civil society', in Oran R. Young (ed.), *Global Governance: Drawing Insights for the Environmental Experience*, Cambridge, Mass.: MIT Press.

Wheeler, Nicholas J. (2000) *Saving Strangers: Humanitarian Intervention in International Society*, Oxford: Oxford University Press.

Young, Oran R. (1994) *International Governance: Protecting the Environment in a Stateless Society*, Ithaca: Cornell University Press.

Young, Oran R. (1999) *Governance in World Affairs*, Ithaca: Cornell University Press.

Zacher, Mark W. and Sutton, Brent A. (1996) *Governing Global Networks: International Regimes for Transportation and Communications*, Cambridge: Cambridge University Press.

Zaring, David (1998) 'International law by other means: the twilight existence of international financial regulatory institutions', *Texas International Law Journal*, 33, pp. 281–330.

3

Governance in a
New Global Order

James N. Rosenau

So dominant in contemporary consciousness is the assumption that authority must be centralized that scholars are just beginning to grapple with how decentralized authority might be understood. . . . [T]he question of how to think about a world that is becoming 'domesticated' but not centralized, about a world after 'anarchy', is one of the most important questions today facing not only students of international relations but of political theory as well.

Alexander Wendt, 1999

We live in a messy world. There are far too many people who survive on or below the poverty line. There are far too many societies paralysed by division. There is too much violence within and between countries. Terrorists are too successful. In many places there is too little water and too many overly populated, pollution-ridden cities. And, most conspicuously, there is all too little effective governance capable of ameliorating, if not resolving, these and numerous other problems that crowd high on the global agenda. Perhaps even more troubling, our generation lacks – as the above epigraph implies – the orientations necessary to sound assessments of how the authority of governance can be brought to bear on the challenges posed by the prevailing disarray.

Consequently, with the end of the Cold War and the stability inherent in the superpower rivalry, the messiness of world and domestic affairs has led to pervasive uncertainties. People are unsettled by the realization that deep changes are unfolding in every sphere of life, that events in any part of the world can have consequences for developments in every other part of the world, that the internet and other technologies have collapsed time and distance, that consequently national states and their governments are not as competent as they once were, that their sovereignty and boundaries have become increasingly porous, and that therefore the world has moved into a period of extraordinary complexity. In effect, diverse and contradictory forces have been unleashed that can be summarized in the clash between globalization, centralization and integration on the one hand, and localization, decentralization and fragmentation on the other. The clashes between these forces – what I call 'fragmegration' in order to capture the intricate links between the polarities (Rosenau, 1997, ch. 6) – underlie the many huge challenges to humankind's capacity to lessen the messiness unfolding throughout the world and intensify movement towards acceptable levels of peace and prosperity.

In short, reinforced by the collapse of time and distance, the weaknesses of states, the vast movements of people and the ever greater complexities of modern life, the question of how to infuse a modicum of order, a measure of effective authority and a potential for improving the human condition into the course of events looms as increasingly urgent. It is being asked at every level of community as fragmegrative tensions intensify and as citizens and officials alike ponder how to conduct their affairs in the face of transformative dynamics that are often bewildering and seemingly out of control.

Much of the bewilderment derives from the fast-paced dynamics of fragmegration. As suggested by linking in a single phrase the interactions between worldwide forces pressing for fragmentation and those exerting pressure for integration, fragmegrative dynamics are pervaded with contradictions and tensions. They tug people and institutions at every level of community in opposite directions, often forcing choices favouring localizing or globalizing goals. Indeed, it can be reasonably postulated that every increment of fragmentation gives rise to an increment of integration, and vice versa. This pervasiveness of fragmegrative dynamics is readily traceable in a wide variety of situations, from cultural sensitivities to inroads from abroad to fears of jobs lost through the demise of trade barriers, from linguistic distortions fostered by the Internet to environmental degradation generated by expanded productive facilities, and so on across all the situations that mark our transformative epoch. To grasp the underpinnings of modern life, in other words, there is considerable clarity to be had in viewing all its issues through fragmegrative lenses.

To proceed in this fashion, however, is not to answer the question of how to develop the order and authority needed for an improvement of the human condition. Perhaps the most frequent answer to the question is a two-word phrase that may appear to make sense, but that upon reflection can seem vague and vacuous. The phrase is 'global governance'. What does the phrase mean, one can reasonably ask? Does it refer to a central authority that can exercise control over far-flung situations on a global scale? Or is it limited to the exercise of authority in particular situations, such as environmental threats or outbreaks of widespread violence, which may be global in scope and especially dire? Or does it connote the sum of all the diverse efforts of communities at every level to move towards goals while preserving their coherence from one moment in time to the next? The ensuing pages are founded on a clear-cut response to these alternatives: global governance is a summarizing phrase for all the sites in the world where efforts to exercise authority are undertaken. It neither posits a highest authority nor anticipates that one is likely to evolve in the long run. On the contrary, it argues that an irreversible process is underway wherein authority is increasingly disaggregated, resulting in a system of global governance comprised of more and more centres of authority in every corner of the world and at every level of community.

The Concept of Global Governance

If one appreciates that widespread use of the word 'governance' is essentially a recent phenomenon – indeed, it does not exist in some languages (such as German) – it is not surprising that its wider usage has paralleled the advent of globalization. With but few exceptions, in fact, governance tends to be employed when it is modified by the adjective 'global'. Otherwise, for any scale short of the global – whether local, provincial, national or regional – 'government' is usually treated as the entity through which order is sought and goals framed and implemented. And why have 'global' and 'governance' become inextricably linked in public discourse? The answer strikes me as rather obvious: for a long time the world was described as increasingly interdependent, but only since the end of the Cold War have the dynamics of interdependence tended to have consequences that are global in scope. The problem of global warming, for example, knows no boundaries and reaches into every corner of the globe. Likewise, genocidal policies and practices in Rwanda and Kosovo have been experienced as challenges to all of humankind, as have financial crises and a growing gap between the rich and poor in developing countries. As the advent of such situations have accelerated at a seemingly ever more rapid rate, the notion has quickly spread that interdependence is characteristic of the world as a whole. Accordingly, persuaded that many problems cannot be allowed to fester and endanger the well-being of people everywhere, and eager to bring a modicum of order and direction to the uncertainties and dislocations inherent in the vast degrees of interdependence, analysts have quite naturally begun to talk of the need for global governance and the processes and structures that might foster and sustain it.

Both governance and government consist of rule systems, of steering mechanisms through which authority is exercised in order to enable systems to preserve their coherence and move towards desired goals. While the rule systems of governments can be thought of as structures, those of governance are social functions or processes that can be performed or implemented in a variety of ways at different times and places (or even at the same time) by a wide variety of organizations. To govern, whether as structure or function, is thus to exercise authority. To have authority is to be recognized as having the right to govern, to issue directives that are heeded by those encompassed by the directives. Rule systems acquire authority in a variety of ways. These range from steering mechanisms that are structures endowed with authority through constitutions, bylaws and other formally adopted instruments of rule, to those that are processes informally created through repeated practices that are regarded as authoritative even though they may not be constitutionally sanctioned. Both the formal and informal rule systems consist of what I call 'spheres of authority' (SOAs) that define the range of their capacity to generate compliance on the part of those persons towards whom their directives are issued. Compliance, in other words, is the key to ascertaining the presence of an SOA.

Viewed in terms of their compliance-generating capacities, the steering mechanisms that undertake governance may be just as effective (or ineffective) as those of governments. While governments generate compliance through formal prerogatives such as sovereignty and constitutional legitimacy, the effectiveness of governance rule systems derives from traditional norms and habits, informal agreements, shared premises, and a host of other practices that lead people to comply with their directives. Thus, as the demand for governance increases with the proliferation of complex interdependencies, rule systems can be found in non-governmental organizations, corporations, professional societies, business associations, advocacy groups, and many other types of collectivities that are not considered to be governments.

It follows that world affairs can be conceptualized as governed through a bifurcated system – what can be called the two worlds of world politics – one an interstate system of states and their national governments that has long dominated the course of events, and the other a multicentric system of diverse types of other collectivities that has lately emerged as a rival source of authority with actors that sometimes cooperate with, often compete with, and endlessly interact with the state-centric system (Rosenau, 1990, ch. 10). Viewed in the context of proliferating centres of authority, the global stage is thus dense with actors, large and small, formal and informal, economic and social, political and cultural, national and transnational, international and subnational, aggressive and peaceful, liberal and authoritarian, who collectively form a highly complex system of global governance.

To repeat, despite the vast differences among them, what the disparate collectivities in the two worlds of world politics have in common is that they all sustain rule systems that range across the concerns of their members and that constitute the boundaries of their SOAs (Rosenau, forthcoming, ch. 13). When collectivities in the two worlds cooperate across the divide between them, as often they must, to advance shared interests in particular issue areas, the hybrid institutions they form to coordinate their SOAs are considered to constitute a 'regime' (Krasner, 1983, p. 2).

Does the advent of a bifurcated system imply that states are in a process of disintegration? Not at all. Doubtless the interstate system will continue to be central to world affairs for decades and centuries to come. To stress that collectivities other than states have emerged as important SOAs is not in any way to suggest that states are headed for demise. Analysts differ over the degree to which the national state has been weakened by the dynamics of fragmegration, but few contend that the weakening amounts to a trend line that will culminate in total collapse. States are still among the main players on the global stage, but they are no longer the only main players.[1] Many of them are deep in crisis, by which I do not mean pervasive street riots, but rather cross-cutting conflicts that paralyse policy-making processes and result in stalemate and stasis, in the avoidance of decisions that would at least address the challenges posed by a fragmegrative world undergoing vast and continuous changes. Yes, most states still control their banking systems and maintain legitimate monopoly over the use of force. Yes, states have undergone transformation into managerial entities and are thus still able to exercise a measure of control over the course of events. And yes, the aspiration to statehood is still shared widely in many parts of the world. But for all its continuing authority and legitimacy, key dimensions of the power of the modern state have undergone considerable diminution. In the words of one analyst, 'As wealth and power are increasingly generated by private transactions that take place across the borders of states rather than within them, it has become harder to sustain the image of states as the preeminent actors at the global level' (Evans, 1997, p. 65).

Analysts also differ over the notion of global governance as disaggregated centres of authority. Some argue that positing the global stage as ever more crowded with SOAs is such a broad conception as to make it 'virtually meaningless both for theory construction and social action' (Väyrynen, 1999, p. 25). Here this argument is found wanting. Opting for a narrow conception may facilitate analysis, but doing so is also misleading in that it ignores the vast proliferation of SOAs that has emerged as a prime characteristic of the system of global governance since the end of the Cold War. As noted below, a meaningful route to theory is plausible through a typology of six forms of global governance (see pp. 80–3).

Domestic-Foreign Boundaries

It is not a simple matter to grasp global governance as congeries of diverse collectivities in the two worlds of world politics. Such a perspective requires one to wrench free of the long-standing and unquestioned premise that the boundaries separating countries are firm and impassable without the permission of the states that preside over them. This wrenching task is not easily accomplished. Our analytic capacities are rooted in methodological territorialism (Scholte, 2000, pp. 56–8), in a long-standing, virtually unconscious habit of probing problems in a broad, geographic or spatial context. This habit poses an acute problem because of the ever growing porosity of domestic-foreign boundaries (Rosenau, 1997) that has rendered territoriality much less pervasive than it used to be even as all the social sciences construct their inquiries, develop their concepts, formulate their hypotheses and frame their evidence-gathering procedures through spatial lenses. Nor are officials free to think in alternative contexts: as one analyst put it, 'Trapped by the territoriality of their power, policy makers in traditional settings often have little choice but to address the symptoms rather than the causes of public problems' (Reinicke, 1999–2000, p. 45).

Yet breaking out of the conceptual jail imposed by methodological territorialism is imperative because a prime characteristic of fragmegration is that its processes readily span foreign-domestic boundaries. Fragmegrative dynamics are such that states can exercise little control over the flows of ideas, money, goods, pollution, crime, drugs and terrorism; and they have only slightly greater control over the flow of people. Why? Because their capacities have been weakened by a pervasive trend towards ever greater complexity – by microelectronic technologies that have rendered what used to be remote ever more proximate; by a continuing proliferation of networked organizations; by a variety of incentives that lead huge numbers of people, everyone from the tourist to the terrorist, to move widely around the world; by the globalization of national economies and the neoliberal economic policies that have enhanced the relevance of markets and the power of multinational corporations; by a skill revolution that has everywhere linked people ever more closely to the course of events; and by divisive politics that have fostered authority crises which inhibit many states from framing and implementing goals appropriate to the dilemmas they face. In short, a host of dynamics have greatly increased transborder flows and rendered domestic-foreign boundaries ever more porous. With the collapse of time and distance, sub-national organizations and governments that once operated within the confines of national boundaries are now so inextricably connected to far-off parts of the world that the legal and geographic jurisdictions in which they are located matter less and less. What matters, instead, are the spheres of authority to which their members are responsive.

Compliance

As previously noted, if the world is conceived to be a vast multiplicity of SOAs that collectively constitute a new global order, the key to understanding their various roles in global governance lies not in focusing on their legal prerogatives, but rather in assessing the degree to which they are able to evoke the compliance of the people whom they seek to mobilize through the directives they issue. Achieving compliance is the key to leadership and politics, and it is not readily accomplished. The more complex societies and the world become, the more difficult it is to get people to respond to efforts to generate their compliance. States have an advantage in this regard because they have the legitimate right to employ force if their citizens fail to comply. But to stress this distinctive quality of states is to ignore the underpinnings of compliance. Most notably perhaps, it ignores the large degree to which compliance is rooted in habit, in an unthinking readiness to respond to directives issued by the authorities to which one has been socialized to be committed and loyal, and the large degree to which such habits are no longer encompassed by the clear-cut province of states. With the proliferation of SOAs and the declining relevance of domestic-foreign boundaries, with the emergence of alternative authorities to which people can transfer their compliance habits, states are less and less able to rely on the effectiveness of their directives.

Put differently, many states today are ensconced in paralysing authority crises that inhibit their governing capacities. This is not to refer to those states plagued with internal wars (such as Colombia) or to rioting protesters in the streets of national capitals. Some do experience such moments on occasion (as in Yugoslavia or the Philippines), but more often than not authority crises involve stalemate, an inability to frame goals, to implement them, to realize them. Governments in many countries, from Russia to Israel, from Peru to China, from the Congo to Indonesia, from the United States to Belgium, are riven by deep divisions and thus often have difficulty raising taxes, preserving societal harmony, ameliorating deep-seated conflicts, expanding their economies, recruiting or retaining members of their armed forces, or otherwise maintaining a level of compliance that sustains their effectiveness.

It follows that global governance today is characterized by an extensive disaggregation of authority, by growing numbers of SOAs in the two worlds of world politics that immensely complicate the tasks of coordination necessary to establish a humane and stable world. Put differently, SOAs proliferate because increasingly people are capable of shouldering and managing multiple identities that lessen their allegiance to their states. As they get involved in more and more networks in the multi-centric world, so their loyalties fractionate and become issue and object specific. Yet history in this era of fragmegration does record pockets of successful coordination among states in the state-centric world and among collectivities in the multi-centric world that are able to generate meaningful compliance. Even though SOAs vary widely in their ability to evoke compliance and thus in their contributions to the processes of global governance, some do manage to gain a measure of control over fragmegrative tensions. Rule systems developed through negotiation among national governments – such as the United Nations, the Kyoto Protocol on the Environment, the World Trade Organization, or the European Union – have the widest scope and, consequently, make perhaps the most substantial contribution to governance processes. Steering mechanisms maintained by SOAs in the multicentric world – such as the calculations of credit-rating agencies that estimate the reliability of national economies, the rulings of truth commissions designed to enable countries racked by civil strife to heal their wounds, or the practices of the insurance industry to offset climate changes (Carlsson and Stripple, 2000) – exemplify effective instruments of governance with respect to specific issues.[2] No less important, many successful efforts at global governance result from cooperation among collectivities in the state-centric and multi-centric worlds. In the words of one knowledgeable observer, 'global regimes are increasingly the product of negotiations among state and non-state actors' (Zacher, 1999, p. 48).

For every example of rule systems in the two worlds of world politics that achieve meaningful coordination and compliance, however, innumerable cases can be cited in which efforts to maintain effective steering mechanisms fail to generate the compliance necessary for governance. Indeed, such failures may well be more the rule than the exception in world affairs today. Our messy world is littered with paralysed or stalemated governments and non-governmental SOAs that fall far short of evoking the compliance appropriate to their goals and policies. Given the continuing processes wherein authority is undergoing disaggregation and rendering compliance more elusive, it is easy to be pessimistic about the prospects for global governance and the probabilities of continuing disarray in world affairs.

Leadership

Some analysts contend that the disarray is not as great as it may seem, that tendencies in this direction are held in check – and in some cases reversed – by the leadership of the United States as the dominant actor in the post-Cold War arrangement of world politics. Frequently referred to as 'hegemonic stability' or a 'unipolar structure', the dominance of the United States and the democratic values it espouses is conceived to be a form of global governance. It is a conception that presumes that the capabilities of the US are so unrivalled that it can generate the compliance necessary to preserve stability on a global scale even as it promotes human rights, democracy and open markets. As I see it, such an approach is misguided. Not only does it ignore the reluctance of the American people to play an active role in the processes of global governance – a reluctance which takes the form of not paying in full its dues to the United Nations or otherwise not participating in numerous international rule systems to which most countries have agreed – but even more important it is a perspective that takes no account of the large degree to which authority is undergoing disaggregation. If the preceding analysis is correct that the global stage is ever more crowded with SOAs capable of independently pursuing their goals, then obviously hegemonic leadership can neither flourish nor endure. Much as many people in the US, ordinary citizens as well as leaders, might prefer to pursue unilateral policies, for example, in most situations the country is forced to work within and through multilateral institutions and, in so doing, it often has to accept modification of its goals. And when it does not accept any modifications, when it proceeds unilaterally – as in the case of its war on drugs – its policies tend to flail aimlessly at best, or fail at worst. The world is simply too interdependent, and authority is too dispersed, for any one country to command the global scene as fully as was the case in the past.

The Advent of Networks

While a number of dynamics have contributed to the diminution of state capacities, certainly one of the most important of these has been the shifting balance between hierarchical and network forms of organization, between vertical and horizontal flows of authority. Greatly facilitated by the Internet, people now converge electronically as equals, or at least not as superiors and subordinates. They make plans, recruit members, mobilize support, raise money, debate issues, frame agendas and undertake collective action, amounting to steering mechanisms founded on horizontal rather than hierarchical channels of authority. Indeed, it has been argued, with reason, that:

> The rise of network forms of organization – particularly 'all channel networks', in which every node can communicate with every other node – is one of the single most important effects of the information revolution for all realms: political, economic, social, and military. It means that power is migrating to small, non-state actors who can organize into sprawling networks more readily than can traditionally hierarchical nation-state actors. It means that conflicts will increasingly be waged by 'networks', rather than by 'hierarchies'. It means that whoever masters the network form stands to gain major advantages in the new epoch. (Arquilla and Ronfeldt, 1997, p. 5)

In other words, not only has the advent of network forms of organization undermined the authority of states, but in the context of our concern with global governance, it has also had even more important consequences. Most notably, networks have contributed to the disaggregation of authority as well as the formation of new collectivities not founded on hierarchical principles.

If the notion that new rule systems can be founded on horizontal as well as vertical structures of authority seems awkward, it warrants reiterating that the core of effective authority lies in the compliance of those towards whom it is directed. If people ignore, avoid, or otherwise do not heed the compliance sought by 'the' authorities, then it can be said that for all practical purposes the latter are authorities in name only, that their authority has evaporated. Authority is thus profoundly relational. It links – or fails to do so, or does so somewhat – those who issue directives and those for whom the directives are intended. Stated more elaborately, authority needs to be treated as a continuum wherein at one extreme full compliance is evoked and at the other extreme it is not. The viability of all collectivities can be assessed by ascertaining where they are located on the continuum. The closer they are to the compliance extreme, the greater will be their viability and effectiveness, just as the nearer they are to the non-compliance extreme the greater is the likelihood that they will be ineffective and falter. Accordingly, it becomes possible to conceive of collectivities held together through horizontal flows of authority – through compliance with electronic messages cast as requests rather than as directives – and it is precisely this possibility that underlies the bifurcation of global structures into state-centric and multi-centric worlds, the proliferation of SOAs, the growing relevance of NGOs, and the increased attention paid to the possibility that a global civil society may be emerging.

The Governance of Fragmegration

As previously indicated, there is no lack of either variety or number in the extant systems of governance. On the contrary, it is difficult to overestimate how crowded the global stage has become as the world undergoes a multiplication of all kinds of governance, from formal to multilevel governments, from formally sanctioned entities such as arbitration boards to informal SOAs, from emergent supranational entities such as the European Union to emergent issue regimes, from regional bodies to international governmental organizations (IGOs), from transnational corporations to neighbourhood associations, from humanitarian groups to ad hoc coalitions, from certifying agencies to social movements, and so on across an ever widening array of activities and concerns.

Notwithstanding the increasing difficulty of generating compliance posed by the world's greater complexity, not every fragmegrative situation on the global agenda lacks governance. There are innumerable situations involving localizing responses to globalizing stimuli that are marked by a high, or at least an acceptable, quality of governance and that thus need not be of concern here. The vast proliferation of rule systems in recent decades includes a trend to devolve governance so that its steering mechanisms are closer to those who experience its policies. This trend is most conspicuously marked by the evolution of what has been called 'multilevel' governance, a form of rule system in which authority is voluntarily and legally dispersed among the various levels of community where problems are located and local needs require attention. The European Union exemplifies multilevel governance, as does Scotland, Wales, the French provinces, US welfare programmes, and many other federal systems in which previously centralized authority has been redistributed to provincial and municipal rule systems. Such systems are not lacking in tensions and conflicts, but relatively speaking the quality of governance is such that the tensions do not lead to violence, the loss of life, the deterioration of social cohesion, or the degradation of people. In short, in and of itself no fragmegrative process is inherently negative or destructive.

For all kinds of reasons, however, some fragmegrative situations are fragile, deleterious, violence-prone, and marked by publics who resent, reject or otherwise resist the intrusion of global values, policies, actors or institutions into their local affairs. It is these situations that pose problems for global governance. To be sure, some of the global intrusions can be, depending on one's values, welcomed and applauded. The world's intrusion into the apartheid rule system, for example, was clearly worthwhile. But in many cases – in those where fragmegrative situations involve local reactions to globalizing dynamics that result in internal fighting, external aggression, intensified crime, repressed minorities, exacerbated cleavages, sealed boundaries, glorified but exclusionary ideals, pervasive corruption, and a host of other patterns that run counter to human dignity and well-being – corrective steering mechanisms that upgrade the quality of governance seem urgently needed. Put more moderately, given the worldwide scope of such situations, effective mechanisms for global governance seem eminently desirable.

Part of the problem of achieving governance over deleterious fragmegrative situations, of course, is that often they require the use of external force against local authorities, a practice that has long been contrary to international law and only lately undergone revision, most notably with respect to Kosovo. But international military interventions into domestic arenas are only one part – and a small one at that – of the challenge of establishing rule systems for unwanted fragmegrative conditions. There are many situations in which organized violence is not the response to globalizing dynamics, but which are nonetheless woefully lacking in appropriate steering mechanisms and thus in need of enlightened rule systems. The list of such circumstances is seemingly endless: they can involve situations in which boundaries are sealed, minorities silenced, crime tolerated, majorities deceived, societies ruptured, law flouted, tyrants enhanced, corruption ignored, oppositions jailed, people trafficked, pollution accepted, elections rigged, and thought controlled – to cite only the more conspicuous practices that are often protected by the conventions of sovereignty and that one would like to see subjected to at least some effective and humane mechanisms of global governance. The thwarted aspirations of the Falun Gong, the people of Burma, the women of Afghanistan, and the Kurds are only among the more conspicuous of many examples of continuing fragmegrative situations that elude efforts towards steerage in enlightened directions.

Nor are the protections of sovereignty the only hindrance to decent global governance. Governance on a global scale is also difficult because the globalizing and localizing interactions often occur across both cultures and issue areas. For instance, while national governments can address – though not necessarily alleviate – the fears of their workers over the loss of jobs resulting from foreign trade with relative ease because they have some jurisdiction over both the well-being of their workers and the contents of trade legislation, the global scale of fragmegrative dynamics can also involve situations in which the parties to them are not located in the same jurisdiction, with the result that any attempt to steer them must be undertaken by diverse authorities that often have different interests and goals. Indeed, not infrequently a globalizing political or economic stimulus can provoke localizing cultural reactions far removed from the country, region or issue area in which the stimuli were generated; contrariwise, local events such as protest marches, coups d'état or severe economic downturns can have widespread consequences in distant places. The rapid spread of currency crises, for example, often seems ungovernable because authority for coping with the crises is so widely dispersed in this issue area and because much of the action takes place beyond the reach of any extant governments, in cyberspace. Put more strongly, the processes of imitative, emulative and isomorphic spread, as well as those that are direct and not circuitous, are so pervasive and powerful that developing steering mechanisms that prevent, or at least minimize, their unwanted consequences seems a staggering task under the best of circumstances.

A Typological Scheme

The vast proliferation of rule systems calls for a sorting out, for typological clarification. While the great number and variety of governance entities suggest that parsimonious classification may be unachievable, numerous simplifying typologies have been developed. Unfortunately, none of them fully breaks with the practice of locating the state at the centre of the scheme. Different levels of government and different types of issues, for example, have been offered as typological schemes,[3] but in each case they are amplified in the context of states. In order to account for the diversity, the horizontality, and the sheer number of steering mechanisms in addition to states that now crowd the global stage, here the typological focus is on the structures and processes that sustain the flows of authority.

A Six-Governance Typology

For analytic purposes such a focus points to six general forms of global governance. Three of these reflect the complex and extensive non-linear feedback processes that have accompanied the advent of fragmegration: one can be called 'network' governance, another labelled 'side-by-side' governance, and still another designated as 'mobius-web' governance. These three can, in turn, be distinguished from three other, more straightforward forms that are less complex and more linear and familiar sources of governance: those that can be traced so fully to the cajoling, shaming, noisy pressures or other activities of NGOs and transnational advocacy groups that the governments of states are, in effect, mere policy ratifiers at the receiving end of the flow of authority (the governance-without-government or bottom-up model); those that derive from the downward flow of authority originating within corporations or among national states and their bureaucracies (the governance-by-government or top-down model); and those that stem from the informal horizontal flows whereby economic exchanges occur in the framework of formal regulatory mechanisms (the governance-by-market model).

These six forms of governance come more fully into focus if a key structural attribute of the global governance system (the degree to which authority is formally established) and a key process attribute (the degree to which authority flows in vertical or horizontal directions) serve as analytic bases for classifying the various collectivities active on the global stage. More precisely, the structural attribute can usefully be trichotomized, with governance arrangements consisting of (1a) formal, (1b) informal, or (1c) both formal and informal (mixed) structures, while the process attribute can be dichotomized in terms of whether authority flows in a (2a) single direction (up or down), or (2b) multiple directions (both up and down as well as back and forth horizontally). The resulting 3×2 matrix (see table 3.1) serves to distinguish the six forms of global governance.

Before differentiating more fully among the forms of governance, let us specify the eight types of collectivities that crowd the global stage. These consist of (1) subnational and national governments founded on hierarchical structures formally adopted in constitutions; (2) for-profit private transnational corporations (TNCs) formally and hierarchically structured by articles of incorporation; (3) international governmental organizations (IGOs) based on formal treaties and charters; (4) subnational and national not-for-profit non-governmental organizations (NGOs) sustained by either formal bylaws or informal, undocumented arrangements; (5) international or transnational not-for-profit non-governmental organizations (INGOs) either formally structured as organizations or informally linked together as associations or social movements; and (6) markets that have both formal and informal structures which steer horizontal exchanges between buyers and sellers, producers and consumers. In addition to the variety introduced by different degrees of formal or informal organization, note needs to be taken of unorganized (7) elite groups or (8) mass publics that form briefly in response to specific issues and then disband when the issue is settled.

Unlike top-down, bottom-up, and market governance, the other three forms are not marked by processes that flow in essentially one direction. The fourth form (the governance-by-network model) involves bargaining among equal (that is, non-hierarchical), formally organized collectivities – between governments, within business

Table 3.1 Six types of governance

		PROCESSES *(type of collectivities involved in this form of governance)*	
		unidirectional (vertical or horizontal)	multidirectional (vertical and horizontal)
	formal	**Top-down governance** (*governments, TNCs, IGOs*)	**Network governance** (*governments, IGOs, NGOs, INGOs – e.g. business alliances*)
STRUCTURES	informal	**Bottom-up governance** (*mass publics, NGOs, INGOs*)	**Side-by-side governance** (*NGO and INGO, governments*)
	mixed formal and informal	**Market governance** (*governments, IGOs, elites, markets, mass publics, TNCs*)	**Mobius-web governance** (*governments, elites, mass publics, TNCs, IGOs, NGOs, INGOs*)

alliances, or between NGOs and INGOs – that ensues when the impetus for governance stems from common concerns about particular problems. The fifth form (the side-by-side model) arises not out of the noisy pressures, internal deliberations, or horizontal bargaining that respectively mark bottom-up, top-down, or network governance, but out of cooperative interchanges among transnational non-governmental elites and state officials, interchanges that are so thorough and effective that the distinction between formal and informal inputs breaks down and the two become fully intertwined and indistinguishable. The sixth form (the mobius-web model) occurs when the impetus to steer a course of events derives from networked interactions across levels of aggregation among TNCs, INGOs, NGOs, IGOs, states, elites, and mass publics, interactions that are elaborate and diverse enough to constitute a hybrid structure in which the dynamics of governance are so overlapping among the several levels as to form a singular, web-like process that, like a mobius, neither begins nor culminates at any level or at any point in time.

It is important to reiterate that all six models involve governance and government on a transnational or global scale. One cannot rely on the literature on state–society relationships to distinguish these models, since this literature focuses on national rather than global governance and does not allow for transnational processes and structures of governance that transcend societal and state boundaries. National and subnational actors may be participants in any or all of the six processes, but their participation stems from concerns over developments beyond their national or subnational jurisdictions.

It should also be stressed that while the labels used to designate the different forms of governance are descriptive of hierarchy or its absence, they do not preclude occasional fluctuations and reversals in the patterns of interaction. In other words, the labels are shorthand ways of referring to central tendencies, to the nature and essential direction of the paths along which authority and the impetus for governance flows. But they also allow for nuance. Top-down governance, for example, originates mainly within the halls of state governments, but corporations that dominate an industry can also initiate it. The campaign to get Yugoslavia to desist from ethnic cleansing in Kosovo is illustrative in this regard. Both during its diplomatic and military phases, the campaign was sustained exclusively by governments. To be sure, NATO's efforts were energized and supported by public shock over the scenes depicted by the television media, but the origins and impetus for governance in that situation can be traced readily to the authority exercised by governments. On the other hand, bottom-up governance refers to policies that may be ratified by governments but that are propelled and unfold mainly outside the halls of governments. The processes in which governments eventually yielded to pressures from NGOs to approve a land-mine treaty are a quintessential example of bottom-up governance. The setting of standards for commodities and productive processes is no less a striking example of bottom-up governance. Thousands of standards were authorized for thousands of commodities and productive processes by autonomous and non-governmental organizations well before quasi-state bodies became involved in monitoring and implementing the standards (Loya and Boli, 1999, ch. 7; Mattli, forthcoming). As for market governance, its processes are horizontal in the sense that they involve the day-to-day interactions of traders and investors, and they are both informal and formal in the sense that governments exercise a modicum of formal regulation over the informal flows of trade and investment. In contrast to the three unidirectional types of governance, the network, side-by-side, and mobius-web forms of governance are pervaded with nuance, by interactive and multiple flows of influence in which governments exert their authority even as they are also bypassed by TNCs NGOs, INGOs, elites, or mass publics. Thus the three types of governance in the right-hand column of table 3.1 are too complex and overlapping to justify an essentially unidirectional presumption.

It is hardly surprising that our typology consists of six different forms of global governance. Just as states vary substantially in the structures and processes through which they govern, so has variety evolved at the global level as the tasks of governance have moved ever more fully beyond the territorial boundaries of states. In other words, the existence of six discernible and meaningful forms of global governance speaks to the continuing expansion of complexity in world politics. If the statics of continuity rather than the dynamics of transformation prevailed today, it would be unnecessary to enlarge our analytic antennae beyond the long-standing conceptions in which the boundaries between domestic and foreign affairs are firmly in place and top-down and bottom-up governance serve as the prime means for framing and implementing policies both at home and abroad. As stressed throughout, however, such conceptions are no longer sufficient. More often than not, the global stage is witness to situations unfolding in ways that call for supplementing linear models with models rooted in non-linear feedback and network processes.

The non-linearity of network, side-by-side and complex-web governance derives from the nature of the issues that each, respectively, undertakes to resolve. In the case of network governance, it occurs when interactions take place exclusively among formal actors such as states, NGOs or business alliances (as distinguished from informal aggregations such as social movements) that form feedback loops to address and solve common problems. The 1992 summit meeting on the environment and the parallel and simultaneous, down-the-street meeting of established INGOs and NGOs were marked by extensive feedback loops between leaders at the two meetings – as also occurred at subsequent meetings on human rights, population, habitat, and women's rights – and exemplify network governance in the sense that all the participants who interacted at the meetings held posts in either governmental or non-governmental organizations.

Side-by-side governance, on the other hand, emerges and is sustained in issue areas where the loci of action are so widely dispersed, unrelated and situation-specific that neither the relevant governmental officials nor their non-governmental counterparts can usefully resort to mass mobilization and, instead, must rely on non-confrontational cooperation to achieve control over the diverse and unrelated situations. The global effort to combat corruption is a classic example in this regard. A major INGO devoted to waging this fight, Transparency International (TI), has self-consciously avoided provoking mass publics and confined its efforts to working closely with the officials of both states and IGOs in the hope of persuading them to adopt anti-corruption policies. The efforts would appear to have been successful: eight years of TI's short life has witnessed the World Bank, the OECD, the International Monetary Fund, several regional IGOs and many states formally explicate goals and strategies for reducing corrupt practices within their realms of authority (Wang and Rosenau, 2001).

In a sense mobius-web governance would seem to amount to a vast elaboration of side-by-side governance. The major difference involves resort to mass mobilization. As noted, such processes are unlikely to occur in side-by-side governance. In the case of mobius-web governance, however, the relevant actors are closely linked and neither widely dispersed nor situation-specific, with the result that the relevant agencies are prone to cross the private–public divide by mobilizing mass publics as well as elites on behalf of the values at stake. The environmental issue area is illustrative. It encompasses intricate networks of actors at subnational, national, transnational and international levels who interact in such diverse ways as to render fruitless any attempt to tease out the direction of causal processes. That is, IGOs and most states have yielded to the pressures of NGOs and INGOs on issues pertaining to the environment and cooperatively formed both formal and informal networks through which the spreading norms get translated into mechanisms of governance (Frank et al., 1999, ch. 3). Indeed, mobius-web governance may be marked by a cumulative sequencing in which the pressures generated by bottom-up governance give rise to top-down and side-by-side governance that, in turn, becomes a vast network encompassing all levels of governance and diverse flows of authority. Given the ever greater complexity of our fragmegrative epoch, mobius-web governance may well supersede the other five forms and become the dominant form of governance in the future. On the other hand, one analyst estimates that in the course of these complex sequences the governance of issues will become more formalized under IGOs and states, thereby 'eating into the realms of the INGOs/NGOs' (Boli, 1999).

Admittedly this six-governance typology is complicated and not lacking in overlaps among the types. Given the diversity of new forms of horizontal governance, however, the typology helps bring a modicum of order to the subject even as it highlights the complexity of our fragmegrative epoch. No less important, the typology allows for seemingly similar types of collectivities to be analysed differently to the extent that their structures and processes vary. Indeed, as indicated in table 3.1, each of the various types of collectivities involved in global governance can engage in more than one form of governance if different situations evoke their participation and authority in different ways. Global governance is much too convoluted, in other words, for there to be a perfect fit between the six forms of governance and the eight types of collectivities.

Conclusions

Of course, typologies are only aids to organizing thought. They do not in any way come close to resolving the problems of accountability, transparency and effectiveness that loom large as obstacles to global governance. The other essays in this volume go a long way towards clarifying whether such problems will prove manageable or insurmountable in the long run. To a large degree, however, much depends on one's temperament – on whether one pessimistically stresses the disarray inherent in weakened states or optimistically focuses on humankind's capacities for innovation and adaptation. Will the proliferation of rule systems, the disaggregation of authority and the greater density of the global stage enhance or diminish the effectiveness of the overall system of global governance? While there doubtless will be pockets of ineffectiveness and breakdown, will the emergent system, on balance, make for more humane and sensitive governance? Are the tensions and conflicts fostered by the deleterious aspects of fragmegration likely to prove ungovernable?

As an optimist, I am inclined to note three aspects of an upbeat answer if one is willing to look beyond the immediate present. In the first place, more than a little truth attaches to the aphorism that there is safety in numbers. That is, the more pluralistic and crowded the global stage gets with SOAs and their diverse steering mechanisms, the less can any one of them, or any coalition of them, dominate the course of events and the more will all of them have to be sensitive to how sheer numbers limit their influence. Every rule system, in other words, will be hemmed in by all the others, thus conducing to a growing awareness of the virtues of cooperation and the need to contain the worst effects of deleterious fragmegration.

Secondly, there is a consciousness of and intelligence about the processes of globalization that is spreading widely to every corner of the earth. What has been designated as 'reflexivity' (Giddens and Pierson, 1998, pp. 115–17) and what I call 'the globalization of globalization' (Rosenau, 2000) is accelerating at an extraordinary rate – from the ivory towers of academe to the halls of government, from the conference rooms of corporations to the peasant homes of China (where the impact of the WTO is an intense preoccupation), people in all walks of life have begun to appreciate their interdependence with others as time and distance shrink. For some, maybe even many, the rush into a globalized world may be regrettable, but few are unaware that they live in a time of change and thus there is likely to be a growing understanding of the necessity to confront the challenges of fragmegration and to be open to new ways of meeting them. Put more positively, an endlessly explosive literature on globalization reflects substantial evidence that good minds in government, academe, journalism and the business community in all parts of the world are turning, each in their own way, to the task of addressing and constructively answering the questions raised above. It is difficult to recall another period of history when so many thoughtful people concentrated their talents on the human condition from a worldwide perspective.

Third, the advent of networks and the flow of horizontal communications has brought many more people into one or another aspect of the ongoing dialogue. The conditions for the emergence of a series of global consensuses never existed to quite the extent they do today. The skills of individuals and the orientations of the organizations they support are increasingly conducive to convergence around shared values. To be sure, the battle of Seattle and subsequent skirmishes between advocates and critics of globalization – quintessential instances of fragmegration – point to a polarization around two competing consensuses, but aside from those moments when their conflicts turn violent, the very competition between the opposing camps highlights a potential for dialogue that may lead to compromises and syntheses. Already there are signs that the attention of international institutions such as the World Bank, the World Economic Forum, the WTO and the IMF has been arrested by the complaints of their critics and that they are pondering the challenges posed by the growing gap between rich and poor people and nations.

None of this is to suggest, however, that nirvana lies ahead. Surely it does not. Surely fragmegration will be with us for a long time and surely many of its tensions will intensify. But the collective will to preserve and use the new, horizontal forms of authority is not lacking and that is not a trivial conclusion.

Notes

1 Some analysts suggest that conceptions of the state trace a pendulum-like pattern that swings back and forth between notions of strong and weak states. See, for example, Evans (1997, p. 83), who cites Dani Rodrik as observing that 'excessive optimism about what the state would be able to accomplish was replaced by excessive pessimism.'

2 For a host of other examples of effective governance in the multi-centric world, see Cutler, Haufler and Porter, 1999.

3 The levels-of-government typology – 'called the ladder of governance' – traces the movement of issues on to and around the various rungs of the ladder as they arrest the attention of officials and publics, thereby highlighting the prospect that multilevel governance will prevail in the future. This scheme has been developed by the Workshop on Globalization and the Comprehensive Governance of Water, sponsored by the Commission on Economic, Environmental, and Social Policy of the World Conservation Union (Gland, Switzerland). The state-based typology seeks 'to capture a rather complex reality' through five models that 'constitute a continuum ranging from the [societies] most dominated by the State and those in which the State plays the least role and indeed one in which there is argued to be governance without government' (Peters and Pierre, 2000, pp. 4, 5).

References

Arquilla, John and Ronfeldt, David (1997) 'A new epoch – and spectrum – of conflict', in John Arquilla and David Ronfeldt (eds), *In Athena's Camp: Preparing for Conflict in the Information Age*, Santa Monica: RAND.

Boli, John (1999) Personal correspondence, 30 Apr.

Carlsson, Sverker and Stripple, J. (2000) 'Climate governance beyond the state – contributions from the insurance industry', paper presented at the International Political Science Association, Quebec City, 1–5 Aug.

Cutler, A. Claire, Haufler, Virginia and Porter, Tony (eds) (1999) *Private Authority in International Affairs*, Albany: State University of New York Press.

Evans, Peter (1997) 'The eclipse of the state? Reflections on stateness in an era of globalization', *World Politics*, 50, Oct., pp. 62–87.

Frank, David John, Hironaka, Ann, Meyer, John W., Schofer, Evan and Brandon Tuma, Nancy (1999) 'The rationalization and organization of nature in world culture', in John Boli and George M. Thomas (eds), *Constructing World Culture: International Nongovernmental Organizations since 1875*, Stanford: Stanford University Press.

Giddens, Anthony and Pierson, Christopher (1998) *Conversations with Anthony Giddens: Making Sense of Modernity*, Cambridge: Polity.

Krasner, Stephen A. (ed.) (1983) *International Regimes*, Ithaca: Cornell University Press.

Loya, Thomas A. and Boli, John (1999) 'Standardization in the world polity: technical rationality over power', in John Boli and George M. Thomas (eds), *Constructing World Culture: International Nongovernmental Organizations since 1875*, Stanford: Stanford University Press.

Mattli, Walter (ed.) (forthcoming) *Governance in International Standards Setting*.

Peters, B. Guy and Pierre, Jon (2000) 'Is there a governance theory?', paper presented at the International Political Science Association, Quebec City, 1–5 Aug.

Reinicke, Wolfgang H. (1999–2000) 'The other world wide web: global public policy networks', *Foreign Policy*, Winter, pp. 44–57.

Rosenau, James N. (1990) *Turbulence in World Politics: A Theory of Change and Continuity*, Princeton: Princeton University Press.

Rosenau, James N. (1997) *Along the Domestic-Foreign Frontier: Exploring Governance in a Turbulent World*, Cambridge: Cambridge University Press.

Rosenau, James N. (2000) 'The globalization of globalization', paper presented at the International Studies Association, Los Angeles, 16 Mar.

Rosenau, James N. (forthcoming) *Distant Proximities: Dynamics beyond Globalization*.

Scholte, Jan Aart (2000) *Globalization: A Critical Introduction*, London: Macmillan.

Väyrynen, Raimo (1999) 'Norms, compliance, and enforcement in global governance', in Raimo Väyrynen (ed.), *Globalization and Global Governance*, Lanham: Rowman and Littlefield.

Wang, Hongying and Rosenau, James N. (2001) 'Transparency International and corruption as an issue of global governance', *Global Governance*, 7, Jan., pp. 25–9.

Wendt, Alexander (1999) *Social Theory of International Politics*, Cambridge: Cambridge University Press.

Zacher, Mark (1999) 'Uniting nations: global regimes and the United Nations systems', in Raimo Väyrynen (ed.), *Globalization and Global Governance*, Lanham: Rowman and Littlefield.

4

Global Governance: a Feminist Perspective

Jill Steans

Introduction

The term governance conveys the idea that the 'arena of politics is not captured by the study of the state or governments alone', but embraces 'collective processes of rule-making, monitoring and implementation, conducted by many intertwined social actors and institutions' both within and beyond the nation-state (Goldblatt, 1998, p. 1). Governance refers not just to governmental institutions and policy-making backed by formal authority, but also includes informal non-governmental organizations (NGOs) operating within the public realm that are increasingly involved in decision-making and in the 'implementation and monitoring' of policy.

Any discussion of governance immediately raises these questions: who are the 'actors'; how are they constituted; and how far can these 'actors', be they states, elites within international organizations, or NGOs, influence the decision-making process, or conversely, how far they are constrained by structural forces? To understand processes of governance it is necessary to look beyond individual acts or decisions made by policy-makers, to a structure of power that constrains actions by, among other things, setting the terms in which issues are discussed and determining the parameters of what are deemed to be 'feasible' policy options. This is an essential part of social power[1] that is exercised through institutions, networks and processes of governance.

To simplify somewhat there are three basic approaches[2] to the relative importance of structure and agency that can be used to elucidate how outcomes are determined in the policy-making process (see summary in Scholte, 2000, pp. 91–2). First, that social relations are entirely driven by the aims and decisions of actors, be they states, firms, or civic organizations. Thus, while neoliberal institutionalists see regimes as 'persistent and connected sets of rules and practices that prescribe behavioural roles, constrain activity, and shape expectations', in the final analysis it is states that make the rules and so have the capacity to effect changes (Haas, Keohane and Levy, 1993, p. 5). The neoliberal institutionalist approach to governance is basically state-centric, but others have recognized the role of NGOs in global governance, particularly their potential as agents of social change (Willetts, 1996b).[3]

The diversity of feminist theory has been extensively documented and perhaps one should begin by acknowledging that there are, potentially, a number of quite distinctive feminist approaches to governance (Tong, 1989). Liberal-feminists emphasize the need to increase the representation of women's groups within the global policy-making process at both national and international levels, but adhere to a basically pluralistic, consensus-oriented view of governance. From this perspective, governance is about establishing consensual norms and rules through a process of discussion and bargaining, and the translation of these agreed norms into domestic realities through a variety of policy networks that should include an active role for women's NGOs.

The problem with liberal approaches is that they are often unreflective about how power relations are played out in the making of the rules and the exercise of 'authority'. A second approach in the structure/agency debate suggests that the trajectory of social change is wholly determined by deeply embedded organizing principles of social relations. These configurations of social relations might include the structure of production relations; the embedded nature of gender relations; the dominant-rationalist-knowledge structure; and a governance structure that comprises states and international organizations (Scholte, 2000). In constructing a feminist perspective on governance, therefore, one must first address the embedded nature of gender relations. Marxist-feminists take gender to be a specific form of social inequality rooted in the 'privatization' of women's productive and reproductive labour power. Gender relations are thus 'embedded' through the social/gendered division of labour that underpins the distinction between the public world of 'work' in the national and, increasingly, global economy and the 'private' realm of the home, family and social reproduction (Young, Wolkowitz and McCullagh, 1984; Mies, 1986; Mitter, 1986).

A further structural factor is the dominant form of political organization – in effect, the state. Marxist-feminists and radical feminists have employed the concept of patriarchy to refer to the institutionalization of male power. The state is held to be patriarchal not only in the sense that the institutions and functionary roles of the state tend to be filled by men, but also because the state supports and perpetuates a gendered division between the public/private realms. States engage in ideological activity on issues of sex and gender through, for example, support for the institution of marriage and the family, family planning and sexual health, social policy and welfare, labour legislation, rights of citizenship and so on (Connell, 1987; McIntosh, 1985; Dalerup, 1987; MacKinnon, 1989, p. 157; Standt, 1986; Yuval-Davis and Athias, 1989, pp. 1–14; Whitworth, 1994). Moreover, increasingly, not only states but multilateral economic institutions have been active agents structuring the exploitation of women as a socio-economic resource in postcolonial countries that are increasingly driven by the dictates of economic development programmes (Standt, 1986; Chinkin, 1999).[4]

A third perspective stresses the mutually constitutive nature of agent choices and structural dispositions. Structural forces determine a range of options available to actors in a given historical context and thus encourage agents to take certain steps rather than others, but structures depend on the accumulation of actors' decisions for their creation and perpetuation (Scholte, 2000, pp. 91–2). At moments of structural instability and flux, agents can have considerable influence in reshaping the social order (Giddens, 1994; see also O'Brien, 1999).

It is important not to lose sight of the degree to which 'gender relations are constructed out of the activities of actors and the institutions they create, and as such are open to change' (Whitworth, 1994, p. 4). The opportunities for human intervention or agency are constrained by historical circumstance, but at the same time there is room for some optimism about the possibilities of achieving change through political action. In challenging the notion that gender is social and not 'natural', feminists have shown that gender relations are a matter for politics. Gender issues are politicized as boundaries shift between what is deemed to be 'public' and what 'private'. The feminist slogan that the 'personal is political' both highlights the power dynamic in personal relationships, and draws attention to the way in which demands for women's autonomy are political in nature. As Scott contends, demands for personal autonomy are political demands in the sense that they necessarily involve engaging with the policy-making and legislative apparatus, in everything from divorce law to taxation (Scott, 1990). Gina Vargas argues that during the last decade feminist activists have engaged with the state at the political level to further citizenship rights for women. For example, feminist groups have called the state to account for tolerating violence and discrimination against women. In this way, Vargas claims, women have expanded the state's responsibility to reduce abuse in 'private' situations (Vargas, 1999).

However, feminist politics is not only directed at national governments. There is a 'gender politics' at work in global governance as women's NGOs are increasingly involved in diverse policy-making forums and networks beyond the nation-state (Meyer and Prugl, 1999). As Sandra Whitworth contends, 'the interests around which people organize within international institutions reflect a whole variety of power relations, including gender relations' (1994, p. 7). 'Gender interests' are those 'interests that women and men may develop by virtue of their social positioning through gender attributes' (Goetz, 1995, p. 7). What are deemed to be appropriate roles and relationships between men and women are created, sustained and legitimated by social institutions, states and, increasingly, international institutions, but at the same time the 'naturalization' of gender relations is contested.

A literature on gender in governance is now appearing, preceded by and to some extent drawing on earlier works on the role of NGOs in internationalizing gender issues and advancing the status of women, particularly through UN programmes and, more recently, World Bank development projects (Bystydzienski, 1992; Pietila and Vickers, 1994). The UN Decade for Women (1976–85), and the subsequent Fourth UN Conference on Women held in Beijing in 1995, opened up political spaces for NGOs, which used the preparatory meetings, the UN conferences and parallel NGO forums to raise a number of crucial gender issues. These issues included the impact of structural adjustment on women in indebted countries and economies in transition; continuing sexual discrimination and segregated labour markets; women's (often unrecorded and unrecognized) contribution to economic growth; equal pay for work of equal value; reproductive rights; and domestic violence as a human rights concern. Partly as a consequence of the UN women's conferences, a transnational feminist movement has emerged, pushing a global agenda of women's human rights, and a network of relationships has grown up between NGOs, and between NGOs, states and international institutions (Willetts, 1996a).

This chapter takes these issues of power, structure and agency as a starting point from which to construct a feminist perspective on global governance. The first section sketches the main claims of critical feminism and explains why this is a particularly promising framework for developing a perspective on governance that is cognisant of issues of power and structural constraints on action, but at the same time alert to the possibilities of using existing structures and processes of governance to achieve social and political change. The second section links governance with processes of globalization or 'global restructuring'. This linkage is made because the various mechanisms and networks of governance cannot be understood independently from transformations in economic and social relations as a consequence of the competitive pressures generated by a capitalist world economy, changing forms of political organization and new sites of political struggle. This section focuses on the role played by multilateral institutions, like the United Nations and World Bank, in global governance. The third section elucidates more fully the gender politics at work in global governance, notably the way that women's groups have attempted to both shape agendas and contest the dominant rules and norms. By way of conclusion, the final section of the chapter turns to the 'good governance agenda' adopted by the World Bank in the post-Cold War period. It asks whether recent efforts to increase accountability and transparency within the World Bank and other multilateral institutions provide genuine opportunities for women's NGOs to have an expanded role in international economic and social policy-making, and, if not, what might 'good governance' mean in practice for women?

Institutions, Ideas and the Reproduction of Gender Relations

While there are potentially a number of approaches to women/gender and/in governance, a critical feminist framework is particularly useful. First, critical feminism is helpful in elucidating the structural aspects of gender relations and, crucially, gender inequalities, by situating processes of governance within a broader framework of globalization – the restructuring of global production and changing configurations of social relations. In this respect, critical feminism shares some common ground with an earlier tradition of Marxist-feminist thought in that it emphasizes material structures that support and reproduce social relations of inequality.

Second, critical feminism emphasizes the crucial role played by ideas and ideology in legitimizing unequal social relations. The role of intersubjective meanings and ideas is crucial to the reproduction of gender relations. As Cheng and Hsuing suggest in relation to the NIEs of East Asia, 'the family firm, touted by scholars as the engine of Asian economic success, is rooted in gender ideologies and held together by the waged and unwaged labour of women' (Cheng and Hsuing, 1998, p. 126). The literature on gender and governance specifically is fairly sparse, but a key theme that is emerging from recent work is that both material structures and ideas (about the 'naturalness' of gender roles and women's responsibility for childcare, for example) are integral to understanding processes of governance. Similarly, the rules and 'norms' reflect the preferences of powerful states or dominant social elites, but might be contested by oppositional groups.

While mindful of the importance of structural constraints, critical feminists do not hold such a rigid, deterministic view of the relationship between the economic, political and social system and the dynamic of historical change. The structure (the global capitalist economy, political forms and social relations) imposes constraints on oppositional groups pushing for change, but states and other institutions have a degree of autonomy, reflecting the complex configuration of forces at work in international society. Whitworth argues that it is necessary to examine the position of women in relation to the globalization of economic and social relations and understand how these same forces give rise to dominant and oppositional forces which support or challenge the existing order (Whitworth, 1994). Such an approach takes politics seriously. Whatever the constraints, women are not simply 'victims' of patriarchy, but self-determining agents who are capable of challenging and resisting structures of domination. Feminist politics is in essence about bringing about changes in prevailing forms of gender relations because these are seen to be detrimental to women.

To speak of agency is to presuppose the existence of 'agents' or 'subjects' empowered to act. This might appear rather obvious, but the existence of autonomous female 'subjects' with concrete 'interests' has been problematized in recent feminist theoretical debates (see, for example, Nicholson, 1990). This is why some of the contemporary literature on gender and governance prefers to focus on 'discursive practices' that 'reproduce gender hierarchies and reproduce dominant understandings of masculinity and femininity' rather than on material structures and concrete interests rooted in class, or gender, or ethnic identity perhaps (M. Meyer and Prugl, 1999, p. 5). Critical feminism employs the notion of 'women' as a category of analysis, because women are held to share certain commonalities and interests that arise from their position in the social division of labour and through common experiences of subordination and/or discrimination. However, as Marshall contends, we need to conceive of social relations not as eternally 'fixed' or wholly 'determining' structures, but as constituted and reconstituted through subjectivities and their 'subjective inhabitation' (Marshall, 1994). According to Marshall, the historically specific effectiveness of certain subject positions in either legitimizing or contesting discourses of domination demonstrate that subjectivity cannot be viewed as fixed in relationship to social structures. The placing of subjects in certain subject positions is a key mode of legitimation of unequal social relationships, but there is emancipatory potential in the fluid manner in which interests/identities are formed. At the same time, conceiving of social relations as relations of inequality makes it possible to make certain claims in the name of 'woman' (Marshall, 1994). Focusing on the subject allows an analysis of how women are positioned in relation to dominant power structures and how this forges a sense of identity and a politics of resistance. Thus women are empowered as reflective subjects: autonomous beings capable of defining interests and pursuing strategies to achieve positive changes in their lives. Women are agents by virtue of their economic activity, but agency cannot be understood by reference to public activities and identities alone: the 'private' domain is also a site of struggle.

Historically, feminism (in both theory and practice) has been centrally concerned with the social position of women in specific societies. The social position of women is shaped by gender relations that operate in different situations and, increasingly, is affected by both international and internal factors (Whitworth, 1994). Although gender relations appear to be locked into the realm of the private, the cultural and the affective and so to be less open to change than social relations like class, for example, the global division of labour and the public and private identities and roles which underpin it, are being shaped and reshaped by globalization. Increasingly, gender relations have to be understood in the context of the dynamic between the global and the local and the changing relationship between the two (Steans, 1999). As Whitworth argues, analysing gender relations entails exploring the ways in which meanings and understandings of 'masculinity' and 'femininity' are constructed and maintained locally, nationally and globally. While the minutiae of gender roles differ from society to society and culture to culture, they are constantly being transformed (Runyan, 1996).

Critical feminism expands the purview of feminist analysis to include the interplay between gender relations and the institutional contexts within which they take shape

(Disch, 1991). International institutions not only institutionalize arrangements that distinguish the public from the private, but play a key role in constructing meanings and understandings about gender and thus in legitimizing gender relations (Whitworth, 1994, p. 4). However, states and institutions can potentially serve as vehicles for change and so should not be seen as *inherently* patriarchal, but more as a 'set of power relations and political processes in which patriarchy is both constructed and contested' (Connell, 1995). Critical theorists insist on the relative autonomy of the state (and institutions) from civil society in order to open up a space for exploring the possibilities for an emancipatory politics.

Thus far the discussion of critical feminism and processes of governance has centred on how actors (in this case women's NGOs) are constituted and how they are both constrained and empowered to act. As will be elaborated below, while the feminization of poverty has been a global phenomenon over the past two decades, it is poor women in the South[5] who have felt the worst effects of economic globalization, debt and structural adjustment programmes. The overall position of women – as measured by concrete factors like access to food and resources, employment opportunities and burden of work – has declined. A worsening economic climate and a lack of resources has frequently meant that women's NGOs have been unable to access policy-making bodies, and their needs and interests have been neglected.

Given the central importance that has been placed on power relations in governance it is equally important to ask: who gets to 'act' and who gets to represent and speak for 'women'? There is also a politics at work in what might be broadly labelled the 'global women's movement' which can disguise the diverse interests, concerns and strategies that characterize women's NGOs in both the North and the South. While more women from the global South are finding a voice within, for example, the UN, historically the 'needs' and 'interests' of women in developing countries have been viewed through the prism of Western, mainly liberal, feminism, which is profoundly disempowering (Mohanty, 1988; Mohanty, Rosso and Torress, 1991; Grewal and Kaplan, 1994; Ferree and Martin, 1995; Amos and Parmar, 1984; Spivak, 1996). All too frequently women in the 'third world' have been portrayed as the helpless victims of 'backward' cultural practices, while 'Third World Women' have been represented as a monolithic subject who is passive and voiceless (Mohanty, 1988). Moreover, NGOs in the global South often exclude the poorest women in the role of self-critical agents (Spivak, 1996).

At other times, states have resisted the project of 'advancing' the status of women, insisting on the need to preserve their own sovereign jurisdiction over 'domestic matters' and/or the need to respect cultural difference. Of course, the specificity of gender relations in national and local contexts must be recognized, but 'culture' is not essential and fixed. Culture can be seen as a set of practices and norms that underpin material structures, or a series of constantly contested and negotiated social practices that change over time, in accordance with the needs, demands and circumstances of peoples at particular times in history.

Postcolonial feminist critiques of UN programmes and women's NGOs do raise serious issues of power, representation and participation in both policy-making and in the implementation and monitoring process. This is particularly the case when women's NGOs are treated as direct representatives of a 'female constituency', rather than groups of activists who play a key role in keeping open the channels of communication between international institutions, national governments and those most affected by economic and social policies. Feminist critiques of states and institutions bring into stark relief the problems of male dominance and the patriarchal construction of women's needs and women's roles. However, as Sen and Grown argue, feminism cannot be monolithic in its issues, goals and strategies, since it constitutes the political expression of the concerns and interests of women from different regions, classes, nationalities and backgrounds, and therefore needs to be 'responsive to the different needs and concerns of different women, and defined by them for themselves' (Sen and Grown, 1987). This diversity does not, however, preclude building alliances around common opposition to gender oppression and hierarchy, as a first step in articulating and acting upon a political agenda that challenges structures and relationships that perpetuate and reinforce the subordination of women wherever they are located.

Globalization and Governance

The term 'globalization' has no fixed or agreed meaning, but in relation to the realm of the global economy, it is frequently associated with a loss of state autonomy. Governance beyond the nation-state is often explained in terms of interdependence or the ever deepening integration that globalization fosters, which creates problems of regulation and control for national governments – particularly in relation to economic policy – and so increases the need for collective management, as states endeavour to reassert some control over markets. The consequence of efforts at collective management is not the re-establishment of governmental control, but a further erosion of state autonomy as the state's control and regulation functions become dispersed among different states in the world and across a range of international institutions and regimes.

As Scholte contends, the enhanced position of capitalism as the dominant structure of production has resulted in the state losing its predominance as a site of governance (Scholte, 2000). Moreover, as Murphy points out, globalization, the rise of NGOs, transnational alliances, 'civil society' and mechanisms of governance have together 'added up to the supremacy of the neo-liberal agenda both within and across states' (Murphy, 2000, p. 796). Increasingly it is the International Monetary Fund, the World Trade Organization and the World Bank who 'make the rules', favouring the adoption of neoliberal, pro-market policies. According to Falk, the potency of market forces organized around energies of greed is dominating policy-forming arenas at all levels of social organization and in all regional and global structures of governance. This is further reinforced through ideas of neoliberal economics, which have sapped the normative creativity of states by imposing the discipline of global capital on existing structures of governance (Falk, 1999).

The Gramscian conception of hegemony claims to capture the rich complexity of historical structures, intersubjective meanings and ideas, and production modes that collectively constitute 'world order' and elucidate how power relations between transnational elites and the 'masses' are structured and reproduced. Here states, regional organizations and multilateral institutions are understood primarily in terms of the role and function they play in cementing or legitimizing dominant economic projects. Cox argues that we now live in a state system in which all members are formally equal, but in which different states perform different functions to facilitate the opening up of global markets and the operations of capitalist enterprises, and have different levels of power and influence. In this view, states act as transmission belts of international or global capital. However, states are also being superseded by international organizations that support capitalist hegemony.

In the contemporary global economy a transnational historic bloc has emerged which comprises key institutions, big transnational corporations, major capitalist states and international organizations like the IMF. This process has brought with it new transnational networks. Indeed, the internationalization of the state may in itself have generated cross-cutting coalitions, class alliances and socio-historical blocs of forces across as well as within countries. At the same time, the concept of 'counterhegemony' directs attention to possibilities for resistance and strategies to effect change (Cerny, 1986, 1990; Cox, 1983, 1986; Cox and Sinclair, 1996; Germain and Kenny, 1998; Gill, 1993; Overbeek, 1993; Rupert, 1995; Tooze and Murphy, 1990).

A key concern of feminist international political economy has been the need to develop a richer, more nuanced conception of hegemony that addresses differences within hegemony, marked by gender, race and culture (Ling and Bell, 1998). In order to understand the 'gender politics' at work in global governance, it is necessary first to sketch the broad impact of globalization – including the changing international division of labour, investment patterns, trading structures and, crucially, neoliberal belief systems that play a crucial role in legitimizing dominant economic projects – on women specifically.

Questions about whether globalization is 'good' or 'bad' for women are not always easily answered. First, there is no one single category or group called 'women' who have identical interests, although there are, it seems, unifying problems and experiences among very different groups of women in different local and national locations. Second, women are not ever the 'victims' of global capitalism. Critical feminism emphasizes that women are agents who to some extent shape globalization. As Jacqui True has noted, there has been little analysis of gender as a site of globalization, *that shapes* and is *shaped by* global market forces (True, 1999). As will be elaborated below, women's NGOs are involved in struggles around all of these issues and are thereby 'challenging and refashioning globalization' (Mitter and Rowbotham, 2000, p. 382).

Globalization undoubtedly creates 'opportunities' for women to enter the paid workforce, improve their material circumstances and challenge gender stereotypes. This allows women to carve out new identities for themselves. Neoliberal discourses construct globalization as a brave new world of opportunities for those able and willing to grasp them (Hall, 1992). Indeed, some women are grasping 'opportunities' on offer. Women in many parts of the world are entering the paid workforce in increasing numbers. This gives women access to earned income that might improve their position within the family and in society at large.

However, this is not the whole picture. Women continue to carry a double burden as women's labour stretches to accommodate both a reproductive and productive role (Elson, 1990; Harcourt, 2000). While the ideology of neoliberalism espouses certain egalitarian values, the changes associated with globalization and restructuring have sometimes worked to 'privatize' women's labour and, consequently, resulted in a loss of power and autonomy. The neoliberal emphasis on consumer choice, the rational distribution of resources and the efficacy of the market pays no regard to the socially embedded nature of 'economic' activity. Neoliberalism ignores the significance of unremunerated labour, usually performed by women, to the local, national and global economy. By concentrating on markets and the appropriate role and function of the state, it is possible to overlook how women's activities, though profoundly important to the social welfare of families and communities, have been demoted to the 'private' sphere, and, moreover, how ideas about gender often play a crucial role in tracking and trapping women into conventional, and frequently low-paid and low-skilled jobs and thwart access to education and promotion in work and pay (Waring, 1988; Boserup, 1989; Steans, 1998; Sylvester, 1994; Tickner, 1992).

Moreover, the shift in gender relations which is occurring as young women rather than men are being absorbed into the new jobs has implications for men's traditional roles as 'providers', leading to, in some cases, a relative decline in their power and position, tensions in the home and, studies suggest, increased incidences of violence against women (Harcourt, 2000). In all of these ways dominant gender relations are sustained and reproduced in ways that continue to disadvantage women. While the 'evidence' is mixed, it seems that there is no necessary advantage accruing to women in particular, and economic globalization might simply be resulting in a continuation or even deterioration of an existing relative disadvantage (Birdsall and Graham, 2000).

Feminist Politics in Global Governance

Since the late 1970s, the 'global rules' codified by states and intergovernmental organizations, and the 'informal rules with global reach' promoted by big business and policy think tanks have rested on certain ideas or beliefs about the efficacy and dynamism of open markets and competition (M. Meyer and Prugl, 1999, p. 5; O'Brien et al., 2000). Neoliberal ideology promoted by key groups within the Bretton Woods institutions has been used to justify economic policies which foster the deregulation of capital and labour markets, aid the weakening of trade unions, and give support to the free market. Increasingly states have been compelled to orient their economic policies to the needs of globally mobile capital, and this has provided much of the impetus behind both the dismantling of welfare states in many advanced capitalist societies and the widening income inequalities within those societies (Stopford and Strange, 1991).

The ideology of neoliberalism has informed development theory and development strategies and programmes since the early 1980s. In the wake of the debt crisis, developing countries of the global South have increasingly followed a liberal model of export-led growth combined with cuts in public expenditure; the so-called 'earn more, spend less' approach to development (George, 1988; Riley, 1992; Wood, 1983; Onimode, 1989). Structural adjustment also involves the implementation of pro-grammes and policies by national governments that will create the conditions domes-tically to attract inward investment.[6] Since the collapse of communism, former Eastern bloc states have similarly been encouraged to liberalize their economies. This trend has been enhanced by structural adjustment policies enforced on indebted countries by the World Bank and IMF.

Undoubtedly this has generated increased demands for women's labour, particularly in export production zones (EPZs) and free trade zones (FTZs). Women, mostly young and childless and with some education, make up the majority of the labour force in these zones (Meyer, 1998). However, women's employment outside the home often occurs under inferior conditions (Marchand, 1995). In the case of EPZs women are frequently hired in preference to men because women are constructed as 'vulnerable', 'docile', and so more likely to accept unsafe working conditions and low wages (Enloe, 1989).

Of course, women's groups have tried to shape the global rules and influence the decision-making process. There are two major forums through which women's NGOs have organized to influence the political process, the United Nations and, increasingly, the Bretton Woods institutions, particularly the World Bank. The UN conferences and the parallel NGO forums which have taken place since 1975 have allowed women's NGOs to carve out 'niches for themselves and their interests as women become political agents, framing issues and advancing feminist agendas' (M. Meyer and Prugl, 1999, p. 9; see also Hendessi, 1986).

Meyer and Prugl have identified a number of distinctive ways in which women's NGOs are involved in processes of governance (Meyer and Prugl, 1999). Established women's international non-governmental organizations have worked within the UN system to try to influence directly the political agendas of multilateral institutions. Since the end of the UN Decade for Women in 1985, NGOs have pushed to have gender concerns incorporated into the mainstream of UN policy-making, resulting in the setting up of a number of specialized agencies like the UN Development Fund for Women (UNIFEM) and the International Research and Training Institute for the Advancement of Women (INSTRAW). These agencies have developed considerable technical expertise and the necessary bureaucratic machinery to mainstream a gender perspective into UN development policies.[7] The gradual 'mainstreaming' of gender in other areas of the UN's work has resulted in the emergence of what Kardam has called an 'international women's regime', bringing pressures to bear on states, resulting in a deluge of gender-focused policies over the past three decades (quoted in Alvarez, 1999).

Simmonds argues that NGOs influence governments and institutions in four main ways: agenda setting, outcome negotiations, conferring legitimacy, and helping to implement policies (Simmonds, 1998). Both nationally and internationally, NGOs were active in the preparation for the Fourth United Nations Conference on Women, held in Beijing in 1995.[8] The Draft Platform of Action which formed the basis of negotiations at the Fourth UN Conference on Women in Beijing, and the various regional Expert Reports compiled in preparation for the conference were littered with references to the impact of economic globalization on women around the world, and the impact of structural adjustment on women in developing countries and the former Eastern bloc states (Hooper, 1994a, 1994b, 1994c).

The UN conferences and the preparatory process also helped to consolidate fledgling women's movements in many countries as they prepared for participation in the Beijing NGO Forum.[9] Women's groups are now fairly securely embedded in the UN system or working as an effective and coordinated lobby that exerts pressure on national governments and international institutions.[10] Virginia Vargas argues that it is now possible to identify a series of networks extending to the spaces carved out in multilateral institutions, local and international NGOs and transnational issue networks that constitute the outlines of a global women's movement (Vargas, 1999).

The women's movement has had some successes working within the UN system.[11] However, these have been overshadowed by the disappointments and failures of the UN Decade for Women, and a seemingly ongoing decline in the positions of women globally. At the end of the UN Decade for Women, surveys suggested that the relative status and position of women throughout the world had declined during the previous ten years (Ashworth and Bonnerjea, 1985). To some extent, the failure of the UN Decade can be explained by the reluctance on the part of many states to implement UN recommendations.[12] However, the failure was also attributed to the underlying assumptions of the liberal Women in Development (WID) approach. During the UN Decade, development policies were based on the underlying belief that the problems of Third World women were related to insufficient participation in the process of development. It has been argued that WID rested on a liberal feminist view that the problems of sexual inequality could be largely overcome if women were integrated into the public sphere. Furthermore, the possibility that increasing poverty among women, and the relative decline in the position of women compared to men during the Decade, was the direct result of previous development policies was not considered. Critics argued that WID policy documents avoided and obscured issues of inequalities and power by presenting the issue of assistance to women as a purely technical exercise. It did not address the broader redistributional issues that arise in the project of 'assisting' women. WID also ignored the broader context in which women-specific projects were inscribed. Increases in the productivity of women increased women's overall work load, since there was no relief from traditional reproductive tasks (Ashworth, 1988).

Instead of linking women's issues to global economic forces, or highlighting issues of gender relations and power and problematizing the relationship between women and the state, WID promoted an agenda focused on women's practical needs for health care and education, and as such neglected women's strategic interests (see Molyneux, 1985; Moser, 1991).[13] These short-term practical gains were easily reversed because women lacked the ability to protect them when the economic and political climate was less favourable and resources became scarcer. Arguably, this is occurring in the present day as structural adjustment policies pursued by governments in their efforts to deal with the problems of debt, chronic balance of payment imbalances and budget deficits undermine the position of women, particularly in developing countries. Clearly, it is necessary to understand the broader economic and political context in which global governance takes place and ask whether dominant economic projects really serve the interests of women in both the North and the South.

With regard to processes of 'policy assessment, implementation and monitoring', during the 1990s NGOs have become more closely involved in translating international agreements and norms into domestic policies. There are a number of possible reasons why this has occurred. First, concomitantly with economic globalization and the reassertion of neoclassical economics, there has been a 'privatization' of decision-making in matters relating to the economy and social policy in many countries. Second, the expansion of various mechanisms of global governance has opened up more spaces for participation in the process by civic organizations, including an array of non-governmental organizations, a trend that has intensified in the post-Cold War period.

Third, a number of multilateral institutions have sought to strengthen the linkages with NGO networks, because this is seen as a way of promoting and consolidating democracy. NGOs are often taken to be representatives or 'conduits' of civil society – articulating the needs, wants and preferences of interest groups – and as such vital for a thriving democracy. Moreover, the participation of NGOs in global governance is seen to be an effective means of increasing the accountability to civil society of both national governments and international institutions. Fourth, states and intergovernmental international organizations need specialized knowledge that can be supplied by technically adept professionalized organizations (Ashworth, 1988; Boas, 1999; O'Brien et al., 2000; Alvarez, 1999). Finally, NGOs are often seen to have some advantages over the state in distributing development resources to poor, marginalized groups, because they are more in touch with and knowledgeable about local conditions and needs.

In principle these developments should consolidate the position of women's NGOs in governance networks and strengthen the linkages between women's NGOs and women as a constituency in civil society. Women's NGOs are frequently hailed as key intermediaries for a 'women's constituency' in civil society (O'Brien et al., 2000; Alvarez, 1999). During the Beijing conference many Latin American governments, for example, invited select NGOs to participate in the official preparatory process; a practice also adopted by many European delegations. Certainly, this has played a role in helping women's NGOs to legitimize their claims and to develop further transnational networks to press for further change. However, these developments have to be seen in the broader context of state downsizing and the cutting back of development aid to all but emergency programmes. NGOs, in helping to implement such policies, take on responsibilities that were formerly the responsibility of the state. From this perspective, NGOs might actually play a key role in legitimizing rules, norms and policies that work against the interests of the constituency they claim to represent (O'Brien et al., 2000; Alvarez, 1999).

Arguably, the UN is being eclipsed by the Bretton Woods institutions that increasingly dominate international economic and social policy-making and so it is increasingly important for women's NGOs to access key decision-makers within the World Bank. Wolfensohn became the first World Bank president to attend a UN conference on women when he attended the Beijing meeting. Since 1995, there has also been evidence of a greater commitment to gender equity within the World Bank. O'Brien et al. have pointed to the 'Gender Analysis and Policy' thematic group set up in 1995 and the external Gender Consultative Group, comprised of members of the women's movement across the world, as evidence of a greater willingness by the Bank to engage in dialogue about policy, particularly in relation to structural adjustment. Wolfensohn has pressed for gender equity in the workplace and in private sector development projects, and demanded that gender action plans be incorporated into all of the Bank's regional operations. The World Bank also produces an annual report on gender in development (O'Brien et al., 2000). The Bank's poverty alleviation strategy has promised changes in approach in order to incorporate governance issues, and attention is now focused more closely on participation and improved cooperation with women's NGOs. However, these commitments often amount to no more than vague statements, and most observers seem to agree that the Bank's actual track record of implementation of these 'vague statements' has been less than impressive (Boas, 1999).

While women's groups have had some, albeit limited, successes in securing recognition of women's rights in the UN bodies and agencies, the Bretton Woods institutions are governed by a rather different ideology and set of values, which works against genuine gender equality. Steinstra identifies liberalization and globalization as hegemonic 'comprehensive norms' that severely limit women's advancement (Steinstra, 1999). World Bank policy, ostensibly designed to consolidate democratic spaces in civil society and increase women's visibility and participation in development projects, works to ensure the basic functioning of an economic model that excludes the majority of citizens (Vargas, 1999). Alvarez argues that a discourse of state and civil society co-responsibility for social welfare pervades the neoliberal quest for partnership with women's NGOs. As states 'downsize', NGOs come to be regarded as vehicles of choice, which helps to foster support for currently fashionable development strategies (Alvarez, 1999). NGOs are represented as articulating the interests and concerns of women worldwide, but this engagement with NGOs is intended to build public consensus and support for the work of the Bank, not to facilitate a genuine debate, or generate a critique of the Bank's work (O'Brien et al., 2000).

During the 1980s feminist groups were among the most vocal critics of structural adjustment policies foisted on indebted countries across the South and the former Eastern bloc by the IMF and World Bank. Many developing countries complain that goals agreed at UN conferences on poverty eradication, social progress and equality are being undermined by economic liberalization, Structural Adjustment Programmes (SAPs), the continuing debt crisis, the decline in aid flows to developing countries and the attendant marginalization of countries and poor people. In more recent years, the women's movement has continued to challenge the neoliberal economic development paradigm that the Bank promotes and which is responsible for accelerating rates of female poverty in developing countries particularly. However, while feminist critique has made 'some inroads' in, for example, generating support for women's education and on health issues and micro-credit, it has not seriously challenged neoliberal prescriptions of market-led economic growth despite evidence that these prescriptions have failed (Boas, 1999).

Globalization has had a profoundly significant impact on the ability of NGOs to engage in the political process. On the one hand, rapid technological advances in communications have extended the organizational reach of the women's movement, making it global in scope. An electronic networking system has gradually emerged and this network has facilitated an exchange of information among women's NGOs. On the other hand, as Alvarez points out, neoliberal social and economic adjustment policies, state downsizing and changing international regimes have dramatically altered the conditions under which women's struggles for social justice are unfolding. The 'rolling back' of the state and welfare services has meant that women across the world have taken on a greater burden of care. Dominant ideas of gender mean that men continue to be seen as the head of the household, while women are assumed to be responsible for childcare. Far from extending democratic accountability and expanding participation, in many OECD countries the 'rolling back of the state' has insulated economic policy from the demands of the poor for economic and social security. At the same time, job insecurity has become a feature of economic and corporate restructuring and the dismantling of social protection measures. O'Brien et al. similarly argue that the women's movements, and those visible advocacy NGOs particularly, are wrestling with unfavourable economic climates and are frequently fighting to prevent a major retreat of women from the political arena as they struggle to survive. The degree to which NGOs can follow up on international conferences depends on the national political context, the policy environment and the commitment of governments, but it also depends crucially on the capacities and resources of NGOs.

The World Bank, IMF and the WTO are governed by a set of values drawn from neoliberal economics within which women's concerns with social justice can be seen as attempts to impose market distortions. The mainstreaming of gender concerns occurs only if it increases efficiency and facilitates economic growth. Governance is at best seen as a tool that can facilitate adequate returns and ensure the efficacy of the programmes and projects funded by the Bank (Alvarez, 1999). In this context, gender equality comes to be seen as a technical issue or technical dimension of welfare policy and poverty alleviation. In an age of state downsizing, a range of development agencies are relying on NGOs to advise them, fulfilling the needs for detailed assessment surveys and other forms of empirical data. However, government delegations and international organizations make strategic choices about whom to consult and tend to choose NGOs whose goals coincide with their own policies and agendas (Global Policy Forum, 2001).

This 'engagement' with NGOs seldom extends to a wider political debate with civil society constituencies with the highest stakes in gender-focused programmes. States and multilateral institutions are turning NGOs into 'gender experts' rather than citizens' groups advocating on behalf of women's rights. However, those consulted tend to be the ones who can maximize technical capabilities rather than those most politically able to meaningfully involve women as citizens. This is ultimately disempowering, because it 'frames women as having needs but never choices and agency' (M. Meyer and Prugl, 1999, p. 13). Critics also argue that NGOs that work closely with policy-makers in national and international agencies have deradicalizing effects on the women's movement as a whole. Alvarez argues that in Latin America there has been a reconfiguration of the feminist movement, pushing some sections to public prominence and marginalizing others (Alvarez, 1999).

Conclusion: Can Global Governance be 'Good' for Women?

In summary, institutions, regimes and processes of governance are deeply embedded in power inequalities and ideologies of gender that work to institutionalize arrangements that distinguish the public from the private and perpetuate gender inequalities. However, gender is neither wholly constrained by social structures, nor in some way fixed or essential. The stress on gender, rather than women, draws attention to the socially constructed nature of gender relations and the possibilities of change in the interests of redressing inequalities. In diverse ways women's NGOs and feminist groups[14] have campaigned to put gender issues on the international agenda, and contest dominant norms and rules (Meyer and Prugl, 1999; O'Brien et al., 2000).

A feminist perspective on global governance necessarily involves some scepticism towards the (liberal) view that states and international institutions are impartial by alerting us to structural factors that constrain and limit politics oriented to achieving social and political change. The problems of working within existing institutions should not be underestimated. The creation of separate institutional mechanisms and the adoption of special measures to rectify discrimination against women do not always have the desired effect, often resulting in a 'women's ghetto' endowed with less power and fewer resources, attracting less interest and commanding a lower priority than other national policy goals. On the other hand, efforts to improve the situation of women through general measures addressed to the population as a whole often result in the struggle for equality becoming submerged in global concerns.[15] Moreover, recent developments do not offer grounds for optimism that the situation is likely to improve. Over the last few decades, the UN system has evolved into a disparate structure with little coordination and some duplication, and consequently there have been moves to improve the division of responsibilities among programmes and specialized agencies. Rationalization brings its own potential dangers since it might serve to make macro-economic policy the sole preserve of the World Bank, IMF and WTO.

Some NGOs are even beginning to question the usefulness of participating in UN conferences, or engaging with multilateral economic institutions at all. The outcome of UN conferences is not legally binding, and usually reflects a consensus reached on the basis of the lowest common denominator. NGOs are often not equipped to follow up effectively on such conferences. For NGOs in the South the task of translating agreements reached at UN conferences into the national context is particularly difficult and daunting. Moreover, governments and international institutions often impede NGO participation in various ways (Rao, 1996). Some commentators see global governance as simply a new name for US hegemony or Western imperialism. Spivak, for example, argues that events like the Beijing conference can be seen as a well-organized ideological apparatus used to demonstrate an ostensible unity of North and South, when the North organizes the South and the UN supports development policies which nurture post-Fordism (Spivak, 1996).

Clearly, NGOs are working under difficult conditions and powerful constraints. While some space has been available to advance a pro-woman (and often feminist) agenda, and women's NGOs have made some progress in consolidating their position, it is difficult not to conclude that, overall, gender issues continue to be marginalized within governance networks and processes. It seems that at present the dominant rules and norms effectively mean that women's NGOs are caught up in the dilemma of, on the one hand, entering into a formalized relationship with the state as donors who expect visible, short-term results on gender projects, or, on the other hand, refusing to play by the rules and being effectively silenced in public discourse (Alvarez, 1999).

The Platform of Action negotiated at Beijing noted that 'the advancement of women and the achievement of equality between men and women are a matter of human rights and a condition for social justice', while recognizing that continuing poverty among women, inequalities in women's access to and participation in economic structures, policies and the productive process, and inequalities in the sharing of power and decision-making were all significant obstacles to achieving women's human rights. At the same time NGO forums have insisted that the whole issue of women's human rights must be seen not just in terms of modernization and development strategies in individual countries, but in terms of the current globalization of economic activity and the 'current dominant economic paradigm and resulting economic and social policies inherently detrimental to women's rights'.[16] Globalization is not producing a world of limitless opportunity, as neoliberal advocates of globalization contend, but is contributing to growing levels of poverty and inequality. All these factors severely constrain the opportunities and life chances available to women.

In concluding her reflections on the WID movement, Newland comments that perhaps transnational coalitions can do no more than offer a framework of encouragement and support while doing as much as possible within existing constraints to improve the material conditions of women's lives (Newland, 1991). While recognizing the problems and constraints, UN conferences do at least set standards on which governments are held accountable and it is vital that women's NGOs continue to be involved in the process, if only to prevent the erosion of established principles. Withdrawal might be an unwise strategy for women's NGOs given that historically women have not had access to power and continue to be heavily underrepresented in government and policy-making bodies, despite advances made in the last three decades.

NGOs need to avoid becoming involved in the implementation of policies that might disadvantage women, and need to continually highlight the negative impacts of neoliberalism, privatization and structural adjustment. Women's NGOs must continue to struggle for more resources and better access to policy-makers and policy-making forums. Crucially, women's NGOs must continue to challenge dominant understandings of gender relations, by challenging the language in which 'women's problems' and 'women's needs' – in relation to economic and social policies and development programmes – have been articulated. Finally, while NGOs cannot be said to represent or articulate the demands of women directly, they do strengthen the linkages between policy-makers, major centres of power and those most affected by economic globalization, who are at present often without a voice. In this way, women's NGOs can play an important role in articulating the views of poor, marginalized groups. NGOs provide important channels of communication between women, national policy-makers and international institutions, and can facilitate a wider discussion involving a broader range of women's groups in the process of monitoring and assessment.

If global governance is about forging pathways between society and government, then there is potential for NGOs to play a more active role in setting norms and acting as agents of change. At the same time NGOs have to be aware of the dangers of creating an elite group of insider NGOs that effectively mimic existing structures of power. Simmonds argues that the challenge facing women's NGOs is that, as they acquire the access and influence they have long sought, they must not lose the qualities that have made them a source of protest, innovation and change (Simmonds, 1998).

The adoption of the term 'good governance' by the World Bank and other Bretton Woods institutions has opened up a broader debate about whether such a thing is really possible and what it would entail in practice to make it a useful and meaningful concept for women. The language of 'good governance' has been adopted by oppositional groups and used to articulate a project that is not merely about a technical process of the implementation of a neoliberal agenda, but embraces democratization, accountability and respect for basic human rights. This vision of the good governance project involves constructing an effective system of global governance, as a counterweight to the globalization of the world economic system (UN, 1996).

The best strategy for women's NGOs is, perhaps, to embrace this alternative 'good governance' agenda, insisting that governments and international institutions make good on their promises to foster genuine dialogue and take seriously their own stated objectives of promoting basic human rights. Post-Beijing, human rights has provided the conceptual underpinnings of all other issue areas addressed in the Platform of Action. Moreover, while the diversity of women and, indeed, women's groups has been noted, the Beijing conference was also notable for the degree to which women from both the North and the South agreed on the problems of economic globalization, structural adjustment, economic transition, and the promotion of women's human rights in order to achieve genuine security for women (Chow, 1996). Demands for women's human rights necessarily involve developing a critique of neoliberal programmes which might actually involve the 'rolling back' or even curtailment of economic and social rights. As Bunch argues, good governance demands that women from diverse groups, cultures and societies are represented and participate fully in the global policy-making process; women's voices have been missing for too long (Bunch, 1995).

Notes

1 On the gendered nature of social power, see Connell, 1995.
2 Social constructivism is another, relatively recent, approach to regimes and governance. Here social agents are held to produce, reproduce and redefine the constitutive principles and structures by which they operate. Transnational and international network activity plays a key role in bringing about the internalization of norms – intersubjective meanings – and agreed rules that then become part of the domestic politics of states (Risse and Sikkink, 1999). This provides a promising framework to explore the role of women's NGOs in shaping the rules, perhaps, but unfortunately for reasons of space it cannot be included here.
3 See also Rosenau and Czempiel, 1992; Rosenau, 2000.
4 I do not mean to imply that the authors cited here work within a Marxist-feminist paradigm, only that this work discusses or raises questions about the degree to which the state can be viewed as patriarchal.
5 On the continuing relevance of the concept of the South in a globalizing world, see Thomas and Wilkin, 1996.
6 Birdsall and Graham (2000) claim that in India and Pakistan, and even in China, economic policy changes have been inevitably directed towards liberalization. Throughout Africa and the Middle East, more countries have been moving to market economies because this has been offered as a route out of poverty. Since the end of the Cold War and the collapse of communism in the former Soviet Union and Eastern Europe, there has been a marked consolidation of capitalism throughout the world. The process continued in the 1990s, with the East Asian financial crisis only producing yet another round of market-oriented consolidation.
7 Moreover, since the end of the Second World War there has been a gradual expansion of international human rights law, which includes the Convention on the Elimination of All Forms of Discrimination against Women (CEDAW) and a UN General Assembly Declaration on Violence against Women.
8 In preparation for the Beijing conference, at the UN's request, governments produced national reports in consultation with NGOs, setting out progress on issues of concern to women and strategies for the future. Government delegations also held regular meetings with NGOs to brief them about ongoing negotiations at both regional and international levels in preparation for the conference and, in some cases, throughout its duration. In the follow-up to Beijing, NGOs have played some role in the implementation of the Platform of Action. Consequently, many countries are now committed to mainstreaming a gender perspective into all their policies and operational systems. Moreover, NGOs recorded a 'list of promises' at the Beijing conference that has subsequently been used by national

and local groups to hold governments to account (NGO Forum on Women, 1996). While primary responsibility for advancing the status of women lies with governments, the actions of governments are subject to wider scrutiny as women's NGOs and transnational feminist networks exert pressure on national governments. See Ahmady, 2001.

9   The 1990s saw the formation of a Women's Caucus at the UN Conference on the Environment and Development (UNCED) that went on to become a fixture of subsequent UN conferences, including Beijing. This development has further helped to coordinate the lobbying efforts among women's NGOs and dissemination of information. See Ahmady, 2001.

10 The communications revolution has helped NGOs to coordinate strategies and this has resulted in horizontal links to a wide variety of organized communities and in a more coordinated, effective women's lobby at the UN (Harcourt, 1999).

11 Initially much of the focus of the UN's work was directed towards improving women's status through the development process. In more recent years, the UN women's conferences have made democracy, citizenship and women's human rights central focal points in feminist politics. The Commission on the Status of Women met in New York in March 1999, a meeting attended by over 1,000 delegates from governments, UN agencies and NGOs, to begin a comprehensive review of the Beijing Platform of Action and reach an agreement on a text for an optional protocol to the Convention on the Elimination of Discrimination against Women. The Office of the High Commissioner for Human Rights (OHCHR) has also included a series of measures to advance the issue of gender mainstreaming and women's human rights. In addition, in tandem with the Division on the Advancement of Women (DAW) and UNIFEM, the OHCHR has initiated workshops dedicated to incorporating gender mainstreaming into the UN human rights framework.

12 One survey by INSTRAW at the end of the 1980s found that out of ninety-six countries, only six included women's issues as key aspects of their development strategies.

13 GAD (Gender and Development) and mainstreaming aimed at the institutionalization of gender issues and thus the transformation of institutional structures. See Bryne et al., 1996.

14 Some NGOs may be concerned with single issues that affect women particularly, while feminist groups embrace a broader agenda that is concerned with improving the status of women, or increasing women's access to resources and power. However, for the most part women's groups and more overtly feminist organizations are motivated by a belief that women are in some way disadvantaged and that this disadvantage should be addressed and remedied, and as such are politicizing gender issues. It should be noted, nevertheless, that some 'women's groups' who organize internationally pursue a conservative agenda. See Global Policy Forum, 'NGOs at the UN: discrimination', at www.global policy.org/ngos/doc00/druelle.htm.

15 Attempts to reach consensus at Copenhagen conference in 1980 were scuttled by the second cold war, the rise of a confident New Right that trivialized the issue of gender equality, and by continuing ethnic and national conflicts such as the Palestinian issues and apartheid. See UN, 1995.

16 See *Vienna NGO Forum 94 Call to Action*, Economics Commission for Europe Regional meeting, Vienna, 1994, p. 1.

References

Ahmady, V. (2001) 'Evaluating the impact and effectiveness of the transnational feminist movement: the UN Decade and beyond', Ph.D. thesis, Keele University.

Alvarez, S. (1999) 'Advocating feminism', *International Feminist Journal of Politics*, 2, no. 1, pp. 181–209.

Amos, V. and Parmar, P. (1984) 'Challenging imperial feminism', *Feminist Review*, 17, pp. 13–19.

Ashworth, G. (1988) 'An elf among gnomes: a feminist in North–South relations', *Millennium: Journal of International Studies*, 17, no. 3, pp. 497–537.

Ashworth, G. and Bonnerjea, L. (1985) *The Invisible Decade: UK Women and the UN Decade for Women*, London: Gower.

Birdsall, N. and Graham, C. (eds) (2000) *New Markets, New Opportunities? Economic and Social Mobility in a Changing World*, Washington: Brookings Institution.

Boas, M. (1999) 'Governance as multilateral development bank policy: the case of the African Development Bank and the Asian Development Bank', in C. Lind (ed.), *Development and Rights: Negotiating Justice in Changing Societies*, London: Frank Cass.

Boserup, E. (1989) *Women's Role in Economic Development*, London: Earthscan.

Bryne, B., Kock, L. J., Baden, S. and Marcus, R. (1996) 'National machineries for women in development', paper, Institute of Development Studies, Brighton.

Bunch, C. (1995) 'Transforming human rights from a feminist perspective', in J. Peters and A. Wolper (eds), *Women's Rights, Human Rights: International Feminist Perspectives*, London: Routledge.

Bystydzienski, J. M. (1992) *Women Transforming Politics: Worldwide Strategies for Empowerment*, Bloomington: Indiana University Press.

Cerny, P. (1986) 'What next for the state?', in E. Kofman and G. Youngs (eds), *Globalization: Theory and Practice*, London: Pinter.

Cerny, P. (1990) *The Changing Architecture of Politics*, London: Sage.

Cheng, L. and Hsuing, P. (1998) 'Engendering the economic miracle: the labour market in the Asia Pacific', in G. Thompson (ed.), *Economic Dynamism in the Asia Pacific*, London: Routledge.

Chinkin, C. (1999) 'Gender, inequality and international human rights law', in A. Hurrell and N. Woods (eds), *Inequality, Globalization and World Politics*, Oxford: Oxford University Press.

Chow, E. Ngan-ling (1996) 'Making waves, moving mountains: reflections on Beijing '95 and beyond', *Signs*, 3, Autumn, pp. 185–92.

Clark, A. M. (1995) 'Non-governmental organizations and their influence on international society', *Journal of International Affairs*, 48, no. 2, Winter, pp. 507–25.

Connell, R. (1987) 'The state, gender and sexual politics: theory and appraisal', *Theory and Society*, 19, pp. 507–44.

Connell, R. (1995) *Gender and Power*, Cambridge: Polity.

Cox, R. W. (1983) 'Gramsci, hegemony and international relations: an essay in method', *Millennium: Journal of International Studies*, 12, no. 2, pp. 162–75.

Cox, R. (1986) 'States, social forces and world order', in R. Keohane (ed.), *Neorealism and its Critics*, Princeton: Princeton University Press.

Cox, R. (1987) *Production, Power and World Order: Social Forces in the Making of History*, New York: Columbia University Press.

Cox, R. and Sinclair, T. (eds) (1996) *Approaches to World Order*, Cambridge: Cambridge University Press.

Dalerup, D. (1987) 'Confusing concepts – confusing reality: a theoretical discussion of the patriarchal state', in A. Showstack Sassoon (ed.), *Women and the State*, London: Hutchinson.

Disch, L. (1991) 'Towards a feminist conception of politics', *Political Science Teacher*, Sept. pp. 46–8.

Elson, D. (1990) *Male Bias in the Development Process*, Manchester: Manchester University Press.

Enloe, C. (1989) *Bananas, Beaches and Bases: Making Feminist Sense of International Politics*, London: Pandora.

Falk, R. (1999) 'Humane governance for the world: reviving the quest', *Review of International Political Economy*, 7, no. 2, pp. 317–34.

Ferree, M. and Martin, P. Y. (eds) (1995) *Feminist Organisations: Harvest of the New Women's Movement*, Philadelphia: Temple University Press.

George, S. (1988) *A Fate Worse than Debt*, London: Penguin.

Germain, R. and Kenny, M. (1998) 'Engaging Gramsci: international relations theory and the new Gramscians', *Review of International Studies*, 24, no. 1, pp. 3–21.

Giddens, A. (1994) 'Living in a post-traditional society', in U. Beck, A. Giddens and S. Lash (eds), *Reflexive Modernization: Politics, Tradition and Aesthetics in the Modern Social Order*, Cambridge: Polity.

Gill, S. (ed.) (1993) *Gramsci, Historical Materialism and International Relations*, Cambridge: Cambridge University Press.

Global Policy Forum (2001) 'NGOs and global policy making', at www.global policy.org/ngos/info/ngoun.htm.

Goetz, A. (1995) *The Politics of Integrating Gender to States' Development Processes*, Geneva: United Nations Research Institute.

Goldblatt, D. (1998) 'Politics and governance in the Asia-Pacific: historical and thematic overview', in R. Maidment, D. Goldblatt and J. Mitchell (eds), *Governance in the Asia-Pacific*, London: Routledge.

Grewal, I. and Kaplan, C. (eds) (1994) *Scattered Hegemonies: Postmodernity and Transnational Feminist Practices*, Minneapolis: University of Minnesota Press.

Haas, P. M., Keohane, R. O. and Levy, M. A. (1993) *Institutions for the Earth: Sources of Effective Environmental Protection*, Cambridge, Mass.: MIT Press.

Hall, S. (1992) 'Brave new world', *Socialist Review*, 21, no. 1, pp. 57–64.

Harcourt, W. (1999) *Women@Internet: Creating New Cultures in Cyberspace*, London: Zed Books.

Harcourt, W. (2000) 'Comments on "Bringing women's voices into the dialogue on technology policy and globalization in Asia" by Swasti Mitter and Sheila Rowbotham', *International Feminist Journal of Politics*, 2, no. 3, Autumn, pp. 402–5.

Hendessi, M. (1986) 'Fourteen thousand women meet: report from Nairobi, July, 1985', *Feminist Review*, 23, June, 147–56.

Hooper, E. (1994a) 'Report on the UN ECE regional preparatory meeting for the Fourth World Conference on Women', UN Publications, Geneva.

Hooper, E. (1994b) 'Report on the UN ESCAP regional preparatory meeting for the Fourth World Conference on Women', UN Publications, Jakarta.

Hooper, E. (1994c) 'Report on the UN LAC regional preparatory meeting for the Fourth World Conference on Women', UN Publications, Mexico.

Ling, L. and Bell, N. (1998) 'Theorizing hegemony: a critical examination of gender, race and class in Gramscian globalism', conference paper, IR Standing Group of the ECPR, Vienna, Sept.

Lubeck, P. (1998) 'Winners and losers in the Asia Pacific economic miracle', in G. Thompson (ed.), *Pacific Economic Dynamism in Asia*, London: Routledge.

McIntosh, M. (1985) 'The state as oppressor of women', in A. Kuhn and A. Wolfe (eds), *Feminism and Materialism: Women and Modes of Production*, London: Routledge.

MacKinnon, C. (1989) *Towards a Feminist Theory of the State*, Cambridge, Mass.: Harvard University Press.

Marchand, M. (1995) 'Latin American voices of resistance: women's movements and development debates', in S. Rostow, M. Rupert and A. Samatur (eds), *The Global Economy as Political Space: Essays in Critical Theory and International Political Economy*, Cambridge: Cambridge University Press.

Marshall, B. (1994) *Engendering Modernity*, Cambridge: Polity.

Meyer, M. and Prugl, E. (eds) (1999) *Gender Politics in Global Governance*, London: Rowman and Littlefield.

Meyer, W. H. (1998) *Human Rights and International Political Economy in the Third World*, Westport, Conn.: Praeger Press.

Mies, M. (1986) *Patriarchy and Accumulation on a World Scale*, London: Zed Books.

Mitter, S. (1986) *Common Fate, Common Bond: Women in the Global Economy*, London: Pluto Press.

Mitter, S. and Rowbotham, S. (2000) 'Bringing women's voices into the dialogue on technology policy and globalization', *International Feminist Journal of Politics*, 3, no. 2, pp. 382–401.

Mohanty, C. (1988) 'Under Western eyes: feminist scholarship and colonial discourse', *Feminist Review*, 30, pp. 61–88.

Mohanty, C., Rosso, A. and Torress, L. (1991) *Third World Women and the Politics of Feminism*, Bloomington: Indiana University Press.

Molyneux, M. (1985) 'Mobilization without emancipation? Women's interests, state and revolution in Nicaragua', *Feminist Studies*, 11, no. 2, Summer.

Moser, C. (1991) 'Gender planning in the Third World: meeting practical and strategic needs', in R. Grant and K. Newland (eds), *Gender and International Relations*, Bloomington: Indiana University Press.

Murphy, C. N. (2000) 'Global governance: poorly done and poorly understood', *International Affairs*, 76, no. 4, pp. 789–803.

Newland, K. (1991) 'From transnational relationships to international relations: Women in Development and the International Decade for Women', in R. Grant and K. Newland (eds), *Gender and International Relations*, Milton Keynes: Open University Press.

NGO Forum on Women (1996) *Final Report 1996*, New York: UN Publications.

Nicholson, L. (ed.) (1990) *Feminism/Postmodernism*, London: Routledge.

O'Brien, M. (1999) 'Reflexivity, identity and environment in Giddens' social theory', in M. O'Brien, S. Penna and C. Hay (eds), *Theorising Modernity: Reflexivity, Environment and Identity in Giddens' Social Theory*, London: Longmans.

O'Brien, R., Goetz, A. M., Scholte, J. A. and Williams, M. (2000) *Contesting Global Governance*, Cambridge: Cambridge University Press.

Ohmae, K. (1996) *The End of the Nation State: The Rise of Regional Economies*, London: HarperCollins.

Onimode, B. (1989) *The IMF, the World Bank and the African Debt*, London: Zed Books.

Overbeek, H. (1993) *Restructuring Hegemony in the Global Political Economy: The Rise of Transnational Neo-Liberalism in the 1980s*, London: Routledge.

Pietila, H. and Vickers, J. (1994) *Making Women Matter: The Role of the UN*, London: Zed Books.

Rao, A. (1996) 'Engendering institutional change', *Signs*, 22, no. 3, pp. 218–21.

Riley, S. (ed.) (1992) *The Politics of Global Debt*, Basingstoke: Macmillan.

Risse, T. and Sikkink, K. (1999) *The Power of Human Rights*, Cambridge: Cambridge University Press.

Rosenau, J. (2000) 'Governance in a globalizing world', in D. Held and A. McGrew (eds), *The Global Transformations Reader*, Cambridge: Polity.

Rosenau, J. and Czempiel, E. (1992) *Governance without Government: Order and Change in World Politics*, Cambridge: Cambridge University Press.

Runyan, A. S. (1996) 'The place of women in trading places: gendered global/regional regimes and internationalized feminist resistance', in E. Kofman and G. Youngs (eds), *Globalization: Theory and Practice*, London: Pinter.

Rupert, M. (1995) *Producing Hegemony: The Politics of Mass Production and American Global Power*, Cambridge: Cambridge University Press.

Scholte, J. A. (2000) *Globalization: A Critical Introduction*, Basingstoke: Palgrave.

Scott, A. (1990) *Ideology and the New Social Movements*, London: Unwin Hyman.

Sen, G. and Grown, C. (1987) *Development, Crisis and Alternative Visions: Third World Women's Perspectives*, London: Earthscan.

Simmonds, P. J. (1998) 'Learning to live with NGOs', *Foreign Policy*, 112, Fall, pp. 82–90.

Spivak, G. (1996) ' "Woman" as theatre: United Nations Conference on Women, Beijing 1995', *Radical Philosophy*, 75, Jan.–Feb., pp. 1–7.

Standt, K. (1986) 'Women, development and the state: on the theoretical impasse', *Development and Change*, 17, pp. 325–33.

Steans, J. (1998) *Gender and International Relations*, Cambridge: Polity.

Steans, J. (1999) 'The private is global: global political economy and feminist politics', *New Political Economy*, 4, no. 1, Mar., pp. 113–28.

Steinstra, D. (1999) 'Of roots, leaves and trees: gender social movements, and global governance', in M. Meyer and E. Prugl (eds), *Gender Politics in Global Governance*, London: Rowman and Littlefield.

Stopford, J. and Strange, S. (1991) *Rival States, Rival Firms: Competition for World Market Shares*, Cambridge: Cambridge University Press.

Strange, S. (1996) *The Retreat of the State: The Diffusion of Power in the World Economy*, Cambridge: Cambridge University Press.

Sylvester, C. (1994) 'The emperor's theories and transformations: looking at the field through feminist lenses', in C. Sylvester and D. Pirages (eds), *Transformations in Global Political Economy*, London: Macmillan.

Thomas, C. and Wilkin, P. (1996) *Globalization and the South*, Basingstoke: Macmillan.

Tickner, A. (1992) 'On the fringes of the global economy', in R. Tooze and C. Murphy (eds), *The New International Political Economy*, Boulder: Lynne Rienner.

Tong, R. (1989) *Feminist Thought*, London: Unwin Hyman.

Tooze, R. and Murphy, C. (eds) (1990) *The New International Political Economy*, Oxford: Lynne Rienner.

True, J. (1999) 'Expanding markets and marketing gender: the integration of the post-socialist Czech Republic', *Review of Governmental International Political Economy*, 6, no. 3, pp. 360–89.

UN (1995) 'The United Nations and the advancement of women', New York: United Nations Department of Public Information.

UN (1996) 'The United Nations, NGOs and global governance: challenges for the twenty-first Century', United Nations Non-Governmental Liaison Service, Geneva, Nov.

UN (1999) 'A human face for globalization', Human Development Report Office, United Nations, www.undp.org/hdro/E1.html.

Vargas, G. (1999) 'Latin American feminism in the '90s: reflections', interview with Gina Vargas by Nira Yuval-Davis, October 1998, *International Feminist Journal of Politics*, 1, no. 2, Nov., pp. 300–10.

Waring, M. (1988) *If Women Counted: A New Feminist Economics*, San Francisco: Harper and Row.

Whitworth, S. (1994) *Feminism and International Relations*, Basingstoke: Macmillan.

Willetts, P. (ed.) (1992) *Pressure Groups in the Global System*, London: Pinter.

Willetts, P. (ed.) (1996a) *The Conscience of the World: The Influence of NGOs in the UN System*, London: Hurst.

Willetts, P. (1996b) 'From Stockholm to Rio and beyond: the impact of the environmental movement on the United Nations Consultative Arrangement for NGOs', *Review of International Studies*, 22, no. 1, pp. 57–81.

Wood, R. (1983) 'The debt crisis and North–South relations', *Third World Quarterly*, July.

Young, K., Wolkowitz, C. and McCullagh, R. (1984) *Of Marriage and the Market: Women's Subordination Internationally and its Lessons*, London: Routledge.

Yuval-Davis, N. and Athias, F. (1989) *Woman Nation State*, Basingstoke: Macmillan.

Part II

Governing Global Problems

5

Global Pandemics: HIV/AIDS

Nana K. Poku

Introduction

Improved prevention, awareness and access to better drugs in the more advanced countries have meant that the scourge of the Human Immunodeficiency Virus (HIV) – the cause of Acquired Immune Deficiency Syndrome (AIDS) – has largely slipped from public consciousness. Yet HIV/AIDS remains, in the words of Peter Piot, the head of the Joint United Nations Programme on HIV/AIDS (UNAIDS), 'the single greatest threat to continual global development' (interview 12 September 2001). It is not difficult to see why: last year alone, some 5 million people contracted HIV at a rate of 15,000 a day or 11 infections per minute. This brought the global total of people living with the virus to 35 million – see table 5.1 below. Depending on access to effective anti-retroviral drugs, these people will die in the next 5–10 years, joining the 17 million people who have already lost their lives to the epidemic since the early 1980s (UNAIDS, 2001).

Beyond these grim statistics, the virus is already eroding hard-won improvements in development indicators across the developing world. As a result of HIV/AIDS, many countries are witnessing a deterioration in child survival rates, reduced life expectancy, crumbling and overburdened health systems and the decimation of a generation in the prime of their working lives. Indeed, not since the bubonic plague of the European Middle Ages has there been so large a threat to hundreds of millions of people and the future of entire societies. As one astute observer rightly noted, 'AIDS is the modern incarnation of Dante's inferno.' Predicated on the unfolding HIV/AIDS crisis, this chapter is concerned with its societal causes and global responses to them. The chapter begins with a brief overview of the pandemic's first two decades, and then moves to assess its societal causes. Following this, it addresses the history of governance and concludes by considering the challenges facing the new global AIDS fund proposed by the Secretary-General of the United Nations, Kofi Annan.

Global AIDS: Societal Causes and Consequences

As it enters its third decade, several important observations can be made about the specific challenges posed by the HIV/AIDS epidemic. First, it is at one and the same time both a crisis and an endemic condition. It is a crisis because the speed of spread of the virus has proved to be quite awesome. That it is an endemic condition may best be simply illustrated by the fact that, even if an affected country were to suffer no further cases of infection as from today, the pain and trauma of the deaths of those already infected will continue for the next twenty years and the social and economic repercussions of their deaths will continue on for decades and generations after that. Second, the pandemic manifests itself both as a specific problem and also as a pervasive one. Its specificity is revealed in its associated morbidity and mortality, in increasing numbers of people – mostly healthy, productive young women and men – getting sick and dying. The response of the first decade of the epidemic addressed this quality of the crisis. It focused on the epidemic as a health crisis and on its ramifications for health service delivery. However, the repercussions of these deaths are beginning to permeate and affect every facet of human life and national development in the regions most affected (see Hope, 2001; Poku and Cheru, 2001).

In truth, HIV/AIDS has always been a strikingly patterned pandemic. That is, it is possible to identify different forms of the epidemic in different parts of the world (see table 5.1). In the developed societies of Western Europe, North America and Japan, for example, HIV infections are concentrated principally among injecting drug users and gay men. The available data suggest that there is very low HIV infection rates among heterosexuals in the general population. In Germany, for example, in the mid-1990s fewer than 3 in 10,000 women of childbearing age were infected. Similarly low rates have been recorded across Western Europe (UNDP, 1999, p. 3). The situation is very different among injecting drug users and gay men. Some communities and countries have initiated aggressive HIV prevention efforts among these vulnerable groups (UNAIDS, 2000a, p. 23). In many places, however, the political cost of implementing needle-exchange and other prevention programmes for the gay community has been considered too high for such programmes to be started or maintained. As a result, there are continuing high prevalence rates among injecting drug users in many high-income countries. Take the case of Canada, where nearly half of all new HIV infections occur in this group. Similarly, among gay men, the virus continues to spread despite two decades of targeted prevention campaigns.

Unlike in the higher income countries, the HIV epidemic in the developing world is highly diverse. Here, most transmission occurs through sex between men and women, but there are also very high rates of infection among men who have sex with men, and among injecting drug users. In much of Latin America, for example, HIV infections are confined largely to these subpopulations, while in Africa – where over 70 per cent of the global HIV population resides – the virus is spread primarily through heterosexual and perinatal transmission, with heterosexual activity being the dominant mode of transmission. Already the virus has overtaken malaria as the major killer on the continent, but its structural impact threatens to be even more devastating (UNAIDS, 2001). Across Africa, life expectancy at birth rose by a full 15 years from 44 years in the early 1950s to 59 in the early 1990s; due to AIDS the figure is set to recede between 2005 and 2010 to just 44 years (UNAIDS, 2000a, p. 2). The six countries in southern Africa that now form the global epicentre of the epidemic – Botswana, Namibia, South Africa, Swaziland, Zambia and Zimbabwe – face a particularly bleak future. Within these countries, one in six adults is HIV positive and AIDS is expected to claim the lives of between 8 per cent and 25 per cent of today's educated elite by the year 2005 (UNAIDS, 2000c, p. 23).

The above demonstrates that although the terminal events have been grimly similar across the globe, the course of HIV infections has been highly variable. Yet one determining factor is indisputable. While not restricted solely to poor people, AIDS is

Table 5.1 Regional HIV/AIDS statistics and features, January 2002

Region	Epidemic started	Adults and children living with HIV/AIDS	Adults and children newly infected with HIV	Adult prevalence rate[a]	Percent of HIV-positive adults who are women	Main mode(s) of transmission[b] for adults living with HIV/AIDS
Sub-Saharan Africa	late 1970s–early 1980s	28.1 million	3.4 million	8.4%	55%	Hetro
North Africa and Middle East	late 1980s	440,000	80,000	0.2%	40%	IDU, Hetro
South and South East Asia	late 1980s	6.1 million	800,000	0.6%	35%	Hetro, IDU
East Asia and Pacific	late 1980s	1 million	270,000	0.1%	20%	IDU, Hetro, MSM
Latin America	late 1970s–early 1980s	1.4 million	130,000	0.5%	30%	MSM, IDU, Hetro
Caribbean	late 1970s–early 1980s	420,000	60,000	2.2%	50%	Hetro, MSM
Eastern Europe and Central Asia	early 1990s	1 million	250,000	0.5%	20%	IDU, MSM
Western Europe	late 1970s–early 1980s	520,000	30,000	0.3%	25%	MSM, IDU
North America/Canada	late 1970s–early 1980s	940,000	45,000	0.6%	20%	MSM, IDU, Hetro
Australia and New Zealand	late 1970s–early 1980s	15,000	500	0.1%	10%	MSM, IDU
TOTAL		40 million	5 million	1.2%	48%	

[a] The proportion of adults (15 to 49 years of age) living with HIV/AIDS in 2001, using 2000 population numbers.
[b] MSM (sexual transmission among men who have sex with men), IDU (transmission through injecting drug use), Hetro (heterosexual transmission).
Source: WHO/UNAIDS data.

a disease of poverty. Indeed, poverty structures not only the contours of the pandemic but also the nature of outcomes once an individual is sick with complications of HIV infections (Poku, 2001b, p. 196). Perhaps more than anywhere else, the wealthiest country in the world, the United States – in which at least 20 per cent of the people nevertheless live in poverty – provides an important example of the role of poverty as the main driving force of the epidemic (UNDP, 1999, p. 149). Here, HIV has moved almost unimpeded through poor communities – mostly of colour. By the end of 1999, African-Americans, who comprise approximately 12 per cent of the US population, made up more than 26 per cent of the country's poor and accounted for 37 per cent of all reported cases of HIV/AIDS (CDC, 2000, p. 457).

The link between poverty and vulnerability to HIV/AIDS is brought into an even sharper focus at the global level. The inescapable picture from table 5.1 in this regard is the fact that 95 per cent of the global distribution of HIV infections and AIDS cases are located in the developing world. The following paragraph by Jodi Jacobson dramatizes the complex interconnectivity of poverty, gender and HIV/AIDS:

> Two out of three women in the world presently suffer from the most debilitating disease known to humanity. Common symptoms of this fast-spreading ailment include chronic anaemia, malnutrition, and severe fatigue. Sufferers exhibit an increased susceptibility to infections of the respiratory and reproductive tracts. And premature death is a frequent outcome. In the absence of direct intervention, the disease is often communicated from mother to child, with markedly higher transmission rates among females than males. Yet studies confirm the efficacy of numerous prevention and treatment strategies, to date few have been vigorously pursued. The disease is poverty. (Jacobson, 1992, p. 3)

While poverty itself does not cause AIDS, there are endless potential links between poverty and poor health. From the biomedical literature, we know a great deal about the mechanisms by which malnutrition and parasite infection undermine the body's specific and non-specific immune response. Protein-energy malnutrition (general calorie deficit) and specific micronutrient deficiencies, such as vitamin-A deficiency, weaken every part of the body's immune system, including the skin and mucous membranes, which are particularly important in protecting human beings from sexually transmitted diseases (STDs) – the critical co-factor for transmission of HIV. Parasite infestation plays a dual role in suppressing immune response. It aggravates malnutrition by robbing the body of essential nutrients and by increasing calorie demand. Moreover, the presence of parasites chronically triggers the immune system, impairing its ability to fight infection from other pathogens.

Poverty, however, not only creates the biological conditions for greater susceptibility to infectious diseases such as HIV, it also limits the options for treating these critical diseases. A central feature of HIV infection, for example, is that it clusters in families, with both parents often being HIV positive (and, in time, experiencing morbidity and mortality). Poor families have less capacity to deal with the effects of morbidity and mortality than richer ones, for very obvious reasons. These include the absence of savings and other assets that can cushion the impact of illness and death. The poor are already on the margins of survival and thus are also unable to deal with the consequent health and other costs. These include the costs of drugs – when available – to treat opportunistic infections, transport costs to health centres, reduced household productivity through illness and the diversion of labour to caring roles, losses of employment through illness and job discrimination, funeral and related costs, and so on. In the longer term such poor households never recover even their initial level of living as their capacity is reduced through the losses of productive family members through death and through migration, and through the sales of any productive assets they once possessed. As a result, a true process of immiseration is now observable in many parts of the developing world, particularly Africa.

There is thus enormous strain on the capacity of families to cope with the psycho-social and economic consequences of illness, such that many families experience great distress and often disintegrate as social and economic units (Menon et al., 1999, p. 23). Even where they do not, by eliminating the breadwinners – often the parents – the process further exposes the rest of the family members to poverty which then increases their chances of contracting the virus. This is particularly true of young women, who will often be forced to engage in commercial sexual transactions, some-times as a casual sex worker (CSW) but more often on an occasional basis, as survival strategies for themselves and their dependants. The effects of these behaviours on HIV infection in women are only too evident, and in part account for the much higher infection rates in young women, who are increasingly unable to sustain themselves by other work in either the formal or informal sectors. In the western Kenyan city of Kismusu, for example, 23 per cent of girls aged between 15 and 19 are infected with HIV, as compared with only 8 per cent of boys (Buvé et al., 1999, p. 5). This difference persists among men and women in their twenties as well, although it narrows some-what with age. Some 38 per cent of women aged 20 to 25 tested positive for HIV in Kismusu, against 12 per cent of men of the same age (Williams, Milligan and Odemwingie, 1998, p. 5).

A note of caution must be entered here, however, because there are many reasons why women (particularly young women) are so vulnerable to HIV. A number of recent community-based studies from developing countries have taught us at least two important things about the vulnerability of women to HIV. First, they tell us that African women are having unprotected sex from very young ages. Although this is no surprise to anyone who keeps track of teenage pregnancies, it is a fact often wilfully ignored by most governments when it comes to sex education in schools. Kenya, for example, still has no 'family life' education in schools despite nearly two decades of glaring evidence that young Kenyan women are some five to six times more likely to be infected with HIV than young Kenyan men of comparable age. Recent attempts to introduce such education have been repeatedly defeated following intensive opposition from conservative and religious groups.

Secondly, community-based research indicates that young women are having sex with men much older than they are – a point confirmed by, among others, our ongoing studies in Botswana and Zambia (Poku, 2002, p. 44). Preliminary results indicate that 'these older men' select young girls for sex because they are perceived to be 'clean': that is, unlikely to be infected with HIV or STDs. In reality, this belief is very mis-placed. The very high prevalence rates recorded among teenagers exist alongside the fact that in most African societies a significant proportion of the vulnerable age group (between 14 and 19) is not sexually active (Poku and Cheru, 2001). Out of 2,400 teenagers interviewed in Botswana and Zambia, for example, nearly 48 per cent had never had sex, with only 25 per cent admitting to being sexually active. These results are not too dissimilar to studies from other parts of Africa. In Kismusu, for example,

HIV prevalence among girls of 15 to 19 is 23 per cent, but 29.9 per cent of this age group has never had sex (Buvé et al., 1999, p. 8). What these figures tell us is that the girls who are already sexually active are even more likely to be infected with HIV than the high prevalence rate calculated as an average suggests. Moreover, given that they are close to the start of their sexual lives, these younger girls have probably been infected with HIV relatively recently. This further increases their contagion rates because the virus replicates very quickly at the start of an infection, only gradually being brought under temporary control as antibodies are produced. Having unprotected sex with young women may therefore actually represent a higher risk of acquiring HIV for older men than selecting a partner their own age.

International Response to HIV/AIDS

The architecture of the global response to HIV/AIDS resembles a series of evolving but complexly interdependent regimes centred on the United Nations and related agencies. The first significant regime was created in early 1986 when the World Health Organization (WHO) established the Global Programme on AIDS (GPA) – under the late Jonathan Mann's leadership. Mann resigned dramatically in early 1990, protesting at what he called 'a lack of commitment' to fighting the disease on the part of the WHO's former director-general Hiroshi Natajima. Mann's replacement, Michael Merson, a public health expert who had spent much of his career at the WHO, was widely criticized for unimaginative leadership. This notwithstanding, by the early 1990s at least three fundamental weaknesses had emerged concerning the global response to the societal causes and consequences of the epidemic under GPA. First, it was clear that under GPA the strategy to reduce the overall levels of new infections was failing because the gap between the rate of new infections and the strategic expectations was growing ever wider. Second and relatedly, the gap was expanding because the existing knowledge about the underlying societal factors working to expose people to the virus was limited. Indeed, as late as 1994 – some fifteen years into the epidemic – an editorial in the *Lancet* could comment concerning a new study: 'we are not aware of other investigations which have considered the influence of socio-economic status on mortality in HIV-infected individuals' (Sampson and Neaton, 1994, p. 1100). Finally, there was a growing dissatisfaction among donor governments with the working of GPA, seen as hamstrung by its place within WHO and unable to work effectively with other UN agencies. This was further complicated by the structural weakness of the WHO: particularly in developing effective strategies, coordinating policies and providing financial support for activities at the country level that would slow down the transmission rates of the virus.

Dissatisfaction with GPA's overall performance finally sparked the chiefs of AIDS programmes in other UN agencies to insist on an overhaul and the creation of a separate United Nations Programme on AIDS. The unique nature of this new programme is brought into a sharper focus when one considers the traditional difficulties in creating new regimes under the UN structure. While each regime differs in its substantive details, the process by which each is arrived at has been remarkably similar. It involved first agreeing on the areas where the actions of nations need to be harmonized and international machinery employed. Following this, the process moves to define the norms that set standards of behaviour, defined in terms of rights and obligations that will govern that cooperation. The result of the process is usually a text that is accepted by governments, ranging from a treaty through to a resolution, and which forms the basis for legitimate behaviour by states – and their citizens – to be reflected in public policies and programmes.

At the heart of this process is extended multilateral negotiation. This is a very complex process, which often continues over many years, involving intricate subsidiary negotiations among subgroups of negotiators and over details, with sequential changes in the diagnoses given to problems and a continual restructuring of agendas as differences narrow and the focus of negotiations sharpens. The roles of different actors – governments, civil society and the secretariats of international organizations – also change during the process. The process of negotiating the Framework Convention on Global Climate Change illustrates the complexities. The process began with an extended discussion of the nature (even the existence) of the problem, largely carried out in international scientific unions (civil society) and within the World Meteorological Organization (international secretariats). It was carried to the global level at the General Assembly (governments), which mandated a specific negotiation process on the definition of the problem, the Intergovernmental Panel on Climate Change; and then to the negotiation of a specific framework for the regime and its general acceptance in a larger global context at the United Nations Conference on Environment and Development. The regime is now being further articulated under the terms of the Framework Convention. The process has thus far taken some twenty years, and there is still no clear agreement in sight.

In contrast, the emergence of UNAIDS was remarkably swift. First proposed by the United Nations Economic and Social Council in 1993, by January 1996, UNAIDS had been endorsed by six agencies belonging to, or affiliated with, the United Nations system (see table 5.2 below). Moreover, the wider UN structure had endorsed its mission statement and given the programme its governing structures. The mission statement was specific in laying down the expectations of the programme: 'UNAIDS is committed to co-ordinate, strengthen and support an expanded UN response aimed at preventing HIV transmission, providing care, reducing the vulnerability of individuals and alleviating the impact of the epidemic.' For this to be achieved, the programme was given the following mutually reinforcing roles:

- *HIV/AIDS policy development and research*   To identify, develop and be a major source of international best practice and to promote relevant research on HIV/AIDS;
- *Technical support*   To catalyse and provide selected technical support targeted at strengthening national capacity for an expanded response to HIV/AIDS;
- *Advocacy*   To speak out for and promote a comprehensive, multisectoral response to HIV/AIDS that is technically, ethically and strategically sound, and is provided with adequate resources;
- *Coordination*   To coordinate and rationalize action by the co-sponsors and other UN bodies in support of the national responses to HIV/AIDS.

In the WHO office in Geneva, a UNAIDS secretariat under the leadership of a Belgian microbiologist, Peter Piot, was given its base, along with a permanent staff of 130 people. This was quite modest compared to GPA, which had 275 professional

Table 5.2 The individual response to HIV/AIDS of the co-sponsors of UNAIDS, 2001

	UNICEF	UNDP	UNESCO	UNFPA	WHO	World Bank
Mission	To support promotion of the health of women, particularly their sexual and reproductive health	To strengthen the capacity of member states to respond to the development challenge of the HIV epidemic	To foster development of efficient educational strategies to help young people avoid HIV infection	To provide support in line with national AIDS programme and within the scope of the Global AIDS Strategy	To mobilize an effective, equitable and ethical response to the pandemic; to raise awareness and stimulate solidarity; provide technical and policy guidance; promote and support research	To alleviate poverty (overarching institutional mission)
Comparative advantage	Long-standing relationship with various ministries and NGOs; experience with children in especially difficult circumstances and families affected by emergencies and disasters	Central funding and coordinating mechanisms of UN system's operational activities in the field; extensive network of field offices; multisectoral experience; work with NGOs	Policy and planning in education	Key activity is support training programmes for maternal and child health/family planning providers	Health expertise; technical and policy guidance; socio-behavioural and vaccine-related research; intervention development; surveillance and forecasting; support to NGOs	Largest single source of long-term development finance for poor countries; research on socio-economic impacts and cost-effectiveness of interventions
HIV/AIDS strategy	To promote young people's health, placing HIV/AIDS in the broader context of young people's needs and problems	To increase awareness of the development implications of HIV; enhance community capacity to respond to HIV; promote and assist prevention, care and support programmes for women; assist governments in developing effective multisectoral HIV strategies	To promote technical assistance in developing and implementing AIDS educational prevention strategies that are culturally sensitive	To support AIDS prevention within the larger framework of ongoing programmes in population sector	To prevent HIV infection, to reduce the personal and social impact of HIV infection; to unify national and global efforts against AIDS	To create a better socio-economic environment whereby personal vulnerability to HIV is decreased

Source: Various institutional documents.

employees; moreover, UNAIDS is working with a budget of $60 million per year, roughly 15 per cent lower than GPA had in its last year. These economy measures reflect the desire of the sponsoring UN agencies to spend less supporting the day-to-day operating costs of the programme and more on developing effective mechanisms of dealing with the crisis. Peter Piot puts the position this way: 'the reduced budget is not a bad thing. When we took over the programme we discovered that more than half the money GPA had allocated for many projects had been returned unspent. The need was there, but the money could not be absorbed because the AIDS projects were not well organized' (interview, 12 September 2001).

The new programme aimed to coordinate the work of the co-sponsoring agencies in each country by setting up AIDS 'thematic groups'. Meeting as the host country's United Nations Theme Group on AIDS, representatives of the co-sponsoring organizations share information, plan and monitor coordinated action between themselves and with other partners, and decide on joint financing of major AIDS activities in support of the country's government and other national partners. The principal objective of the Theme Group is to support the host country's efforts to mount an effective and comprehensive response to HIV/AIDS. In most cases, the host government is invited to be part of the Theme Group. Increasingly, other partners, such as representatives of other United Nations agencies and bilateral organizations working in the country, are also included.

In priority countries the Theme Group has the support of a UNAIDS staff member, called a country programme adviser. Elsewhere, a staff member of one of the seven co-sponsors serves as the UNAIDS focal point for the country. In addition to supporting the UN system, these staff endeavour to build national commitment to AIDS action and provide information and guidance to a range of host country partners, including government departments and groups and organizations from civil society, such as people living with HIV/AIDS. (For the roles and responses of the co-sponsors, see table 5.2.) The UNAIDS secretariat makes catalytic funding available for selected AIDS initiatives. Between January 1998 and May 1999, the secretariat approved a total of 87 projects in 77 countries. As of April 2001, the UNAIDS co-sponsors had established 152 United Nations Theme Groups on HIV/AIDS covering 155 countries. For their day-to-day operations, most Theme Groups have set up special working groups that involve donors, NGOs and groups of people living with HIV/AIDS. A cornerstone of this collaboration is a series of manuals published by UNAIDS called the Best Practice Collection, which provides detailed technical advice on subjects ranging from blood safety, to HIV testing, to the use of female condoms. The thematic groups also help local authorities to develop the necessary health infrastructure for expanded use of antiviral therapies, especially the treatment of HIV-positive pregnant women with the antiviral drug AZT – now that clinical trials have demonstrated that even short courses of this drug can sharply cut the transmission of HIV from mother to child.

UNAIDS's Achievement

To be sure, UNAIDS and its predecessor have not turned the epidemic around. In fact, the organization's epidemiologists estimate that more than 5 million people were newly infected with HIV last year. In the face of this onslaught, the organization has had to be content with more modest victories, flanking operations against an enemy whose strongest allies are poverty and ignorance. In this context, a number of successes are worthy of note. With the benefit of hindsight, it appears that GPA had three clear achievements: the establishment of an international discourse around HIV/AIDS which stressed the language of empowerment and participation; technical support for a number of developing countries in a range of policy and programme areas; and mobilization of donor countries to support a multilateral response to the epidemic. In large part due to the GPA, the non-governmental sector was also fully integrated into the global response against HIV/AIDS. Thus, under GPA's aegis, networks developed such as the Global Network of People living with AIDS (GNP plus), the International Council of AIDS Service Organizations (ICASO) and the International Community of Women living with AIDS (ICW). At the same time, these networks enabled links to be made with other transnational social movements, particularly among gay/lesbian organizations, sex worker groups and some development organizations.

Building on these, UNAIDS can be seen as a success on at least four fronts. The first concerns the reliability of information about the nature, intensity and direction of the virus, not only across the globe, but also within individual countries. Due to the activities of the programme, over the past five years HIV surveillance and monitoring has become so sophisticated that it is now not only possible to chart the number of infected persons country by country, but – and perhaps more crucially – also by gender, age, socio-economic class and so on. In turn, this has allowed researchers to gain a deeper understanding of the societal dynamics of the epidemic; particularly, the social, cultural and economic factors that spur or curb the spread of the virus. Collectively, this information has provided a crucial societal context for understanding the spread of the virus. As a result, we now know that economic need and dependency lead to activities that magnify the risk of HIV transmission, and also that many people, particularly women, are powerless to protect themselves against infection. Inequitable power structures, a lack of legal protection and inadequate standards of health and nutrition all further exacerbate the spread of the virus and accelerate the progression from HIV infection to AIDS. Further, the setting of the HIV epidemic – particularly in the developing world – also creates a downward spiral whereby existing social, economic and human deprivation produces a particularly fertile environment for the spread of HIV, and, in turn, the HIV epidemic compounds and intensifies the deprivation already experienced by people.

The second important contribution made by the programme has been the development and monitoring of 'best practice' strategies against the virus (these are primarily effective strategies to curb the spread of the virus). Critical here has been the demonstration that behavioural changes can significantly change the course of the epidemic at the domestic level and, by extension, reduce the number of new infections globally. Take, for example, the case of Uganda and Thailand. In Uganda over the past five years there has been a 40 per cent reduction in the HIV prevalence rate among women of childbearing age. This decline was due to a programme co-sponsored by UNAIDS to encourage young women to delay their first sexual intercourse and to use condoms. In Thailand a UNAIDS-sponsored behavioural survey revealed that the majority of risk activities were associated with commercial sex. This led to the establishment of a national programme to encourage '100 per cent condom use' in the commercial sex industry. Recent figures indicate that the prevalence rate among young military conscripts in Thailand has reduced from 8 per cent in 1993 to less than 3 per cent in 2000 (UNAIDS, 2000b).

The third achievement of the programme has been the way it has raised the epidemic to the top of the political agenda. By encouraging informed debates about the societal forces fanning the epidemic, the organization has significantly contributed towards a reduction in the level of stigma attached to the virus and its sufferers. To put this in context, before the arrival of UNAIDS most societies approached the subject with indifference and often hostile denial. In Africa, for example, politicians frequently arrived at the erroneous conclusion that the moral values of their societies would not permit transmission of an agent such as HIV – which is associated with risky sexual behaviour, homosexuality and injecting drug use (Poku, 2001a). Even where denial was conquered, the type of intervention proposed and pursued by national governments often exacerbated the problem. As recently as 1996 (some fifteen years after the first reported HIV case was recorded in his country) President Bakili Muluzi of Malawi was calling on his police force to restrict the civil liberties of known prostitutes and their clients. In the same year, Tfohlongwane Dlamini, the chairman of the powerful Swaziland National Council Standing Committee, told delegates at a conference that HIV-afflicted people 'should be kept in their own special place if we want to curb the spread of the disease'. The statement followed an earlier parliamentary debate where Swazi King Mswati III called for HIV-positive citizens to be 'sterilized and branded' (*Cape News*, 10 July 2000, p. 23). Against this background, UNAIDS activities such as the annual AIDS conferences and World AIDS Day have all contributed towards demystifying the virus as well as highlighting its current and potential devastating impact if effective strategies are not implemented.

The final key achievement of UNAIDS has been the placement of stakeholders (in affected NGOs) at the heart of HIV/AIDS governance. From the beginning UNAIDS recognized that the nature of HIV infection requires the mobilization of considerable resources and direct intervention in areas of personal behaviour which often infringe on taboos and involve groups who are discriminated against in society. Indeed, this is what sets AIDS apart from other diseases, where the necessary precautions may be difficult and expensive but are not emotionally charged in the way AIDS measures are: providing adolescents with condoms, or drug users with clean needles. Although tensions have often surfaced between the various NGOs regarding issues of legitimacy and representation at the Programme Coordination Board level, it is fair to say that their general inclusion has underpinned almost all the successful examples of UNAIDS response to the pandemic at the national and local levels.

Drugs, Patents and the Global AIDS Fund

Despite the successes of GPA/UNAIDS, there continue to be two epidemics: the one in the rich world, where the latest biomedical techniques have turned HIV into a chronic condition; and the one in the poor, where even the basic treatments for opportunistic diseases are rare and hence HIV remains a death sentence. In the hardest hit countries, for example, over one-quarter of the medical staff needed to help those living with HIV/AIDS are themselves infected with the virus (Poku and

Cheru, 2001, p. 43). Experienced teachers are dying faster than new teachers can be trained, seriously affecting the supply and quality of education. The impact on industry and the military continues to grow rapidly, as the rate of infection among men in the armed forces and those working in heavy industry is often much higher than in the general population. Against this background comes a new proposal from the UN Secretary-General, Kofi Annan, for a global AIDS fund to bolster the work of UNAIDS with essential funds. According to Annan, this multilateral fund will seek 'annual contributions between 7 and 10 billion dollars to address care, treatment, and prevention of HIV/AIDS, tuberculosis and malaria'. How the fund will be governed or operated remains unclear, but Annan has said it would probably be run by a small secretariat outside the UN, with financial operations housed at the World Bank.

The World Bank is already home to the AIDS Trust Fund created by US Congressional action in April 2000. This fund was intended to galvanize international donations, but they have not materialized. However, Kofi Annan's proposal for a global fund sounds very similar to the World Bank's AIDS Trust Fund, leading some to think that the World Bank entity will be revamped to become the big global fund. This makes governance of the fund very important, because the US Treasury Department is in charge of establishing the charter for the World Bank AIDS Trust Fund. The Treasury Department's proposal envisages a governing board made up of donors, with some participation by recipient countries. 'Donors' would include not just governments, but private parties – meaning not just private foundations, but private corporations, including drug companies. Under the Treasury Department's proposal for a contribution of 5 million dollars, the drug companies would be able to buy themselves seats on the Trust Fund's governing board. This would be a morally outrageous and indefensible outcome. There are many parties to blame for the horrible and grotesque AIDS epidemic in the developing world, but drug companies are hugely culpable. That they would be permitted a key role in directing the world's belated response to the unfolding tragedy would dishonour the memories of the millions who have died or are dying from HIV/AIDS without access to effective intervention drugs.

Underlying this moral argument are very practical considerations. The participation of the pharmaceutical companies on the governing board of the new global fund would create an irresolvable, structural conflict of interest. Although Annan has reassured the pharmaceutical companies that the global fund would honour patent rights, while at the same time expanding access to cheap drugs to the poorest, it is far from clear how this can be achieved. Currently generic manufacturers can sell patented triple therapy combination anti-retroviral drugs for $350 per patient per year. By contrast, brand name drugs fetch between $10,000 and $15,000 per patient per year, while annual GDP per capita in developing countries ranges from $140 to $6,190.

This, however, tells only half the story. At the intergovernmental conference held in Nairobi in June 2000, delegates were told that the potent antibiotic ciprofloxacin (one of the most successful anti-retroviral drugs available on the market) was twice as expensive in Uganda as in Norway (Médecins Sans Frontières, 2000, p. 15). An equally disturbing example is the case of fluconazole, a treatment for AIDS-related meningitis. In Thailand, where generic competition has lowered prices, fluconazole costs only US$0.30. However, this same drug costs US$18 in Kenya, where it is patent protected. Similarly, it was noted that comparing retail prices of other essential drugs showed the same disturbing pattern: ten out of thirteen commonly used drugs are more expensive in Tanzania than in Canada. The huge disparity in average income between the two countries also means that a Tanzanian would have to work 215 days (assuming someone lucky enough to be in employment) to buy these thirteen drugs, while a Canadian would only have to work eight days (Médecins Sans Frontières, 2000, p. 23). For many treatments, companies sold the same product very differently in different countries. For example, Pfizer's Diflucan (branded version of fluconazole) costs nearly 49 per cent less in Thailand than in Guatemala. Roche's Rocephine (branded version of ceftriaxone) was 33 per cent less expensive in Colombia than in South Africa. The widely divergent prices for the thirteen selected products within developing countries put into question current pricing practices and highlight the lack of transparency with regard to the relationship between product costs and prices.

Confronted with this absurd reality, the news from UNAIDS on 11 May 2000 that five of the largest global pharmaceutical companies had agreed to 'slash the cost of their AIDS treatment drugs for the developing world' appeared as a much-needed breakthrough at the time. The drug companies themselves – Bristol-Meyer Squibb, Merck, Glaxo-Wellcome, Hoffmann-La Roche and Boehringer Ingelheim – issued a flurry of press releases, but provided few details of how much they will charge for the drugs. The details that have since emerged give every reason for disillusionment – particularly with the role of UNAIDS. It appears that UNAIDS had agreed for pharmaceutical companies to negotiate price reduction bilaterally. Moreover, neither the companies nor their partners – local governments, international donors and agencies – have committed themselves in practical terms to bringing an effective treatment to the majority of the poor who are dying from HIV. The only consummated agreement thus far is in Senegal, though Uganda is said to be close. Ibra Ndoye, Senegal's AIDS coordinator, said in an interview with the *Washington Post* that the discount will enable his country to offer an unspecified 'range of therapeutic choices . . . at access costs ranging from about $1,000 to $1,800 a year', down from the $10,000 or more at previous market prices. 'The number of patients treated will increase eightfold,' he said. In real terms, that increase is likely to add between 420 and 889 patients to the rolls of the privileged, depending on whose figures are used. There are an estimated 79,000 Senegalese men, women and children infected with the AIDS virus. Because that number continues to grow, the target rate of coverage in 2006 is, at best, under 1 per cent. Other countries in the developing world – particularly Africa – which generally have a much higher prevalence of AIDS and less effective efforts to fight it, are likely to fall short of even that mark.

In this sense, the real tragedy of the 11 May deal is that UNAIDS has unwittingly provided legitimacy for the pharmaceutical companies to put profits before life. In the words of one observer, the agreement was a farce because 'it redefined the meaning of bad faith' (*Toronto Globe and Mail*, 15 Jan. 2001, p. 23). Not surprisingly, the programme has since been viewed by many as just another UN agency collecting and disseminating information, albeit very well. The hope is that the new global AIDS fund will champion the struggle for equity in the provision of services – medical and otherwise – for people already living with the HIV virus, particularly the 95 per cent of victims who are in the developing world. The inescapable challenge in this regard is ensuring that the poor have access to essential life-sustaining drugs. At the heart of this challenge is the fact that the Agreement on Trade-Related Aspects of Intellectual Property Rights (TRIPS), administered by the World Trade Organization, does not free up trade in pharmaceutical products (see chapter 8 by Susan Sells below). Rather, it imposes restrictive, US-style patent laws on WTO member countries in order to protect the pharmaceutical companies' market for a minimum of twenty years. These monopolies sustain prices that far exceed the average income of most of the people in the world dying from AIDS.

Boehringer Ingelheim, one of the most powerful pharmaceutical companies in the world, summarized the industry's position in the following way: 'infringement of intellectual copyright laws to allow poor countries cheap access to AIDS drugs would be the thin end of a dangerous wedge. Pirating would run riot across the world – and global [read American] business would suffer' (*Washington Post*, 27 December 2000, p. 7). Raymond V. Gilmartin, the chairman of Merck (another of the giant pharmaceutical companies), pursues the theme further, noting that 'if copyright is not protected, who will bother investing in the research and development necessary to continue the fight against AIDS?' In truth, nobody disputes that some protection is necessary to enable private companies to recoup their investments and to encourage them to sustain their efforts in developing new and effective drugs against HIV/AIDS. This said, a number of factors make the industry's current position hard to justify. First, pharmaceutical companies refuse to disclose research and development expenditure on a drug-by-drug basis, so their claims about the costs of developing new drugs are not subject to independent verification. Second, the profits of these companies are so huge that the argument that patent protection is needed to ensure a return on companies' investment amounts to mere greed. Médecins Sans Frontières, for example, reported last year that Glaxo-Wellcome made $589 million on one AIDS drug in 1999 alone, recouping more than twice its research and development costs in just one year (Médecins Sans Frontières, 2000, p. 45).

Against this background of exploitation and greed, Annan's reassuring words to the pharmaceutical industry look particularly out of place. Even after a series of reluctant and not universally available price reductions in recent years, the lowest priced anti-retroviral drug combinations from the leading pharmaceuticals are about three times the cost of the dollar-a-day versions offered by generic companies like the Indian manufacturer Cipla. In the face of this, the choice facing the new global AIDS fund is unambiguous. A decision to permit generics to bid on procurement contracts will institutionalize market competition and drive down prices – including those of new drugs. The exclusion of generics will help consolidate the brand-name cartel and perpetuate their hideously indefensible strategy of putting profits before lives.

Conclusion

Over the past two decades it has been the position of many observers of this grotesquely pervasive HIV crisis that politics, not medicine, has been its dominant feature. Consequently, it is in political terms that a solution must be couched, as much as it must be searched for in medical terms. The United Nations General Assembly session on AIDS in June 2001 finally confirmed this, with global leaders' acquiescence. The headline of the *New York Times* reporting on the United Nations AIDS session captured the essence of recent political changes that have occurred in considering the pandemic: 'UN redefines AIDS as issue of rights and peril to poor' (*New York Times*,

28 June 2001). The Director of the United Nations Programme on HIV/AIDS (UNAIDS), Peter Piot, is quoted as pronouncing the final Declaration an 'instrument of accountability'. This belated acknowledgment by political leaders has served to heighten the expectations for an effective global strategy against HIV/AIDS. Yet it is still far from axiomatic that the existing institutional frameworks will be empowered to deal with the multiplicity of challenges posed by the pandemic.

References

Altman, D. (1994) *Power and Community: Organization and Cultural Responses to AIDS*, London: Taylor and Francis.

Altman, D. (1999a) 'AIDS and global governance', *Pacifica Review*, 11, no. 2, pp. 195–211.

Altman, D. (1999b) 'Globalization, political economy and HIV/AIDS', *Theory and Society*, 28.

Barnett, T. and Blaikie, P. (1992) *AIDS in Africa: Its Present and Future Impact*, London: Bellhavan Press.

Buvé, A. et al. (1999) *Differences in HIV Spread in Four Sub-Saharan African Cities*, UNAIDS Special Report 12, Lusaka.

CDC (Centers for Disease Control) (2000) 'AIDS in America: a report to the Joint Council on Health', 17 Sept.

Farmer, P. (1999) *Infections and Inequalities: The Modern Plagues*, Berkeley: University of California Press.

Hooper, E. (1999) *The River: A Journey Back to the Source of HIV and AIDS*, London: Allan Lane.

Hope, R. K. (1995) 'The socio-economic context of AIDS in Africa', *Journal of Developing Societies*, 11, no. 2, pp. 179–88.

Hope, R. K. (ed.) (1999) *AIDS and Development in Africa: A Social Science Perspective*, Binghamton, N.Y.: Haworth Press.

Hope, R. K. (2001) 'Africa's HIV/AIDS crisis in a development context', *Journal of International Relations*, 15, no. 6, pp. 15–36.

Jacobson, J. L. (1992) 'Women's health: the price of poverty', in M. Koblinsky, J. Timyan and J. Gay (eds), *The Health of Women: A Global Perspective*, Boulder: Westview Press.

Kanu, M. (1989) 'Traditional abuse on women and children', *Guardian* (Nigeria), 4 July.

Kirumira, E. K. (1992) 'Uganda: why a re-think is needed of AIDS control', *AIDS Analysis Africa*, 2, no. 5, Sept.

Mann, J., Tarantola D. and Netter, T. (1992) *AIDS in the World*, Cambridge Mass.: Harvard University Press.

Médecins Sans Frontières (2000) 'Price of essential drugs for HIV/AIDS', paper presented at African Development Forum 2000 conference in Ethiopia.

Medilinks (2001) 'African statistics: cost of HIV/AIDS, Malaria and TB to Africa', at www.medilinks.org/Features/Articles/Statistics%20in%20Africa%202001.htm.

Menon, R. et al. (1999) 'The economic impact of adult mortality on households in Rakai District, Uganda', EU HIV Paper 15.

Morar, N. S., Ramjee, G. and Abdool Karim, S. S. (1998) *Safe Sex Practices among Sex Workers at Risk of HIV Infection*, Poster 332871, 12th World AIDS Conference, Geneva, 28 June–3 July.

Poku, N. K. (2000) 'Poverty, AIDS and the politics of response in Africa', *International Relations*, 15, no. 3, Dec.

Poku, N. K. (2001a) 'Africa's AIDS crisis in context: how the poor are dying', *Third World Quarterly*, 22, no. 2.

Poku, N. K. (2001b) *Regionalisation and Security in Southern Africa*, Basingstoke: Palgrave.

Poku, N. K. (ed.) (2001c) *Security and Development in Southern Africa*, Westport, Conn.: Greenwood Press.

Poku, N. K. (2002) *The Political Economy of HIV/AIDS in Africa*, Basingstoke: Ashgate.

Poku, N. K. and Cheru, F. (2001) 'The politics of poverty and debt in Africa's AIDS crisis', *International Relations*, 15, no. 6, Dec.

Policy Project (1999) 'The economic impact of AIDS', draft, The Futures Group International.

Rungana, R. M. et. al. (1992) 'The use of herbal and other agents to enhance sexual experience', *Social Science and Medicine*, 35, pp. 1037–46.

Sampson, J. and Neaton, J. (1994) 'On being poor with HIV', *Lancet*, 344, pp. 1100–1.

Seidel, G. (1993) 'Women at risk: gender and HIV in Africa', *Disasters*, 17, no. 2, pp. 133–42.

Simmon, J., Farmer, P. and Schoepf, B. G. (1996) 'A global perspective', in P. Farmer, M. Connors and J. Simmon (eds), *Women, Poverty and AIDS: Sex, Drugs and Structural Violence*, Monroe: Common Courage Press.

Topouzis, D. (1998) *The Implications of HIV/AIDS for Rural Development Policy and Programming: Focus on Sub-Saharan Africa*, Rome: Sustainable Development Department, Food and Agriculture Organization.

UN (2000) 'Security Council holds debate on impact of AIDS on peace and security in Africa', press release SC/6781, 8 Jan.

UNAIDS (1998) 'New initiative to reduce HIV transmission from mother to child in low-income countries', press release, Geneva, 29 June.

UNAIDS (1999a) 'AIDS epidemic update', Geneva, Dec.

UNAIDS (1999b) 'Early data from mother-to-child transmission study in Africa finds shortest effective regimen ever', press release, Geneva, Feb.

UNAIDS (2000a) 'AIDS epidemic update', Geneva, Feb.

UNAIDS (2000b) 'Framework for global leadership on HIV/AIDS', UNAIDS/PCB(10)/00.3 Geneva, June.

UNAIDS (2000c) 'AIDS in Africa: country by country', Geneva, 15 Nov.

UNAIDS (2001) 'AIDS epidemic update', Geneva, Feb.

UNDP (1998) *Human Development Report, 1998*, Oxford: Oxford University Press.

UNDP (1999) *Human Development Report, 1999*, Oxford: Oxford University Press.

Williams, G., Milligan, A. and Odemwingie, T. (1998) *A Common Cause: Young People, Sexuality and HIV/AIDS in Three African Countries*, ACTIONAID.

World Bank (1990) *World Development Report*, New York: Oxford University Press.

World Bank (1996a) *Poverty Reduction and the World Bank: Progress and Challenges in the 1990s*, Washington DC: World Bank.

World Bank (1996b) *World Bank Annual Report 1996*, Washington DC: World Bank.

World Bank (1997) *Confronting AIDS: Public Priorities in a Global Epidemic*, New York: Oxford University Press.

6

Global Governance, Transnational Organized Crime and Money Laundering

Phil Williams and Gregory Baudin-O'Hayon

For most of the Westphalian era, the central issue of interstate relations has revolved around the competing concepts of anarchy versus society (Bull, 1995). On the one side was a society of states with its own institutions, rules, norms and procedures; on the other side, interstate relations in the absence of a central authority to maintain order were characterized by insecurity, military competition and warfare. The mix of anarchy and society differed at different periods and in different regions. Yet the consistent tension between the cooperative efforts to establish order and stability on the one side and the competing impulse towards competition, confrontation and conflict did much to shape the evolution of the international system through the nineteenth and twentieth centuries. Such tension remains today. In the twenty-first century, however, this traditional dialectic is being superseded by a new dialectic between the forces of disorder on the one side and the efforts to establish global governance on the other. And just as anarchy and warfare were the dominant motifs of the twentieth century, so is disorder likely to be the dominant motif of the twenty-first century.

This new disorder, however, does not replace anarchy so much as subsume it. The security dilemma, the arms races, and the military clashes among states that were so prevalent in the twentieth century have not disappeared. Increasingly, though, they are accompanied by other problems, many of them created by transnational or subnational forces. James Rosenau has argued very persuasively that one of the most important determinants of global politics in the future is the relationship between the state-centric world and the multicentric one (Rosenau, 1990). In the realm of security, states not only have to contend with each other and with traditional geopolitical imperatives and national rivalries, they also face threats from transnational 'sovereignty-free actors' (Rosenau, 1990, 1994) who can mobilize sufficient resources to challenge state power and legitimacy.

The terrorist attacks of 11 September 2001 on the World Trade Center and the Pentagon provided a dramatic illustration of this new reality in which 'the power to hurt' (Schelling, 1967) is no longer a monopoly of states but is also exercised by transnational networked actors. The need to incorporate this into a new paradigm for understanding global politics is evident. The debate over hegemony, for example, needs to be broadened beyond its exclusive focus on states. Traditionally the emergence of a single hegemonic power has provoked efforts by other states to develop countervailing alliances that allow them to challenge the hegemon. The terrorist attacks on the United States combine with the al-Qaeda rhetoric, however, to suggest a very different locus for efforts to counter United States hegemony in the post-Cold War world. Indeed, the thrust of the al-Qaeda campaign is directed at both United States cultural hegemony and United States military hegemony manifested in the military presence in Saudi Arabia.

If the new terrorism is one of the most dramatic forms of the tension between governance and disorder, however, it is far from the only one. Transnational organized crime also poses a major challenge to efforts at global governance. Indeed, large parts of the world since the 1980s have witnessed what can be termed a criminalization syndrome. This involves the rise of several closely related and mutually reinforcing phenomena – drug trafficking, transnational organized crime, illegal markets, corruption and rent-seeking, and money laundering.

Although these phenomena have had an impact on many countries, they have been most obvious in states in transition and in developing states, generally reflecting gaps in state capacity and the inability of states to function effectively in meeting the needs of their citizens. The presence of functional holes in government extends from the legal system to economic management – and provides both spaces in which organized crime can operate virtually unhindered, and needs, such as business protection and arbitration of disputes, that organized crime can meet, thereby enhancing its legitimacy. Charles Tilly, in an oft-quoted comment, once noted that the state was simply the most efficient and effective form of organized crime (Tilly, 1985). In effect, the state transcended organized crime by transforming extortion into taxation, brute force into authority, and rule by fear into rule by consent of the governed. Yet in the last decade or so there have been signs that organized crime has been fighting back and that the state is not as successful as it was in the period of state-building so trenchantly dissected by Tilly. States are held to be in retreat or in decline, to be failing or collapsing, and organized crime seems to be spreading to more countries.

It is hardly surprising, therefore, that there has been, in Kenichi Ohmae's terms, a gradual displacement of the 'Westphalian cartographic illusion' by a new economic map and, in particular, the emergence of natural economic zones that are rarely congruent with state boundaries (Ohmae, 1995). Yet other observers have described the emerging system of global politics in terms of a new medievalism (Ruggie, 1993), a coming anarchy (Kaplan, 1994), or zones of turmoil (Singer and Wildavsky, 1996). Indeed, the new geography is studded with an increasing number of anomalous but powerful sovereignty-free transnational entities on the one side, and weak and penetrated states on the other. Domestic and global pressures have accelerated a process of deterritorialization – the creation of disconnects and lacunae between states and portions of territory nominally under their control. Many states no longer have exclusive sovereignty, or exercise exclusive authority over their territories. The emergence of no-go zones where the state has no authority and little power has been accompanied by a decline in the extractive power of states. More economies are becoming criminalized, with burgeoning informal sectors and black markets that are subject to neither regulation nor taxation. In addition, organized crime has taken on a transnational dimension, with the smuggling of illicit, regulated and stolen goods across national boundaries in search of large markets and high prices. In the twenty-first century, organized crime is fighting back with a vengeance.

This does not mean that the state is likely to disappear. Nor does it mean that individual states are helpless against the onslaught of organized crime. In both

Colombia and Italy, during the late 1980s and early 1990s, organized crime declared war on the state – and lost. Moreover, states have been increasingly developing global governance mechanisms in an effort to combat organized crime as both a national and a transnational challenge. Against this background this chapter seeks to do three things. Initially it elucidates the phenomenon of transnational organized crime, and examines its emergence as a major issue requiring efforts at global governance. Second, the chapter identifies the efforts of states to confront the challenge posed by transnational organized crime, focusing on international cooperation for governance in response to transnational organized crime – with particular emphasis on the United Nations and the Financial Action Task Force. The third section of the chapter looks at the problems with such cooperation and with global governance efforts more generally in the area of combating transnational crime. It suggests that governance mechanisms in the area of transnational crime are particularly fraught with complications and deficiencies, the overall result of which is likely to be a lack of effectiveness. The concluding section offers a brief indication of what can be done to strengthen global governance in relation to transnational organized crime.

Transnational Organized Crime, Globalization and the New Disorder

The Bundeskriminalamt, the German equivalent of the United States Federal Bureau of Investigation, defines organized crime as

> the planned violation of the law for profit or to acquire power, which offenses are each, or together, of a major significance, and are carried out by more than two participants who cooperate within a division of labor for a long or undetermined time span using: (a) commercial or commercial-like structures; or (b) violence or other means of intimidation; or (c) influence on politics, media, public administration, justice and [the] legitimate economy. (Van Duyne, 1996, p. 343)

While this definition is helpful, organized crime can be understood rather more simply in Clausewitzian terms as the continuation of business by criminal means. And just as business has become transnational in scope as part of globalization, so has organized crime. Although it is tempting to suggest that organized crime operates as if the world were borderless, this is not in fact the case. For criminals, borders provide demarcations of markets and differential prices for products that are regulated or prohibited. Border crossings themselves can involve the perpetrators, their illicit products, people (either illegal migrants or women and children being trafficked illegally for commercial sex), their profits, or digital signals (a virtual border crossing). Although the border crossing circumvents state controls, it usually results in a substantial price increase. Moreover, significant parts of the profits also cross borders, with the flow moving in the opposite direction to the products. Paradoxically, criminals simultaneously ignore and violate borders for product trans-shipment and movement, yet exploit borders and the price differentials that go with them for marketing purposes. They also exploit borders defensively, by operating from home states that have been deeply penetrated and act as safe havens. Efforts to extradite them are sometimes met with nationalist campaigns and claims that extradition to another country (especially the United States) would be a violation or abdication of national sovereignty.

The rise of transnational organized crime – and associated phenomena such as black markets, drug trafficking, money laundering, and corruption – can be understood as a response to opportunities provided by failures of domestic governance and by globalization, as well as to economic and social imperatives that have also been driven by state failures and inadequacies, and by the inequities and fallout from globalization. If the criminalization of societies and the pervasiveness of transnational crime are symptoms of a new global disorder, however, they also intensify and exacerbate that disorder. Indeed, transnational organized crime is both a reflection of and a contributor to a new form of geopolitics that is almost transcendental in nature. The geopolitical realities of today are not simply about power, boundaries and territory; they are about transnational flows – of money, commodities and people – and linkages, about networked organizations, about ethnic connections and loyalties that transcend national borders, about wire transfers and underground banking systems, about global communications and the internet, and about megacities and global transportation links.

The emergence of transnational organized crime during the 1990s is sometimes dismissed as little more than a reflection of the end of the Cold War and the natural transition to a new and different international agenda. Certainly, the end of the Cold War meant that in the West a more honest look could be taken at politicians and political parties who were linked to organized crime but whose relationships had been overlooked or tacitly excused because they were anti-communist. In one respect, the organized crime problem was simply more obvious and more disturbing because it was now examined more closely than ever before. To acknowledge this, however, is not to deny that there was a real increase in the scale of the problem: the demise of the Soviet Union and the end of the Cold War had major substantive effects. First, the collapse of one-party states in which corruption and organized crime had been endemic but controlled allowed organized crime to expand at an unprecedented rate: the removal of social and political controls and constraints combined with a plethora of new opportunities generated by moves towards market economies provided a perfect incubator. Indeed, the failure of most states in transition to provide a legal framework for business regulation and mechanisms for the arbitration of disputes and debt collection created a functional hole that was filled by organized crime, which stepped in and fulfilled these functions. Second, the breakdown of barriers between East and West encouraged new flows of goods and services, both legal and illegal. Women being trafficked for commercial sex, illegally exported raw materials, nuclear materials, and both criminal proceeds and capital flight poured out of the former Soviet Union, while stolen cars, drugs and 'dirty money' went in. Organized crime from the former Soviet Union expanded into Western Europe, Israel and the United States. For their part, Italian criminal organizations – the Sicilian Mafia, the Camorra based in and around Naples and the 'Ndrangheta from Calabria – expanded eastward, engaging in collaborative ventures with the new organizations and establishing a triangular relationship involving Russian organized crime and Colombian drug-trafficking organizations.

If the end of the Cold War gave a boost to organized crime, however, the rise of transnational criminal organizations can also be understood as a reflection of long-term secular trends, and in particular increasing economic and social globalization. Just as a globalized economy provided new opportunities for business, it also provided major new opportunities for criminal enterprises. Yet it was more complex than this: the growth of transnational organized crime was a response to both successes and failures – to both the opportunities and the inequities of globalization, to the new opportunities for illegal activity provided by the growth of global trade and financial systems, and to the failure of both governments and the market to provide for basic needs in many countries (Mittelman and Johnston, 1999). In effect, organized crime was able to exploit the mechanisms of globalization while also feeding off the dislocation, discontent and alienation that accompanied it.

The opportunities are very obvious. The growth of global markets and the existence of surplus incomes in wealthy developed countries, for example, provided a huge demand for recreational drugs that was met by the growth of transnational trafficking networks. At the same time, it is no accident that the major producers of cocaine and heroin – Colombia, Burma and Afghanistan – were all torn by ethnic strife, insurgency, or civil war. Drug production became a means of funding political and military struggle; control of growing areas, routes and markets became a form of political power and the prize of political-military competition; and power became concentrated in the hands of warlords and militias, or powerful criminal organizations willing to use violence and corruption – both within and outside the country – to maintain their dominance over an enormously lucrative trade in what had become ubiquitous, if illicit, global commodities.

If drug trafficking was the most obvious manifestation of the rise of transnational organized crime, it was far from the only one. Trafficking in drugs has been accompanied by the growth of trafficking in various other products. Immigration regulations in many developed countries, for example, encouraged the development of illegal alien smuggling. Well-organized networks from China and elsewhere established themselves as intermediaries, providing false documentation, transportation, and guidance in circumventing border and immigration controls. Closely linked to alien smuggling in methods, but in many ways distinct from it, was the trafficking of women and children for commercial sex. This has become a global market, with Russian, Moldovan and Ukrainian women trafficked to Western Europe, Israel, the United States and Japan; Burmese women and girls trafficked to Thailand; Thai women trafficked to Japan; and women from Nigeria trafficked to Western Europe. In some cases the women go voluntarily, but deception and coercion are also prevalent – and the result, in any case, is a life of sexual servitude. The smuggling of aliens and trafficking in women reflect the dynamics of demand and supply in a global market, and also the perverse consequences of regulation. Indeed, transnational trafficking generally involves products that are regulated, prohibited, differentially taxed, or stolen. In addition to human commodity trafficking, transnational organized crime is also involved, among other things, in the theft and trafficking of cars, antiquities and cultural property, fauna and flora (endangered species), intellectual property, and arms and ammunition.

Trafficking networks of all kinds exploit the growth of global transportation and trade links and the inability of governments to scrutinize more than a small portion of the goods they import and export. A critically important but often neglected dimension of the growth of global trade has been the development of intermodal containers that are moved easily from ship to rail or road transportation. Most countries are able to inspect only a small percentage (somewhere between 2 and 8 per cent) of the containers that come into their countries. Not surprisingly, therefore, transnational criminal organizations are able to embed illicit commodities within the vast array of licit goods that are shipped across borders.

When transnational organized crime is successful in trafficking, extortion, fraud or theft, it generally makes a large profit. As a UN study pointed out, something has to be done about the proceeds for two reasons. 'The first is that the money trail itself can become evidence against the perpetrators of the offence; the second is that the money *per se* can be the target of investigation and action' (Blum et al., 1999). If the investigation is successful then there is a real danger that the money will be seized. It is for this reason that transnational criminal organizations have developed sophisticated money-laundering schemes. 'Strictly speaking money laundering should be construed as a dynamic three-stage process that requires firstly, moving the funds from direct association with the crime; secondly disguising the trail to foil pursuit; and, thirdly, making the money available to the criminal once again with its occupational and geographic origins hidden from view' (Blum et al., 1999, p. 4). Put more succinctly, money laundering takes dirty money, hides its origins and ownership, and makes it appear to be the proceeds of legitimate economic activity. In some cases, it is not necessary to go through the whole money-laundering cycle, and the proceeds of crime are either placed in the financial system through apparently legitimate companies that provide adequate rationales for the earnings, or they are simply moved to where they are safe from seizure. In other instances, however, criminals – often with the assistance of financial professionals – develop elaborate steps to cleanse the money. In many cases, the money is moved through multiple jurisdictions, making it very difficult for investigators to follow a trail that is characterized by what a New Mexican lawyer, Alexis Johnson, has termed 'jurisdictional confusion' and Jeremy Kinsell has termed 'jurisdictional holes' (Kinsell, 2000).

Indeed, the movement of criminal proceeds is greatly facilitated by a deregulated global financial system characterized by the prevalence of what has been termed 'megabyte money' (Kurtzman, 1993). Most money takes the form of bits and bytes on computer screens and can be transferred across multiple jurisdictions with speed, ease and often with anonymity. Moreover, it is possible – and this is where criminals once again exploit the continued respect of states for the principle of national sovereignty – to park the money in financial safe havens, offshore financial centres that have bank secrecy regulations and do not ask hard questions about the source of incoming money. Several Caribbean islands such as Antigua and the Caymans, and some South Pacific jurisdictions such as Nauru, Niue and Vanuatu are among offshore financial centres that have been highlighted as safe havens for dirty money.

If criminal enterprises – like all other enterprises – use wire transfer systems to move their profits, they also use underground banking systems, known as the hawala in South Asia, and fie-chien (flying money) in South East Asia and China. These systems, which initially developed as coping mechanisms in immigrant communities, are based on social trust, allow money movement from one country to another without having to carry or declare large amounts of currency, and are not intrinsically criminal in nature. Their great virtue for criminals, and indeed for terrorists, is that they do not create a paper trail. For those wanting to obscure the money trail there are few mechanisms more attractive than underground banking systems.

Another component of the new geopolitics that feeds into organized crime is the emergence of megacities and global cities (Sassen, 1994, 1996). Global cities can be understood as the major nodes of the global economy, providing communications and transportation links, banking and financial systems. They are also wonderful hosts within which organized crime can operate effectively and anonymously. In contemporary Italy, for example, Milan, with its critical location on regional and international transportation routes, and its financial significance, is probably far more important to organized crime than is Palermo. Cities such as São Paolo, Johannesburg, Moscow, Hong Kong, and both Bangkok and Pattaya in Thailand provide safety and sanctuary for criminals, while also facilitating cooperation in new enterprises. In some cases, they breed a criminal cosmopolitanism, facilitating cooperative ventures among individuals and groups with different ethnicities and nationalities but a common interest in expanding their activities and profits.

If cooperation among criminal groups occasionally crosses ethnic divisions, however, national, ethnic or tribal identities remain – along with family and kinship – some of the most significant bonding mechanisms and sources of trust in criminal organizations (Ianni, 1974). Indeed, to understand the rise of transnational criminal organizations, it is necessary to understand not only the diasporas and migration patterns that have taken place during recent decades, but also – in a few cases at least – those that are of longer standing. Immigrants are more often victims than perpetrators of crimes. Nevertheless, transnational networks of immigrants provide an important set of resources and a basis from which organized crime can operate (Bovenkerk, 2001). Ethnic communities within host countries provide cover, recruitment, targets, and support structures for criminal organizations based within them. To understand the global rise of Nigerian criminal networks, or the importance of Turkish and Albanian criminal clans in heroin trafficking in Western Europe, for example, it is necessary to examine the transnational distribution of ethnic communities within which and from which they operate. Similarly the rise of Russian and Ukrainian organized crime in Western Europe, the United States and Israel followed the trail of Russian and Ukrainian migration, especially after the collapse of the Soviet Union. In much of the literature on transnational forces and phenomena, considerable attention is given to networks of NGOs, networks that are believed to represent at the very least the genesis of a global civil society. But transnational networks are efficient and effective not only in providing advice and pursuing causes such as political reform or the banning of land-mines; they are equally adept at providing illicit goods and services that have to be moved from source states to market states in which there is lucrative consumer demand.

Organized crime also links to other forms of change, disorder and conflict in world politics. In general terms, the decline of territorial control and the loss of extractive capacity in many states has been accompanied by the re-emergence of 'grey zones', *terrae incognitae* where order has vanished and lawlessness returned (Minc, 1993, p. 67), where the écorcheurs (Tuchman, 1978, p. 223), highwaymen and pirates of medieval Europe have returned, and where new and extremely ruthless breeds of criminals, terrorists and insurgents dominate political and economic life. Indeed, organized crime feeds on conflict and disorder. As suggested above, it is no accident that the major drug-growing regions of the world are also among the most violent and dangerous. Insurgents such as the FARC in Colombia tax drug cultivators and traffickers and sometimes engage in trafficking, usually involving drugs for weapons deals. Stolen diamonds from Angola and Sierra Leone help to fund African wars and even the al-Qaeda terrorist network. Ethnic conflicts such as those in the Balkans also produce a large number of specialists in violence who make an easy transition from slaughtering ethnic opponents for pleasure to killing businessmen or rival criminals for profit. None of this is meant to suggest that there is an organized crime terrorism nexus – as some observers claim. There is ad hoc cooperation between organized crime and terrorist and insurgency organization, but this is neither as prevalent nor as important as the way in which terrorists and insurgents have appropriated the methods of organized crime to raise money. Organized crime activities, for example, are used by competing ethnic factions, civil war belligerents, insurgency groups and terrorist organizations to fund their political and military campaigns.

For its part, organized crime often acts as supplier to civil conflicts, circumventing arms embargoes and thereby helping to perpetuate the fighting. In addition, organized crime can act as a spoiler to peacekeeping efforts and post-civil war reconstruction. Nowhere has this been more obvious than in Bosnia where the Dayton Accords, which presumed the gradual creation of a central authority, have been consistently and systematically undermined by symbiotic linkages between the major nationalist parties and organized crime groups (GAO, 2000). Criminal groups in conjunction with nationalist politicians control black markets, various trafficking activities and engage in corruption and rent-seeking – all of which simultaneously robs the envisaged central authority of resources, and provides funds for separatist agendas. Ironically, criminal cooperation sometimes transcends the nationalist divisions, although the profits earned thereby serve to accentuate them.

If organized crime both feeds off and feeds into political violence, the violence perpetrated directly by organized crime is selective rather than indiscriminate, contract killings of selected and targeted individuals rather than violence against innocent civilians or particular ethnic groups. Although it cannot be dismissed, this violence is perhaps less important than organized crime-related corruption. The global campaign against corruption generally treats corruption as a condition to be eradicated. For organized crime, however, corruption is an instrument designed to break down the defences of the body politic, to neutralize the criminal justice system by undermining the effectiveness of law enforcement and the judiciary, and to buy information and support. In this sense, organized crime embodies a concentration of illegal power in society that can pose a direct threat to the viability and independence of state structures. When this is added to the inherently harmful nature of organized crime activities such as drugs and arms trafficking, or trafficking in women and children, it is easy to see why some observers increasingly regard organized crime as a threat to national and international security – and why drug trafficking, transnational organized crime, and money laundering have become the target of global governance efforts. The next section identifies and assesses two of the most important of these efforts.

Global Governance and Transnational Organized Crime

Although particular crimes such as trafficking in women for sexual servitude have been the focus of conventions for some time, efforts to establish global governance norms and principles, mechanisms and procedures, and implementation and enforcement agencies to combat transnational organized crime really developed only in the late 1980s and the 1990s. In some cases, such as Interpol, which has been in existence since 1923, there was something to build on. In other instances, however, the process had few antecedents and even fewer building blocks in place. Yet governance efforts were relatively quick to emerge and did so at several distinct levels.

The most obvious – and the main focus of this analysis – is the global level, where efforts were made to create norms and to provide a framework for international cooperation. This was done largely through the United Nations, but also through the G7's Financial Action Task Force established in 1989. A second level is more operational and involves information-sharing for law enforcement. Traditionally, Interpol has been the major player at this level, but during the 1990s it was joined on a regional basis by Europol. The third level is through informal networks of trust that are created among national law enforcement agencies. As more and more crimes have a transnational or cross-border dimension, informal cooperation through trust networks has become an imperative – especially given some of the difficulties of cooperation in an area that most states continue to regard as an exclusive matter of national sovereignty. The discussion here focuses primarily on the evolution of norms and standards – along with accompanying efforts to strengthen the capacity of states to meet these standards.

The Convention against Transnational Organized Crime

During the 1990s the United Nations took the lead in placing transnational organized crime on the international agenda and in developing a set of principles and procedures that would be of help as governments began to take the threat more seriously. The first major gathering was the World Ministerial Conference on Organized Transnational Crime, held in Naples in 1994. Developed as a result of an idea of Judge Giovanni Falcone, the Italian anti-Mafia magistrate who was later killed by the Mafia, the conference was attended by 142 delegations and 86 ministers. Not surprisingly, it helped focus attention on the issue, crystallized concerns and resulted in a declaration and action plan emphasizing the need for greater international cooperation and technical assistance to countries that were particularly vulnerable to transnational organized crime. In the aftermath of the conference, in a process that was enormously assisted by the secretariat in the Crime Division (subsequently a Centre) at the United Nations Office Vienna, moves began to develop a convention against transnational organized crime. In part, this reflected the importance of the Vienna Convention of 1988, to combat the trafficking and abuse of narcotics and psychotropic drugs, in mobilizing the international community against drug trafficking. The desire to emulate this earlier initiative was a powerful impulse, but the negotiations to create the Convention against Transnational Organized Crime were protracted and difficult. With the Polish and Argentinian governments proving particularly helpful in facilitating negotiations, and one or two key figures in the secretariat providing specialist knowledge and guidance, however, the process gradually moved towards completion. The convention was finally unveiled for signature in Palermo, Sicily – a symbolic venue given the traditional importance of the Mafia in the city – in December 2000.

The intention of the convention was spelt out in Article 1, which made it explicit that the purpose was 'to promote cooperation to prevent and combat transnational organized crime more effectively'. In accordance with this, specific provisions of the convention were designed to provide instruments that law enforcement agencies and prosecutors could use, as well as to encourage and coordinate prevention efforts and the protection and support of victims. At the same time, the convention encouraged states with gaps in legislation against organized crime to develop the necessary measures, thereby facilitating international standardization or coordination at the policy, legislative, administrative and enforcement levels.

The convention and accompanying protocols oblige countries which sign and ratify them to adopt what are described as 'basic minimum measures' against organized crime so that there are 'no safe havens' where organizational activities or the concealment of evidence or profits can take place. Beyond this, many provisions are intended to ensure that the approaches taken by different states under their domestic legislative and law enforcement regimes are as coordinated as possible to 'make collective international measures both efficient and effective'.

Article 2 defines an organized criminal group in terms of at least three members who take some action in concert to commit a 'serious crime' for the purpose of obtaining a financial or other benefit. The group must have some internal organization or structure, and exist for some period before or after the actual commission of the offence(s) involved. Having set out the definition, the convention identifies four specific crimes – participation in an organized criminal group (Article 5), money laundering (Article 6), use of corruption (Article 8), and obstruction of justice (Article 23) – to combat areas of criminality linked to transnational organized crime activities. These crimes provide the basis for extradition and mutual legal assistance subject to the requirement of dual criminality in separate jurisdictions. The convention also provides a basis for conducting joint investigations (Article 19) and for cooperation among law enforcement agencies, including the use of special investigative procedures such as electronic surveillance.

The convention also has attached protocols against Trafficking in Persons, Smuggling of Migrants, and Illicit Trafficking in Firearms. The Protocol on Trafficking in Persons was intended to create obligations on the signatories to combat the traffickers, but also to offer protection and support to the victims of trafficking. This was consistent with the general theme of the convention and for some states would mark a significant change in the approach to women involved in commercial sex, who are typically treated as perpetrators of crime rather than the victims of trafficking or duress.

Overall, the convention can be understood as a major step forward in the effort to combat transnational organized crime. Its emphasis on international cooperation reflects the inability of any single state to combat a transnational phenomenon, the need to remove or lessen the traditional inhibitions on cooperation in areas where respect for sovereignty remains a sensitive issue, and the need to think not only about the perpetrators but also the victims. It is an attempt to place the international community in a position where the risks faced by transnational criminal organizations are both higher and more evenly distributed than in the past (Williams and Savona, 1996). The removal of safe havens and even low-risk jurisdictions would strike at the heart of transnational criminal organizations that traditionally have operated from home bases that have been – often because of lack of state capacity – sanctuaries and placed their funds in financial havens that use bank secrecy provisions to inhibit international investigations or efforts to follow the money trail. The financial dimension of transnational organized crime, of course, has been a focus for international agencies other than the UN for some years.

The Financial Action Task Force

Foremost among the international anti-money laundering efforts and agencies is the Financial Action Task Force, set up in 1989. In April 1990 the FATF issued a set of forty recommendations for its twenty-six members to implement. These recommendations focused on the need for legislative measures that would enable authorities to detect money laundering activities, to trace the assets of criminals and to confiscate laundered money or property of corresponding value. Anonymity was to be replaced by transparency in financial transactions, with banks – put on the front line by the new approach – being expected to exercise 'due diligence' and to ensure that they 'knew their customers' and the beneficial owners of all accounts. The forty recommendations – and this was an important precursor to the approach subsequently adopted in the Convention against Transnational Organized Crime – envisaged both a domestic and an international component to the regime it sought to establish. At the domestic level, governments were expected to establish a reporting system for cash transactions above $10,000 (or its equivalent in other currencies), and for suspicious transactions. They were also encouraged to set up Financial Intelligence Units to monitor these transaction reports. At the international level, the recommendations emphasized cooperation through extradition and mutual assistance in investigations, information-sharing, and responsiveness to requests by foreign countries to identify, freeze, seize and confiscate proceeds. Following the promulgation of the forty recommendations the FATF developed a threefold role:

- Monitoring the progress of the member states in implementing measures to counter money laundering through annual self-assessments and more detailed mutual evaluations. The review processes make it possible to put considerable moral and political pressure on governments not meeting their obligations to comply with the recommendations.
- Reviewing money laundering trends, techniques and countermeasures and sharing this information among the members so as to enhance their capacity to counter innovations and new trends in laundering. The annual typologies exercise has become an important source for determining new directions in money laundering and disseminating this information so that law enforcement agencies know what to look for.
- Extending the regime by broadening membership to include new countries and by facilitating the creation of regional groupings such as the Caribbean Financial Action Task Force and the Eastern and Southern African Anti-Money Laundering Group (ESAAMLG) to operate as a regional variant of the FATF.

As well as seeking to extend the scope of its activities geographically, the FATF has also tried to encompass more financial sectors under its umbrella. In 1996, for example, it recommended that laws and regulations developed for the banking sector be extended to non-bank financial institutions. More significantly, in 1999 FATF attempted to give teeth to its efforts, beginning what was to become a name and shame campaign. In 2000 it identified fifteen 'non-cooperative jurisdictions' including Bahamas, Cayman Islands, Israel, Liechtenstein, Nauru, Panama, Philippines, Russia, and St Kitts and Nevis. This was followed by technical assistance and encouragement to those regimes making serious efforts to meet the new norms and standards in the financial sphere. The Bahamas, for example, introduced new legislation that radically overhauled its banking system and made beneficial ownership of international business corporations (previously based on anonymity) transparent. Not surprisingly, therefore, the Bahamas, along with the Cayman Islands, Liechtenstein and Panama, was removed from the list in 2001. Russia and Israel remained on the list, however, and serious deficiencies were also identified in Egypt, Guatemala, Hungary, Indonesia, Myanmar and Nigeria – all of which were added to the list.

In October 2001, in an extraordinary Plenary on the Financing of Terrorism held in Washington, as part of the aftermath of 11 September and the effort by the United States to combat terrorism, the FATF formally expanded its mission to include an assault on terrorist financing. It issued an immediate set of recommendations (accompanied by a plan of action) that urged its members to freeze and confiscate terrorist assets; report suspicious transactions linked to terrorism; provide the widest possible range of assistance to other countries' law enforcement and regulatory authorities for terrorist financing investigations; impose anti-money laundering requirements on alternative remittance systems (such as the hawala described above); strengthen customer identification measures in international and domestic wire transfers; and ensure that entities, in particular non-profit organizations, cannot be misused to finance terrorism.

Ironically, terrorists do not actually launder much money. For the most part they take clean money and use it to fund terrorist operations rather than cleanse dirty money. Nevertheless, they use many of the same mechanisms and modalities for moving money as do transnational criminal organizations. One of the likely ironies is that the effort to go after terrorist financing will actually lead to a more vigorous and extensive anti-money laundering regime as great urgency is given to requirements to know customers and exercise due diligence, and to freeze and confiscate terrorist funds. Even so, it is far from clear that governance will triumph over disorder, that law will triumph over crime, or that probity will triumph over corruption. Indeed, the next section assesses these approaches to governance and highlights a number of intractable problems they encounter.

Governance and Transnational Organized Crime: an Assessment

The Financial Action Task Force is perhaps the most venerable example of international cooperation designed to combat transnational organized crime, albeit with a focus only on the profits. It is both a necessary and important component of the overall response and one that – as suggested – is likely to be strengthened significantly. Yet there are several problems with the FATF. Fortunately, these do not apply to anything like the same extent to the Convention against Transnational Organized Crime.

Ironically, a major problem for global governance in relation to transnational organized crime is the intended spillover effect from other areas of governance – a spillover effect that creates both perverse incentives and new opportunities for organized crime. As one of us has written elsewhere,

> governance in certain domains can provide criminal organizations with major opportunities to expand their activities and enhance their profits. The creation of regulatory regimes in areas such as environmental management and the protection of cultural property, efforts to punish states violating norms of international behavior or engaging in massive transgressions of human rights through the imposition of sanctions, create perverse incentives for criminal organizations to engage in entrepreneurial activities that undermine regimes and embargoes. This is to be expected; after all, one of the things that most criminal organizations do is to supply goods and services that are prohibited or restricted. (Williams, 2001)

A second shortcoming is that global governance focuses exclusively on interstate cooperation to combat transnational organized crime. Yet some states are themselves part of the problem rather than part of the solution. Indeed, it is possible to identify several kinds of states that are problematic when it comes to combating transnational organized crime:

Weak states   It is not coincidental that organized crime has flourished in states in transition where traditional legitimacy and authority structures have collapsed and social control systems have disappeared. As well as being the result of a sudden collapse of an old regime, however, state weakness can also reflect a more long-term failure to develop viable, legitimate and effective state institutions. Whatever the short- or long-term causes of weakness, however, weak states are characterized by low levels of state legitimacy; weak border controls; ineffective rules; institutions and people representing the state who place personal, tribal, clan or factional goals above the public interest; a lack of economic or social provision for the citizenry; a failure to regulate or protect businesses; the absence of a fair and efficient criminal justice system; and an inability to carry out typical state functions with either efficiency or effectiveness. Not surprisingly, these weaknesses provide a greenhouse for organized crime. Weak states provide excellent sanctuaries in which and from which transnational criminal organizations can operate with impunity. In effect – and this is hardly surprising – weak states provide large holes in global governance.

Corrupt states   In some states organized crime has exploited weaknesses in state institutions, penetrating and coopting government personnel, agencies and departments. The culmination of this process is the emergence of what Roy Godson has termed the political-criminal nexus, a symbiotic relationship between criminals and politicians where they provide mutual benefits: personal enrichment or electoral support for the politicians, and information and protection for the criminals. Successive PRI (Partido Revolucionario Institucional) governments in Mexico, for example, clearly had collusive relationships with major drug traffickers, while in Russia there is actually a political-criminal-business nexus, undergirded in part by a failure to distinguish clearly between what is public and what is private or between what is criminal and what is legal. In other cases, the problem is not so much collusive networks of this kind as dictators who use the state as their own personal treasury and extend the spoils to cronies. In Africa, the era of the single dictator seems to have waned, but there has not been a fundamental shift in the way the state is viewed. And so long as the state is still seen as a prize of politics, the main difference in the future is likely to be in the wider distribution of corruption pay-offs. Indeed, the more the benefits of corruption are diffused, the greater the vested interests in maintaining the spoils system. The point about corrupt states is that they have either already been bought off by organized crime, or provide a ready and willing partner for such an approach. Although they do not necessarily lack a capacity to contribute to governance efforts, they certainly lack the inclination or will to do so.

Criminal states   If weak and corrupt states are pervasive, there is yet a third kind of state that is unlikely to play a supportive role in global efforts to combat transnational organized crime. This is the criminal state, a state in which the authorities have taken over crime. North Korea fits this model, and was aptly described by David Kaplan as a 'wiseguy state' (Kaplan, 1999). Another good example was Serbia under Milosevic. The president and his family and cronies had monopolies on all legitimate imports such as food and fuel, as well as on contraband such as untaxed cigarettes for sale on the black markets in the Balkans and elsewhere in Europe.

As suggested above, the implication of all this is that some states are part of the problem rather than part of the solution. States are the instruments for attacking the targets – transnational criminal organizations – and unless the instruments are effective, the targets are relatively secure. In other words, the response of the international community to transnational organized crime is inevitably partial, incomplete and characterized by gaps and deficiencies. In some cases, these are obvious; in others they are more subtle but no less pernicious in their effects. Some states overtly defect from regulatory regimes or from efforts at governance. In the case of conventions or other efforts to establish norms and standards they simply do not sign on. It is hard to hold them accountable for not meeting obligations when they have not accepted that they have obligations. The more subtle shortcoming is covert defection – where states pretend to be participating or contributing, but at a minimum are acting as free riders. Governments sometimes play games, engaging in cosmetic forms of conformity but doing little to implement their obligations. This is particularly the case in the efforts to combat money laundering where Potemkin villages abound. Many nations have established reporting requirements for cash transactions and suspicious transactions, and even created financial intelligence units to process these reports. In some cases, however, this is almost as far as it goes. The system does not extend to investigations, indictments and successful prosecutions. On the one hand, such jurisdictions can claim to be meeting FATF requirements; on the other hand, they are doing very little in substantive terms to combat money laundering or transnational organized crime.

   This suggests a third problem in the efforts to establish governance norms and mechanisms to combat transnational organized crime and money laundering – an emphasis on procedural norms, standards and patterns of behaviour rather than the creation of substantive norms with real impact. Nowhere is this more obvious than FATF. International cooperation against money laundering has become a goal in its own right rather than simply a means to the end of removing criminal profits and putting criminal enterprises out of business. Even more important, the cooperative venture has become fundamentally flawed by elevating form over substance. The FATF has established a set of standards and practices that require considerable effort but do not yield commensurate results. The imposition of procedural requirements that states adopt certain forms of regulation designed to inhibit or detect money laundering has had far less impact than might be expected, and in substantive terms has been disappointing. The reason is that the wrong questions are being asked by the FATF. The focus is exclusively on whether or not the participating states meet FATF standards rather than the far more important question of whether or not these standards are effective in combating money laundering. The result is self-delusion.

The lesson is that in combating transnational organized crime and money laundering, it is essential to know what works and what does not – and to develop measures of effectiveness that reflect real rather than ostensible results. Until this is done, the FATF will continue to operate on a flawed concept that emphasizes procedural norms – and the need to have them in place – but never addresses the substantive effectiveness of the procedural norms in combating money laundering. And so long as this is the case some states will manage to be simultaneously wonderful launderettes and in good standing with the FATF. Fortunately, the Convention against Transnational Organized Crime does not place the same emphasis on peer review and evaluation, and has also drawn more carefully on effective practice rather than legalistic reporting requirements. Consequently, it is unlikely to be as flawed as the FATF approach.

A fourth problem – and one that confronts all governments that are serious about combating transnational organized crime – is what might be termed the dialectic of governance. In the area of transnational organized crime this is particularly pronounced: transnational criminal organizations are smart adversaries with a capacity for learning (Kenney, forthcoming), high levels of adaptation, and a ruthlessness and nimbleness that governments are rarely able to replicate. In addition, they often operate through network structures that give them many advantages over the formal hierarchies and bureaucracies that are trying to disrupt or destroy them or put them out of business. Whenever governments introduce new laws, regulations and efforts at control, transnational criminal organizations find ways of circumventing them. They are adept at risk management, developing strategies that combine risk prevention, risk control and risk absorption. Often they succeed in neutralizing or disarming international efforts to control them. And even when law enforcement succeeds in inflicting considerable harm on them, they are able to offset the consequences through well-designed mitigation strategies. As networks, for example, they have considerable redundancy so that they can still function effectively even after suffering some degradation of their capabilities. The other important characteristic of criminal networks is that they can be extended into legal businesses and financial institutions. Embedded networks are difficult to identify and to expel. The Bank of New York scandal that erupted in August 2000 provides a good example of a criminal network that crossed into the legal domain and, for some time at least, successfully circumvented banking regulations. Indeed, regulators think in terms of 'know the customer', due diligence, and so on; criminals think in terms of know the banker, become the banker, marry the banker, or own the bank – and then ignore, violate or transcend banking norms and regulations.

This leads directly to yet another problem of global governance – states do not consist solely of governments and a political sector. They also embody business and financial institutions and an economic sector – and there is not always congruence between the two. Once again, this is nowhere more evident than in the efforts to combat money laundering. Banks themselves are often complicit institutions in laundering activities. Citibank, through its private banking sector, for example, helped Raul Salinas, whose brother at the time was President of Mexico, to deposit well over 100 million dollars in Swiss bank accounts. No questions were asked about the origins of the money. Bank officials assumed they knew the customer even though they did not know the source of the money. Similarly, the Bank of New York in the mid-1990s appeared to do little due diligence before entering a very high risk banking environment and developing correspondent relations with Russian banks. In Congressional testimony in the US in 1994 it was revealed that approximately 40 per cent of Russian banks were controlled by organized crime. Such revelations should have been sufficient to give pause to Western banks seeking correspondent relationships with banks in Russia. Significantly, Republic Bank pulled out of the Russian market because of the risks involved. Bank of New York, in contrast, vigorously pursued such relationships with little regard to risk. When the scandal broke in August 2000 about both criminal money and flight capital moving through the bank, the excuse was a lapse in supervision. This was disingenuous – the failure was a policy and institutional failure rather than simply a personnel failure. Yet it should not be surprising. In the final analysis banks are commercial institutions whose primary aim is profit. Increasingly, however, they being asked to become adjuncts to law enforcement. This is a responsibility that is not welcomed, that is not central to their role and mission, and that they would prefer not to be burdened with. Consequently, it is a responsibility that is often not fully met. Global governance efforts sometimes fail to adjust to this basic reality.

None of this is meant to suggest that governments should abandon their efforts to combat transnational organized crime and money laundering. It does suggest, though, that these efforts will continue to encounter major obstacles, some of which might prove to be insuperable. Even acknowledging that the forces of disorder might be impossible for governments to control, however, it is clear that there are several relatively simple ways in which the efforts to combat transnational organized crime can be strengthened. These are discussed briefly in the final section.

Towards More Effective Governance

One of the deficiencies in governance efforts directed at combating transnational organized crime has been that, although there are many initiatives, there is no overall strategy. If governance is to be effective, it needs to be strategic. Any chance of real success requires an integrated comprehensive approach for attacking transnational organized crime. In some respects the Convention against Transnational Organized Crime provides the basis for such an approach. It recommends measures that could at least provide the building blocks for a strategic approach by the international community. Such a strategy needs to target criminal leaders, organizations (whether traditional hierarchies or more prevalent criminal networks) and profits. Furthermore, efforts against money laundering, against transnational organized crime and against corruption need to be coordinated in ways that create synergies for governments and law enforcement agencies.

As part of this strategy it is critical to develop real measures of effectiveness. As indicated above, it is essential to go beyond the procedural assessments currently in place to ask what measures have most effect in disrupting and damaging transnational organized crime and money laundering. In terms of the effectiveness of anti-money laundering measures, for example, there are at least five dimensions that need to be considered:

* What is the effect in terms of facilitating detection of money laundering?
* What is the effect in terms of prosecutions and convictions?
* What is the effect in terms of increasing the costs of doing business to the criminals?
* What is the effect in terms of removing the profits from criminal activities?
* What is the effect in terms of deterrence?

It appears – at least from outside – that none of these questions is asked by the Financial Action Task Force. The Convention against Transnational Organized Crime, in contrast, does draw on best practices in ways that offer some prospect of developing a strategic approach. Indeed, the convention can be understood as an effort to provide the elements that now need to be integrated into an overall strategic framework. Such a framework would also have to take into consideration the problems identified in the previous section, especially the defection issue. It is critical to recognize that in the competition between states and sovereignty-free actors, some states are on the other side. A strategy for dealing with these states, and either developing capacity (where the problem is weakness) or changing their incentive structure (where the problem is will or inclination), is essential. Even if all these things are done, there is of course no guarantee of success. Without a strategic approach to governance, however, the forces of disorder can hardly fail to emerge triumphant.

References

Blum, Jack, Levi, Michael, Naylor, R. Thomas and Williams, Phil (1999) *Financial Havens, Bank Secrecy and Money Laundering*, New York: United Nations.

Bovenkerk, Frank (2001) 'Organized crime and ethnic minorities: is there a link?', in Phil Williams and Dimitri Vlassis (eds), *Combating Transnational Crime: Concepts, Activities and Responses*, London: Cass.

Bull, Hedley (1995) *The Anarchical Society*, 2nd edn, New York: Columbia University Press.

GAO (General Accounting Office) (2000) *Bosnia Peace Operation – Crime and Corruption Threaten Successful Implementation of the Dayton Peace Agreement*, Report to Congressional Requesters, Washington DC: GAO, www.gao.gov/new.items/ns00219t.pdf

Ianni, Francis A. J. (1974) *Black Mafia: Ethnic Succession in Organized Crime*, New York: Simon and Schuster.

Kaplan, Robert D. (1994) 'The coming anarchy', *Atlantic Monthly*, Feb., pp. 44–75.

Kaplan, David (1999) 'The wiseguy regime: North Korea has embarked on a global crime spree', *US News and World Report*, 15 Feb., pp. 36–9.

Kenney, Michael (forthcoming) 'When criminals out-smart the state: understanding the learning capacity of Colombian drug trafficking organizations', *Transnational Organized Crime*, 5, no. 1.

Kinsell, Jeremy (2000) 'The conductivity of transnational crime', *Cross Border Control*, 16, p. 38.

Kurtzman, Joel (1993) *The Death of Money*, New York: Simon and Schuster.

Minc, Alain (1993) *Le Nouveau Môyen Age*, Paris: Gallimard.

Mittelman, James and Johnston, Robert (1999) 'The globalization of organized crime, the courtesan state, and the corruption of civil society', *Global Governance*, 5, pp. 103–26.

Ohmae, Kenichi (1995) *The End of the Nation State: The Rise of Regional Economies*, New York: Free Press.

Rosenau, James N. (1990) *Turbulence in World Politics*, Princeton: Princeton University Press.

Rosenau, James N. (1992) 'The relocation of authority in a shrinking world', *Comparative Politics*, Apr., pp. 253–72.

Rosenau, James N. (1994) 'New dimensions of security', *Security Dialogue*, 25, no. 3, pp. 255–81.

Rosenau, James N. (1996) 'The dynamics of globalization', *Security Dialogue*, 27, no. 3, pp. 247–62.

Ruggie, John Gerrard (1993) 'Territoriality and beyond: problematizing modernity in international relations', *International Organization*, Winter, pp. 139–74.

Sassen, Saskia (1994) *Cities in a World Economy*, Thousand Oaks: Pine Forge Press.

Sassen, Saskia (1996) *Losing Control*, New York: Columbia University Press.

Schelling, Thomas C. (1967) *Arms and Influence*, New Haven: Yale University Press.

Singer, Max and Wildavsky, Aaron B. (1996) *The Real World Order: Zones of Peace, Zones of Turmoil*. New York: Chatham House Publishers.

Tilly, Charles (1985) 'War making and state making as organized crime', in Peter Evans, Dietrich Rueschemeyer and Theda Skocpol (eds), *Bringing the State Back In*, Cambridge: Cambridge University Press.

Tuchman, Barbara W. (1978) *A Distant Mirror: The Calamitous Fourteenth Century*, New York: Ballantine Books.

Van Duyne, Petrus C. (1996) 'The phantom and threat of organized crime', *Crime, Law and Social Change*, 24, pp. 341–77.

Williams, Phil (2001) 'Transnational organized crime, illicit markets, and money laundering', in P. J. Simmons and Chantel Ouderen (eds), *Challenges in International Governance*, Washington: Carnegie Endowment.

Williams, Phil and Savona, Ernesto (eds) (1996) *The United Nations and Transnational Organized Crime*, London: Cass.

7
Global Digital Communications and the Prospects for Transnational Regulation
Perri 6

Introduction

For much of the 1990s, one could hardly pick up a magazine or a newspaper without reading that regulating the internet was like nailing jelly to the ceiling. 'The internet interprets censorship as damage and routes around it' was the catchphrase of that decade. This was, by turns, hailed as the great hope for liberty (the libertarian Barlow, 1996a, 1996b, or the neoliberal Dyson, 1997), or as the great disaster for social order (Carr, 1999, 2001), or simply as increasing the already disaster-prone character of technology (Brown, 1997).

Today, the catchphrase already seems quaint, and now specialist internet lawyers are writing huge and detailed tomes on how businesses can exploit loopholes in every kind of regulatory activity in any country they may have reason to operate in (for one of the shorter and more readable, see Edwards and Waelde, 2000). No serious writer now argues that the internet and other digital networks[1] are in general ungovernable, anarchic, or overgoverned or crushed under the heel of public authority, *tout court*. Indeed, there were major social conflicts through the 1990s over the regulation of encryption, and over the demand by law enforcement authorities for mandatory key escrow,[2] directly or indirectly, and a variety of settlements have been made in different countries. However, in practice, law enforcement authorities do not expect to exercise comprehensive surveillance over all traffic, still less enforce the law everywhere.

After the collapse of the dot.com gold rush in early 2000 and the tumbling of telecommunications stocks in 2001, and after the evident fact of the persistence of most of institutions of governance that were supposedly threatened by these technologies, the debate about governance of digital technologies and the transnational aspects of this has become rather sober, practical, even legalistic and certainly fragmented into a series of specialist debates, despite the convergence between computing and television technologies and hence of regulatory issues (Lessig, 1999; Lees, Ralph and Langham Brown, 2000; Barnett et al., 2000).[3] With the specialization of debate about regulation and online activity has come the recognition that there is little about the technology of the internet that presents genuinely new and distinctive challenges to regulation – or rather, about the convergence or at least increasing interdependence between the internet, proprietary data exchange systems, telephony and television. By 'regulation of the internet and other internationally publicly accessible electronic networks', I shall argue, we actually mean the application to a new field of the regulation of personal information, intellectual property rights, rationing of scarce resources such as certain kinds of carrying capacity, restrictive practices and abuse of monopoly power, freedom of expression or censorship on such grounds as obscenity, libel, advertising, tax law, privacy, police powers in respect of surveillance, technical standards and so on. These are all bodies of law in which the principles long predate the advent of the internet (see Edwards and Waelde, 2000). The central challenges the internet presents for regulation are, I shall argue, fourfold, and in no way unique to this technology or even to the most recent decades; indeed, all were familiar to nineteenth-century international lawyers and political economists. The four types of challenge are those of

- *Jurisdiction*: resolving uncertainty and conflict over which sets of national laws are to be applied;
- *Sovereignty*: ensuring capability of effective enforcement;
- *Free riding*: preventing excessive development of capabilities for some states to adopt standards that encourage malefactors and tortfeasors to operate internationally with relative impunity from a base within their territory; and
- *Relevance*: determining the appropriate geographical unit for the application of laws.

All these four raise issues of efficacy in regulation, while the second and the fourth raise issues of legitimacy with key publics about even the domestic application of regulation. Efficacy and legitimacy can, however, also come into conflict: there are many reasons to be as concerned at the possibility of excessively efficacious and intrusive overregulation as about underregulation.

In this chapter, I review the complex division of regulatory labour and a network of regulatory institutions which reflect a wide variety of types of mechanism of global governance. I first set out the range and complexity of the regulatory issues and agencies, before examining the extent to which the setting of rules is actually done transnationally. I argue that there is more transnationalization of regulation than first meets the eye, for there are many more horizontal mechanisms at work than are often recognized. The chapter then discusses the question of how effective this regulation really is, before considering whether any of the standard off-the-peg theories help us understand its nature, origins or efficacy. If none of the standard theories of global governance describe all the variations we observe across the vast network of regulatory challenges, this is, I argue, not surprising. For most standard theories argue for the pre-eminence of a single power mechanism of regulation. The sensible question for social science is not to pick one of these and try to stretch it to cover the whole system, but to examine the viability of the particular mix of such mechanisms that we have inherited, across this complex and ramified division of labour (on the concept of the regulatory mix, see Raab, 1997, 1999, 2000; Raab and Bennett, forthcoming; Industry Canada, 1994; 6, 1998, chs 10 and 19). I conclude with a discussion of the future prospects for effective and acceptable transnational regulation.

The Challenge for Global Governance of the Uses of Digital Networks

It is now clear that there is and will be no *single* thing called 'internet regulation' or 'internet governance'. Most of the legal fields of regulation that are applied to the internet are not peculiar to that technology, but are quite generic, and even those regulatory issues that seem to be specific to the technology are in fact ones that reflect provisional and much less than universal balances between technologies.[4] Without attempting to be exhaustive, one can classify in the following manner the main areas of risk in relation to which regulatory action either is already being taken or is under negotiation nationally or internationally or at least is frequently called for.[5] Table 7.1 gives the titles for ten of the main areas of regulatory activity that people have in mind when they talk of 'regulating the internet'.

Table 7.1 There is no such thing as regulating the internet: risks and areas of regulatory interest in public access digital networks – the internet, public interactive digital television, etc.

1 Investment
1a Tax treatment of companies providing telecommunications, routers and servers, internet services, etc.
1b Pricing of scarce intangible resources, e.g. bandwidth spectra for broadcasting and for next generation mobile telephony

2 Access to services
2a Universal service obligations
2b Levies to finance initiatives to extend access (mainly in the US)
2c Price regulation on telecommunications and (in some countries) internet service providers
2d General freedom to trade internationally, including over digital networks (as enforced, for example, by the World Trade Organization)

3 Content
3a Rights to supply content
    3a.i Freedom of expression
        3a.i.1 Protection for investigative journalism
3b Negative restrictions on rights to supply content
    3b.i Intellectual property
        3b.i.1 Passing off
        3b.i.2 Rationing and prevention of conflict of scarce content rights. e.g. domain names
        3b.i.3 Document copyright
        3b.i.4 Ownership of other assets e.g. software licences, film and video material rights
    3b.ii Obscenity
        3b.ii.1 Censorship
        3b.ii.2 Rating and classification
    3b.iii Sedition – mainly in China, Myanmar (Burma), to a lesser extent in Singapore, but also occasionally in Western countries
    3b.iv Blasphemy
    3b.v Libel
    3b.vi Privacy and data protection
3c Positive restrictions on rights to supply content: content standards
    3c.i Quality thresholds
    3c.ii Internal diversity requirements for channel programming
    3c.iii Taste standards

Cont'd

Table 7.1   (*Cont'd*)

3d Duties to supply content
   3d.i Freedom of information laws upon government
   3d.ii Product labelling and warnings online
   3d.iii Subject access rights in data protection: duty to supply personal records for information and possible correction only to the subject of those records
3e Duties to carry content supplied elsewhere
   3e.i Public information services
   3e.ii Duty to publish corrections; 'right to reply'
3f Content authorization
   3f.i Accreditation

4 Market organization and competition
4a General competition law e.g. abuse of monopoly power, monopoly power *per se*, restrictive practices
4b Cross-media ownership and media pluralism
4c Duties on monopoly infrastructure owners to 'unbundle' some assets and make them available to competitors e.g. requiring monopoly operating system providers to provide open source code, or unbundled applications from operating systems software; requiring monopoly or dominant telecommunications companies to make local loop systems available to competitors

5 Consumer protection
5a Protection of online purchasing: general consumer protection law
5b Online contract specific rules, e.g. consumer information and authorization procedures required before contract is deemed to have been entered into
5c Spam control

6 Contract law
6a Legal status of digital signatures
6b Recognition and authority of arbitration systems

7 Criminal law
7a Detection: regulation of access to and use of encryption software, duties to provide decryption keys; requirements to put in place alerting systems for certain kinds of traffic
7b Prosecution: status of certain kinds of digital content as evidence
7c Prevention: requirements on code to be robust against certain kinds of crime

8 Law of torts
8a Application of nuisance and negligence to viral and Trojan Horse attack
8b Duties of care to consumers placed upon telecommunications and internet service providing companies

9 Technical standards
9a Content standards e.g. mark-up languages such as XML
9b Data movement protocols, e.g. TCP/IP
9c Application compatibility systems standards, e.g. Java

10 Tax law
10a Tax treatment of goods and services traded internationally over digital networks
10b Tax treatment of funds moved internationally over digital networks

There are some well-known conflicts in regulatory policy between some of these ten categories, but hardly any of these conflicts are specific to the digital technologies or networks. Within content regulation, conflicts between freedom of expression on the one hand, and libel, privacy or obscenity on the other long predate these networks. What has changed with the change of medium is that regulators have to work harder to trace those they consider violators. Again, conflicts between incentives to invest in infrastructure and the importance of competition are perennial problems of economic policy-making. Conflicts between commercial freedom and universal service obligations for access are as old as the idea of a utility. Even the conflict between freedom of expression and the rights of law enforcement authorities that has been fought out over more than a decade in respect of encryption is neither new nor specific to the internet, but goes back as far as crime itself. Encryption has been used by organized criminals as much as by the military for decades: the original restriction of trade in cryptography as a 'munition' (under the US International Traffic in Arms Regulations, or ITAR) of which Phil Zimmerman, inventor of the PGP (Pretty Good Privacy) algorithm which offered cheap and modestly strong cryptography around the world initially at no cost but now available commercially, famously fell foul, reflects both these long-standing concerns (Phillips, 1997).

Institutions and Levels of Digital Governance

Just how globalized, then, are the systems of regulation on each of the ten issue categories, and just how far are problems of jurisdiction, sovereignty, free riding and relevance overcome? And how far are these systems of regulation expressions of public power, and how far do they reflect genuinely private self-regulation? These questions are not straightforward. In the case of the degree of globalization by contrast with continental regional or national governance, this is because it is important to distinguish the level at which regulatory rules are formulated and agreed, the level at which they are formally set, the level at which they are enforced, and the level at which there is mobilization to try to seize and change the agenda. In the case of the second question, again the same distinctions need to be made, but in addition, there are well-known difficulties in telling true self-regulation from something behind which governmental or other public power stands, albeit with a decorously low profile; there are also ways to combine differing degrees of self-regulation with governmental regulation (Majone, 1996, pp. 23–6; Mayer, 1995).

Focusing just on the level at which rules are formally set, table 7.2 provides a very rough-cut brief summary of the levels at which the main regulation-making institutions are located. In what follows, it will be of central importance to recognize the crudity of the picture presented, which represents only the conventional wisdom, which will be qualified in the course of this chapter.

Table 7.2 shows, for example, rather few global bodies that are formal regulation-making authorities, and that most regulation remains nationally set. Indeed, contrary to the popular myth, national regulation even for censorship is not necessarily entirely ineffective, as the experience of China in blocking access to at least some sites deemed politically unacceptable there has shown (Economist, 2000a). To the extent that this has been successful, it has been due to the willingness of major foreign companies to

Table 7.2 How global and how private is the regulation of digital networks? A very crude, first-cut view of the levels at which rules are formally set

	Global regulation	Continental regulation	National regulation	Public regulation	Private self-regulation
Tax incentives to invest			✓	✓	
Bandwidth pricing			✓	✓	
Universal service obligations			✓	✓	
Freedom of expression		✓ EU, Council of Europe		✓	
General intellectual property	✓ WIPO, ITU			✓	
Domain names	✓ ICANN, ITU				✓ (currently strong, but under threat)
Obscenity			✓	✓	✓ (modest)
Libel			✓	✓	
Data protection		✓ OECD, EU		✓	✓ (modest)
Quality, diversity, taste			✓	✓	✓ (modest)
Freedom of information		✓ EU	✓	✓	
Accreditation			?		✓
Competition law		✓ EU		✓	
Cross-media ownership		✓ EU	✓	✓	
Unbundling			✓	✓	
Consumer protection			✓	✓	✓ (modest)
Recognition of digital signatures		✓ OECD	✓	✓	
Arbitration	✓ ICC, UNCITRAL				✓ (quite strong)
Criminal law		✓ Council of Europe	✓	✓	
Law of tort			✓	✓	
Technical standards	✓ IETF				✓ (strong)

remove content that might offend the government in Beijing, in order to gain access to the huge Chinese market.

However, there are important global authorities. The World Intellectual Property Organization (WIPO), based on international treaty law, represents a powerful force for convergence in national legal treatments of a wide range of types of intellectual property. It works within the overarching regulatory system set by the World Trade Organization. Nevertheless, the importance of the national level, at least for the nearly-but-not-quite hegemon nation, the United States, should not be underestimated. The Napster case is instructive here. Napster provided a website that supported peer-to-peer exchange of data, allowing millions of people to exchange music files (among others) for free, undermining musicians' and record companies' revenues (Rapp, 2000). Napster.com was bought by Bertelsmann, but was finally ordered by the US courts to find some way to operate legally and to police its subscribers or else face being shut down (Standage, 2000). There are now many other peer-to-peer sites offering similar access to music, and they are attracting many people. Some may be found to be no more legal than Napster – such as MP3.com (see BBC News Online, 2001c) – but others are operating for the longer term on the right side of the law. Despite the court decision, some legal form of peer-to-peer will probably emerge and the music industry will have to adapt its business model to accept this and secure revenues from its intellectual property in other ways (Economist, 2000b). Peer-to-peer technology is unlikely to make intellectual property rights unenforceable: in practice, regulation and technology will no doubt come to an accommodation around some new pricing and property protection model that can be used within a peer-to-peer environment (Economist, 2001c).

In this field, the roots of the regulatory importance of the US are as much economic as anything else. Napster could, at least in theory, have locked out US users and taken its servers offshore. But with so much of its consumer base located in the world's largest economy, this was hardly a serious option. This fact, as much as the timidity of European and other authorities, means that the Napster case could only be handled in the US courts. There are differences between European and US approaches to intellectual property law (Edwards and Waelde, 2000, chs 6–10). The fact that only the US can really enforce against major violations extends the global reach, in practice, of US intellectual property rules. Conversely, the relative weakness of the EU as a regulator reflects the greater attractiveness of the US market to many companies.

Also in this field – but more specifically concerned with 'passing off' rules – although more modest, the importance of the International Trademark Association should not be underestimated as a rule-influencing body. In the governance of domain names, the Internet Corporation for Assigned Names and Numbers (ICANN) is, at least formally, both global and private. In practice, both those classifications should probably be very heavily qualified (Mueller, 1999). In fact, ICANN is largely a creature of its licence from the US government, which stands behind much of its authority. The degree of international influence is limited, and indeed limiting it may have been one of the motives for which the Clinton administration created the system as a formally private body in the way and at the speed that it did (Mueller, 1999). ICANN's charging and allocation policies for new top level domain names are now subject to heavy Congressional investigation (Mueller, 2001). In fact, there are a number of commercial initiatives under way to offer domain names outside the ICANN system, and their success depends only on the willingness of the net community to connect to their servers: 'New.net', an independent rival, is one important potential challenger (BBC News Online, 2001b).

However, the hegemony of the US is crucially limited by both commercial and international legal factors. The fate of key escrow is a good example of the former: the decision of the Clinton administration to pull back from mandatory key escrow reflected the US software industry's need to sell its products internationally. For the latter, we need look no further than the World Trade Organization: having worked so hard to set the body up, the US has been forced to abide by its rules even when it has operated against its medium-term economic interests.

International arbitration in commercial disputes arising from online transactions is subject to a structure – formally global, but in practice dominated by the developed world – under the International Chamber of Commerce (ICC), although the influence of the United Nations Commission on International Trade Law (UNCITRAL), a public body, in shaping the rule base cannot be underestimated (Reinicke, 1998; Wiener, 1999; Ronit and Schneider, 1999). Again, the International Organization for Standardization (ISO) and its relationship with European, other continental and national standards systems is formally private, and global, but in practice its rule-making is heavily influenced by intergovernmental activity. The Internet Engineering Task Force (IETF) – regulating technical standards – is a private body, but the degree to which it can claim truly global reach is limited by the origins of the contemporary internet, its infrastructure financing etc. The IETF's remarkably egalitarian, open and unanimity-based decision system survives largely because of the tightly defined nature of its responsibilities.

Qualifications need to be made, too, to the assignment of regulatory roles to the continental and national levels. For the Organization for Economic Cooperation and Development (OECD), which spans continents without being truly global, has provided the basis for national rule-making in many areas, including data protection, legal recognition of digital signatures, and telecommunications standards, and has devoted a high-level initiative to policy coordination in this field (Ypsilanti, 1999). Standing somewhere between the global and the continental and somewhere between advisory and binding rule-making, the OECD complicates the picture greatly.

Although freedom of expression is regulated at continental level through, for example, the European Convention on Human Rights, behind that convention stands the United Nations Declaration. Competition policy rules are set principally at the national level – and most importantly in the United States, as was seen in the Justice Department's celebrated case against Microsoft (Standage, 2001), and at continental level in Europe. Nevertheless, there is increasing interest within the World Trade Organization in the interaction between GATT rules on non-tariff barriers and national or continental competition policy; although the WTO has no competition policy jurisdiction, it is likely that in coming years it will attempt to use its trade policy tools to influence competition policy.

At first blush, table 7.2 seemed to be suggesting that most rule-making and rule-setting in digital network regulation is in fact national or at most continental and public, but the qualifications already made are beginning to suggest that there is already more that is global or at least intergovernmental within the developed world than first meets the eye. They also suggest that even behind those global and inter-governmental institutions, in many cases, there stands the central fact of the hegemon nation and heart of the digital economy, the United States. Finally, wholly private self-regulation is harder to find than first sight suggests. The sharp distinctions between levels and forms are in fact misleading. There is much greater variety in the system of regulation, seen as a whole, than table 7.2 suggests.

However, to see just how far regulation is being transnationalized, we need a richer system of classifying regulatory structures than simply the geographical level at which rules are formally set. We need to bring into the picture the implementation, priorities, degree of effort, and the nature of and responsibility for enforcement. Secondly, we need to explore the ways in which, irrespective of the level of formal rule-setting, regulatory processes adjust to each other internationally, or fail to. For this purpose, table 7.3 provides a richer account of the dimension of transnationalization (for a less

Table 7.3 Transnational ordering strategies for regulation systems

Type of ordering	Examples	Cases
A1 Hierarchically harmonized	A1.a *Supranational law- and scheme-making*: setting of laws by international authority, e.g. international treaty or other formal multilateral adjustment (Wiener, 1999)	WIPO, UNCITRAL, WTO; aspirations for Council of Europe treaty on cybercrime
A2 Hierarchically nested – public	A2.a *Nested regulation*: harmonization of regulatory standards through international agreement, enforced nationally, within which national systems operate and with which the details are expected to comply, and where sanctions and incentives are in place (Aggarwal, 1998: for an example from another field, see Vogel, 1998)	OECD statements on digital signatures and encryption, European Convention on Human Rights; within Europe, much of the EU Directive on data protection
A3 Hierarchically nested – public/private	A3.a *Supervised self-regulation*: encouragement of transnational self-regulation: for example, the encouragement of voluntary standards bodies, backed up by the long-stop threat of statutory regulation in the event of the failure of self-regulation, as in the case of domain names control, or quasi-voluntary systems of alternative dispute resolution (Perritt, 1997)	ICANN; sections in EU Directive on data protection creating approval mechanism for private codes of practice
B1 Horizontally geographically separated	B1.a *Catchment area regulation*: agreement separately to regulate, either through executive regulatory agencies or in the courts, transnational flows on their domestic manifestations, either on	Data protection, consumer protection

Cont'd

Table 7.3   (Cont'd)

Type of ordering	Examples	Cases
	the destination or source principle, but agreeing to eschew attempts to enforce national laws extraterritorially	
	B1.b *Comity, or permitted extra-territoriality in case of recognized greater interest*: a right for regulators from one state to enforce in another if they can show the greater interest than that of the state in the jurisdiction of which they seek to enforce (Johnson and Post, 1997); this is not unlike the principle behind extradition in criminal matters	None as yet, but some extra-territorial applications of US and EU law might come to be stabilized under such a principle
	B1.c *Regulation lending*: or agreement by one state to adopt another's regulatory standards specifically in respect of flows of information trade between the two countries	1999–2000 'Safe harbour' agreement between US and EU on US companies conforming to EU data protection law when providing services using European citizens' personal data
B2 Horizontally syndicated	B2.a *Syndication of regulation*: national regulators engaging in mutual adjustment, dialogue, coordination on timing of enforcement, sharing information about violators and new technologies to be promoted, taking each other into account, agreeing joint priorities, creating international colleges of regulators to conduct joint training, policy development and advice	International Conference of Privacy Data Protection Commissioners; regulator conferences for telecommunications, and within Schengen system
B3 Horizontally competitive	B3.a *Mutual recognition, mutual adjustment and toleration of some jurisdiction shopping*: here, within a span of broadly similar national laws, there is some discretion both for regulators and regulated about where enforcement is done	Some intercorporate contract and tort litigation

ramified classification, see Reinicke, 1998; see also the taxonomy presented in 6, 2001). We can distinguish at the first level between *hierarchical* systems, which introduce order into the mix of different national, continental and sectoral regulatory structures by means of some overarching authority, and *horizontal* systems, which allow order to emerge through channelling attention to problems, effort, innovation and flows of information between regulatory bodies. In any given field, there may be a mix of hierarchical and horizontal systems.

There is an important orthogonal dimension, not shown on table 7.3, along which would be arrayed the specific instruments of regulation that can be agreed upon hierarchically or horizontally, ranging from the most mandatory – such as 'code' (Lessig, 1999), or hard-wired mandatory systems built into all systems (such as the TCP/IP protocol) through to systems that are currently more voluntary (such as privacy-enhancing technologies: Information and Privacy Commissioner and Registratiekamer, 1995).

Although it would be tedious to reproduce, a roughly similar classification can be presented for private sector self-regulation, with hierarchical systems reflecting the dominance of the interests of major monopolists or oligopolists in defining self-regulatory standards and controlling patent exploitation rights, and horizontal systems being those that emerge from forms of adjustment in more competitive markets. Although the more hierarchical ordering systems have attracted more attention, because of their greater visibility, the horizontal systems have proliferated because of the lower costs of their establishment and the fact that they make smaller demands on existing regulatory and political institutions (raising serious questions about their democratic accountability), and because it is easier for national governments to represent them to their populations as consistent with national sovereignty, although in reality all these systems represent strategic pooling of sovereignty in the hope of an exchange for greater efficacy of regulation.

Table 7.3 shows that there are examples of each type of transnationalization, and no type and neither of the overarching categories can be said to be the one to which regulatory activity and change is generally tending. However, it would be wrong to tell the story of the governance of digital networks as one of simple trendless variation. Rather, we can see a general trend towards the use of all the approaches to transnationalization, and one which has built on trends in regulation of all these ten issue areas that long predated the internet or digital television.

More importantly, however, table 7.3 corrects a key misleading impression given in table 7.2, which still tends to be the conventional wisdom. That is the idea that there are necessarily zero-sum relationships between control over regulatory rule-making or enforcement at global, continental and national levels. Table 7.3 demonstrates the wide variety of ways in which, within the field of regulation of digital networks, efforts are being made to create institutions under which these relationships can be positive sum games. Nation-states – and the hegemon nation-state least of all – do not in general hand over power in the regulation making or enforcing process to supranational bodies, nor are they passively allowing technologies to be used in ways that evade their regulatory goals. On the contrary, they follow an impressive range of strategies for innovation in securing their regulatory goals transnationally, and in securing influence over the content and enforcement of those regulatory systems. They are making digital regulatory globalization work for them, but without typically confining themselves to classical intergovernmentalism or simple obedience to rule-making by bloc-leading hegemon states.

Consideration of table 7.2, with all the qualifications, and table 7.3 together should also put paid to the still-popular myth of a 'race to the bottom' in regulatory capability, levels of standards, or regulatory effectiveness. The idea that there is anything about either globalization or about digital systems that turns regulatory interaction between states necessarily into a system of competitive deregulation is quite clearly wrong. It may be that this might have occurred but for the work of certain continental and global institutions (Golub, 2000), but the fact is that they have successfully supported high environmental, health and safety, welfare and other standards, just as they have sustained high standards of formal legal privacy protection and other information standards. However, there are some business interests – both 'good' and 'bad' – that can lead to 'race to the top' phenomena, including imperatives to overcome consumer and media distrust, and for incumbents to create barriers to entry or restrictive practices (Clarke, 2000, ch. 7).

It should be recalled just how recently it is in the history of government that many of the ten issue areas have been the subject of regulation at all. Intellectual property was first regulated in the nineteenth century; passing off in the late nineteenth and early twentieth; data protection only in the 1970s; quality thresholds were imposed on terrestrial private broadcasting only in the postwar years; freedom of information laws are a creature of the 1970s in most of the world (except, admittedly, for some of Scandinavia, which can trace them back to the eighteenth century); and bandwidth allocation is a creature of the second half of the twentieth century. On the measure of fields and issues in which regulation has been undertaken, it has to be said that the age of globalization, far from being the age of retreating regulatory ambition, has been one of the great ages of regulatory expansion by nation-states. Moreover, the range of means of achieving regulatory aims has been enormously expanded in this period. The means available in the late nineteenth century were much more limited, as the simple instrumentation deployed in the creation of the International Telegraph Union (ITU) bears witness. Most of the repertoire identified in the middle column of table 7.3 has been developed relatively recently.

The Effectiveness of Regulation

Someone could reply to the argument of the previous section that none of this shows that all this regulation of transnational digital networks actually *works*. The 'nailing jelly to the ceiling is pointless' school of thought might argue that much of this effort is either sham, in order to keep up appearances for citizens who demand the comforting illusion that public power remains intact, or, if it is sincere, then it is typically in vain. While that might be true, it leaves unanswered the question of why governments cannot tell citizens what its advocates insist is the unvarnished truth, and why they persist with what would, on their argument, be high and rising costs of failing regulatory institution-building (cf. Keohane and Martin, 1995, p. 40). However, the challenge deserves to be addressed more fully.

What then are the specifically global dimensions and transnational dimensions of the problems of effectiveness in the ten regulatory issues and challenges? Essentially,

Table 7.4 Global and transnational dimensions of the regulatory challenge

A Jurisdiction: application of laws in litigation
A.i   Uncertainty, e.g. inability to locate geographically any place where a regulable activity is conducted
A.ii   Conflict, e.g. between source and destination principles

B Sovereignty: capability of effective laws in legislation and executive action
B.i   Power of any individual states to achieve goals through regulation
B.ii   Power of smaller, poorer states or states remote from metropolitan Western centres to gain effective leverage on market forces

C Free riding: capability for some states to adopt standards that encourage malefactors and tortfeasors to operate with relative impunity from their territory, but committing acts that affect people, companies and governments in other countries

D Relevance: appropriate (efficient) geographical unit for design of laws
For determination of market condition (especially defining the scope of the relevant market for applying competition law principles: Scherer, 1994)

we can distinguish four types of transnational problem that can arise in at least several of the ten categories identified in table 7.1. They may be called, for the sake of convenience, problems of jurisdiction, sovereignty, free riding and relevance: each is briefly defined in table 7.4.

In the mid to late 1990s, issues of uncertainty of and conflict of jurisdictions were expected to be the key problem in regulating digital networks, and much thought was given to them by academic commentators and practising policy-makers (Kahin and Nesson, 1997). In the early to mid 1990s, there were a number of high profile cases in which cases were brought in the US, German and other courts in an effort to apply obscenity and other content laws extraterritorially. There are still a few such cases every year. In response to the anticipation of a major problem here, there have been advocates of voluntary horizontal solutions such as online arbitration (Perritt, 1997), of technological solutions such as forcing the disclosure of the country of origin of all addresses (Lessig, 1999), and, of course, of more hierarchical solutions such as a vast programme of multilateral treaty-based lawmaking. Indeed, there are not only regulatory but ordinary commercial reasons, for marketing and for fraud or laundering detection in particular, for being interested in country-disclosure systems, or 'geolocation', and software that can identify country of origin of website visitors is now a rapidly growing sector (Economist, 2001d).

Certainly, these problems have not disappeared. Working out just where certain online crimes, breaches of contract or tort were committed, and in which jurisdiction they are actionable, is not easy, and the comprehensiveness of the available techniques raise civil liberties concerns. There will no doubt be attempts in future by courts and even by legislatures to make laws apply extraterritorially in ways that prove unacceptable to other countries. Applying the destination principle, but in effect applying French law extraterritorially, a French court recently ordered the portal company Yahoo!.com to find a way of preventing French net users from seeing the sales of

Nazi memorabilia available on its US-based sites (Economist, 2001a): the First Amendment to the US constitution would prevent the US courts from requiring Yahoo!.com to do such a thing in that country. Lessig's proposal for forcing the country-coding of users and automated filtering by country code might yet come to seem a natural solution to problems of this kind (Lessig, 1999). Indeed, the proposal for the IPV6 standard put forward by the Internet Engineering Task Force which would, controversially, provide identifying information about every user, thus raising privacy and anonymity concerns, could be expanded for this purpose; however, the IETF also supports much more effective encryption. As so often, what is really at issue in response to jurisdiction problems is not unregulability, but the conflict of different values and regulatory goals.

However, what is striking is just how manageable the problem has, in fact, been in the context of the growth of online international business-to-business commerce, and the slower but still significant growth of online international business-to-consumer sales. Uncertainty and conflict of jurisdictions are not new problems in international law: they were the subject of detailed textbooks, bodies of supreme court case law in many countries, and no little effort in bilateral and multilateral treaty-making for more than a century prior to the advent of the internet as a mass communication medium. The internet has not presented fundamentally new problems of legal principle, or ones to which no relevant legal principles are already institutionalized in the bodies of law in most developed countries. What it has raised is the challenge of working out how to apply those procedural principles to only a few substantive areas of law that have not previously been litigated using those principles, such as data protection and obscenity. In fact, of course, problems of jurisdiction in intellectual property law troubled Dickens, whose writings were plagiarized in the US in his lifetime, and problems of jurisdiction in libel are as old as the legal concept itself.

In response to the jurisdiction problems, there have been a number of strategies deployed. The Council of Europe is seeking 'approximation' – which may or may not mean harmonization – of the laws of member states on hacking, online fraud and pornography (le Goueff, 2000), although the proposals have raised civil liberties concerns (BBC News Online, 2001a). The G8 has been working on a convention on the same issues. A similar fifty-country process is being used with the aim of producing a Hague Convention on Jurisdiction and Foreign Judgments during 2002, despite earlier failures that resulted in negotiations being abandoned in 1999. The convention would, if agreed, deal with the civil law problems of jurisdiction and extraterritoriality in respect of patents, intellectual property law, patents and defamation. The intention is to build on the principle of mutual recognition of judgments, although there are many technical legal problems to be overcome as well as political ones (Economist, 2001b). It remains to be seen whether this will sink in the way that the proposed Multilateral Agreement on Investment did (Calabrese, 1999).

By contrast with these hierarchical and multilateral approaches, what I have called regulation lending is currently being tried between the US and the EU in data protection, in the recent 'safe harbour' agreement. In other aspects of data protection and in many other fields, the destination principle is being affirmed more strongly, because of its (relative) ease of application, although there remain questions about its enforceability. The use of both hierarchical and horizontal systems of ordering regulation in order to encourage convergence in the content of regulation can have the effect, where these strategies are successful, of reducing the importance of the question of in which jurisdiction a litigant issues proceedings, or a complainant applies to a regulator, because collaboration is possible on the basis of roughly common standards or laws to ensure some action is taken.

Turning to sovereignty problems, it seems hard to argue that there is a *general* problem of declining efficacy, for the major states do seem to capable of creating and innovating regulatory institutions. If there is a problem here, it is, rather, the problem of *inequality* of sovereignty. When only the United States can even attempt to use public power to enforce competition law on Microsoft, and even then with limited effect, or when only the United States can effectively act to enforce intellectual property law on Napster, it should be clear that the key problem is not that no one is enforcing public power upon private power, but that even the states of the developed world are dependent on the hegemon state's ability and willingness to act on behalf of them all, in some of the really landmark cases. Poorer states and those most remote from the metropolitan centres of the world economy are indeed in the weakest position here.

Problems of free riding are indeed real ones, but again these are hardly special problems to digital governance: there have been tax havens as long as there have been taxes, and regulation havens as long as there has been a political culture of civil regulation. Moreover, the range of instruments presented in table 7.3 have, at least in some cases, been deployed imaginatively to try to overcome these problems. The European Union has long regarded the United States as a data haven in data protection law, because of the US's long-standing refusal to enact any general privacy legislation covering its commercial sector, and the American insistence (although increasingly inconsistently applied: 6, 1998) that to do so would violate the higher value of commercial freedom. However, the deal finally struck on regulation lending represented a reasonably satisfactory way forward, limiting the effect of what the EU saw as the US's free riding. The EU Directive provision that personal data on European citizens may not be exported to countries with inadequate protection may be, in a strict sense, unenforceable, but by setting a norm for other countries, and by enabling citizens to ask important questions of the organizations that handle their personal information, it represents a kind of public pedagogical strategy for responding to problems of free riding. The EU's aim here is perhaps best thought of as trying to get a 'race to the top' process moving by offering a standard of respectability, much like the one which produced the 'California effect' among US states in environmental standards in the 1980s as they followed California's example (Vogel, 1995). There are other ways to create clubs of goods between states in regulation and public policy from which free-riding states can be excluded, including a variety of mutual recognition systems. These have long been used in relation to tax havens; and in the context of intellectual property the United States's protracted blocking of China's full entry into the WTO until China took steps to control piracy of US-based companies' software and content products was an example of exactly this kind of strategy. In some part, of course, this reflects the near-hegemon economic status of the US: like Taiwan in previous decades, China allowed its enterprises to violate US intellectual property until the overriding national economic interest was to export to Western markets.

In some areas of regulation, relevance problems persist. It can be argued on sound economic grounds that in the context of global software and media industries, neither the European Union nor the United States, nor even any future and much developed North American free trade zone, represents the right geographical unit over which to measure monopoly and anti-competitive practices. However, resistance is widespread to proposals that the WTO should acquire a new and global competence directly over competition policy, and indeed, that resistance is not confined to the United States. In a sense, however, the fact of the United States acting as a near-hegemon in the international regulatory system is both part of the problem and part of a provisional solution here. To the extent that the United States's regulatory practice protects its own companies from challenge, it makes it very difficult for others to challenge mergers and acquisitions between them. Although the EU has occasionally flexed its muscles in this regard, and did threaten to examine the Time Warner–AOL merger, in practice it is very difficult for it to apply its competition laws on a destination principle basis. On the other hand, to the extent that the United States Justice Department is at least occasionally willing to attempt to discipline US-based monopolists such as Microsoft, albeit with mixed results, its hegemon regulator position provides some kind of substitute for a global regulator that might apply considerations of monopoly and anti-competitive practice on a more relevant global scale.

Those who argue that regulating global digital networks is bound to be ineffective need to make clear what yardstick or standard of comparison they are using. What, after all, are reasonable expectations for regulation of this kind? Surely, the relevant comparison is not the effectiveness with which a national utility regulator can regulate prices set by a single monopoly company per area. That regulation of that kind is generally effective is hardly surprising. After all, such a regulator needs only to research one company's behaviour, has the attention of a defined group of consumers, and has a single variable which it seeks to influence. Surely the more appropriate comparison and set of appropriate expectations are those of health and safety or environmental or data protection regulation within a country, where a regulator has multiple objectives, vaguely defined and qualitatively expressed principles on which to base regulation, a huge and indefinite number of organizations regulated, an indefinite number of consumers affected in many ways, and very limited information. In that situation, complete enforcement is not to be expected. Rather, such regulators aim to detect and deter the most egregious violations, respond as best they can to issues and events, and seek to influence the wider commercial culture towards more respect for health and safety, consideration for the environment, or privacy. Regulators of these kinds cannot expect to ensure that no one violates the principles. They can be expected to make best efforts to work with the media, with major companies and with consumer activist groups, to ensure that the problem of violation is maintained at a manageable level and to prevent outbursts of excessive enthusiasm leading to regulatory action that is self-defeating or that leads to rules becoming dead letters.

If it is accepted that these are roughly the right order of reasonable expectations that we might have for a transnational order of regulation, too, then it is possible to answer the critics. For what surely strikes any reasonably balanced observer of the state of our digital networks is how surprisingly orderly they are, at least in part due to the interests that many actors have in observing rules that coincide with many of those actually regulated. It is not otiose to point out, to change metaphor, that the regulatory glass is at least half full. E-commerce in the developed world is, by and large, not very much like an online equivalent of the 'wild east capitalism' observed in some parts of Russia or the Balkans or central Asia. Although predatory activity and some money laundering has indeed intruded from these regions into the digital networks from time to time (including a famous Moldovan web phone scam), its effects have been surprisingly contained. On the contrary, where e-commerce is wild, it is because commerce generally in those parts of the world is wild, rather than because of anything inherently wild about e-commerce.

Theoretical Frameworks

If the argument of this chapter so far is accepted, then none of the conventional theories of global governance on offer in the study of international relations is entirely adequate.

First, the well-known tale of the retreat of the state and of public power generally before the advance of private commercial power (Strange, 1996) does not really describe the range or the sophistication with which governance systems have in fact responded to the development of transnational digital networks. The model that posits global governance as being essentially based on private self-regulation, whatever its merits in explaining self-regulation in the pharmaceutical and chemical dyes industries or in marketing ethics (Ronit and Schneider, 1999), if applied to this field, would overstate both the extent and the autonomy from government of self-regulation.

Again, the simple story of unregulability, conflict of jurisdictions, constant attempts at blocking the extraterritorial application of laws, and general anarchy is clearly inadequate: there is both more collaboration, more effectiveness and more transnational order in regulation than the theory would predict.

Conventional neo-realism – the theory that nation-states are essentially autonomous and pursuing their own interests in regulation, making collaboration at best provisional and typically fragile, and convergence in regulatory regimes fortuitous and unstable – would also predict rather less institutionalization of collaboration between national regulatory systems than described in the previous sections of this chapter. Neither can these theories adequately account for the fact that the age of globalization has also been the great age of regulatory innovation by nation-states, both in range of topics regulated and in styles of transnational adjustment.

Hegemon theory (Ikenberry, 1999), in pointing to the pre-eminence of the United States, captures something of importance, but misses the limitations of the hegemon's regulatory capabilities, and the enormous range of transnational regulatory innovation – for example in data protection – that has developed and been institutionalized more in spite of than because of the hegemon state. It also tends to exaggerate the effect of the hegemon state in stabilizing the regulatory order into a regime.

On the other hand, pure neoliberalism – the theory that growing international trade and political interdependence are creating the conditions for ever more pooling of sovereignty – would not predict the central role for the hegemon regulator state, acting with greater autonomy than neoliberal models of interdependence would suggest likely, that has been detected in several key areas. Of the qualified forms of neoliberalism, intergovernmentalism does not adequately account for the range of relatively autonomous activity by regulatory agencies in developing horizontal collaboration in regulatory strategies and institutions, or the degree to which their discipline has been accepted and their rule-making authority has become institution-alized. Regime theory, in both neo-realist and neoliberal variants, posits a stabler and more institutionalized structure. This makes it difficult to account for the rapid evolu-tion of the international regulatory system, for this change exhibits such deep con-tinuities with the inherited legal order that it cannot be considered a regime change. The neoliberal version of 'neomedievalism' (Kobrin, 1999: the original neomedievalist theory was, of course, Bull's 1977 neo-realist version) faces a very similar problem: although it may be able to account for the role of the hegemon regulatory state in the system, the legal continuities with the inherited order are too great for its positing of a new era to appreciate. The currently fashionable 'social constructivist' theories of evolutionary institutional change (Haas, 1999) depend on mechanisms of variation and the independence of ideas that do not seem to explain either the deep institutional continuities or to be able to cope with the way in which ideas have followed rather than led organization in the transnational regulatory process in respect of digital networks.

At first sight, a promising account with which to explain what we observe in this field may seem to be the liberal institutionalist theory – the view that states can and will cooperate when they have, or at least when their elites come to believe that they have, interests in doing so; that in those circumstances where distributional conflicts are not too severe, the absolute gains from cooperation will weigh more heavily than will relative gains; that, provided the transaction costs are not too great, institutions can assist in providing information about defectors as well as deterring defection, providing salience for possible future agreements; and that institutions will have effects independently of the favourable background conditions (Keohane, 1988; Keohane and Martin, 1995; Snidal, 1991; Martin, 1999). At first sight, this approach might appear to help explain the importance of horizontal mechanisms, because of their lower trans-action costs, and the fact that the multilateral hierarchical mechanisms proposed at the G8, the Council of Europe and The Hague not only involve investment of both resources and effort, but also great difficulties in achieving agreement there. To the extent that sovereignty is itself seen as an institution (Keohane, 1988, p. 385), this approach might also help explain those difficulties as themselves an institutional effect. The problem is that, depending on how one operationalizes such terms as the transaction costs being 'too' high, together with such issues as what cognitive forces shape elites' beliefs about their own interests, the amount of information yielded by institutions and so on, the theory might easily predict either less or more cooperation than we in fact observe. This vagueness may be no worse than that found in, say, realist theories, but it remains a problem. Most crucially, unless the theory is made more specific on these issues, it is hard to know whether it accounts for the ambiguities in global regulatory processes of the not-quite-hegemon state, the USA, at once trying to secure international acceptance for some principles and willing to submit to those rules, for example in intellectual property, while unilaterally evading others, notably in data protection, and effectively seizing control over further regulatory mechanisms that might otherwise have become globally accountable – as in the case of the creation of ICANN (Mueller, 1999). Some neoliberal institutionalist accounts suggest that there is some automatic connection between the development of international flows and the emergence of transnational institutions of governance (Sandholtz, 1999), but these accounts do not give enough weight to the contingency with which the regulatory process reflects regulators feeling their way in many of the areas discussed in this article (Raab, 1993).

Theories of the rising power of international non-governmental organizations to shape the nature of global governance and to disrupt the club model of multilateralism (Keohane and Nye, 2000) do not, at least as yet, have a huge grip in this field. Privacy, intellectual property, obscenity, freedom of expression, anti-monopoly concerns do indeed all attract the passions of many pressure groups, including some international ones. They have not been entirely absent from the debates about regulation, and indeed some protest actions – such as that by users of Lotus Notes against the software company's intention to sell its global database of users – have had some impact on policy-makers' sense of urgency. Indeed, such protest groups increasingly use the net to organize (Browning, 1996; Locke, 1999). However, the impact of such groups and such spontaneous protests on the development of transnational regulation in these fields has been modest indeed, and certainly none of these bodies has achieved anything like the mobilization or profile of the environmental and general anti-capitalist groups that have filled the streets in Seattle, Prague and Davos in recent years. The high point of protest mobilization was over mandatory key escrow, yet even here the really important motive for retreat by law enforcement authorities was not popular resistance but the importance of strategic commercial interests. However, it is quite possible that the significance and power of protest movements to influence regulation may increase if present trends in mobilization around anti-capitalism and anti-globalization causes continue.

Most of these theories are essentially 'one club' approaches: they point to a single process when what is needed is something that recognizes that there are several processes going on, and that they need not all point in the same direction. The development of transnational digital networks is something to which governments – and most especially the US government, with its crucial role in the early stages of the development of the internet – have acted as midwives, as they have for most of the major processes of internationalization (Weiss, 1998). Nevertheless, by overseeing the birth of transnationalization, states have created a series of institutional dynamics that place some disciplines on them (Martin, 1999). There is not only multilayered governance (Held et al., 1999, pp. 62–77), but multiple strands within layers.

However, amid this complexity, there are ways to simplify without doing too much violence to the phenomena. The disciplines affect states in different zones of the world differently, as Cooper (1996) has argued. In the zone of the developed world where sovereignty pooling has become most deeply institutionalized, and which a qualified neoliberalism can understand to some degree, inevitably the hegemon state occupies an ambivalent position, at once centrally enmeshed in that system of transnational governance, and needing constantly to assert its hegemonic relationship to it. Conversely, the other states in that region both depend on it and feel threatened by its tendency, on occasion, to free ride. In the zone that neorealism describes best, that of conventional autonomous nation-states such as Iran, Iraq or much of Latin America until the second half of the 1990s, the processes of transnational governance of digital networks have their weakest grip. In the zone where nation-states have either failed and collapsed or never successfully been built, such as Haiti, Somalia or Kosovo, to the extent that the digital networks are important (just as social networks are), their use (like that of most social networks) may indeed be for essentially anarchic and criminal purposes, either in rebellion (consider the web and e-mail strategy used, mainly for securing publicity in the developed world, by Subcomandante Marcos and his Zapatista rebels in Chiapas, which has at times looked not altogether unlike a collapsed province, even though Mexico has never been a failed state) or in organized crime (as in the use of the encryption by Mafias in some parts of the Balkans and in Colombia).

Prospects, Scope and Limits of Global Digital Governance

For the future prospects for the transnational governance of global digital networks, just as for the transnational governance of anything else discussed in other chapters of this volume, it is possible to paint a pessimistic or an optimistic scenario, based on exactly the same evidence about recent trends. A key recent trend stressed here has been the importance of more horizontal systems of emerging institutional development in transnational regulatory order. Basically, those commentators who distrust horizontal and less formal forms of ordering regulation, and who see in the strength, transparency and availability of redress that hierarchical systems afford the only possibility for effective and fair regulation, tend to be more alarmed about the 'regulatory deficit' and the prospect of covert nationalism and mercantilism lurking in the horizontal systems (for instance, Cable, 1999). By contrast, those who have more faith that less formal systems of mutual adjustment can in practice lead to reasonably tolerable and reasonably liberal systems, and who doubt the political feasibility of achieving formal, hierarchical multilateral treaties on all the important issues, (for instance, Reinicke, 1998) tend to be slightly more optimistic about the efficacy and acceptability of regulation.

Considering efficacy first, it is worth reflecting on the history of previous zones of anarchy, and why those histories are comparatively brief. The American 'wild west' did not remain lawless for very long. The commercial interests of those who lived there in creating and extending zones of regulation, and the imposition of private hegemonic power by the railway barons and public hegemonic power by the police and army, combined to introduce effective regulation in a relatively short period of time.

The period of internet history which resembled the lawless nineteenth-century west is probably already coming to an end, and for many of the same reasons. Consider the technologically most sophisticated, most innovative, best capitalized and most profitable industry on the internet, which is also the one that is still suspected by many of being the enemy of regulation: I mean, of course, the sex industry. It is worth noting the speed with which the industry has accepted many forms of self-regulation, including those imposed by hegemonic power, due to its own commercial interest. Age certification, site rating by standard filter software systems, separate zoning, intellectual property rights in products have all been adopted with great speed by the online sex industry, not only in the hope of avoiding statutory regulation, but precisely in order to stabilize its own commercial position. Conversely, although there are certainly data equivalents of tax havens, most portal and internet service providing companies have not relocated to them, because their commercial interests keep them operating within the main metropolitan centres, not despite regulation but precisely because acceptance of at least some regulation has a positive effect on reputation and on attractiveness to investors (Vogel, 1995).

Again, the key issue about the effectiveness of transnational regulation is to consider what would be reasonable expectations. Not everything can or will be heavily regulated, nor can or will all rules be enforced absolutely. Complete regulatory coverage of all risks is impossible – there will always be some free riding. Nor does practical politics generally permit complete logical consistency of regulation between the conflicting goals. Likewise, complete harmonization between countries is not likely. However, the scale of commitment to regulatory effort and the innovations made in new techniques of regulation, such as those identified in table 7.3, suggests that we need not expect in future to rely entirely on hierarchical tools, and at least a reasonable amount of regulated global order should be possible. The question is whether it will be an order worth celebrating.

Finally, therefore, we must ask whether, on normative grounds, we can expect to want to welcome the range both of horizontal and hierarchical processes of securing transnational order, and whether the contents of the regulations agreed through these processes are likely to be reasonable. This is too large a question to address in any detail here. However, the general argument against the regulation of digital networks ought to be rejected: that any power is illegitimate if it might be abused by an illiberal government or regulator (as argued, for example, by *The Economist* in a special report, Economist, 2001a). There are many powers that are required – even to police the kinds of conditions that liberals value as necessary for orderly operations of the market – including intellectual property rights, technical standards and anti-fraud and money laundering controls – that could be abused in the hands of malign authorities. The key issue, both for the prospects for acceptability of the processes and for their contents, is their accountability. At present, it is surely a reasonable criticism of the ways in which at least the horizontal, and perhaps also the hierarchical system of ordering transnational collaboration in regulation actually work that they exhibit inadequate transparency and inadequate accountability to consumers and wider publics, and in some cases even to special interests. If transnational regulatory capture is to be avoided, and if nested or syndicated regulatory processes, whether of a race to the top or to the bottom, are not to become a system of protection for incumbents (Sun and Pelkman, 1998, pp. 460–1), then the regulatory systems need to be open to public deliberation before rules are institutionalized, and open to public accountability after enforcement. Of course, those liberals who are most suspicious that democracy and accountability will empower special interests inimical to good liberal governance, and who prefer some guidance of democratically accountable governance by liberal elites, will disagree (Brittan, 1988; Hayek, 1973–82; Olson, 1982). However, the evidence of the recrudescence of liberal programmes of both de- and reregulation with popular support in the 1980s and 1990s suggests that their fears may be premature. No doubt, there will always be both over- and underregulation, transnationally as there is within nations. But in global as in local politics, in general, it is better to design decision-making institutions that get things very roughly right over the long run than those that will get them either very precisely right or else catastrophically wrong. And it is those institutions that lack wider accountability which typically fall in the latter category. It remains to be seen just how effective nation-states will continue to be in supplying the institutional basis of that accountability for the very transnational processes of ordering regulation that they have embarked on, especially given the difficulties of imposing wider transnational accountability on the hegemon regulatory state.

Liberal institutionalist theories do not imply that cooperation between states is necessarily benign (Keohane, 1988, p. 380): there are, after all, quite explicable but malign conspiracies. This is as true of horizontal as it is of hierarchical mechanisms of policy coordination. Even if the absolute gains from cooperation are sufficiently great to motivate agreement between states, and compliance, there is no guarantee that what is agreed between elites will not represent a game for relative gains domestically with those states' own citizens. That would be a rather vicious form of the two-level game (Evans, Jacobson and Putnam, 1993). Such vicious two-level games are not particularly stable, because the growth of media and access to information systems has reduced the transaction costs to citizens of making efforts to hold to account the horizontal international institutions that are emerging in this field. What is now required is an institutional framework for an open transnational debate about the accountability to citizens of the new clubs through which the regulation of information systems is now conducted.

Notes

I am grateful to the following people for comments on an earlier draft of this chapter: Colin Blackman, Caspar Bowden, David Held, Tony McGrew, Charles Raab, Shaun Riordan and Paula Tiihonen. None of these people should be accused of agreeing with me, still less of bearing any responsibility for my errors.

1   In very simple terms, the internet is that system of linking other networks for which the basic protocol is TCP/IP (and its successors approved by the Internet Engineering Task Force, or IETF), which provides routing – i.e. sends messages by several circuitous routes and reassembles the pieces at the other end – rather than switching – the system of sending a single version of a message over a defined route, as traditional telephony exchange systems do. The internet, understood in this sense, currently supports several different types of application, including e-mail, the UseNet system of newsgroups, a plethora of multi-user environments, and the World Wide Web; loosely but incorrectly, many people use the word 'internet' when they mean little more than the web and e-mail. Clearly, there are many digital networks that do not use TCP/IP, and now there are many more that integrate seamlessly between broadcast transmission and internet-based information and traditional telephony. In this chapter, I am concerned with the regulatory issues raised by the internet and other international publicly accessible digital networks, but for readability I shall often speak loosely but incorrectly of regulatory issues arising in connection with 'the internet'; readers should bear in mind that the application of the argument is broader than just the systems supported by TCP/IP.

2   Mandatory key escrow is a system for the governance of the use of encryption (that is, software that encodes a message so that unauthorized persons cannot decipher it), in which anyone using cryptographic software is required to provide a copy of their private key for decryption either to law enforcement authorities or else to a trusted third party, who will not disclose it to anyone else but who would make it available to law enforcement authorities in the event that those authorities could show that they needed access to that key for the purposes of conducting an investigation. An early proposal of this kind was made by the Clinton administration which would have required all US computers to use the 'Clipper chip', a hardware implementation of cryptographic capability which effectively provided the

US law enforcement agencies with a copy of the key automatically. Eventually, the proposal was defeated. There were proposals for mandatory key escrow in the UK. The highly controversial Regulation of Investigatory Powers Act 2000 now governs the codes under which British law enforcement agencies can require individuals to divulge their keys for decryption. For an accessible review of the key escrow debate, see Singh, 1999; for a slightly more technical discussion, see Phillips, 1997; for a discussion of policy principles, see 6, 1998, pp. 116ff. and 300ff.; for a review of the international controversy and major documents from the conflicts over key escrow, see www.fipr.org, which hosts a comprehensive databank of materials from the perspective of a civil liberties organization; for an academic perspective in support of the law enforcement agencies' case for mandatory key escrow, see Denning, 1997.

3   The British government has now announced that there will be a merged regulator for all electronic media, to be called OfCom, combining the regulatory bodies for telephony, television and radio: see Secretaries of State for Trade and Industry and for Culture, Media and Sport, 2001.

4   It is sometimes said that even if there is no distinctive subject of regulation raised by the internet, what is distinctive is the speed at which technological developments happen in this field, which allegedly raises unique challenges for regulators. I know of no metric for measuring speed of technological change between industries or periods. However, it seems difficult to make out the claim that innovation in this field is faster than in, say, contemporary materials science or biotechnology, or indeed than in internal combustion engine technology a century ago, or in antibiotics in the 1950s, in military technologies between 1905 and 1955, or indeed in a wide range of industrial technologies in the 1840s. For some historical evidence on this point, see e.g. Pool, 1997 and Buchanan 1992. At the very least, regulators in this field, it can surely be argued, have responded with no worse a lag behind the technological innovations than other regulators have in other industries.

5   For the present purpose, I understand regulation widely to mean the use of authorized but coercive public power under the definition of law in order to discipline private behaviour. That is, I do not observe Clarke's distinction between regulation and the criminal law (2000, pp. 1–5).

References

Aggarwal, V. K. (ed.) (1998) *Institutional Designs for a Complex World: Bargaining, Linkages and Nesting*, Ithaca: Cornell University Press.

Barlow, J. P. (1996a) 'Declaration of the independence of cyberspace', *Cyber Rights Electronic List*, 8 Feb.

Barlow, J. P. (1996b) 'Declaring independence', *Wired*, June, www.wired.com/wired/archive/4.06/independence.html.

Barnett, S., Bottomley, V., Cave, M., Graham, A., Hughes, J., Inglewood, R., Leadbeater, C., Mather, G., McNally, T., Oliver, M., Seaton, J., Shooshan, H. M. and Stevenson, W. (2000) *E-Britannia: The Communications Revolution*, Luton: University of Luton Press.

BBC News Online (2001a) 'Treaty "could stifle online privacy"', 11 June, at http://news.bbc.co.uk/hi/english/sci/tech/newsid_1378000/1378482.stm.

BBC News Online (2001b) 'Novel net domains court controversy', 19 June, at http://news.bbc.co.uk/hi/English/sci/tech/newsid_1396000/1396456.stm.

BBC News Online (2001c) 'More legal trouble for MP3.com', 23 Aug., at http://news.bbc.co.uk/hi/english/entertainment/new_media/newsid_1505000/1505572.stm.

Brittan, S. (1988) 'The politics of excessive expectations' (1974), in S. Brittan, *Economic Consequences of Democracy*, 2nd edn, Aldershot: Wildwood.

Brown, D. (1997) *Cybertrends: Chaos, Power and Accountability in the Information Age*, Harmondsworth: Penguin.

Browning, G. (1996) *Electronic Democracy: Using the Internet to Influence American Politics*, Wilton, Conn.: Pemberton Press.

Buchanan, R. A. (1992) *The Power of the Machine: The Impact of Technology from 1700 to the Present*, Harmondsworth: Penguin.

Bull, H. (1977) *The Anarchical Society: A Study of Order in World Politics*, New York: Columbia University Press.

Cable, V. (1999) *Globalisation and Global Governance*, London: Pinter with Royal Institute for International Affairs, London.

Calabrese, A. (1999) 'Communication and the end of sovereignty?', *Info: The Journal of Policy, Regulation and Strategy for Telecommunications, Information and Media*, 1, no. 4, pp. 313–26.

Carr, J. (1999) 'Anarchy.com: can we tame the net?', *Prospect*, June.

Carr, J. (2001) 'Microsoft's money: we can't leave the debate about the internet to business and the techies', *Prospect*, Jan.

Clarke, M. (2000) *Regulation: The Social Control of Business between Law and Politics*, Basingstoke: Macmillan.

Cooper, R. (1996) *The Post-modern State and the World Order*, London: Demos.

Denning, D. (1997) 'The future of cryptography', in B. D. Loader (ed.), *The Governance of Cyberspace: Politics, Technology and Global Restructuring*, London: Routledge.

Dyson, E. (1997) *Release 2.0: A Design for Living in the Digital Age*, London: Viking.

Economist (2000a) 'The files swarm in: wired China', *The Economist*, 22 July, special report, pp. 23–5.

Economist (2000b) 'If you can't beat 'em . . .', *The Economist*, 4 Nov., leader article, p. 22.

Economist (2001a) 'Stop signs on the web: the Internet and the law', *The Economist*, 13 Jan., special report, pp. 25–7.

Economist (2001b) 'Tied up in knots', *The Economist*, 9 June, p. 97.

Economist (2001c) 'Big music fights back', *The Economist*, 16 June, pp. 75–6.

Economist (2001d) 'Putting it in its place: geography and the net', *The Economist*, 11 Aug., special report, pp. 18–20.

Edwards, L. and Waelde, C. (eds) (2000) *Law and the Internet: A Framework for Electronic Commerce* (1997), 2nd edn, Oxford: Hart.

Evans, P., Jacobson, H. K. and Putnam, R. D. (eds) (1993) *Doubled-Edged Diplomacy: International Bargaining and Domestic Politics*, Berkeley: University of California Press.

Golub, J. (2000) 'Globalisation, sovereignty and policy-making: insights from European integration', in Holden, B. (ed.), *Global Democracy: Key Debates*, London: Routledge.

Haas, P. M. (1999) 'Social constructivism and the evolution of multilateral environmental governance', in A. Prakash and J. A. Hart (eds), *Globalisation and Governance*, London: Routledge.

Hayek, F. A. von (1973–82) *Law, Legislation and Liberty: A New Statement of the Liberal Principles of Justice and Political Economy*, 3 vols, London: Routledge and Kegan Paul.

Held, D., McGrew, A., Goldblatt, D. and Perraton, J. (1999) *Global Transformations: Politics, Eonomics and Culture*, Cambridge: Polity.

Ikenberry, G. J. (1999) 'Liberal hegemony and the future of the American postwar order', in T. V. Paul and J. A. Hall (eds), *International Order and the Future of World Politics*, Cambridge: Cambridge University Press.

Industry Canada (1994) *The Canadian Information Highway*, Ottawa: Ministry of Supply and Services, Canada.

Information and Privacy Commissioner and Registratiekamer (1995) *Privacy Enhancing Technologies: The Path to Anonymity*, vols 1 and 2, Toronto and Rijswijk: Information and Privacy Commissioner, Ontario, Canada and Registratiekamer, The Netherlands.

Johnson, D. R. and Post, D. G. (1997) 'The rise of law on the global network', in B. Kahin and C. Nesson (eds), *Borders in Cyberspace: Information Policy and the Global Information Infrastructure*, Cambridge, Mass.: MIT Press.

Kahin, B. and Nesson, C. (eds) (1997) *Borders in Cyberspace: Information Policy and the Global Information Infrastructure*, Cambridge, Mass.: MIT Press.

Keohane, R. O. (1988) 'International institutions: two approaches', *International Studies Quarterly*, 32, no. 4, pp. 379–96.

Keohane, R. O. and Martin, L. M. (1995) 'The promise of institutionalist theory', *International Security*, 20, no. 1, pp. 39–51.

Keohane, R. O. and Nye, J. S. Jr (2000) 'Introduction', in J. S. Nye Jr and J. D. Donahue (eds), *Governance in a Globalizing World*, Washington DC: Brookings Institution Press.

Kobrin, S. J. (1999) 'Back to the future: neomediaevalism and the postmodern digital world economy', in A. Prakash and J. A. Hart (eds), *Globalisation and Governance*, London: Routledge.

le Goueff, S. (2000) 'The draft cyber crime convention: creating an international law enforcement standard', *Info: The Journal of Policy, Regulation and Strategy for Telecommunications, Information and Media*, 2, no. 6, pp. 605–6.

Lees, T., Ralph, S. and Langham Brown, J. (eds) (2000) *Is Regulation Still an Option in a Digital Universe? Papers from the 30th University of Manchester International Broadcasting Symposium*, Luton: University of Luton Press.

Lessig, L. (1999) *Code and Other Laws of Cyberspace*, New York: Basic Books.

Locke, T. (1999) 'Participation, inclusion, exclusion and netactivism: how the internet invents new forms of democratic activity', in B. N. Hague and B. D. Loader (eds), *Digital Democracy: Discourse and Decision Making in the Information Age*, London: Routledge.

Majone, G. (1996) 'Regulation and its modes', in G. Majone (ed.), *Regulating Europe*, London: Routledge.

Martin, L. (1999) 'An institutionalist view: international institutions and state strategies', in T. V. Paul and J. A. Hall (eds), *International Order and the Future of World Politics*, Cambridge: Cambridge University Press.

Mayer, C. (1995) 'The regulation of financial services: lessons from the UK for 1992', in M. Bishop, J. Kay and C. Mayer (eds), *The Regulatory Challenge*, Oxford: Oxford University Press.

Mueller, M. (1999) 'ICANN and internet governance: sorting through the debris of "self-regulation"', *Info: The Journal of Policy, Regulation and Strategy for Telecommunications, Information and Media*, 1, no. 6, pp. 497–520.

Mueller, M. (2001) 'Domains without frontiers', *Info: The Journal of Policy, Regulation and Strategy for Telecommunications, Information and Media*, 3, no. 2, pp. 97–9.

Olson, M. (1982) *The Rise and Decline of Nations*, New Haven: Yale University Press.

Perritt, H. H. Jr (1997) 'Jurisdiction in cyberspace: the role of intermediaries', in B. Kahin and C. Nesson (eds), *Borders in Cyberspace: Information Policy and the Global Information Infrastructure*, Cambridge, Mass.: MIT Press.

Phillips, D. J. (1997) 'Cryptography, secrets and the structuring of trust', in P. E. Agre and M. Rotenberg (eds), *Technology and Privacy: The New Landscape*, Cambridge, Mass.: MIT Press.

Pool, R. (1997) *Beyond Engineering: How Society Shapes Technology*, New York: Oxford University Press.

Raab, C. D. (1993) 'The governance of data protection', in J. Kooiman (ed.), *Modern Governance: New Government–Society Interactions*, London: Sage.

Raab, C. D. (1997) 'Co-producing data protection', *International Review of Law, Computers and Technology*, 11, no. 1, pp. 11–24.

Raab, C. D. (1999) 'Governing privacy: systems, participants and policy instruments', paper presented at the Ethicomp fifth international conference, Rome.

Raab, C. D. (2000) 'ICT and governance, and the governance of ICT', paper given at the conference, Public Management and Governance in the New Millennium: Lessons from the Past and Challenges for the Future, City University of Hong Kong, 10–11 Jan.

Raab, C. D. and Bennett, C. (forthcoming) *Private Information and Public Policy* (working title), Aldershot: Ashgate.

Rapp, L. (2000) 'The "Napsterisation" of the European content industry', *Info: The Journal of Policy, Regulation and Strategy for Telecommunications, Information and Media*, 2, no. 6, pp. 551–72.

Reinicke, W. H. (1998) *Global Public Policy: Governing without Government?* Washington DC: Brookings Institution.

Ronit, K. and Schneider, V. (1999) 'Global governance through private organisations', *Governance*, 12, no. 3, pp. 243–66.

6, P. (1998) *The Future of Privacy*, vol. 1: *Private Life and Public Policy*, London: Demos.

6, P. (2001) 'Governing by technique: judgment and the prospects for governance of and with technology', in OECD, *Governance in the Twenty-First century*, Paris: Organization for Economic Cooperation and Development.

Sandholtz, W. (1999) 'Globalisation and the evolution of rules', in A. Prakash and J. A. Hart (eds), *Globalisation and Governance*, London: Routledge.

Scherer, F. M. (1994) *Competition Policies for an Integrating World Economy*, Washington DC: Brookings Institution.

Singh, S. (1999) *The Code Book: The Science of Secrecy from Ancient Egypt to Quantum Cryptography*, London: Fourth Estate.

Snidal, D. (1991) 'Relative gains and the pattern of international cooperation', *American Political Science Review*, 85, no. 3, pp. 701–26.

Standage, T. (2000) 'Why Napster matters: special report', *Prospect*, Oct., pp. 50–3.

Standage, T. (2001) 'Understanding Microsoft: special report', *Prospect*, Mar., pp. 50–4.

Strange, S. (1996) *The Retreat of the State*, Cambridge: Cambridge University Press.

Sun, J.-M. and Pelkman, J. (1998) 'Regulatory competition in the single Market', in R. Baldwin, C. Scott and C. Hood (eds), *A Reader on Regulation*, Oxford: Oxford University Press, repr. in slightly abridged form from *Journal of Common Market Studies*, 33 (1995), pp. 67–89.

Vogel, D. (1995) *Trading Up: Consumer and Environmental Regulation in a Global Economy*, Cambridge, Mass.: Harvard University Press.

Vogel, D. (1998) 'The globalisation of pharmaceutical regulation', *Governance*, 11, no. 1, pp. 1–22.

Weiss, L. (1998) *The Myth of the Powerless State: Governing the Economy in a Global Era*, Cambridge: Polity.

Secretaries of State for Trade and Industry and for Culture, Media and Sport (2001) *A New Future for Communications*, London: Stationery Office, available at www.communicationswhitepaper.gov.uk.

Wiener, J. (1999) *Globalisation and the Harmonisation of Law*, London: Pinter.

Ypsilanti, D. (1999) 'A borderless world: the OECD Ottawa Ministerial Conference and initiatives in electronic commerce', *Info: The Journal of Policy, Regulation and Strategy for Telecommunications, Information and Media*, 1, no. 1, pp. 23–33.

8

Intellectual Property Rights
Susan K. Sell

The last two decades have ushered in a dramatic change in the global environment for the protection of intellectual property (patents, copyrights, trade marks, trade secrets) rights. Up until recently, nations enjoyed extensive discretion in the adoption and implementation of domestic intellectual property regulation that suited their comparative advantages in either imitation or innovation. Previous multilateral conventions governing intellectual property protection, the Paris Convention for the Protection of Industrial Property, and the Berne Convention for copyrights, only set minimum standards that signatories had to uphold. By contrast, the 1994 Agreement on Trade-Related Aspects of Intellectual Property Rights (TRIPS hereafter) introduced a brand new era that extends the global reach of intellectual property regulation based on the concepts of protection and exclusion rather than dissemination and competition. Unlike the earlier conventions, TRIPS does not merely circumscribe the range of acceptable policies governments may practise, but requires states to take positive steps to protect these property rights. I argue that TRIPS is a significant instance of global rule-making by a small handful of well-connected corporate players and their governments. However, it is important to note that TRIPS represented the high water mark of 'hard law' for the commercial intellectual property agenda in a multilateral context and that the momentum of the TRIPS protests, particularly with regard to patents, has created a much more difficult political environment for industry.

In the process that led to TRIPS, private sector advocates of high protectionist norms based in the United States mobilized to lobby their government to take action to stop the widespread appropriation of their intellectual property abroad. The American government was responsive and supportive, in part due to institutional changes. The state adopted policies to increase its and its firms' abilities to compete in the global economy. The changing structure of global capitalism helped to constitute new agents of particular importance, delivering high technology corporate actors to the forefront of global business regulation. The American TRIPS story reveals a process in which the changing structure of global capitalism constituted newly powerful agents and altered institutions in ways that compounded the agents' power, American power, and structural power to alter outcomes for others. Institutional change empowered intellectual property owners, and these agents drove institutional change. But that is not the end of the story. The very fact of TRIPS has spawned new actors who are mobilizing to contest the high protectionist agenda that won so handily in the TRIPS negotiations. If at time 1, private sector agents constructed the problem as one of weak and poorly enforced property rights, at time 2 (post-TRIPS) they continue to see enforcement problems as central. However, at time 2 opposition also has emerged to define the problem as one of overly broad property rights at the expense of other more crucial values such as public health. This contestation is as much a part of the new global intellectual property regime as the negotiated rules administered by the World Trade Organization.[1] TRIPS is not merely an incremental change in international regulation, but rather the embodiment of a new 'constitutive principle' in so far as it creates new property rights that create or define new forms of behaviour and generate structures (Dessler, 1989, p. 455; Burch, 1994). In short, it reconstitutes both agents and structures, reproducing and transforming them, and thereby redefines winners and losers. In this sense it is not an end-point, but rather another beginning.

Indeed, we are already seeing the consequences of the increasingly effective protests against overly broad intellectual property rights in pharmaceutical and agricultural products. For instance, the HIV/AIDS crisis in Thailand and sub-Saharan Africa has provided an opportunity for an alternative framing of patent 'rights' as a public health issue rather than a trade issue. While public resistance is on the rise, and has achieved some impressive victories, one must be careful not to overstate its significance. The ink is dry; TRIPS is here to stay. Interested parties will do battle over implementation and interpretation, and opponents will fight hard to prevent any further attempts to ratchet up levels of protection within WTO. In order to understand global governance in intellectual property it is necessary to focus on the relationships between those private sector activists favouring high protectionist norms, states, international organizations, and in the aftermath of TRIPS, the citizen groups that are mobilizing to challenge the high protectionist norms.

The first section below provides a brief overview of TRIPS, highlighting the fact that a handful of American-based corporations constructed the problem as a trade issue. The second section discusses the emergence of intellectual property governance, focusing on institutional structures and dynamics leading to the adoption of TRIPS. The third section discusses the effectiveness of global regulation, and in particular, post-TRIPS efforts to compel compliance. The fourth section places the case in broader analytic perspective and suggests that the notion of structured agency[2] is well suited for apprehending the contours and possibilities of governance in intellectual property. The final section speculates on the future of intellectual property governance by examining two broad citizen campaigns protesting TRIPS and championing people's rights in agriculture and medicine.

TRIPS

TRIPS was a stunning triumph for commercial interests and industry lobbyists who had worked so tirelessly to achieve the global agreement. TRIPS institutionalized a conception of intellectual property based on protection and exclusion rather than competition and diffusion. By extending property rights and requiring high substantive levels of protection, TRIPS represented a significant victory for US private sector activists from knowledge-based industries. TRIPS is part of the multilateral trade agreements that were made binding on members in the Final Act of the Uruguay Round. Adhering to the TRIPS Agreement is obligatory for all states that wish to join the WTO, and is part of the WTO's common institutional framework. The Agreement covers all intellectual property rights, patents, trademarks, copyrights and trade secrets, including relatively new ones such as semiconductor chip rights. It incorporates the Berne Convention for copyright norms, and adds additional copyright protection for computer software, databases and sound recordings. TRIPS adopts a patent law minimum well above the previous standards of the 1883 Paris Convention, extending both subject-matter covered and term of protection. Patent rights are extended to virtually all subject-matter (with the exception of plants and animals other than micro-organisms), including pharmaceutical products, chemicals, pesticides and plant varieties, and are to be granted for twenty years. Semiconductor chips and the layout designs of integrated circuits are protected under a *sui generis* (special or more specific) system. States are required to provide adequate and effective enforcement mechanisms both internally and at the border. States must also provide for both civil and criminal penalties for infractions. The Agreement makes the WTO's dispute settlement mechanism available to address conflicts arising under TRIPS, and significantly provides for the possibility of cross-sectoral retaliation for states that fail to abide by WTO's Dispute Settlement Body's rulings. Proponents of TRIPS helped to devise an enforcement mechanism linking intellectual property protection to trade leverage in order to compel developing countries to respond. Now infractions in intellectual property can lead to sanctions on goods. The WTO is empowered to monitor compliance to ensure that defendants carry out their obligations within a reasonable time period. If the defendants fail to comply, the WTO will authorize the complainant to impose retaliatory trade sanctions if requested to do so. This gives the WTO power to enforce the TRIPS Agreement.[3]

This far-reaching agreement has important implications for innovation, economic development, the future location of industry and the global division of labour. Indeed, the dramatic expansion of the scope of intellectual property rights embodied in the TRIPS Agreement reduces the options available to future industrializers by effectively blocking the route that earlier industrializers followed. It raises the price of information and technology by extending the monopoly privileges of rights-holders, and requires states to play a much greater role in defending them. The industrialized countries built much of their economic prowess by appropriating others' intellectual property; with the TRIPS Agreement, this option is foreclosed for later industrializers.

The agreement codifies the increasing commodification of what was once the public domain, 'making it unavailable to future creators' (Aoki, 1996, p. 1336). States and firms whose comparative advantage lies in imitation stand to lose under the new regime. In all, the long-term redistributive implications of TRIPS are not yet fully understood. The short-term impact of stronger intellectual property protection will undoubtedly be a significant transfer of resources from developing country consumers and firms to industrialized country firms (Rodrik, 1994, p. 449). TRIPS increases the range of regulatory standards that states are obliged to implement; specifies in greater detail what those standards must be; requires states to implement those standards; mandates and institutionalizes greater substantive convergence of national intellectual property systems; and ties the principle of national treatment to a higher set of standards for intellectual property (Drahos, 1997, pp. 202–3). Overall, TRIPS has 'added solidly to the property power around the world of corporations with high technology resources' (Arup, 1998, p. 376).

How Governance Came About

Without private sector activism there would be no TRIPS today. However, it is important to place this activism into a broader economic, historical and political context. In this section I will focus on the United States, where the quest for TRIPS began. Several trends, emerging in the 1970s and accelerating in the early 1980s, began to weigh heavily on US policy-makers' minds. First of all, policy-makers were preoccupied by perceived American 'decline', as reflected in twin budget and trade deficits. Worries over trade deficits elevated the importance of trade in American policy-making. Competitiveness concerns dominated policy debates as Japan and East Asia appeared to be overtaking the United States in trade competition. Second, the increasing importance of high technology sectors in the global economy heightened US policy-makers' interest in intellectual property as an important component of competitive advantage. Traditional industries in decline as a result of aggressive import competition from low-wage labour sites enjoyed reduced political power. High technology, intellectual property-based industries began to eclipse formerly powerful sectors such as steel and textiles. The high technology intellectual property-based sectors, such as the pharmaceutical, entertainment and software industries, could claim trade surpluses in their products and services, in sharp contrast to the overall US trade deficit. Third, in response to emerging trade pressures, US support for 'free trade' was weakening. Successful proponents of a new conception – 'free-but-fair-trade' – endorsed a strategy of easing competitive pressures on US exporters 'by asking for, not higher import barriers against others, but lower import barriers by others' (Bhagwati, 1989, p. 452).

Institutional changes in American trade policy-making expanded private sector access throughout the 1970s and 1980s. Amendments to Section 301 of the US Trade Act provided important opportunities for proponents of high protectionist norms for intellectual property protection. Section 301 allows the President to deny benefits or impose duties on products or services of countries unjustifiably restricting US commerce. The amendments fortified a cooperative relationship between the private sector and government by institutionalizing consultations between the private sector and the United States Trade Representative (USTR) throughout the process of a 301 investigation. With 301 the US began to employ market access as a bargaining chip in exchange for investment liberalization and increased intellectual property protection abroad.

In the late 1970s private sector activists initially sought government help in pressuring foreign governments to adopt and enforce more stringent intellectual property protection. They sought, and won, changes in US domestic laws and urged the government to get tough on violators of US-held intellectual property rights. They were encouraged by the elevated role of the USTR and its sympathetic stance towards industry concerns. The government's new focus on market access and the trade deficit was gratifying in so far as some of the countries that posed the biggest piracy problems were heavily dependent on trade with the US (Gadbaw, 1989, p. 228).

In 1984, eight trade associations representing over 1,500 copyright-based companies came together as an umbrella lobbying group, the International Intellectual Property Alliance (IIPA), advocating stronger protection and enforcement of US-held copyrights abroad. In the years leading up to TRIPS, the IIPA vigorously supported the use of bilateral and unilateral diplomacy to promote strong intellectual property protection. The IIPA promoted revisions to the US Trade and Tariff Act in 1984 and 1988 that extended the intellectual property components and served to increase US trade leverage against countries that failed adequately to protect US-held intellectual property. The IIPA and the powerful and well-organized Pharmaceutical Manufacturers Association (PMA, now called the Pharmaceutical Research and Manufacturers of America, PhRMA) successfully lobbied to include inadequate intellectual property protection as grounds for suspending trade privileges under programmes such as the Generalized System of Preferences (GSP, non-reciprocal trade benefits for developing countries), and regional initiatives such as the Caribbean Basin Initiative and the Andean Trade Preferences Act. The US government increasingly responded to these demands and frequently used threats to get targeted countries to increase their intellectual property protection and enforcement (Sell, 1998, ch. 6).

The institutional, economic and political context provided a favourable environment for advocates of high protectionist norms in intellectual property to press their case. These private sector representatives enjoyed superb access to the highest levels of policy-making. In particular, the Advisory Committee for Trade Negotiations (ACTN) provided an official channel for these business people to present their views on trade policy. The President appoints its members and it serves as an official channel for private sector advice on trade policy. From 1981 Edmund Pratt, then chief executive of Pfizer pharmaceutical, chaired this influential committee, ensuring that intellectual property concerns would gain a hearing at the top policy-making level. John Opel, then chief executive of IBM, and Pratt engaged in extensive lobbying activity. These proponents of high protectionist norms urged industry associations and companies to get involved in the issue, and played a crucial role in developing support for incorporating intellectual property into the talks in the Uruguay Round of GATT (General Agreement on Tariffs and Trade).

Pratt and Opel were both founding members of the Intellectual Property Committee (IPC), comprised of chief executives from a handful of well-connected and economically powerful American-based multinational corporations.[4] This group came together in March 1986 to push for an intellectual property agreement in GATT. The IPC sought a multilateral agreement to strengthen global protection of its members' intellectual property.[5] As technological prowess has increasingly spread throughout the world economy, certain types of technology have become easy and relatively inexpensive to appropriate. The American-based firms with comparative advantage in software, pharmaceuticals, music and film feared losing that advantage without government help. These intellectual property activists redefined inadequate intellectual property protection abroad as a barrier to legitimate trade. Adding inadequate enforcement of intellectual property rights as actionable under existing trade statutes, such as 301, brought intellectual property under the normative umbrella of trade policy. Private sector intellectual property rights activists effectively cast intellectual property rights as equivalent to general property rights, hence essential to free trade. Behaviour that was once tolerated was now redefined as objectionable and unfair. Linking intellectual property to trade and advocating this conception for the multilateral trading order, the IPC was able to appeal to an existing international institution, GATT, and emphasize the benefits of the new approach not just for the IPC but for the world trading system as a whole.

The IPC had just six months before the September 1986 start of the Uruguay Round. It immediately contacted its peers in Europe (Union of Industrial and Employers' Confederations of Europe – UNICE) and Japan (Keidanren) and worked hard to develop a transnational private sector consensus. The IPC stressed that the issue of intellectual property was too important to leave to governments, that industry needed to decide on the best course of action and then tell governments what to do. These private sector actors agreed that getting intellectual property on the Uruguay Round agenda was a worthy goal and pledged to lobby their home governments to support it. They quickly arrived at a consensus that the three critical components of an international intellectual property agreement would be: (1) a code of minimum standards for copyrights, patents, trademarks, and appellation of origin issues; (2) an enforcement mechanism; and (3) a dispute settlement mechanism. This 'trilateral group' succeeded in its quest to get intellectual property on the agenda by the outset of the Round. Throughout the next eighteen months this private sector coalition met frequently to negotiate its wish list. By the summer of 1988 the group had achieved sufficient consensus to issue a trilateral document outlining its specific goals for intellectual property (IPC, UNICE and Keidanren, 1988). This document was widely circulated and the United States government distributed 100 to 150 copies indicating that it reflected its views.[6] Throughout the Uruguay Round negotiations the IPC and the IIPA stayed in close contact with government negotiators and helped to shape specific proposals and successfully pressed their demands. Indeed, in the TRIPS negotiations the IPC had a potent ally in Pratt of Pfizer, who was an adviser to the US Official Delegation at the Round in his capacity as chairman of the ACTN. This was auspicious because the private sector has no official standing at GATT. When TRIPS was adopted in 1994 Jacques Gorlin, a consultant to the IPC who drafted its position papers, said that he was surprised by how much the IPC had achieved, and stated that 'we got 95 per cent of what we wanted'.[7]

In intergovernmental negotiations, such as the multilateral Uruguay Round, only states have formal standing. No matter how actively engaged private sector actors may be, bargains are ultimately struck between states. And realist logic suggests that the more powerful the state, the more likely it is to prevail in negotiations. In the case of the new global intellectual property regime, the United States was indisputably the most powerful state and possessed abundant negotiating power. The United States, at the behest of the private sector, had engaged in extensive coercive economic diplomacy leading up to and during the Uruguay Round. The United States had been using access to its large domestic market as a coercive means to goad other countries into adopting and enforcing stricter intellectual property policies. Many countries assented to TRIPS in the hopes that a multilateral rule-based system would eliminate the US's coercive economic diplomacy.

Effectiveness of Global Regulation: TRIPS Compliance

The new global regulation of intellectual property rights requires a 'web of surveillance' (Braithwaite and Drahos, 2000, p. 87), particularly since initially the vast majority of countries signing on to TRIPS will be negatively affected. The web of surveillance operates on multiple levels. Since the adoption of TRIPS the American intellectual property activists have remained vigilant in monitoring implementation and compliance. They have continued to avail themselves of the US 301 apparatus to pressure developing countries to alter their domestic intellectual property policies. They have also utilized the mechanisms of the WTO, through USTR, to file complaints over TRIPS. This section discusses post-TRIPS industry strategies and actions for ensuring compliance through the WTO process and the continued use of Section 301.

Intellectual property industry activists originally hoped that incorporating intellectual property and dispute settlement mechanisms into the WTO would reduce firms' transactions costs by eliminating, or at least sharply reducing, the need for costly and time-consuming bilateral and unilateral negotiations and coercive diplomacy. However, Jacques Gorlin, adviser to the IPC, admitted that one of the biggest surprises in the wake of TRIPS was the extent of wholesale non-compliance.[8] The IPC initially expected most countries to bring their laws into compliance, and then it would use the WTO dispute settlement mechanism for fine-tuning or to address those few countries whose laws needed further adjustment. Not surprisingly, the US has been the most aggressive country in the intellectual property area. It has filed fifteen WTO TRIPS complaints, more than all other member countries combined. However, Gorlin suggested that using the WTO to address so many flagrant and extensive violations of TRIPS would threaten to overload the system. Therefore, litigation and continued use of Section 301 are guaranteed.

Charles Levy, a lawyer and lobbyist for the IPC, spelled out the IPC's post-TRIPS strategy. Bemoaning the 'significant noncompliance' with TRIPS, he suggested that TRIPS supporters use litigation 'selectively, bringing, in the first instance, those cases they know they can win, and that present strategic issues that will develop the necessary body of precedent' (Levy, 2000, pp. 789, 790). True to the strategy advocated by Levy, fourteen of the fifteen US TRIPS cases have been straightforward violation complaints where states simply failed to enact the TRIPS provisions (Samahon, 2000, p. 1059). As predicted by Bello, the early intellectual property cases have been easy wins to help build support for the system (Bello, 1997). Levy hoped that by pursuing dispute settlement in WTO, high profile cases would serve as powerful examples that would bring other more lax countries in line. Levy also stressed the benefits of both intergovernmental and private sector diplomacy, urging the business community, and in particular 'companies with a major presence in a country' to highlight the benefits of TRIPS compliance (Levy, 2000, p. 794).

Eric Smith of the IIPA endorsed the dispute settlement route and advocated exploiting the opportunity the TRIPS Council[9] provides through its practice of reviewing implementation and obligations to point out deficiencies in various countries' laws. For the review process, states must notify the TRIPS Council of the steps they have taken to implement TRIPS, and then must respond to questions put to it by other TRIPS Council members. The IIPA, along with other interested parties, prepares questions and detailed enforcement information that it then submits to USTR for the TRIPS Council review process. In Smith's words, 'this is an important means to put pressure on countries that have not yet fully implemented their obligations to do so immediately or risk the commencement of a formal consultation and dispute settlement process' (Smith, 1996, p. 5). Indeed, in 1998 the USTR reported that it had been using the TRIPS Council meetings as 'an opportunity to educate developing country members as to how these provisions must be implemented in their laws'

(USTR, 1998a, p. 60). The USTR sees these meetings as useful for keeping pressure on developing country members and providing a valuable forum for confirming US interpretations of the TRIPS Agreement.

In its implementing legislation the US expressly retained its prerogatives to suspend GSP benefits, and benefits under various regional initiatives. The US has sought to accelerate TRIPS compliance by developing countries prior to the negotiated deadlines, or transition periods, largely through bilateral treaties. This reflected widespread industry dissatisfaction with the negotiated transition periods. Smith further underscored the continued importance of Special 301[10] identification of intellectual property rights priority countries, 'which has done more than any other provision of US trade law to improve the level of worldwide protection of US products embodying copyright' (Smith, 1996, p. 3). Many countries finally assented to the inclusion of intellectual property in the Uruguay Round agenda, expecting that it would make 301 disappear. But this expectation remains unmet. To the delight of intellectual property activist industries, in its implementing legislation the US strengthened Special 301 by requiring the USTR to take into account a country's prior status under Special 301, the history of US efforts under Special 301 and the country's response to such efforts in order to help highlight persistent recalcitrance in the face of Special 301 pressure. This increases the information requirements for USTR and will make the USTR even more dependent on private sector groups for data and analysis. Furthermore, in 1996 the USTR established an Office of Monitoring and Enforcement to oversee trade agreement implementation. It pursues enforcement actions, 'aggressively' litigating disputes to 'compel compliance' with the WTO agreements, NAFTA, and other regional and bilateral agreements (USTR, 1998b, p. 235). This same office also addresses problems outside the framework of the multilateral and regional treaties by invoking Section 301 and Special 301 of the Trade Act. It is likely no coincidence that 1997 saw a 25 per cent increase in the number of trading partners named under Special 301 in 1996 (USTR, 1998b, p. 244).

Overall, industry strategies have been to press the USTR to invoke 301 and WTO dispute settlement measures, and to use trade leverage and the TRIPS Council forum to achieve full-scale compliance with TRIPS. Industry has engaged in extensive monitoring of global intellectual property protection. Despite all this, there is undoubtedly room for some foot-dragging, so-called passive aggression, slowness in implementation and the like.[11]

Structures, Institutions and Agents

The global governance of intellectual property is best understood as a product of structured agency. The changing structure of global capitalism provided a permissive condition for TRIPS by delivering advocates of high protectionist norms for intellectual property to the forefront of global business regulation, and exacerbating the US government's concerns over competitiveness. This prompted institutional change within the United States that heightened access for these private sector actors (agents). The institution of the US state, embedded in this broader structure, mediated between domestic private sector actors and international institutions. One can consider the agent as the proximate cause, who is embedded in larger and larger structures, including material causes, state institutions, and the structure of global capitalism, that both constrain and empower.

This perspective endeavours to bring politics back into the analysis of global political economy. Who gets what, when and why? The structure of global capitalism helps to determine who the most important actors will be: representatives of leading economic sectors tend to enjoy enhanced political power. This power is compounded if they happen to reside in the most powerful state. For all the power of market actors and 'knowledge brokers', transnational private sector mobilization and emerging citizen campaigns to check corporate power, states are still centrally important in this arena. State power matters a great deal in determining who gets to make the rules, how compliance is pursued once the rules are in place, and how international institutions (in this case the World Trade Organization) operate. However, structure shapes but does not dictate outcomes.

Institutions, including legal norms, also play an important role. In the TRIPS case the legal norm of property rights was well established, as was the propensity for free trade. These norms are an integral part of the identity of the United States in the global political economy. In the years immediately prior to TRIPS, neither of these norms was effectively contested. Indeed, part of the genius of the IPC's framers was this synthesis of two hallowed principles, making such a synthesis appear both natural and necessary.

The relationship between institutions and agents is crucial. In this case the US state came to have strong positive views of the private sector's goals and became tangibly supportive by offering superb access to the top levels of policy-making both at domestic and multilateral levels. The IPC members enjoyed excellent access by virtue of their members' economic might and importance to American competitiveness goals. The agents and institutions were mutually dependent in so far as the government relied extensively on the agents' expertise and surveillance, and the agents needed state sanction for promoting the enforcement of other governments' intellectual property laws. Government support was also necessary in the intergovernmental multilateral arenas of GATT and the WTO.

Finally, at the most micro level, agents' skills in translating arcane issues into political discourse are important. Certain kinds of knowledge are concentrated and exclusive; this gives its purveyors additional power. By contrast, in instances in which required knowledge is accessible and disseminated, power is more widely dispersed, or at least not based on access to knowledge. Pre-TRIPS, advocates of high protectionist norms effectively set the agenda in part due to the arcane nature of intellectual property. Post-TRIPS, citizen campaigns are striving to educate the global public about the implications of TRIPS in order to mobilize opposition and reduce the formerly glaring information asymmetries. Post-TRIPS, alternative framing of the issues is beginning to weaken the public sense of legitimacy about the achievements of TRIPS – especially in the HIV/AIDS context. Indeed, legitimacy was not a major issue until well after the ink was dry. Even the compatibility of TRIPS with US goals has been called into question: the government has articulated that public health may well be an equally important competing goal.

Structural factors tipped the scale in the direction of privileged agents and their preferred policies, but it took the actions of agents to ensure the TRIPS outcome. The global governance of intellectual property is a dynamic process; focusing on the relationships between micro and macro level factors helps to show how agents reproduce and transform the structure through their actions.

Limits to Governance, Opportunities and Challenges

As the impact of TRIPS has become more palpable, new pockets of resistance and social mobilization have emerged to challenge TRIPS. With the exception of initial developing country resistance, opposition to TRIPS emerged rather late – after its adoption. This implies that while TRIPS cannot be 'undone' in any direct sense, the fight over loopholes, alternative interpretations of vague language and, perhaps most importantly, effective resistance to further expansion of global intellectual property rights lie ahead. This suggests some limits to the type of governance that the architects of TRIPS had in mind, but it also opens up the possibilities for more balanced and democratic governance of intellectual property. The deck is still stacked in favour of a commercial, as opposed to social agenda, but two emerging civil society campaigns have made an impact and are gaining significant momentum. If these campaigns can join forces, they could serve as a more potent counterweight to the existing system.

Two of the most important challenges to TRIPS address agriculture and medicine. Opposition groups are constructing 'the problem' in a different way by appealing to a competing set of rights and duties in the context of intellectual property. Farmers' rights, the rights of indigenous peoples and their knowledge, and rights to essential medicines challenge the claims of property holders who advocated the high protectionist norms embodied in TRIPS.

Agriculture and plant varieties

Grass roots activists, farmers' groups, environmental groups, development groups, human rights groups and consumer groups have mobilized to oppose global biotechnology, pharmaceutical, agricultural chemical and seed industries and their increasingly aggressive approach to intellectual property. Among the central concerns of this campaign are farmers' rights to save, reproduce and modify seeds. As early as 1993, when the TRIPS negotiations were still underway, hundreds of thousands of Indian farmers demonstrated against TRIPS proposals claiming that these rights could be jeopardized by the required implementing legislation (Sutherland, 1998, p. 293). Vandana Shiva, an Indian grass-roots activist, has helped mobilize the campaign against what she calls 'biopiracy' (Shiva, 1997). Biopiracy is seen as a new form of Western imperialism in which global seed and pharmaceutical corporations[12] engage in the unauthorized and uncompensated expropriation of genetic resources and traditional knowledge. This turns the discourse of piracy upside down in so far as these activists seek to demonstrate that America's global corporations are the biggest 'pirates' on the planet.

TRIPS permits the exclusion of plants and animals from patentability, but Article 27.3(b) requires that members provide protection for plant *varieties* either by patents or an 'effective *sui generis*' system. However, there really is no consensus on what qualifies as an effective *sui generis* system. American industries are pushing for the adoption of the Union for the Protection of New Varieties of Plants (UPOV) as the appropriate model *sui generis* system. UPOV is very generous to the corporate plant breeder and sharply limits farmers' rights.

Opponents argue that patenting and *sui generis* plant variety protection based on UPOV have led to extensive economic concentration in the past decade. The vertical integration of plant breeding, agrochemical and food processing corporations has led to a situation in which 'the top ten seed companies currently control 30 per cent of the world's US$23 billion commercial seed market' (GRAIN, 1998, p. 13). Corporate plant breeders are patenting entire species (cotton), economic characteristics (oil quality), plant reproductive behaviour (apomixis) and basic techniques of biotechnology (gene transfer tools) (Gaia/GRAIN, 1998, p. 13). This combination of economic concentration with extensive and broad patenting concentrates control of the world's food supply and entangles farmers and indigenous peoples in an onerous web of licensing and royalty obligations.

Developing countries and NGOs have been pursuing alternative approaches to *sui generis* protection that respect farmers' rights and communal and indigenous forms of knowledge. In December 1997 a number of developing country NGOs issued the Thammasat Resolution calling for a revision of TRIPS to expressly permit countries to exclude life forms and biodiversity-related knowledge from intellectual property monopolies, and asserting the primacy of the 1993 Convention on Biological Diversity (CBD) over TRIPS.[13] The CBD expressly incorporates farmers' rights, which has become an important metric for developing countries' approaches to TRIPS Article 27.3(b).[14] It highlights the contribution of traditional practices, such as seed saving, trading and hybrid experimentation, to biological diversity (Tejera, 1999, p. 981). Numerous countries have joined the *sui generis* 'rights movement' by proposing legislation that addresses the concerns raised by the anti-biopiracy activists (GRAIN, 1999).[15]

When TRIPS was negotiated, participants agreed to revisit Article 27.3(b) four years after the date of entry into force. Going into the Seattle Ministerial, the US agenda included the deletion of exclusions to patents on life forms, and the incorporation of UPOV into TRIPS. Developing countries were prepared to resist this agenda and insist on the primacy of CBD over TRIPS. However, the Seattle meeting yielded very little. Putting a positive spin on the Seattle deadlock, IPC lawyer Levy stated that 'the good news is that members did not have a chance to tinker with TRIPS. Because there was no Ministerial Declaration, they did not have to deal with the cross-currents that were building on intellectual property' (Levy, 2000, pp. 794–5). Those 'cross-currents' will not disappear any time soon. Future efforts to negotiate multilateral TRIPS-plus provisions will meet with resistance.

Pharmaceutical patents

In the face of the devastating HIV/AIDS crisis in sub-Saharan Africa and Thailand, the 'access to essential medicines' campaign has mobilized to highlight the public health consequences of overly broad patent rights. The campaign supports developing countries' rights to avail themselves of compulsory licensing provisions under TRIPS to produce and export generic equivalents of life-saving HIV/AIDS drugs. US trade pressure on both South Africa and Thailand has galvanized criticism of TRIPS. Ralph Nader's Consumer Project on Technology (CPT), headed by James Love, Amsterdam-based Health Action International (HAI),[16] and the Nobel prize-winning group Médecins Sans Frontières (MSF)[17] have joined forces to protest against American trade policy in intellectual property and the TRIPS trade-off in favour of commercial interests over public health concerns. Public health activists have scored some important victories, and considerable momentum appears to be building globally in favour of a public health perspective on patent rights.

Faced with debilitating HIV/AIDS crises, South Africa and Thailand sought to employ compulsory licensing to manufacture AIDS drugs more cheaply. When a state grants a compulsory licence, rights to produce a product are licensed to another party without the patent-holder's permission. Compulsory licensing allows states to produce generic drugs which are more affordable to increase access. USTR pressured Thailand on behalf of PhRMA in 1997 and 1998; US trade officials threatened sanctions on core Thai exports and Thailand dropped its compulsory licensing plans. The December 1997 South African Medicines and Medical Devices Regulatory Authority Act allowed the Minister of Health to revoke patents on medicines and to allow for broad-based compulsory licensing to manufacture generic versions of HIV/AIDS drugs. PhRMA complained to USTR that the South African law posed a direct challenge to TRIPS (PhRMA, 1999, pp. 10–11). The USTR placed South Africa on the 301 'watch list' and urged the South African government to repeal its law. Despite USTR pressure, South Africa refused to repeal its law. The US advocacy group ACT-UP took up South Africa's cause and repeatedly disrupted Vice President Al Gore's campaign appearances in 1999. Shortly thereafter, the US removed South Africa from the USTR watch list (Vick, 1999, p. A18).

The access to essential medicines campaign, spearheaded by Love's CPT, HAI and MSF, undertook a number of activities leading up to the WTO Seattle Ministerial of December 1999. The campaign participated in drafting a historic resolution that the World Health Assembly (governing body of the World Health Organization) unanimously enacted in May 1999,[18] calling on member states to ensure equitable access to essential drugs and review options under international agreements to safeguard access to these medicines (MSF, HAI and CPT, 1999). This incensed the pharmaceutical industry in so far as it elevated public health issues above property rights in trade. In its open letter to WTO member states, the Campaign for Access to Essential Medicines urged states to make public health their highest priority in implementing TRIPS obligations, explore the extension of grace periods for developing countries, and to encourage developing countries to actively invoke the public health and public interest considerations of TRIPS Articles 7 and 8. The Campaign strongly advocates generic drug competition and urged WTO member states to prevent the use of trade sanctions against countries that do not implement TRIPS-plus obligations on policies concerning access to essential medicines.

Significantly, at the Seattle WTO Ministerial, President Clinton signalled a major change in US policy that responded to the goals of the access campaign. He announced that the US would alter its trade policy to support African access to HIV/AIDS drugs (MSF, 2000). He also introduced institutional collaboration between USTR and the US Department of Health and Human Services on trade cases involving public health issues.

On 10 May 2000 the Clinton administration went even further by issuing an execut-ive order that prohibited the USTR from pressuring sub-Saharan African countries into foregoing legitimate strategies, such as compulsory licensing and parallel import-ing, aimed at increasing access to affordable HIV/AIDS drugs. This was a notable departure from past US policy in so far as it elevated public health into the framing of trade issues, and marked a retreat from the government's previously unqualified support for its global pharmaceutical firms. Furthermore, after taking office the Bush administration indicated that it would not rescind Clinton's executive order.

Companies have begun to offer drugs to African countries at reduced prices, as individual companies and under the auspices of the Joint United Nations Programme on HIV/AIDS. Companies fear that cut-rate drugs provided for developing countries will begin to flood developed country markets and reduce profit margins, but public pressure in the face of what appears to be a treatable crisis is demanding a response. The companies hope that their counterparts will match their price reductions, and that OECD governments will offer funds to help the Africans buy the drugs. They also hope to pre-empt any compulsory licensing of their products.

In early March 2001, a three-year-old lawsuit that thirty-nine global pharmaceutical companies brought against South Africa over its 1997 Act was scheduled to begin. The trial quickly became a high profile event marked by protestors, grim images of dying mothers and babies, street demonstrations and extensive media coverage. The powerful imagery conjured up memories of apartheid, and all but demonized global pharmaceutical companies. Amid intense public outcry the companies withdrew their South African lawsuit. This was widely hailed as an important victory for the citizen groups' campaign against the global pharmaceutical industry.

Events in early 2001 seemed to overwhelm the pharmaceutical companies' earlier public relations efforts to reduce prices. In a deal negotiated between Love of CPT and Cipla, an Indian generic drug firm, Cipla pledged to offer a three-drug AIDS 'cocktail' to governments for $600 a year per patient, and to MSF for $350 a year (versus the $10,000–15,000 that American patients pay) (Stolberg, 2001).[19] This offer made all previous price reductions look insignificant. Subsequently, a number of phar-maceutical firms reduced their prices even more sharply and Pfizer began to offer one drug for free.

The campaign scored another important victory in 2001 by pressuring Yale Univer-sity, which holds the patent on an important AIDS drug, d4T, to promote African access to generic versions of the drug. Yale's patent contract with Bristol-Myers Squibb brings in $40 million a year in licensing fees for the drug (McNeil, 2001). A group of Yale law students organized campus protests and one of the drug's developers, Yale Pharmacology Professor William Prusoff, supported the students. He said, 'I wish they would either supply the drug free or allow India or Brazil to produce it cheaply for underdeveloped countries' (quoted in McNeil, 2001). On 14 March, Bristol-Myers Squibb announced that it would cut the cost of d4T to 15 cents for a daily dose (1.5 per cent of the cost to an American patient). In an editorial after the Bristol-Myers Squibb announcement Dr Prusoff wrote, 'I am struck by all the steps that led us to today . . . I find it hard to see any pattern in all this, except perhaps that there is a moral urge among people that, however coincidentally, can sometimes bring results' (Prusoff, 2001).

The momentum generated by these developments accelerated into the summer. At the behest of the group of African countries, the TRIPS Council convened a special session on 20 June 2001 to address the access to medicines issues and to listen to member delegations present their positions. A building consensus emerged, including the European Union, that TRIPS should not interfere with the protection of public health, although the US continued to defend its global drug companies (Boseley and Capella, 2001). Developing countries sought official confirmation that measures to protect public health would not make them subject to dispute settlement procedures in the WTO. The TRIPS Council resolved to continue analysing the degree of flexibility afforded by TRIPS in the context of public health, planned future meetings on the issue and pledged to convene another special session on trade and pharmaceuticals in September 2001 (Capdevila, 2001). At the June meeting, the delegation from Brazil highlighted Brazil's dramatically successful programme of distributing HIV/AIDS medicines at very low or no cost to patients. Its access to medicines programme has decreased AIDS-related deaths by half and reduced hospital admissions brought on by opportunistic infections by 80 per cent (CPT, 2001). Brazil has become a beacon of hope in the struggles of developing countries against the HIV/AIDS pandemic.

Intellectual property disputes between Brazil and the US have been rancorous since 1987 when, in a PMA-initiated dispute over Brazil's lack of patent protection for pharmaceuticals, the US placed a 100 per cent retaliatory tariff (totaling $39 million) on imports of an array of Brazilian goods (Sell, 1998, p. 190). US-initiated WTO cases against Brazil and Argentina go to the heart of the access to medicines campaign. Unlike the other relatively bloodless WTO cases, a US-initiated Brazilian WTO case and an Argentine case currently in the consultation stage, have become political lightning rods for the access campaign. PhRMA pressed the USTR to object to both countries' policies that serve to increase access to affordable medicines. For example, Brazil's law provides 'that if a patented product is not manufactured within three years of the issuance of the patent, the Brazilian government can compel the patent holder to license a competitor' (Yerkey and Pruzin, 2001). Brazil has maintained that the threat of compulsory licensing has helped it negotiate reasonable drug prices with global pharmaceutical corporations; it has used this threat effectively against Roche and Merck in its quest for affordable access to AIDS drugs. In particular, the CPT and MSF maintain that Brazil's approach has permitted it to pursue its stunningly successful policies to reduce AIDS deaths by making generic equivalents of life-saving drugs (MSF, 2001). On 1 February 2001, the WTO acceded to a US request for the establishment of a WTO panel to rule on its complaint against Brazil's compulsory licensing provisions. Yet the US dragged its heels in pursuing the appointment of panelists and in moving the process forward. In the wake of the South Africa spectacle and the increasingly vociferous NGO criticism the case became a political embarrassment. On 25 June the US announced that it was officially withdrawing its WTO case against Brazil; Robert Zoellick of the USTR noted that 'litigating this dispute before a WTO dispute panel has not been the most constructive way to address our differences, especially since Brazil has never actually used the provision at issue' (quoted in Yerkey and Pruzin, 2001). The US withdrawal of the Brazilian WTO case may portend reconsideration of the Argentine case as well.

The US announcement came on the first day of the first United Nations General Assembly Special Session devoted to a public health issue (HIV/AIDS). The special session culminated in 'The Declaration of Commitment' on HIV/AIDS of 27 June 2001. Applauded by the access to essential medicines campaigners such as MSF, the declaration framed the issue as not merely medical but as a 'political, human rights, and economic threat' (Steinhauer, 2001). The declaration emphasized both prevention and treatment, and there was a call to generate about $9 billion for a Global AIDS and Health fund that UN Secretary-General Kofi Annan hopes will be fully operational by the end of 2001. Governance of the fund is bound to be controversial: NGO activists have warned that global pharmaceutical companies have conflicts of interest and should not be making spending decisions, whereas industry insists on a substantial role in the fund. Nonetheless, while numerous controversies remain, progress on the access campaign has come a long way even since the beginning of 2001.

What is new is that public health issues are finally becoming linked to trade and intellectual property. There is evidence of movement away from the industry-sponsored intellectual property orthodoxy that animated deliberations leading up to the TRIPS accord. To the extent that public health activists are succeeding in persuading others of the merits of this way of framing the issues, they could have a significant impact indeed in redressing the imbalance between private and public interests in the context of intellectual property.

Overall, the post-TRIPS picture is mixed. TRIPS has energized industry to press further for TRIPS-plus policy changes in foreign countries. At the same time, TRIPS has galvanized an increasingly vociferous and mobilized civil society campaign to temper the previously unchecked industry dominance over the intellectual property agenda. At the very least, the post-TRIPS trends have revealed new areas of contestation and portend a more difficult political environment for industry.

Notes

1   The World Intellectual Property Organization is another important institution in this context, but due to space limitations will not be discussed here. For a good treatment of WIPO as an institution see Doern, 1999.
2   Important scholarship addressing the relationship between agents and structures includes Giddens, 1986 and Wendt, 1999. My treatment of these issues directs more attention to the micro level than does Wendt's.
3   For a useful guide to the TRIPS provisions, see Blakeney, 1996.
4   The IPC membership has fluctuated between eleven and fourteen members. At the time that the Uruguay Round of GATT negotiations got underway in 1986 its members were Bristol-Myers, CBS, Du Pont, General Electric, General Motors, Hewlett-Packard, IBM, Johnson & Johnson, Merck, Monsanto, and Pfizer.
5   For a more detailed treatment of this discussion see Sell, forthcoming.
6   Author's interview with Jacques Gorlin, 22 Jan. 1996, Washington DC.
7   Ibid. The 5 per cent the IPC did *not* get included transition periods for developing countries; the IPC was vehemently opposed to these.
8   Jacques Gorlin's comments presented at Yeshiva University's Benjamin Cardozo School of Law Symposium, Intellectual Property, World Trade, and Global Elites, New York, 7 Mar. 2001.
9   Formally known as the Council for Trade-Related Aspects of Intellectual Property Rights.
10 While widely known as 'Special 301', this provision is Section 182 of the Trade Act of 1974, added by Section 1303 of the Omnibus Trade and Competitiveness Act of 1988. It

requires the USTR to identify countries abusing US intellectual property rights, negotiate with them, and impose retaliatory sanctions on recalcitrant states.

11 For examples of this in the Special 301 context see Sell, 1998, ch. 6.

12 In many instances, owing to extensive merger activity in the past decade, these corporations are one and the same. For example, when Sandoz and Ciba-Geigy completed their $63 billion merger in 1996 the new firm, Novartis, became 'the world's number-one agrochemical corporation, second largest seed firm, third largest pharmaceutical firm, and fourth largest veterinary medicine company' (Shulman, 1999, p. 49). Additionally, Monsanto was acquired by Pharmacia.

13 The Thammasat Resolution is reprinted in GRAIN, 1997.

14 In 1985 the Rural Advancement Foundation International (RAFI), a Canadian-based international NGO, developed the concept of farmers' rights as a counterweight to plant breeders' rights. RAFI introduced this principle in the United Nations Food and Agriculture Organization's deliberations over plant genetic resources in the so-called 'seed wars' of the 1980s (Braithwaite and Drahos, 2000, p. 572; Sutherland, 1998, p. 292).

15 For examples see GRAIN, 1998.

16 Health Action International is an informal network of over 150 consumer, health, development and other public interest groups involved in health and pharmaceutical issues.

17 Also known as Doctors Without Borders.

18 WHA52.19. Notably, the US did not have a seat on the World Health Assembly board that year, which helps account for the unanimity. Author's interview with James Love, 6 April 2001, Washington DC.

19 Author's interviews with James Love, 24 March 2001, Gainesville, Florida and 6 April 2001, Washington DC.

References

Aoki, K. (1996) '(Intellectual) property and sovereignty: notes toward a cultural geography of authorship', *Stanford Law Review*, 48, no. 5, May, pp. 1293–1356.

Arup, C. (1998) 'Competition over competition policy for international trade and intellectual property', *Prometheus*, 16, no. 3, pp. 367–81.

Bello, J. H. (1997) 'Some practical observations about WTO settlement of intellectual property disputes', *Virginia Journal of International Law*, 37, pp. 357–67.

Bhagwati, J. (1989) 'United States trade policy at a crossroads', *The World Economy*, 12, Dec., pp. 439–79.

Blakeney, M. (1996) *Trade-Related Aspects of Intellectual Property Rights: A Concise Guide to the TRIPS Agreement*, London: Sweet and Maxwell.

Boseley, S. and Capella, P. (2001) 'US defends drug companies', *Guardian*, 21 June; accessed 29 June 2001 at www.commondreams.org/headlines01/0621-01.htm.

Braithwaite, J. and Drahos, P. (2000) *Global Business Regulation*, Cambridge: Cambridge University Press.

Burch, K. (1994) 'The "properties" of the state system and global capitalism', in S. Rosow, N. Inayatullah and M. Rupert (eds), *The Global Economy as Political Space*, Boulder: Lynne Rienner.

Capdevila, G. (2001) 'WTO concedes developing world's plea for access to low-cost drugs', *Dawn: The Internet Edition*, 24 June, at www.dawn.com/2001/06/24/intl l.htm, accessed 29 June 2001.

CPT (Consumer Project on Technology) (2001) 'Policy position of Brazil at the Trips Council on access to medicines', 20 June, at www.cptech.org/ip/wto/tc/brazil.html, accessed 29 June 2001.

Dessler, D. (1989) 'What's at stake in the agent-structure debate?', *International Organization*, 43, no. 3, Summer, pp. 441–73.

Doern, C. B. (1999) *Global Change and Intellectual Property Agencies: An Institutional Perspective*, London: Pinter.

Drahos, P. (1997) 'Thinking strategically about intellectual property rights', *Telecommunications Policy*, 21, no. 3, pp. 201–11.

Gadbaw, M. (1989) 'Intellectual property and international trade: merger or marriage of convenience?', *Vanderbilt Journal of Transnational Law*, 22, no. 2, pp. 223–42.

Gaia/GRAIN (Gaia Foundation/Genetic Resources Action International) (1998) 'Intellectual property rights and biodiversity: the economic myths', *Global Trade and Biodiversity in Conflict*, no. 3, pp. 1–20, available at www.grain.org/publications/gtbc/issue3.htm, accessed 25 July 2000.

Giddens, A. (1986) *The Constitution of Society: Outline of a Theory of Structuration*, Berkeley: University of California Press.

GRAIN (Genetic Resources Action International) (1997) 'Towards our sui generis rights', *Seedling*, Dec., pp. 4–6, available at www.grain.org/publications/dec97/dec971.htm, accessed 24 June 1999.

GRAIN (Genetic Resources Action International) (1998) 'The TRIPS review takes off', Dec., available at www.grain.org/publications/dec98/dec983.htm, accessed 24 June 1999.

GRAIN (Genetic Resources Action International) (1999) 'Beyond UPOV: examples of developing countries preparing non-UPOV sui generis plant variety protection schemes for compliance with TRIPS', July, available at www.grain.org/publications/reports/nonupov.htm, accessed 7 Aug. 2000.

IPC, UNICE and Keidanren (1988) 'Basic framework of GATT provisions on intellectual property', MS.

Levy, C. S. (2000) 'Implementing TRIPS: a test of political will', *Law and Policy in International Business*, 31, no. 3, pp. 789–95.

McNeil, D. (2001) 'Yale pressed to help cut drug costs in Africa', *New York Times*, 12 Mar., p. A3.

MSF (Médecins Sans Frontières) (2000) 'MSF reaction to UNAIDS proposal', 11 May, available at www.msf.org/un/reports/2000/05/pr-unaids/, accessed 7 Aug. 2000.

MSF (Médecins Sans Frontières) (2001) 'US action at WTO threatens Brazil's successful AIDS programme', 1 Feb. available at www.msf.org in the Content section, accessed 19 Mar. 2001.

MSF (Médecins Sans Frontières), HAI and CPT (1999) 'An open letter to WTO member states', 8 Nov., available at http: //msf.org/advocacy/accessmed/wto/reports/1999/letter, accessed 11 July 2000.

PhRMA (Pharmaceutical Research and Manufacturers of America) (1999) 'Submission of the Pharmaceutical Research and Manufacturers of America for the "special 301" report on intellectual property barriers', 16 Feb., available at www.phrma.org/issues/nte/html, accessed 12 Aug. 1999.

Prusoff, W. (2001) 'The scientist's story', *New York Times*, 19 Mar., p. A23.

Rodrik, D. (1994) 'Comments on Maskus and Eby-Konan', in A. Deardorff and R. Stern (eds), *Analytic and Negotiating Issues in the Global Trading System*, Ann Arbor: University of Michigan Press.

Samahon, T. N. (2000) 'TRIPS copyright dispute settlement after the transition and moratorium: nonviolation and situation complaints against developing countries', *Law and Policy in International Business*, 31, no. 3, pp. 1051–75.

Sell, S. (1998) *Power and Ideas: The North-South Politics of Intellectual Property and Antitrust*, Albany: State University of New York Press.

Sell, S. (forthcoming) *Private Power, Public Law: The Globalization of Intellectual Property Rights*.

Shiva, V. (1997) *Biopiracy: The Plunder of Nature and Knowledge*, Boston: South End Press.

Shulman, S. (1999) *Owning the Future*, Boston: Houghton Mifflin.

Smith, E. H. (1996) 'Testimony of Eric H. Smith, President of the International Intellectual Property Alliance representing the International Intellectual Property Alliance before the Committee on Ways and Means, United States House of Representatives', 13 Mar., available at: www.iIPa.com/html/rbi_trips_tstmn_31396.html, accessed 26 Oct. 1998.

Steinhauer, J. (2001) 'UN redefines AIDS as political issue and peril to poor', *New York Times*, 28 June, p. A1.

Stolberg, S. (2001) 'Africa's AIDS war', *New York Times*, 10 Mar., p. A1.

Sutherland, J. (1998) 'TRIPS, cultural politics and law reform', *Prometheus*, 16, no. 3, pp. 291–303.

Tejera, V. (1999) 'Tripping over property rights: is it possible to reconcile the convention on biological diversity with Article 27 of the TRIPS agreement?', *New England Law Review*, 33, Summer, pp. 967–87.

USTR (US Trade Representative) (1998a) '1998 trade policy agenda and 1997 annual report of the President of the United States on the trade agreements program', available at www.ustr.gov, accessed 26 Oct. 1998.

USTR (US Trade Representative) (1998b) 'USTR announces results of special 301 annual review', 1 May, available at www.ustr.gov accessed 26 Oct. 1998.

Vick, K. (1999) 'African AIDS victims losers of a drug war', *Washington Post*, 4 Dec., p. A18.

Wendt, A. (1999) *Social Theory of International Politics*, Cambridge: Cambridge University Press.

Yerkey, G. and Pruzin, D. (2001) 'United States drops WTO case against Brazil over HIV/AIDS patent', *WTO Reporter*, Bureau of National Affairs, Inc., 26 June, accessed 5 July 2001 at www.cptech.org/ip/health/c/brazil/bna6262001.htm.

9
Governing Global Finance
Jan Aart Scholte

Introduction

In contemporary history, 'global crisis' has as often as not referred to the field of finance. Over the past two decades the world has experienced continual problems with heavy transborder debt burdens, major disruptive swings in foreign exchange values, a perpetual roller-coaster in the securities markets of global financial centres, and a string of crashes among global derivatives players. Understandably, therefore, taming transworld financial flows has ranked as one of the top priorities of governance in an emergent global polity.

This chapter examines the regulation of global finance. The first section below identifies the forms and extent of contemporary financial globalization: that is, how monetarily denominated savings and investments now increasingly move in transworld spaces. A range of evidence is cited to indicate that finance has acquired a very substantial global character. The second section of the chapter reviews the various institutional mechanisms that currently serve to govern global finance. This regulation is shown to be multilayered and diffuse: across local, national, regional and global levels; and across public and private sectors. The third section considers the effectiveness of present regulatory arrangements, with reference to criteria of efficiency, stability, social equity, ecological integrity and democracy. Current frameworks are found to be seriously wanting on all of these counts. The fourth section reflects on the relevance of various analytical frameworks in understanding the governance of global finance. Rather than ally with one of the theoretical approaches discussed elsewhere in this book and oppose the others, the chapter opts to note the insights (sometimes complementary) that different theories offer, as well as certain limitations of each perspective as it relates to global finance. Finally, the chapter assesses future challenges and prospects in the governance of global finance. It is argued here that considerably more proactive and socially progressive public regulation of global finance is possible and desirable.

Global Finance

Finance is the part of an economy that links savings with investments through a variety of instruments denominated in monetary values. Finance is the intermediating activity that makes savings available for investments while generating income from those investments for savers. (See Bryant, 2002 for an accessible account of basic economics of finance; and Held et al., 1999, ch. 4 for a comprehensive survey of global finance.)

A host of mechanisms have developed to connect savings and investments. Many take the form of deposits in and loans from banks. Others are securities: that is, stocks and debt instruments like bonds, notes and money market tools. Then there are financial derivatives: that is, forwards, options, swaps and other such contracts that relate to future levels in foreign exchange rates, interest charges, securities prices, stock market indices, and other financial indicators. Insurance arrangements constitute still another large field of financial activity, where people pay in today to cover possible needs for payouts tomorrow.

The scale of contemporary finance is quite astounding. The levels of transactions often dwarf those in the so-called 'real' economy of primary production, manufacturing, transport, communications, etc. For example, the average volume of foreign exchange dealings rose from $15 billion per day in 1973 to $1,490 billion per day in 1998, before dropping to $1,210 billion per day in 2001 (Gilpin, 2000, p. 261; BIS, 2001a; BIS, 2001d, pp. 98–100). At today's level it takes wholesale foreign exchange markets just a month to trade the value of annual world GDP, at some $30,000 billion (UNDP, 2001, p. 181). Likewise, turnover on the world's securities exchanges exceeds many times over the value of the 'real' assets behind those stocks and bonds. As for financial derivatives, a tool first developed in 1972, the notional amount of outstanding over-the-counter contracts alone (thus excluding exchange-based derivatives) stood at $99,800 billion in 2001 (BIS, 2001b). In short, finance is big – indeed, extremely big – business.

Finance can transpire in diverse geographical settings. It can be a local affair, for example, with banks that operate only within certain districts or provinces. Several localities have even adopted 'community currencies' as a statement of their wish to delink from high finance (cf. www.ratical.org/many_worlds/cc/). However, contemporary finance usually unfolds more in a country context, with national money forms, national institutions, and national financial markets. Meanwhile, international finance occurs when savings and investments are transferred between one country and another. More recently we have seen the rise of regional finance with, for example, the creation of distinct regional currencies like the euro in most of the European Union and the CFA franc covering fourteen countries in West and Central Africa. Regional financial institutions like the Asian Development Bank and the Euronext securities exchange have also appeared. Then there is global finance: namely, monetary savings and investments that flow through world networks.

The terms 'globality' (the condition) and 'globalization' (the trend of increasing globality) mean many things to many people; however, most will agree that, broadly speaking, 'globalness' involves social connections in a planetary realm. In other words, global aspects of social relations are those that unfold in a transworld space. This global arena can be distinguished from – though it also coexists and interlinks with – local, national, international and regional spaces.

Globality has at least four interrelated aspects: internationality, liberality, universality and supraterritoriality. With its international quality, globality entails interaction and interdependence between countries. So global relations involve intensive cross-border communication, investment, trade and travel. With its liberal quality, globality is marked by a low level (or even absence) of statutory barriers to cross-border flows, such as tariffs, foreign exchange restrictions, capital controls and visa requirements. With its universal quality, globality prevails when objects, symbols and experiences spread to most if not all corners of the inhabited earth. The many examples include postcards, Arabic numerals and Hollywood films. Finally, in a feature that has mainly arisen in recent history, globality connects people in ways that largely transcend territorial geography, for instance, in respect of telecommunications and global ecological changes. Such supraterritorial links exist with little if any regard to fixed territorial locations, territorial distances and territorial borders. Supraterritorial phenomena can span any points on earth simultaneously, and they can move between any points on earth instantaneously. (For more on supraterritoriality, see Scholte, 2000, ch. 2.)

Globalization – that is, increasing globality – has marked contemporary finance in all four of these ways. In terms of increased cross-border financial flows, for example, the world total of bank deposits owned by non-residents of a given country rose from $20 billion in 1964 to $9,600 billion in 2001 (IMF, 1993, pp. 60–70; BIS, 2001c, p. 10). Concurrently, outstanding balances on syndicated international commercial bank loans rose from under $200 billion in the early 1970s to well over $8,000 billion in 2001 (BIS, 1998, p. 144; BIS, 2001c, p. 10). New borrowings of this kind amounted to $1,465 billion in 2000, as compared with $372 billion in 1995 and just $9 billion in 1972 (OECD, 1996; BIS, 2001c, p. 68). In addition, governments and multilateral institutions like the International Monetary Fund (IMF, or 'the Fund') and the World Bank have extended several hundred billion further dollars in official cross-border loans to medium- and low-income countries. The capital base of the IMF has risen tenfold since the 1960s, to almost $300 billion in 1999.

In the securities area, the net issuance of international bonds and notes rose from $1 billion in 1960 to $461 billion in 1995 and $1,246 billion in 2000 (OECD, 1996; BIS, 2001c, p. 71). The total of outstanding cross-border debt securities stood at over $7,000 billion in 2001 (BIS, 2001c, p. 71). In addition, over $300 billion in new equities were issued to non-residents in 2000 (BIS, 2001c, p. 86). Before 1980, resident and non-resident investors rarely traded securities with each other, but by 1997 the value of such transactions was equivalent to 672 per cent of GDP in Italy, 253 per cent of GDP in Germany, and 213 per cent of GDP in the USA (BIS, 1998, p. 100). The two main clearing houses for cross-border securities trading, Euroclear and Clearstream (formerly Cedel), both founded in the early 1970s, together accumulated an annual turnover of nearly $60,000 billion in 1999, up from $10,000 billion in the late 1980s (Kirdar, 1992, p. 2; Euroclear, 2000).

Much of this increased internationalization of finance has gone hand in hand with liberalization. For example, starting with the USA in 1974, over 150 states have now removed official restrictions on foreign exchange movements related to the current account of the balance of payments, in accordance with Article VIII of the Articles of Agreement of the IMF. Many states have also relaxed (though rarely completely eliminated) capital controls: that is, regulatory limitations on transfers related to the capital account of the balance of payments (including stocks, bonds, short-term credits, derivatives, foreign direct investments, etc.). In addition, increasing numbers of states have lifted restrictions on non-residents holding bank accounts or dealing in securities within their jurisdictions, thus encouraging the increased cross-border activity mentioned above. Likewise, more and more states now allow externally based banks, securities houses and insurance companies to operate within their territory, sometimes on an equal footing with domestic companies. Only a few securities markets – such as the relatively small exchanges in Saudi Arabia and the United Arab Emirates – prohibit foreign participation altogether. Additional liberalization of the financial industry is anticipated through further development of the General Agreement on Trade in Services (GATS) of the World Trade Organization (WTO).

Universality has also become a widespread feature of contemporary finance. Several national denominations like the US dollar and the Japanese yen have become universal currencies, circulating just about everywhere on earth. In addition, the euro and – on a much more limited scale – the Special Drawing Right (SDR) have emerged through the EU and the IMF, respectively, as monies with transworld use. Meanwhile credit cards like Visa and MasterCard offer universal commerce, with acceptance at tens of millions of establishments across some 200 countries (www.visa.com; www.mastercard.com). Likewise, many insurance policies now extend worldwide coverage. Recent years have also seen the institution of a securities exchange spread to most countries on earth, including seemingly unlikely sites such as Albania and Burma.

As noted earlier, supraterritoriality is arguably what makes contemporary global finance qualitatively different from previous eras. For example, electronic transfers now permit huge sums in financial transactions to be moved instantly between any points on earth. With telephones and computer links, foreign exchange trading today occurs through a round-the-world, round-the-clock market that connects dealing rooms in London, New York, Tokyo, Zurich, Frankfurt, Hong Kong, Singapore, Paris and Sydney. Electronic payments through the Society for Worldwide Interbank Financial Telecommunication (SWIFT), founded in 1977, averaged more than $6,000 billion per day in 2000, linking over 7,000 financial institutions in 194 countries (www.swift.com). In retail banking, many plastic cards (such as those connected to the Cirrus network) can extract cash in local currency from over 400,000 automated teller machines (ATMs) across the planet. Electronic communications also enable securities brokers instantly to transmit and execute orders to buy and sell stocks and bonds anywhere in the world. Several derivatives exchanges (for example, London–Singapore and Chicago–Sydney) have established direct links to enable round-the-world, round-the-clock dealing in certain futures and options. Meanwhile insurance brokers have developed networks that allow them to transact business across the planet from their office computers.

In addition, supraterritorial organization today enables many financial actors to operate simultaneously across the globe. A number of commercial banks and insurance companies operate as transworld enterprises with affiliates in dozens of countries. Prominent examples include Citicorp, Lehman Brothers, and Winterthur Worldwide. Several global multilateral development banks (MDBs) have also emerged since the 1940s, including the five components of the World Bank Group and the Islamic Development Bank. Meanwhile, membership of the IMF has grown from 62 states in 1960 to 183 in 2000.

As well as financial communications and financial organizations, a number of financial instruments have acquired a supraterritorial quality that substantially delinks them from a particular locality or country. For example, in so-called 'eurocurrency' banking, begun in the 1950s, deposits and loans are denominated in money that is different from the official currency in the country where the funds are held. Thus a citizen of country A, resident in country B, can hold an account in country C, in the currency of country D. Likewise, in so-called 'eurobonds' the debt is denominated in a currency different from that of the country of issue. So a borrower in country A, with headquarters in country B, can obtain a bond in the currency of country C, arranged by brokers in countries D and E, for listing on an exchange in country F. From its inception in 1963, the eurobond market grew to \$371 billion in new issues in 1995 (Kerr, 1984; OECD, 1996). In stock markets, too, various companies have developed global share listings, that is, on up to a dozen exchanges spread across the world. The 1990s also saw the advent of American Depository Receipts (ADRs) and Global Depository Receipts (GDRs). These instruments bundle together shares of companies in Asia, Latin America and Central and Eastern Europe for trading at the world's main financial centres. On the side of investors, a number of mutual funds, pension funds, hedge funds and individuals hold global portfolios and trade simultaneously on financial markets across the world.

In these circumstances of supraterritorial communications, organization and instruments, much of contemporary finance is marked by a veritable global consciousness. Countless savers, investors, borrowers and brokers think of – and act on – the world as a single field of financial operations. Innumerable slogans and logos in the financial sector incorporate explicit references to and symbols of globality. Most major players aspire to global reach as a key mark of success.

In sum, contemporary finance has a significant global character, including substantial supraterritorial features that were barely if at all evident before the middle of the twentieth century. Localities, countries and regions are by no means irrelevant in today's banking, securities, derivatives, and insurance industries: twenty-first century finance has not become purely global and non-territorial. However, many financial activities are now considerably global, including in ways that largely transcend territorial geography. As such, they also transcend the traditional scope of the territorial state and pose considerable challenges for effective governance.

Current Governance of Global Finance

Global finance is obviously not 'controlled', in the sense of being ruled by a sovereign world government on the model of a modern territorial state writ large. Nevertheless, these activities are subject to considerable if imperfect governance. Recent developments in the regulation of global finance largely conform to general trends in contemporary governance under the influence of globalization (cf. Scholte, 2000, ch. 6; Scholte, 2001). In other words, states remain key, but they have increasingly adopted strategies of multilateral management of transworld finance, through a host of interstate, transstate and suprastate mechanisms. In addition, substate actors have begun to figure in the regulation of global finance, albeit still marginally. Also, regulatory mechanisms based in private sector agencies have gained substantial significance in the governance of global finance. The following paragraphs elaborate on these features in turn.

States are still, on the whole, the primary actors in the governance of finance under conditions of contemporary globalization. Any examination of the regulation of global finance must therefore consider the activities of national central banks, national treasuries and ministries of finance, national securities and exchange commissions, and national insurance supervisors. In general states have more resources (staff, funds, technology and legitimacy) to regulate global finance than any other authorities.

Of course some states have figured more prominently and powerfully in the governance of global finance than others. Thus France and the USA have exercised far greater influence than Uzbekistan and Zambia. Indeed, limited capacity for financial regulation at national level has left many states in a weak position *vis-à-vis* global finance. The government of Bolivia has been little match for the eurobond market, and authorities in the Philippines have enjoyed little room for manoeuvre in relation to the IMF.

Yet even the best resourced states have not been able to tackle the governance of global finance alone. The intensely international, liberalized, universal and above all supraterritorial character of these flows has made it impossible for even the strongest states to handle global finance by themselves. Thus various networks of intergovernmental consultation and cooperation have developed in tandem with the accelerated globalization of finance during recent decades.

For example, central bank governors of the so-called Group of Ten (G10) advanced industrial countries have met regularly at Basel since 1962 to discuss monetary and financial matters of mutual concern. (The G10 actually encompasses eleven states: namely, Belgium, Canada, France, Germany, Italy, Japan, the Netherlands, Sweden, Switzerland, the UK and the USA.) An Intergovernmental Group of Twenty-Four on International Monetary Affairs (G24) was established in the early 1970s as a South-based counterpart to the G10, although it has made far less policy impact (Mayobre, 1999).

The Group of Seven (G7) summits, held annually since 1975, have also frequently discussed issues related to global finance (Hajnal, 1999; www.g7.utoronto.ca). The G7 comprises Canada, France, Germany, Italy, Japan, the UK and the USA. The European Union (previously European Community) has participated in these proceedings since 1977, and Russia was added in 1998 to form the G8. A separate G7 finance ministers' group was established in 1986 and normally meets three to four times per year. In September 1999 the G7 finance ministers created the Group of Twenty (G20) in order to include governments of so-called 'emerging markets' like Argentina, China and South Africa in structured discussions concerning global financial stability (www.g20.org/indexe.html).

Both the G10 and the G7 have from time to time set up working parties to explore specific issues related to global finance. The best-known example is the Basel Committee on Banking Supervision (BCBS), formed as a standing group of the G10 in 1975 (Dale, 1994; Kapstein, 1994, ch. 5; Norton, 1995). Most significantly, the BCBS has formulated the Basel Capital Accord, a framework first issued in 1988 for assessing the capital position of transborder banks, and Core Principles for Effective Banking Supervision, published in 1997. On a more specific problem, the G7 created the Financial Action Task Force (FATF) in 1989 to combat drug-related money laundering (Reinicke, 1998; www.oecd.org/fatf). More recently, the G7 has promoted the establishment of a Financial Stability Forum (FSF), first convened in April 1999. The FSF aims to enhance information exchange and cooperation among states in the supervision and surveillance of commercial financial institutions (www.fsforum.org).

As the existence of such working groups indicates, much intergovernmental collaboration on policy regarding global finance has occurred among civil servants rather than at a ministerial level. Indeed, the governance of global finance offers a prime example of transgovernmental networks, where civil servants from parallel agencies in multiple states develop close regulatory collaboration in a particular policy area (Slaughter, 2000). Other significant transstate links among financial technocrats have developed through the so-called Paris Club. Started in 1956 and maintaining a secretariat in the French Treasury since 1974, this informal group has convened from time to time to make some 350 rescheduling agreements for the bilateral debts of 77 countries (clubdeparis.org). Further transgovernmental groups of civil servants have met under the auspices of the Organization for Economic Cooperation and Development, for example, to formulate measures in respect of financial liberalization, offshore finance centres, taxation of transborder portfolio investments, and development assistance. The OECD has also housed the secretariat of the FATF. In respect of bond and stock markets more particularly, the International Organization of Securities Commissions (IOSCO) was created as an inter-American body in 1974, went global in 1983, and now involves nearly a hundred national securities authorities (Porter, 1993; Steil, 1994; www.iosco.org). In addition, the International Association of Insurance Supervisors (IAIS) was formed in 1994 and has quickly grown to link regulators in over a hundred countries (www.iaisweb.org). Since 1996 the BCBS, IAIS and IOSCO have convened a Joint Forum on Financial Conglomerates to promote cooperation between banking, securities, and insurance supervisors, given that global financial corporations increasingly operate across the three sectors.

As the work of the OECD, IOSCO and IAIS illustrates, intergovernmental collaboration in respect of global finance has been increasingly institutionalized in separate permanent bodies. These agencies might be characterized as 'suprastate' organs. That is, they correspond to regional and transworld jurisdictions that are larger and to some extent beyond the state. 'Suprastate' does not mean 'non-state', in the sense that the institutions in question have gained full independence from, and control over, their state members. However, like most organizations, suprastate bureaucracies and the rules they produce have acquired some initiative and power of their own, particularly in respect of weaker states.

The oldest major suprastate agency for governance of global finance, the Bank for International Settlements, dates back to 1930, but it has become especially active in recent decades. The voting membership of the BIS has increased to 45 national central banks, and the institution has other dealings with several score more. The BIS undertakes major research work and convenes several influential working groups, including the Committee on the Global Financial System and the Committee on Payment and Settlement Systems. The organization also houses secretariats for the BCBS, the IAIS and the FSF. With this proliferation of activities, the staff of the BIS has grown to exceed 500 (www.bis.org).

The IMF has undergone even more striking expansion in conjunction with the globalization of finance. In addition to its previously mentioned increases in membership and quota subscriptions, its staff numbers have quadrupled from 750 in 1966 to 3,082 in 1999 (IMF, 1966, p. 133; IMF, 2000, p. 95). The Fund took a leading role in the management (some say mismanagement) of the Third World debt crisis in the 1980s and the emerging market financial crises of the 1990s. More generally, IMF surveillance of its members' macroeconomic situations has expanded since 1997 to include assessments of the financial sector. In several countries the Fund has taken a substantial role in restructuring the finance industry after a crisis. Since 1996 the IMF has promoted data standards that aim to make information on and for financial markets more reliable and accessible (http://dsbb.imf.org). Recently the Fund's International Monetary and Financial Committee (formerly called the Interim Committee) has served as an important forum for intergovernmental consultations regarding the so-called 'global financial architecture', drawing on discussions in the FSF and the G20.

The IMF's Bretton Woods twin, the World Bank, has played a less prominent role in the governance of global finance (as opposed to lending activity itself). The Bank's main intervention in respect of regulatory frameworks has involved loans and technical assistance for financial sector development in various countries of the South and the East. In recent years the Bank's policies in this area have focused on sector restructuring with programmes of privatization and legal reform.

Several other permanent multilateral agencies have also served as forums for intergovernmental discussion of global financial issues. The OECD has done so through its Economic Policy Committee and Working Party Three of that body, which between them meet six times per year. Within the United Nations system the General Assembly, the Economic and Social Council, the regional economic and social commissions, the Department of Economic Affairs, the United Nations Conference on Trade and Development (UNCTAD), the United Nations Development Programme (UNDP) and the United Nations Children's Fund (UNICEF) have all addressed issues of global financial governance. However, UN intergovernmental forums have adopted mainly hortatory resolutions in this area, as opposed to formulating and implementing specific regulatory measures. The Financing for Development (FfD) Initiative at the United Nations, launched in late 1997 and culminating in a global conference in March 2002, has attempted to integrate wider economic and social concerns into the governance of global finance (Herman, 2002; www.un.org/esa/ffd).

Some further suprastate governance of global finance has emerged in recent years through the WTO. The Uruguay Round of intergovernmental trade talks (1986–94) produced the GATS, which extended multilateral liberalization of international commerce *inter alia* to finance (Underhill, 1993). Since 1995 a WTO Committee on Financial Services has overseen the operation of GATS in respect of finance. In 2000 the WTO launched further multilateral negotiations on trade in services, including in the financial area.

Contemporary globalization has often encouraged a rise of substate as well as suprastate competences in governance; however, devolution has been less apparent in respect of finance than in other areas of regulation. True, various provincial and municipal governments have turned to global sources like the eurobond market for credits. However, these substate authorities have rarely participated in the regulation of global finance. A few exceptions might be noted, such as the inclusion of agencies from two Canadian provinces as Associate Members of IOSCO and the membership of bureaux from Hong Kong, Labuan, New South Wales and Ontario in the IAIS. However, for the moment official governance of global finance remains almost entirely in state and suprastate hands.

On the other hand, the financial sector presents an outstanding example of another major trend in contemporary governance, namely, the turn to non-official mechanisms of regulation (cf. Cutler, Haufler and Porter, 1999; Ronit and Schneider, 2000). A number of national securities and exchange commissions have lain in the private sector for some time, of course, and IOSCO also includes over fifty securities exchanges and dealers associations as Affiliate Members. Meanwhile several industry associations have promoted the transworld harmonization of standards and devised a number of self-regulatory instruments for bond and equity business in global financial markets. These bodies include the International Council of Securities Associations (ICSA), the World Federation of Exchanges (known by the French acronym FIBV), the International Primary Market Association (IPMA), and the International Securities Market Association (ISMA). The ISMA indeed describes its task as 'regulation by the market, for the market' (www.isma.org/about1.html). In addition, bond-rating agencies like Moody's Investors Service and Standard & Poor's – and the financial markets whose sentiments they reflect – have come to exercise considerable disciplining authority over many national governments (Sinclair, 1994; Friedman, 1999, pp. 32–3, 91–2).

Private sector inputs to the governance of global finance have also figured outside the securities area. For example, non-governmental groups like the Group of Thirty (composed of economists and businesspeople) and the Derivatives Policy Group (with members drawn from major investment banks) have taken a lead in developing rules for derivatives markets (G30, 1993; DPC, 1995). Two other private sector bodies, the International Accounting Standards Committee (IASC) and the International Federation of Accountants (IFAC), have devised the main accountancy and auditing norms currently in use for global business. Since 1999 the IAIS has welcomed insurance industry associations, companies and consultants as observer members, now numbering over sixty.

In sum, then, current governance of global finance is both multilayered and dispersed. It involves complex networks of state, suprastate, substate, and private sector actors. As such, developments in respect of global finance conform to the broad patterns of post-statist governance in the context of large-scale globalization.

Key Issues for the Governance of Global Finance

Not only is the governance of global finance complex, but it has also been particularly challenged to meet goals of efficiency, stability, social justice, ecological integrity and democracy. Almost no one argues that current regulatory arrangements for transborder finance are satisfactory, although the diagnoses of problems and the prescriptions of solutions vary widely. The next paragraphs assess measures taken to date towards these five objectives and remaining shortcomings. Possible responses to these flaws are considered in the final section of this chapter.

Among efficiency problems, many observers have worried that global finance currently functions with substantial data deficits. Indeed, missing data, rumour and harmful manipulations of information have often hampered the operation of transborder financial markets. Requirements for greater publication of financial company information and data dissemination efforts by the IMF have attempted to improve this situation, but ill-informed panics and herd behaviour persist, frequently with destructive consequences. Moreover, the IMF programme only gathers country-based data, and participation is voluntary. Nor is it evident that the information collected there is widely and effectively used. Meanwhile, no mechanisms for complaint and compensation exist when, for example, faulty analysis by credit-rating agencies damages the financial position of governments and corporations.

Limited competition has presented another major efficiency problem for the current governance of global finance. According to conventional economic theory, liberalization should promote a more optimal allocation of world financial resources; however, the theory also presumes conditions of open and equal competition among a multiplicity of actual and prospective market participants. Yet in practice contemporary global finance has seen a progressively smaller number of corporate conglomerates come to dominate the banking, securities, and insurance industries: both within countries and in global markets. Neither national governments nor multilateral arrangements have done anything of note to check this trend towards concentration and monopoly, which raises various issues of excess profits, reduced incentives to innovation, and consumer protection.

A further efficiency problem in global finance that present governance arrangements have largely ignored is the increased divorce of finance from the 'real economy'. Savings and investment are meant to stimulate economic activities that promote human welfare, for example, by creating employment and increasing stocks of goods and services. Yet much contemporary global finance is mainly self-referential, where finance becomes an end in its own right rather than a means to general material betterment. Thus, for example, most foreign exchange business does not relate to 'real' trade, and most financial derivatives relate at best only indirectly to 'real' production. No regulations of note are in place to discourage financial behaviour that does not serve – and indeed may detract from – the 'real' economy.

The multifaceted character of governance arrangements for global finance, as described above, raises additional efficiency concerns. In various cases several forums address the same problems, and do so in a loosely coordinated and fairly ad hoc fashion. In recent years some multilateral agencies have undertaken greater efforts at communication and coordination: for instance, between the IMF and the World Bank; between the Bretton Woods institutions and the rest of the UN system; and in the previously mentioned Joint Forum on Financial Conglomerates. However, little serious consideration has been given to a rationalization of governance through a curtailment of some agencies or a merger of certain bodies, for example, into a World Financial Authority.

In respect of stability, many commentators have argued that current global financial markets are inordinately volatile, creating insecurities that range well beyond normal investor risk to damage livelihoods of the public at large. Some of these harmful instabilities have arisen from large and rapid speculative swings in foreign exchange values (as occurred, for example, in the European exchange rate mechanism in 1992). Other excessive volatility has come from enormous and swift withdrawals of transborder investments, especially short-term credits (as in the crises in Asia, Latin America and Russia during the late 1990s). In addition, many securities markets have since the late 1980s experienced wildly unstable courses of steep climbs and precipitous downturns. The global derivatives business, too, has suffered a series of debacles: as in the Metall Gesellschaft and Orange County affairs in 1994; Barings in 1995; Sumitomo in 1996; and Long Term Capital Management in 1998.

As noted earlier, many public and private governance initiatives have sought to reduce instability in global finance to acceptable levels: G7 consultations, the BCBS, the FSF, the G20, the ISMA, the DPG, and so on. However, we remain far short of a global central bank, a global securities and exchange commission, a global derivatives supervisor, or other such bodies with effective powers of intervention and sanction. Likewise, authorities have so far rejected the introduction of charges (like the so-called Tobin tax on foreign exchange business) that could discourage excessive speculation. (For more on the Tobin tax, see Patomaki, 2001.) Most market players and many policy-makers have argued that more interventionist measures of this kind are impracticable and undesirable; yet financial companies have usually not been shy to call for help from regulatory quarters when instability has come at their expense, and it cannot be said that a global public policy for finance has really been tried.

This tendency to cater regulation of global finance mainly to commercial interests also raises questions of social equity. For one thing, current governance arrangements for global finance have often sustained or even widened arbitrary inequalities of opportunity in the world economy between Northern and Southern countries. Prevailing frameworks have on the whole given people living in the North far better access to and far more benefits from global financial flows than people resident in the South. Moreover, it is now almost universally acknowledged that onerous transborder debt burdens have substantially hampered the development potentials of poor countries. Paris Club rescheduling, the cancellation of a few bilateral debts, and the IMF/World Bank programme of relief for Heavily Indebted Poor Countries (HIPCs) have arguably only begun to address the debt problem. More broadly, the previously mentioned FfD initiative of the United Nations aims to make finance work for development in the South rather than – as has often seemed to be the case – the other way around. However, at the time of this writing the impact of FfD is – to put it charitably – uncertain.

Meanwhile, current rules of global finance have exacerbated injustice between income groups through so-called 'offshore' centres (cf. Hampton and Abbott, 1999). Around sixty jurisdictions across the world (including Bahrain, the Cayman Islands, Jersey and Singapore) now offer low taxation and high confidentiality that are mainly geared to what are euphemistically termed 'high net-worth individuals' (hinwis). Offshore banks now hold an estimated $5 trillion in deposits that escape normal regimes of taxation and regulation (www.transnationale.org/anglais/association/bulletin_modif.asp). The FATF has explored ways to halt criminal money laundering through offshore finance, and the OECD Committee on Fiscal Affairs has since 1998 undertaken some initial steps to combat tax evasion in these centres. However, few concrete measures have yet curtailed what has in effect been a global subsidy to wealthy people, with no efficiency justification.

More generally, too, the gains of participation in global financial markets have flowed disproportionately to those who already control the greatest resources. Income gains from foreign exchange trading, eurobonds, hedge funds and the like have largely gone to small circles of wealthy investors and their brokers. Proposals to impose redistributive taxes on such transactions have so far got nowhere, at a time when regressive value-added taxes on the transactions of everyday life have proliferated across the world. True, unprecedented numbers of ordinary working people now participate in global finance through pension funds; however, a vast majority of the world's people still do not invest in global financial markets in any way.

One promising market-generated regulatory mechanism for greater social justice has appeared in recent years with the rise of so-called 'socially responsible investment' (SRI). These 'ethical' funds guarantee that monies will only be placed in businesses that respect core labour conventions and human rights. However, to date use of SRI schemes remains comparatively small, all the more so in the absence of special taxation or other measures to promote this alternative model of investment.

As for gender equity, feminist critiques have highlighted limited access for women to global credit markets relative to men. In addition, women have occupied few management positions in global finance. Women have also suffered disproportionate hardships in the economic crises that have been induced (at least partly) by global finance. (Evidence for these and other uneven gender consequences is summarized in Staveren, 2002.) Countervailing measures like women-centred micro-credit schemes, while welcome, have done little to address the deeper structural gender inequalities that have marked contemporary global finance.

Relatively little research has explored the relationship between global finance and ecological integrity, but various indications suggest that the environmental consequences can be negative (Durbin and Welch, 2002). For example, a number of governments have condoned ecological damage as they struggle to repay transborder debts or meet the conditions of structural adjustment loans (Reed, 1996). Following concerted campaigns from civil society groups, the World Bank has since the 1990s instituted environmental impact assessments for its development projects. However, few commercial bankers, brokers or investors have stopped to consider the repercussions of their global financial activities for climate change, biological diversity, toxic waste production, and other ecological degradation. Recent years have seen the inauguration of some environmentally sensitive investment instruments, often as part of SRI initiatives, but as yet these programmes account for but a miniscule fraction of global financial activities (Bouma, Jeucken and Klinkers, 2001).

In respect of democracy, considerable unease has developed that current arrangements governing global finance are insufficiently participatory and publicly accountable. For one thing, most states have been excluded from the G7, the G10, the G20, the OECD, and transstate networks of national officials. At the same time weighted votes have in effect given a handful of states a collective veto in the Bretton Woods institutions. Most of the world's people have therefore been only marginally, if at all, represented by their states in the governance of global finance.

In all countries, democratically elected bodies like parliaments and local councils have had little direct involvement in, or exercised much supervision over, the transstate networks, suprastate institutions and private regimes that have largely governed global finance. National legislatures in France, Ireland and the USA have taken a few initiatives to influence policy at the Bretton Woods institutions, but these exceptions prove the rule of parliamentary passivity in respect of global finance. Nor have suprastate and private regulatory bodies like the BIS and the ISMA acquired any democratically representative organs of their own. Apart from a poll in 1992 on Switzerland's membership of the IMF and the World Bank, states have not conducted popular referendums on questions of global finance either.

Indeed, largely unaccountable technocrats hold sway over global finance to an extent found in few other areas of contemporary governance. Central bankers, finance ministry officials, and staffers in suprastate financial institutions have tended to live in a regulatory world largely of their own. These civil servants have usually emerged from similar educational backgrounds, use a specialist language that is poorly accessible to most outsiders, and often spend their entire careers circulating within the limited circle of financial agencies, rarely experiencing other sectors of governance. These circumstances have (mostly inadvertently) encouraged narrow visions, a culture of secrecy, and considerable immunity from democratic scrutiny in much regulation of global finance.

True, several suprastate institutions involved in the regulation of global finance have in recent years become more publicly transparent. In particular, the Bretton Woods institutions and the WTO have published many more internal documents and details of their decision-taking procedures, including on extensive and continuously updated websites. Also, in recent years the World Bank and, to a lesser extent, the IMF have consulted civil society organizations as a direct way to gauge public views of their policies. The two bodies have also implemented independent evaluation mechanisms that increase their public accountability, albeit not sufficiently in the eyes of some critics. Meanwhile, other suprastate financial institutions have done far less to improve their transparency and accountability, and transstate networks and private regimes in the governance of global finance remain more or less completely divorced from public participation and public accountability.

Indeed, the vast majority of citizens across the world have scarce if any awareness of the rules and regulatory institutions that govern global finance. Few governments, mass media organs or schools have taken initiatives of public education to improve this sorry situation. Likewise, limited efforts by civil society groups to inform citizens about global finance have generally not reached large circles. Even academic textbooks on globalization often omit a chapter on the governance of global finance.

Mounting concerns about these various challenges to efficiency, stability, ecological sustainability, social justice and democracy have generated much discussion in recent years about change in the so-called 'global financial architecture'. In official circles, the G7, the G20, the FSF, the IMF and the OECD have all put the question of reform prominently on their agendas. At the same time, academic researchers have published numerous studies to diagnose the problems and prescribe solutions. (For examples of these analyses from different theoretical and ideological perspectives, see Bond and Bullard, 1999; Eichengreen, 1999; Eatwell and Taylor, 2000.) Meanwhile citizens have mobilized in larger numbers than ever concerning questions of global finance. One outstanding instance of this recent civic activism has been the transborder campaign for debt relief of poor countries. Another striking example has been the ATTAC movement for greater global public regulation of financial markets. ATTAC started in 1998 and now encompasses some tens of thousands of members in around thirty countries (www.attac.org). With all this agitation, it is likely that the coming years will bring change in the governance of global finance; however, the extent, speed and direction of reconstruction remain to be determined.

Theoretical Frameworks

Before reflecting on future trends, though, we do well to pause and relate the above discussion of current governance of global finance to the theories presented elsewhere in this book. All too often, theoretical and empirical treatments of global governance issues develop separately, without systematic interconnections. Yet neither conceptual nor substantive research has much merit in isolation from the other.

The account given above suggests that the governance of global finance is not well understood by rigidly applying a single theory from the conventional menu. Each approach explored in other chapters (as well as other theories like constructivism, poststructuralism and eco-centrism that have been omitted) offers substantial insights. Otherwise people of sharp mind and good will would not have devoted so much energy to developing and defending these perspectives. On the other hand, all of these frameworks tend to oversimplify the messiness of actual global social practices and thereby neglect other significant forces at play. Arguably a multifaceted understanding and multicausal explanation offer a fuller (if less easily managed) knowledge of global finance and its regulation.

To look at various available theories, realist conceptions of international relations have the merit of highlighting the importance of states and struggles for state power in the governance of global finance. As emphasized earlier, recent accelerated globalization has not dislodged states from a central position in the regulation of transborder finance. States continue to figure importantly in several ways: as unilateral actors; as participants in multilateral networks; and as members of suprastate institutions. Moreover, states show no sign of transferring all of their regulatory roles regarding money and investment to other actors. Realist theory also rightly highlights the competitive character of much interstate activity in the regulation of global finance. The G7 and its policies, the ascendancy of the Bretton Woods institutions over other parts of the UN system, and membership in (and exclusion from) the OECD are all in good part assertions of state power.

On the other hand, the realist premise that states are the *only* veritable actors in world politics is clearly flawed when it comes to the regulation of global finance. True, the existence of suprastate institutions and private governance mechanisms depends in part on state endorsement; however, these arrangements do not operate under the close, constant and complete control of states. Indeed, states often depend on the BIS and Moody's as well as vice versa. In addition, the notion that the logic of governing global finance boils down to nothing more than interstate competition is oversimplistic. Other theories are right to note the concurrent and sometimes greater relevance of interstate cooperation, technological developments, capitalism, gender relations and more.

Functionalist international relations theory also has some applicability to the governance of global finance, *inter alia* by addressing the interstate cooperation that realism neglects. Also in conformity with functionalist ideas, technological innovations (especially in telecommunications and data processing) have figured significantly in enabling recent large-scale growth of foreign exchange dealing as well as transborder banking, securities, derivatives and insurance businesses. As functionalism suggests, these developments have generated needs for rules to bring order and predictability: that is, to stabilize exchange rates, to limit banking crises, to prevent derivatives debacles, etc. The emergence of rules has in turn encouraged the construction of permanent institutions like the IMF and the IAIS that can effectively formulate, monitor and administer regulatory frameworks for global finance. To this extent the contemporary history of global financial governance has followed the functionalist dictum that 'form follows function'.

On the other hand, functionalism fails to consider that function has also followed form in the regulation of global finance. We saw earlier that certain rules and institutions (like various types of liberalization and the IMF) have played a central role in *enabling* the globalization of finance. In other words, governance has not always come afterwards, but has been part and parcel of the process from the start. The relevance of functionalism is also limited in so far as the theory concentrates on the development of permanent suprastate institutions; yet much contemporary regulation of global finance has taken shape in multilateral conferences, transstate networks and private governance mechanisms. In addition, functionalist explanations are insufficient in saying nothing about the deeper social forces that have propelled technological change and the construction of rules and institutions in global finance. Furthermore, functionalism only addresses the efficiency and stability dimensions of effective governance; it offers no guidance on criteria of social justice, ecological integrity and democracy. Indeed, functionalism altogether overlooks questions of power and conflict, when in practice the governance of global finance is riven with hierarchy and competition as well as cooperation.

Liberal institutionalism avoids some of these flaws of functionalism: for example, by addressing the complex mix of interstate cooperation and conflict; and by considering transgovernmental as well as suprastate sites of regulation. True, liberal institutionalist writings have to date given little attention to private governance arrangements, but the theory could in principle accommodate these mechanisms inasmuch as it recognizes the significance of non-state actors. Moreover, liberal institutionalist concepts of 'regimes' correspond to the currently prevailing situation in the governance of global finance, where a number of multilateral rules and institutions have acquired some life of their own, separate from the states that originally created them.

For the rest, however, liberal institutionalism suffers from many of the same shortcomings as functionalism in relation to the regulation of global finance. Liberal institutionalism has a limited account of causality: we cannot explain the globalization of finance in terms of market forces, technological change and regimes alone, without asking questions about the deeper social conditions that yield those circumstances. In a similar vein, liberal institutionalism omits many key questions about power in the governance of global finance. There is more to power in global finance than the relative influences of actors: that is, the various states, firms and international institutions. Liberal institutionalism neglects embedded hierarchies of power between North and South, between classes, between faiths, between races, between sexes and so on. These structures also substantially determine the character of the arrangements that govern global finance. With its severely limited account of power, liberal institutionalism is poorly equipped to address questions of social equity and democracy in the regulation of global finance. Similarly, liberal institutionalism can only address environmental degradation as a market failure, without examining the deeper social conditions that might undermine ecological integrity.

Like functionalism and liberal institutionalism, radical theories are helpful in understanding the governance of global finance inasmuch as they avoid realist flaws of neglecting non-state actors and interstate cooperation. In addition, radicalism avoids functionalist and liberal institutionalist failures to examine deeper causality and structural power. Thus Marxist accounts highlight the centrality of capitalism as an underlying force that has generated the globalization of finance and shaped the way that this development has been governed. Much of what has transpired in global finance has indeed conformed to a logic of surplus accumulation. Moreover, traditional Marxist concepts of class and neo-Marxist notions of core–periphery relations highlight key configurations of power that have significantly shaped developments in the governance of global finance. At the same time these concepts identify certain key forces that militate against social justice and democracy in the regulation of global banking, securities, etc.

Yet these radical theories have their limitations, too. For one thing, Marxist analyses often incline towards a methodological structuralism that neglects the importance of the particular features and internal dynamics of institutions and other actors. In addition, radical theories hold a narrow conception of social structure that tends to reduce all political economy to a function of capitalism. Arguably structures of knowledge (as highlighted by poststructuralist theories) and structures of the state system (as highlighted by neo-realist and some historical-sociological theories) have also had an important bearing on the governance of global finance. Likewise, we can question whether class and core–periphery configurations always hold primacy in global finance over hierarchies on gender, nationality, race, urban/rural and other lines. Class does not explain why women and people of colour have met systemic barriers in accessing global finance. Nor do traditional Marxist theories offer much guidance on improving efficiency and stability in global finance; nor do these approaches provide much insight into ecological aspects of global finance, except to say the obvious that strivings for surplus accumulation tend to override environmental considerations. Finally, radical theories have to date proved better at diagnosing shortcomings in the governance of global finance than at specifying desirable changes and the means to achieve them.

Feminist thought provides a helpful antidote to the gender-blindness of most theory on global governance. As noted earlier, social constructions of femininity and masculinity have shaped the regulation of global finance in various ways. Indeed, feminism can alert us to the predominance of masculine behaviour in the financial sector, for example, in terms of aggressive competition, means–ends rationality, drives to subordinate nature, and an unwillingness to entrust women with positions of power. In turn, these and other manifestations of masculinism could help to explain why current rules of global finance tend to encourage the dominance of technical expertise, environmental degradation and gender inequality in this sector.

However, it would seem inadequate to analyse the governance of global finance in terms of gender relations alone. Like neo-realism and Marxism, feminist theory is limited inasmuch as it focuses narrowly on one structure of world politics, important though that structure might be. The dominance of masculinity over femininity is not the only force shaping the character of rules and the operation of regulatory institutions in global finance. Feminism provides an important corrective to the oversights of other theories, but most gender-sensitive researchers prefer to integrate feminist concepts with insights from other theories.

As for the theoretical framework of cosmopolitanism discussed in part III, it has the decided strength of placing normative questions of social equity and democracy to the fore. Cosmopolitan issues of the community of humanity, world citizenship, the avoidance of serious harm and the amelioration of urgent need are most certainly implicated in principle in the governance of global finance. However, as David Held notes in his chapter, to date cosmopolitan inspirations have figured at best secondarily in the construction of global economic governance. Certain leaders of suprastate finan-cial institutions like Michel Camdessus at the IMF and Robert McNamara and James Wolfensohn at the World Bank have amply invoked cosmopolitan-like language, but these principles have been far from comprehensively embedded in the constitu-tional instruments and everyday practices of the agencies. To this extent cosmo-politanism is more an exhortation for the future than an explanation of the past in the governance of global finance. To become a politically practicable proposition, the theory would need to take more account of cultural diversity, national allegiances, state power and capitalist interests than its proponents have tended thus far to do.

And so this discussion of theory could continue. As mentioned at the start of this section, the range of theories available for studies of global finance and its governance extends beyond the frameworks of analysis addressed in this book. Thus, for example, eco-centric social theory could reveal more about the environmental dimensions of global governance in the area of finance. In addition, constructivist and poststructuralist theories of world politics could identify some of the ways that ideational forces like modes of communication and structures of knowledge operate in respect of the regulation of global finance. From another angle, historical sociology in the vein of theorists like Anthony Giddens and Michael Mann might suggest ways that the governance of global finance could be understood as an interplay of actors with multiple (sometimes complementary and sometimes opposing) structural forces (Giddens, 1985; Mann, 1986, ch. 1).

In short, no single or simple theoretical formula is available to make full sense of the governance of global finance (or any other aspect of globality for that matter). Most analysts adopt a perspective that highlights few variables, on the argument that parsimony makes for more readily practicable research and policy. Others like the present author prefer an approach that tries to handle greater complexity in terms of the interplay of multiple social forces (cf. Scholte, 2000, ch. 4). Whatever methodology one adopts, however, choices of theory reflect the analyst's personal background, socio-cultural and historical position, and (implicit or explicit) political commitments.

Conclusion: Future Challenges

This chapter has described the globalization of finance, the arrangements made to govern these activities, the achievements and limitations of these regulations, and the different theories that elucidate (parts of) these developments. All of this brings us to policy prescription: what, in the light of the preceding empirical and theoretical discussion, should be done for the future governance of global finance? Full con-sideration of these issues goes beyond the scope of this chapter, but a few pointers may be given.

Prescriptions for the future governance of global finance depend on one's assess-ment of the severity of current problems and the practicability of various responses. As said earlier, pretty well every observer agrees that change is needed. However, analysts interpret the 'global financial architecture' metaphor differently. For their part, modest reformers want only to upgrade the wiring and plumbing. More ambi-tious reformers want to break down various walls and reconstruct the interior of the building. Radicals want to create an altogether new building on different foundations.

Modest reformers do not in fact aim for a new global financial 'architecture'. Their eyes are set on a limited renovation of existing arrangements. In this vein, for example, such commentators have suggested that governments should take greater care in liberalizing the capital account. In addition, they suggest that debt relief for poor countries could be larger, faster and/or less conditional. Likewise, modest reformers variously promote further initiatives on money laundering, micro-credits for women, transparency, and parliamentary oversight of financial regulators. On this analysis, the global financial architecture can be fixed with limited repairs.

More ambitious reformers argue that modest changes will not suffice to address the shortfalls in efficiency, stability, ecological integrity, social justice and democracy that mark existing governance arrangements in global finance. These advocates look for major new regulatory initiatives in the vein of a global public policy for finance. Such innovations might include the aforementioned Tobin tax on foreign exchange transactions, as a way to reduce speculation and raise funds for poverty alleviation and other human development purposes. Other possible ambitious reforms include the abolition of offshore finance arrangements; new voting mechanisms in suprastate financial institutions; a code of conduct to govern transgovernmental networks of finance officials; assembly and publication of gender statistics regarding all aspects of global finance; measures to make ethical investment the rule rather than the exception; a global bankruptcy procedure for governments that cannot meet their obligations on transborder loans; a global competition office to monitor and where necessary counteract concentration in financial markets; a world financial authority; and fully fledged formal complaints mechanisms for the public regarding the effects of suprastate financial policies.

A third general alternative is the still more radical prescription of a full-scale social revolution to alter the basic character of governance of global finance (and the rest of society). Such a transformation could turn back the historical clock with deglobalization and a return to statist governance. Or a fundamental reconstruction could transcend the capitalist mode of production or make some other such comprehensive change to a new world order of some as yet hazy nature. However, given the scale of contemporary forces behind increasing globality, proposals for a return to a statist and territorialist world of finance seem quite impracticable. Likewise, a full-scale transcendence of primary social structures like capitalism and rationalism seems unlikely in the short or medium term.

If this diagnosis is correct, then progressive politics would do best to pursue a strategy of ambitious reform. Achievement of such a programme would require large-scale active political mobilization with substantial levels of cosmopolitan vision. Happily, developments like the debt campaign and the ATTAC movement suggest that sizeable public constituencies for major reform of global finance do exist. Nevertheless, proposals for public policies that seek deliberately to harness transborder financial markets to a human development agenda face substantial resistance from large sectors of established commercial and official interests, particularly in the G7 countries. Moreover, when it comes to taking challenging and visionary decisions to remould globalization in finance or other sectors, most politicians today are afflicted with the NIMTO syndrome ('not in my term of office'). In these circumstances it will – as in any political struggle – require concerted efforts to realize the potentials for large-scale and lasting progressive change.

References

BIS (1998) *68th Annual Report*, Basel: Bank for International Settlements.

BIS (2001a) 'Central Bank survey of foreign exchange and derivatives market activity in April 2001: preliminary global data', Bank for International Settlements press release, 9 Oct.

BIS (2001b) 'The global OTC derivatives market at end-June 2001', Bank for International Settlements press release, 20 Dec.

BIS (2001c) *Quarterly Review, December 2001*, Basel: Bank for International Settlements.

BIS (2001d) *71st Annual Report*, Basel: Bank for International Settlements.

Bond, P. and Bullard, N. (1999) *Their Reform and Ours: The Balance of Forces and Economic Analysis that Inform a New Global Financial Architecture*, Bangkok: Chulalongkorn University Press.

Bouma, J. J., Jeucken, M. and Klinkers, L. (eds) (2001) *Sustainable Banking: The Greening of Finance*, Sheffield: Greenleaf/Deloitte and Touche.

Bryant, R. C. (2002) *Turbulent Waters: Cross-Border Finance and International Governance*, Washington DC: Brookings Institution.

Cutler, A. C., Haufler, V. and Porter, T. (eds) (1999) *Private Authority in International Affairs*, Albany: State University of New York Press.

Dale, R. (1994) 'International banking regulation', in B. Steil (ed.), *International Financial Market Regulation*, Chichester: Wiley.

DPC (1995) *A Framework for Voluntary Oversight of the OTC Derivatives Activities of Securities Firm Activities to Promote Confidence and Stability in Financial Markets*, Washington DC: Derivatives Policy Group.

Durbin, A. and Welch, C. (2002) 'The environmental movement and global finance', in J. A. Scholte with A. Schnabel (eds), *Civil Society and Global Finance*, London: Routledge.

Eatwell, J. and Taylor, L. (2000) *Global Finance at Risk: The Case for International Regulation*, Cambridge: Polity.

Eichengreen, B. (1999) *Toward a New International Financial Architecture: A Practical Post-Asia Agenda*, Washington DC: Institute for International Economics.

Euroclear (2000) '1999: another record year as Euroclear market share shows marked increase', Euroclear press release, 16 Feb.

Friedman, T. (1999) *The Lexus and the Olive Tree*, London: HarperCollins.

G30 (1993) *Derivatives: Practices and Principles*, Washington DC: Group of Thirty.

Giddens, A. (1985) *The Nation-State and Violence,* Cambridge: Polity.

Gilpin, R. (2000) *The Challenge of Global Capitalism*, Princeton: Princeton University Press.

Hajnal, P. I. (1999) *The G7/G8 System: Evolution, Role and Documentation*, Aldershot: Ashgate.

Hampton, M. P. and Abbott, J. P. (eds) (1999) *Offshore Finance Centres and Tax Havens: The Rise of Global Capital*, Basingstoke: Macmillan.

Held, D., McGrew, A., Goldblatt, D. and Perraton, J. (1999) *Global Transformations: Politics, Economics and Culture*, Cambridge: Polity.

Herman, B. (2002) 'Civil society and the financing for development initiative at the United Nations', in J. A. Scholte with A. Schnabel (eds), *Civil Society and Global Finance*, London: Routledge.

IMF (1966) *Annual Report 1966*, Washington DC: International Monetary Fund.

IMF (1993) *International Financial Statistics Yearbook*, Washington DC: International Monetary Fund.

IMF (2000) *Annual Report 2000*, Washington DC: International Monetary Fund.

Kapstein, E. B. (1994) *Governing the Global Economy: International Finance and the State*, Cambridge, Mass.: Harvard University Press.

Kerr, I. M. (1984) *A History of the Eurobond Market: The First 21 Years*, London: Euromoney.

Kirdar, U. (1992) 'Issues and questions', in U. Kirdar (ed.), *Change: Threat or Opportunity for Human Progress, Volume 3: Globalization of Markets*, New York: United Nations.

Mann, M. (1986) *The Sources of Social Power, Volume 1: A History of Power from the Beginning to AD 1760*, Cambridge: Cambridge University Press.

Mayobre, E. (ed.) (1999) *G-24: The Developing Countries in the International Financial System*, Boulder, Colo.: Rienner.

Norton, J. J. (1995) *Devising International Bank Supervisory Standards*, London: Graham and Trotman.

OECD (1996) *International Capital Market Statistics 1950–1995*, Paris: Organization for Economic Cooperation and Development.

Patomaki, H. (2001) *Democratising Globalisation: The Leverage of the Tobin Tax*, London: Zed.

Porter, T. (1993) *States, Markets and Regimes in Global Finance*, Basingstoke: Macmillan.

Reed, D. (ed.) (1996) *Structural Adjustment, the Environment and Sustainable Development*, London: Earthscan.

Reinicke, W. H. (1998) *Global Public Policy: Governing without Government?* Washington DC: Brookings Institution.

Ronit, K. and Schneider, V. (eds) (2000) *Private Organisations in Global Politics*, London: Routledge.

Scholte, J. A. (2000) *Globalization: A Critical Introduction*, Basingstoke: Palgrave.

Scholte, J. A. (2001) 'The globalization of world politics', in J. Baylis and S. Smith (eds), *The Globalization of World Politics: An Introduction to International Relations*, Oxford: Oxford University Press.

Sinclair, T. J. (1994) 'Passing judgement: credit rating processes as regulatory mechanisms of governance in the emerging world order', *Review of International Political Economy*, 1, pp. 133–59.

Slaughter, A. M. (2000) 'Governing the global economy through government networks', in M. Byers (ed.), *The Role of Law in International Politics: Essays in International Relations and International Law*, Oxford: Oxford University Press.

Staveren, I. van (2002) 'Gender and global finance', in J. A. Scholte with A. Schnabel (eds), *Civil Society and Global Finance*, London: Routledge.

Steil, B. (1994) 'International securities markets regulation', in B. Steil (ed.), *International Financial Market Regulation*, Chichester: Wiley.

Underhill, G. R. D. (1993) 'Negotiating financial openness: the Uruguay Round and trade in financial services', in P. G. Cerny (ed.), *Finance and World Politics: Markets, Regimes and States in the Post-Hegemonic Era*, Aldershot: Elgar.

UNDP (UN Development Programme) (2001) *Human Development Report 2001*, New York: Oxford University Press.

10
Maintaining Peace and Security
Michael Pugh

Introduction

The 'maintenance of peace and security' – in the phraseology of the UN Charter – is an aspect of global governance that refers to ad hoc multinational responses to breakdown in parts of the international system. Such operations have been frequent (thirty-nine new missions were launched by the UN alone in the 1988–99 period), and they have been underpinned by political and administrative processes and structures. It will be argued here that, in spite of their improvised character, 'peacekeeping', 'peace support operations' and related 'humanitarian' relief missions have become institutionalized and structurally embedded in the system. They have also been agents for maintaining it.

The paucity of theoretical debate about them belies their significance as elements in sustaining a particular representation of the norms of global governance. Yet international relations theorists have paid little attention to how and why this is constructed, and students of these activities have tended to assume, rather than contest, the relevance of the foundational theoretical frameworks of liberal internationalism and realism. This is not to deny the importance of conceptual work and debates on, for example: a new generation of 'peacekeeping' (Mackinlay and Chopra, 1992); emancipatory theories and conflict resolution (Galtung, 1976; Fetherston, 1994, 2000); and 'peacekeepers' and sovereignty (James, 1995). But much of the focus has been on the diplomatic politics and techniques of peacekeeping, lessons learned from operations, and prescriptive analysis for improving performance in these areas (see, for instance, Durch, 1997).

Studies informed by neo-Marxism (Chandler, 1999, 2001), utopian realism (Kinloch, 1997), critical theory (Pugh, 2001b), cosmopolitanism (Williams, 1999) and constructivism (Paris, 2001) have been relatively few. Given the actual and potential role of individuals and functional organizations to contribute to such activities in a non-statist framework this gap is perhaps surprising. The contention here is that although post-foundational theories are applicable in this research area, 'peacekeeping' and humanitarian missions have moved in from the periphery of world politics to reflect and legitimize the neoliberal values, statism and economic structure of the international system.

As the field is littered with disputed labels, it is appropriate to examine some of the key terms. The traditional term 'peacekeeping' had a generally accepted definition: a multinational force, sometimes with a civilian element, mandated to administer, monitor or patrol in conflict areas in a neutral and impartial way, usually with the consent of the parties to a dispute. UN management was not essential, as the Multinational

Force and Observers in the Sinai since 1982 testifies, but peacekeeping conjures up the image of highly visible, lightly armed soldiers in blue berets who pose no threat to local combatants. Peacekeepers were nearly always deployed under the provisions of Chapter VI of the UN Charter (that is, a procedure involving the pacific settlement of a dispute). Since the end of the Cold War attempts to fix definitions of more coercive operations (sometimes under the enforcement provisions of Chapter VII) have spawned a host of new descriptors such as 'multi-dimensional peacekeeping', 'second generation peacekeeping', 'peace-making', and 'peace enforcement' (Schmidl, 2000, pp. 18 n1, 20 n31; Mackinlay, 1996; Jakobsen, 1998). The intellectual intention behind these neologisms is sound enough: to distinguish between different types of mission that have become more demanding and complex, and also to differentiate all these missions from war. The distinction between a 'peace enforcement' operation and war rests mainly on the assumption that the former entails localized mitigation of conflict without discrimination against *whoever* disrupts a peace arrangement. 'Victories' against 'spoilers' who attempt to undermine an agreement are assumed to be victories for a peace. By contrast, a war assumes the existence of particular enemies who have to be defeated.

'Peace support operations' (PSOs) will be used here because it incorporates peace-keeping and peace enforcement, and is a common generic term used in British Army and NATO doctrine. However, it should be borne in mind that 'peace support' is a value-laden signifier, conveying the sense that external actors actually engage in main-taining or creating peace. Their involvement (as in Somalia and the conflicts of South-East Europe for example) may be alternatively interpreted as exacerbating a situation.

The term 'humanitarianism' is used in a variety of ways, but modern principles of humanitarianism stem from the work of Henry Dunant after the battle of Solferino (in 1859) and the establishment of the International Committee of the Red Cross (ICRC). Humanitarian missions in this sense depend on civilian actors being *hors de combat*. They act neutrally and impartially according to the needs of prisoners, the sick and wounded, refugees and others suffering from the consequences of disaster and conflict. These missions should not be confused with 'humanitarian intervention' which has its foundations in the Just War tradition, and concerns 'the legitimacy of using force against states that grossly violate human rights' (Wheeler, 2000, p. 6; Ramsbotham and Woodhouse, 1996, pp. 8–18).

This chapter considers how PSOs and humanitarian missions are interlocked and have increasingly merged into humanitarian intervention. But before examining how the issue is currently constructed and framed, it is relevant to note *both* its antecedents in the cooperative management of European security and its conceptual evolution.

Dynamics of Management and Conceptual Shifts

The modern antecedents are rooted in nineteenth-century European cooperative security management and regime development. Several multinational operations grew out of attempts by major powers to manage the collapse of the Ottoman Empire, including a subdivision of the Balkans in 1913 that created Albania as a neutral international protectorate secured by a multinational force of 2,000 (Schmidl, 1999,

p. 8). There were no permanent institutional mechanisms before the First World War, but intergovernmental cooperation foreshadowed the peace enforcement, interim administration and humanitarian missions in the Balkans of the present day.

The interwar and immediate post-Second World War years in Europe witnessed further instances of multinational governance. Ad hoc forces were deployed to calm situations, monitor elections, supervise territorial transfers and observe truces – from the plebiscite in Schleswig-Holstein (1920) to the military observation mission in Greece (1947–51). Subsequent operations dealt with the legacies of European imperial rule and liberation processes in, for example, Palestine, Lebanon and Cyprus (actually legacies of the Ottoman question), Kashmir, Indonesia, Namibia, Angola and East Timor (Schmidl, 2000, pp. 9–10; James, 1999). The event that gave rise to the first occasion when blue berets were worn and when the term 'peacekeeping' first came into existence also had an imperial provenance: the UN Emergency Force (UNEF) of 1956 sent to supervise the withdrawal of British, French and Israeli troops who had invaded Egypt. The UN thus began to institutionalize peacekeeping as an extension of its diplomacy. However, in the former Belgian colony of the Congo (1960–4), the size of the UN force reached 20,000 and engaged in combat. Dogged by strategic controversies among the external actors, financial bankruptcy and operational problems, the experience discouraged further risky deployments. However, in its degree of complexity and in providing humanitarian and administrative assistance, the Congo operation was a precursor of current protectorate governance in Bosnia-Herzegovina, Kosovo and East Timor.

Elsewhere, as in Cyprus, peacekeeping froze rather than resolved disputes (Richmond, 1998). And, for much of the Cold War, political and military establishments barely raised a flicker of interest in peacekeeping. For some militaries, counterinsurgency in Algeria, South East Asia and Northern Ireland provided operational experience, but even these were subordinate to spending, planning and exercising for a world war directed by the superpowers. No one advanced their career through peacekeeping.

In some respects security concerns have been modified only hesitantly and half-heartedly since the demise of bipolarity. Military establishments in the permanent five members of the UN Security Council are still geared to preparing for combat and war, albeit in a 'post-heroic' and 'casualty-free' mode. PSOs are ancillary to the main military business of achieving 'escalation dominance' over potential threats and rivals, and there have been complaints, for example, that the British Army is gradually turning into a full-time peacekeeping force (Bowcott and Norton-Taylor, 2001). Nevertheless, peacekeeping has been reconfigured as 'peace support operations' closer to the central security focus of rich and powerful states. Missions are no longer mainly the expression of Nordic, Canadian, Indian and Fijian foreign policy (see Berdal, 1993).

A disposition on the part of the United States and its closest allies to divide the world into 'friends' and 'rogues', prominent at certain times in the Cold War and reinforced by triumphalism as communism collapsed, has also infiltrated peace support operations. As candidate for the American presidency in 2000, George Bush admitted that he didn't know who the enemies were, but they were out there somewhere. It is probably no coincidence that this kind of Manichaean approach informed US involvement in multinational operations and not simply where one might expect it (as in the Coalition war against Iraq). It was evident in Somalia where General

Aideed was declared an enemy, and carried over into Bosnia-Herzegovina and Kosovo where the Serbians were thus identified. By contrast, UN peacekeeping had no enemies. PSOs have thus purveyed the worldview of the hegemonic power and its allies, and furthermore identified the UN and the 'international community' with their norms of governance.

As part of the process of generating a model of global governance, governments have also constructed their involvement in PSOs with an eye to legal or moral legitimation and authoritative appeals to international practice. Without losing sight of perceived state power and interests, they have adapted their representations of PSOs to the discourses of ethics, humanitarianism, justice and the 'will of the international community'. Thus the UK Prime Minister declared in 1999 that the conflict in Kosovo was a fight for values and a world where dictators who abused their own people would have nowhere to hide (Blair, cited in *Newsweek*, 1999). The formulation of new concepts for the 'maintenance of peace and security' has been an essential escort for bringing peacekeeping in from the cold.

With the Security Council freed from Cold War manoeuvring and with abatement in the use of the veto, peacekeeping enjoyed a revival in the late 1980s and early 1990s, proving useful in contexts as divergent as the ceasefire between Iran and Iraq in 1988–91 and the transition to independence in Namibia in 1989–90. The UN's peacekeeping budget rose steadily from $464 million in 1990 to $3,364 million in 1995, before steadily falling back to $900 million in 1999 (McDermott, 2001, p. 186). At a peak in 1993–4, UN forces numbered nearly 80,000. Awarded the Nobel Peace Prize in 1988, the UN was even described as being a victim of its own success and suffering from too much credibility (Tharoor, 1995a, p. xvi). (See tables 10.1 and 10.2 for UN and non-UN peace support operations from the beginning of 1990 to the end of 2001.)

Most of the conflicts demanding attention have been multifaceted and displayed cross-cutting dynamics that affect sovereignty, political economies and personal identity (Woodhouse and Ramsbotham, 1998, pp. 42–9). A breakdown in central authority, atrocities against civilian populations, large-scale refugee movements and predatory economic activity characterize these conflicts. Prominent stakeholders in the wars include corporate interests and private security companies, and to some extent these conflicts are deterritorialized: being fought through control over trade, crime and money laundering (Duffield, 1998, 2001). The UN has encountered formidable operational, command and conceptual difficulties in coping with them.

Although relatively successful in stabilizing Cambodia, El Salvador and Nicaragua, UN forces were unable to contain determined 'spoilers' and warlords in Angola, Somalia, Yugoslavia and Rwanda. The old 'blue beret' concept no longer seems generally serviceable in situations where consent for an international presence is unstable. Demands on the capacity of intervention forces to conduct a range of functions from escorting humanitarian convoys to demining has grown and the civilian element of missions has received a higher priority than during the Cold War, especially in postwar peacebuilding. Above all, the requirement for soldiers to enforce peace arrangements and protect civilians where there is 'no peace to keep' has gone well beyond the traditional role of unarmed or lightly armed peacekeepers. It has become part of the doctrine, imported into operations by the UK, France and the United States, that PSOs have to be prepared for conflict, even if they are not expected to defeat an enemy.

Table 10.1 New UN peace support operations, 1 January 1990–31 December 2001

Operation	Tasks	Dates
Africa		
• Mission for the Referendum in Western Sahara (MINURSO)	Conduct referendum on independence from Morocco	April 1991–
• Angola Verification Mission (UNAVEM II & III)	Verify ceasefire, demilitarization and elections, mediate implementation of Lusaka accord, monitor national police	May 1991–Feb. 1995; Feb. 1995–June 1997
• Observer Mission in Angola (MONUA)	Assist stability, confidence-building, reconciliation	June 1997–Feb. 1999
• Operation in Mozambique (ONUMOZ)	Verify demobilization, disarmament and troop withdrawals, monitor elections, coordinate relief	Dec. 1992–Dec. 1994
• Operation in Somalia (UNOSOM I & II)	Monitor ceasefire, safeguard relief provision, assist reconciliation and reconstruction	April 1992–Mar. 1993; Mar. 1993–Mar. 1995
• Observer Mission for Uganda Rwanda (UNOMUR)	Monitor border, verify halt to military aid to Rwanda	June 1993–Sept. 1994
• Assistance Mission in Rwanda (UNAMIR I & II)	Monitor ceasefire and Arusha Accords, secure Kigali, monitor refugee returns	Oct. 1993–Mar. 1996
• Observer Mission in Liberia (UNOMIL)	Monitor ceasefire and observe ECOMOG (see table 10.2), verify demobilization, prepare elections	Sept. 1993–Sept. 1997
• Aouzou Strip Observer Group Chad/Libya (UNASOG)	Verify Libyan withdrawal	May–June 1994
• Mission in the Central African Republic (MINURCA)	Replace MISAB (see table 10.2), monitor Bangui Accords, stabilize capital, demilitarization, assist police, elections	Apr. 1998–Feb. 2000
• Observer Mission in Sierra Leone (UNOMSIL) and Assistance Mission in Sierra Leone (UNAMSIL)	Monitor security situation and respect for humanitarian law, monitor ceasefire, secure key locations, demilitarization, law enforcement and elections, facilitate relief, human rights monitoring	July 1998–Oct. 1999; Oct. 1999–
• Democratic Republic of the Congo (MONUC)	Monitor ceasefire, protect civilians from violence	Dec. 1999–
• Mission in Ethiopia and Eritrea (UNMEE)	Monitor ceasefire and security agreements	July 2000–
Americas		
• Observer Mission in El Salvador (ONUSAL)	Monitor ceasefire, human rights, demobilization, elections	July 1991–April 1995
• Mission in Haiti (UNMIH)	Oversee transition to civilian rule	Sept. 1993–June 1996
• Support Mission in Haiti (UNSMIH), Transition Mission (UNTMIH), Civilian Police Mission (MIPONUH)	Institution building, supervision and training of national police	July 1996–July 1997; Aug.–Nov. 1997; Dec. 1997– Mar. 2000

Cont'd

Table 10.1 *Cont'd*

Operation	Tasks	Dates
• Verification Mission in Guatemala (MINUGUA)	Verify ceasefire, demilitarization	Jan.–May 1997
Asia		
• Advanced Mission in Cambodia (UNAMIC) and Transitional Authority in Cambodia (UNTAC)	Supervise government functions, demobilization, elections, human rights, refugee returns	Oct. 1991–Mar. 1992; Mar. 1992–Sept. 1993
• UN Mission in East Timor (UNAMET) and Transitional Administration in East Timor (UNTAET)	Conduct referendum on independence from Indonesia, administer territory with legislative and executive authority	Oct. 1999–
Central Asia/Middle East		
• Iraq/Kuwait Observer Mission (UNIKOM)	Monitor demilitarized zone	Apr. 1991–
• UN Guards Contingent in Iraq (UNGCI)	International police protect aid deliveries to Kurds and Shiites in Iraq	May 1991–
• Observer Mission in Georgia (UNOMIG)	Monitor separatist conflict and observe CIS force (see table 10.2)	Aug. 1993–
• Observer Mission in Tajikistan (UNMOT)	Monitor implementation of Teheran Agreement, ceasefire, political liaison, coordinate relief	Dec. 1994–May 2000
Europe		
• Protection Force in Former Yugoslavia (UNPROFOR)	Monitor ceasefire in Croatia, supervise Federal Army withdrawal, demilitarize and safeguard 'protection areas', assist UNHCR aid delivery in Bosnia-Herzegovina	Feb. 1992–Mar. 1995 UNCRO and UNPREDEP separated from UNPROFOR in Mar. 1994
• Preventive Deployment in FYROM (UNPREDEP)	Deter spread of Yugoslav conflict into Macedonia	Mar. 1995–Feb. 1999
• Mission in Bosnia and Herzegovina (UNMIBH)	Supervise law enforcement, coordination of relief, refugee returns, demining, human rights observance, elections, reconstruction	Dec. 1995–
• Confidence Restoration Operation in Croatia (UNCRO)	Foster territorial settlement	Mar. 1995–Jan. 1996
• Mission of Observers in Prevlaka (UNMOP)	Replaced UNCRO, monitor demilitarization	Feb. 1996–
• Transitional Authority In Eastern Slavonia, Baranja and Western Sirmium (UNTAES)	Demilitarization, administration, monitor refugee returns, establish police, elections	Jan. 1996–Jan. 1998
• Police Support Group in Croatian Danube area (UNPSG)	Monitor Danube region policing, after UNTAES withdrawal	Jan.–Oct. 1998
• Mission in Kosovo (UNMIK)	Administration, foster autonomy, coordination with UNHCR, OSCE, EU in relief, reconstruction, law and order, human rights, refugee returns	June 1999–

Table 10.2   New non-UN peace support operations, 1 January 1990–31 December 2001

Operation (leading body)	Tasks	Dates
Africa		
• Monitoring Group (ECOMOG) in Liberia and Sierra Leone (Economic Community of West African States)	Establish truce, disarm factions, eliminate Taylor's forces. Drawn into Sierra Leone April–July 1999	Aug. 1990–
• Unified Task Force in Somalia (UNITAF) (US)	Secure relief distribution points, installations and supplies	Dec. 1992–May 1993
• Neutral Military Observer Group in Rwanda (NMOG I & II) (OAU)	Supervise respect for civil war ceasefire and Arusha Accords	July 1992–Aug 1993; Aug.–Oct. 1993
• Operation *Turqoise* in Rwanda (France)	End massacres, control Goma airport, establish 'humanitarian zone'	June–Aug. 1994
• Observer Mission in Burundi (OMIB) (OAU)	Restore confidence, assist re-establishment of order	Dec. 1993–July 1996
• Observer Mission in Comoros (OMIC) (OAU)	Monitor unrest	Nov. 1997–
• Operation *Boleas* in Lesotho (South Africa)	Secure key locations and prevent mutiny by Lesotho Army	Sept.–Oct. 1998
• Inter-African Mission to Monitor the Bangui Agreements in Central African Republic (MISAB) (Francophone West Africa and France)	Restore order, disarm rebels	Jan. 1997–Apr. 1998
• Monitoring Group in Guinea-Bissau (ECOWAS)	Secure key locations, assist relief access, patrol Senegal border, demilitarization	Dec. 1998–
• Sierra Leone (UK)	Evacuate nationals, assist UNAMSIL, secure Freetown, rescue UN and UK hostages, train and assist SL army	May 2000–
Americas		
• Multinational Force in Haiti (US)	Establish stable environment for transfer to civilian rule and elections, end refugee crisis	Sept. 1994–Jan. 1995
Asia/Pacific		
• Truce Monitoring Group (NZ) and Peace Monitoring Group (Australia) in Bougainville	Monitor implementation of ceasefire and peace accord	Dec. 1997–Apr. 1998; May 1998–
• Operation *Stabilize* International Force East Timor (INTERFET) (Australia)	Restore order, protect and support UNAMET (see table 10.1), facilitate relief	Sept. 1999–Feb. 2000

Cont'd

Table 10.2 *Cont'd*

Operation (leading body)	Tasks	Dates
• International Peace Monitoring Team in Guadalcanal (Australia and NZ)	Implement Townsville Peace Agreement, monitor ceasefire; collect weapons	Nov. 2000–
Central Asia/Middle East		
• Operation *Provide Comfort* for Kurdish 'Safe Haven' in Iraq and enforcement of no-fly zones (US)	Establish and secure Kurdish refugee camps, secure relief, eject Iraqi forces, prevent Iraqi aircraft flying in northern and southern zones of Iraq	Apr. 1991–
• Operation in Trans-Dniester/ Moldova (Russia with OSCE Observers)	Enforce ceasefire; protect Russian speaking population	1992–
• CIS Collective Peacekeeping Forces in Tajikistan (Russia)	Border patrols, enforce security	Sept. 1992–
• CIS Collective Peacekeeping Forces in Georgia (Russia with OSCE Observers)	Ceasefire observance, refugee returns	May 1994–
• International Security Assistance Force in Afghanistan (ISAF) (US/UK)	Support interim government, assist security measures	Dec. 2001–
Europe		
• European Community/Union Monitoring Mission in former Yugoslava (EUMM) (EU and Canada)	Stabilize ceasefires, monitor humanitarian situation, no-fly zone and external borders, assist confidence building and relief	July 1991–
• Operations *Maritime Monitor* and *Maritime Guard* (NATO), *Sharp Vigilance* and *Sharp Fence* (WEU), *Sharp Guard* (NATO-WEU), *Deny Flight* and *Deliberate Force* (NATO)	Monitor and enforce sanctions in Adriatic, enforce no-fly zone, air support to UNPROFOR and 'safe areas', air attacks on Bosnian Serb facilities, monitor Yugoslav sanctions against Bosnian Serbs	July 1992–Dec. 1995
• Spillover Monitor Mission to Skopje (OSCE)	Monitor FYROM's borders	Sept. 1992–
• Sanctions Assistance Missions on River Danube (OSCE/WEU)	Monitor trade embargo in Bulgaria, Romania, Hungary.	Apr. 1993–Dec. 1995
• Mostar Commission and Police Support (EU/WEU)	Administration and policing of Mostar, conduct election	July 1994–Oct. 1996
• Rapid Reaction Forces (UK/ France)	Protect UNPROFOR (BiH) in Bosnia-Herzegovina (see table 10.1)	June 1995–Dec. 1995

Cont'd

Table 10.2 *Cont'd*

Operation (leading body)	Tasks	Dates
• Implementation Force (IFOR) and Stabilization Force (SFOR) (NATO)	Implement territorial and military provisions of Dayton Accords	Dec. 1995–Dec. 1996; Dec. 1996–
• Multinational Protection Force in Albania, Operation *Alba* (Italy) and Police Advisory Element (WEU)	Secure humanitarian relief, election preparation, police advice	Apr.–Aug. 1997
• Kosovo Verification Mission (KVM) (OSCE)	Verify ceasefire	Oct. 1998–Mar. 1999
• Operation *Allied Force* in Kosovo-Yugoslavia (NATO)	Attack Serb forces and military-civilian infrastructure, support KLA, build refugee camps	Mar.–June 1999
• Kosovo Force (KFOR) (NATO)	Enforcement of ceasefire, demilitarization, secure situation for civilian tasks	June 1999–
• Operation *Essential Harvest* in Macedonia (NATO)	Collect weapons from rebels	Aug. 2001–

In the context of the crisis in Bosnia-Herzegovina, a special adviser in the UN's Department of Peacekeeping Operations (DPKO) referred to:

> the deployment of United Nations peacekeepers tasked to mitigate the nature and course of an ongoing conflict by limiting the parties' recourse to certain military means (. . . interdiction on the use of aircraft for combat purposes) or to attacks upon certain cities (protection of 'safe areas'), in both cases backed by the threat of military force provided by a regional organisation [NATO]. (Tharoor, 1995b, p. 44)

NATO's combat orientation was to push enforcement even closer to war in the case of Kosovo. NATO elites refused to label the 1999 bombing campaign as a war and claimed to be distinguishing between the ruling regime in the Federal Republic of Yugoslavia and the Yugoslav people (with whom there was supposedly no quarrel). Drawing general lessons from the 1990s, a UN Panel on Peace Operations issued a report in August 2000 (the Brahimi Report). It recognized that impartiality was incompatible with the use of force and proposed dropping it in UN operations: 'In some cases, local parties consist not of moral equals but of obvious aggressors and victims and peacekeepers may not only be operationally justified in using force but morally compelled to do so' (UN Doc., 2000b, ch. E, sec. 50). As Berdal points out, however, the lessons from Somalia, Rwanda and Yugoslavia are that expecting PSOs to escalate and de-escalate along a spectrum of force enables politicians to avoid hard choices about which kind of mandate to devise and what kind of force to send. It also encourages false hopes of a military fix to deep political problems (Berdal, 1995, 1999, 2001; also James, 1993). Moreover, contrary to the view that peacekeeping died in the 'new wars', it remains a viable proposition for non-enforcement operations (Jakobsen, 2000, p. 171). These have included the ceasefires in rare interstate conflicts, such as the UN Mission in Eritrea and Ethiopia (UNMEE) from March 2001, and also in internal conflicts where a peace process has become self-perpetuating, as in the unarmed, New Zealand-led Truce Monitoring Group in Bougainville (Rolfe, 2001).

Where considerable coercive power is considered necessary, the chief management device, beginning in Somalia and Yugoslavia, has been to subcontract to regional bodies and coalitions of the 'willing and able' (as discussed below). It represents a shift into coercive engineering by states armed with a moral design to safeguard human rights, for which purpose humanitarian missions and humanitarian intervention have been increasingly integrated.

The Integration of Humanitarianism and Humanitarian Intervention

The great bulk of humanitarian relief activity is not conducted in the context of PSOs. However, an attempt to mark out a middle ground, where military and non-military humanitarianism overlap, has been a key feature of the dynamics of global governance, and the propagation of a normative, essentially Western, model of civilization. The Security Council's mandate for the Unified Task Force (UNITAF) in Somalia (Resolution 794 of 3 December 1992) was the first resort to Chapter VII of the UN Charter within a sovereign state: 'to establish as soon as possible a secure environment for humanitarian relief operations'. Humanitarian organizations and the ICRC were themselves resorting to hiring local gunmen for protection. Subsequently Chapter VII was invoked to secure Sarajevo airport, and in Rwanda, Haiti, Albania and Kosovo (Weiss and Campbell, 1991; Jackson, 1993). However, both the UN and military proxies have been vulnerable to charges of not responding adequately to the needs of civilian protection and humanitarian relief. The humanitarian organization Médecins sans Frontières campaigned for military intervention in Rwanda and was highly critical of the way peacekeepers were 'shackled' in Bosnia by the restrictive interpretations of their mandate, which supposedly relegated them to the status of mere observers of ethnic cleansing (Jean, 1993, pp. 94–5; Hermet, 1995, pp. 91–6). Independent reports heavily criticized the UN for inaction over Rwanda and failure to secure 'safe areas' in Bosnia-Herzegovina in 1994. Additionally the UN High Commissioner for Refugees (UNHCR) was censured for her weak showing over Kosovo in 1999.

In response to these failings, the Brahimi Report contends that:

> peacekeepers – troops or police – who witness violence against civilians should be presumed to be authorised to stop it, within their means, in support of basic United Nations principles and, as stated in the report of the Independent Inquiry on Rwanda, consistent with the perception and the expectation of the protection created by [an operation's] very presence. (UN Doc., 2000b, ch. F, sec. 61)

The presumption of authorization on such vague grounds and without reference to a Chapter VII mandate challenges the normative principles of rules of engagement that restrain the use of force (Van Baarda, 2001). This is not only an ethical issue but a practical one as well. Although lives have undoubtedly been saved where enforcement has occurred, the capacity of external actors to do more than soften the consequences of 'new wars' for civilians has been limited in the face of determined local rivalries (Mayall, 2000, pp. 324–7). Enforcement shifts the focus away from the humanitarian protection of civilians (which relies on *minimizing* the strategic value of aid), towards the protection of aid itself and ultimately to the protection of other soldiers or to retaliatory action that kills civilians. The failure of NATO's bombing campaign in Kosovo to reverse or prevent the humanitarian crisis suggests that humanitarian PSOs do not necessarily produce a humanitarian outcome (Woodward, 2001, p. 343).

And, as Larry Minear notes, 'a host of conceptual considerations points to major problems inherent in the assumption of wider humanitarian roles by the military in internal armed conflicts' (Minear, 1994, p. 24). For those directly involved in humanitarian assistance, the trend towards a dominance of security over humanitarian concerns has been alarming (Griffiths, Levine and Weller, 1995, p. 35). The NGO, Save the Children, argued that the effect of the military actions in pursuit of Aideed in Somalia disrupted aid programmes, dissuaded donors from making funds available, diverted forces from convoying activities and produced such strain that the Humanitarian Unit moved out of military headquarters to distance itself from the military operations (Visman, 1993; Hinton, 1993).

The roles of external military and civilian components in humanitarian action appear to have blurred even further in the Balkan emergencies. But coercion and humanitarian intervention also exposed divergent philosophies and allegiances. The UNHCR, who coordinated the humanitarian operation in Bosnia-Herzegovina and who could call on military protection for relief work, highlighted the benefits of military assistance, but also noted that NATO airstrikes had increased the risk to the lives of humanitarian staff and to the perceived impartiality and neutrality of humanitarian missions associated with the operation (Ogata, 1994). The Kosovo crisis heightened the dilemma. The UNHCR, along with virtually all other aid agencies, was obliged to abandon its work in Kosovo on the eve of the bombing. Humanitarianism was subordinated to humanitarian intervention. Military priorities and member governments protecting refugees independently of each other made the coordination of relief problematic. Many NGOs worked closely with their national military forces, in effect jeopardizing their independence through a close association with the intervention operation. The work of humanitarian organizations, notably the UNHCR, was co-opted into the strategic goals of state elites (Rieff, 1999; Pugh, 2000).

Although official and private humanitarian groups do not hold unanimous or rigid views about humanitarian intervention, they worry that association with the military can be compromising. Although conducted as a war rather than humanitarian intervention, the US air campaign in Afghanistan in 2001 was accompanied by a warning to Afghans that unexploded bombs and air-dropped aid packages could be confused because of their similar colouring. Many humanitarians have called for semi-detachment, even withdrawal, from such operations to maintain their credibility (Bryer, 1995, p. 25). It would seem that the principles of humanitarianism, including relief according to need, are at greatest risk when a force is engaged in humanitarian intervention.

We might question, also, whether the combination of humanitarianism and enforcement does actually reflect a normative shift towards humanitarian intervention (which is politically determined and inconsistent in its application anyway). Rather, it may represent the use of humanitarians by states to address issues of poverty and redistributive justice. By the mid-1980s, development support to governments had begun to give way to donor policies of funding NGOs whose role was essentially to provide welfare safety netting, particularly in conflict zones where NGOs were gaining unprecedented access (Operation *Lifeline Sudan* in 1989, for example). In this respect, subcontracted NGOs have been the handmaidens of a shift from development to safety netting for areas excluded from, or on the borders of global integration. Civilian agencies deeply resent the use of humanitarian action as an alibi for political inaction that prolongs emergencies. The phenomenon is not sustainable development but sustained emergency. In effect, humanitarians are structured into conflict by acting as subcontractors of states that have adopted a kind of semi-detached engagement (Duffield, 1999). States are not especially heroic about humanitarianism, but nervous about incurring casualties, cautiously weighing up a range of variables, including intangibles such as credibility and prestige (Jakobsen, 1996). In effect, rational, civilized 'humanitarian intervention' may be part of the packaging in which Western security culture, self-perception and self-interest are wrapped.

Constructions

Traditional peacekeeping tended to be constructed by UN officials and participants as an unsung but worthwhile contribution to world peace. Peacekeepers were represented as disinterested in the outcome of a dispute, neutral and impartial towards the disputants. Indeed, one study was entitled *Soldiers without Enemies* (Fabian, 1971). The benign image can be seen on book covers and postage stamps and a sculptured monument in Ottawa. A particularly striking UN publicity photo, reproduced on book jackets, shows a black peacekeeper in Namibia holding a white child who is wearing the soldier's blue beret (Weiss, 1999). Soldiers operating under Chapter VI of the UN Charter can thereby mimic humanitarians in their lack of military significance and their rapport with the innocent. To the extent that the presence of peacekeepers prevents people from being attacked, humanitarianism could be portrayed as the raison d'être of peacekeeping, 'underpinning and transcending the mere settlement of disputes' (Vieira de Mello, 1994, p. 18).

Humanitarian organizations themselves have a more direct claim to representations of being 'above politics' and answering to basic human needs. The construction of a moral calling was moulded most effectively by the Red Cross and Crescent movements. Although specifically mandated by the 1949 Geneva Conventions and 1977 Protocols to supervise and implement the humanitarian law of war, the ICRC has taken on a broader remit to provide assistance to refugees and victims of conflict. It has been responsible, more than any other organization, for implanting and cherishing principles of humanitarian action: neutrality, impartiality, provision according to need and independence from politics. The notion that humanitarian actors would permeate borders also derived from the stance that non-military humanitarians were acceptable to warring parties. By the mid-1990s, there were estimated to be a hundred, overwhelmingly Western, non-state groups actively working for humanitarian relief in conflict zones with unprecedented access to some areas such as the Sudan (Natsios, 1996, p. 68).

Humanitarians may of course develop institutionalized commitments to this form of governance so that they are structured into the political economy of zones where emergencies are endemic. Representations of humanitarian emergencies tend to reinforce a victim–rescuer model. Innocent and helpless women and children are projected as visual emblems of crisis, suggesting that there is particular power in this representation to catch our attention and jog the liberal conscience (Campbell, forthcoming). Aid workers, usually from wealthy parts of the world, who are often the mediators between the victims and media reportage, stand for an external response that is not only sympathetic but seemingly essential to survival. For example, a television documentary on the Mozambique floods of February 2000 devoted significant film footage to interviews with aid workers and dramatic helicopter rescues by the outsiders. In reality the vast majority of those affected rescued themselves (Barratt, 2000). Furthermore, constructions that focus on the immediacy of a crisis distance us from underlying causes in the workings of the global economy and from political acts and negligence (Campbell, forthcoming).

Indeed the elevation of PSOs in global governance is accompanied by representations that attempt to legitimize the right to use military force to protect populations within states. Images of altruism and merciful assistance seem to have become potent enough to match or offset the symbols and images of national power that glorify the defence of state interests. In the new construction, strategic and political considerations are curbed and interventions configured as the application of 'natural laws' of economics, state creation and human rights protection. Appropriation of this representation has been detected in the way that during the Kosovo conflict NATO purposefully developed a 'humanitarian' image through its website (Hansen, 2001). NATO represented the Kosovo operation as combining 'humanitarianism' and 'preventive diplomacy'. From a realist perspective this construction camouflaged a war. NATO's military commander, General Wesley Clark, complained that he was prevented from conducting a proper military campaign (Clark, 2001). From critical perspectives, NATO's construction was pitched to capture the moral high ground for maintaining public support, to legitimize an action that was illegal (UN Security Council authorization was not sought on the grounds that it would have been vetoed by Russia and China), and to disguise hollow diplomacy (in that negotiations at Rambouillet produced an ingenuous ultimatum rather than an accord or peace to be enforced). Furthermore, 'humanitarianism' masked an imperative to impose internal alliance discipline. Disputes over handling the Bosnia-Herzegovina crisis had damaged NATO's credibility, and US unilateralism (including secretly supplying arms to the Bosnian Muslim army) had driven the European members to forge closer military cooperation among themselves (Booth, 1999; Gowan, 2000, pp. 3–4; Hebditch and McDonald, 2001; Chomsky, 1999, ch. 1).

The discourse of 'humanitarianism' has become structurally embedded in this way because, although diffuse, it has become – in the words of Astri Suhrke – 'a principal normative reference for states and organisations to clarify their international obligations, or against which to hold others responsible' (Suhrke, 1999, pp. 268–9). The phrase 'to clarify' disguises the sophistry and representational purpose of humanitarian rhetoric. The US political elite has refused to ratify rights conventions, has attacked the universal principles of the International Criminal Court, and has introduced draconian curtailment of civil liberties and legal processes as part of the 'war against terrorism'. Ironically, in May 2001 the United States was voted off the UN Human Rights Commission. Thus the prominence of humanitarianism in the representation of PSOs has several functions other than benchmarking. It promotes moral values and responses that demonstrate and reinforce the superiority of liberal ideology, while avoiding having to deal with the structural injustices that cultivate instabilities in the system.

Second, in Western societies that need to be convinced of the sacrifices implied in stabilizing or isolating unruly parts of the world it has the function of striking an ethical chord with media and public opinion. Third, because ethical considerations alone are insufficient to compel action by states in the absence of more specific motives (Mayall, 2000, p. 326; Gibbs, 2000), it may serve as a veneer to cover base interests (Chomsky, 1999, ch. 3). Fourth, the 'new humanism' and the demonization of 'rogue states' have been key elements of the 'West's script for reconstituting security so as to fill a threat vacuum and maintain a "Selves and Others" duality in the post-cold war world' (Krause and Latham, 1998). Finally, it has become a conscious tactic of insurgent factions to employ humanitarian and human rights rhetoric to trigger international assistance (Woodward, 2001, pp. 334–5). In realist and neo-realist interpretations, this mobilization of external support relies on a coincidence between the 'liberation' goals of insurgents and the geopolitical interests of the external powers. Apparently, the criminal operations and human rights abuse by Croats in the Krajina, the Kosovo Liberation Army or the Northern Alliance in Afghanistan were discounted in the process of making ethical judgements about supporting them. 'Humanitarianism', then, has mainly emblematic status as a legitimizing principle attached to PSOs.

Institutional Mechanisms and their Effectiveness

The most prominent global mechanism for mobilizing responses to crises, the United Nations, often stands accused of institutional incompetence. It experienced overstretch in its capacity in the 1990s; the humanitarian agencies, the Department of Political Affairs and the DPKO were slow to adapt to the demands placed on them. But the portrayal of an arthritic UN is contradicted by structural changes introduced by the middle of the decade. The post of Military Adviser was created and the number of seconded military officers increased dramatically (though these were from Western countries and unpaid secondment was ended at the insistence of Third World states). A situation centre was set up so that field commanders could be in contact with New York outside standard working hours. Early warning of crises and conflict prevention was given greater attention, a lessons-learned unit was formed and the recycling of equipment from one operation to another was undertaken. Slow responsiveness to crises was addressed by creating a 'stand-by database' of pledges by member states to make forces and equipment available to the UN. By 1999, a group of like-minded states led by Denmark had formed a Standby High Readiness Brigade (SHIRBRIG), with earmarked units available at short notice to the UN, Organization for Security and Cooperation in Europe (OSCE) and other regional organizations for Chapter VI operations. However, the participating states have to agree to release their contributions in any particular case and the components have to be acceptable to the disputants.

The UN's operations have been a relative success in some instances (Central America and Cambodia), and a relative failure in others (Somalia, Angola) because PSOs remain largely improvised. Reform has been piecemeal, lacking a constitutional overhaul that would integrate the response system (Childers and Urquhart, 1994, pp. 33–5). In such formal but poorly articulated regimes, political variables are too great to promote a consistent and adequate reaction to crises. Response has to be negotiated to fit each situation. At bottom, the UN's defects are largely attributable to the way it is managed by the most powerful members (Parsons, 1995, p. x). Perhaps the only consistency that one can anticipate is that the hegemonic power and its allies will be the chief determinants of how the regime will function in each case. This is not restricted to use of the Security Council veto, the design of mandates and the withholding of funds and support. The smaller Western states and developing countries that dominated Cold War peacekeeping contributions have now been joined by states that were largely ruled out. France and the UK were the largest troop contributors in 1993, and domestic constitutional restraints on Germany and Japan have been gradually lifted. Wealthy industrialized states are allocated two-thirds of the 170 professional posts in the DPKO. The United States, which has persistently defaulted on its dues and is unwilling to place its forces in harm's way, has 29 posts, three times more than Canada, the next most favoured. Third World representatives are concerned that Western states find it difficult to accommodate the views of experienced and committed peacekeeping countries (Krishnasamy, 2001, pp. 69–73). Although the Brahimi Report anticipates further reforms to decision-making, UN members are deeply divided over the desirability of challenging domestic jurisdiction through Chapter VII enforcement measures. China, Mexico, Pakistan, Peru, Russia, South Africa and Tunisia are among the states that reject the use of humanitarian emergencies as a pretext for international intervention (UN Doc., 2000a).

Regional organizations and coalitions have long been engaged in dispute resolution and PSOs, and are required to resolve disputes peacefully under Chapter VIII of the UN Charter. Indeed the Organization of American States (OAS) was already fostering US-approved democratic norms in the 1980s, before acting as partner to the UN in Haiti in 1991. An ad hoc 'Contadora group' of Central American states acting outside the OAS eventually helped to bring disputes in Nicaragua, El Salvador and Guatemala to a close. A US-sponsored force began operating in the Sinai after the Camp David agreement. Inter-African forces have attempted to deal with problems in Chad and the Central African Republic. West African states led by Nigeria set up a monitoring group in Liberia, which transposed into enforcement and spilled over into Sierra Leone. In Europe, Italy led a coalition into Albania, and the OSCE has institutionalized a role in conflict prevention and dispute settlement, particularly in Central Asia. The OSCE is also a UN partner for elections, human rights and democracy building in Albania, Bosnia-Herzegovina and Kosovo alongside the EU and NATO (McKenzie, 2001, pp. 155–61). A combination of underfunding and overcommitment in the 1990s obliged the UN to mobilize regional organizations, in spite of the opportunities this presents for ambitious regional powers to meddle in crises.

Security Council members had an opportunity after a summit in January 1992 to secure and expand the organization to cope with new demands. But the failure of member states to pay their contributions, operational problems in Angola, Cambodia and Somalia and the Security Council's delinquency in failing to recommend a wholesale review of the rationale and management of PSOs crippled the UN's capacity. Tensions over the Somalia operations then led the United States to become dogmatically opposed to placing its forces under a UN commander. In addition, the Clinton administration responded to the ideological and tactical hostility towards the UN among right-wing fundamentalists in Congress by issuing a presidential directive, PDD25 of February 1996, to lay down stringent conditions for participation in UN operations (MacKinnon, 2000, pp. 116–18). The Security Council also had a tendency, evident in Bosnia-Herzegovina, to pass resolutions but fail to provide the wherewithal to fulfil them. Nevertheless the UN has relied on US and NATO military capability to enforce the Dayton Accords in Bosnia-Herzegovina and to maintain stability in Kosovo. The Brahimi Report gave its imprimatur to subcontracting Chapter VII operations to military coalitions, such as NATO.

NATO has never been a regional organization for purposes of cooperation with the UN, its leaders having been concerned that this would reduce its autonomy of action as a defence alliance. Nor do NATO leaders want the UN to lead coercive actions. In demanding a military fix to the conflict in Bosnia-Herzegovina and by circumventing explicit Security Council authorization for its war against Yugoslavia, NATO's 'exceptionalism' has raised alarm that this presages global policing by the West. Enforcement operations, such as the UK-led International Security Assistance Force in Afghanistan of December 2001, require Security Council authorization. NATO's failure to abide by this norm over Kosovo has raised an issue that will have to be considered in any future enforcement action by the nascent European rapid reaction force. Due to become operational in 2003, this force can be made available to the UN, but the United States will have a veto over its use for non-NATO purposes. Whether one interprets this regionalization as a sensible division of labour (Jakobsen, 2000), or as either a marginalization or subversion of the UN by the hegemon and its allies (Bennis, 1996), the political cohesion, infrastructure and military competence available in Europe cannot be replicated elsewhere. African states have debilitating problems of their own. Generally, the North has been reluctant to send military forces to the South, preferring 'indirect' assistance to develop African capabilities, but reinforcing African dependence on external equipment and expertise (Berman, 1998, pp. 13–14).

Limitations on the UN's autonomous capacity have also been evident in reforms in the humanitarian field. The Department of Humanitarian Affairs (DHA) was replaced in 1998 by the Office for the Coordination of Humanitarian Affairs (OCHA) in a major UN reform package designed to save money and cut posts. Several states, including the UK and the United States, had frowned on the way that the DHA had become a new layer of bureaucracy in the UN system. OCHA has powerful standing in New York through its responsibility for chairing the UN's cabinet-style Executive Committee for Humanitarian Affairs, but it does not have the field presence of relief agencies such as UNHCR or the World Food Programme. It was virtually bypassed in East Timor, and its efforts in Kosovo were overshadowed by NATO's involvement in refugee protection.

Questions about the purpose and impact of humanitarianism, as opposed to humanitarian intervention, also create uncertainty in the NGO world. Long-standing accusations that emergency relief can do more harm than good by fuelling war economies were addressed if not resolved by increased professionalism. Codes of conduct have been developed including an ICRC/NGO Code. An International Steering Committee for Humanitarian Response comprising the major umbrella organizations also published a manual to set minimum standards of aid provision in disaster response (Sphere Project, 2000). The civilian voluntary sector is increasingly aware of the possibilities of monitoring and evaluating its procedures and impacts.

But the main troubling issue has been the drive for coherence with political goals. A new kind of paradigm has meant that the effectiveness of humanitarian relief is judged by how it contributes to Western notions of rights and conflict resolution. A crisis broke in 1994–6 when agencies were accused of feeding Hutus who were allegedly using Zairean refugee camps as bases for genocidal attacks on Rwanda. The Rwandan Army attacked the camps and, so as to serve a political agenda, the UNHCR and some NGOs assisted in an involuntary repatriation to Rwanda of over a million refugees. The ensuing slaughter and diaspora generated further conflict in Rwanda and Zaire/Democratic Republic of Congo. Few would deny that humanitarian aid is politically manipulated and has political impacts, but its conscious subordination to political goals through aid conditionality is arguably a betrayal of humanitarianism (Fox, 2001, pp. 5–7). The explanation of this politicization can be framed in both foundational and alternative frameworks of international relations.

Foundational and Alternative Frameworks

For the most part PSOs and humanitarian missions have been analysed within the foundational theories of realism/neo-realism and liberal internationalism. The foundational theories emphasize the management of PSOs by state and intergovernmental bodies whose immediate preoccupations are not necessarily with advancing an equitable global society.

In the realist framework, the international system is governed according to the precepts of self-help (which is moulded by system structures in the view of neo-realists). For example, realists view participation in PSOs as attempts by governments to increase their international clout or to subsidize the maintenance of armed forces (Neack, 1995). And because permanent members of the UN Security Council can veto decisions about deployments there is no possibility of PSOs being used against their interests. On the contrary, reports that US intelligence agents penetrated the UN Special Commission on Iraq and the OSCE's Kosovo Verification Mission suggest that PSOs have been harnessed to support strategic goals (Johnstone, 2000, p. 162; Gellman, 1999; Walker and Laverty, 2000). However, realists sometimes harbour a misconception that peacekeeping was a realistic substitute for the idealist collective security system as prescribed in the UN Charter (Kegley, 1998, pp. 17–18). On the contrary, whereas collective security was supposed to provide overwhelming resistance to aggression, peacekeeping emerged with distinctively diplomatic purposes – to reduce the scope of dispute escalation, allowing imperial powers to save face and inhibiting wider conflict (James, 1990, p. 5).

Within the realist framework, the focus of interest in PSOs is not, as with peace researchers for example, on 'the crisis' and the adequacies or otherwise of the missions. The crisis itself takes second place to domestic considerations, foreign policy agendas and the allocation of power and responsibility among elites (Pouligny, 2001; Hughes,

2001). In this respect, for example, critics of the humanitarian construction of the arrival of US Marines on a Somali beach in December 1992 argue that it may have had less to do with the Somali crisis than with George Bush Sr bequeathing a poisoned chalice to his successor (Bennis, 1996); boosting defence plans for a military intervention force (Chomsky, 1999, p. 69); or supporting commercial and strategic interests in the region (Gibbs, 2000).

A Grotian, liberal-internationalist approach to normative development has gained ground to rationalize the PSO–humanitarian nexus. Nicholas Wheeler, for example, adopts the assumption of English School theorists that states form an international society with key rules to constrain and legitimize action (Wheeler, 2000, pp. 8–10; Wheeler, 2001). Since the Cold War the legitimation of intervention has shifted towards humanitarian claims and justice rather than the maintenance of order. Contrary to the neo-realist view that states use regimes as arenas for competition and establish norms to reflect power and interests, powerful states are restrained by such norms. Further, the humanitarian outcomes of action are as important as the motives (Teson, 1988), which may indeed be non-humanitarian and include the repatriation of refugees and the advancement of economic and strategic goals. The case that states have a moral duty to express solidarity by using force against state perpetrators of massive rights violations, in spite of the absence of legal criteria for determining legitimate humanitarian intervention, is an influential one that has been echoed by the UN Secretary-General (Annan, 1999; Wheeler, 2000, pp. 12–13). Known as a 'solidarist' position, its minimum ethical requirement is that the means used must adhere to recognized *jus in bello* criteria such as banning civilian targeting. Complementary practical steps to 'solidarism' include strengthening international law, shaming financial defaulters, and regulating the principles and practice of intervention – in effect regulating the regulators (Knudsen, 1999).

This is still a long distance from a radical cosmopolitan framework (see chapter 15 below), since it remains firmly within the foundations of statism. Individuals within states will be offered external protection, but it will be states that do the protecting. Solidarism assumes that states, or governments, can be divided into 'abusers' and 'protectors' of rights, and expects the latter to abide by their own standards. It concentrates on the ethics of intervention rather than deep-seated structural problems which give rise to the urge to police and engineer.

Although foundational theories are prominent, the issue can also be understood through alternative frameworks – and by probing beyond the mere exposure of statist hypocrisy. From a critical theory perspective, PSOs and humanitarian missions illustrate the disempowering effects of statist sovereignty and capitalist globalization. Rich and powerful states and institutions are the sources of key decisions about policing the world and provide the mass of humanitarian experts and assistance. PSOs and humanitarian missions are manifestations of stresses in the international system for which corporations, states and the international financial institutions are in large measure culpable. In advancing the globalization of a capitalist manifest destiny – the 'Washington consensus' of neoliberal market economy – these institutions advance a top-down socio-economic model that disempowers communities in the periphery.

Duffield's analysis modulates theories of structural violence to contend that metropolitan states have adapted governance through innovative forms of subcontracting, partnership and regime building (Duffield, 2001). The 'borderlands' of the global economy, where development has collapsed into brutal competition between warring factions, no longer correspond to the Westphalian sovereign state model. Conflict fractures territory and governance into pseudo-state polities (Republika Srpska for example). The metropolitan capitalist centres are reluctant to police this unruliness at great cost to national treasures or in soldiers' lives. They thus attempt to govern borderlands by projecting authority through networks of non-state assistance and by creating international regimes to control warlord criminality. Where inhabitants are deemed unable to determine their future without paternalistic guidance, external actors are so intrusive that the imposition is tantamount to establishing protectorates, as in the Balkans. International financial institutions, UN administrators, NGOs, inter-governmental aid agencies, private companies, foreign 'peace support' forces, foreign civilian police and judges attempt to control territory, economic resources and public policy. This form of protectorate aims to establish the values of neoliberal market economics, statism and political plurality, and itself therefore represents the ideals of global liberal governance (Duffield, 2001; Paris, 1997, 2001). However, Western agencies charged with peacebuilding in war-torn societies encounter local resistance in specific contexts and, as in the Balkans, resident war entrepreneurs capture aspects of the model, such as economic privatization, for their own purposes (Chandler, 1999; Pugh, 2001a; Sörensen, 2002).

Finally, cosmopolitan approaches are both relevant to intrastate conflicts and a potential modification of prevailing statist responses. In rejecting a future where non-state actors have become complicit in the projects of states to govern borderlands, radical cosmopolitanism seeks expressions of solidarity with 'alterities' (alternatives that practise tolerance) that are suppressed by power-holders (Campbell, 1998). NGOs and other non-state actors may be co-opted into statism – through contract funding, performance-related codes and auditing, and through integration with military PSOs. But they also represent a potential for crossing frontiers to empower alterities and develop global society. By contrast, military forces have been the servants and instru-ments of state par excellence and have been a key to constructing identity with the state. But let us suppose that even a soldier's identity and allegiance was reconstructed to develop global society. In adopting an alternative stream of thinking about global governance in this field Kinloch postulates a utopian realism, deriving from Kantian thought, in proposing a permanent international volunteer armed force (Kinloch, 1997). With a strong historical pedigree, the idea resurfaced in various configurations in the late 1980s and early 1990s, when the UN was becoming overstretched. It claimed to offer practical advantages in enabling the UN to mobilize a rapid response to crises without having to beg from states (Righter, 1995, p. 350; Urquhart, 1993). It also bridges the frameworks of international society and cosmopolitanism: the UN's autonomy would be enhanced through the allegiance of individuals.

Humanitarians consider that primary responsibility for coping with emergencies lies with state governments, but radical cosmopolitanism can be an appropriate com-plement to their ethical philosophies for three main reasons. First, they seek more inclusive governance both within and beyond frontiers through processes that mitigate the tendencies of the state and global capitalism to marginalize and impoverish entire social groups. Second, cosmopolitans regard social movements from below as essential to the transformation of global politics, pointing to the impact of the environmental and anti-globalization movements. Third, the theory regards basic values of human life, security and 'freedoms' as preconditions for world citizenship. Many humanitarians can doubtless identify with such goals. The first four of the ten points in the ICRC code fit with a cosmopolitan approach: '(1) The humanitarian imperative comes first; (2) Aid is given regardless of race, creed or nationality on the basis of need alone; (3) Aid will not be used to further a particular political or religious standpoint; (4) We shall endeavour not to act as instruments of government foreign policy' (ICRC, n.d., Annex II(2)). French humanitarian organizations, for example, use the phrase 'sans frontières' in a political as well as an ethical sense, and thereby challenge the orthodox concepts of sovereignty that stress the centralizing and monopoly roles of the state. The framework exhibits problems, concerning, for example, the meaning of empowering 'alterities' and assessing the significance of transnational social movements. It may underestimate the persistence of state forms and the dilemmas arising when two or more 'suppressed' groups abuse each other. But radical cosmopolitanism is as much about process as form, about the accountability of leaders, the representation and participation of social groups, the tolerance of dissent and links across state boundaries.

Conclusion

By the beginning of this century, instruments for maintaining peace and security, order and justice had not only been institutionalized but were integral to the structure of global governance. Peacekeeping and humanitarian missions came in from the margins of the former bipolar system to occupy a more central role in the management of disorder as leading states redefined their security interests after the Cold War. But more than this, the evolution of PSOs and the integration of humanitarian intervention and humanitarianism have reflected and reinforced the structure of the system and promoted the globalization of a particular ideology of good governance.

The limits of the current forms of peacekeeping and humanitarianism lie in the inherent contradictions of an unstable interstate capitalist system attempting to govern its instability. Peace support operations and humanitarianism deal with the manifestations of that instability, marking the extent to which the system fails to benefit large parts of the world. The issue certainly reflects a concern about the abuse of people by state and substate elites, and many war-torn societies have benefited from relief aid and military protection. But they pay a price for that assistance in their dependency on the wealthy parts of the world and in their subjection to the demands of an economic globalization that arguably fails to work for the poor.

Democracy and neoliberalism may be assumed by its proponents to provide an ethically superior model to authoritarian alternatives. But they need to consider fundamental questions about the extent to which the statist structure and neoliberal value system fosters the political and social instability that requires policing, protection or exclusion. PSOs and humanitarian missions are as much manifestations of flawed politico-economic structures as vehicles of system management. Soldiers and humanitarians are trouble-shooters for an international society structured to sustain inequality and denial of human needs. PSOs and humanitarian missions are value-laden in reproducing, or attempting to reproduce, the state system and the normative and ideological assumptions that enable dominant states to manage it.

This chapter has contended that liberal internationalist and realist/neo-realist orthodoxies legitimize the structure of the international system and the ideology of the states that benefit from it. For the time being, and in the absence of structural upheaval and without prevalent values based on local human needs, the system is policed by states whose hubris may fit comfortably within a liberal-international society framework, but which must remain suspect to critical theorists and advocates of cosmopolitan global society.

References

Annan, K. (1999) 'Annual report of the Secretary-General', UN Doc. SG/SM7136 GA/9596, 20 Sept.

Barratt, C. (prod.) and Anderson, H. (dir.) (2000) 'The real story of the Mozambique flood', shown on Channel 4, 24 Mar.

Bennis, P. (1996) *Calling the Shots: How Washington Dominates Today's UN*, New York: Olive Branch Press.

Berdal, M. (1993) *Whither UN Peacekeeping?* Adelphi Paper 281, London: IISS/Brassey's.

Berdal, M. (1995) 'United Nations peacekeeping in the Former Yugoslavia', in D. C. F. Daniel and B. Hayes (eds), *Beyond Traditional Peacekeeping*, Basingstoke: Macmillan.

Berdal, M. (1999) 'UN peacekeeping and the use of force: no escape from hard decisions', in R. Patman (ed.), *Security in a Post Cold War World*, Basingstoke: Macmillan.

Berdal, M. (2001) 'Lessons not learned: the use of force in "peace operations" in the 1990s', in A. Adebajo and C. L. Sriram (eds), *Managing Armed Conflicts in the 21st Century*, London: Frank Cass.

Berman, E. G. (1998) 'The Security Council's increasing reliance on burden-sharing: collaboration or abrogation?', *International Peacekeeping*, 5, no. 1, pp. 1–21.

Booth, K. (1999) 'NATO's republic: warnings from Kosovo', *Civil Wars*, 2, no. 3, pp. 89–95.

Bowcott, O. and Norton-Taylor, R. (2001) 'Braving hostilities in the name of peace', *Guardian*, 28 Aug., p. 4.

Bryer, D. (1995) 'Comment', in *World Disasters Report*, Geneva: International Federation of Red Cross and Red Crescent Societies.

Campbell, D. (1998) *National Deconstruction: Violence, Identity, and Justice in Bosnia*, Minneapolis: University of Minnesota Press.

Campbell, D. (forthcoming) 'Salgado and the Sahel: documentary photography and the imaging of famine', in F. Debrix and C. Weber (eds), *Mediating Internationals*, Minneapolis: University of Minnesota Press.

Chandler, D. (1999) *Bosnia: Faking Democracy after Dayton*, London: Pluto Press.

Chandler, D. (2001) 'The people-centred approach to peace operations: the new UN agenda', *International Peacekeeping*, 8, no. 1, pp. 1–19.

Childers, E. and Urquhart, B. (1994) *Renewing the United Nations System*, Uppsala: Dag Hammarskjöld Foundation.

Chomsky, N. (1999) *The New Military Humanism: Lessons from Kosovo*, London: Polity Press.

Clark, W. (2001) *Waging Modern War: Bosnia, Kosovo and the Future of Combat*, New York: Public Affairs.

Dellaire, R. A. (1996) 'The changing role of UN peacekeeping forces: the relationship between UN peacekeepers and NGOs in Rwanda', in J. Whitman and D. Pocock (eds), *After Rwanda: The Coordination of United Nations Humanitarian Assistance*, Basingstoke: Macmillan.

Duffield, M. (1998) 'Post-modern conflict: warlords, post-adjustment states and private protection', *Journal of Civil Wars*, 1, no. 1, pp. 65–102.

Duffield, M. (1999) 'NGO relief in war zones: towards an analysis of the new aid paradigm', *Third World Quarterly*, 18, no. 3, pp. 527–42.

Duffield, M. (2001) *Global Governance and the New Wars: The Merging of Development and Security*, London: Zed Books.

Durch, W. J. (ed.) (1997) *UN Peacekeeping, American Policy, and the Uncivil Wars of the 1990s*, Basingstoke: Macmillan.

Fabian, L. L. (1971) *Soldiers without Enemies: Preparing the United Nations for Peacekeeping*, Washington DC: Brookings Institution.

Fetherston, A. B. (1994) *Towards a Theory of United Nations Peacekeeping*, Basingstoke: Macmillan.

Fetherston, A. B. (2000) 'Peacekeeping, conflict resolution and peacebuilding: a reconsideration of theoretical frameworks', in T. Woodhouse and O. Ramsbotham (eds), *Peacekeeping and Conflict Resolution*, London: Frank Cass.

Fox, F. (2001) 'New humanitarianism: does it provide a moral banner for the twenty-first century?', *Disasters*, 25, no. 4, pp. 275–89.

Galtung, J. (1976) 'Three approaches to peace: peacekeeping, peacemaking, and peacebuilding', in *Peace, War and Defense: Essays in Peace Research*, vol. 2, Copenhagen: Christian Eljers.

Gellman, B. (1999) 'UN official believes evidence shows inspectors helped US eavesdrop on Iraq', *Washington Post*, 6 Jan., p. 1.

Gibbs, D. N. (2000) '*Realpolitik* and humanitarian intervention: the case of Somalia', *International Politics*, 37, no. 1, Mar., pp. 41–55.

Gowan, P. (2000) 'The Euro-Atlantic origins of NATO's attack on Yugoslavia', in T. Ali (ed.), *Masters of the Universe? NATO's Balkan Crusade*, London: Verso.

Griffiths, M., Levine, I. and Weller, M. (1995) 'Sovereignty and suffering', in J. Harriss (ed.), *The Politics of Humanitarian Intervention*, London: Pinter.

Hansen, L. (2001) 'Visualizing security institutions: NATO and the Internet', paper at 42nd annual International Studies Association Convention, Chicago, 20–24 Feb.

Hebditch, D. (prod./dir.) and McDonald, S. (reporter) (2001) 'Allies and lies', *Correspondent*, SFI production for BBC, NRK and WDR, shown on BBC2, 24 June.

Hermet, G. (1993) 'Peacekeeping operations above humanitarian law', in F. Jean (ed.), *Life, Death and Aid: The Médecins Sans Frontières Report on World Crisis Intervention* (English edn), London: Routledge.

Hermet, G. (1995) 'Rwanda: why Médecins Sans Frontières made a call to arms', in F. Jean (ed.), *Populations in Danger* (English edn), London: MSF.

Hinton, N. (Director-General of Save the Children) (1993) Letter in the *Independent*, 10 June.

Hughes, A. (2001) '(Im)partiality a key principle of peacekeeping? United Nations Observation Group in Lebanon 1958', Ph.D. thesis, Keele University.

ICRC (n.d.) *The Code of Conduct for the International Red Cross and Red Crescent Movement and NGOs in Disaster Relief*, Geneva: International Committee of the Red Cross.

Independent International Commission on Kosovo (2000) *The Kosovo Report: Conflict, International Response, Lessons Learned*, Oxford: Oxford University Press.

Jackson, R. H. (1993) 'Armed humanitarianism', *International Journal*, 68, no. 4, pp. 579–606.

Jakobsen, P. V. (1996) 'National interest, humanitarianism or CNN: what triggers UN peace enforcement after the Cold War?', *Journal of Peace Research*, 33, no. 2, pp. 44–76.

Jakobsen, P. V. (1998) *Western Use of Coercive Diplomacy after the Cold War: A Challenge for Theory and Practice*, Basingstoke: Macmillan.

Jakobsen, P. V. (2000) 'Overload, not marginalization, threatens UN peacekeeping', *Security Dialogue*, 13, no. 2, pp. 167–77.

James, A. (1990) *Peacekeeping in International Politics*, Basingstoke: Macmillan.

James, A. (1993) 'Internal peacekeeping: a dead end for the UN?', *Security Dialogue*, 24, no. 4, pp. 359–68.

James, A. (1995) 'Peacekeeping, peace-enforcement and national sovereignty', in R. Thakur and C. Thayer (eds), *A Crisis of Expectations: UN Peacekeeping in the 1990s*, Boulder, Colo.: Westview Press.

James, A. (1999) 'The peacekeeping role of the League of Nations', *International Peacekeeping*, 6, no. 1, pp. 154–60.

Jean, F. (1993) 'The paradoxes of armed protection', in F. Jean (ed.), *Life, Death and Aid: The Médecins Sans Frontières Report on World Crisis Intervention* (English edn), London: Routledge.

Johansen, R. C. and Mendlovitz, S. H. (1980) 'The role of enforcement of law in the establishment of a new international order: a proposal for a transnational police force', *Alternatives*, 6, pp. 307–38.

Johnstone, D. (2000) 'Humanitarian war: making the crime fit the punishment', in T. Ali (ed.), *Masters of the Universe? NATO's Balkan Crusade*, London: Verso.

Kegley, C. W. Jr (1998) 'Thinking ethically about peacemaking and peacekeeping', in T. Woodhouse, R. Bruce and M. Dando (eds), *Peacekeeping and Peacemaking: Towards Effective Intervention in Post-Cold War Conflicts*, Basingstoke: Macmillan.

Kinloch, S. P. (1997) 'Utopian or pragmatic? A UN permanent military volunteer force', in M. Pugh (ed.), *The UN, Peace and Force*, London: Frank Cass.

Knudsen, T. B. (1999) 'Humanitarian intervention and international society: contemporary manifestations of an explosive doctrine', Ph.D. thesis, University of Aarhus, Denmark.

Krause, K. and Latham, A. (1998) 'Constructing non-proliferation and arms control: the norms of Western practice', in K. Krause (ed.), *Culture and Security: Multilateralism, Arms Control and Security Building*, London: Frank Cass.

Krishnasamy, K. (2001) 'Recognition for Third World peacekeepers: India and Pakistan', *International Peacekeeping*, 8, no. 4, pp. 56–76.

McDermott, A. (2001) 'UN finances: what are the costs and who pays the bills?', in E. Newman and O. P. Richmond (eds), *The United Nations and Human Security*, Basingstoke: Palgrave.

McKenzie, M. M. (2001) 'The UN and regional organizations', in E. Newman and O. P. Richmond (eds), *The United Nations and Human Security*, Basingstoke: Palgrave.

Mackinlay, J. (ed.) (1996) *A Guide to Peace Support Operations*, Providence: Thomas J. Watson Institute for International Studies.

Mackinlay, J. and Chopra, J. (1992) 'Second generation multinational operations', *Washington Quarterly*, 15, no. 3, pp. 113–31.

MacKinnon, M. G. (2000) *The Evolution of US Peacekeeping Policy under Clinton: A Fairweather Friend?* London: Frank Cass.

McNulty, M. (1997) 'France's role in Rwanda and external military intervention: a double discrediting', *International Peacekeeping*, 4, no. 3, pp. 24–44.

Mayall, J. (2000) 'The concept of humanitarian intervention revisited', in A. Schnabel and R. Thakur (eds), *Kosovo and the Challenge of Humanitarian Intervention: Selective Indignation, Collective Action and International Citizenship*, Tokyo: UN University Press.

Minear, L. (1994) 'Humanitarians and intervention', in Å. Eknes and A. McDermott (eds), *Sovereignty, Humanitarian Intervention and the Military*, Oslo: Norwegian Institute of International Affairs.

Natsios, A. S. (1996) 'NGOs and the UN system in complex humanitarian emergencies', in T. G. Weiss and L. Gordenker (eds), *NGOs, the UN, and Global Governance*, Boulder, Colo.: Rienner.

Neack, L. (1995) 'UN peace-keeping: in the interest of community or self?', *Journal of Peace Research*, 32, no. 2, pp. 181–96.

Newsweek (1999) 'A new generation draws the line', *Newsweek*, 19 Apr.

Ogata, S. (1994) 'Humanitarianism in the midst of armed conflict', address at the Brookings Institution, Washington DC, 12 May.

Paris, R. (1997) 'Peacebuilding and the limits of liberal internationalism', *International Security*, 22, no. 2, pp. 54–89.

Paris, R. (2001) 'Echoes of the *mission civilisatrice*: peacekeeping in the post-cold war era', in E. Newman and O. P. Richmond (eds), *The United Nations and Human Security*, Basingstoke: Palgrave.

Parsons, A. (1995) *From Cold War to Hot Peace: UN Interventions, 1947–1995*, London: Penguin.

Pouligny, B. (2001) 'Les opérations de paix: mieux maîtriser les paramètres et contextes d'intervention', paper at seminar on 'Gestion des sorties de crise', Institut Diplomatique, Paris, 25 June.

Pugh, M. (2000) 'Civil–military relations in the Kosovo crisis', *Security Dialogue*, 31, no. 2, pp. 229–42.

Pugh, M. (2001a) 'Elections and "protectorate democracy" in Southeast Europe', in E. Newman and O. P. Richmond (eds), *The United Nations and Human Security*, Basingstoke: Palgrave.

Pugh, M. (2001b) 'Peacekeeping and humanitarian intervention', in B. White, R. Little and M. Smith (eds), *Issues in World Politics*, 2nd edn, Basingstoke: Palgrave.

Ramsbotham, O. and Woodhouse, T. (1996) *Humanitarian Intervention in Contemporary Conflict: A Reconceptualization*, Cambridge: Polity.

Richmond, O. P. (1998) *Mediating in Cyprus: The Cypriot Communities and the United Nations*, London: Frank Cass.

Rieff, D. (1999) 'Did truly independent relief agencies die in Kosovo?', *Humanitarian Affairs Review*, 7, pp. 28–31.

Righter, R. (1995) *Utopia Lost: The United Nations and World Order*, New York: Twentieth Century Fund Press.

Roberts, A. (1993) 'Humanitarian war: military intervention and human rights', *International Affairs*, 69, no. 3, pp. 429–49.

Rolfe, J. (2001) 'Peacekeeping the Pacific way in Bougainville', *International Peacekeeping*, 8, no. 4, pp. 38–55.

Rufin, J.-C. (1993) 'The paradoxes of armed protection', in F. Jean (ed.), *Life, Death and Aid: The Médecins Sans Frontières Report on World Crisis Intervention* (English edn), London: Routledge.

Schmidl, E. A. (1999) 'The international operation in Albania, 1913–14', *International Peacekeeping*, 6, no. 3, pp. 1–10.

Schmidl, E. A. (2000) 'The evolution of peace operations from the nineteenth century', in E. A. Schmidl (ed.), *Peace Operations between War and Peace*, London: Frank Cass.

Sörensen, J. S. (2002) 'Balkanism and the new radical interventionism: a structural critique', *International Peacekeeping*, 9, no. 1, pp. 1–22.

Sphere Project (2000) *Humanitarian Charter and Minimum Standards in Disaster Response*, Oxford: Oxfam.

Suhrke, A. (1999) 'Human security and the interests of states', *Security Dialogue*, 30, no. 3, Sept., pp. 265–76.

Teson, F. (1988) *Humanitarian Intervention: An inquiry into Law and Morality*, Dobbs Ferry, N.Y.: Transnational.

Tharoor, S. (1995a) 'Foreword', in D. C. F. Daniel and B. Hayes (eds), *Beyond Traditional Peacekeeping*, Basingstoke: Macmillan.

Tharoor, S. (1995b) 'The role of the United Nations in European peacekeeping', in E. B. Eide (ed.), *Peacekeeping in Europe*, Peacekeeping and Multinational Operations Series, No. 5, Oslo: Norwegian Institute for International Affairs.

UN Doc. (2000a) 'Peacekeeping Operations Committee 160th mtg', press release GA/PK/166–7, 14–15 Feb.

UN Doc. (2000b) 'Report of the Panel on United Nations Peace Operations', A/55/305 and S/2000/809, 21 Aug.

Urquhart, B. (1993) 'For a UN volunteer military force', *New York Review of Books*, 10 June, pp. 3–4.

Van Baarda, T. A. (2001) 'Conscience, military law and peacekeeping: an uneasy relationship in view of the Brahimi report', paper to 4th Canadian Conference on Ethical Leadership, Royal Military College, 7–9 Nov.

Vieira de Mello, S. (1994) 'Humanitarian and military interface in peace-keeping. Cambodia and Bosnia-Herzegovina: a comparative overview', in U. Palwankar (ed.), *Symposium on Humanitarian Action and Peace-Keeping Operations*, Geneva: ICRC, 22–24 June.

Visman, E. (1993) *Military Humanitarian Intervention in Somalia*, London: Save the Children.

Walker T. and Laverty, A. (2000) 'CIA aided Kosovo guerrilla army', *Sunday Times*, 12 Mar.

Weiss, T. G. (1999) *Military–Civilian Interactions: Intervening in Humanitarian Crises*, Lanham, Mass.: Rowan and Littlefield.

Weiss, T. G. and Campbell, K. M. (1991) 'Military humanitarianism', *Survival*, 33, no. 5, pp. 451–65.

Wheeler, N. J. (2000) *Saving Strangers: Humanitarian Intervention in International Society*, Oxford: Oxford University Press.

Wheeler, N. J. (2001) 'Humanitarian intervention after Kosovo: emergent norm, moral duty or the coming anarchy?', *International Affairs*, 77, no. 1, pp. 113–28.

Williams, J. (1999) 'The ethical basis of humanitarian intervention, the Security Council and Yugoslavia', *International Peacekeeping*, 6, no. 2, pp. 1–23.

Woodhouse, T. and Ramsbotham, O. (1998) 'Peacekeeping and humanitarian intervention in post-cold war conflict', in T. Woodhouse, R. Bruce and M. Dando (eds), *Peacekeeping and Peacemaking: Towards Effective Intervention in Post-Cold War Conflicts*, Basingstoke: Macmillan.

Woodward, S. L. (2001) 'Humanitarian war: a new consensus?', *Disasters*, 25, no. 4, pp. 331–4.

Part III

Theories of Global Governance

11

A Realist Perspective on International Governance

Robert Gilpin

The idea of a realist theory of international governance is a contradiction in terms, at least as many scholars employ the term 'international governance' in contemporary discourse. The fundamental proposition of political realism is that the international system is anarchic. 'Anarchy,' as most realists use this term, means the absence of a legitimate authority to which sovereign states are subordinate and give allegiance. If such an authority were established, then, the defining anarchic nature of international affairs, as realists believe, would no longer exist and the fundamental difference between domestic and international affairs, that is, the presence or absence of authority, would disappear. As the basic premise of realism is that the domestic and international realms do differ in kind rather than in degree, the doctrine of realism would cease to have any relevance. For this reason, this article is essentially a critique of the idea of international governance. But first, what do I mean by 'realism' and, subsequently, by 'international governance?'

The Nature of Political Realism

Political realism, or simply realism, is the oldest perspective on international affairs. It traces its roots to Thucydides, Machiavelli and Thomas Hobbes. In the contemporary era, among the most important realist thinkers have been Hedley Bull, E. H. Carr, Hans Morgenthau, Reinhold Niebuhr, Kenneth Waltz and Martin Wight. Although these influential thinkers disagreed on many aspects of contemporary affairs and foreign policy, they shared fundamental perspectives or assumptions regarding the nature of international politics. Thus understood, realism constitutes a way of thinking about and analysing international affairs.

Realism, as I use the term, is a philosophical position; it is not a scientific theory. As a philosophical or intellectual perspective, realism is not subject to the Popperian criterion of falsifiability and, like other philosophical positions such as liberalism and Marxism, realism can neither be proved nor disproved by empirical research. However, international relations scholarship in the realist tradition has led to theories or hypotheses regarding international affairs, including theories of the balance of power and of hegemonic stability, theories that can be and have been subjected to empirical testing to determine their validity.

The realist interpretation of international affairs makes several basic assumptions regarding the nature of international affairs. Because it assumes that the international system is anarchic and has no supreme political authority, realism regards the state as the principal actor(s) in international affairs; the state is said to be sovereign and not subordinate to any higher temporal power. The existence of anarchy, however, does not mean that international politics is characterized by a constant and universal Hobbesian war of one against all; states obviously do cooperate with one another and do create international institutions in those areas where their interests coincide. Anarchy means rather that there is no higher authority that compels them to cooperate and to which a state can appeal for succour in times of trouble. In addition, although the state is the primary actor in international affairs, realism does not ignore the importance of such non-state actors as multinational firms, international organizations and non-governmental organizations in the determination of international affairs. Realism insists, however, that the state continues to be the principal actor in both economic and political affairs.

The central concerns of the state are its national interests, as defined principally in terms of military security and political independence; realism does not necessarily reject the importance of moral and value considerations in determining national behaviour. However, realists do warn against basing a nation's fate on moral persuasion. Power and power relations play the major role in international affairs; as E. H. Carr has pointed out, power can assume the form of military, economic, and even psychological relationships among states (Carr, 1951). Moreover, despite realism's emphasis on power, other factors such as ideas, values and norms can play an important role in interstate affairs. The idea, for example, that all realists are unaware of the role of ideas or intellectual constructs in international affairs is patently false. As Hans Morgenthau argued in his classic *Scientific Man vs. Power Politics* (1946), the liberal beliefs of the Western democracies made them incapable of recognizing and being able to react decisively to the threat of Nazism and fascism in the 1930s. Recognizing the importance of ideas, Morgenthau warned that it was unwise to place one's faith solely in the power of ideals.

Realism assumes that national security is and always will be the principal concern of states. In a 'self-help' international system, to use Kenneth Waltz's apt expression, states must constantly guard against actual or potential threats to their political and economic independence. Concern with security means that power is vitally important in international affairs; states must be continuously attentive to changes in power relations and to the consequences for their own national interests of shifts in the international balance of power among the members of the international political system.

Realists believe that the territorial state continues to be the primary actor in both domestic and international affairs. However, the state is not the only important actor. Today other significant players include the World Bank, the International Monetary Fund and the Commission of the European Union. Despite the importance of these other actors, however, national governments still make the primary decisions regarding economic and political matters; the states still set the rules within which other actors function, and they use their considerable power to influence economic and political outcomes. Even in such a highly integrated international institution as the European Union, the role of the major political players, namely Germany, France and the United Kingdom, is central. Whatever the ultimate shape of the European Union, national governments will continue to be important actors within this regional arrangement.

Although realists recognize the central role in international affairs of the state, of security and of power, individual realists do not necessarily approve of this situation.

Martin Wight, the author of one of the most important tracts on realism in this century, 'Power politics' (Wight, 1986), was a Christian pacifist. Even Hans Morgenthau in his influential *Politics among Nations* (1972), having Adolph Hitler in mind, condemned as immoral 'universal nationalism', that is, imperialistic behaviour; one of his basic messages was that states should try to respect the interests of other states. It is possible, I believe, as in my own case, to analyse international affairs from a realist perspective and, at the same time, to have a normative commitment to liberal and humanitarian ideals.

Many scholars and others believe that economic and technological forces have eclipsed the nation-state and are creating a global economy and society in which political boundaries and national loyalties are no longer relevant; the realist inter-pretation of international affairs rejects that popular belief. It is certainly true that economic and technological forces are profoundly reshaping international affairs and influencing the behaviour of states; however, even in a highly integrated global economy, states continue to use their power and to implement policies to channel economic forces in ways favourable to their own national interests and the interests of their citizenry. National economic interests include receipt of a fair or even favourable share of the gains from international economic activities as well as preservation of national autonomy. Movement towards such regional arrangements as the European Union and the North American Free Trade Agreement exemplify collective national efforts to reach these shared goals.

The nation-state has certainly come under attack from within and from without; both transnational economic forces and ethnic nationalisms are tearing at the economic and political foundations of the nation-state. Yet the nation-state remains of supreme importance even though there is no certainty that it will exist forever. Like every human institution, the nation-state was created to meet specific needs. The state arose at a particular moment in time in order to provide economic and political security and to achieve other desired goals; in return, citizens gave the nation-state their loyalty. When the nation-state ceases to meet the needs of its citizens, the latter will withdraw their loyalty and the modern state will disappear as did the feudal kingdoms, imperial systems and city-states that it displaced. However, there is no evidence that such a transformation in human affairs has yet occurred or is even occurring. On the con-trary, the world is witnessing a rapid increase in the number of nation-states, and this increase is accompanied by intense nationalisms and the creation of powerful military forces. Moreover, if and when the nation-state does disappear, it will be displaced by some new form of formal political authority. However, it is highly unlikely that the nation-state will, at any time soon, be replaced by a global governing mechanism.

The next section will consider, from a realist perspective, the most important attempts to formulate a system or mechanism of international governance for the international economy: neoliberal institutionalism, new medievalism, and transgovern-mentalism. The emphasis in each approach is economic cooperation. Certainly, if international governance is to be achieved, it will come first in the realm of economic affairs. This is the area where a common interest in stability and in effective rules is most obviously apparent; trade, foreign investment, and other commercial activities are of mutual benefit and require binding obligations. Yet, as I shall argue, even though trade, foreign investment and other commercial activities make contributions to the goal of greater order in international economic affairs, they do not overcome the fundamental anarchic nature of the international system. They fail to create an international or suprastate authority that can govern the behaviour of self-centred and self-seeking states. If an effective governance mechanism in economic affairs is unlikely to be achieved, then, the prospects for greater order in the far more difficult area of international political and security matters are not promising.

Governance of the Global Economic and Political System

Although many scholars have addressed the problem of international governance, no generally accepted definition of the term exists. However, a very useful analysis of the issue is found in Wolfgang H. Reinicke's *Global Public Policy: Governing without Government*? (1989). The central proposition of Reinicke's interesting book is that government and the functions of governance can be disentangled from one another. In the modern world, 'government' refers to formal institutions that enjoy national sovereignty, possess a monopoly of power over a particular territory, and are not answerable to an external authority. Governments have been able to make domestic public policy and also to be politically independent actors in international affairs. Governance, on the other hand, is a social function such as the regulation of economic affairs, and is not necessarily the same as government. Governance, according to Reinicke, need not be equated with government but can be achieved through networks of public and private groups or institutions at national, regional and international levels. Thus the global system can enjoy the benefits of government without the existence of a formal governing structure.

Despite Reinicke's formulation, governance requires the exercise of power, and we still live in a world where (following Max Weber) governments continue to be the only institutions with the legitimacy to employ force to achieve social objectives and to enforce agreements. More specifically, the three principal functions of government and the ones on which all other functions must rest are still largely the monopoly of states. These sovereign rights are: (1) coinage (money creation); (2) taxation; and (3) safeguarding national and individual security. The importance of money creation speaks for itself; yet it is worth noting that the state's control over the money supply is the basis of its capacity to manage the economy through the use of monetary policy; this source of leverage over the economy makes governments very reluctant to give up the sovereign right of coinage. The European Economic and Monetary Union embodies the only significant effort to transfer control over the money supply away from individual states. However, the ultimate success of this experiment has yet to be determined, and many experts believe that the common currency (euro) will not work without greater European political unity. The possibility of transferring the function of money creation to a global governance mechanism is inconceivable at this time.

With respect to the sovereign right of taxation, the European Union has been reluctant to assert a right to levy taxes on members of the Union; the right to tax remains vested in national governments. The EU has even been slow to harmonize tax policies across the Union. Without a Europe-wide tax, the EU cannot easily assume one of the principal welfare functions of government in the modern world, namely, income redistribution among classes and regions. Regarding the provision of security, the EU has of course committed itself to a more unified security policy and creation of a rapid deployment force. While this is a welcome initiative, one must ask if the peoples of Western Europe are willing to pay its accompanying high cost. In short, it is doubtful that government and the functions of governance can be separated from one another even at the level of the European Union, and if governance cannot supplant government among these highly integrated nations, it is doubly doubtful that it can be achieved at the much more fragmented global level.

Despite the strong reservations expressed here regarding international governance, it is useful to consider three prominent proposals for international governance that have been set forth by American and some other scholars: neoliberal institutionalism, 'new medievalism', and transgovernmentalism. Neoliberal institutionalism, based on the continued importance of the state, assumes that formal international regimes, rules and institutions can govern international affairs, or at least, significant aspects of it. The new medievalism is based on the assumption that the state and the state system have been undermined by economic, technological and other developments; the state and state system are being eclipsed, it is alleged, by non-governmental actors and by emergence of an international civil society. New medievalists believe that the end of national sovereignty and the resulting diffusion of power will enable selfless NGOs to solve the world's pressing environmental and other problems. Transgovernmentalism argues that international cooperation through subnational government units or agencies in specific functional areas is rapidly replacing the decision-making functions of centralized national governments in the management of the global system.

Neoliberal Institutionalism

Neoliberal institutionalism, which accepts the continued importance of the nation-state, has been concerned primarily with the governance of the international economy. Its proponents believe that international rules, regimes and institutions have become sufficiently strong to meet the challenges of a globalized international economy. Moreover, if existing international institutions and regimes are found to be deficient, new ones can be created or easily modified as they have been in the past. The 1995 replacement of the General Agreement on Tariffs and Trade by the World Trade Organization provides an important example of a substantial reform of an international institution. The newer WTO has greater authority over trade matters, more resources, and more power to enforce its decisions than did the GATT. The World Bank and the International Monetary Fund are also being reformed in the first years of the twenty-first century. In addition, new international conventions on environmental and other important matters are being implemented.

There are formidable obstacles to the achievement of the neoliberal institutionalist ideal of a rule- or regime-based international economy; the issue of compliance is particularly challenging. Regardless of the many books and articles on the compliance problem, it continues to limit the effectiveness of international organizations. Moreover, there are few generally accepted principles and policy prescriptions on which regimes can be constructed. The post-Second World War Bretton Woods regimes dealing with trade and monetary affairs, for example, were based on such Western legal and economic ideas as the transparency of commercial dealings and limited state intervention in the economy; the triumph of neoliberalism in the 1980s reinforced such liberal principles. However, as economic integration among national economies has deepened around the world, fundamental differences among national systems of political economy regarding economic principles and legitimate policy have challenged Western legal and economic ideals. For example, American and Japanese notions of fairness in international economic competition are divergent. Increasing regionalization of the global economy has become a popular way to deal with problems created by national differences.

Although the clash between different national systems of political economy has intensified, most American economists and public officials expect that a process of convergence will eventually lead to worldwide acceptance of the policy prescriptions of neoclassical economics and of a free market based on the American economic model. Some aspects of the Asian state-centred economic model, they point out, have already been discredited, and many states have retreated from aggressive government intervention in the economy. Yet in many countries there is deep suspicion that leaving society's welfare and a nation's position in the global system to the vicissitudes of the market will be very harmful to society and national well-being. Several concerns voiced by sceptics should be noted. Some countries bitterly resent the constraints imposed on economic policy by emphasis on the 'market'; notable examples of such resentment have appeared in Malaysia and South Korea. In defiance of free market ideology, Malaysia in the 1990s imposed capital controls, and South Korea has strongly resisted American demands to liquidate the *chaebol* form of industrial organization. There have also been serious revolts against trade liberalization in the West. An important example is the continuing failure of the US Congress to give the President negotiating power with respect to new rounds of trade negotiations.

International institutions are faced with a number of immediate issues whose outcome will determine their future. One pressing issue given public prominence by the Seattle protestors against the WTO in November 1999 is the 'democratic deficit': international economic institutions are criticized because they are not directly accountable to any democratic electorate. But if they are not to be responsible to national governments, then to whom or to what should international organizations be accountable? If it were a governance system based on 'one person, one vote', then Indians and Chinese would rule the world. It is difficult to believe that many Americans, Japanese or West Europeans would accept such a solution to the democratic deficit; they would undoubtedly prefer a system of weighted voting that takes into account their share of global wealth.

Closely tied to the issue of the democratic deficit is the increasing mismatch between the distribution of authority within and among existing institutions and the changing distribution of power in the international system. Despite the significant shift in global economic power towards East Asia and certain developing economies that has occurred over the last half-century, decision-making authority in the IMF, WTO and World Bank continues to reside mainly with the United States and Western Europe; the United States has a strong voice in the World Bank and Western Europe in the IMF (although American influence in this institution is strong, much to the annoyance of West Europeans). As the power of these institutions has grown, Japan, the industrializing economies of East Asia, and the developing countries have intensified their demands for a greater say. Resolution of this conflict over who controls the world's international economic institutions will not be achieved easily.

The third issue regarding the IMF, the World Bank, and similar bodies is that of institutional reform. The demand for reform has become very strong. In the United States, these institutions have been attacked by both the political left and political right. More and more Americans believe that these institutions should be weakened or even eliminated rather than strengthened. The left argues that these institutions serve only the interests of multinational corporations and the ruling capitalist elite. The right argues that the functions of these organizations are unnecessary in a global economy based on free markets. Opinion in the United States is moving away from and not towards the idea of international governance, unless of course it suits one's own particular interests. Indeed, the most important issue to be resolved is determination of the purpose of international governance.

The New Medievalism

The 'new medievalism', a term attributed to Hedley Bull, assumes that the world is experiencing the end of national sovereignty. Adherents of this position believe that this historic moment has been reached because of transnational economic forces (trade, finance, etc.) and because of such contemporary technological developments as the computer, information technologies, and advances in transportation. Proponents of the new medievalism allege that, in the era of the internet, governments have lost their monopoly over information and can therefore be successfully challenged by non-governmental actors. Concluding that such changes erode hierarchical organizations and undermine centralized power structures, new medievalists see the once-dominant hierarchic order of nation-states being supplanted by horizontal networks composed of states, non-governmental organizations and international institutions. This revolutionary development, in turn, is leading to cooperative problem-solving by concerned individuals and groups from around the world. They envision a world of multiple allegiances and responsibilities replacing the undivided loyalty formerly owed by the citizenry to the sovereign. Subnational, national and supranational institutions will share authority over individuals in this new world.

An example of the new medievalism at work is provided by Reinicke in the work cited above. He discusses the negotiations and establishment of the Basel Accord of 1988 to develop international regulatory standards for international banks. Specification of minimum capital adequacy requirements was particularly important; that is, the Accord specified the size of the monetary reserves that international banks had to maintain to prevent bank failures and to decrease the risk of destabilizing financial crises. Reinicke argues that the Accord resulted from complex and successful negotiations among national governments, private interests and the Bank for International Settlements. Although he himself does not use the term, he concludes that new medievalism worked successfully as governments, NGOs and international institutions cooperated and were able to create an international governance mechanism in this particular area of international finance.

Although Reinicke's example does illustrate that national, private and international organizations can cooperate to solve an international economic problem, his argument does not provide convincing support for the idea that governance (as opposed to government) by itself can deal with the many pressing problems created by the increasing integration of the world economy. As Reinicke himself shows, the Basel Accord was achieved largely through strong American pressure. American 'money centre banks' in New York and California had complained to the American central bank (the Federal Reserve) that, because foreign international banks were permitted to maintain bank reserves lower than those required for American banks, the former enjoyed a competitive advantage over the latter. Responding to this concern, the Federal Reserve put pressure on foreign governments to raise reserve requirements; the resulting Basel Accord required European and Japanese banks to increase their reserves. Although it was undoubtedly desirable that a universal standard be established for reserve requirements, it came about only in response to American pressure. This episode suggests that international governance cannot work in the absence of power and a willingness to use that power. Unfortunately, Reinicke's proposed policy networks lack the power required to achieve compliance with their decisions.

The new medievalism asserts that non-governmental organizations have, or at least should have, a central role in the governance of international (or 'post-national') affairs. Organized primarily around such specific issues as safeguarding the environment, protecting human rights and promoting a safer world, NGOs have indeed become a significant force in particular issue areas. The number of non-governmental organizations has greatly increased in recent decades to the level of approximately 30,000 at the beginning of the twenty-first century. Among the most important of these grass-roots organizations are the Worldwide Fund for Nature, the Sierra Club, and Doctors Without Borders (Médecins Sans Frontières). Most NGOs are located in the United States and, to a lesser extent, in Western Europe. Japan appears to have few important NGOs, but NGOs have become increasingly active in some less developed countries. Although NGOs were initially involved primarily with domestic issues, they have become increasingly concerned over the allegedly negative effects of globalization on the environment and other matters.

NGOs have successfully influenced the policies of national governments and international institutions in a number of areas. One of the most important accomplishments was the Earth Summit (1992) in Rio de Janeiro where NGOs exerted enough pressure to achieve agreements intended to eliminate greenhouse gases. Two years later, NGO protestors besieged the World Bank and forced the latter to reconsider some of its policies. Other examples of effective NGO campaigns have included the treaty to eliminate land mines, the agreement to reduce the huge indebtedness of many less developed countries, and derailment of the American-sponsored Multilateral Agreement on Investment. Whatever one may think about the wisdom or effectiveness of one or another of these successes, it is certain that NGOs have become a force in the contemporary world.

It is much too soon to know what the long-term impact of NGOs will be on the management of a more integrated global economy. At present, the observer should keep in mind that the modern state has been around for over three centuries, that generally effective international institutions have existed for half a century, and that the active era of NGO activity on an international level began only two decades ago. Moreover, it is possible that the highly favourable picture that we have today of NGOs will become quite different in the future. It is in the nature of politics – and politics is what we are talking about – for power to beget countervailing power and for the tactics of the politically successful to be imitated by others. Therefore, the 'good' NGOs of today pursuing noteworthy objectives may one day be joined by NGOs whose goals are much less praiseworthy. Such a possibility was foreshadowed by the unholy alliance in Seattle between the 'good' NGOs seeking to achieve such selfless objectives as human rights and environmental protection, with American organized labour NGOs that cynically exploited the former's goals in their own campaign to keep the exports of less developed countries out of the American economy.

Transgovernmentalism

Like liberal internationalism and unlike the new medievalism, transgovernmentalism accepts the continued existence of nation-states. However, like the new medievalism, it assumes that the governance functions of the state can be separated from one another and delegated to intergovernmental bodies or networks dealing with specific policy issues. Many transgovernmental organizations already exist to deal with such matters as banking regulations (the Basel Accord), anti-trust regulation, and judicial matters. Transnational networks composed of technical experts, business executives and public officials are needed to manage an increasingly complex and integrated world in which extensive technical input is required.

Transgovernmentalism assumes that technical issues can be separated from politics and then solved independently by technocrats; regulatory matters, for example, can be isolated from national economic priorities and from the pressures of powerful interests. This approach to international governance may apply to certain relatively depoliticized areas. However, proponents of transgovernmentalism have ignored more sensitive matters such as national security and foreign policy. They also appear to assume that there is no hierarchy of national interests in which some issues, of vital interest to governments, cannot be delegated to transnational bodies. Proponents of transgovernmentalism argue as if concerns over proliferation of nuclear weapons and the future of the NATO alliance were of no greater importance than the regulation of ocean fisheries.

Transgovernmentalism foresees a world stripped of power, national interests and interstate conflict; its proponents envision a world nearly devoid of either domestic or international politics, a world in which technocrats, bureaucrats and experts can solve issues outside the realm of domestic and international politics. While stressing the absolute gains from transgovernmental cooperation, transgovernmentalism is silent on the equally important matter of relative gains and of the issues of distributive consequences that arise in almost every serious international discussion of substantive issues.

To be sure, transgovernmental networks can be very useful in solving many different issues. However, this approach to governance of the international system is severely limited by the political rivalries and conflicting interests of both nation-states and their domestic constituencies. As we have already seen, even such a technical matter as the Basel Accord on banking practices (frequently cited as an example of successful intergovernmentalism at work) was laced with intense political/economic conflicts, and resolution of these conflicts required the exercise of power. Any effort to resolve the governance issue must recognize that this is still a world of states, power and national interests.

Each of the above approaches to governance of the global economy makes a useful contribution. As proponents of neoliberal institutionalism correctly argue, formal international institutions and agreed-on rules or regimes have greatly facilitated cooperation among sovereign nation-states and been a significant factor in the management of the international economy over half a century. Yet the continuing resistance of states to restrictions on their sovereignty, the limited coverage of international regimes/institutions, and serious problems of compliance mean that neoliberal institutionalism alone cannot govern the global economy. The argument of the new medievalism that NGOs are becoming more important in solving the world's pressing problems gains support from the fact that the strong commitment and concentrated energy of these associations have been, on the whole, a positive force for dealing with the world's many serious issues. Yet these groups cannot function without the national governments and international institutions on which they must bring pressure to achieve their goals. It is much too early to know the true long-term significance of the NGOs.

Finally, the approach of transgovernmentalism is an important complement to the other two approaches. Cooperation and information-sharing among the agencies and branches of national governments can be an effective means to deal with many complex technical issues at both the domestic and international levels. However, the legalistic and technocratic approach of transgovernmentalism suffers not only from a democratic deficit, but its usefulness declines steeply as issues become more entwined with matters of national security, domestic partisan politics and distributive matters.

Although all three approaches can facilitate the governance of the global economy, none of these approaches can fulfil the many demands placed on international governance. Most importantly, each lacks the one crucial component of government, that is, the capacity to enforce decisions. The nation-state continues to be the only institution in the contemporary world that has this capacity. This situation is not one that I personally find pleasing. Although the nation-state ensures domestic peace and, in democratic societies, an element of justice, at the international level the rivalries and jealousies of states too frequently result in war and in many injustices.

Three Challenges to Proposals for International Governance

Every system of governance must deal with what, for lack of a better term, can be called 'the problem of power'; this expression refers to the necessity to control government or governance to prevent the abuse of power. In addition, the institution of a system of government or governance reflects existing power relations and the status quo; as change in human affairs is inevitable, a mechanism must be incorporated in the system of governance to facilitate peaceful change. The most fundamental issue facing proposals for international governance is 'governance for what?' What are the social, political and economic purposes that governance is to serve? Unless these issues can be resolved, proposals for international governance must be greeted with considerable scepticism.

In *The Anarchical Society: A Study of Order in World Politics* (1977), Hedley Bull raised a very serious challenge to the idea of international governance. In this important study of the nature and problem of international order, Bull devoted many pages to a detailed and effective critique of Richard Falk's proposal for moving swiftly to international governance. An important argument made by Bull against Falk's concept of 'central guidance' of the global system based on international law and organization was that Falk neglected the central problem of politics, that is, the problem of power. Falk's system of centralized governance, Bull pointed out, would be dominated and controlled by the world's most powerful state, namely, the United States. In Bull's judgement, such a concentration of power in one state would be dangerous and would eventually lead to tyranny. For Bull, as for other writers in the realist tradition, the power of one group over others can never be eliminated from human affairs, and it is therefore far wiser to rely on a balance of power among states in a decentralized international system.

Bull's argument against Falk's system of centralized guidance hearkens back, of course, to Thomas Hobbes and his proposal for a leviathan – the centralization of power in the hands of one individual – as the solution to the problem of conflict and social disorder. However, Hobbes was unable to conceive of a solution to the dangers of concentrating power in the leviathan. For realists, the existence of power and the danger that such power will be abused constitute the core problems of political affairs. As Morgenthau warns in *Scientific Man vs. Power Politics*, there is no 'once and for all time' solution to this problem. Any proposal for international governance must necessarily address this fundamental fact of the human condition. Instead, the tendency is to wish the problem of power away by declaring that we now live in a new and better world based on universal and humane values.

In addition to the problem of controlling or balancing power, every system of government must rest on a social, political and economic foundation. The rules and institutions of the governing system reflect these underlying social, political and economic arrangements regarding such matters as who owns what and the distribution of rights and obligations. With the passage of time, demographic, technological and other changes undermine this status quo and give rise to demands for changes in these arrangements and in the government that has sustained them. Obviously, adjustment to these changes may be painful for some and could be strongly resisted. As E. H. Carr argued in *The Twenty-Years' Crisis*, the problem of adjusting to change is as applicable to international as it is to domestic affairs. For this reason, any system of international governance must incorporate what Carr calls a mechanism to ensure 'peaceful change'. Recognition of the problem of change and of the fundamental adjustments that change makes necessary is seldom incorporated in proposals for international governance.

In response to that important challenge of 'governance for what?' the Preamble to the American Constitution makes its objectives quite explicit. One should ask no less of proposals for international governance. Is the goal simply world peace? Or is it peace with justice for all? Or is it justice even if this goal means the sacrifice of peace? These three objectives are obviously very different and may even be opposed to one another. Yet for various groups of people, which answer is chosen to these questions is supremely important. Thus, if any proposal for international governance is to be taken seriously, it must attempt to address the issue of the purpose(s) to be served.

References

Bull, Hedley (1977) *The Anarchical Society: A Study of Order in World Politics*, New York: Columbia University Press.

Carr, E. H. (1951) *The Twenty-Years' Crisis, 1919–1939*, 2nd edn, London: Macmillan.

Morgenthau, Hans (1946) *Scientific Man vs. Power Politics*, Chicago: University of Chicago Press.

Morgenthau, Hans J. (1972) *Politics among Nations*, New York: Knopf.

Reinicke, Wolfgang H. (1989) *Global Public Policy: Governing without Government?* Washington: Brookings Institution.

Wight, Martin (1986) 'Power politics', in *Power Politics*, ed. Hedley Bull and Carsten Holbraad, Harmondsworth: Penguin Books.

12
Marxism and Global Governance
Alex Callinicos

It has become a cliché to say that Marx anticipated the emergence of what we now call economic globalization nearly 150 years before the term came into common currency. Thus in the midst of his celebration in the *Communist Manifesto* (1848) of the dynamic and revolutionary character of the capitalist mode of production, he writes: 'The bourgeoisie has through its exploitation of the world market given a cosmopolitan character to production and consumption in every country.' Marx goes on to describe the destruction of 'national industries' by rivals that import raw materials and export finished products across the world. Not simply do we develop material wants whose satisfaction depends on this globally integrated production system, but culture itself is transformed: 'from the numerous national and local literatures, there arises a world literature' (Marx and Engels, 1976, p. 488).

Marx says little about the immediate political implications of these processes of economic and cultural transformation, but his few remarks on this subject in the *Manifesto* would place him among the 'hyperglobalizers' in contemporary debates who argue that economic globalization is producing the effacement of the nation-state: 'National differences and antagonisms between peoples are daily more and more vanishing, owing to the development of the bourgeoisie, to freedom of commerce, to the world market, to uniformity in the mode of production and in the conditions of life corresponding thereto' (Marx and Engels, 1976, p. 503).[1] It is in general unwise to treat the *Manifesto* as a definitive statement of Marx's views: rather it must be seen as a set of brilliant intuitions based on his initial encounter with political economy that were later developed, and in some cases revised or even abandoned as a result of his further economic studies. Yet the emphases of Marx's later writings did not, with respect to economic globalization and its political consequences, shift significantly from those so famously made in the *Manifesto*. Thus, on the one hand, he continued to insist on the intrinsic connection between capitalism and economic globalization, writing, for example: 'The tendency to create the *world market* is directly given in the concept of capital itself' (Marx, 1973, p. 408). On the other hand, in *Capital* he abstracts from the existence of national differences, 'treat[ing] the whole world of trade as one nation' (Marx, 1976, p. 727 n2). Whether or not this assumption was necessary in order to analyse the capitalist economy, it constituted an obstacle to any attempt by Marx to thematize the existence of an international system of states, let alone to explore the forms of global governance which this system might generate (Luporini, 1979).

Nevertheless, it is at least arguable that the analytical framework of *Capital* contained the conceptual resources from which a theory of the international could be developed. Marx argued that the capitalist mode of production is constituted by two fundamental dimensions – the exploitation of wage-labour by capital in the process of production, and the competitive struggle among rival capitals. Far from being an epiphenomenal expression of the class struggle, the competition between capitals imposes capitalism's distinctive tendencies on them: 'The influence of individual capitals on one another has the effect precisely that they must conduct themselves as capital' (Marx, 1973, p. 657; see Rosdolsky, 1977). From this perspective, the development of the European state system from the late Middle Ages onwards and its world-wide extension in the nineteenth and twentieth centuries, defined by endemic military and territorial conflicts between politically sovereign actors, could be seen as part of the same process as the emergence of a capitalist economic system driven by competition between 'many capitals'.[2] Marxist theorization of world politics as it developed after Marx's death in 1883 sought systematically to explore the relations between these two forms of competition, economic and geopolitical, though, as we shall see, one of the main points of debate concerned the possibility that the further evolution of capitalism might bring these anarchic struggles to an end. It is through these explorations that what one might retrospectively describe as specifically Marxist claims about the nature of global governance began to emerge, though, till very recently, these have done so obliquely, in the context of discussions of international political economy.

Ultra-imperialism or Global Anarchy?

Marx and his successors had to confront the political effects of the international state system even if they initially failed to conceptualize it. For the Marxists of the Second International (1889–1914) this took the form mainly of discussion of what would later be called the national and colonial question – on the one hand, responding to the demands for national self-determination that were increasingly stridently asserted particularly within the multinational empires still dominant in central and eastern Europe; on the other hand, weighing the moral rights and wrongs and the political significance of the reduction of the non-European world to formal or informal colonies of the European powers and their American and Russian extensions (Haupt et al., 1974). The distribution of these colonies was, of course, one of the main stakes in the geopolitical conflicts that produced the First World War: the search for the economic roots of these rivalries helped to stimulate the efflorescence of Marxist political economy at the turn of the century whose masterworks were Rudolf Hilferding's *Finance Capital* (1910) and Rosa Luxemburg's *The Accumulation of Capital* (1913).

But it was the implosion of the state system in August 1914 that prompted leading Marxist theoreticians to draw together these economic analyses and political arguments into what we might retrospectively think of as theses about global governance. Two principal positions, sharply opposed to one another, emerged. The first was formulated by Karl Kautsky, leading theorist of the German Social Democratic Party (SPD), and, thanks to his editorship of the weekly *Neue Zeit*, the main intellectual reference point of the entire international socialist movement. Kautsky's theory of ultra-imperialism amounted to a Marxist version of the then widely current idea – it was put forward, for example, by Norman Angell in his best-selling book *The Great Illusion* (1910) – that the dramatic trends towards economic integration that the world experienced at the end of the nineteenth century had rendered military competition and war irrational from a capitalist point of view.[3]

Kautsky's version of this argument focused on the trend towards cartellization through which leading industrial firms bound themselves together in order to protect themselves from competition. Marxist economists such as Hilferding saw this as one facet of a larger process in which nationally organized capitalisms emerged on the basis – of which Wilhelmine Germany offered the classic example – of the integration of investment banks, industrial firms, and the nation-state. But, asked Kautsky, why should this process not be extended from the national to the international scale?

> What Marx said about capitalism can also be applied to imperialism: monopoly creates competition and competition, monopoly. The frantic competition among the huge firms, giant banks, and multimillionaires compelled the great financial groups, who were absorbing the small ones, to devise the cartel. Similarly the World War between the great imperialist powers may result in a federation of the strongest, who renounce their arms race.
>
> From the purely economic standpoint it is therefore not impossible for capitalism to live through yet another phase, the transferral of this process of forming cartels into foreign policy; a phase of *ultra-imperialism*. (Kautsky, 1984, p. 181)

Kautsky understood 'imperialism' here as it was generally used in the Second International, namely to refer to the entire process of geopolitical competition among the Great Powers of which the construction of colonial empires was merely one facet. His view of it as a passing phase in the evolution of capitalism fitted in with Kautsky's broader historico-political view of socialism as an organic process of development out of a capitalism that was itself becoming progressively more civilized thanks to the development of welfare politics and liberal democracy in the advanced countries. This outlook survived the First World War, allowing Kautsky to anticipate that the League of Nations could – as part of this civilizing process – institute a more pacific world order.

It was understandable that this worldview should come under challenge from the revolutionary wing of the Second International that went on to form, after the Russian Revolution of October 1917, the Third, or Communist International. The analytical basis of this challenge was provided by the theory of imperialism chiefly associated with Lenin but most rigorously formulated by his fellow Bolshevik leader Nikolai Bukharin. Lenin's pamphlet *Imperialism, the Highest Stage of Capitalism* (1916) was never intended as a piece of original research. Rather, its aim was to situate theoretically and politically the work of others – notably Hilferding and the radical Liberal economist J. A. Hobson. The main point was provided by the pamphlet's title: imperialism was no mere policy, as the Marxists of the Second International had tended to see it, nor was it a transitory phase of capitalist development – on the contrary, it represented the highest stage to which that mode of production could attain. This appreciation implied the complete rejection of Kautsky's speculations about ultra-imperialism: for Lenin, Kautsky was the ultimate renegade, the visible symbol of the Second International's failure to offer a revolutionary response to the outbreak of the First World War. The notion of ultra-imperialism served, on this view, as a means of justifying this failure by suggesting that capitalism itself could rid the world of geopolitical competition and war, without the need for socialist revolution.

Lenin nevertheless started from the same premises as Kautsky: he saw imperialism as the consequence of the growing concentration of economic power – 'imperialism is the monopoly stage of capitalism' – and he largely accepted Hilferding's picture of an increasingly organized national capitalism in which the banks tended to control industry. But national organization was, according to Lenin, mirrored by international anarchy: he took over from Hobson the idea that modern imperialism involved '(1) the competition between *several* imperialisms; and (2) the predominance of the financier over the merchant.' The ultimate formation of 'a single world monopoly' was theoretically conceivable, but to base political analysis on such a possibility was profoundly misleading. International agreements and cartels registered the existing correlation of forces among the capitalist powers, but – given that the dynamism of capitalist development was constantly altering the global distribution of power – such arrangements were necessarily temporary and liable to give way to periods of instability in which the new correlation could only be established through the proof of force:

> The only conceivable basis under capitalism for the division of spheres of influence, interests, colonies, etc., is a calculation of the *strength* of those participating, their general economic, financial, military strength, etc. And the strength of these participants in the division does not change to an equal degree, for the *even* development of different undertakings, trusts, branches of industry, or countries is impossible under capitalism. Half a century ago Germany was a miserable insignificant country, if her capitalist strength is compared with that of the Britain of that time; Japan compared with Russia in the same way. Is it 'conceivable' that in ten or twenty years' time the relative strength of the imperialist powers will have remained *un*changed? It is out of the question. (Lenin, 1964, pp. 266, 269, 271, 295)

The resemblance of this view of imperialism to the classical realist conception of international relations as an anarchic structure, what Martin Wight calls 'a multiplicity of independent sovereign states acknowledging no political superior, whose relations are ultimately regulated by warfare', should be obvious (Wight, 1991, p. 7). Lenin sometimes showed himself willing to countenance the possibility of the fusion of national capitalist classes into a global finance capital (for example, Lenin, 1972). But his hostility to the theory of ultra-imperialism involved more than his rejection of its apparent political implication that future capitalist development could take a peaceful course; it can be seen as a reaffirmation of Marx's insistence on the constitutive role of competition in the capitalist mode of production. It implied an ultra-realist view of global governance: international institutions represented the temporary and inherently unstable arrangements reached by imperialist powers engaged in an endless struggle to repartition the world among themselves. Notoriously Lenin dismissed the League of Nations as a 'thieves' kitchen'; by contrast Kautsky predicted that it would 'ultimately be taken control of by elements that transform it into an effective tool against the power politics of the large states and for the international union of peoples; into a tool for the peaceful settlements of problems arising from their living together and for the regulation of economic life' (Kautsky, 1988, p. 449).

A more developed economic analysis supportive of Lenin's conclusion was provided by Bukharin, notably in his *Imperialism and World Economy* (1917). Bukharin took as his starting point the formation of a capitalist world economy but argued that this process involved in fact two apparently contradictory tendencies – on the one hand, 'the internationalization of capitalist interests' expressed in the growth of foreign trade and investment, the formation of multinational corporations and international cartels, etc., and, on the other, 'the nationalization of capitalist interests'. For Bukharin, the process of national organization of capital analysed by Hilferding culminated, not in the form of finance capital (that is, the fusion of the circuits of money and productive capital, normally under the domination of the banks), and certainly not in the shape of ultra-imperialism, but rather as state capitalism: the increasing involvement of the state in economic life (for example, the growth of public enterprise and the increasing economic significance of tariff policy) represented 'a very strong tendency towards transforming the entire national economy into one gigantic combined enterprise under the tutelage of the financial kings and the capitalist state, an enterprise which monopolizes the national market and forms the prerequisite for organized production on a higher non-capitalist level' (Bukharin, 1972, pp. 62, 73–4).

The outcome of this process was an alteration in the nature of competition:

> Every one of the capitalistically advanced 'national economies' has turned into some kind of a 'national trust'. This process of the organization of the economically advanced sections of world economy, on the other hand, has been accompanied by an extraordinary sharpening of their mutual competition. The overproduction of commodities, which is connected with the growth of large enterprises; the export policy of the cartels, and the narrowing of the sales markets in connection with the colonial and tariff policies of the capitalist powers; the growing disproportion between tremendously developed industry and backward agriculture; the gigantic growth of capital export and the economic subjugation of entire regions by 'national' banking combines – all this has thrown into the sharpest possible relief the clash of interests between the 'national' groups of capital. Those groups find their final argument in the force and power of the state organization, first of all in its army and navy. A mighty state military power is the last trump in the struggle of the powers. The fighting force in the world market thus depends upon the power and consolidation of the 'nation', upon its financial and military resources. A self-sufficient national state, and an economic unit limitlessly expending its great power until it becomes a world kingdom – a world-wide empire – such is the ideal built up by finance capital. (Bukharin, 1972, pp. 108–9)

The geopolitical rivalries among the Great Powers thus reflected the transformed structure of capitalism, the domination of the world economy by competing blocs of nationally organized capital. This analysis allowed Lenin and Bukharin to infer that the First World War did not reflect some avoidable failure of statecraft, or even (as liberal and social democratic opponents of the war tended to argue) the aristocratic and unaccountable character of foreign policy-making in *fin-de-siècle* Europe, but arose from the anarchic structure of capitalism in its imperialist phase. This analysis supported the Bolsheviks' revolutionary socialism. But it also provided a more accurate guide than did Kautsky's rival theory to the years between 1914 and 1945 – what Arno Mayer has called 'the General Crisis and Thirty Years War of the twentieth century', an era marked not only by the two world wars but also by the disintegration of the world into rival trade blocs during the Great Depression of the 1930s and by the Holocaust (Mayer, 1990, p. 31). A conception of world politics that highlighted the primacy of conflict within the international state system had, on the face of it, greater explanatory power than one that claimed to discern the emergence of a growing propensity for international cooperation. Nevertheless the polarity that emerged during the First World War between these two views – one perceiving the world as increasingly integrated into a single entity, the other highlighting the centrifugal tendencies produced by the ceaseless dynamism of capitalist competition – has dominated Marxist thinking about the interstate system ever since.

American Hegemony and its 'Decline'

Even during the years of crisis complexities began to make themselves felt. There was an ambiguity in Kautsky's notion of ultra-imperialism. He had expected to see rival centres of imperialist power converge on a single cartel as a result of rational calculations revealing that geopolitical competition was no longer in their economic interest. But what if the same process were achieved through a process of conquest and assimilation in which one imperialist power established its global domination, creating what Bukharin calls in the passage last cited a single 'world kingdom'? This was not, of course, merely a theoretical possibility. The Second World War involved, among other things, a German drive to dominate the Eurasian landmass. The failure of this enterprise left the area divided between two great blocs of which that headed by the United States enjoyed, thanks both to the domestic resources of the American super-power and to its success in integrating the rest of the advanced capitalist world, a commanding lead in economic and military strength.

America's emergence as the arbiter of Eurasian geopolitics had already been noted by Marxists in the interwar period. Trotsky notably argued in 1924 that '[t]he basic world antagonism occurs along the lines of the conflict of interests between the United States and England', as a result of the growing industrial, financial, and naval lead that the US had developed over Britain by the end of the First World War. Trotsky indeed argued that the development of the American economy set the US well ahead of all the other Great Powers: 'The national income of the United States is two and a half times greater than the combined national incomes of England, France, Germany, and Japan. These figures decide everything. They will cut a road for themselves on land, on sea and in the air' (Trotsky, 1971, pp. 22, 25).

Trotsky's stress on the antagonistic relationship between the US and Britain accords well with what has become a historical commonplace – the extent to which the Roosevelt administration used the wartime alliance against Hitler to remove obstacles to the pursuit of US interests such as the fragmentation of the world economy into closed trading blocs, chief among them the British Empire.[4] But the political conditions under which Trotsky's prognoses were confirmed were hardly propitious to the formulation of serious Marxist analyses of the structure of world politics (or indeed of anything else). On the one hand, the installation and postwar expansion of the Stalinist system evacuated the intellectual content of the 'official' Marxism of the Communist parties: the commentaries on international affairs by figures such as the British Communist leader R. Palme Dutt faithfully followed the vagaries of Soviet foreign policy; on the other hand, critical Marxism in the West found itself reduced to the margins of intellectual and political life during the 'Golden Age' of economic boom in the 1950s and 1960s, and tended towards abstract philosophical reflection rather than historico-political analysis (Anderson, 1976).

Such analysis revived as part of the more general renaissance of Marxist and radical thought at the end of the 1960s in a new historical conjuncture. In the first place, the long postwar boom was coming to an end, ushering in a succession of world recessions that, while not as serious as the Great Depression of the 1930s, nevertheless represented a significant deterioration in the international economic environment. Secondly, this crisis manifested itself within the international financial institutions set up after the Second World War – notably the International Monetary Fund and the World Bank – that formed what has come to be known as the Bretton Woods System (BWS) based on a set of exchange rates fixed relative to the US dollar, which itself was on a gold exchange standard. Thirdly, the decline of this system reflected the increasing economic difficulties faced by the US as a result of its growing balance of payments deficits – themselves a consequence of more intense competition from West Germany and Japan – and the consequent pressure the dollar came under in the international currency markets. Finally, the American economic crisis was itself closely bound up with the costly and politically unpopular war the US waged in Vietnam from the early 1960s to the fall of Saigon in 1975.[5]

This conjuncture set the agenda for Marxist writing about the international state system. Perhaps the critical issue concerned the position of the US: did the crisis manifestly developing at the end of the 1960s represent the relative decline of American power? In his contribution to an important debate in *New Left Review*, Bob Rowthorn identified three possible positions:

> *US super-imperialism* in which all other capitalist states are dominated by the United States and have comparatively little freedom to choose their policies and control their economies in ways opposed by the American state. America acts as the organizer of world capitalism, preserving its unity in the face of socialism. This domination may not, of course, operate smoothly – for antagonisms will not be eliminated but merely contained.
> *Ultra-imperialism* in which a dominant coalition of relatively autonomous imperialist states performs the organizing role necessary to preserve the unity of the system. For this to work the antagonisms between the members of the coalition must not be so severe that they overcome the interest they have in maintaining the coalition.
> *Imperial rivalry* in which the relatively autonomous states no longer perform the necessary organizing role, or perform it so badly that serious conflicts break out between them and the unity of the system is threatened. For this to happen the antagonisms between states must be severe. (Rowthorn, 1971, pp. 31–2)[6]

In the debates of the 1970s genuine commitment to the theory of ultra-imperialism was rare. Argument polarized between the other two positions. Writers notably associated with the journal *Monthly Review* tended to see the US as the dominant imperialist power operating in a manner very similar to that portrayed by Hobson and Lenin by seeking to control the sources of raw materials and to secure the widest opportunities for the export of American capital and commodities. The Vietnam War fell into place as reflecting a more general strategy aimed at maintaining access to key commodities and markets in the Third World (for example, Magdoff, 1969). The alternative position – argued with particular force by the Belgian Trotskyist theorist and activist Ernest Mandel – located the main arena of conflict within the advanced capitalist countries themselves. Mandel, Rowthorn and others argued that the principal trends were the relative economic decline of the US as West Germany and Japan

re-emerged as major exporters of manufactured goods, and a return to a more pluralistic world economy. The future of Western Europe was seen as a particularly
important site of contestation, given the huge increase there in foreign direct investment by US-owned multinational corporations and the efforts by national capitalisms
to construct through the European Economic Community supranational institutions
capable of pooling their resources in face of the American challenge (for example,
Mandel, 1970). For Michael Kidron and Chris Harman, European and Japanese competition was also the driving force undermining the Long Boom, since it compelled
the US to divert investment to civilian industries and therefore to reduce the high
levels of military expenditure that had played a crucial role in stabilizing postwar
capitalism (Kidron, 1970; Harman, 1984).

It is probably fair to say that the debate was largely won by the theorists of imperial
rivalry. The evidence of American decline – the crises of the dollar during the 1960s
and 1970s, the inroads made even into the US home market by Japanese and European firms (for example, the investment boom of the 1980s that saw symbols such as
the Rockefeller Center and Columbia Pictures succumb to Japanese takeovers), and
the setbacks suffered by US foreign policy, culminating in the Iranian and Nicaraguan
revolutions and the Soviet invasion of Afghanistan at the end of the 1970s – seemed
decisive. Moreover, the theorists of American ultra-imperialism tended to portray
advanced capitalism as dependent on the exploitation of cheap labour in the Third
World. This was certainly consistent with Lenin's belief that part of the Western
working class had been bought off with imperialist super-profits, and it fed into the
climate of Third Worldism that flourished on the post-1968 left, in which China and
Cuba were seen as the vanguard of anti-imperialist struggle. But this analysis fitted ill
with a world in which trade and investment increasingly flowed between the advanced
capitalist economies: the Third World, with the exception of a handful of Newly
Industrializing Countries, was not so much exploited as ignored by what Michael
Mann has recently called 'ostracizing imperialism' (Mann, 2001, pp. 53–5).[7]

A more sophisticated defence of the thesis of US domination was offered by Nicos
Poulantzas. Its main thrust was to argue that this represented imperialist domination
of a new type, less an imposition based on external force than the restructuring of the
other advanced economies along lines that mirrored the structures of the dominant
capitalism:

> this hegemony of the United States is neither analogous to that one of metropole over
> the others in preceding phases, nor does it differ from a simple 'quantitative' point of
> view: it passes by the establishment of the relations of production characteristic of Amer-
> ican monopoly capitalism and its domination *at the very interior* of the other metropoles,
> and by the reproduction *at their heart* of this new relation of dependence . . . This new
> dependence *must not be identified* with those characteristic of the relations between
> metropoles and dominated formations, and absolutely cannot be treated in an *analogous*
> fashion to these, precisely to the extent that these metropoles continue on the one hand
> to constitute distinct centres of capital accumulation, and on the other hand themselves
> to dominate the dependent formations on the other. (Poulantzas, 1974, pp. 44–5)

This internalization of American capitalism within its European counterparts
(Poulantzas does not discuss the Japanese case) produced a distinctive class fraction,
the 'interior bourgeoisie', neither a 'national' bourgeoisie pursuing its interests

independently of and if necessary against the US, nor a 'comprador' bourgeoisie acting as the mere agent of American designs. Both dependent on US capitalism and in conflict with it, the 'interior bourgeoisie' represented the *internal disarticulation* of the European capitalist classes, their disaggregation into diverse fractions pulled in different directions (Poulantzas, 1974, p. 73).[8] If Poulantzas's analysis was suggestive but left largely undeveloped, Kies van der Pijl pursued a somewhat analogous theme in an ambitious historical study that traced successive efforts to integrate the capitalist classes of the North Atlantic area under US leadership – a process that culminated after the Second World War on the basis of 'corporate liberalism', an ideological synthesis of free-market economics and state interventionism that permitted the incorporation of American and European industrial working classes reshaped by the articulation of mass production and consumption characteristic of Fordism (Van der Pijl, 1984).

Both Poulantzas and van der Pijl represented versions of Marxism hostile to economic reductionism. Poulantzas was himself one of the most eloquent defenders of the idea formulated by Louis Althusser that the politico-ideological superstructure is relatively autonomous of the economic base (Althusser, 1969; Poulantzas, 1973). Van der Pijl was influenced by the French Regulation School, which (again, partly under Althusser's inspiration) sought to conceptualize the institutional conditions necessary to coordinate production and consumption and thereby to secure economic equilibrium (Aglietta, 1979). Both by contrast highlighted the primarily economic focus of the debate on US decline. Discussion of what from some perspectives might be thought of as proto-forms of political globalization was relatively limited: BWS institutions such as the IMF received some attention, but were interpreted primarily as means through which US hegemony was maintained or contested by its rivals; analysis of the European Economic Community tended to be sceptical of its capacity genuinely to transcend competing national interests (for example, Mandel, 1975).

One strategy for moving beyond a purely economic analysis was to take the idea of hegemony seriously. The concept was after all well established in Marxist theory: Gramsci had used the term to refer to the intellectual and moral leadership that he believed was a necessary condition of any class attaining social domination (Gramsci, 1971). Why not transpose this theory to the international arena? This was the approach undertaken by Robert W. Cox. He was in two respects faithful to Gramsci. First, the main historical actors are social classes: 'class is important as the factor mediating between production on the one hand and the state on the other. The building and disintegration of historic blocs is the process whereby class formation can transform both states and the organization of production' (Cox, 1987, p. 356). Secondly, hegemony is understood primarily in ideological terms. Thus, unlike the conventional understanding of hegemony in international relations theory, where it is equated with 'dominance by a state', for Cox 'a hegemonic structure of world order is one in which power takes primarily a consensual form' (Cox, 1986, p. 251 n16). A world order thus depended on its capacity to justify itself in normative terms acceptable to the dominated. This perspective could comfortably accommodate international institutions such as those constituting the BWS:

> international organization functions as the process through which the institutions of hegemony and its ideology are developed. Among the features of international organization

which express its political role are the following: (1) they embody the rules that facilitate the expansion of hegemonic world orders; (2) they are themselves the product of the hegemonic world order; (3) they ideologically legitimate the norms of the world order; (4) they co-opt the elites from peripheral countries and (5) they absorb counter-hegemonic ideas. (Cox, 1983, p. 172)

The obvious merit of Cox's appropriation of Gramsci was that it permitted a non-reductive interrogation of world politics as precisely politics. But the very loosening of Marxist categories that made this possible also introduced new difficulties. Cox distinguished between three structural levels – the organization of production and the social forces it generates; state forms and the specific relationships to civil society that they embodied; and world orders, 'the particular configurations of forces which successively define the problematic of war or peace for the ensemble of states'. The three levels interact without any having causal priority (Cox, 1986, pp. 220–1). The resulting indeterminacy could simply be accepted, leaving Cox open to the accusation of embracing an explanatory pluralism closer to Weber than to Marx. Alternatively some unifying factor could be invoked. Given Cox's stress on social forces, classes were the obvious candidate for this role. But then the totalizing force became a class subject imposing its will on the world. Some of the difficulties familiar in the application of Gramscian concepts to individual societies – for example, a reliance on culturalist explanations of state policies – reappeared; at the same time, Marx's strongest analytic card, his emphasis on the structural constraints imposed on actors by the global process of capital accumulation, disappeared.[9]

Empire's Apogee

All the same, no Marxist analysis that hoped to make sense of world politics after the end of the Cold War could avoid engagement with ideological representations. The world after 1989 presented two apparently contradictory aspects. On the one hand, rumours of American decline turned out to be greatly exaggerated. Not only did the US win its forty-year contest with the Soviet Union, but it proceeded in the subsequent decade to see off the challenge presented by the 'stakeholder capitalisms' of Western Europe and Japan, which experienced serious economic difficulties in the 1990s. The IMF and World Bank found a new role as enforcers of a Washington consensus whose name was evidence enough of the normative power of the Anglo-American model of free-market capitalism championed by Reagan and Thatcher. The three wars waged by the US between 1991 and 2001 underlined its military supremacy: by the year 2000, the Pentagon accounted for 36 per cent of global military expenditure, more than the next nine powers combined (*Financial Times*, 8 Dec. 2001). On the other hand, even the wars of the post-Cold War era seemed to represent a transcendence of purely national interest: the Gulf War of 1991 was authorized by the United Nations and waged by an international coalition, while the Balkan War of 1999 was conducted by NATO and legitimized by appeal to a notion of humanitarian intervention that overrode national sovereignty. Meanwhile, multilateral organizations – whether old like the IMF, new like the World Trade Organization, or expanded like the G8 summit of the leading capitalist powers and Russia – seemed to be exercising an increasingly prominent role in policy-making. Greater international economic integration was thus accompanied by processes of political globalization involving new forms of governance apparently irreducible to the old Westphalian state system.[10]

The main thrust of Marxist discussion has again polarized between two principal positions. The first bears some resemblance to the thesis of 'US ultra-imperialism' that Rowthorn distinguished in the early 1970s. Leo Panitch, for example, argues that the worldwide triumph of neoliberalism in the 1980s and 1990s was a consequence, not of the impersonal workings of market forces, but of a successful political intervention by the American state intended to maintain 'a hierarchically organized international political economy' under US domination. This development has vindicated Poulantzas: 'His framework allowed him to discern, as few others were able to do, the American capacity to manage the radical restructuring of global capitalism in forms that reproduced their [sic] imperial dominance' (Panitch, 2000, pp. 13–14). Panitch makes explicit the implication of this analysis that greater international economic integration has not, as hyperglobalizers claim, fundamentally undermined the capacities of states – though some states were more equal than others.

A similar analysis has been developed with great force and mastery of detail by Peter Gowan (1999). He argues that globalization in fact represented 'Washington's Faustian bid for world dominance'. Its origins lie not in economic or technological changes, but rather in the political strategy pursued by successive US administrations after the collapse of the BWS at the beginning of the 1970s. Their policies brought into being a new Dollar–Wall Street Regime (DWSR). The Nixon administration's decision to take the dollar off gold in August 1971 placed the international monetary system on a pure dollar standard. Not simply did this give the American state a significant degree of political control over its currency's exchange rate and thereby enormous leverage over the other advanced capitalist countries, but the world of floating currencies that it helped to produce gave much greater salience to international financial markets in which US investment banks played the largest role. Washington and Wall Street were able to manage the greatly increased global flows of private finance to compel other states to adopt neoliberal policies that opened up their economies to foreign capital. The resulting socio-economic restructurings strengthened the domestic constellations of interests aligned to internationally mobile money capital. Even the increasingly frequent financial crises unleashed by the DWSR – most notably in East Asia in 1997–8 – form part of this system of positive feedback mechanisms: the capital scared out of the affected states usually fled to the US, further strengthening American financial capitalism, while the 'rescue' packages mounted by the IMF and the G7 required these states to take further doses of neoliberalism, thereby allowing multinational corporations to cherry-pick their most attractive assets.

This appreciation implies a robustly realist view of political globalization. Gowan sets the development of what have frequently been seen as forms of global governance in the 1990s in the context of the struggle of the US to maintain its dominant position with respect to the other 'Triad' powers – the European Union and Japan. He stresses that the relations among the advanced capitalist states are conflictual rather than harmonious. Maintaining US hegemony over allies that were also rivals crucially depends on political and ideological conditions: 'Much discussion of this US hegemony misses the specifically *political* form that this dominance took and imagines that US dominance was anchored only in its preponderance of quantitative power resources – economic and military above all.' To grasp this political form Gowan invokes Carl Schmitt's theory of sovereignty, according to which the sovereign is he who decides the exception, who determines when a state of emergency obtains (Schmitt, 1985). 'Thus, for the US to have sovereign hegemony over Western Europe, it would have to be able to impose a state of emergency upon the region if it wished: it would have, in other words, to call the political community to order and to discipline it under its undivided leadership, untrammelled by restrictions.' The crises of the Cold War permitted the US to play this role, as did the Iraqi seizure of Kuwait in August 1990. Gowan interprets the Clinton administration's efforts to maintain and indeed to expand NATO – in particular, to deal with 'out-of-area' threats – as an effort to maintain the conditions under which Washington could continue to act as Eurasia's Schmittian sovereign (Gowan, 2000, pp. 15–16).

It is interesting that another ambitious Marxist interpretation of world politics after the Cold War should also offer a theory of sovereignty: political structures and ideological discourses play a large part in contemporary Marxist writing on the international dimension. In other respects, however, Michael Hardt's and Toni Negri's *Empire* (2000) represents the polar opposite of Gowan's analysis, a position that in certain respects resembled Kautsky's thesis of ultra-imperialism. Hardt and Negri accept that 'an irresistible and irreversible globalization of economic and cultural exchanges' over the past few decades has undermined the sovereignty of nation-states, but deny that this amounts to the disappearance of sovereignty *tout court*. On the contrary, a new form of sovereignty has emerged – or rather, been revived: imperial sovereignty. 'In contrast to imperialism, Empire establishes no territorial centre of power and does not rely on fixed boundaries or barriers. It is a *decentred* and *deterritorialized* apparatus of power that progressively incorporates the entire global realm within its open, expanding frontiers' (Hardt and Negri, 2000, pp. xi, xii; emphasis in the original).

This conception of Empire is plainly inconsistent with any notion of American hegemony: '*The United States does not and indeed no nation-state can today, form the centre of an imperialist project*. Imperialism is over. No nation will be world leader in the way modern European nations were.' Thus 'what used to be conflict or competition among several imperialist powers has in important respects been replaced by the idea of a single power that overdetermines them all, structures them in a unitary way and treats them under one common notion of right that is decidedly postcolonial and postimperialist.' The new juridical concepts that legitimize the exercise of power on the international arena are explicitly transnational: in the 1991 Gulf War the US acted '*not as a function of its national motives but in the name of global right*'. The concept of humanitarian intervention that developed in the 1980s and the 1990s is a symptom of the shift in sovereignty. The NGOs that pioneered this concept are less the agents of a global 'civil society' than 'some of the most powerful pacific weapons of the new world order – the charitable campaigns and the mendicant orders of Empire'. Indeed, intervention by the 'international community' in 'failed states' at the margins of Empire is 'the logical form of the exercise of force that follows from a paradigm of legitimation based on a state of permanent exception and police action', where conflict occurs not between states but as a result of forms of deviance internal to a morally integrated world order (Hardt and Negri, 2000, pp. xiii–xiv, 9, 180, 36, 39; emphasis in the original).

Despite the consolation offered by ideologies of human rights and democratic governance, Empire is the latest form taken by capitalist exploitation, even 'the highest stage of imperialism' (Negri 2001). Yet it has precedents, notably in the ancient empires where power also knew no territorial boundaries. Hardt and Negri draw on Polybius' theory of the mixed constitution of the Roman republic in order to analyse contemporary forms of global governance. They argue that these constitute a three-tier pyramid corresponding to the three forms of legitimate government distinguished by ancient political thought – at the apex, the US, the G7 and various other key bodies that perform the function of monarchy; below it, an aristocracy of transnational corporations and nation-states; and finally a constellation of bodies – the UN General Assembly, NGOs, churches, etc. – that play the democratic role in the imperial order (Hardt and Negri, 2000, ch. 3.5).

Empire has with astonishing rapidity captured the contemporary radical imagination. In particular, its portrayal of an empire that is permanently in crisis – already decadent, to use the language of the historians of Rome's fall, above all because of the constant resistance of the multitude whose creative labour is the source of imperial productivity – has provided many within the movement against corporate globalization with a ready-made theoretical language.[11] From an analytical point of view, *Empire* represents the most sustained Marxist attempt critically to analyse contemporary forms of political globalization.[12] In this respect it is most persuasive in its account of the changing forms of sovereignty: here the shift is undeniable. Thus Gowan – whose overall theoretical stance is very different from that of Hardt and Negri – comments that during the 1990–1 crisis that led to the US-led invasion of Iraq,

> the dominant language of public debate was that of rights, justice and law. This discourse was triggered primarily by the use the Bush administration made of UN Security Council resolutions. These were interpreted in an idiom that was in fact metaphorical: the transfer of the discourse that serves the domestic legal system within a liberal democratic state to the realm of world politics. In the perception of millions, international affairs became a depoliticized process of crime and judicial punishment. (Gowan, 1999, p. 142)

The critical question is whether or not this discursive shift corresponds to the kind of transformation in the distribution and indeed the nature of power postulated by Hardt and Negri.[13] There are good reasons for doubting this, as is suggested by the international crisis that followed the attacks on New York and Washington on 11 September 2001. In declaring a 'war against terrorism' the administration of George W. Bush sought to appeal to an international constituency and not merely to assert American national interests: in this sense, the crisis was indeed presented as 'a depoliticized process of crime and judicial punishment'. Moreover, the US strove, for both political and logistical reasons, to construct an international coalition to pursue those deemed responsible for the attacks. At the same time, however, the Bush administration sought firmly to maintain control over the response and indeed to use it to demonstrate American capacity for power projection and thereby to reassert US hegemony. The war it launched in Afghanistan was directed by US Central Command, while any suggestion to bring the culprits before an instance of international justice was firmly rebuffed: if captured, they would instead appear before military commissions convened by the American President. The idea that the United States had somehow dissolved as a centre of power into the impersonal 'smooth space' of Empire seems, at best, premature. We are confronted with a hybrid form of sovereignty, in which appeals to universal principles coexist in complex ways with assertions of national interest.

The basis for a Marxist understanding of contemporary world politics can be summed up under the following headings:[14]

1   The context of world politics is provided by processes of capital accumulation occurring on a global scale. Neither Gowan's preoccupation with state strategies nor Hardt and Negri's rhapsodies of Empire take sufficient account of the rhythms of growth and crisis governing all the major capitalist economies.[15]

2   The competitive struggle between a plurality of centres of capital accumulation remains a constitutive dimension of contemporary capitalism. The US enjoys major economic and military advantages relative to the other leading powers, but its position is permanently contested.

3   The forms taken by this competition are complex. Western capitalism after the Second World War underwent a partial dissociation of military and economic competition. Whereas before 1945, competition over territory and economic resources tended to be a mutually reinforcing process in the manner depicted by Bukharin, during the Cold War the Western bloc was politically and militarily unified under US leadership against the geopolitical and ideological challenge represented by the Soviet bloc; nevertheless serious economic rivalries developed in the West, between the US, Western Europe and Japan. This pattern persists to this day: Russia and China are America's main geopolitical rivals, while economic conflict, notably over trade, occurs primarily within the advanced capitalist Triad (though it is clear many US policy-makers fear that China has the potential to develop into an economic as well as a military rival).

4   Maintaining US hegemony is not an automatic process but requires a continuous and determined struggle on the part of American political and economic elites. One of the merits of Gowan's work is to highlight the considerable efforts made by the Clinton administration in particular to ensure that the US continues to be the dominant power in the Eurasian landmass. That this kind of strategy is no mere projection by Marxist commentators but is actively pursued by US policy-makers is indicated by the writings of influential figures such as Zbigniew Brzezinski and Henry Kissinger (for example, Brzezinski, 1997 and Kissinger, 1994). One of the most striking geopolitical developments in the 1990s was the manner in which the US used its commanding military lead over other powers – notably by intervening to settle the wars that followed the disintegration of Yugoslavia – in order to see off the danger that the EU might assert itself as an independent political force. US oscillations between multilateralism and unilateralism reflect the tensions inherent in building and maintaining international coalitions whose ultimate objective is to perpetuate American hegemony over even its closest and most powerful allies.

5   The developing forms of global governance are no mere ideological screen, but nor are they an embryonic 'cosmopolitan democracy'. For the US to secure its objectives, the cooperation of other powers must be secured, and potential rivals must be isolated, divided, or incorporated. The major international institutions – G7/8,

UN Security Council, IMF, WTO, NATO, etc. – provide arenas in which the US can brigade together the other leading powers behind its policy goals, conflicts among the leading capitalist powers are argued out and compromises reached, and the smaller states are bullied or bribed into falling in line. The result is unprecedentedly developed forms of institutionalized policy-coordination and cooperation among the main states. But these forms represent not the abolition, but the continuation of the economic and political conflicts that have driven global capitalism since its inception.

6 The development of these forms of global governance has involved the formulation of legitimizing discourses – not merely the ideology of humanitarian intervention but also increasingly strident affirmations of liberal democracy as the only acceptable political form throughout the world. Here we observe the rational kernel in Cox's attempt to extend Gramsci's theory of hegemony to the international arena: the prevailing global distribution of power must to some degree be legitimized in the eyes of the ruled as well as the rulers. But, as always, the effects of such ideological discourses are ambivalent: arguably, the contrast between the value that they attribute to democratic institutions and the highly centralized and unaccountable way in which decisions are actually taken in the international arena has provided one of the main stimuli to the development of the movement against capitalist globalization (Rupert, 2000).

7 One unanticipated consequence of the rise of global governance is therefore that its main institutions have themselves become objects of political contestation, particularly as the destabilizing and impoverishing consequences of neoliberal economic policies have made themselves felt. Since the demonstrations at Seattle in November 1999, the international gatherings supposed to affirm the development of global community have become targets for those who wish to protest against the effective absence of any such community. A globalized capitalism has generated globalized opposition to its effects, and demands for its reform or replacement.

Whether or not this summary view of world politics adequately captures the main contemporary trends remains to be seen. But the debates surveyed here indicate the vitality of the Marxist tradition of thinking about these topics, which has sought to locate the patterns of global politics within the broader development of the capitalist mode of production, to analyse the shifting distribution of world power, and to trace the political trajectories through which humankind can escape from the relentless process of economic and political competition that is capitalism.

Notes

In writing this essay I have greatly benefited from Sam Ashman's help as a source of ideas, references, and criticism.

1 See, on the contemporary scholarly debate about globalization, Held et al., 1999, pp. 2–14.
2 This argument is systematically developed in Rosenberg, 1994.
3 On *fin de siècle* global economic integration see, for example, Hobsbawm, 1987.
4 For a pathbreaking work of radical scholarship that explores this theme, see Kolko, 1970.
5 For a historical account of the development of this crisis that is itself an instance of the Marxist renaissance under review here, see Block, 1977. It is a limitation of the literature

surveyed in this section that it tended to abstract from the geopolitical rivalries between the American and Soviet empires, focusing instead on the conflicts within the former. For two exceptions to this pattern, from divergent theoretical and political perspectives, see Binns, 1983, and Halliday, 1983.

6   Rowthorn's and the other contributions to this debate were reprinted in Radice, 1975.
7   For two important attempts to rethink the changed nature of imperialism after 1945, see Kidron, 1974 and Harris, 1971.
8   For a recent reassessment of Poulantzas's analysis, see Panitch, 2000, esp. pp. 8–10.
9   For critical discussion of Cox's 'neo-Gramscianism' see Burnham, 1991 and Germain and Kenny, 1998.
10   See Held et al., 1999, ch. 1, on political globalization.
11   For a critique of *Empire* that sets it in the context of Negri's broader intellectual and political development, see Callinicos, 2001b.
12   Though contemporary Marxist writing on the European Union should not be discounted: see, for example, Bonefeld, 2001 and Carchedi, 2001.
13   In what follows I have greatly benefited from the discussion at a forum on *Empire* led by Michael Hardt, Simon Bromley and me that the journal *Historical Materialism* organized in London on 26 October 2001.
14   See Callinicos et al., 1994; Callinicos, 2001a, ch. 3; Achcar 2000a, 2000b; Rees, 2001.
15   The most influential recent Marxist analysis of these rhythms is provided by Robert Brenner: see his highly controversial 1998 article and the symposium devoted to it in *Historical Materialism*, 4 and 5 (1999).

References

Achcar, Gilbert (2000a) 'Rasputin plays at chess', in T. Ali (ed.), *Masters of the Universe?* London: Verso.
Achcar, Gilbert (2000b) 'The strategic triad', in T. Ali (ed.), *Masters of the Universe?* London: Verso.
Aglietta, Michel (1979) *A Theory of Capitalist Regulation*, London: New Left Books.
Althusser, Louis (1969) 'Contradiction and overdetermination', In Althusser, *For Marx*, London: Allen Lane.
Anderson, Perry (1976) *Considerations on Western Marxism*, London: New Left Books.
Binns, Peter (1983) 'Understanding the new cold war', *International Socialism*, 2, no. 19, pp. 1–48.
Block, Fred (1977) *The Origins of International Economic Disorder*, Berkeley: University of California Press.
Bonefeld, Werner (ed.) (2001) *The Politics of Europe*, Houndmills: Palgrave.
Brenner, Robert (1998) 'The economics of global turbulence', *New Left Review*, series I, no. 229, pp. 1–265.
Brzezinski, Zbigniew (1997) *The Grand Chessboard*, New York: Basic Books.
Bukharin, N. I. (1972) *Imperialism and World Economy*, London: Merlin.
Burnham, Peter (1991) 'Neo-Gramscian hegemony and the international order', *Capital and Class*, 45, pp. 73–93.
Callinicos, Alex (2001a) *Against the Third Way*, Cambridge: Polity.
Callinicos, Alex (2001b) 'Toni Negri in perspective', *International Socialism*, 2, no. 92, pp. 33–61.
Callinicos, Alex et al. (1994) *Marxism and the New Imperialism*, London: Bookmarks.
Carchedi, Guglielmo (2001) *For Another Europe*, London: Verso.
Cox, Robert W. (1983) 'Gramsci, hegemony and international relations', *Millennium*, 12, pp. 162–75.

Cox, Robert W. (1986) 'Social forces, states and world order', in R. O. Keohane (ed.), *Neorealism and its Critics*, New York: University of Columbia Press.

Cox, Robert W. (1987) *Production, Power and World Order*, New York: University of Columbia Press.

Germain, Randall M. and Kenny, Michael (1998) 'Engaging Gramsci: international relations theory and the new gramscians', *Review of International Studies*, 24, pp. 3–21.

Gowan, Peter (1999) *The Global Gamble*, London: Verso.

Gowan, Peter (2000) 'The Euro-Atlantic origins of NATO's attack on Yugoslavia', in T. Ali, (ed.), *Masters of the Universe?* London: Verso.

Gramsci, Antonio (1971) *Selections from the Prison Notebooks*, ed. Q. Hoare and G. Nowell-Smith, London: Lawrence and Wishart.

Halliday, Fred (1983) *The Making of the Second Cold War*, London: Verso.

Hardt, Michael and Negri, Antonio (2000) *Empire*, Cambridge, Mass.: Harvard University Press.

Harman, Chris (1984) *Explaining the Crisis*, London: Bookmarks.

Harris, Nigel (1971) 'Imperialism today', in N. Harris and J. Palmer (eds), *World Crisis*, London: Hutchinson.

Haupt, Georges et al. (1974) *Les Marxistes et la question nationale 1848–1914*, Paris: Maspero.

Held, David, McGrew, Anthony, Goldblatt, David and Peratton, Jonathan (1999) *Global Transformations*, Cambridge: Polity.

Hobsbawm, E. J. (1987) *The Age of Empire 1875–1914*, London: Weidenfeld and Nicolson.

Kautsky, Karl (1984) 'Imperialism', in J. Riddell (ed.), *Lenin's Struggle for a Revolutionary International: Documents: 1907–1916*, New York: Monad.

Kautsky, Karl (1988) *The Materialist Conception of History*, ed. John H. Kautsky, New Haven: Yale University Press.

Kidron, Michael (1970) *Western Capitalism since the War*, Harmondsworth: Penguin.

Kidron, Michael (1974) 'Imperialism: highest stage but one', in Kidron, *Capitalism and Theory*, London: Pluto.

Kissinger, Henry (1994) *Diplomacy*, New York: Simon and Schuster.

Kolko, Gabriel (1970) *The Politics of War*, New York: Vintage.

Lenin, V. I. (1964) *Imperialism, the Highest Stage of Capitalism*, in Lenin, *Collected Works*, vol. 22, Moscow: Progress.

Lenin, V. I. (1972) 'Introduction', in N. I. Bukharin, *Imperialism and World Economy*, London: Merlin.

Luporini, Cesare (1979) 'Le Politique et l'étatique: une ou deux critiques?', in E. Balibar et al., *Marx et sa critique de politique*, Paris: Maspero.

Magdoff, Harry (1969) *The Age of Imperialism*, New York: Monthly Review Press.

Mandel, Ernest (1970) *Europe vs America*, New York: Monthly Review Press.

Mandel, Ernest (1975) 'International capitalism and "Supranationality"', in Radice 1975.

Mann, Michael (2001) 'Globalization and September 11', *New Left Review*, series II, no. 12, pp. 51–72.

Marx, Karl (1973) *Grundrisse*, Harmondsworth: Penguin.

Marx, Karl (1976) *Capital*, vol. 1, Harmondsworth: Penguin.

Marx, Karl and Engels, Friedrich (1976) *Manifesto of the Communist Party*, in Marx and Engels, *Collected Works*, vol. 6, London: Lawrence and Wishart.

Mayer, Arno J. (1990) *Why Did the Heavens Not Darken?* New York: Pantheon.

Negri, Antonio (2001) 'L'"Empire", stade suprême de l'impérialisme', *Le Monde Diplomatique*, 3.

Panitch, Leo (2000) 'The new imperial state', *New Left Review*, series II, no. 2, pp. 5–20.

Poulantzas, Nicos (1973) *Political Power and Social Class*, London: New Left Books.

Poulantzas, Nicos (1974) *Les Classes sociales dans le capitalisme aujourd'hui*, Paris: Seuil.

Radice, Hugh (ed.) (1975) *International Firms and Modern Imperialism*, Harmondsworth: Penguin.

Rees, John (2001) 'Imperialism: globalization, the state and war', *International Socialism*, 2, no. 93, pp. 3–30.

Rosdolsky, Roman (1977) *The Making of Marx's 'Capital'*, London: Pluto.

Rosenberg, Justin (1994) *The Empire of Civil Society*, London: Verso.

Rowthorn, Bob (1971) 'Imperialism in the 1970s – Unity or Rivalry?', *New Left Review*, series I, no. 69, pp. 31–54.

Rupert, Michael (2000) *Ideologies of Globalization*, London: Routledge.

Schmitt, Carl (1985) *Political Theology*, Cambridge Mass.: MIT Press.

Trotsky, L. D. (1971) *Europe and America: Two Speeches on Imperialism*, New York: Pathfinder.

Van der Pijl, Kies (1984) *The Making of an Atlantic Ruling Class*, London: Verso.

Wight, Martin (1991) *International Theory*, London: Leicester University Press.

13

Liberal Internationalism: Between Realism and Cosmopolitanism

Anthony McGrew

Introduction

Since the end of the Cold War, liberal internationalism has experienced a renaissance as a new generation of Western scholars and political elites seek either to understand, or to manage, world affairs in a globalizing era. Just as the hubris of the 'end of history' produced a resurgence of liberal internationalist rhetoric, expressed in President George Bush Sr's vision of a 'new world order', so globalization has encouraged a revival of liberal international thought. To this extent, liberal internationalism no longer appears, as E. H. Carr once described it, a 'utopian edifice' but on the contrary constitutes, in the absence of any secular ideological competitors, the dominant discourse of the emerging post-Cold War world order (Carr, 1981, p. 26; Clark, 2001). As Howard reminds us, however, it is also a deeply flawed discourse since it is 'marred by naiveté, by intellectual arrogance, by ignorance, by confused thinking and sometimes, alas, by sheer hypocrisy' (1981, p. 134). Whether the current renaissance in liberal internationalist thinking has overcome or simply perpetuated these flaws remains to be judged. To this end the existence and vitality of global governance constitutes a crucial indicator of the robustness and continuing relevance of liberal internationalist theory in the twenty-first century.

In elaborating the origins, development and principal arguments of the liberal internationalist tradition, this chapter seeks to present a critical assessment of liberal theories of global governance. The chapter has four principal sections, commencing with an overview of the intellectual history – the philosophical origins, core assumptions and arguments – of the liberal internationalist tradition. Section two examines the current renaissance of liberal international theory – the clash of liberal internationalisms – while section three reviews the major ambiguities and controversies to which it has given rise. In conclusion, section four assesses Stanley Hoffman's claim that the new circumstances of twenty-first century global politics require a 'complex and sophisticated rethinking of liberal internationalism' (Hoffman, 1995).

Liberal Internationalism: Origins and Legacies

Liberal internationalism,[1] as Doyle asserts, 'lays a special claim to what world politics is and can be: a state of peace' (1997, p. 302). Since the early twentieth century, the discourse of liberal internationalism has constituted a principal intellectual alternative to realism and geopolitics not only for explaining world order as it is, but also prescribing how it should be. For it offers an account of the possibility of the transcendence of power politics – or the anarchy problematic – in international relations. This primacy attached to peace arises from a conviction that the achievement of ultimate human freedom is only feasible in the absence of war or the conditions that give rise to it.[2] Since conflict and war are an endemic feature of a system of states in which sovereigns seek to maximize their power, liberal internationalism holds that it is only through the governance or transcendence of power politics that the necessary conditions for the promotion and realization of human freedom can be effectively achieved. This argument rests on several presumptions, including:

- First, that reason and rationality are necessary and sufficient requirements for the effective conduct and management of international affairs. In essence, through the pursuit of enlightened self-interest and rational deliberation, conflicts of interests between states can be resolved or mediated without recourse to force or war.
- Second, international cooperation is rationally, as well as ethically, preferable to conflict. Furthermore, growing material interdependence between states and peoples promotes the necessity for the international regulation of their common affairs as well as the rational and cognitive basis for increased cooperation.
- Third, international institutions[3] contribute to peace and world order in two ways: they tame the powerful by creating international norms, incentives and new patterns of multilateral politics which limit the scope for power politics; and they also provide mechanisms for preventing or managing interstate conflict.
- Fourth, progress is possible in world politics in so far as power politics (and thereby war) is not regarded as an immutable property of the interstate order (as realism presumes) but on the contrary can be mitigated, if not transcended, through the progressive reform or domestication of international affairs (the rule of law, universal human rights, etc.). In this respect liberal internationalism reflects a distinctly Enlightenment commitment to the improvement of the human and global condition.

These assumptions inform the central explanatory logic of the liberal internationalist argument captured in the simple notion of the virtuous circle. This asserts that the mutually reinforcing dynamics of transnational economic integration, the diffusion of liberal democracy and the growth of international governance creates the conditions for an expanding liberal zone of peace in which war increasingly becomes an irrational or unthinkable instrument of interstate politics (Russett and Oneal, 2001). Under these conditions, liberty and prosperity can be fully realized. As an account of the postwar evolution of the Western security community the virtuous circle has considerable explanatory power and appears to present a convincing alternative to realism in its various forms.[4] However, beyond the peculiar Western zone of peace its explanatory power or normative appeal may be less apparent. The relevance of liberal internationalism to an understanding of the current global condition is therefore open to question.

As Richardson observes there is no singular tradition of liberal internationalism but, on the contrary, a series of contending approaches (Richardson, 1997). E. H. Carr, in his classic *The Twenty Years' Crisis*, created the myth of a monolithic liberal internationalist tradition, imposing 'more coherence on his contemporary internationalists than actually existed' (Franceschet, 1999). This rhetorical device may have reinforced Carr's intelligent demolition of the liberal case, but in so doing it gave lie to the myth that liberal internationalism was purely synonymous with a form of idealism or utopianism characterized (if not caricatured) by the doctrine of the natural harmony of interests – namely that through the pursuit of enlightened self-interest by peoples and governments the global public good and international harmony would be advanced (Lynch, 1999). What is absent from this otherwise brilliant analysis is a recognition of the distinctive voices within the liberal internationalism of the period.[5] In many respects, liberal internationalism has been stigmatized by its 'idealist' legacy, not to mention its historical association with the collapse of the interwar order and the failure of collective security, namely the League of Nations.

There are various classifications of liberal internationalist thought, including among others, classical and new forms; institutional, commercial and republican variants; conservative versus cosmopolitan forms; and individual versus state-centric variants (Doyle, 1997; Hobson, 2000; Howard, 1981; Long, 1995; Richardson, 1997). Of course any classification can be contested, but all nevertheless serve to emphasize the rich diversity within the liberal tradition. Drawing on a more historical approach it is possible to discern three great waves of liberal internationalist theorizing from the period of the Enlightenment to the present day: the classical wave; the new wave; and the contemporary (renaissance) wave. Although there are obvious continuities among the three waves in respect of their underlying philosophical premises and principal arguments, significant differences of interpretation and emphasis are also detectable. In particular, not only does the normative significance attached to international governance (its necessity, desirability or appropriate design) vary among these three waves, but there are also different explanatory accounts relying on different epistemologies. Each wave has a distinct intellectual identity and trajectory, although all have evolved from a common pool of values and ideas.

The first wave: classical liberal internationalism (eighteen to nineteenth centuries)

Classical liberal-internationalist thought embraces two related but nevertheless distinctive discourses: the political and the commercial (Doyle, 1997). What they share in common is both a methodological concern for the domestic sources of war or international conflict, and a remarkable faith in the power of human reason. War, for Thomas Paine, Immanuel Kant, Jeremy Bentham and J. S. Mill, could be traced principally to the failings of domestic political structures: absolutist states and monarchies characterized by centralized power, secrecy, public ignorance and the absence of effective mechanisms of political accountability made war a frequent instrument of state policy. For Adam Smith, Richard Cobden and John Bright the prevailing mercantilist organization of the economy encouraged wars for economic gains or imperial ambitions since it subjugated production and trade to the political requirements of state interests. Both the political and economic versions of classical liberal internationalism considered that the determinants of peace, in the first instance, lay more in transforming the domestic structures of states than in reforming the international society of states. In general, a liberal suspicion of government and arbitrary state power was reflected in a rejection of ideas of international or world government to enforce the peace.

By rejecting the notion of a global leviathan, the intellectual route to perpetual peace was sought instead in republican forms of government, the market and free trade. Kant[6] considered that a liberal republican form of government (that is, constitutional government based on the consent of citizens) was an essential building block of a peaceful international order. Liberal republics, although not democracies in the contemporary sense, were less likely to engage in war since citizens, he argued, would be inclined to 'great hesitation in embarking on so dangerous an enterprise' (Kant, 1795). Bentham, too, placed great faith in the capacity of public opinion, or at least educated public opinion, to recognize that war was irrational – the product of the machinations of government – proclaiming that 'between the interests of nations there is nowhere any real conflict, if they appear repugnant anywhere it is only in proportion as they are misunderstood' (Hinsley, 1967, p. 83). This theme is also evident in Smith's and Cobden's works. Both argued that trade and commerce encouraged material interdependence between peoples and nations, making war less likely because citizens, as well as governments, would calculate that its potential economic costs would outweigh any prospective benefits (Doyle, 1997, p. 234; Hinsley, 1967, pp. 96–7; Howard, 1981, p. 41). In multiplying the economic connections between societies, commerce and market forces are considered the harbingers of world peace by making war irrational and ultimately obsolete.

Despite an emphasis on the domestic determinants of peace, Kant and Bentham, in particular, nevertheless advocated the importance of international law to the maintenance of international order. Just as liberal republican government required a constitutional order, so international politics required a codification of states' rights and duties. Kant proposed a framework of cosmopolitan law that sought to secure peace by entrenching the rights and duties of both individuals and nations within a confederation of republican states (see chapter 15 below)(Boucher, 1998, p. 283). Although there is considerable ambiguity with respect to Kant's position on the question of world government, his proposed confederation constituted, in the first instance, a select club of republican states which by general agreement prohibited war among its members – some regard this as the forerunner to the idea of collective security (Boucher, 1998; Cavallar, 1999, 2001; Doyle, 1997; Williams, 1992). Within this select club states become socialized, rather than coerced, into peaceful relations, contributing to a virtuous circle of growing interdependence, the strengthening of democracy, and the realization of peace and prosperity (Huntley, 1996). To the extent to which the confederation is successful, argued Kant, it will acquire an inclusivist logic as other states aspire to membership and in the process conform unilaterally (as for instance in the case of aspirant members of the European Union) to its rules and norms. Moreover, as liberal values are diffused, and global economic integration intensifies, the potential membership of the liberal zone of peace will correspondingly expand. Even so, for Kant, perpetual peace was a largely separate peace in that republican states remained 'in a state of war with non-republics' (Doyle, 1997, p. 258).

World order, for Bentham, was not associated with world government or even strong international institutions. On the contrary, Bentham advocated that 'there should be as little government as possible so there should be as little international government as possible' (Hinsley, 1967, p. 87). At most, all that was required was a Common Court of Judicature to provide a framework for arbitration between states, since reasoned deliberation could resolve all disputes (Howard, 1981, p. 33). Similarly, for economic liberals such as Smith, Cobden and Bright, minimal government within the state demanded minimal government beyond the state or, as Cobden remarked, 'as little intercourse as possible between Governments, as much connection as possible between the nations of the world' (Howard, 1981, p. 43). As will become apparent, this suspicion of public power and belief in limited government remain an important theme in contemporary liberal internationalist thinking about global governance and the proper form of world order.

The second wave: the new liberal internationalism (1900–1960s)

Faith in the classical liberal idea that a more peaceful world order would automatically arise from growing interdependence between nations and enlightened public opinion was discredited by the Great War of 1914–18. It was somewhat of a cruel irony that at the turn of the twentieth century, liberal theorists, such as Norman Angell, had proclaimed the transformation of the international predicament such that 'war, even when victorious, can no longer achieve those aims for which peoples strive' (Angell, 1933, p. 78). Paradoxically, however, the mass mobilization of societies demanded by industrial warfare altered liberal attitudes to state intervention. If the state could mobilize societal resources for the war effort, then government could act to improve the human condition. This new liberal internationalism advocated the need for strong international government to secure both the conditions for world peace and a liberal world order of self-governing nations (Dunne, 2001; Richardson, 1997).

If classical liberal theory had sought international peace primarily in the transformation of the domestic organization of societies, the new liberal internationalism sought peace through the domestication of world order. It was inspired by, among other factors, the success of the international public unions (such as the International Telegraph Union and the Universal Postal Union) which were established in the late nineteenth century to facilitate international cooperation in technical or functional areas of common interest; and the legalism of the classical theorists which relied on the power of international norms and the rule of law as an instrument for overcoming the logic of power politics. Accordingly, the new liberalism advocated a form of international government with appropriate powers and authority to enforce the peace. This did not presuppose a single vision but, on the contrary, a spectrum of institutional designs: from world federation or confederation, implying a world government with supranational authority; through functionalism (see chapter 14 below), which advocated a decentralized and pluralistic system of international governance; to reformism (in the spirit of Woodrow Wilson and the League of Nations), which envisaged a system of enhanced international cooperation and collective security (Claude, 1971; Long, 1996, ch. 8; Mitrany, 1975). Two convictions, however, informed all these visions: first, a moral and philosophical idealism inasmuch as ideas, norms and adherence to moral principles were considered central to the generation of social and political change; and second, that peace required not just, as Kant had argued, democracy within states but also democratic forms of international government. In the aftermath of the Great War, this new liberal internationalism, as Carr documented, became an influential alternative to the discredited discourse of geopolitics (Carr, 1981). Its most authoritative expression came in Woodrow Wilson's Fourteen Points, which shaped the entire design (some might say fatally) of the interwar global order.

Central to the Wilsonian world order were two key liberal principles: the spread of democracy or self-determination; and the creation of a 'democratic' system of collective security in the form of the League of Nations – the first great experiment in modern international governance. As Claude comments, 'Wilson had fought his war to make the world safe for democracy; he created his League to make the world safe by democracy' (Claude, 1971, p. 52). The League, in principle, was democratic in two limited senses: in the deliberative sense of seeking to bring about international change through dialogue rather than force; and in so far as the doctrine (rather than the practice) of collective security presumed the equality of states ('all for one and one for all'). Its design combined elements of Kant's confederation of republican states and Bentham's proposals for a Common Court of Adjudication. For more radical liberal internationalists in this period, however, it was never designed to be sufficiently democratic or authoritative enough to overcome the entrenched privileges and political manipulation of the great powers of the day. In failing ignominiously to realize its Wilsonian mandate, the history of the League has come to symbolize for many students of international relations the deluded and utopian character of liberal internationalist thought (Carr, 1981).

Despite the failure of the liberal experiment in international government, the architects of the post-1945 world order were not convinced that it should be abandoned entirely. On the contrary, the historical experiences of the interwar period, notably the Great Depression and the catastrophe of world war, reinforced the perceived demand for some form of international government, most especially (as John Maynard Keynes and other liberals argued) in respect of economic and social affairs: 'what distinguished the reformist efforts of the Second from those of the First World War was the much greater attention paid to economic and social policy . . . Most of those who pondered on such matters believed it was defective economic arrangements which had made such a "hash", as Keynes put it, of the inter-war years' (Skidelsky, 2000, p. 179). Establishing the United Nations and a raft of specialized agencies, including the Bretton Woods institutions to promote global trade and commerce, reflected the desire of the US, as the liberal hegemon, to establish a liberal world order in which democracy and capitalism could flourish. Paradoxically, these developments appeared to undermine key tenets of liberal internationalist theory since they all but confirmed the realist argument that international government could only exist at best by grant of the hegemonic power, or at worst as simply an instrument for the promotion of its interests. This seeming paradox came to be addressed directly by the third wave of liberal internationalist scholarship.

The Renaissance of Liberal Internationalism: Contending Approaches (1980s to the present)

The third wave of liberal internationalism has its origins in attempts to confront two issues: the essential liberal logic of international cooperation; and the implications of globalization for world order. Throughout the 1970s and 1980s increased global interdependence, as classical liberal analysis predicted, appeared to be transforming international relations. It created simultaneously the potential for a more cooperative world order and, as the new liberal internationalists had advocated, a proliferation of new regimes of international governance to manage collective problems. As the Cold War ended and globalization further intensified, 'the liberal inheritors of the Enlightenment seemed once again poised to establish peace' (Howard, 2000, p. 91). This was reflected in a significant renaissance of liberal internationalist scholarship (Franceschet, 1999).

Several themes characterize this burgeoning literature. First, a primary interest in explicating, by contrast with realism, the specifically liberal logic of international cooperation and international governance. For realists, international governance is to be explained principally as a product of hegemonic power (see chapter 11 above): the establishment of a multilateral world order in the postwar era is understood as an expression of US hegemony and its drive to create a liberal world. Other than appealing to altruism, or a natural harmony of interests, liberal internationalism had difficulty in explaining how international cooperation materialized in a world of power politics. Put simply, why, in the absence of coercion, would states subject themselves voluntarily to the constraints of international institutions or international government?

Second, associated with the above, there is an expressed desire to re-establish the credibility of liberal theory by reformulating it in ways that meet the requirements of more formal and positivistic social science. One consequence of this development has been the tendency for overtly normative analysis to be displaced in favour of more descriptive or empirically verifiable theory.

Third, there is widely held assumption that the state-centric conception of world politics is no longer adequate for understanding the complexities of post-Cold War global politics, and even less for understanding how the world is actually governed. States are no longer considered the dominant or even the principal agents in global politics but operate alongside a plurality of bodies, from international organizations through multinational corporations to the agencies of transnational civil society, embracing NGOs, advocacy networks and transnational pressure groups of all kinds. Central to the management of global affairs is an evolving system of global governance, with the UN and its agencies at its core, coordinating and regulating extensive areas of transnational and global activity.

Fourth, and finally, though global governance is generally considered a progressive force there is genuine concern with its poor democratic credentials and the unrepresentative nature of transnational civil society. For liberals this situation creates what Keohane refers to as the governance dilemma: namely, that institutions are necessary but also dangerous (Keohane, 2001).[7] This ambivalence towards international public power has its roots in the second wave of liberal internationalism and is addressed in a growing literature on the reform and democratization of global governance.

Contemporary liberal internationalist scholarship can be divided into four main variants: liberal institutionalism; structural liberalism; liberal reformism; and liberal cosmopolitanism. Though these labels define relatively discrete schools of thought, the work of any particular scholar rarely fits neatly into any single category. Of course, while the classification itself can be contested, it nevertheless offers a useful heuristic framework for exploring the cacophony of liberal voices. These variants will be reviewed briefly before turning to a critical evaluation.

Liberal institutionalism

Drawing on the importance of institutions within liberal thought, Robert Keohane in particular has advanced a seminal theory of why, and how, international cooperation or governance flourishes even in the absence of a hegemonic power imposing order on states (Keohane and Martin, 1995; Keohane, 1984). Though his argument recognizes that US hegemony may have been necessary to initiate international cooperation, it questions whether hegemony alone can really explain the continuing widening and deepening of multilateral cooperation throughout the postwar period (Keohane, 1984, p. 55). Nor does hegemony appear able to explain why, despite the end of the Cold War, multilateralism continued to expand and flourish most especially when the principal institutional rationales had disappeared (for instance, NATO). Central to liberal institutionalist theory is a line of reasoning which suggests that far from international cooperation being a product of hegemony or an altruistic motivation on the part of states, it is a rational response to conflict between states among whom there is considerable interdependence (Keohane, 1984). Conflict drives cooperation for in its absence – a condition of international harmony – there would be no need for states to cooperate to achieve their objectives since this would occur automatically (Keohane, 1984). As Keohane puts it, 'Harmony is apolitical. No communication is necessary, and no influence need be exercised. Cooperation, by contrast is highly political . . . without the spectre of conflict, there is no need to cooperate' (Keohane, 1984, p. 54).

Of course, cooperation is easier to achieve in areas where there are mutual interests, but even in such conditions, conflict over means rather than ends is endemic. In this respect, Keohane dismisses the classical liberal notion of a harmony of interests as an explanation for international cooperation. Furthermore, he demonstrates, using rational choice theory and realist assumptions about state motivation, why cooperation is both rational and functional for states and thus why, in the absence of hegemony, it will continue to develop (Keohane, 1984). International institutions provide important benefits for states since they facilitate the achievement of national goals while also reducing uncertainty, enhancing trust and generally minimizing the risks of cooperation. In these respects, international institutions, whether formal organizations such as the WTO or looser arrangements of international regimes, such as that covering the prevention of international terrorism or the proliferation of nuclear weapons, 'empower governments rather than shackle them' (Keohane, 1984, p. 13).

Realism, by contrast, predicts that states will always resist being constrained by international arrangements because the self-help or anarchic structure of the international system is such that states constantly seek to maximize their relative advantage or superiority over their competitors. Liberal institutionalism, however, demonstrates that states, as rational actors, are satisficers: that is, comfortable with realizing absolute gains (that is, with ensuring that they improve their own position irrespective of whether others do better) from cooperative arrangements (Hobson, 2000, p. 100). Liberal institutionalism therefore provides a rationalist validation of the classical liberal assumption that power politics – the condition of anarchy in the international system – can be mitigated, by demonstrating why and how international institutions 'are necessary . . . in order to achieve state purposes' (Keohane, 1984, p. 245). However, Keohane is careful to point out that the theory is principally applicable to relations among states which share a high degree of interdependence (such as the Western zone of peace) and may be less relevant in explaining cooperation where there are considerable disparities of power, for instance, between North and South.

Since the original publication of Keohane's theory in *After Hegemony* in 1984, the world has witnessed profound structural changes, including the ending of the Cold War, unprecedented globalization with a concomitant deepening of international interdependence, and the global spread of democracy. In these circumstances, liberal institutionalism appears to have acquired much greater explanatory power and therefore wider relevance than its many advocates and critics anticipated (Doyle, 2000; Hasenclever, Mayer and Rittberger, 1997; Hobson, 2000; Keohane and Martin, 1995; Long, 1995). Accordingly, it has come to constitute the principal liberal theory of why and how governance beyond the state is such a dominant feature of the current global political landscape.

Structural liberalism

Although liberal institutionalism presents a distinctively liberal theory of international institutions, according to structural liberalism it fails adequately to explain the origins of the existing system of global governance (Deudney and Ikenberry, 1999; Ikenberry, 1998, 2001a). Taking issue with liberal institutionalism's dismissal of hegemony and its functional account of cooperation, structural liberalism seeks to show why hegemony matters and why international institutions, precisely because they do constrain state power, have prospered in the postwar era (Ikenberry, 2001a). It does so relying on a historical institutionalist approach – rather than the rational choice approach of liberal institutionalism – which contends that institutions have to be understood as structures which evolve over time, constraining and shaping patterns of state behaviour, and which tend to persist even after the original reasons for their establishment have expired (Peters, 1999; Pierson, 1998; Steinmo, Thelen and Longstretch, 1992). Institutions, in this view, lock states into patterns of cooperation that acquire their own imperatives.

In explaining the origins of the postwar multilateral order, structural liberalism highlights the importance of the specifically *liberal* character of US hegemony (Ikenberry, 2001b, 2001c). This is hardly a novel claim. It is, however, crucial to explaining why, despite its hegemonic power, the US chose an institutional strategy – the construction of a multilateral order – as opposed to a strategy of domination (hegemonic control) or alternatively a return to the balance of power in order to maintain international order (Ikenberry, 2001a, ch. 1). As Ikenberry emphasizes, 'The liberal character of American hegemony allows the United States unusual capacities to make commitments and restrain power' (Ikenberry, 2001b). In effect, its sheer dominance gave the US the capacity 'to employ institutions to lock in a favourable order' while simultaneously being in an 'advantaged position to exchange restraints on its power for institutional agreements and to trade off short-term gains for long-term gains' (Ikenberry, 2001a, p. 5). As a democratic state, it was also in a strong position to legitimize to its citizens an institutional order which would necessarily restrain its power. This restraint, in turn, created significant incentives for less powerful states to participate in a multilateral order given that for them it significantly 'reduced the risks of domination or abandonment' (Ikenberry, 2001a, p. 5). In contrast to the liberal institutionalist argument, significant power asymmetries are an important component of the liberal structuralist explanation of why global governance structures arise to regulate international order.

Liberal structuralism is not just interested in explaining why the postwar order took an institutional form but also why, despite the end of the Cold War, it has remained so durable. In a context in which US hegemony remains unchallenged and in which, until 11 September, there was no significant external threat binding together Western states, the durability of the postwar order appears puzzling. For liberal institutionalism it is the functional logic of international cooperation which explains its persistence. By contrast, for structural liberalism the explanation is to be found in the way in which the postwar multilateral institutional order has become embedded or constitutionalized. Constitutions set the rules of the power game and set constraints on power. As it has evolved over the postwar era, the Western multilateral order has increasingly taken on the characteristics of a constitutional order in so far as it is 'an institutionalised settlement that binds states together so as to limit and constrain state power, including the power of the leading or hegemonic state' (Ikenberry, 2001a, p. 7).

Moreover, the evolution of this constitutional order is facilitated by the mutually reinforcing relationship between the democratic character of Western states, their growing economic interdependence and their deepening political bonds (Deudney and Ikenberry, 1999). In effect, the durability and stability of the Western postwar order is a product of both the way in which its constitutionalization constrains hegemonic power, and the way in which its institutionalization creates 'mutual dependencies that make . . . the costs and constraints on replacing those institutions grow considerably' (Ikenberry, 2001a, p. 269). States become systematically socialized, rather than coerced, into conformity with this constitutional order (Huntley, 1996).

This socialization process is developed more systematically within the expanding literature of democratic peace theory (Doyle, 1999; Huntley, 1996; Mesquita and Lalman, 1992; Russett, 1993). In effect, this literature seeks to test the empirical validity of the central propositions of the classical liberal argument, namely that peace and world order are a product of the mutually reinforcing dynamics of democratic government, market capitalism and effective international organizations. In general the democratic peace theorists conclude that rigorous statistical analysis of the empirical evidence indicates positive correlations between these factors, suggesting that liberal democracies tend not to engage in war with one another but inhabit a separate liberal or democratic peace (Russett, 1993). There is evidence that democratic states do tend, on the other hand, to engage in conflict with non-democratic states. More recent work, however, suggests that international organizations reduce the propensity for all states to engage in military conflict, while trade and economic interdependence are linked to more pacific relations between states whether democratic or not (Russett and Oneal, 2001, ch. 5). Where democracy, economic interdependence, and multilateralism reinforce each other, as in the Western community of states, a distinctively liberal zone of peace can be identified in which, according to this account, war has become obsolete (Mueller, 1989; Russett, 1993; Russett and Oneal, 2001).

These empirical findings vindicate structural liberalism in so far as they appear to confirm the validity of the deductive and normative analysis of classical liberal internationalist theory that a virtuous circle of republican (democratic) government, free trade and international law does create the necessary conditions for a universal and perpetual peace (Russett and Oneal, 2001, p. 272). Given a liberal faith in the possibilities of progress, the logical extrapolation of this argument is that a more peaceful world can be engineered by expanding the zone of peace. Structural liberalism is thus motivated ultimately by a normative concern with extending the liberal peace beyond its Western core. Russett, for instance, concludes that:

> A different kind of world can be nurtured, one in which most conflicts of interests are not managed primarily by the threat of violence . . . The benefits of liberalism need not be confined, therefore, to the powerful. Nor should the powerful seek to impose liberalism on others. . . . Extending the Kantian system will require cooperation. Multilateralism will be crucial . . . If multilateralism is to be effective, international organizations will have to play an important role. (Russett and Oneal, 2001, pp. 303–4)

Structural liberalism is an explanatory account of how power politics (anarchy) has been tamed, if not transcended, within the contours of the postwar Western liberal international order. It is not simply concerned, as is liberal institutionalism, with explaining the functional imperatives of international cooperation *per se* but rather with explaining the structural factors which have given rise to the distinctive Western liberal international order and its corresponding system of global governance (Deudney and Ikenberry, 1999). It is a theory which, in simpler language, explains how the liberal international order came to be – and is – governed. But it also explains why, as the balance between liberal and non-liberal states in the global system shifts in favour of the former, the governance and constitutionalization of world order is likely to be universalized (Moravcsik, 1997). To the extent to which the liberal order has been globalized, structural liberalism is therefore implicitly an account of why contemporary global governance is necessarily best described as *liberal* global governance.

Liberal reformism

Reform of liberal global governance is a key theme in contemporary studies of international organization (Cable, 1999; Commission on Global Governance, 1995; Edwards, 2000; Keohane, 2001; Reinicke, 1999; Rosenau, 2000a; Slaughter, 2000; Weiss and Gordenker, 1996; Woods, 1999). In part, this is because globalization imposes significant new burdens on international agencies with respect to managing transnational forces in ways which enhance human security and global social justice. It is also because of a growing political awareness that the prevailing system of liberal global governance, as anti-globalization protests attest, is widely perceived as having limited political legitimacy and limited effectiveness. Liberal reformism is concerned with elucidating the key defects of the present system and elaborating the necessary conditions for more effective and legitimate global governance.

Among those key defects is the structural dominance of the most powerful states in shaping the institutions, patterns and outcomes of global governance. Key aspects of global governance are also distorted by the imperatives of nurturing, legitimizing and sustaining the global market. Furthermore, the technocratic nature of global institutions removes many issues from public scrutiny and thus creates a growing backlash against globalization. These distortions are reinforced by several critical gaps in the governance capacity of the system, most especially in respect of its welfare, human security and poverty reduction functions (UNDP, 1999). The most strategically important of these gaps, from the perspective of liberal reformism, is the democratic deficit (Commission on Global Governance, 1995; UN Secretary-General, 2000; Keohane, 1998, 2001). As the Commission on Global Governance report asserts:

> It is fundamentally important that governance should be underpinned by democracy at all levels and ultimately by the rule of enforceable law . . . as at the national level, so in the global neighbourhood: the democratic principle must be ascendant. The need for greater democracy arises out of the close linkage between legitimacy and effectiveness . . . as the role of international institutions in global governance grows, the need to ensure that they are democratic also increases. (1995, pp. 48, 66)

Democratic reform, however, tends to be conceived principally in limited procedural terms, as creating slightly more representative, transparent and accountable international institutions (Falk, 1995; Commission on Global Governance, 1995). National governments remain crucial in this regard for representing citizens' interests and bringing to account the decision-makers in global and regional bodies. In effect, states are considered the primary units of democratic accountability such that democratizing global governance is conceived as synonymous with creating a democratic order between (democratic) *states* (rather than in relation to *peoples*). Creating more representative, responsive, transparent and accountable international institutions by widening the participation of states in key global forums and strengthening existing lines of accountability are central to this reformist vision (Commission on Global Governance, 1995).

Transnational civil society is nevertheless part of this vision. Given the associational revolution and the power shift towards the agencies of civil society, new forms of democratic accountability and transparency arise (Matthews, 1997; Rosenau, 1997). Accordingly liberal reformism tends to conceive of the prevailing system of global governance as exhibiting the characteristics of a form of polyarchy or pluralist order in which states share power with international organizations, transnational civil society, the corporate sector and other agencies (Rosenau, 1997, 2000b). In this pluralist order, global public policy results from the deliberations of diverse agencies within the context of global public policy networks (Reinicke, 1998). Making this system operate both more transparently and more effectively is a principal ambition (Keohane, 2001; Reinicke and Witte, 1999; Woods, 1999). As Keohane asserts, global governance requires a more enhanced system of 'voluntary pluralism under conditions of maximum transparency' (Keohane, 1998). A more pluralistic system of global governance, in this view, implies more democratic global governance.

In effect, liberal reformists advocate the reconstruction of aspects of liberal-pluralist democracy at the international level shorn of the requirements of electoral politics. In place of parties competing for votes, a vibrant transnational civil society channels its demands to the decision-makers, while in turn also making them accountable for their actions. Accordingly, 'accountability will be enhanced not only by chains of official responsibility but also by the requirement of transparency. Official actions, negotiated amongst state representatives in international organizations, will be subject to scrutiny by transnational networks' (Keohane, 1998). This reflects some of the ideas of the new liberal internationalism of the early twentieth century: 'open covenants openly arrived at', as Woodrow Wilson proposed. Democratizing global governance is conceived principally in rather limited terms as enhancing the procedures for making and legitimizing global public policy (see chapter 16).

Global governance, in the liberal reformist view, constitutes the key arena within which the interests of both states and the agencies of civil society are articulated and reconciled in the process of global policy formulation. A proliferation of transnational policy networks and multilateral institutions give form and substance to global governance and are central to the formulation and implementation of effective and legitimate global public policy. Liberal reformism accepts that this system has defects but that, nevertheless, it is vital to the effective management of global affairs and the maintenance of world order. Its principal advocates believe that democratic reform of global governance is not only feasible and desirable but that it is also absolutely necessary, since only a more democratic system of global governance can ensure that the benefits of globalization are more widely diffused and that its undesirable consequences are mitigated (UNDP, 1999).

Intrinsic to liberal reformist thinking is a deeply rooted liberal anxiety, which has some rational basis in the events of the 1930s, that '[international] institutions, especially those created to tackle the problems of globalism, come at particular moments of crisis under strains that are so great as to preclude their effective operation. They become the major channels through which the resentments against globalization work their destruction' (James, 2001, p. 5). Whether liberal reformism constitutes an intellectually persuasive or politically feasible project capable of addressing this fear remains, as will become apparent, in doubt.

Liberal cosmopolitanism

For advocates of liberal cosmopolitanism, however, liberal reformism is not radical enough. Liberal cosmopolitanism questions the very purposes and practices of liberal global governance, not just its institutional form. As a discrete theory, liberal cosmopolitanism must be distinguished from other variants of cosmopolitanism, especially democratic cosmopolitanism or cosmopolitan democracy (discussed in chapter 15 below). The significant differences are of four kinds:

- *Substantive* Whereas liberal cosmopolitanism is concerned principally with the matter of global justice, cosmopolitan democracy is principally concerned with the question of (global) democracy.

- *Philosophical*   Whereas liberal cosmopolitanism develops a purposive and analytical distinction between moral cosmopolitanism (that all individuals are members of a universal moral community) and institutional or political cosmopolitanism (that global political structures are essential to the realization of cosmopolitan principles), cosmopolitan democracy presupposes that the former necessarily implies the latter such that in ethical (although not necessarily analytical) or practical political terms they are inseparable or mutually constitutive (Held, 1995; Hutchings, 1999; Jones, 1999; O'Neill, 2001).
- *Methodological*   Whereas liberal cosmopolitanism tends to be 'agnostic . . . about the proper political constitution of international relations', cosmopolitan democracy adopts an institutionalist analysis of the proper form of a democratic world order (Beitz, 1999).
- *Prescriptive*   Whereas liberal cosmopolitanism seeks to establish justificatory arguments for global social justice, rather than designs for its realization, by contrast cosmopolitan democracy seeks to identify the requirements of a democratic system of global governance and the necessary conditions for its effective realization (Doyle, 1999, 2000; Held, 1995; Russett, 1993; Russett and Oneal, 2001).

Liberal cosmopolitanism is a normative theory of global justice. It is, in Beitz's words, 'a doctrine about the basis on which institutions and practices should be justified or criticized. It applies to the whole world the maxim that choices about what policies we should prefer, or what institutions we should establish, should be based on an impartial consideration of the claims of each person who would be affected' (Beitz, 1999). Since it takes the well-being of individuals as central, it accords primacy to global distributive justice not just to 'bounded justice' within societies or international justice between states (Beitz, 2001). In so doing, it presents a radical critique of the existing world order and global governance arrangements in so far as they perpetuate global inequalities and therefore global injustices. As Caney observes, the argument is 'that the current system is extremely unjust and that a redistribution of wealth from the affluent to the impoverished is required' (Caney, 2001).

Although it is associated with Rawlsian notions of distributive justice, liberal cosmopolitanism takes issue with Rawls's restricted conception of the scope of justice, and some of the principal justifications for its pursuit (Beitz, 1999; Hutchings, 1999; Jones, 1999). In particular, Beitz and others argue that the demands of social justice cannot be limited by relatively arbitrary national, ethnic or territorial boundaries, but on the contrary transcend them (Beitz, 2001; Jones, 1999). This is because, in part, globalization and the structures of global politics have bound the fate of communities and individuals together such that it is increasingly 'misleading to describe the international environment as a realm of states knit together by an array of mutual assistance schemes in which any individual state may participate, or not, as it wishes' (Beitz, 1999).

Taking account of this new reality of a globalized world order, liberal cosmopolitanism is therefore concerned with establishing the principal philosophical justifications and ethical grounds 'for the redistribution of wealth from rich to poor across the globe' (Hutchings, 1999, p. 37). It is, as Hutchings acknowledges, only 'secondarily concerned with how this redistribution, justly, might be achieved' (1999, p. 37). Even so, the implications of this critique for the existing world order are dramatic for it implies the need for a fundamental transformation if the principles of global distributive justice are to be fully realized. More ambiguous are its implications for global governance, conceived both as an instrument of global injustice and an instrument for global redistribution (Hurrell, 2001; Jones, 1999; O'Neill, 2001). Liberal cosmopolitanism is a normative theory which, in privileging the principle of global distributive justice, delivers a radical critique of the current constitution and conduct of global governance. In this respect, it shares with some of its classical liberal progenitors a genuine commitment to the emancipation of humankind from arbitrary power and injustice of all kinds.

Ambiguities and Controversies: the Clash of Liberal Internationalisms

Each of these schools of contemporary liberal internationalist thought demands further reflection. Considered conjointly they give expression to deeper ambiguities and inconsistencies rooted within the substantive reasoning and ethical foundations of the liberal internationalist tradition.

In a recent review of liberal international theory, Burchill concludes optimistically by suggesting that 'in many ways international relations at the dawn of the new century fulfils the dream of eighteenth and nineteenth century liberals' (Burchill et al., 2001, p. 63). This observation reflects a sense that patterns of globalization are creating a unified world for some, even if not for the majority of humankind. In this context, and indeed precisely because of the events of 11 September, global governance has become rather more indispensable than its detractors acknowledge. As this examination of the three great waves of liberal internationalist thought demonstrates, while consistent themes surface across the centuries, theoretical diversity is its hallmark. As with liberal political theory, there is no single coherent narrative but rather a veiled intellectual unity disguising considerable theoretical pluralism (Mason, 2000; Richardson, 1997). This diversity is a source of significant ambiguities. These ambiguities invite reflection on both the theoretical reasoning and the continuing relevance of liberal internationalism, especially its contemporary variants, to an understanding and explanation of global governance.

Three principal sources of ambiguity are endemic to liberal internationalist thought, most particularly in its third wave. These ambiguities express logical tensions between different sets of ethical principles or philosophical assumptions within liberal internationalist reasoning, including, in particular, statism versus cosmopolitanism; economics versus politics; and minimal governance versus active governance. Each will be considered briefly in turn.

Statism versus cosmopolitanism

Liberal internationalism embodies an ambiguous attitude to the state and sovereignty. At issue is a deductive and ethical argument as to whether the sovereign state is a barrier to, or the building block of, a genuine liberal world order. As Franceschet argues, a crucial division in liberal internationalist thought is 'ethical and is concerned with whether or not the sovereign state is compatible with the highest of liberal goals, individual freedom' (Franceschet, 1999). Liberals of a statist persuasion tend to answer this question in the affirmative, while those of a cosmopolitan persuasion respond in the negative (Hutchings, 1999). This leads to quite different, if not incompatible, ethical conceptions of world order: cosmopolitan arguments presuppose or advocate the transcendence of the interstate order, while statists argue for its reform.

Humanitarian intervention is one crucial issue where this tension is expressly visible and produces contradictory prescriptions. Whereas the cosmopolitan position sanctions humanitarian intervention, given that universal human rights must ultimately trump state sovereignty, the statist argument leads to a defence of non-intervention (and thereby the doctrine of sovereign self-determination) over the application of universal principles (Hoffman, 1995). This tension between statism and cosmopolitanism can be traced through the history of liberal internationalist thought, reflecting a critical ambiguity at its ideological core. It remains a central unresolved issue with profound implications for contemporary liberal discourses on the proper role and legitimate purposes of global governance.

Economics versus politics

The relationship between the economic and the political in liberal internationalist thought is complicated. At one level, the philosophical separation of the political and economic spheres is decidedly problematic (Carr, 1981; Gray, 2001; Polanyi, 1944). In its crudest formulation it leads to a separation of political and economic power and thus to a rather naive pluralist account of global governance and global institutions as simply neutral mechanisms for the articulation and pursuit of the global interest or global public good. As Halliday observes, 'There remains a strand of optimism, but also naivety, about the liberal agenda in regard to international organizations . . . For all the proclamations of a global interest, there is a serious question as to whether, in most areas, such an interest exists' (2000, pp. 37, 39). Such an approach fails to acknowledge what Schattschneider argued many years ago, that institutions represent, in effect, 'the mobilization of bias'.

Even when this is recognized, as in the cosmopolitan and liberal reformist accounts which seek to address the distorted nature of global governance, there remains an a priori assumption that institutions can be engineered to realize progressive purposes: that the politics of international institutions can be understood as (or made) relatively autonomous from wider structures of global economic and social power. In this view, institutions develop distinctive internal structures and political processes which moderate power politics, ensuring that they are never simply the captives of dominant powers or sets of interests (Nordlinger, 1981). Rarely, in the liberal view, by contrast with realism and Marxism, do institutions function as mechanisms simply to reproduce the structure of global power relations. That institutions matter is not in doubt. But the separation of the political and the economic in liberal thought leads to ambiguous or vacuous answers (the global interest) to the really important questions about global institutions: governance in whose interests and for what purposes? On the one hand, institutions are held to constrain the powerful (as in structural liberalism) and empower the weak (liberal institutionalism); on the other hand, they are held to be the products of hegemony (structural liberalism) and are distorted by global power relations (liberal reformism). These ambiguities, however, are associated with a more fundamental philosophical disagreement concerning the purposes of public power and the state's role in the realization of human freedom.

Minimal governance versus active governance

There is a long-standing disagreement within liberal political theory with respect to the role of the state in social life (Held, 1996; Richardson, 1997; Sandel, 1996). The sources of this disagreement can be traced, in part, to different ethical conceptions of freedom. Whereas the classical conception of freedom emphasizes negative liberty (freedom from undue constraint), the modern conception emphasizes positive liberty (freedom to act). This distinction produces different conceptions of the proper role of government as either non-intervention (negative liberty) or empowerment (positive liberty). The result is disagreement about the proper role of government in a liberal society: a contest between the proponents of limited government (negative liberty) and active government (positive liberty). Although far more nuanced than this binary opposition suggests, the implications for liberal internationalism are nevertheless quite profound. At issue is a disagreement about the proper scope and the rationale for liberal international governance.

This disagreement threads its way through the three great waves of liberal internationalist scholarship. It takes the form of a recurring dialogue concerning the scope of international governance as reflected, for instance, in the arguments of nineteenth-century liberal internationalists for minimal international governance and the arguments of the new liberal internationalism of the mid-twentieth century for a multilateral system of global governance extending to the economic and social spheres. Furthermore, the disagreement is also about the ends of international governance: whether it should be principally concerned with dismantling the barriers to individual liberty (negative freedom) or to creating the conditions for the universal realization of individual liberty (positive freedom). This tension is explicit in differences between liberal cosmopolitanism, which harbours an ambivalent attitude towards international institutions because of their potential role as agents of injustice and tyranny, and liberal reformism, which considers global governance to be essential to ensuring greater global social justice (Cable, 1999; O'Neill, 2001).

These ambiguities appear intrinsic to liberal international theory. To the extent to which liberal theory validates contradictory or inconsistent (explanatory and normative) accounts of global governance, its theoretical coherence is significantly undermined. These ambiguities are amplified further by other more substantive critiques from beyond the liberal tradition.

As an enduring theory of world order, liberal internationalism has attracted justifiable and vehement criticism. Among its most impassioned critics, E. H. Carr dismissed it as utopian and untenable, Karl Polanyi considered it delusory, and Stanley Hoffman condemns it as fallacious in 'believing that all good things can come together' (Hoffman, 1995; Carr, 1981; Polanyi, 1944). These critiques have concentrated on several aspects of the liberal tradition, but the predominant theme is its essentially ideological nature.

Ideologies can be understood as belief systems that both reflect and distort social reality (Bernstein, 1976, p. 108). They are connected in complex ways to the exercise of power. As an ideology, liberal internationalism stands accused, by realists and Marxists alike, of such extensive distortion of international reality that it is nothing short of utopian – understood in E. H. Carr's words as the attempt to make 'political theory a norm to which political practice ought to conform' (Carr, 1981, p. 12). Likewise, for many realists, the current discourse of global governance is a similarly utopian project (see chapter 11), while Halliday too identifies 'a naivety about the liberal agenda in regard to international organization' (Halliday, 2000, p. 37). In particular, it retains a naive faith in the logic of international cooperation and the capacity of global institutions ultimately to transcend power politics. This naiveté, argue its critics, issues from the principal intellectual failure of liberal internationalism: an inability to confront the effective sources of power in world politics and the real, as opposed to nominal, power structures which effectively govern world order. As Carr succinctly put it: 'Power is an indispensable instrument of government. To interna-tionalise government is to internationalise power; and international government is, in effect, government by that state which supplies the power necessary for the purpose of governing' (Carr, 1981, p. 107). Liberal internationalism is fatally flawed, argue its critics, because it conceals the true sources of power in world politics.

To the extent that liberal theories respond to such critiques by incorporating notions of hegemony into their explanatory schema, as with structural liberalism, they become hard to distinguish from the realist analyses they seek to transcend. Sophist-icated as it has become, liberal internationalism, its principal realist and Marxist critiques suggest, functions less as an explanatory theory than the vital ideology (see chapter 12) which legitimizes a liberal multilateral world order, concealing the domina-tion of the powerful, whether hegemonic states or hegemonic global capitalism (or both), over the rest of humanity (Zolo, 1997). Historically, liberal internationalism has been and remains the ideology of the powerful and not the weak (Carr, 1981; Polanyi, 1944). It has sanctioned both empire in the nineteenth century and the first war of the twenty-first century, Afghanistan. The liberal order is peaceful at home but 'dangerous and culturally imperialist' beyond the 'zone of peace' (Hutchings, 1999, p. 166). At best it is hypocritical, at worst menacingly arrogant (Gowan, 2001; Mayall, 2000). To its critics, *liberal* global governance is a dangerous delusion which 'will not work: it is more likely to plunge the planet into increasingly divisive turmoil' (Gowan, 2001, p. 92).

From Crisis to Renaissance: the Remaking of Liberal Internationalism

Following the end of the Cold War, Stanley Hoffman suggested that the hubris of liberal internationalism might be somewhat misplaced. In a provocative gesture he posed the simple question: 'Communism is dead, but is the other great postwar ideo-logy, liberal internationalism, also dying?' (Hoffman, 1995). Ironically his question coincided with the publication of *Our Global Neighbourhood*, the final report of the 'last of the great liberal commissions', which introduced into the political lexicon the concept of global governance (Commission on Global Governance, 1995). While the Commission delivered a definitive 'no' response to Hoffman's question, the author himself presented a more pessimistic conclusion. Hoffman made much of the inconsistencies and naiveties of the liberal internationalist tradition, as well as its hypocrisies. His conclusions have been influential such that there is a widespread acceptance among students of international relations that the post-Cold War renaissance of liberal internationalism represents not its ascendancy but rather its intellectual dissolution (Dunne, 2001; Ishay, 1995; Lynch, 1999; Rengger, 2000; Richardson, 1997).

There are good reasons for taking issue with Hoffman's assessment. Not least among them is the fact that liberal internationalism is not uniquely vulnerable to intellectual critique: neither realism nor Marxism provide consistent or coherent analyses of, let alone answers to the political and moral dilemmas of contemporary global politics. Both embrace, as does liberal internationalism, quite diverse schools of thought. Realist and radical analyses of world politics – just like liberal internationalist analyses – have defended as well as decried the humanitarian interventions of the 1990s. In a different age, at the height of the Korean War, Hans Morgenthau, the principal advocate of the postwar realist tradition, opposed US intervention on the grounds that it violated the logic of realism, while others defended it on equally solid realist reasoning (Morgenthau, 1951). In analysing contemporary global governance, the tendency of both realism and Marxism to dismiss international institutions as epiphenomenal seems overly reductionist, dismissing too hastily the vast literature within social science that shows that institutions do matter (Peters, 1999; Steinmo, Thelen and Longstretch, 1992). Nor do these traditions necessarily provide convincing frameworks for understanding or explaining the institutional logic or governance of the liberal international order (Clark, 2001; Ikenberry, 2001a). Furthermore, the postmodernist critique of the possibility of human progress applies as much to Marxism, and the eternal 'truths' of realism, as it does to liberal internationalism (George, 1994). The current crisis of liberal internationalist thought is somewhat exaggerated. Nor, as the radicalism of liberal cosmopolitanism demonstrates, is it accurate to depict it – as many critics do – as having lost its ethical commitment to human emancipation (Franceschet, 2001).

There is much in the current renaissance of liberal internationalist scholarship that is to be valued. In certain respects it provides a middle way between realism and cosmopolitanism (see chapter 15), for it takes governance and politics beyond the state seriously. In doing so, it offers significant insights into the origins, form, logic and defects of contemporary liberal global governance. As a theory of global change, it also provides a normative account, limited as it might be, of the possibility of genuine global governance. However, it embodies two significant defects: a visible tension between its explanatory and normative ambitions; and a disjuncture between an ethical radicalism and an institutional conservatism, or even agnosticism, concerning 'the best institutional structure for international politics' (Beitz, 1999). In the first regard, the normative gap between liberal institutionalism, liberal structuralism and liberal reformism, liberal cosmopolitanism is particularly instructive.[8] With respect to the second, whereas Paine, Kant and Hobson, among others, sought to confront arbitrary power through both an ethical and an institutional radicalism, there is a reluctance, evident among advocates of liberal cosmopolitanism, to engage directly with issues of global institutional design for a more just and democratic world order (Beitz, 1999; O'Neill, 2001). Whereas in its explanatory versions, liberal internationalism tends to be purged of ethical content, in its more radical normative versions it tends to be purged of institutional content. If there is a crisis of liberal internationalism, it is not due to its lack of relevance or radicalism, as Hoffmann and other critics suggest, but on the contrary to a failure to combine, in a systematic or convincing way, its explanatory and radical ethical ambitions.

Situated precariously between realism and cosmopolitanism, contemporary liberal internationalism will have to reconnect its explanatory and radical ethical projects if its intellectual renaissance is to flourish. As E. H. Carr remarked, 'Utopia and reality are . . . the two facets of political science. Sound political thought and sound political life will only be found where both have their place' (1981, p. 10).

Notes

The chapter has benefited from the advice and comments of my colleagues at Southampton University: Andy Mason, Caroline Thomas and David Owen.

1   Liberal internationalism conjoins two rather discrete discourses: that of liberalism and that of internationalism. Liberalism, as a political philosophy seeks to explicate the conditions for the realization of political liberty and liberal government, while internationalism is concerned with the promotion of transnational or global solidarity and international government. Though related, in so far as human freedom is conceived as a universal value, neither necessarily implies the other: not all liberals are internationalists, while not all internationalists are liberals (for example, socialist internationalism) (Ishay, 1995); and whereas liberalism advocates limited government, internationalism seeks government's extension to the international sphere. Furthermore, internationalism is compatible with a variety of different political philosophies (Hutchings, 1999, p. 154; Lynch, 1999). Intellectually and ethically, the conjunction of liberalism and internationalism is therefore not surprisingly somewhat problematic.
2   Liberal internationalism, however, is not a pacifist doctrine since just wars, in the defence of liberal values or humanitarian intervention, are sanctioned by many leading liberal theorists, including Immanuel Kant, J. S. Mill, John Locke and J. A. Hobson.
3   Used here in its broadest sociological sense as durable sets of rules, roles, norms, routines and expectations defining appropriate behaviour, thereby encompassing everything from formal international organizations and international law to informal international regimes.
4   Realism, as chapter 11 argues, is deeply sceptical of the notion that the virtuous circle has, or even can, overcome the central structural feature of the modern states system, namely anarchy. Instead, realists explain the present liberal world order as a product of US hegemonic power and the absence of any serious challengers to the status quo.
5   On this diversity see, for instance, Long and Wilson, 1995.
6   Kant is regarded as the principal figure in liberal internationalist thought. His legacy for international theory is complicated for his work is also central to critical theory and aspects of the international society approach. Accordingly, the fact that liberal internationalism claims Kant's legacy for itself should be treated with some caution (Cavallar, 1999; Neufeld, 1995; Onuf, 1998).
7   'Although institutions are essential for human life, they are also dangerous' (Keohane, 2001).
8   This is not to argue that explanatory theories have no normative agenda since, for instance, Keohane addresses the ethical issues of liberal institutionalism in the final chapter of *After Hegemony* (1984) and in chapter 16 here. What is at issue is the attempt of explanatory theory to purge liberal internationalism of its radical ethical content and this to some degree applies to liberal reformism. See Cavallar, 1999; Hobson, 2000.

References

Angell, N. (1933) *The Great Illusion* (1908), London: Heineman.

Beitz, C. R. (1999) 'Social and cosmopolitan liberalism', *International Affairs*, 75, pp. 347–77.

Beitz, C. R. (2001) 'Does global inequality matter?', in T. W. Pogge (ed.), *Global Justice*, Oxford: Blackwell.

Bernstein, R. J. (1976) *The Restructuring of Social and Political Theory*, London: Methuen.

Boucher, D. (1998) *Political Theories of International Relations*, Oxford: Oxford University Press.

Burchill, S. et al. (2001) *Theories of International Relations*, 2nd edn, London: Palgrave.

Cable, V. (1999) *Globalization and Global Governance*, London: Royal Institute of International Affairs.

Caney, S. (2001) 'International distributive justice', *Political Studies*, 49, pp. 974–97.

Carr, E. H. (1981) *The Twenty Years' Crisis 1919–1939*, London: Papermac.

Cavallar, G. (1999) *Kant and the Theory and Practice of International Right*, Cardiff: University of Wales Press.

Cavallar, G. (2001) 'Kantian perspectives on democratic peace: alternatives to Doyle', *Review of International Studies*, 27, pp. 229–49.

Clark, I. (2001) *The Post-Cold War Order*, Oxford: Oxford University Press.

Claude, I. (1971) *Swords into Ploughshares*, New York: Random House.

Commission on Global Governance (1995) *Our Global Neighbourhood*, Oxford: Oxford University Press.

Deudney, D. and Ikenberry, G. J. (1999) 'The nature and sources of liberal international order', *Review of International Studies*, 25, pp. 179–96.

Doyle, M. (1997) *Ways of War and Peace*, New York: Norton.

Doyle, M. (1999) 'A liberal view: preserving and expanding the liberal pacific union', in J. A. Hall and T. V. Paul (eds), *International Order and the Future of World Politics*, Cambridge: Cambridge University Press.

Doyle, M. (2000) 'A more perfect union? The liberal peace and the challenge of globalization', *Review of International Studies*, 26, pp. 81–95.

Dunne, T. (2001) 'Liberalism', in K. Booth and S. Smith (eds), *The Globalization of World Politics*, Oxford: Oxford University Press.

Edwards, M. (2000) *Future Positive: International Cooperation in the Twenty First Century*, London: Earthscan.

Falk, R. (1995) 'Liberalism at the global level: the last of the independent commissions?', *Millennium*, 24, pp. 563–78.

Franceschet, A. (1999) 'The ethical foundations of liberal internationalism', *International Journal*, 54, pp. 463–81.

Franceschet, A. (2001) 'Sovereignty and freedom: Immanuel Kant's liberal internationalist legacy', *Review of International Studies*, 27, pp. 209–28.

George, J. (1994) *Discourses of Global Politics*, Boulder, Colo.: Lynne Reiner.

Gowan, P. (2001) 'Neoliberal cosmopolitanism', *New Left Review*, series II, no. 11, pp. 79–93.

Gray, J. (2001) *The Two Faces of Liberalism*, Cambridge: Cambridge University Press.

Halliday, F. (2000) *The World at 2000*, London: Palgrave.

Hasenclever, A., Mayer, P. and Rittberger, V. (1997) *Theories of International Regimes*, Cambridge: Cambridge University Press.

Held, D. (1995) *Democracy and Global Order*, Cambridge: Polity.

Held, D. (1996) *Models of Democracy*, Cambridge: Polity.

Hinsley, F. H. (1967) *Power and the Pursuit of Peace*, Cambridge: Cambridge University Press.

Hobson, J. M. (2000) *The State and International Relations*, Cambridge: Cambridge University Press.

Hoffman, S. (1995) 'The crisis of liberal internationalism', *Foreign Policy*, 98, pp. 161–77.

Howard, M. (1981) *War and the Liberal Conscience*, Oxford: Oxford University Press.

Howard, M. (2000) *The Invention of Peace*, Princeton: Princeton University Press.

Huntley, W. L. (1996) 'Kant's third image: systematic sources of the liberal peace', *International Studies Quarterly*, 40, pp. 45–76.

Hurrell, A. (2001) 'Global inequality and international institutions', in T. W. Pogge (ed.), *Global Justice*, Oxford: Blackwell.

Hutchings, K. (1999) *International Political Theory*, London: Sage.

Ikenberry, G. J. (1998) 'Constitutional politics in international relations', *European Journal of International Relations*, 4, pp. 147–77.

Ikenberry, G. J. (2001a) *After Victory*, Princeton: Princeton University Press.

Ikenberry, G. J. (2001b) 'American power and the empire of capitalist democracy', *Review of International Studies*, 27, pp. 191–213.

Ikenberry, G. J. (2001c) 'America's liberal grand strategy: democracy and national security in the postwar era', in M. Cox, G. J. Ikenberry and T. Inoguchi (eds), *American Democracy Promotion*, Oxford: Oxford University Press.

Ishay, M. R. (1995) *Internationalism and its Betrayal*, Minneapolis: University of Minnesota Press.

James, H. (2001) *The End of Globalization*, Princeton: Princeton University Press.

Jones, C. (1999) *Global Justice: Defending Cosmopolitanism*, Oxford: Oxford University Press.

Kant, I. (1795) 'To perpetual peace: a philosophical sketch', in *Perpetual Peace and Other Essays*, Indianapolis: Hackett.

Keohane, R. O. (1984) *After Hegemony*, Princeton: Princeton University Press.

Keohane, R. O. (1998) 'International institutions: can interdependence work?', *Foreign Policy*, Summer, pp. 82–96.

Keohane, R. (2001) 'Governance in a partially globalized world', *American Political Science Review*, 95, pp. 1–13.

Keohane, R. O. and Martin, L. (1995) 'The promise of institutionalist theory', *International Security*, 20, pp. 39–51.

Long, C. D. and Wilson, P. (eds) (1995) *Thinkers of the Twenty Years' Crisis: Inter-war Idealism Reassessed*, Oxford: Oxford University Press.

Long, D. (1996) *Towards a New Liberal Internationalism*, Cambridge: Cambridge University Press.

Long, P. (1995) 'The Harvard School of Liberal International Theory: the case for closure', *Millennium*, 24, pp. 489–505.

Lynch, C. (1999) 'The promise and problems of internationalism', *Global Governance*, 5, pp. 83–107.

Mason, A. (2000) *Community, Solidarity, and Belonging*, Cambridge: Cambridge University Press.

Matthews, J. T. (1997) 'Power shift', *Foreign Affairs*, Jan., pp. 50–66.

Mayall, J. (2000) 'Democracy and international society', *International Affairs*, 76, pp. 61–75.

Mesquita, B. B. de and Lalman, D. (1992) *War and Reason*, New Haven: Yale University Press.

Mitrany, D. (1975) 'The progress of international government (1932)', in P. Taylor (ed.), *The Functional Theory of Politics*, London: Martin Robertson.

Moravcsik, A. (1997) 'Taking preferences seriously: a liberal theory of international politics', *International Organization*, 51, pp. 513–33.

Morgenthau, H. J. (1951) *In Defense of the National Interest*, New York: University Press of America.

Mueller, J. (1989) *Retreat from Doomsday: The Obsolescence of Major War*, New York: Basic Books.

Neufeld, M. (1995) *The Restructuring of International Relations Theory*, Cambridge: Cambridge University Press.

Nordlinger, E. A. (1981) *On the Autonomy of the Democratic State*, Boston: Harvard University Press.

O'Neill, O. (2001) 'Agents of justice', in T. W. Pogge (ed.), *Global Justice*, Oxford: Blackwell.

Onuf, N. (1998) *The Republican Legacy in International Thought*, Cambridge: Cambridge University Press.

Peters, B. G. (1999) *Institutional Theory in Political Science*, London: Pinter.

Pierson, P. (1998) 'The path to European integration: a historical-institutionalist analysis', in W. Sandholtz and A. Sweet (eds), *European Integration and Supranational Governance*, Oxford: Oxford University Press.

Polanyi, K. (1944) *The Great Transformation*, Boston: Beacon Press.

Reinicke, W. H. (1998) *Global Public Policy: Governing without Government?* Washington DC: Brookings Institution.

Reinicke, W. H. (1999) 'The other world wide web: global public policy networks', *Foreign Policy*, Winter, pp. 44–57.

Reinicke, W. H. and Witte, J. M. (1999) 'Globalization and democratic governance: global public policy and trisectoral networks', paper.

Rengger, N. (2000) *International Relations, Political Theory and the Problem of Order*, London: Routledge.

Richardson, J. L. (1997) 'Contending liberalisms: past and present', *European Journal of International Relations*, 3, pp. 5–33.

Rosenau, J. N. (1997) *Along the Domestic-Foreign Frontier: Exploring Governance in a Turbulent World*, Cambridge: Cambridge University Press.

Rosenau, J. N. (2000a) 'Change, complexity, and governance in globalizing space', in J. Pierre (ed.), *Debating Governance: Authority, Steering, and Democracy*, Oxford: Oxford University Press.

Rosenau, J. N. (2000b) 'Governance in a globalizing world', in D. Held and A. McGrew (eds), *The Global Transformations Reader*, Cambridge: Polity.

Russett, B. (1993) *Grasping the Democratic Peace: Principles for a Post-Cold War World*, Princeton: Princeton University Press.

Russett, B. and Oneal, J. (2001) *Triangulating Peace*, New York: Norton.

Sandel, M. (1996) *Democracy's Discontent*, Cambridge, Mass.: Harvard University Press.

Skidelsky, R. (2000) *John Maynard Keynes*, vol. 3: *Fighting for Britain 1937–1946*, London: Macmillan.

Slaughter, A.-M. (2000) 'Governing the global economy through government networks', in M. Byers (ed.), *The Role of Law in International Politics*, Oxford: Oxford University Press.

Steinmo, S., Thelen, K. and Longstretch, F. (1992) *Structuring Politics: Historical Institutionalism in Comparative Analysis*, Cambridge: Cambridge University Press.

UN Secretary-General (2000) *Renewing the United Nations*, New York: United Nations (www.un.org).

UNDP (1999) *Globalization with a Human Face: UN Human Development Report 1999*, Oxford: UN Development Programme/Oxford University Press.

Weiss, T. G. and Gordenker, L. (1996) *NGOs, the UN, and Global Governance*, Boulder, Colo.: Lynne Rienner.

Williams, H. (1992) *International Relations in Political Theory*, Milton Keynes: Open University Press.

Woods, N. (1999) 'Good governance in international organization', *Global Governance*, 5, pp. 39–61.

Zolo, D. (1997) *Cosmopolis: Prospects for World Government*, Cambridge: Polity.

14
Functionalism
Mark F. Imber

Sovereignty cannot in fact be transferred by a formula, only through a function.
David Mitrany, *The Functional Theory of Politics*

Functionalism deserves re-examination. Functionalism, as the term is used in international relations, rather than sociology, was the dominant theory of the new multilateral institutions of post-Second World War reconstruction. It was especially associated with the economic, scientific and humanitarian programmes of the new United Nations, and of the specialized agencies created, or brought into relationship with the UN at that time. Their emphasis on reconstruction and development, managing technological innovation, and creating an enlarged concept of welfare and security were the 'functions' that this use of the term sought to identify (Jones, 1967). Functional theory argues that these functions are beyond the scope of national governments to provide, and so intergovernmental cooperation is necessary for the more efficient provision and delivery of these services. Functionalism provided a highly effective explanation of the process underlying the *growth* of these agencies during the period 1945–75, into a system of international organizations which promoted the economic, scientific and humanitarian dimensions of international stability and order during a period of exceptional economic growth and prosperity. This contrasted with the acute tension of the nuclear armed and bipolar division of the international system in that same period, during which the UN Charter's provisions for collective *military* security were almost wholly ineffective. As Third World self-determination came to replace the colonial system, so the states of the global South acquired majority voting rights within the UN General Assembly, its functional programmes such as the UN Development Programme (UNDP) and the UN High Commissioner for Refugees (UNHCR), and the legally separate specialized agencies such as the International Labour Organization (ILO) and the UN Educational, Scientific and Cultural Organization (UNESCO). The mission and mandate of these functional agencies was thereafter progressively enlarged to embrace the developmental dimension.

After 1975, the period of growth and high expectations concerning the UN agencies faded. Allegations of declining relevance, 'politicization', and even corruption, led certain Western powers to de-emphasize the specialized agencies, and thus implicitly the functional theory on which their activities rested. To the US at least, the agencies' espousal of Third World rhetoric and causes devalued their original scientific, humanitarian and developmental purposes. The realities of the US budgetary constraints on the UN system after 1980 effectively froze the growth of the specialized agencies, as well as rendering their existing programmes and reputations hostage to a singularly parochial and hostile US Congress. The low point of functionalist endeavour was typified by the US withdrawal from UNESCO in December 1984, shortly followed by that of the UK. Both had acted as co-founders of the organization (Imber, 1989).

Conditions were therefore ripe, *after* 1990, for a resurgence of functional activity as part of post-Cold War global governance. As the US President spoke of a New World Order, reviving the collective security role of the UN in the Gulf War of 1990–1, so the pressing agenda of environmental diplomacy, sustainable development and persistent poverty received post-Cold War endorsement. Indeed the mooted 'peace dividend' would be available to direct to functional activities. The high point of *this* brief transformation in functional thinking was the June 1992 pledge delivered by the world's largest ever conference of heads of government, the Rio UNCED (UN conference on Environment and Development) or 'Earth Summit'. The Agenda 21 rededicated the participants to meet the 0.7 per cent of GDP target for aid, and itemized an *annual* spending plan of $600 billion for the years 1993–2000 (UN, 1992, ch. 33). For the first time in over twenty years, a new UN initiative, the Agenda 21, included ambitious plans for new, additional UN programmes and enlarged powers for existing agencies. A new Commission on Sustainable Development was proposed, along with a new tri-agency fund, the Global Environmental Facility, a joint creation of the World Bank, the UN Environment Programme (UNEP) and UNDP. The latter two agencies were scheduled for major growth (UN, 1992, ch. 38).

However, the UN agencies have not benefited from this opportunity. The failure of ambitious and overdue reform programmes has led to continuing US hostility, and budgetary sanctions in a decade of rising needs. On 31 May 2000, the US owed the UN $1,774 million (UN Association of the USA, 2000, p. 275). Something of the 1970s adheres to the *dirigiste* image of the UN agencies, promoting regulation, intervention and redistribution, in a millennial decade of globalization, deregulation and entrepreneurship. But we should not throw out the Functional baby with the Fabian bath-water. The functional *idea* needs re-explaining to a neoliberal generation and a new century. It is an especially exciting opportunity because Mitrany's own elegant model proposed a sparse institutional furniture, of which the more pompous, state-centric UN agencies are, in fact, a bad illustration. As we will show, Mitrany advocated a polycentric field of functional activities; the agencies were one element, NGOs another, direct collaboration among technical and scientific elites yet another. Mitrany also identified early the borderless creativity and organizational skills of transnational corporations. In addition to his academic and civil service careers, Mitrany was retained by Unilever as a political consultant from 1944 to 1960 (Mitrany, 1975, p. 31).

Functionalism: a Working Peace System?

Since the 1980s, those searching for a continuing rationale of cooperation under anarchy (see chapter 13) have tended to look to ever more complex explanations, to the neglect of the simpler functional explanation (Rochester, 1993, pp. 19–20).

Mitrany's injunction was to proceed by 'binding together those interests which are common, where they are common, to the extent that they are common' (Mitrany, 1966, pp. 115–16). This would never win a sound-bite competition, but does convey the limited and realistic aspirations of the functionalist idea. Functionalism is closely identified with the writings of David Mitrany, the most often quoted being his 1943 Chatham House monograph, *A Working Peace System*, reprinted, with an introduction by Morgenthau, in 1966. The clear precursor of that work can be seen in the 1933 essay, *The Progress of International Government*. His works were very conveniently collected in a 1975 volume under the title *The Functional Theory of Politics*, with a distinguished introduction by Paul Taylor. Haas's compendious 1964 study of the ILO, and Sewell's 1965 study of the World Bank linked case studies of two major agencies to theoretical developments in Mitrany's scheme (Sewell, 1966). Charles Pentland (1973) focused on the European dimension of functional cooperation. Others such as Keohane, while clearly influenced by Mitrany, have chosen to develop their own vocabulary of complex interdependence and regime formation to emphasize the informal, normative and non-institutional aspects of an essentially similar process. Among British scholars, John Groom and Paul Taylor did most during the unfashionable years to keep Mitrany's work and reputation in view (Groom and Taylor, 1975; Taylor and Groom, 1988). Others such as Wells (1987) on UNESCO, Imber (1989) on the ILO, the International Atomic Energy Agency (IAEA) and UNESCO, and Siddiqi (1995) on the World Health Organization (WHO) continued the case-study approach to the functional agencies into the problematical and contested 1980s, focusing on programme failures and criticisms of the agencies' performance and politicization.

Mitrany, a Romanian born, naturalized British scholar, was closely involved personally in the Allied planning of the postwar reconstruction. He took the New Deal of the Roosevelt period in general, and major cooperative public works schemes such as the Tennessee Valley Authority (TVA), in particular, as examples of creating new governmental institutions, dedicated to the provision of a particular service, which were crucially decoupled from the territorial basis of state authority. In the TVA case, seven US states renounced their parochial authority over the river to enable one specific agency to plan and execute an extraordinarily ambitious plan of dam construction, hydraulic engineering, electricity generation and job creation in an economically blighted area subject to regular flood damage. The 'functions' to which functionalists allude are therefore the economic, welfare and social security responsibilities of the state. To internationalize the domestic analogy of the TVA, Mitrany advocated the creation after 1944 of a range of technical and scientific agencies, with *potentially* global reach, to implement across *national* frontiers the sort of hard science-led public works and infrastructural programmes typified domestically by the TVA.

> The functional approach emphasises the common index of need. Very many such needs cut across national boundaries. Not a few are universal, and an effective beginning for building up an international community of interest could be made by setting up joint agencies for dealing with these common needs. (Mitrany, 1948, p. 356)

The allies created the Food and Agriculture Organization (FAO) in 1944 in anticipation of the need to totally support a European emergency food programme after the final defeat of Germany. The WHO, UNESCO and the whole family of agencies associated with the postwar growth of the UN system may therefore be explained by this analysis. 'Full powers for a limited purpose' was Mitrany's own description of the authority to be invested in the agencies (1975, p. 26).

> By entrusting an authority with a certain task, carrying with it command over requisite powers and means, a slice of sovereignty is transferred from the old authority to the new;

and an accumulation of such transfers over time brings about a translation of the true seat of authority. (Mitrany, 1966, p. 31)

Many of these organizations *predate* Mitrany's writing. He did not claim to do more than synthesize visible trends and was especially concerned that the nascent UN be fully equipped with these supporting functions; the lack of which was one of the great failings of the League of Nations.

The Universal Postal Union (UPU) and the International Telegraph Union (ITU) indeed date from the middle of the nineteenth century, and the origins of the WHO may be traced to Anglo-French collaboration in the late nineteenth century for regulations to prevent the transmission of disease among colonial populations. Other new agencies developed with new technologies such as civil aviation (ICAO) and nuclear energy (IAEA). In parallel to these autonomous specialized agencies, the UN itself created numerous welfare programmes on functional lines such as the UNHCR and the UN Children's Fund (UNICEF).

Mitrany argued that further stages in the development of the functional agencies and programmes could assist in transforming the nature of global governance in favour of a stable peace. Sewell coined the term 'task-expansion' (1966, pp. 55–6) for the progressive transfer of political authority to these agencies. This process would enlarge the mandate and competence of the agencies, relative to those of national governments. 'The transference of functions from the domestic to the international field has been apt to run further and faster than the corresponding change in legal doctrine' (Mitrany, 1975, p. 96).

Organizations that are judged to be competent will gain additional powers, those that are not will be unlikely to enjoy task-expansion. Jacobsen describes the process in terms of international organizations progressively acquiring normative, rule-creating, rule-enforcing and finally programmatic responsibilities (Jacobsen, 1979, p. 88). An example would be the IAEA's gradual assumption of ever more sensitive tasks, from technical assistance since 1957 through to administering the NPT safeguards system since 1970 – the latter representing the most intrusive legal powers of on-site inspection allowed to an international organization.

In the event of defiance against international order, the same agencies could apply economic sanctions, depriving recalcitrant states of the advantages of membership. 'Just as it would be their function to give service wherever it was needed, so it would clearly be their duty to deny service where it was not obviously needed, or might be abused' (Mitrany, 1975, p. 183).

Building on its experience with the Nuclear Non-Proliferation Treaty, the IAEA was eventually deeply involved in the UN Special Commission (UNSCOM) programme to detect and destroy Iraq's chemical and biological weapons programme after 1991.

The end-state or eponymous 'working peace system' of Mitrany's title anticipated the 'complex interdependence' of Keohane and Nye (1977), and was built on the enlightened self-interest of a community of states, in which the level of prosperity and ability to deliver welfare to their peoples relied on the maintenance of a complex, peaceful web of functional relations across international borders:

> not a peace that would keep the nations quietly apart but a peace that would bring them actively together, not the old static and strategic view, but a social view of peace. One

might say that we must put our faith not in a protected peace but in a working peace; it would be nothing more or less than the idea and aspiration of social security taken in its widest sense. (Mitrany, 1966, p. 92)

Or, as Claude puts it,

Functionalism proposes not to squelch but to utilize national selfishness; it asks governments not to give up the sovereignty which belongs to their peoples but to acquire benefits for their peoples which were hitherto unavailable, not to reduce their power to defend their citizens, but to expand their competence to serve them. (1964, p. 352)

In addition to explaining the rise of the global, specialized agencies, functionalism also contributed to understanding the process of European integration in the 1960s through its derivative 'neo-functional' approach. Reversing the logic of the federalists such as Altiero Spinelli, who argued for binding integration at the level of 'high politics', that is political and security affairs, neo-functionalists advocated using the 'low politics' of functional, technical and economic cooperation, as more suitable for promoting integration. The European federalists' best chance was vitiated in 1954, when the French National Assembly voted against the creation of a European Defence Force. The original European Economic Community, whose agenda would be initiated by a permanent civil service or Commission, appeared an altogether more credible route to eventual union. Neo-functionalists argued that an irreversible process of 'spillover' could be sustained as the Commission initiated ever more progressive policies (Lindberg and Scheingold, 1970; Pentland, 1973). Electorates would come to identify Brussels with progressive government and be weaned from their residual nationalism – which, it was argued, would already have been weakened by the catastrophic experience of Nazi occupation before 1945. In this way, a sort of creeping federalism could carry the process of cooperation and integration over the threshold of low politics into the realm of high politics. This approach was successively defeated by de Gaulle in 1965 and by Margaret Thatcher after 1979. We are all sceptics now. Neo-functionalism made a surreptitious return in the guise of the single European currency, which, it is hoped by its proponents, can overcome economic sovereignty without anyone noticing.

Neo-functionalists therefore *used* the functional method, but linked the growth of the European institution's authority to an ultimately federalist goal. In this scheme 'low politics' constituted issue areas such as transport, infrastructure, agricultural subsidy and tariff policy. 'High politics' was reserved to citizenship, macroeconomic and monetary policy, foreign and defence policy. This federalism by stealth was a briefly fashionable strategy of integration, especially with American political scientists trained in the federalist culture. Neo-functionalism carried a lot of optimistic interpretations of the early period of the European Economic Community, from approximately 1958 to 1965. The Gaullist crisis of 1965, the economic dislocation after the oil shock of 1973, and the Thatcherite resistance to further integration after 1979 falsified any lingering thought that functional cooperation could somehow slip past the guardians and handbags of sovereignty, to deliver 'peace in pieces' or a federal Europe by the backdoor. The discrediting of neo-functionalism has left little political or theoretical space between the alternatives of completing the federal project, or continued scepticism in the framework of a Europe of states.

Functionalism: a Critical Evaluation

The functional scheme has attracted a number of criticisms. These may be grouped for current purposes into two. Those who question the theory, especially its methodology and assumptions; and those who question the record of achievement of the functional scheme. This section looks at the former criticisms, and the next section at the practical issues.

It should be noted that some of the critics raise problems with Mitrany's scheme that he would probably have happily conceded. Some of the accusations of determinism, teleology and induction, while cogent, are essentially misplaced. Mitrany travelled light, theoretically speaking. He set out not to write international relations theory, but to influence the British and US foreign policy elites at the zenith of their wartime planning. Other criticisms are only possible in hindsight; the ecological critique of functionalist faith in big technology, such as the developmental potential of hydroelectric dam schemes, would raise a wry smile from those NGO campaigners who, in the years between the TVA and Pergau, have developed a particular critique of dam projects.

Induction

McLaren (1985) argues that Mitrany's scheme is inductive. Certainly Mitrany did not claim to be *predictive*. He clearly acknowledged that his scheme was to promote the wider application of an approach to post-1945 planning that would generalize and expand the 'New Deal' experience, building on the work and example of numerous, *existing* international organizations. The UPU and ITU were both founded in the middle of the *nineteenth* century, and the ILO, created in 1919, was cited by many as an exemplar of functional practice in the field of workers' welfare. As we shall show below, the ILO pioneered the direct representation of NGOs in international organizations. Also, the larger Bretton Woods institutions, the IMF, World Bank and the mooted, but failed International Trade Organization, were created in 1944. Mitrany wrote from experience and did not claim to be original in his analysis.

Separability-priority

Claude uses this term to describe the twin assumptions made by functionalists in believing it is possible to *separate* the political and the technical, and thereafter to *prioritize* the latter in the formation and work of international organizations (Claude, 1964, pp. 348–50). The most fundamental challenge to functionalism is the counterassertion that in the realm of public policy, all decisions concerning fundraising, resource allocation and prioritization in so-called technical issue areas have political implications. In international society, it is less likely that this strict calculation of costs and benefits will be foregone than within the political community of one state, where appeals to common identity can be made. Functionalism must therefore demonstrate either that separability is possible, or show that goals exist which are only attainable by cooperative endeavour, and which will *require* states to engage in cooperation.

Functionalism does not propose to make a distinction, as some have argued, between 'political' and 'non-political', but rather to emphasize the possibilities of technical cooperation for common purposes. As Mitrany himself put it: '"Politics" would remain as now the debate for deciding grand policy and priorities in general and for the guidance and cooperation of functional activities in particular' (1975, p. 266).

By the 1980s the 'separability-priority' problem had become more acute, in the context of US accusations of 'politicization' leading to the US withdrawal from the ILO, in 1977, and from UNESCO in 1984, and a curious suspension of participation in the IAEA for some months in the period September 1982 to February 1983 (Imber, 1989). This will be discussed later as an operational limitation of functionalism.

Sovereign equality

'Representation is imperative, equality is impossible' (Mitrany, 1975, p. 99). Functionalism is unambiguous in its critique of the doctrine of sovereign equality. Mitrany himself argued for a functional elitism, restricting the membership and voting rights in the proposed functional organizations to maintain an acceptable relationship between responsibility and authority. The present Antarctic treaty system would typify this. He specifically criticized the one-member-one-vote assumption of the UN agencies: 'Instead of the legal fiction of equality there would thus be an evident and factual inequality in certain spheres springing from real differences in capacity and interest with regard to some specific function but also limited to that function' (Mitrany, 1966, p. 65).

This one provision, if implemented, would alienate Third World member states, which have used the twentieth century's overriding concern for sovereign equality to establish majority control of the UN-linked agencies. Those agencies that remain outside this scheme of government, most obviously the weighted-majority voting organs of the multilateral development banks (MDBs), attract vituperative criticism. On the other hand, Mitrany advocated both parliamentary and NGO participation in the decision-making of the functional agencies; the ILO is the prime, indeed the only example to permit this. Mitrany explicitly rejected the need for a supranational political mechanism, regarding this as part of the error of federalism, preferring reliance on indirect representation and the presumed cosmopolitanism of science and scientists as a precursor of what are now termed epistemic communities (Haas, 1990).

The only potential reconciliation lies in the expectation that as the fourth wave of democratization passes through a number of Eastern European, Latin American, East Asian and African countries, this will raise the technocratic quality of participation on their part. The 'majority of tyrannies' assembled in the 1960s and 1970s cannot be assumed to have always had the greater good of their citizens to the forefront of the so-called 'development programmes'.

> While it is admittedly self-serving for the haves in a political system to give more attention to order than to justice, it is equally self-serving for the have-nots to trumpet the ethical superiority of justice (defined as egalitarianism) over order and to reject a 'morality of states' paradigm in favour of a 'cosmopolitan morality' paradigm. My own sense is that neither order nor justice is served by 1 million Omanis possessing the same formal power in international governance as 1 billion Chinese, although this is somewhat of a moot point so long as both people live under dictatorships. (Rochester, 1993, p. 243)

Liberalism

Is functionalism limited in its appeal to a core of liberal democratic, developed states, a self-fulfilling subset of the now fashionable 'democratic peace theory'? Functionalism clearly appealed to developing states, which perceived the UN system of agencies as a major source of development assistance, and the task of development itself as a functional task par excellence. The breakdown of democracy in many postcolonial countries during the period 1970–90 shifted majority control of the agencies away from their founding core of Western powers. This does not undermine the functionalist case that certain functional 'needs' are truly universal, since elected political leaders, dictators and commissars have a common interest in standardized systems of air traffic control, early warning of nuclear accidents, and the containment of pandemic diseases.

Materialism and rationalism

Functionalism requires that participants take a variable-sum analysis of their shared predicament; such as in the case of France and Germany after 1945 over Alsace-Lorraine and the formation of the European Coal and Steel Community. A zero-sum analysis may lead one party to a rational calculation in favour of unilateral action, such as Iraq's seizure of Kuwait in 1990. Functionalism *is* an expressly rationalist and materialist theory of human behaviour. Nothing in the functional scheme would serve to deter warfare prosecuted for non-rational motives, especially religious beliefs. (Anyone who believes in an afterlife will discount the value of the one they are presently living.) No amount of shared infrastructure between, say, Iran and Iraq, Serbs and Bosnian Muslims, Hutu and Tutsi could ever serve to moderate the use of violence in these situations. They remind us how comparatively rare such episodes of 'Jihad' are relative to the more general, global pursuit of 'McWorld'. We are shocked by events in Kigali and Srebrenica precisely *because* such behaviour is exceptional. These occurrences do not invalidate the functional case that cultures and societies of very diverse natures can nonetheless have a shared interest in survival, development and risk-aversion. Eastby (1985) makes much of the materialist and rationalist exclusion of the spiritual dimension. Mitrany answers his own rhetorical question thus: 'the functionalist way may seem a spiritless solution – and so it is, in the sense that it detaches from the spirit the things that are of the body.' He likens this to the earlier separation of church and state. 'Separation of religious belief from political allegiance was one way to freedom of conscience, removing from the jurisdiction of the State a function for which it is clearly unfit' (Mitrany, 1966, p. 99). The point being that spiritual freedom for all *requires* a secular constitution and a disestablished church.

Determinism, transferability and task expansion

Sewell, Pentland and others suggest that functionalists are torn between an 'almost mystical belief' in the automatic nature of growing functional cooperation, and a contradictory tendency to advocate new attitudes and new political will to promote international cooperation (Sewell, 1966; Pentland, 1973, p. 79). Haas made much of these supposed teleological elements in functionalism (Haas, 1964). This is unreasonable. Functionalism certainly advocates a positivistic and technocratic enthusiasm, but it is clear on the balance of Mitrany's writings that his faith in technological progress is a dated 'gee-whiz' or 'can-do' *optimism* in the potential of human society to apply science to its comfort and prosperity, not a *deterministic* view. Scientism and faith in progress were liberal values of the early to mid twentieth century. The emergence of a postmodern, post-Chernobyl anti-science outlook creates massive intellectual problems for modern liberal democracies, but does not blunt the developmental mandate of functionalism. Indeed, it may create new rationales for functional cooperation, in, for example, a policing by FAO of the trade in genetically modified organisms (GMOs) along the lines that fissile materials are monitored by IAEA, and endangered species by the Convention on International Trade in Endangered Species (CITES).

The emergence of a UN system of sixteen legally autonomous specialized agencies in addition to the various programmes and funds directly controlled by the General Assembly, such as UNICEF and UNDP, suggests a sort of international Keynesianism, clearly empirically substantiating the task-expansion hypotheses. However, the period during which this system *expanded* in terms of *functions*, as opposed to the automatic numerical growth of membership in the wake of decolonization, was quite short. Measured for instance in terms of the 0.7 per cent Overseas Development Assistance target, growth was with hindsight limited to a period approximately from 1945 to 1970, before political dispute, budgetary limitations and the problems of coordination froze the growth of the UN system until 1990. In terms used by students of the European Community, the system continued to *widen* but not to *deepen*. The NPT–IAEA safeguards would serve as a high water mark of intrusive, sovereignty-challenging task-expansion.

Functionalism in Practice: Limits and Tensions

Some of the practical criticisms – of politicization, corruption and sectoralism – are issues that only became apparent in the UN agencies after the 1970s, and some are of particular contemporary concern, such as the issue of 'needs' and costs.

Politicization

Politicization was the term given by the Americans to the alleged diversion of the UN agencies from their functional purposes by an extraneous political agenda during the 1970s and 1980s. US hostility was most vigorously expressed during the two Reagan administrations, 1981–8, although the policy had its origin in circles related to the Democratic Party a decade earlier. Moynihan's denunciation of the UN's anti-Israeli positions dates from 1975, and it was the Democratic labour elite of George Meany and the AFL-CIO (American Federation of Labor and Congress of Industrial Organizations) which precipitated the first withdrawal from a UN agency when, in 1977, the newly elected Jimmy Carter carried through Kissinger's notice to quit the ILO given two years earlier. The American charges rested on some quite elastic definitions of *politicization*. This author alone identified eight, not wholly consistent varieties, ranging from the intellectually sustainable to the contrived (Imber, 1989, pp. 29–30). The proper sense in which the term was used to describe the diversion of the functional agencies from their founding purposes focused on *ultra vires* activities, contrived credentials disputes and the harassment of member states' rights of membership. These invariably concerned attempts to unseat Israel and South Africa from membership of the functional agencies. A more dubious cluster of accusations concerned managerial quality, what Kissinger called 'extraneous issues', and related budgetary disputes. These were contestable, and frequently turned on American sensitivities to criticism of its allies. For example, UNESCO *would* seem an appropriate place in which to debate Israel's alleged destruction of Islamic archaeological artifacts in the occupied territories (Imber, 1989, p. 103). The IAEA *would* seem to be the appropriate place to debate Israel's attacks on IAEA-safeguarded facilities in Iraq in 1981 (Imber, 1989, p. 73). However, to successive US administrations these were inappropriate places, and extraneous debates. An almost hysterical and partisan flavour attached to denunciations of 'anti-Western bias' using Moynihan's 'tyranny of the majority' (Moynihan, 1975, p. 41).

US hegemony

The ironical countercharge to that of the Americans is that functionalism was not so much subverted by Soviet and Third World 'politicization' as by US domination. Claude pays considerable attention to this, detailing the extraordinary degree of financial and ideological domination of the UN system by America in the quarter-century 1945–70. The answer is that both charges are right, the apparent contradiction being explained partly by chronology, and partly by sector. The Americans were and remain highly selective in their accusations. The Bretton Woods agencies, and those like GATT/WTO broadly identified with the neoliberal project, remained firmly under Western control. The period of Third World rhetorical ascendancy has passed. All are now seemingly engaged in the neoliberal project, and the agencies are now perceived as facilitating globalization. This creates *other* issues, most obviously the conflict of interest between those organs such as the World Bank lending billions to fund neoliberal models of growth, and those like UNICEF, UNDP and UNEP expending mere millions on correcting some of the grosser consequences of indebtedness and structural adjustment. This is the real failure of functionalism, to be addressed in the conclusion.

Sectoralism

Sectoralism refers to the fragmentation, duplication of efforts and failures of coordination that have characterised the growth of the specialized agencies and UN programmes over the last half century. From Jackson (1969) and Bertrand (1985), to the Agenda 21 of 1992, many have identified the issue and recommended reforms which the membership, while often advancing the same criticism, has repeatedly failed to execute. As Righter notes: 'sectoralization, in practice, also put the UN out of step with two great post-war trends; the integration of economic activities both nationally and internationally, and the growing impact of social issues on political security' (1995, p. 38).

Disregard for costs

McLaren (1985, pp. 139–52) is especially acute in criticizing functionalism's laxness on cost control. This cuts across the theoretical and the operational issues. Based on 'needs' and prone to moral and fiscal inflation during thirty years of Keynesian welfare spending, high costs raise the issue of just who is to determine the costs, efficiency and *opportunity costs* of functional cooperation? It is no coincidence that budgetary inflation and inefficiency were linked to the American complaint of politicization in the period 1975–88. Critics on the right would argue that this inattention to costs, as seen by Western donors, stems from the Third World appropriation of the functional agencies during the 1970s. Therefore, budgetary sanctions against the UN and its agencies are central to the continuing New Right obstruction of *growth* in the post-Cold War responsibilities of the agencies.

Functionalism and the Reform of Global Governance

While the war–peace area may hold unprecedented potential for global institution building, it remains a far more delicate thread upon which to hang the UN's future than the functional one. (Rochester, 1993, p. 197)

In this way we would not have to wait, as Mr Bertrand Russell would have us do, until the masses discard their supposedly narrow selfish loyalty to the nation, and become instead imbued with sentiments of abstract justice embracing humanity as a whole. (Mitrany, 1975, p. 104)

The first post-Cold War decade saw a flurry of proposals for comprehensive reform of global governance. These ranged from the grand, structural proposals of the Commission on Global Governance, to Kofi Annan's internal managerial and staffing reforms styled 'Track 1'. By the end of the 1990s the enthusiasm had cooled. No less an optimist than Richard Falk opined that 'the widely endorsed project for United Nations Reform disappointed even before it failed' (Paolini, Jarvis and Reus-Smith, 1998, p. 296).

Let me advance two, more or less heretical propositions. Firstly, the UN itself will *not* be reformed in any of its essentials. Secondly, this does not actually matter much, especially to functionalists. It *won't* happen because the political coalition that has to be assembled to achieve an amendment of the UN Charter under Article 108 cannot be assembled in any foreseeable future. This requires a two-thirds majority vote in the General Assembly, and the ratification of any amendment by the five permanent members of the Security Council. Effectively this doesn't matter because, as the entire ad hoc saga of peacekeeping has shown, the lack of a legal provision in the Charter is no obstacle to innovation if the political will to do so exists. In contrast, as the negligible progress in areas such as human rights enforcement and the moribund provision in Article 45 for 'ready forces' show, no *existing* UN Charter requirement can *create* something when there is *no* will to do so. Rather, like the 'unwritten' British constitution, UN reform should perhaps be best conceived in terms of evolving custom and practice, and the route of Charter amendment should be abandoned as futile. Stripped of more grandiose pretensions to new world orders, the parts of the UN system that work most effectively are those that most uncontroversially follow the functional path.

Although, curiously, the Charter contains no provisions for withdrawal, membership of the organization is not *compulsory*. Many organs and arrangements exist outside the UN which offer the developed countries in particular a more congenial environment in which to conduct multilateral diplomacy. The G7/G8 forum, the IMF and World Bank, the Bank for International Settlements, and the cosy and discreet Davos/Trilateral Commissions represent a sort of private 'stretched limo' service compared to riding the crowded, strap-hanging, all-stops bus service provided by the UN. The essence of multilateralism is having to ride the bus with people you might not invite to dinner. Have ten years of post-Cold War democratization, sustainable development and globalization enlarged the scope of functional agencies?

Rochester (1986) traces the decline of international institutional studies; an argument expanded in *Waiting for the Millennium* (1993). He takes a critical view of much 1980s neo-realist scholarship for its cynicism, and of the laboured efforts of Keohane (1984) and colleagues to demonstrate a rational basis for 'cooperation under anarchy' as if this was an original contribution to knowledge (1993, pp. 12–17). Wolfers (1962) and Claude (1964) had already demonstrated this quite satisfactorily. Rochester refers at length to the functional approach in his conclusions. Another contemporary attempt to foreground the functional scheme can be found in Rosemary Righter's *Utopia Lost* (1995). Righter, an eloquent and informed critic of the United Nations, is exasperated by the very poor delivery of economic development revealed in UN aid programmes.

The contribution that functional theory can make is to reinvigorate the case for the provision of international public goods, by a means more transparent to the major donors, and more attuned to the basic needs of the major users. Globalization needs this public goods framework. As capital, technology and culture become increasingly borderless, their *use* of global infrastructure in telecommunications, transport and related facilities suggests a revitalized case for global agencies. The neoliberal logic is to furnish these facilities by privatized provision. However, renewed public goods problems have emerged in this decade. The most obvious is in the environment. A mechanism is needed to implement the Framework Convention on Climate Change (FCCC) and the Kyoto Protocol. UNEP, UNDP and the Global Environmental Facility have enormous potential to fill the need for funding the additional costs of compliance for developing countries that are parties to global environmental agreements such as the Montreal Protocol. Market-led mechanisms such as tradeable permits for carbon dioxide emissions require an agreed normative and legal framework. The humanitarian crises of migration and refugees have worsened, strengthening the case for the activities of UNHCR and UNICEF. Other issues such as AIDS, and the health effects and agricultural impact of climate change, have expanded the potential agenda of long-established agencies such as WHO, FAO and the World Meteorological Organization (WMO).

Leaner, more client-focused functional agencies could learn many lessons from the private sector. Their essentially borderless activities function more efficiently for being able to ignore the shibboleths of nationality, race and gender, in favour of efficiency, rationality and a medium-term planning horizon. These are all concentrated in the mind by the need to return a profit, a discipline not acting on civil servants, UN staff or, indeed, political theorists.

Indeed, all forms of global public goods provision are under intense pressure to rethink their relationship with state authority, and the lingering Fabianism of the original functionalists needs to do this more than most. The staff practices, the jobs-for-life culture, well-attested bureaucratization and not a little corruption have all harmed the reputation and quality of UN programmes. Out-sourcing, internal markets and competitive tendering for consultancies would sharpen the performance and improve the willingness of donors to fund programmes.

> Putting the UN's 'operational' activities on a competitive, self-financing basis would help to reduce the confusion about the types of functions that global organizations can reasonably be expected to perform. . . . It would force them to ask what, in a world in which governments themselves are subject as never before to competition from other economic and social actors, the organizations that bring governments together and thus will inevitably be subject to similar competition, can still achieve. It would concentrate the energies of the UN on those aspects of the international agenda for which coopera-tion between governments remains indispensable, and where they need the mediating touch of common institutions. (Righter, 1995, pp. 279–80)

It is possible to imagine two kinds of functionalism; one, assisting global capital to implement a truly borderless global, liberal economy of a kind only imagined by Hume and Smith and other advocates of peace through free trade, an argument developed over two centuries ago. The 'other functionalism' would continue to oper-ate as a global welfare net, assisting those left behind by the first. This is not without contradictions. O'Brien et al. identify the 'hegemonic approach to multilateralism' (2000, p. 4), and the response of '*complex multilateralism*' (p. 5), against the back-ground of popular revolt against MDBs and the WTO at Seattle and Geneva.

The reconciliation of this contradiction lies in the fact that globalization does not advocate *complete* deregulation and complete free trade. Narcotics, plutonium, pro-stitution, pornography and paedophile tourism are typical of the issues on which the most ardent free trade advocate demands intervention and regulation of the market-place. When joined by liberal demands to regulate child labour, to limit drug profits from AIDS treatment, to promote research on renewable energy contributions, debt for nature swaps and to target disasters relief more effectively, the functional agenda for the twenty-first century becomes clearer.

Would Third World states accept the diminution of sovereignty that a revived functionalism would imply? The majority voting systems and the doctrine of sovereign equality that formally characterize the UN system flatter to deceive. Hurrell and Woods note that 'weaker states face heavily constrained choices or an agenda which they have little influence in defining' (1995, p. 456). But domestically *all* governments face much greater difficulties in getting their constituencies to adapt to the changes required by agreements struck in international negotiations, for example, the UK and the euro, the USA and Kyoto, Germany and the right of asylum. Certainly the benefits of globalization are concentrated in the countries with the greatest capacity to absorb and adapt to the new types of transactions referred to by Hurrell and Woods as 'coercive socialisation' rather than the 'progressive enmeshment' of Larry Lipschutz (Hurrell and Woods, 1995, p. 457).

> the struggles and silences within international institutions can only be understood by recognising that institutions do not emerge solely for utilitarian reasons. Although international institutions ostensibly arise among states concerned with solving common problems and promoting overall welfare, in fact they reflect a pattern of structural power which is central to the management of interdependence. . . . In the end it is powerful states that will shape the agenda, decide who can play the game, define the rules and enforce outcomes which are favourable to themselves. (Hurrell and Woods, 1995, p. 461)

Functionalism is at risk of claiming too many antecedents. It can be Fabian in order to appeal to old-fashioned developmentalists, neoliberal and facilitative to appeal to corporate globalizers, and yet realistic enough to appeal to realists. A doctrine so ubiquitous may try to please all and offend none. Indeed, part of the pervasive nature of functionalism is its status as the unwritten constitution of international order.

This last decade has seen the promotion of a number of much grander schemes for global governance. From Bush's 'new world order' of 1990, and the Rio formula of 'sustainable development' from 1992, to cosmopolitan democracy, each has claimed attention. The first of these sought to expand the security role of the UN, as in the 'new' peacekeeping. Sustainable development attempts to reconcile economic growth with environmental protection. Cosmopolitan democracy attempts to apply the post-Cold War expectations for the democratization of domestic politics to the organs of the UN and other international organizations.

The end of Cold War held out the promise that the long-sought international control of the use of force might emerge in a veto-free Security Council. The story from Srebrenica to Kosovo, 1995–9 is a story of retreat and eventual complete *avoidance* of UN mechanisms to achieve a (highly dubious) measure of humanitarian intervention in Kosovo. Secondly, ten years after the Rio Earth Summit sustainable development is in retreat, not in advance. Crucial indicators of sustainability are worse than then. The impasse in the negotiation of binding, quantitative targets for the FCCC as contained in the Kyoto Protocol is the most telling case. Thirdly, proponents of cosmopolitan democracy have sought over a decade to reform the UN itself, to render it more responsive and accountable to the 6 billion persons who constitute *we the peoples*, in whose name the Preamble and Charter are couched. That ten years have elapsed without any Charter reform of the organization founded in 1945 might attest to its perfection, or its irrelevance, but cannot be advanced as evidence of any willing engagement on the part of leading members to advancing the democratization of international organizations. That leaves the functional programmes and agencies still 'binding together those interests which are common, where they are common, to the extent that they are common' (Mitrany, 1966, pp. 115–16), and still our best chance for advancing environmental, medical and developmental welfare into the twenty-first century.

References

Bertrand, M. (1985) 'Some reflections on the reform of the UN', *Joint Inspection Unit Report JIU/REP/85/9*, Geneva: United Nations.

Claude, I. (1964) *Swords into Plowshares*, New York: Random House.

Eastby, J. (1985) *Functionalism and Interdependence*, Lanham: University Press of America.

Groom, A. J. and Taylor, P. (1975) *Functionalism*, London: London University Press.

Haas, E. (1964) *Beyond The Nation-State*, Stanford: Stanford University Press.

Haas, M. (1990) 'Obtaining international environmental protection through epistemic consensus', *Millennium*, 19, no. 3, pp. 347–64.

Hurrell, A. and Woods, N. (1995) 'Globalization and inequality', *Millennium*, 24, no. 3.

Imber, M. (1984) 'Re-reading Mitrany: a pragmatic assessment of sovereignty', *Review of International Studies*, 10, no. 2, pp. 103–24.

Imber, M. (1985) 'A comment', *Review of International Studies*, 11, pp. 153–5.

Imber, M. (1989) *The USA, ILO, UNESCO and IAEA*, Basingstoke: Macmillan.

Jackson, R. (1969) *A Study of the Capacity of the UN Development System*, Geneva: United Nations.

Jacobsen, H. K. (1979) *Networks of Interdependence*, New York: Knopf.

Jones, R. E. (1967) *The Functional Theory of Politics*, London: Routledge.

Keohane, R. (1984) *After Hegemony*, Princeton: Princeton University Press.

Keohane, R. and Nye, J. (1977) *Power and Interdependence*, Boston: Little, Brown.

Lindberg, L. and Scheingold, S. (1970) *Europe's Would-Be Polity*, Englewood Cliffs: Prentice Hall.

McLaren, R. (1985) 'Mitranian functionalism: possible or impossible?' *Review of International Studies*, 11, no. 2.

Mitrany, D. (1948) 'The functional approach to world order', *International Affairs*, 24.

Mitrany, D. (1966) *A Working Peace System*, Chicago: Quadrangle.

Mitrany, D. (1975) *The Functional Theory of Politics*, London: Martin Robertson.

Moynihan, D. P. (1975) 'The United States in opposition', *Commentary*, 59, no. 3, pp. 31–44.

O'Brien, R., Goetz, A. M., Scholte, J. A. and Williams, M. (2000) *Contesting Global Governance: Multilateral Economic Institutions and Global Social Movements*, Cambridge: Cambridge University Press.

Paolini, A., Jarvis, A. and Reus-Smith, C. (1998) *Between Sovereignty and Global Governance*, Basingstoke: Macmillan.

Pentland, C. (1973) *International Theory and European Integration*, London: Faber.

Righter, R. (1995) *Utopia Lost*, New York: Twentieth Century Fund.

Rochester, J. M. (1986) 'The rise and fall of International Organization as a field of study', *International Organization*, 40, pp. 777–813.

Rochester, J. M. (1993) *Waiting for the Millennium: The United Nations and the Future of the World Order*, Columbia: University of South Carolina Press.

Sewell, J. P. (1966) *Functionalism and World Politics*, Princeton: Princeton University Press.

Siddiqi, J. (1995) *World Health and World Politics*, London: Hurst.

Taylor, P. and Groom, A. J. (eds) (1988) *International Institutions at Work*, London: Pinter.

UN (1992) *Agenda 21, the Programme of Action from Rio*, New York: United Nations.

UN Association of the USA (2000) *A Global Agenda: Issues before the 55th General Assembly of the UN*, New York: Rowman and Littlefield.

Wells, C. (1987) *The UN, UNESCO and the Politics of Knowledge*, Basingstoke: Macmillan.

Wolfers, A. (1962) *Discord and Collaboration*, Baltimore: Johns Hopkins University Press.

15

Cosmopolitanism: Ideas, Realities and Deficits

David Held

The struggle over the accountability of the global economic order has become increasingly intense. Violence in Seattle, Prague, Genoa and elsewhere has marked a new level of conflict about globalization, democracy and social justice. The issues which have been raised are clearly fundamental, concerned as they are with the nature of free markets, the relation between corporate and public agendas, and the type and scope of political intervention in economic life. These matters are complex and extremely challenging, although they are not new to political debate and political analysis. What is new is the way the issues are framed, disseminated and fought over – in transnational and global contexts.

In this chapter I want to draw out some of the concerns underlying these controversies by reflecting on the changing nature and form of global processes, networks and connections, and on the meaning and significance today of cosmopolitan ideas and theories. The essay has five parts. It begins with an initial section on globalization and then, in section 2, traces its relevance for the locus and home of democracy, accountability and social justice. Against this background, the meaning of cosmopolitanism is set out in philosophical and institutional terms, in sections 3 and 4 respectively. The argument is made that not only is cosmopolitanism increasingly important to politics and human welfare, but that it ought also to be embraced further in thinking about the proper form of globalization and global governance. A final section explores some basic gaps between cosmopolitan principles and cosmopolitan institutions that need to be overcome if cosmopolitanism is to extend its purchase on governance structures and, thus, on the conditions for greater accountability, democracy and social justice in global politics.

Globalization

Globalization has become the 'big idea' of our times, even though it is frequently employed in such a way that it lacks precise definition. Moreover, it is so often used in political debate that it is in danger of becoming devoid of analytical value. Nonetheless, if the term is properly formulated, it does capture important elements of change in the contemporary world which can usefully be specified further.

Globalization can be understood best if it is conceived as a spatial phenomenon, lying on a continuum with 'the local' at one end and 'the global' at the other. It implies a shift in the spatial form of human organization and activity to transcontinental or interregional patterns of activity, interaction and the exercise of power (Held et al., 1999). Today globalization embraces at least four distinct types of change. First, it involves a stretching of social, political and economic activities across political frontiers, regions and continents. But if these are something other than occasional or random, then something else is suggested: intensification. Thus, second, globalization is marked by the growing magnitude of networks and flows of trade, investment, finance, culture and so on. Third, globalization can be linked to a speeding up of global interactions and processes, as the evolution of worldwide systems of transport and communication increases the velocity of the diffusion of ideas, goods, information, capital and people. And, fourth, it involves the deepening impact of global interactions and processes such that the effects of distant events can be highly significant elsewhere and even the most local developments can come to have enormous global consequences. In this particular sense, the boundaries between domestic matters and global affairs become fuzzy. In short, globalization can be thought of as the widening, intensifying, speeding up and growing impact of worldwide interconnectedness.

Globalization is made up of the accumulation of links across the world's major regions and across many domains of activity. It can be related to many factors including the rapid expansion of the world economy. International trade has grown to unprecedented levels, both absolutely and relatively in relation to national income. In comparison with the late nineteenth century – an era of rapid trade growth – export levels today (measured as a share of GDP) are much greater for OECD states. As barriers to trade have fallen across the world, global markets have emerged for many goods and, increasingly, services (Held et al., 1999, ch. 3).

The growing extensity, intensity and speed of trade has led to the increasing enmeshment of national economies with each other. Key elements of the production process are being sliced up, dispersed, and located in different countries, especially in developing and emerging economies. Thus, not only do countries increasingly consume goods from abroad, but their own production processes are significantly dependent on components produced overseas. Economic activity in any one country is, accordingly, strongly affected by economic activity in other countries. Alongside transnational production networks, the power of global finance has become central to economic globalization. World financial flows have grown exponentially, especially since the 1970s. Daily turnover on the foreign exchange markets exceeds $1.2 trillion, and billions of dollars of financial assets are traded globally, particularly through derivative products. Most countries today are incorporated into rapidly growing global financial markets, although the nature of their access to these markets is markedly unequal.

Processes of economic globalization have not, however, occurred in an empty political space; there has been a shift in the nature and form of political organization as well. The sovereign state now lies at the intersection of a vast array of international regimes and organizations that have been established to manage whole areas of transnational activity (trade, financial flows, risk management and so on) and collective policy problems. The rapid growth of transnational issues and problems has spawned layers of governance both within and across political boundaries. This has resulted in the transformation of aspects of territorially based political decision-making, the development of regional and global organizations and institutions, and the emergence of regional and global law. In addition, a denser pattern of interconnectedness also prevails as a result of changes in migration patterns, communications, the environment, and many other factors. Although these developments fall far short of creating an integrated world order, they have significant political and democratic consequences.

The world is no longer composed of relatively 'discrete civilisations' or 'discrete political communities' (Fernández-Armesto, 1995, ch. 1); rather, it is a world of 'overlapping communities of fate', where the fates of nations are significantly entwined. Political communities are enmeshed and entrenched in complex structures of overlapping forces, processes and movements. During the period in which the nation-state was being forged – and the territorially bounded conception of democracy was consolidated – the idea of a close mesh between geography, political power and democracy could be assumed. It seemed compelling that political power, sovereignty, democracy and citizenship are simply and appropriately bounded by a delimited territorial space. These links were by and large taken for granted, and generally unexplicated in modern political theory (Held, 1995). Globalization raises issues concerning the proper scope of democracy, or democratic jurisdiction, given that the relation between decision-makers and decision-takers is not necessarily symmetrical or congruent with respect to the territory.

Globalization and Democracy: Five Disjunctures

The changing relation between globalization and the modern nation-state can be characterized by five disjunctures. All indicate an increase in the extensiveness, intensity, velocity and impact of globalization. And all suggest important questions about the evolving character of the democratic political community in particular.

First, the idea of a self-determining national collectivity – which delimits and shapes a community of fate – can no longer be simply located within the borders of a single nation-state. Many of the most fundamental economic, social, cultural and environmental forces and processes that determine the nature of the political good and political outcomes now lie – in terms of their operation and dynamics – beyond the reach of individual polities. The current concern about genetic engineering and its possible regulation is a case in point.

Second, it can no longer be presupposed that the locus of effective political power is synonymous with national governments and the nation-state; national states and national governments are now embedded in complex networks of political power at regional and global levels (see Keohane, 1995, 2001; Rosenau, 1997, 1998). In other words, political power is shared and negotiated among diverse forces and agencies at many levels, from the local to the global. The link between effective government, self-government and a bounded territory is being broken.

Third, while significant concentrations of power are found, of course, in many states, these are frequently embedded in, and articulated with, new and changing forms of political authority. The power and operations of national government are altering, although not all in one direction. The entitlement of states to rule within circumscribed territories – their sovereignty – is not on the edge of collapse, but the practical nature of this entitlement – the actual capacity of states to rule – is changing its shape (Held et al., 1999, Conclusion). A new regime of government and governance is emerging which is displacing traditional conceptions of state power as an indivisible, territorially exclusive form of public power.

Fourth, the nurturing and enhancement of the public good increasingly requires coordinated multilateral action (for instance, to ensure security or to prevent global recession). At the same time, the resolution of transboundary issues (such as respons-ibility for carbon emissions) may often impose significant domestic adjustments. In this respect, political and social agents are witnessing a shift in the operation and dynamics of state power and political authority. This has become most apparent as states have become locked into regional and global regimes and associations. The context of national politics has been transformed by the diffusion of political authority and the growth of multilayered governance (see Nye and Donahue, 2000).

Fifth, the distinctions between domestic and foreign affairs, internal political issues and external questions are no longer clear cut. Governments face issues such as the international drugs trade, AIDS, BSE (Bovine Spongiform Encephalopathy), the use of non-renewable resources, the management of nuclear waste, the spread of weapons of mass destruction, and global warming, which cannot meaningfully be categorized in these terms. Moreover, issues like the location and investment strategy of multinational corporations, the regulation of global financial markets, the threats to the tax base of individual countries in the context of a global division of labour and the absence of capital controls all pose questions about the continued value of some of the central instruments of national economic policy. In fact, in nearly all major areas of policy, the enmeshment of national political communities in regional and global flows and processes involves them in intensive transboundary coordination and regulation.

In the context of these complex transformations, the meaning of accountability and democracy at the national level is altering. In circumstances where transnational actors and forces cut across the boundaries of national communities in diverse ways, where powerful international organizations and agencies make decisions for vast groups of people across diverse borders, and where the capacities of large companies can dwarf many a state, the questions of who should be accountable to whom, and on what basis, do not easily resolve themselves. The mesh between geography, political power and democracy is challenged by the intensification of regional and global relations.

Cosmopolitanism: Ideas and Trajectories

The problems and dilemmas of contemporary national politics, just described, can be referred to, following Jeremy Waldron, as the 'circumstances of cosmopolitanism' (2000, pp. 236–9); that is, the background conditions and presuppositions which inform and motivate the case for a cosmopolitan framework of accountability and regulation. It is not just that we are 'unavoidably side by side' (as Kant put it), but that the degrees of mutual interconnectedness and vulnerability are rapidly growing. The new circumstances of cosmopolitanism give us little choice but to consider the possibility of a common framework of standards and political action, given shape and form by a common framework of institutional arrangements (Held, 1995, part III).

How should cosmopolitanism be understood in this context? There are three broad accounts of cosmopolitanism which are important to bear in mind and which con-tribute to its contemporary meaning. The first was explored by the Stoics, who were the first to refer explicitly to themselves as cosmopolitans, seeking to replace the central role of the *polis* in ancient political thought with that of the *cosmos* in which humankind could live in harmony (Horstmann, 1976). Stoics developed this thought by emphasizing that we inhabit two worlds – one which is local and assigned to us by birth, and another which is 'truly great and truly common' (Seneca). Each person lives in a local community and in a wider community of human ideals, aspirations and argument. The basis of the latter lies in what is fundamental to all – the equal worth of reason and humanity in every person (Nussbaum, 1997, pp. 30, 43). Allegiance is owed, first and foremost, to the moral realm of all humanity, not to the contingent groupings of nation, ethnicity and class. Deliberations and problem-solving should focus on what is common to all persons as citizens of reason and the world; collective problems can be better dealt with if approached from this perspective, rather than from the point of view of sectional groupings. Such a position does not require that individuals give up local concerns and affiliations to family, friends and fellow inhabitants of the country they live in; it implies, instead, that they must acknowledge these as morally contingent and that their most important duties are to humanity as a whole and its overall developmental requirements.

The basic idea of classical cosmopolitanism involves the notion that each person is 'a citizen of the world' and owes a duty, above all, 'to the worldwide community of human beings' (Nussbaum, 1996, p. 4). While there are many difficulties with this classical formulation (for instance, its link to a teleological view of nature: see Nussbaum, 1997), the main point of the Stoics contained a most significant idea: 'that they were, in the first instance, human beings living in a world of human beings and only incidentally members of polities' (Barry, 1999, p. 35). The boundaries of polities are understood to be historically arbitrary, and most often the result of coercion and violence. Borders obscured the common circumstances of humankind and, thus, could not have the moral significance frequently ascribed to them (Pogge, 1994b, p. 198). The individual belongs to the wider world of humanity; moral worth cannot be specified by the yardstick of a single political community.

The second conception of cosmopolitanism was introduced in the eighteenth century when the term *weltbürger* (world citizen) became one of the key terms of the Enlightenment. The most important contribution to this body of thought can be found in Kant's writings (above all, 1970, pp. 41–53, 54–60 and 93–130). Kant linked the idea of cosmopolitanism to an innovative conception of 'the public use of reason', and explored the ways in which this conception of reason can generate a critical vantage point from which to scrutinize civil society (see Schmidt, 1998, pp. 419–27). Building on a definition of enlightenment as the escape from dogma and unvindicated authority, Kant measured its advance in terms of the removal of constraints on 'the public use of reason'. As one commentator eloquently remarked, Kant grounds reason 'in the reputation of principles that preclude the possibility of open-ended interaction and communication. . . . The principles of reason are those that can secure the possibility of intersubjectivity' (O'Neill, 1990, p. 194). Locked into the roles, practices and organizations of civil society, people, Kant argued, do not have the opportunity to explore fully the nature and limits of existing rules, prejudices and beliefs. But people are also, if only potentially, members of a 'cosmopolitan society', and as members of this society they can 'enjoy a right to the free and unrestricted public use of their reason' (Schmidt, 1998, p. 424). Individuals can step out of their entrenched positions in civil and political life and enter a sphere of reason free of 'dictatorial authority' – which Kant associated (rather uncritically) with the world of writers, readers and intellectuals – and can, from this vantage point, examine the one-sidedness, partiality and limits of everyday knowledge, understanding and regulations. In this context, individuals can learn to think of themselves as participants in a dialogue – a critical process of communication – in which they can come to an understanding with others about the nature and appropriateness of the demands made upon them (cf. Arendt, 1961, pp. 220–1).

Kant conceived of participation in a cosmopolitan (*weltbürgerlich*), rather than a civil (*bürgerlich*), society as an entitlement – an entitlement to enter the world of open, uncoerced dialogue – and he adapted this idea in his formulation of what he called 'cosmopolitan right' (1970, pp. 105–8). Cosmopolitan right connoted the capacity to present oneself and be heard within and across political communities; it was the right to enter dialogue without artificial constraint and delimitation. He emphasized that this right extended to the circumstances which allow people to enjoy an exchange of ideas (and goods) with the inhabitants of other countries, but that it did not extend as far as the right to permanent settlement or to citizenship in their homelands (1970, pp. 105–8).

Cosmopolitan right, thus understood, transcends the particular claims of nations and states and extends to all in the 'universal community'. It connotes a right and duty which must be accepted if people are to learn to tolerate one another's company and to coexist peacefully. It is the condition of cooperative relations and of just conduct. These arguments also lead Kant to make a striking rejection of colonialism: 'the *inhospitable* conduct of the civilised states of our continent, especially the commercial states' and 'the injustice they display in *visiting* foreign countries and peoples (which in their case is the same as *conquering* them)' (1970, pp. 105–6). Cosmopolitan right is a 'necessary complement' to the codes of existing national and international law, the basis on which cultural, religious and political dogmas can be tested in order to help construct a cosmopolitan order – where all relationships, political and social, should be bound by a willingness to enter into dialogue and interaction constrained only by elementary principles of reason, impartiality and the possibility of intersubjective agreement (see Held, 1995, pp. 266ff.; McCarthy, 1999). In this sense, individuals can be citizens of the world as well as of existing states; citizenship can become an attribute not just of national communities but of a universal system of 'cosmo-political' governance in which the freedom of each person underpins the freedom of all others (Kant, 1970, pp. 47–53 and 128–30).

The third conception of cosmopolitanism is more recent and is expounded in the work of Beitz, Pogge and Barry, among others (see, in particular, Beitz, 1979, 1994, 1998; Pogge, 1989, 1994a; and Barry, 1998a and 1999, although they by no means agree on many matters: see, for instance, Miller, 1998). In certain respects, this work seems to explicate, and offer a compelling elucidation of, the classical conception of belonging to the human community first and foremost, and the Kantian conception of subjecting all beliefs, relations and practices to the test of whether or not they allow open-ended interaction, uncoerced agreement and impartial judgement. This third conception of cosmopolitanism involves three key elements. The first is that the ultimate units of moral concern are individual human beings, not states or other particular forms of human association. Humankind belongs to a single moral realm in which each person is regarded as equally worthy of respect and consideration (Beitz, 1994, 1998; Pogge, 1994a). This element can be referred to as the principle of individualist moral egalitarianism or, simply, egalitarian individualism. To think of people as having equal moral value is to make a general claim about the basic units of the world comprising persons as free and equal beings (see Kuper, 2000). This broad position runs counter to the view of moral particularists that belonging to a given community limits and determines the moral worth of individuals and the nature of their autonomy. It does so because, to paraphrase (and adapt) Bruce Ackerman, there is no nation without a woman who insists on equal liberties, no society without a man who denies the need for deference, and no country without a person who does not yearn for a predictable pattern of meals to help sustain his or her life projects (see Ackerman, 1994, pp. 382–3). The principle of egalitarian individualism is the basis for articulating the equal worth and liberty of all humans, wherever they were born or brought up. Its concern is with the irreducible moral status of each and every person – the acknowledgement of which links directly to the possibility of self-determination and the capacity to make independent choices.

The second element emphasizes that the status of equal worth should be acknowledged by everyone. It is an attribute of every living person, and the basis on which each person ought to constitute their relations with others (Pogge, 1994a, pp. 89f.). Each person has an equal stake in this universal ethical realm and is, accordingly, required to respect all other people's status as a basic unit of moral interest (Pogge, 1994a, p. 90). This second element of contemporary cosmopolitanism can be called the principle of reciprocal recognition. To be satisfactorily entrenched in everyday life it necessitates that all people enjoy an equality of status with respect to the basic decision-making institutions of their communities. Agreed judgement about rules, laws and policies should ideally follow from the 'force of the better argument' and public debate – not from the intrusive outcome of non-discursive elements and forces (Habermas, 1973; Held, 1995, ch. 7). If people are marginalized or fall outside this framework, they suffer disadvantage not primarily because they have less than others in this instance, but because they can participate less in the processes and institutions that shape their lives. It is their 'impaired agency' that becomes the focus of concern (Doyal and Gough, 1991, pp. 95–6; see Raz, 1986, pp. 227–40).

The third element of contemporary cosmopolitanism stresses that equality of status and reciprocal recognition require that each person should enjoy the impartial treatment of their claims – that is, treatment based on principles upon which all could act. Accordingly, cosmopolitanism is a moral frame of reference for specifying rules and principles that can be universally shared; and, concomitantly, it rejects as unjust all those practices, rules and institutions anchored in principles not all could adopt (O'Neill, 1991). At issue is the establishment of principles and rules that nobody motivated to establish an uncoerced and informed agreement could reasonably reject (see Barry, 1989; cf. Scanlon, 1998).

To test the generalizability of claims and interests involves 'reasoning from the point of view of others' (Benhabib, 1992, pp. 9–10, 121–47). Attempts to focus on this 'social point of view' find their most rigorous explication in Rawls's original position, Habermas's ideal speech situation and Barry's formulation of impartialist reasoning (see Rawls, 1971; Habermas, 1973, 1996; Barry, 1989, 1995). These formulations have in common a concern to conceptualize an impartial moral standpoint from which to assess routine forms of practical reasoning. The concern is not overambitious. As one commentator aptly explained:

> All the impartiality thesis says is that, if and when one raises questions regarding funda-
> mental moral standards, the court of appeal that one addresses is a court in which no
> particular individual, group, or country has *special* standing. Before the court, declaring
> 'I like it', 'it serves my country', and the like, is not decisive; principles must be defensible
> to anyone looking at the matter apart from his or her special attachments, from a larger,
> human perspective. (Hill, 1987, p. 132, quoted in Barry, 1998b, pp. 226–7)

This social, open-ended moral perspective is a device for focusing our thoughts, and a
basis for testing the intersubjective validity of our conceptions of the good. It offers a
way of exploring principles, norms and rules that might reasonably command agreement (cf. Nussbaum, 1997, pp. 29–36).

Impartialist reasoning is a frame of reference for specifying rules and principles
that can be universally shared. In order to meet this standard a number of particular
tests can be pursued, including an assessment of whether all points of view have been
taken into consideration; whether there are individuals in a position to impose on
others in such a manner as would be unacceptable to the latter, or to the originator of
the action (or inaction), if the roles were reversed; and whether all parties would be
equally prepared to accept the outcome as fair and reasonable irrespective of the
social positions they might occupy now or in the future (see Barry, 1989, pp. 372 and
362–3).

Impartialist reasoning will not produce a simple deductive proof of the ideal set of
principles and conditions which can overcome the deficiencies of the global economy
or global political order; nor can it produce a deductive proof of the best or only
moral principles that should guide institutional formation. Rather, it should be thought
of as a heuristic device to test candidate principles of moral worth, democracy and
justice and their forms of justification (see Kelly, 1998, pp. 1–8). These tests are concerned with a process of reasonable rejectability, in a theoretical dialogue that is
always open to fresh challenge and new questions and, hence, in a hermeneutic sense,
can never be complete (Gadamer, 1975). But to acknowledge this is not to say that
the theoretical conversation is 'toothless' with respect either to principles or the
conditions of their entrenchment.

One 'biting' principle is the principle of the avoidance of serious harm and the
amelioration of urgent need. This is a principle for allocating priority to the most vital
cases of need and, where possible, trumping other, less urgent public priorities until
such a time as all human beings enjoy the status of equal moral value and reciprocal
recognition, and have the means to participate in their respective political communities and in the overlapping communities of fate which shape their needs and welfare.
A social provision which falls short of this can be referred to as a situation of manifest
'harm' in that the recognition of, and potential for, active agency will not have been
achieved for all individuals or groups; that is to say, some people would not have
adequate access to effectively resourced capacities which they might make use of in
particular circumstances (see Sen, 1999). This practical and participative conception
of agency denotes, in principle, an 'attainable' target – because the measure of optimum
participation, and the related conception of harm, can be conceived directly in terms
of the 'highest standard' presently achieved in a political community (see Doyal and
Gough, 1991, p. 169). But attainable participative levels are not the same thing as
the most pressing levels of vulnerability, defined by the most urgent need. It is only

too clear that within many, if not all, countries, certain needs, particularly cc health, education and welfare, are not universally met (Held and McGre chs 31, 32 and 37). The 'harm' that follows from a failure to meet such need, denoted as 'serious harm', marked as it often is by immediate, life-and-dea sequences. Accordingly, if the requirements specified by the principle of the avoidance of serious harm are to be met, public policy ought to be focused, in the first instance, on the prevention of such conditions; that is, on the eradication of severe harm inflicted on people 'against their will' and 'without their consent' (Barry, 1998b, pp. 231, 207).[1]

I take cosmopolitanism ultimately to connote the ethical and political space which sets out the terms of reference for the recognition of people's equal moral worth, their active agency and what is required for their autonomy and development (see Held, 2003).[2] It builds on principles that all could reasonably assent to in defending basic ideas which emphasize equal dignity, equal respect, the priority of vital need, and so on. On the other hand, this cosmopolitan point of view must also recognize that the meaning of these cannot be specified once and for all. That is to say, the connotation of these basic ideas cannot be separated from the hermeneutic complexity of traditions, with their temporal and cultural structures. The meaning of cosmopolitan regulative principles cannot be elucidated independently of an ongoing discussion in public life (Habermas, 1996). Accordingly, there can be no adequate specification of equal liberty, rights and vital interests without a corresponding institutionalization of 'the public use of reason' in uncoerced national and transnational forms of public dialogue and debate (McCarthy, 1999). The institutionalization of cosmopolitan principles requires the entrenchment of accessible and open public forums.

Cosmopolitan Realities

After over two hundred years of nationalism, sustained nation-state formation and intensive geopolitics, cosmopolitan principles and political positions could be thought of as out of place. Yet, in certain respects, cosmopolitanism defines a set of norms and legal frameworks in the here and now – and not in some remote future. Cosmopolitanism is already embedded in rule systems and institutions which have transformed the sovereign states system in a number of important respects. States have been the initiators of, and have been pressed into, the creation of rights and duties, powers and constraints, and regimes and organizations which impinge on and react back upon them. These transformations go to the heart of the privileged moral and legal position once claimed on behalf of states.

In the first instance, the principle of universal belonging and the relativization of the polity as an independent source of rights and obligations, expounded by the Stoics, find echoes today in the international realm. In a number of international treaties and customary rules, it is what people share – as human beings *simpliciter* (Benhabib, 2000) and as creatures in a common, global habitat – that has guided the foundation and formulation of certain governing principles, norms and rules. However tentative and fragile its entrenchment might be, the emerging regional and universal regulatory order takes what all human beings have in common (the human rights regime) and their ecosystems (the environmental regimes) as a starting point

(Crawford and Marks, 1998; Weller, 1997). Human beings are recognized as active members of the world whose political structures may, or may fail to, contribute to their well-being. This is a view of the public sphere which some classical thinkers might have recognized. Of course, against this, the continuing powerful place of state sovereignty in international law and regulation, and the continuing central role of great powers, would mean that such thinkers would certainly need a helping hand in tracing universal tendencies (cf. Gilpin, chapter 11 above).

Second, the Kantian concern with membership both of national communities and of a wider cosmopolitan order, constituted by the unrestricted use of public reason and universal hospitality (cosmopolitan right), finds expression in a number of articles of the Universal Declaration of Human Rights (UD), and in regional human rights agreements. Those of particular relevance have sought to entrench a common structure of rights and duties in relation to self-determination and the democratic principle (see UD, Article 21, and the Convention on Civil and Political Rights (CCPR), Article 25); full liberty of conscience, thought, speech and the press (see, for example, Articles 18 and 19 of the UD, and Articles 18 and 19 of the CCPR); participation in educational, cultural and scientific realms (see, for instance, UD, Article 27, and Article 15 of the Convention on Economic, Social and Cultural Rights); freedom of movement and travel (UD, Article 13, CCPR, Article 12); and freedom to seek asylum from persecution (UD, Article 14).

For Kant, cosmopolitan society was the realm of critical reason, into which all were, in principle, free to enter; republican national polities, on the one side, and the possibility of a universal dialogue across borders, on the other, were its essential preconditions. However, despite political and legal progress in this direction, we see now that an enlightened public life is even harder to achieve than Kant thought. Even though liberal democracy has spread to most regions of the world, many democracies are still best described as 'partial' (marked by some accountability of government to citizens through elections, but with curtailed and limited election procedures, rights and associational autonomy); they are far from 'full' liberal democracies (with accountable governments, free and fair competitive elections, civil and political rights, associational autonomy and so on) (see Potter et al., 1997). Accountable government, together with freedom of speech, association and movement, remains a fragile achievement or simply unattained in many countries and regions. But even if the Kantian conditions were fully met, they would still not adequately specify the conditions of a 'cosmopolitan society'; and this for three reasons.

First, formal commitments to allow each person to become part of a cosmopolitan society take no account of the complexity of power, power relations and inequality which turn 'the free realm of reason' all too often into a market-driven sphere marked by massive inequalities of access, distribution and outcome (see Held and McGrew, 2000, parts III and V). For example, new information and communication systems are helping to establish a global communication system, while, at one and the same time, creating new divisions between the informed, connected and isolated (UNDP, 1999). International rules and procedures do not address the gulf between assigned rights and effective power or opportunities. Second, participants in a cosmopolitan society of reason can find themselves entering a world of discourse often shaped by sectional interests, private priorities or particular substantive commitments. Existing forms of international law do not address the hiatus between every person's right to participate in diverse deliberative forums and the *modus operandi* of these, which can too often marginalize the concerns and interests of the least powerful. The diverse and often eccentric voting systems of leading intergovernmental organizations (IGOs) is a case in point; for example, the operations of the Bretton Woods institutions are heavily weighted in favour of the industrialized states, while the WTO rules require a wider consensus. Third, the Kantian conception of cosmopolitan right is too weak to underpin the free movement of people and ideas. For universal hospitality, even when guaranteed, is too limited a notion to clarify the dilemmas and proper treatment of, for instance, refugees and asylum seekers (see Benhabib, 2000). In a world where goods and services have greater opportunity for mobility than people (see Held et al., 1999, chs 3 and 6), cosmopolitan right alone will not open sufficient doors to strangers and aliens in need of entry, sanctuary or membership in another country.

Finally, the principles of egalitarian individualism, reciprocal recognition and impartialist reasoning – the principles of what I earlier referred to as contemporary cosmopolitanism – find direct expression in significant post-Second World War legal and institutional initiatives and in some of the new regulatory forms of regional and global governance (Held, 2002). To begin with, the 1948 UN Declaration of Human Rights and subsequent 1966 covenants of rights raised the principle of egalitarian individualism to a universal reference point: the requirement that each person be treated with equal concern and respect, irrespective of the state in which they were born or brought up, is the central plank of the human rights worldview (see UN, 1988). In addition, the formal recognition in the UN Declaration that all people have 'equal and inalienable rights', and that this constitutes 'the foundation of freedom, justice and peace in the world', marked a turning point in the development of cosmopolitan legal thinking (UD, preamble). Single persons are recognized as subjects of international law and, in principle, the ultimate source of political authority (see Crawford and Marks, 1998; Weller, 1997). Moreover, the diverse range of rights found in the Universal Declaration and regarded as integral to human dignity and autonomy – from protection against slavery, torture and other degrading practices to education and participation in cultural, economic and political life (irrespective of race, gender or religious affiliation) – creates the basis of a cosmopolitan orientation to politics and human welfare. Human rights entitlements can trump, in principle, the particular claims of national polities; they set down universal standards against which the strengths and limitations of individual political communities can be judged.

The human rights commitment to the equal worth of all human beings finds reinforcement in the acknowledgement of the necessity of a minimum of civilized conduct and of specific limits to violence found in the laws of war and weapons diffusion; in the commitment to the principles of the Nuremberg and Tokyo war crimes tribunals (in 1945–6 and 1946–8), the Torture Convention (in 1984) and the statute of the International Criminal Court (in 1998) which outlaw genocide, war crimes and crimes against humanity; in the growing recognition of democracy as the fundamental standard of political legitimacy which finds entrenchment in the Universal Declaration of Human Rights and regional treaties; in the development of new codes of conduct for intergovernmental and international non-governmental organizations, concerning the transparency and accountability of their activities; and in the unprecedented flurry of regional and global initiatives, regimes, institutions, networks and treaties seeking to tackle global warming, ozone depletion, the pollution of oceans and rivers, and nuclear risks, among many other factors (see Held, 2002 for a survey).

Cosmopolitan ideas are, in short, at the centre of significant post-Second World War legal and political developments. The idea that human well-being is not defined by geographical or cultural location, that national or ethnic or gendered boundaries should not determine the limits of rights or responsibilities for the satisfaction of basic human needs, and that all human beings require equal respect and concern are notions embedded in aspects of contemporary regional and global legal and political thinking, and in some forms of transnational governance (Beitz, 1994, p. 127; see Held et al., 1999, ch. 1 and Conclusion). There has been a significant shift in emphasis, as one observer has noted, 'in the character and goals of international society: away from minimalist goals of co-existence towards the creation of rules and institutions that embody notions of shared responsibilities, that impinge heavily on the domestic organization of states, that invest individuals and groups within states with rights and duties, and that seek to embody some notion of the planetary good' (Hurrell, 1995, p. 139). Yet, while there may be cosmopolitan elements to existing international law, these have, of course, by no means generated a new deep-rooted structure of cosmopolitan accountability and regulation. The principle of egalitarian individualism may be widely recognized, but it scarcely structures much political and economic policy, north, south, east or west. The principle of universal recognition informs the notions of human rights and other legal initiatives such as 'common heritage of humankind' (embedded in the Law of the Sea (of 1982)), but it is not at the heart of the politics of sovereign states or corporate colossi; the principle of impartial moral reasoning might be appealed to to justify limits on reasons of state and the actions of IGOs, but it is, at best, only an incidental part of the institutional dynamics that have created such chronic political problems as the externalities (or border spillover effects) generated by many national economic and energy policies, overlapping communities of fate in areas as diverse as security and the environment, and the global polarization of power, wealth and income.

This should not be a surprise. In the first instance, the global legal and political initiatives of 1948 onwards, referred to above, do not just curtail sovereignty, they clearly support and underpin it in many ways. From the UN Charter to the Rio Declaration on the environment, international agreements have often served to entrench, and accommodate themselves to, the sovereign international power structure. The division of the globe into powerful nation-states, with distinctive sets of geopolitical interests, has often been built into the articles and statutes of IGOs (see Held, 1995, chs 5 and 6). The 'sovereign rights of states' are frequently affirmed alongside more cosmopolitan leanings. Moreover, while a case can be made that cosmopolitan principles are part of 'the working creed' of officials in some United Nations agencies such as UNICEF, UNESCO and the WHO, and non-governmental organizations such as Amnesty International, Save the Children and Greenpeace, they can scarcely be said to be constitutive of the conceptual world of most modern politicians, democratic or otherwise (Barry, 1999, pp. 34–5; cf. Held and McGrew, 2000, pp. 31–9).

Second, the cosmopolitan reach of contemporary regional and global law rarely comes with a commitment to establish institutions with the resources and clout to make declared cosmopolitan intentions and objectives effective. The susceptibility of the UN to the agendas of the most powerful states, the partiality of many of its enforcement operations (or the lack of them altogether), the underfunding of its organizations, its continued dependency on financial support from a few major states, the weaknesses of the policing of many environmental regimes (regional and global) are all indicative of the disjuncture between cosmopolitan aspirations and their partial and one-sided application.

Finally, the focus of cosmopolitan political initiatives since 1945 has been on the domain of the political. These efforts have had only a tangential impact on the regulation of economic power and market mechanisms. The emphasis has been on checking the abuse of political power, not economic power. Cosmopolitan international politics has developed few, if any, systematic means to address forms of economic domination. Its conceptual resources and leading ideas do not suggest or push towards the pursuit of self-determination and autonomy in the economic domain; they do not seek the entrenchment of democratic rights and obligations outside the sphere of the political. Issues concerning corporate power, corporate governance and flourishing economic inequalities have to be brought back into the centre of cosmopolitan practice if this lacuna – at the heart of the struggle over globalization today – is to be addressed. Cosmopolitan theory, with its emphasis on illegitimate and unacceptable structures of power, and on vital need, has to be reconnected to cosmopolitan institution-building.[3]

Addressing the Institutional Deficit: Reframing the Market

The impact of developing cosmopolitan standards is highly differentiated and uneven across the world's regions. This creates moral and competitive problems for socio-economic agents and institutions of economic governance, and generates a conundrum: how to uphold cosmopolitan standards and values without eroding sound economic practice and legitimate corporate interests? Outside of a cosmopolitan framework there is, I think, no escape from this conundrum.

Onora O'Neill has argued recently that in the context of political turbulence, that is, against the background of rogue states or imploding polities, corporations can find that they are 'the primary agents of justice'; that is, the primary agents with responsibility for maintaining and sustaining cosmopolitan standards and virtues (2000, pp. 21–2). She holds that both states and companies can be judged by the principles and standards they claim to uphold; and that such a judgement today must be made in relation to the principles and standards which are already developing as the universal basis of action – as a result of the spread of democratic values, human rights agreements, environmental regimes and so on. This already provides a tough matrix of social requirements even before the cosmopolitan thinker presses it further.

There is much in this position to affirm: the particular culture and practices of companies matter; the difference between a responsible or a rogue corporation with respect, for example, to pollution is of great significance; and the involvement of companies in the infrastructural development of local communities can be of marked import. None the less, corporations can find themselves extremely vulnerable to shifting competitive circumstances if they bear the burdens and costs of certain environmental or social standards alone. In my view, business men and women object less to political regulation and social reform *per se* than to the intrusion of regulatory mechanisms that upset 'the rules of the game' solely in a certain place or country. Stringent environmental conditions, tough equal opportunities requirements, high labour standards, more accommodating working hours, for example, are particularly objectionable to companies if they handicap the competitive edge of those companies in relation to enterprises from areas not subject to similar constraints. Under such circumstances, companies will be all too tempted to do what they can to resist such standards or depart for more 'hospitable shores'; and this will be perfectly rational from their economic point of view.

Accordingly, if economic interaction is to be entrenched in a set of mechanisms and procedures that allow markets to flourish in the long run within the constraints of cosmopolitan principles and processes, the rules of the game will have to be transformed systematically, at regional and global levels (for instance, at the level of the EU and the WTO). This target for political and economic change provides a potentially fruitful focus, I believe, for both corporate interests and social movements concerned with widespread poverty, social standards and environmental degradation. What are the institutional and procedural implications of these considerations? The requirements of the cosmopolitan framework of accountability and regulation are many and various: there are legal, political, economic and cultural preconditions. But I only have the space here to focus on the economic (see Held, 2002, 2003).

The market system is highly indeterminate – often generating costly or damaging externalities with regard to health, welfare, income distribution or the environment. The 'anti-globalization' protesters are at their clearest and most articulate on these issues. These challenges can only be adequately addressed, and market economies can only function in a manner fully commensurate with cosmopolitan principles and virtues, if the market system is reframed. This should not be taken, as it is all too often, as an argument for either abandoning or undermining the market system – not at all. The market system has distinct advantages, as Hayek has emphasized, over all known alternative economic systems as an effective mechanism to coordinate the knowledgeable decisions of producers and consumers over extended territories (Hayek, 1976). But it is an argument for restructuring – or 'reframing', as I prefer to put it – the market itself. A bridge has to be built between international economic law and human rights law, between commercial law and environmental law, between state sovereignty and transnational law, and between cosmopolitan principles and cosmopolitan practices (see Chinkin, 1998). Precedents exist in, for instance, the Social Chapter of the Maastricht Agreement or in the attempt to attach labour and environmental conditions to the NAFTA regime, for the pursuit of this objective.

This position generates a rationale for a politics of intervention in economic life, not to control and regulate markets *per se* but to provide the basis for reforming and regulating those forms of power which compromise, disrupt or undermine fair and sustainable conditions for economic cooperation and competition – the necessary background conditions for the particular choices of human agents in a world of overlapping communities of fate. What is required is not only the firm enactment of existing human rights and environmental agreements and the clear articulation of these with the ethical codes of particular industries (where they exist or can be developed), but also the introduction of new terms of reference into the ground rules or basic laws of the free market and trade system.

At stake, ultimately, are two interrelated sets of transformations. The first is the entrenchment of revised rules, codes and procedures – concerning health, child labour, trade union activity, environmental protection, stakeholder consultation and corporate governance, among other matters – in the articles of association and terms of reference of economic organizations and trading agencies. The key groups and associations of the economic domain will have to adopt, within their very ways of working, a structure of rules, procedures and practices compatible with cosmopolitan social requirements, if the latter are to prevail. The second set of transformations concerns the institutionalization of cosmopolitan principles as the basis of rightful public authority, at local, national, regional and global levels. Recognizing the complex structures of an interconnected world, cosmopolitanism views certain issues as appropriate for delimited (spatially demarcated) political spheres (the city, state or region), while it sees others – such as the environment, genetic engineering, the terms of trade and financial stability – as requiring new, more extensive, regional and global institutions to address them (see Archibugi, Held and Köhler, 1998, chs 1, 10, 14).

Only by introducing new rules, standards and mechanisms of accountability throughout the global economic system, as a supplement and complement to collective agreements and measures in national and regional contexts, can an enduring settlement be created between business interests, regulatory capacity and cosmopolitan concerns (cf. Lipietz, 1992, pp. 119–24). While the advocacy of such a position clearly raises enormous political, diplomatic and technical difficulties, and would need a substantial period to pursue and, of course, implement, this is a challenge that cannot be avoided if people's equal interest in cosmopolitan principles and outcomes is to be adequately protected.

There are many possible objections to such a scheme and advocacy position. Among these are pressing cultural concerns that the standards and values being projected are those of Western origin and, concomitantly, mask sectional interests – to the advantage, for example, of entrenched corporate and labour interests in the developed world. This point is often made in relation to ILO standards vis-à-vis child labour, freedom to join trade unions, equal pay for men and women for work of equal value. However, this concern is, in my judgement, misplaced and hits the wrong target.

In the first instance, dissent about the value of ideas such as equal consideration, equal liberty and human rights is often related to the experience of Western imperialism and colonization. The way in which these ideas have been traditionally understood in the West – that is, the way in which they have been tied to political and civil rights, above all, and not, for example, to the satisfaction of fundamental human need – has fuelled the view that the language of liberty and democracy is the discourse of Western dominance, especially in those countries which were deeply affected by the reach of Western empires in the nineteenth and twentieth centuries. There are many good historical reasons why such language invokes scepticism. Understandable as they are, however, these reasons are insufficient to provide a well-justified critique: it is a mistake to throw out the language of equal worth and self-determination because of its contingent association with the historical configurations of Western power. The origins of principles should not be confused with their validity (Weale, 1998).

A distinction must be made between those political discourses which obscure or underpin particular interests and power systems, and those which seek explicitly to test the generalizability of claims and interests, and to render power, whether it be political, economic or cultural, accountable (see the section on cosmopolitan ideas and trajectories, pp. 308–13 above). The framework of cosmopolitan principles and values is sound, preoccupied as it is with the equal liberty and development possibilities of all human beings, but it cannot be implemented plausibly without addressing the most pressing cases of economic suffering and harm. Without this commitment, the advocacy of cosmopolitan standards can descend into high-mindedness, which fails to pursue the socio-economic changes that are a necessary part of such an allegiance.

At a minimum, this means linking the progressive implementation of a cosmopolitan regulative framework with efforts to reduce the economic vulnerability of many developing countries by eliminating debt, reversing the outflow of net capital assets from the South to the North, and creating new economic facilities at organizations like the World Bank, the IMF and the UN for development purposes (see Lipietz, 1992, pp. 116ff.; Falk, 1995, ch. 6). In addition, if such measures were combined with a (Tobin) tax on the turnover of financial markets, and/or a consumption tax on energy usage, and/or a shift of priorities from military expenditure to the alleviation of severe need, then the developmental context of Western and Northern nation-states could begin to be accommodated to those nations struggling for survival and minimum welfare (see Held, 1995, ch. 11; Giddens and Hutton, 2000, pp. 213ff., for a fuller account of these proposals).

Improbable? Unrealistic? Two points should be made in this regard. First, a cosmopolitan covenant is already in the making as political authority and new forms of governance are diffused 'below', 'above' and 'alongside' the nation-state, and as new forms of international law, from the law of war to human rights law and environmental regimes, begin to set down universal standards. Second, these standards can be built on, locking cosmopolitan principles into economic life, in developed and developing countries. To meet the requirements of impartialist reasoning, they have, of course, to be pressed much further. The intense battles about globalization are helping to create an environment in which questions about these matters can be pursued in the public domain. Entrenched geopolitical and economic interests are more likely to respond to a mix of pressure and argument, rather than to argument alone. But the risk of a severe backlash (championed already by the Bush administration) is clear. Certainly, the protesters need to come to understand the complexity of the issues they are seeking to address, the diversity of legitimate viewpoints (the difference, for example, between those who object to unbridled free trade and the positions of many developing countries seeking greater access to developed markets), and the extraordinary complexity of institutional solutions. Unless this happens, the gulf between confrontation and constructive engagement will not be bridged. In the end, whether cosmopolitan rules and regulations can be pursued successfully in the long term remains to be seen. But one thing is certain: the modern territorial state was not built in a generation, and one should not expect major and equally significant transformations – in this case to a multilevel, multilayered cosmopolitan polity – to take less time.

Notes

A version of this essay first appeared in *Contemporary Political Theory*, 1, no. 1 (2002), under the title 'Globalization, corporate practice and cosmopolitan social standards'. It appears here in a much amended and developed form.

1   Another way to put this point is to ask whether anyone would freely choose a 'principle of justice' which determined that people (present and/or future generations) suffer serious

harm and disadvantage independently of their consent, such as, for instance, the 30,000–35,000 children who die each day of malnutrition and disease. In the face of impartialist reasoning, this principle is wholly unconvincing. The impartialist emphasis on the necessity of taking account of the position of the other, of only regarding political outcomes as fair and reasonable if there are good reasons for holding that they would be equally acceptable to all parties, and of only treating the position of some socio-economic groups as legitimate if they are acceptable to all people irrespective of where they come in the social hierarchy does not provide grounds on which this principle could be accepted. And yet this is the principle of justice people are asked to accept, de facto, as a, if not the, principle of distribution in the global economic order. No wonder protest levels are so intense.

2 Contemporary cosmopolitans, it should be acknowledged, are divided about the demands that cosmopolitanism lays upon the individual and, accordingly, upon the appropriate framing of the necessary background conditions for a 'common' or 'basic' structure of individual action and social activity. Among them there is agreement that in deciding how to act, or which rules or regulations ought to be established, the claims of each person affected should be weighed equally – 'no matter where they live, which society they belong to, or how they are connected to us' (Miller, 1998, p. 165). The principle of egalitarian individualism is regarded as axiomatic. But the exact moral weight granted to this principle depends heavily on the precise modes of interpretation of other principles (see Nussbaum, 1996; Barry, 1998a; Miller, 1998; Scheffler, 1999). I shall not pursue these issues here, although the position suggested below indicates one way of linking cosmopolitan universalism with the recognition of the irreducible plurality of forms of life (see Habermas, 1996).

3 There are many good reasons why cosmopolitan reasoning must be combined with cosmopolitan institutional design. However sound cosmopolitan reasoning might be, the full meaning of cosmopolitan principles cannot be specified independently of the conditions of their enactment. Different thinkers give priority to 'cosmopolitanism' but, even when they agree about its contemporary conceptual specificity, they often differ over its practical efficacy and implications. Differences about how to secure cosmopolitanism in legal, political and economic terms can reveal differences in how to interpret its meaning. The specification of a principle's 'condition of enactment' is a vital matter; for if a theory of the most appropriate form of cosmopolitanism is to be at all plausible, it must be concerned with both theoretical and practical issues, with philosophical as well as organizational and institutional questions. As I have put the point elsewhere, 'without this double focus, an arbitrary choice of principles and seemingly endless debates about them are encouraged' (Held, 1996, p. 304). A consideration of principles, without an examination of the conditions for their realization, may generate a strong sense of virtue, but it will leave the actual meaning of such principles barely spelt out at all. A consideration of legal arrangements and political institutions, without reflecting upon the proper principles of their ordering, might, by contrast, lead to an understanding of their functioning, but it will barely help us to come to a judgement as to their appropriateness and desirability.

References

Ackerman, B. (1994) 'Political liberalisms', *Journal of Philosophy*, 91, pp. 364–86.

Archibugi, D., Held, D. and Köhler, M. (eds) (1998) *Re-imagining Political Community: Studies in Cosmopolitan Democracy*, Cambridge: Polity.

Arendt, H. (1961) 'The crisis in culture', in *Between Past and Future: Six Exercises in Political Thought*, New York: Meridian.

Barry, B. (1989) *Theories of Justice*, London: Harvester Wheatsheaf.

Barry, B. (1995) *Justice as Impartiality*, Oxford: Clarendon Press.

322 David Held

Barry, B. (1998a) 'International society from a cosmopolitan perspective', in D. Mapel and T. Nardin (eds), *International Society: Diverse Ethical Approaches*, Princeton: Princeton University Press.

Barry, B. (1998b) 'Something in the disputation not unpleasant', in Kelly 1998.

Barry, B. (1999) 'Statism and nationalism: a cosmopolitan critique', in I. Shapiro and L. Brilmayer (eds), *Global Justice*, New York: New York University Press.

Beetham, D. (1999) *Democracy and Human Rights*, Cambridge: Polity.

Beitz, C. (1979) *Political Theory and International Relations*, Princeton: Princeton University Press.

Beitz, C. (1994) 'Cosmopolitan liberalism and the states system', in Brown 1994.

Beitz, C. (1998) 'Philosophy of international relations', in *Routledge Encyclopedia of Philosophy*, London: Routledge.

Benhabib, S. (1992) *Situating the Self*, Cambridge: Polity.

Benhabib, S. (2000) 'Transformations of citizenship: dilemmas of political membership in the global era', presented at the Conference on Globalization, Yale University, New Haven, 31 Mar.–2 Apr.

Brown, C. (ed.) (1994) *Political Restructuring in Europe: Ethical Perspectives*, London: Routledge.

Chinkin, C. (1998) 'International law and human rights', in T. Evans (ed.), *Human Rights Fifty Years On*, Manchester: Manchester University Press.

Cohen, J. (ed.) (1996) *For Love of Country: Debating the Limits of Patriotism*, Boston: Beacon Press.

Crawford, J. and Marks, S. (1998) 'The global democracy deficit: an essay on international law and its limits', in Archibugi, Held and Köhler 1998.

Doyal, L. and Gough, I. (1991) *A Theory of Human Need*, London: Macmillan.

Eleftheriadis, P. (2000) 'The European constitution and cosmopolitan ideals', *Columbia Journal of European Law*, 7, pp. 21–39.

Falk, R. (1995) *On Humane Governance*, Cambridge: Polity.

Fernández-Armesto, F. (1995) *Millennium*, London: Bantam.

Gadamer, H. G. (1975) *Truth and Method*, London: Sheed and Ward.

Giddens, A. and Hutton, W. (2000) *On the Edge: Living with Global Capitalism*, London: Jonathan Cape.

Goldblatt, D., Held, D., McGrew, A. and Perraton, J. (1997) 'Economic globalization and the nation-state: shifting balances of power', *Alternatives*, 22, pp. 269–87.

Habermas, J. (1973) 'Wahrheitstheorien', in H. Fahrenbach (ed.), *Wirklichkeit und Reflexion*, Pfüllingen: Neske.

Habermas, J. (1996) *Between Facts and Norms: Contributions to a Discourse Theory of Law and Democracy*, Cambridge: Polity.

Hayek, F. (1976) *The Road to Serfdom*, London: Routledge.

Held, D. (1995) *Democracy and the Global Order: From the Modern State to Cosmopolitan Governance*, Cambridge: Polity.

Held, D. (1996) *Models of Democracy*, 2nd edn, Cambridge: Polity.

Held, D. (2002) 'Law of states, law of peoples', *Legal Theory*, 8, no. 2, pp. 1–44.

Held, D. (2003) *Cosmopolitanism*, Cambridge: Polity.

Held, D. and McGrew, A. (eds) (2000) *The Global Transformations Reader*, Cambridge: Polity.

Held, D., McGrew, A., Goldblatt, D. and Perraton, J. (1999) *Global Transformations: Politics, Economics and Culture*, Cambridge: Polity.

Hill, T. (1987) 'The importance of autonomy', in E. Kittay and D. Meyers (eds), *Women and Moral Theory*, Totowa, N.J.: Roman and Allanheld.

Horstmann, A. (1976) 'Kosmopolit, Kosmopolitismus', in *Historisches Wörterbuch der Philosophie*, vol. 4, Basel: Schwabe.

Hurrell, A. (1995) 'International political theory and the global environment', in K. Booth and S. Smith (eds), *International Relations Theory*, Cambridge: Polity.

Kant, I. (1970) *Kant's Political Writings*, ed. and introd. H. Reiss, Cambridge: Cambridge University Press.

Kelly, P. (ed.) (1998) *Impartiality, Neutrality and Justice: Re-reading Brian Barry's Justice as Impartiality*, Edinburgh: Edinburgh University Press.

Keohane, R. O. (1995) 'Hobbes' dilemma and institutional change in world politics: sovereignty in international society', in H. Holm and G. Sorensen (eds), *Whose World Order?* Boulder, Colo.: Westview Press.

Keohane, R. O. (2001) 'Governance in a partially globalized world', *American Political Science Review*, 95, pp. 1–13.

Kuper, A. (2000) 'Rawlsian global justice: beyond the law of peoples to a cosmopolitan law of persons', *Political Theory*, 28, pp. 640–74.

Lipietz, A. (1992) *Towards a New Economic Order*, Cambridge: Polity.

McCarthy, T. (1999) 'On reconciling cosmopolitan unity and national diversity', *Public Culture*, 11, pp. 175–208.

MacIntyre, A. (1981) *After Virtue*, London: Duckworth.

MacIntyre, A. (1988) *Whose Justice? Whose Rationality?* London: Duckworth.

Miller, D. (1988) 'The ethical significance of nationality', *Ethics*, 98, pp. 647–62.

Miller, D. (1998) 'The limits of cosmopolitan justice', in D. Mapel and T. Nardin (eds), *International Society: Diverse Ethical Approaches*, Princeton: Princeton University Press.

Nozick, R. (1974) *Anarchy, State and Utopia*, Oxford: Blackwell.

Nussbaum, M. C. (1996) 'Patriotism and cosmopolitanism', in Cohen 1996.

Nussbaum, M. C. (1997) 'Kant and cosmopolitanism', in J. Bohman and M. Lutz-Bachmann (eds), *Perpetual Peace: Essays on Kant's Cosmopolitan Ideal*, Cambridge, Mass.: MIT Press.

Nye, J. S. and Donahue, J. D. (2000) *Governance in a Globalizing World*, Washington DC: Brookings Institution Press.

O'Neill, O. (1990) 'Enlightenment as autonomy: Kant's vindication of reason', in L. Jordanova and P. Hulme (eds), *The Enlightenment and its Shadows*, London: Routledge.

O'Neill, O. (1991) 'Transnational justice', in D. Held (ed.), *Political Theory Today*, Cambridge: Polity.

O'Neill, O. (2000) 'Agents of justice', MS.

Pogge, T. (1989) *Realizing Rawls*, Ithaca, N.Y.: Cornell University Press.

Pogge, T. (1994a) 'Cosmopolitanism and sovereignty', in Brown 1994.

Pogge, T. (1994b) 'An egalitarian law of peoples', *Philosophy and Public Affairs*, 23, pp. 195–224.

Potter, D., Goldblatt, D., Kiloh, M. and Lewis, P. (eds) (1997) *Democratization*, Cambridge: Polity.

Rawls, J. (1971) *A Theory of Justice*, Cambridge, Mass.: Harvard University Press.

Raz, J. (1986) *The Morality of Freedom*, Oxford: Oxford University Press.

Rosenau, J. N. (1997) *Along the Domestic-Foreign Frontier*, Cambridge: Cambridge University Press.

Rosenau, J. N. (1998) 'Governance and democracy in a globalizing world', in Archibugi, Held and Köhler 1998.

Scanlon, T. M. (1998) *What We Owe to Each Other*, Cambridge, Mass.: Belknap.

Scheffler, S. (1999) 'Conceptions of cosmopolitanism', *Utilitas*, 11, pp. 255–76.

Schmidt, J. (1998) 'Civility, enlightenment and society: conceptual confusions and Kantian remedies', *American Political Science Review*, 92, pp. 419–27.

Sen, A. (1999) *Development as Freedom*, Oxford: Oxford University Press.

UN (1988) *Human Rights: A Compilation of International Instruments*, New York: United Nations.

UNDP (1999) *Globalization with a Human Face: Human Development Report*, New York: Oxford University Press.

Waldron, J. (2000) 'What is cosmopolitan?', *Journal of Political Philosophy*, 8, pp. 227–43.

Walzer, M. (1983) *Spheres of Justice: A Defence of Pluralism and Equality*, Oxford: Martin Robertson.

Weale, A. (1998) 'From contracts to pluralism?', in Kelly 1998.

Weller, M. (1997) 'The reality of the emerging universal constitutional order: putting the pieces together', *Cambridge Review of International Studies*, 10, Winter/Spring, pp. 40–63.

16

Governance in a Partially Globalized World

Robert O. Keohane

Talk of globalization is common today in the press and increasingly in political science. Broadly speaking, globalization means the shrinkage of distance on a world scale through the emergence and thickening of networks of connections – environmental and social as well as economic (Held et al., 1999; Keohane and Nye, 2001). Forms of limited globalization have existed for centuries, as exemplified by the Silk Road. Globalization took place during the last decades of the nineteenth century, only to be reversed sharply during the thirty years after the First World War. It has returned even more strongly recently, although it remains far from complete. We live in a partially globalized world.

Globalization depends on effective governance, now as in the past. Effective governance is not inevitable. If it occurs, it is more likely to take place through interstate cooperation and transnational networks than through a world state. But even if national states retain many of their present functions, effective governance of a partially – and increasingly – globalized world will require more extensive international institutions. Governance arrangements to promote cooperation and help resolve conflict must be developed if globalization is not to stall or go into reverse.

Not all patterns of globalization would be beneficial. It is easy to conjure up nightmare scenarios of a globalized world controlled by self-serving elites working to depress wages and suppress local political autonomy. So we need to engage in normative as well as positive analysis. To make a partially globalized world benign, we need not just effective governance but the *right kind* of governance.

My analysis begins with two premises. The first is that increased interdependence among human beings produces discord, since self-regarding actions affect the welfare of others. At worst, the effects of international interdependence include war. As international relations 'realists' have long recognized, interdependence and lack of governance make a deadly mixture. This Hobbesian premise can be stated in a more positive form: globalization creates potential gains from cooperation. This argument is often seen as 'liberal' and is associated with Adam Smith and David Ricardo, but it is actually complementary to Hobbes's point. The gains of cooperation loom larger relative to the alternative of unregulated conflict. Both realists and liberals agree that under conditions of interdependence, institutions are essential if people are to have opportunities to pursue the good life (Hobbes, [1651] 1967; Keohane, 1984; Keohane and Nye, 2001).

My second premise is that institutions can foster exploitation or even oppression. As Judith Shklar expresses it, 'no liberal ever forgets that governments are coercive' (1984, p. 244). The result is what I will call the governance dilemma: although institutions are essential for human life, they are also dangerous. Pessimistic about voluntary cooperation, Hobbes firmly grasped the authoritarian horn of the governance dilemma. We who are unwilling to accept Hobbes's solution incur an obligation to try to explain how effective institutions that serve human interests can be designed and maintained. We must ask the question that Plato propounded more than two millennia ago: Who guards the guardians?

Clearly, the stakes are high: no less than peace, prosperity and freedom. Political science as a profession should accept the challenge of discovering how well-structured institutions could enable the *world* to have 'a new birth of freedom' (Lincoln, 1863). We need to reflect on what we, as political scientists, know that could help actors in global society design and maintain institutions that would make possible the good life for our descendants.

In the first section of this essay I sketch what might be called the 'ideal world'. What normative standards should institutions meet, and what categories should we use to evaluate institutions according to those standards? I turn next to what we know about real institutions – why they exist, how they are created and maintained, and what this implies about their actual operation. In the concluding section I try to bring ideal and reality together to discuss institutional design. Are there ways by which we can resolve the governance dilemma, using institutions to promote cooperation and create order, without succumbing to exploitation or tyranny?

Desirable Institutions for a Partially Globalized World

Democratic theorists emphasize that citizens should reflect on politics and exercise their collective will (Rousseau, [1762] 1978), based on what Jürgen Habermas has called 'a culturally established background consensus shared by the citizenry' (1996, p. 296). Governments derive their just powers from the consent of the governed, as the American Declaration of Independence proclaims, and also from their reflective participation.

To the potential utopianism of democratic thought I juxtapose what a former president of the American Political Science Association, who was also my teacher, called the liberalism of fear (Shklar, 1984). In the tradition of realistic liberalism, I believe that the people require institutional protection both from self-serving elites and from their worst impulses, from what James Madison in *Federalist* 10 called the 'violence of faction' (Madison, [1787] 1961). Madison and Shklar demonstrate that liberalism need not be optimistic about human nature. Indeed, at the global scale the supply of rogues may be expected to expand with the extent of the market. Institutional protection from the arbitrary exercise of coercion, or authoritative exploitation, will be as important at the global level as at the level of the national state.

The discourse theory of Habermas restates liberal arguments in the language of communicative rationality. Legitimacy, in this view, rests on institutionalized procedures for open communication and collective reflection. Or, as Habermas quotes John Dewey, 'the essential need is the improvement of the methods and conditions of debate, discussion, and persuasion' (Habermas, 1996, p. 304; Dewey, [1927] 1954, p. 208). The ideal that Habermas, John Rawls (1971), Robert Dahl (1976, pp. 45–6) and many other political philosophers have upheld is that of rational persuasion – changing others' minds on the basis of reason, not coercion, manipulation or material sanctions. Persuasion in practice is much more complex than this ideal type, but seeking to move towards this ideal seems to me to be crucial for acceptable governance in a partially globalized world.

With these normative considerations in mind, we can ask: What political institutions would be appropriate for a partially globalized world? Political institutions are persistent and connected sets of formal and informal rules within which attempts at influence take place. In evaluating institutions, I am interested in their consequences, functions and procedures. On all three dimensions, it would be quixotic to expect global governance to reach the standard of modern democracies or polyarchies, which Dahl (1989) has analysed so thoroughly. Instead, we should aspire to a more loosely coupled system at the global level that attains the major objectives for which liberal democracy, or polyarchy, is designed at the national level.

Consequences

We can think of outcomes in terms of how global governance affects the life situations of individuals. In outlining these outcome-related objectives, I combine Amartya Sen's concept of capabilities with Rawls's conception of justice. Sen begins with the Aristotelian concept of 'human functioning' and defines a person's 'capability' as 'the alternative combinations of functionings that are feasible for her to achieve'. A person's 'capability set represents the freedom to achieve: the alternative functioning combinations from which this person can choose' (1999, p. 75). Governance should enhance the capability sets of the people being governed, leading to enhancements in their personal security, freedom to make choices, and welfare as measured by such indices as the UN Human Development Index. And it should do so in a just way, which I think of in the terms made famous by Rawls (1971). Behind the 'veil of ignorance', not knowing one's future situation, people should regard the arrangements for determining the distribution of capabilities as just. As a summary set of indicators, J. Roland Pennock's (1966) list holds up quite well: security, liberty, welfare, and justice.

Functions

The world for which we need to design institutions will be culturally and politically so diverse that most functions of governance should be performed at local and national levels, on the principle familiar to students of federalism or of the European Union's notion of 'subsidiarity'. Five key functions, however, should be handled at least to some extent by regional or global institutions.

The first of these functions is to limit the use of large-scale violence. Warfare has been endemic in modern world politics, and modern 'total warfare' all but obliterates the distinction between combatants and non-combatants, rendering the 'hard shell' of the state permeable (Herz, 1959). All plans for global governance, from the incremental to the utopian, begin with the determination, in the opening words of the United Nations Charter (1945), 'to save succeeding generations from the scourge of war'.

The second function is a generalization of the first. Institutions for global governance will need to limit the negative externalities of decentralized action. A major implication of interdependence is that it provides opportunities for actors to externalize the costs of their actions on to others. Examples include 'beggar thy neighbour' monetary policies, air pollution by upwind countries, and the harbouring of transnational criminals, terrorists or former dictators. Much international conflict and discord can be interpreted as resulting from such negative externalities; much international cooperation takes the form of mutual adjustment of policy to reduce these externalities or internalize some of their costs (Keohane, 1984). Following the convention in the international relations literature, I will refer to these situations, which resemble classic prisoners' dilemmas, as collaboration games (Martin, 1992; Stein, 1983).

The third function of governance institutions is to provide *focal points* in coordination games (Fearon, 1998; Krasner, 1991; Martin, 1992; Schelling, 1960). In situations with a clear focal point, no one has an incentive to defect. Great efficiency gains can be achieved by agreeing on a single standard – for measurement, technical specifications, or language communication. Actors may find it difficult, for distributional reasons, to reach such an agreement, but after an institutionalized solution has been found, it will be self-enforcing.

The fourth major function of governance institutions for a partially globalized world is to deal with system disruptions. As global networks have become tighter and more complex, they have generated systemic effects that are often unanticipated (Jervis, 1997). Examples include the Great Depression (Kindleberger, 1973); global climate change; the world financial crisis of 1997–8, with its various panics culminating in the panic of August 1998 following the Russian devaluation; and the Melissa and Lovebug viruses that hit the internet in 2000. Some of these systemic effects arise from situations that have the structure of collaboration games in which incentives exist for defection. In the future, biotechnology, genetic manipulation, and powerful technologies of which we are as yet unaware may, like market capitalism, combine great opportunity with systemic risk.

The fifth major function of global governance is to provide a guarantee against the worst forms of abuse, particularly involving violence and deprivation, so that people can use their capabilities for productive purposes. Tyrants who murder their own people may need to be restrained or removed by outsiders. Global inequality leads to differences in capabilities that are so great as to be morally indefensible and to which concerted international action is an appropriate response. Yet the effects of globalization on inequality are much more complicated than they are often portrayed. Whereas average per capita income has vastly increased during the last forty years, cross-national inequality in such income does not seem to have changed dramatically during the same period, although some countries have become enormously more wealthy, and others have become poorer (Firebaugh, 1999). Meanwhile, inequality within countries varies enormously. Some globalizing societies have a relatively egalitarian income distribution, whereas in others it is highly unequal. Inequality seems to be complex and conditional on many features of politics and society other than degree of globalization, and effective action to enhance human functioning will require domestic as well as international efforts.

Whatever the economic effects of globalization, social globalization certainly increases the attention paid to events in distant places, highlighting abuses that are widely abhorrent. Such issue advocacy is not new: the transnational antislavery movement between 1833 and 1865 is an important historical example. Yet the expansion of concern about human rights during the past two decades has been extraordinary, both in the scope of rights claimed – and frequently codified in UN agreements – and in the breadth of transnational advocacy movements and coalitions promoting such rights (Keck and Sikkink, 1998). Concern about poverty, however, has not been matched by effective action to eliminate the source of human misery (World Bank, 2000).

Procedures

Liberal democrats are concerned not only with outcomes but also with procedures. I will put forward three procedural criteria for an acceptable global governance system. The first is *accountability*: publics need to have ways to hold elites accountable for their actions. The second is *participation*: democratic principles require that some level of participation in making collective decisions be open to all competent adults in the society. The third is *persuasion*, facilitated by the existence of institutionalized procedures for communication, insulated to a significant extent from the use and threats of force and sanctions, and sufficiently open to hinder manipulation.

Our standards of accountability, participation and persuasion will have to be quite minimal to be realistic in a polity of perhaps 10 billion people. Because I assume the maintenance of national societies and state or state-like governance arrangements, I do not presume that global governance will benefit from consensus on deep substantive principles. Global governance will have to be limited and somewhat shallow if it is to be sustainable. Overly ambitious attempts at global governance would necessarily rely too much on material sanctions and coercion. The degree of consensus on principles – even procedural principles, such as those of accountability, participation and persuasion – would be too weak to support decisions that reach deeply into people's lives and the meanings that they construct for themselves. The point of presenting ideal criteria is to portray a direction, not a blueprint.

Now that these normative cards are on the table, I turn to some of the positive contributions of political science. In the next section I ask how we can use our knowledge as political scientists to design sustainable institutions that would perform the functions I have listed. In the final section I explore how these institutions could facilitate the democratic procedural virtues of accountability, participation and persuasion. These issues are all part of one overriding question: How can we design institutions that would facilitate human functioning, in the sense of Aristotle or Sen?

Institutional Existence and Power

How can authoritative institutions exist at all? This is a question that Rousseau claimed not to know how to answer ([1762] 1978, 1, 1) and that students of international politics have recently debated. No student of international relations is likely to forget that institutions are fragile and that institutional success is problematic.

To address this issue, I begin with the contributions of rational-choice institutionalism, which has insistently sought to raise the question of institutional existence and has addressed it with the tools of equilibrium analysis (Shepsle, 1986). To design appropriate and legitimate global institutions, we need to fashion a rich version of institutionalist theory, which uses the power of the rationality assumption without being hobbled by a crude psychology of material self-interest. But before discussing such a theory, it is important to indicate briefly why a simple functional answer is not sufficient.

The inadequacy of functional theories

One can imagine a simple functional theory of global institutions by which the demand for governance, generated by globalism, creates its own supply. Such an account has the defining characteristic that the real or anticipated effects of a process play a causal role (Cohen, 1978). A functional account can only be convincing if the causal mechanism for adaptation is clearly specified. In biology, one such mechanism is Darwinian evolution, which in its strong form implies environmental determinism. The selection environment determines which individual organisms, or other units, survive. Although the individual units may undergo random mutations, they do not act in a goal-directed fashion, and they do not fundamentally affect the environment that selects them. But environmental determinism and the absence of goal-seeking behaviour are not assumptions that seem to fit human social and political reality (Kahler, 1999). Hence, evolutionary arguments in the social sciences have mostly stayed at the level of metaphor. They certainly do not provide us with warrant for a functionalist account of how governance arrangements for globalization would emerge, since the causal mechanism for selection seems even weaker at the global level than with respect to competition among states.

The other causal mechanism for functional theories involves rational anticipation. Agents, seeing the expected consequences of various courses of action, plan their actions and design institutions in order to maximize the net benefits that they receive. Ronald Coase (1960) and Oliver Williamson (1985) use functional theory in Cohen's sense to explain why firms exist at all. 'Transactional economies' account for choices of markets or hierarchies (Williamson, 1975, p. 248). That is, more efficient organizational arrangements will somehow be selected.

But there is a micro–macro problem here, since arrangements most efficient for society are not necessarily optimal for the leaders of the organization. At the level of societies, as Douglass North has pointed out, the history of real economies is one of persistent *inefficiency*, which he explains essentially in terms of the free rider problem. Even if an institutional innovation would increase efficiency, no one may have the incentive to develop it, since institutional innovation is a public good (North, 1981, p. 68; 1990, p. 93). Indeed, rent-seeking coalitions have incentives to resist socially beneficial institutional innovations that would reduce their own advantages (Olson, 1982).

Functional solutions to the problem of institutional existence are therefore incomplete. There must be political entrepreneurs with both the capacity and the incentives to invest in the creation of institutions and the monitoring and enforcement of rules. Unless the entrepreneurs can capture selective benefits from their activities, they will not create institutions. And these institutions will not be effective unless sufficient compliance is induced by a combination of material and normative incentives. To use economic language, problems of supply (Bates, 1988; Shepsle and Weingast, 1995) as well as demand have to be solved.

Mancur Olson's (1965) analysis of the logic of collective action has two major implications for the governance of a globalized world. First, there is no guarantee that governance arrangements will be created that will sustain high levels of globalism. As Western history reveals, notably in the collapse of the Roman Empire and in the First World War, extensive social and economic relations can be undermined by a collapse of governance. At the global as well as national level, political scientists need to be as concerned with degrees of governance as with forms of governance (Huntington, 1968, p. 1).

The second implication of Olson's insight is that we cannot understand why institutions vary so much in their degree of effectiveness simply by studying institutions. To focus only on existing institutions is to select on the dependent variable, giving us no variance and no leverage on our problem. On the contrary, we need to explore situations in which institutions have *not* been created, despite a widespread belief that if such institutions were created, they would be beneficial. Or we can compare situations in which institutions exist to earlier ones in which they were absent (cf. Tilly, 1975, 1990).

Institutional theory and bargaining equilibria

Rational-choice institutionalism in political science insists that institutions, to persist, must reflect bargaining equilibria of games in which actors seek to pursue their own interests, as they define them. This perspective, stated elegantly by Kenneth Shepsle (1986), is not new in its essentials. Indeed, in investigating the effects of constitutions, Aristotle held that those vesting authority in the middle class will promote rationality and the protection of property rights (*Politics*, IV, xi, pp. 4–15).[1] He sought to explain variations in constitutional forms by referring to variations in social conditions (IV, iii, pp. 1–6). And he argued that a stable constitution is not only one that a majority seeks to maintain but also one for which 'there is no single section in all the state which would favour a change to a different constitution' (IV, ix, p. 10).

In the terms of rational-choice institutionalism, Aristotle was interested both in institutional equilibrium and equilibrium institutions. So were Adam Smith and James Madison (Smith, [1776] 1976; Madison, [1787] 1961). The eighteenth-century view, which resonates with rational-choice institutionalism, was that the 'passions' of people in bourgeois society can be interpreted in terms of their interests (Hirschman, 1977, p. 110) and can be moderated by wise institutions.

Yet, rational-choice institutionalism has been more rigorous and more relentless than its predecessors in insisting on explaining, by reference to incentives, why institutions exist. Because rational-choice theorists seek to explain in formal terms why institutions exist, they have to confront directly two critical questions. (1) Under what conditions will political entrepreneurs have incentives to create institutions? (2) What makes such institutions stable?

Since institutions are public goods, they are likely to be underproduced and, at the limit, not produced at all. Hence there must be selective incentives for politicians to invest in institutional innovations (Aldrich, 1995). In addition, significant advantages must accrue to institutional innovators, such as conferring on them control over future rules or creating barriers to entry to potential competitors. Otherwise, late-comers could free ride on the accomplishments of their predecessors, and anticipation of such free riding would discourage institutional innovation. Another barrier to entry for latecomers may be ideology. In so far as only a few ideologies, quite distinct from one another, can exist, first movers would gain an advantage by seizing favour-able ideological ground (cf. Hinich and Munger, 1994). The implication for our prob-lem of institutional design is that first-mover advantages are essential if institutional innovation is to occur.

The European Union provides a compelling example of first-mover advantages in international organizations. New members of the EU have to accept, in their entirety, the rules already established by their predecessors. As a result, the innovators of the European Community – the six founding members – gain persistent and cumulative advantages from having written the original rules. These rules are important. Even if implementation is often slow, during the 1990s all members of the EU had imple-mented more than 75 per cent of EU directives, and more than half had implemented more than 85 per cent (Martin, 2000, p. 174). First-mover advantages are also evident in the processes of writing national electoral rules: those who win an earlier election create rules that subsequently favour their party, policy positions, and personal careers (Bawn, 1993; Remington and Smith, 1996).

The second key question is that of stability. If institutional rules constrain majorities, why do these majorities not simply change the institutional rules to remove the con-straint? If they do, what happens to the 'structure-induced equilibrium' that solves Arrow's paradox of social choice (Riker, 1980)? In other words, why do institutions not simply 'inherit' rather than solve Arrow's paradox (Aldrich, 1993)?

The general answer seems to be that institutions generate rules that resolve Arrow's paradox, for example by giving agenda-setting power to particular agents (Shepsle, 1986) or by requiring supermajorities to change institutional arrangements. These rules ensure that majorities cannot alter them easily when the median voter's prefer-ences change.

First-mover advantages and agenda control provide incentives for institutional innovation and help to stabilize institutions. They operate somewhat differently, however, in coordination and collaboration situations, as described above. In situ-ations of coordination, institutions, once accepted, are in equilibrium. Participants do not have incentives to deviate unilaterally from widely accepted standards for internet connectivity or airline traffic control. Institutions to solve collaboration problems are much more fragile. After an agreement on institutions to solve collaboration problems is reached, participants typically have incentives to defect if they expect to avoid retaliation from others (Martin, 1992).

Students of international relations have used this distinction to show how much more difficult it is to maintain collaboration institutions. Monitoring and enforcement are essential. Furthermore, during the bargaining process 'hold-outs' may be able to negotiate better terms for themselves in collaboration than in coordination situations, since threats to remain outside collaboration-oriented institutions are more credible than threats to remain outside a widely accepted coordination equilibrium. In inter-national relations, the side-payments negotiated by China and India to join the ozone regime, and the refusal so far of developing countries to be bound by emissions restrictions in a climate change regime, illustrate this point.

If we keep our normative as well as positive lenses in focus, we will see that this apparent advantage of coordination institutions has a dark side. Initiators of coordination institutions can exercise great influence over the choice of focal points, thereby gaining an enduring first-mover advantage over their rivals (Krasner, 1991). Collaboration institutions do not offer such first-mover advantages, since participants can defect at lower cost. Collaboration institutions therefore provide fewer opportunities, as compared to coordination institutions, for coercion of latecomers. Real institutions usually combine coordination and collaboration functions, and therefore also contain a mixture of destabilizing (or liberating) elements and stabilizing (or potentially oppressive) ones.

Institutions, whether emphasizing coordination or collaboration, necessarily institutionalize bias, in favour of groups that have agenda control or wish to maintain the status quo. It is therefore not surprising that advocates of social equality such as Thomas Jefferson, and democrats such as Rousseau, are often suspicious of institutions. Barriers to competition confer monopolistic privileges and therefore create normative problems. Yet institutions are essential for the good life.

Normatively, those of us who believe in Shklar's (1984) 'liberalism of fear' both support institutions and are cautious about them. We support them because we know that without well-functioning political institutions, life is indeed 'nasty, brutish, and short'. But we are suspicious, since we understand how self-serving elites can use institutions to engage in theft and oppression. In a partially globalized world, we will need institutions of broader scope. But as in national democracies, eternal vigilance will be the price of liberty.

Rational-choice theory has led to fruitful inquiries into the issue of why institutions exist, because it relentlessly questions any apparent equilibrium. The sceptical question – why should institutions exist at all? – has ironically led to a deeper understanding of institutions than has the assumption that we could take their existence for granted and focus on how they work.

The limits of rational egoism

Commenting on Tocqueville, Albert Hirschman has pointed out a normative problem with the emphasis on self-interest that I have thus far emphasized: 'Social arrangements that substitute the interests for the passions as the guiding principle of human action for the many can have the side effect of killing the civic spirit' (1977, p. 125). There is also an analytical problem: we know from a variety of work that this egoistic picture is seriously incomplete.

Rationalist theory often carries with it the heavy baggage of egoism. People are viewed as self-interested individuals whose incentives are strictly shaped by their environment, including the rules of the institutions in which they are located. The most sophisticated version of this argument does not make the essentialist claim that 'human nature' is fundamentally egoistic but gives priority instead to an instrumentalist logic. Hans J. Morgenthau (1967, ch. 1), for example, argues that since power is a necessary means to other goals in international politics, we can analyse leaders' behaviour in terms of power even if they do not seek power for its own sake (see also Wolfers, 1962, ch. 7). For rationalist students of American and comparative politics, political leaders may have a multiplicity of goals, but since continuation in office is a necessary means to achieve any of them, it can be regarded as a universal objective of politicians, whether purely instrumental or consummatory (Geddes, 1994; Mayhew, 1974).

Thoughtful theorists of rational choice recognize that the assumption of egoism oversimplifies social reality. Norms of reciprocity and fairness often affect social behaviour (Levi, 1997; Ostrom, 1990). The theoretical predictions derived from the assumption of egoism encounter serious predictive failure in experimental settings (Ostrom, 1998). And survey research shows that citizens evaluate the legitimacy of the legal system on the basis not only of their own success in dealing with it but also of their perceptions of its procedural fairness (Tyler, 1990).

Sometimes the assumption of egoism is defended on the ground that only with such simple models can solutions be found to strategic games. But the folk theorem of game theory demonstrates that an essentially unlimited number of equilibria appear in all interesting games. When the equilibrium rabbit is to be pulled from the hat, we are as likely to get a thousand rabbits as one. Equilibria multiply like rabbits in Australia and are about as useful. As Elinor Ostrom (1998, p. 4) commented in her address to the American Political Science Association three years ago, the assumptions of rationality, amoral self-interest, and lack of influence from social norms lead to explanatory chaos: 'Everything is predicted: optimal outcomes, the Pareto-inferior Nash equilibria, and everything in between.'

In addressing the problems of institutional design, it is a good thing that people are not purely egotistical. It would be difficult to understand the creation of major political institutions – from the US Constitution to UN-sponsored human rights agreements – if we took egotism and the free-rider problem too seriously. We are indeed wise to assume that institutions, to be in long-term equilibrium, must be broadly consistent with the self-interest of powerful actors. But we cannot understand the origins of institutions if we banish principled action from our analytic world.

Egoists have a hard time overcoming problems of mistrust, because they know that everyone has an incentive to disguise his or her preferences. Only costly signals will be credible; but the cost of signalling reduces the prospective value of cooperation and limits the agreements that can be reached. Egoists also have difficulty solving bargaining problems, since they do not recognize norms of fairness that can provide focal points for agreement. Cool practitioners of self-interest, known to be such, may be less able to cooperate productively than individuals who are governed by emotions that send reliable signals, such as love or reliability (Frank, 1988). In Sen's phrase, people in purely rational-choice models are 'rational fools' (1977, p. 336), incapable of distinguishing among egoistic preferences, sympathy and commitments.

As Sen makes clear, rejecting the premise of egoism does not imply rejecting the assumption of rationality – more or less bounded in Herbert Simon's (1985) sense. Nor does it imply altruism: people can empathize with others without being self-sacrificing. What it does is demand that norms and values be brought back into the picture. Committed individuals, seeking policy goals as well as office for its own sake, and constrained by norms of fairness or even by more transcendental values, can nevertheless calculate as rationally as the egoists of economic theory.

In thinking about a partially globalized world, one might be tempted to dismiss half the governance dilemma by pointing out that because international institutions are very weak, they are unlikely to be oppressive. For example, contemporary opponents of globalization and associated international institutions have sought to portray the World Trade Organization as some sort of bureaucratic monster, although my own university's budget allocates more money in two weeks than WTO spends in a year.[2]

True as it is, this appeal to institutional weakness is not fully convincing. The problem is not that international organizations are huge and oppressive but that they are seen as serving the vested interests of the powerful and privileged. And they do. Indeed, they are institutions of the privileged, by the privileged, and all too often for the privileged. There are severe restraints on the powers of the international civil servants who lead these organizations, but few such checks limit the ability of the strongest states, such as the United States, to dictate policies and veto personnel. Yet, in the absence of such institutions, dictation by strong states would be even more direct, less encumbered by rules. Like Churchill's aphorism about democracy, an institutionalized world is probably the worst form of governance – except for the alternatives.

Ironically, it is the privileged who often appeal to altruism – their own, of course – as the guarantee against the abuse of power. Political scientists have spent too much time debunking altruism as a general motivating factor in politics to be detained long by such claims. Anyone my age has lived through the disastrous failures of social systems, notably in Russia and China, based on the premise that human nature can be remoulded. The reality is that the worst people thrive under the cover of such grand visions. In any event, the heterogeneity of the world's population makes it impossible to imagine any single ideology providing the basis for a coherent, value-based system of global governance. The answer to global governance problems does not lie in revelation.

Faced with the governance dilemma, those of us interested in governance on a world scale could retreat to the pure self-interest model. With that set of assumptions, we would probably limit world governance. We would sacrifice gains that could result from better cooperation in order to guard against rule by undemocratic, self-serving institutions responsive, in opaque ways, to powerful elites. If we were successful, the result would be to limit global governance, even at the expense of greater poverty and more violent conflict. We might think ourselves wise, but the results would be sad. Due to excessive fear, we would have sacrificed the liberal vision of progress.

Institutions, expectations and beliefs

It may seem that we are at an impasse. Sober reliance on limited institutions based on pure self-interest could lead to a low-level 'equilibrium trap'. But we may be tempted to settle for such an equilibrium rather than accept oppressive global institutions.

There may be a way out of this impasse. That path is to pay more attention than we have to expectations of how others will behave and, therefore, to underlying values and beliefs. Expectations are critical determinants of action. They depend heavily on trust, reputation and reciprocity, which depend in turn on networks of civic engagement, or social capital. Building such networks is an incremental process. Engagement in just such a set of social relations helps create personal integrity, which is the basis for consistent principled action (Grant, 1997). Networks of civic engagement are not easily divided into 'international' and 'domestic' but, rather, cross those lines (Keck and Sikkink, 1998). Rational strategic action depends on the expectations and incentives that these networks create.

Until recently, students of international politics paid too little attention to beliefs. The realists insisted on the dominance of interests and power, which they traced to material factors. Marxist and neoclassical political economists also relied on material forces for their explanations. Students of institutions, such as I, sought to gain credibility by showing that our theories are as realistically based in interests and power as those of our realist adversaries, that we are not tainted by the idealist brush. Ironically enough, however, the theory of strategic interaction on which we all rely has insistently argued that beliefs are crucial to understanding any game-theoretic situation (Morrow, 1994; Wendt, 1999).

The fact that strategic action depends on expectations means that understanding historical and cultural context is critical to any analysis of how institutions operate. Peter Katzenstein (1993, 1996) has used the differing responses of Germany and Japan to military defeat and economic revival to make this point in a cogent and forceful way. Historical explorations of institutional phenomena and negotiations may draw effectively on rational-choice theory, but they must go well beyond its premises to describe multidimensional human behaviour (Bates et al., 1998). Indeed, political scientists have quite a bit to learn from international law, which studies rational strategic action in the context of rules and rule-making, deeply structured by interests and power but also reflecting the influence of ideas on interests and on how power is exercised (Grewe, 2000).

A major task before our discipline is how to connect rational strategic action with beliefs and values. In her presidential address three years ago, Ostrom (1998) linked rational-choice theory with the laboratory experiments of cognitive science to show that institutional incentives, fundamental norms of trust and the practice of reciprocity (Axelrod, 1984; Ostrom, 1990) all provide crucial foundations of cooperation. 'At the core of a behavioral explanation', Ostrom said, 'are the links between the trust that individuals have in others, the investment others make in trustworthy reputations, and the probability that participants will use reciprocity norms' (1998, p. 12). That is, principled values, 'congealed' in institutions, provide the basis for meaningful rational actions and direct such actions in ways that we can describe and explain (Riker, 1980).

Robert Putnam's *Making Democracy Work* exemplifies a productive analysis of the connections among values, social norms and rational behaviour. Putnam argues that 'networks of civic engagement' produce better government. Why does he think so? Not because engaged people necessarily work altruistically for the common good but because these networks increase costs of defection, facilitate communication and create favourable expectations of others' likely actions (Putnam, 1993, pp. 173–4).

Understanding beliefs is not opposed to understanding interests. On the contrary, interests are incomprehensible without an awareness of the beliefs that lie behind them. Indeed, even the financial self-interest so dear to political economists implies acceptance of norms that would be incomprehensible in many societies, whether those imagined by Jean-Jacques Rousseau or those studied by twentieth-century anthropologists. The values and beliefs that are dominant within a society provide the foundations for rational strategy.

Even beliefs about beliefs can be as solid as any material interests. As Barry O'Neill shows brilliantly in a book awarded the Woodrow Wilson Prize, prestige refers to 'beliefs about beliefs' – whether people think that others hold a high opinion of someone (O'Neill, 1999, p. 193). Prestige is a 'social fact', like a dollar bill (Searle, 1995): although it is genuinely real, its importance does not lie in its material manifestation but in the beliefs people hold. Both money and prestige matter a great deal in politics, but only in so far as people hold beliefs about others' beliefs.

To see how beliefs relate to issues of institutional design, think about two possible worlds of the future. In one of them, the 'normative anarchy' portrayed by the 'political realism' of the late twentieth century (Waltz, 1979) prevails. That is, there is no consensus about principled beliefs on the basis of which governance across national boundaries can take place, and transnational networks of people with similar beliefs are virtually non-existent. The only norm on which there is general agreement is the 'antinorm' of sovereignty: the principle that the rulers of each state are supreme internally and independent from external authority (Bull, 1977). Since I expect self-interested agents to continue to dominate among politicians, I would expect, in this world, familiar patterns of modern Western international politics to persist. Rationally egoistic politicians would have few incentives to fight for principles of human rights, since to do so they would have to overcome both collective action problems and ridicule from 'realistic' statesmen and academics.

Now consider another world, in which certain principles have become generally accepted – as opposition to slavery became generally accepted in the nineteenth century and as certain human rights seem to be becoming accepted now (Keck and Sikkink, 1998). In this world, transnational advocacy networks would be active. Behaviour in this world would, of course, be different from that in the first world. Even those who do not subscribe to these principles would have to calculate the costs of acting counter to them.

Now let us go a step farther and imagine that the principled innovators of the new principles, and the value-based transnational networks, disappear, to be replaced by purely rational egoists. Would the egoists seek immediately to overturn these norms of human rights? Probably not, unless they had compelling internal reasons, as tyrants, to do so. Ordinary egoists, governing non-tyrannically, would have interests in mimicking the principled leaders whom they succeed. Furthermore, the egoists would face serious collective action problems in overturning norms of human rights: Their counterpart egoists would have an interest in defending those rights in order to enhance their reputation as principled agents. As a result, egoistic self-interest would counsel them to uphold the norms established and even to bear some costs in order to send credible signals that they believe in the norms (even though, by assumption, they do not). The effect of former principles would persist for a while, although it would eventually fade.

What this thought-experiment illustrates is a simple but fundamental point. Beliefs in norms and principles – even beliefs only held in the past – can profoundly affect rational action in the present. Joseph Schumpeter (1950, p. 137) made the famous argument sixty years ago that capitalism requires precapitalist values: 'The stock exchange is a poor substitute for the Holy Grail.' The facile response to his argument at millennium's end could be: 'Yes, but he didn't take into account NASDAQ.' More seriously, however, the varieties of capitalism in the world today, from Japanese corporatism to American legalism to Russian organized theft, make it clear that what is economically rational in each context varies enormously. Schumpeter was wrong about the staying power of capitalism but right about the dependence of institutions, capitalism included, on beliefs.

Institutional Design: Bringing Ideals and Reality Together

I began by sketching an ideal vision – a liberal and democratic vision of how institutions should work. On the liberal side, it includes what one might call the liberalism of progress, represented by such eighteenth-century thinkers as Smith and Madison. But it also includes Shklar's liberalism of fear, which emphasizes the potential depravities of human nature and the pathologies of human institutions and is deeply cognisant of imperialism, totalitarianism, and the Holocaust (Arendt, 1958). The liberalism of fear is horrified by the atrocities of Rwanda and Bosnia, but these atrocities do not shake its liberalism, which was forged in the searing recognition that human action can be horrible.

The liberalism of progress and the liberalism of fear are two sides of the same coin. They both seek to understand how otherwise unattractive human passions can nevertheless promote the general good. Madison is the American father of such a realistic liberalism, but it has deep roots both in English utilitarianism, going back to Hobbes, and in French thought (Hirschman, 1977; N. O. Keohane, 1980). Neither Madison nor Smith indulged in the more utopian dreams of the liberalism of progress. Even though potential gains from trade, combined with advancing technology, make it possible for all economies to prosper simultaneously, the Hobbesian desire for 'power after power' gets in the way. So does greed. People often seek to gain distributional advantages not by being more productive but by gaining control of public policies in order to capture rents. Nevertheless, mercantilist theory has been proved bankrupt, and the institutions of liberal democracy have limited, although they have not eliminated, the success of rent-seeking. Smith and Madison would not be fully satisfied, but they would be gratified by the partially successful institutionalization of their ideas.

Together the liberalism of progress and the liberalism of fear emphasize the need for institutions. Smith's liberalism calls for institutions to promote exchange; Shklar's for institutions to control the human vices of those individuals among us whose vices are most dangerous to others. For these institutions to be morally acceptable, they must rest both on humane beliefs and substantial mutual trust. The Mafia is not better than anarchy; the people who live under either find themselves impaled on one horn or the other of the governance dilemma.

Democratic theory is even more demanding. From a democratic standpoint it is not enough to have non-oppressive institutions that enforce rules. Accountability, participation and persuasion are also essential. International institutions will probably never meet the standards of electoral accountability and participation that we expect of domestic democracies (Dahl, 1999), so at best they will be low on a democratic scale. It is unfair to demand too much of them. But in the liberal democratic tradition that I embrace, voluntary cooperation based on honest communication and rational persuasion provides the strongest guarantee of a legitimate process. In this section, I return to the issues of accountability, participation and persuasion that I introduced earlier.

Accountability is not necessarily electoral, so it is essential to explore other forms of it if we are to increase accountability in global governance. Participation will probably continue to be largely local, so global governance implies viable forms of local self-governance. Finally, for global governance to be legitimate, global institutions must facilitate persuasion rather than coercion or reliance on sanctions as a means of influence. Here there seems to be considerable scope for improvement, so I will emphasize persuasion in the following discussion.

Accountability

The partially globalized world that I imagine would not be governed by a representative electoral democracy. States will remain important; and one state/one vote is not a democratic principle. National identities are unlikely to dissolve into the sense of a larger community that is necessary for democracy to thrive. Accountability, however, can be indirectly linked to elections without a global representative democracy. Control by democratic states over international institutions can be exerted through chains of delegation. A complementary measure is to strengthen mechanisms of domestic accountability of governments to publics. Such practices can reinforce accountability in so far as transparency ensures that people within the several states can make judgements about their own government's performance.

Non-electoral dimensions of accountability also exist.[3] Some international regimes seek to regulate the activities of firms and of governments, although they are weaker than their domestic counterparts, and they do not meet democratic standards as well as the 'best practices' domestically. Global governance, combined with modern communications technology (including technologies for linguistic translations), can begin to generate a public space in which some people communicate with one another about public policy without regard to distance. Criticism, heard and responded to in a public space, can help generate accountability. Professional standards comprise another form of non-electoral accountability.

Finally, markets provide a third dimension of non-electoral accountability. Since people do not bring equal wealth to the marketplace, markets are not democratic. But they do hold firms and other institutions with hard budget constraints accountable to their consumers and investors in ways that are often more rapid and effective than electoral democracy. Advocates of principle-based change have learned to use markets on issues as diverse as the promotion of infant formula in poor countries, environmental protection, and labour standards.

These mechanisms of accountability exist, in fragmented ways, at the global level, but they are *disarticulated*. They do not come together in a clear pathway by which laws are enacted and implemented. Chains of delegation are long, and some of their links are hidden behind a veil of secrecy. Incentives for politicians to hold leaders of other governments accountable are lacking. The public, professional groups, and advocacy networks can only punish leaders inconsistently. Governments, non-governmental organizations, and firms that do not rely on brand names may be immune from market-based sanctions. In devising acceptable institutions for global governance, accountability needs to be built into the mechanisms of rule making and rule implementation.

Participation

Individual participation is essential to democratic governance. In the past, meaningful participation has only been feasible on a face-to-face basis, as in the New England town meeting, and it has been argued that, 'in its deepest and richest sense, community must always remain a matter of face-to-face intercourse' (Dewey, 1954, p. 211). Yet, the costs of communication between any two points of the world no longer depend on distance, and within fifty years we can expect the forms of such communication to change in extraordinary ways. Although it is difficult to imagine good substitutes for the multiple dimensions – verbal, visual and tactile – by which communication occurs when people are close to one another, the potential of communications technology should not be underestimated.

More serious barriers to global democratic participation can be found in numbers and cultural diversity. Meaningful collective participation in global governance in a world of perhaps 10 billion people will surely have to occur through smaller units, but these may not need to be geographically based. In the partially globalized world that I am imagining, participation will occur in the first instance among people who can understand one another, although they may be dispersed around the world in 'diasporic public spheres', which Arjun Appadurai calls 'the crucibles of a post national political order' (1996, p. 22).

Whatever the geographical quality of the units that emerge, democratic legitimacy for such a governance system will depend on the democratic character of these smaller units of governance. It will also depend on the maintenance of sufficient autonomy and authority for those units, if participation at this level is to remain meaningful.

Persuasion and institutions

Since the global institutions that I imagine do not have superior coercive force to that of states, the influence processes that they authorize will have to be legitimate. Legitimacy is, of course, a classic subject of political philosophy and political science (Rousseau, [1762] 1978, book 1, ch. 1; see also Hobbes, [1651] 1967, chs 17–18; Locke, [1689] 1967, ch. 9; Weber, [1920] 1978, p. 214). In the liberal tradition that I embrace, voluntary cooperation based on honest communication and rational persuasion provides the strongest guarantee of a legitimate process (Habermas, 1996; Rawls, 1971). To understand the potential for legitimate governance in a partially globalized world, we need to understand how institutions can facilitate rational persuasion. How do we design institutions of governance so as to increase the scope for reflection and persuasion, as opposed to force, material incentives, and fraud?

'Persuasion' means many things to many political scientists. I will define it with reference to two other processes, *bargaining* and *signalling*. In a bargaining situation, actors know their interests and interact reciprocally to seek to realize them. In a signalling situation, a set of actors communicates to an audience, seeking to make credible promises or threats (Hinich and Munger, 1994). Both processes essentially involve flows of information. If successful, these flows enable actors to overcome informational asymmetries (Akerlof, 1970) as well as private information (Fearon, 1995) and therefore reach mutually beneficial solutions. Neither bargaining nor signalling as such involves any changes *in preferences over attributes*, that is, over the values involved in choices.

If targets of influence change their choices as a result of bargaining and signalling, they do so by recalculating their own strategies as a result of new information they received about the strategies of others. That is, they become aware that others will not behave as they had previously expected. In bargaining, a quid pro quo is involved; in signalling, threats and promises may be unilateral.

Persuasion, as I will use it, involves changing people's choices of alternatives *independently of their calculations about the strategies of other players*. People who are persuaded, in my sense of the word, change their minds for reasons other than a recalculation of advantageous choices in light of new information about others' behaviour. They may do so because they change their preferences about the underlying attributes. They may consider new attributes during processes of choice. Or they may alter their conceptions of how attributes are linked to alternatives.

Unlike bargaining on the basis of specific reciprocity, persuasion must appeal to norms, principles and values that are shared by participants in a conversation. Persuasion requires giving reasons for actions, reasons that go beyond assertions about power, interests and resolve (Elster, 1998; Risse, 2000). Karl Deutsch argued long ago that to be susceptible to persuasion, people 'must already be inwardly divided in their thought', that there must be 'some contradictions, actual or implied, among their habits or values' (1953, p. 52). These contradictions, sharpened by discussion, may lead to reflection and even attitude change.

Persuasion is a major subject of study in social psychology (McGuire, 1985; Petty and Wegener, 1998). Thousands of experiments later, the essential message from this field is that, even in the laboratory, it is difficult to find strong and consistent relationships that explain attitude change. As William McGuire puts it, 'human motivation is sufficiently complex so that multiple and even contradictory needs may underlie any act' (1985, p. 304).

What we do know about persuasion in politics indicates that it consistently involves various degrees of agenda control and manipulation. Rational or open persuasion, which occurs when people change their choices of alternatives voluntarily under conditions of frank communication, is an interesting ideal type but does not describe many major political processes. Yet, the ideal is important, since it is so central to the liberal democratic vision of politics. Indeed, thinking about persuasion helps restate the central normative question of this address: How can institutions of governance be designed so as to increase the scope for reflection, and therefore persuasion, as opposed to force, material incentives, and fraud?

If governance were exercised only by those with direct stakes in issues, such a question might have no answer. Actors could be expected to use their resources and their guile to achieve their desired objectives. And the institutions would themselves 'inherit' the inequalities prevalent in the societies that produced them, as Rousseau and many successors have pointed out (Aldrich, 1993; Riker, 1980). Indeed, choices of electoral institutions can often be traced to the policy, party and personal preferences of the politicians who created them (Bawn, 1993; Remington and Smith, 1996).

One feature of both democratic governance and contemporary international institutions, however, is that decision-making is not limited to the parties to a dispute. On the contrary, actors without a direct stake in the issues under consideration may play important roles, as members of the mass public in democracies and legislators often do on issues arising for decision through voting. In general, the legalization of rules – domestically, and more recently in international politics – requires the formation of durable rules that apply to classes of cases and puts interpretation and rule application into the hands of third parties, whose authority depends on maintaining a reputation for impartiality (Goldstein et al., 2000). Legalization also increases the role of precedents. Precedents matter, not because loopholes are impossible to find or because they cannot be overruled, but because the status quo will prevail in the absence of a decision to overturn it.

Some third parties will have calculable interests that closely parallel those of the principal disputants or advocates. Others may have strongly held beliefs that determine their positions. Some may accept side-payments or succumb to coercive pressure. But still others may lack both intense beliefs and direct stakes in the outcome. Legal requirements or internalized normative standards may inhibit them from accepting inducements for their votes. Even more important, uncertainty about the effect of future rules may make it difficult for them to calculate their own interests. Rule-makers face a peculiar form of 'winner's curse': they risk constructing durable rules that suit them in the immediate instance but will operate against their interests in the unknown future.

In so far as uncertainty is high, actors face a situation similar to one covered by a 'veil of ignorance' (Rawls, 1971). In game-theoretic terms, the actors may still have preferences over outcomes, but these preferences over outcomes do not directly imply preferences over strategies, since actors do not know their future situations. In experiments, introducing a veil of ignorance in prisoners' dilemma games without communication induces a dramatic increase in the willingness of subjects to cooperate (Frohlich and Oppenheimer, 1996). It is reasonable to hypothesize that under conditions of uncertainty in the real world, the chain of inheritability will be broken, and actors' preferences about future outcomes will not dictate their choices of alternatives in the present.

Under conditions of authority for impartial third parties, or high uncertainty about future interests, opportunities for persuasion are likely to appear, even if everyone is a rational egoist. Egoists have a long-term interest in rules that will correspond to an acceptable general principle, since they may be subject to these rules in the future. Various principles could be chosen – expected utility maximization, the maximum principle (Rawls, 1971, p. 152), minimax regret (Riker, 1980), or utility maximization subject to a floor minimum, which is the prevailing choice in laboratory experiments (Frohlich and Oppenheimer, 1992). In so far as the consequences and functions of institutions are not seriously degraded, institutions that encourage reflection and persuasion are normatively desirable and should be fostered.

Conclusion

I have asked how we can overcome the governance dilemma on a global scale. That is, how can we gain benefits from institutions without becoming their victims? How can we help design institutions for a partially globalized world that perform valuable functions while respecting democratic values? And how can we foster beliefs that maintain benign institutions? My answers are drawn, mostly implicitly, from various schools of work in political science.

From rational-choice institutionalism, we learn both the value of institutions and the need for incentives for institutional innovation. These incentives imply privileges for the elite, which have troubling implications for popular control.

From a variety of perspectives, including game theory, the study of political culture, and work on the role that ideas play in politics, we learn how important beliefs are in reaching equilibrium solutions, and how institutionalized beliefs structure situations of political choice.

From traditional political theory, we are reminded of the importance of normative beliefs for the practice of politics – and for institutions. It is not sufficient to create institutions that are effective; they must be accompanied by beliefs that respect and foster human freedom.

From historical institutionalism and political sociology, we understand how values and norms operate in society. Without such understanding, we can neither comprehend the varying expectations on which people rationally act nor design institutions based on normative views. We abdicate our responsibility if we simply assume material self-interest, as economists are wont to do.

From democratic theory, we discover the crucial roles of accountability, participation, and especially persuasion in creating legitimate political institutions.

These lessons are in tension with one another. Institutional stability is often at odds with innovation and may conflict with accountability. Protection against oppression can conflict with energetic governance; a practical reliance on self-interest can conflict with the desire to expand the role of persuasion and reflection. Governance, however, is about reconciling tensions; it is Max Weber's 'boring of hard boards' (Weber, [1919] 1946).

As students of political philosophy, our objective should be to help our students, colleagues and the broader public understand both the necessity for governance in a partially globalized world and the principles that would make such governance legitimate. As positive political scientists, we need to continue to analyse the conditions under which different forms and levels of governance are feasible. As practitioners of a policy science, we need to offer advice about how institutions for global governance should be constituted. This advice must be realistic, not romantic. We must begin with real people, not some mythological beings of higher moral capability. But we need also to recognize, and seek to expand, the scope for reflection and the normative principles that reflective individuals may espouse. We should seek to design institutions so that persuasion, not merely interests and bargaining, plays an important role.

The stakes in the mission I propose are high, for the world and for political science. If global institutions are designed well, they will promote human welfare. But if we bungle the job, the results could be disastrous. Either oppression or ineptitude would likely lead to conflict and a renewed fragmentation of global politics. Effective and humane global governance arrangements are not inevitable. They will depend on human effort and on deep thinking about politics.

As we face globalization, our challenge resembles that of the founders of America: how to design working institutions for a polity of unprecedented size and diversity. Only if we rise to that challenge will we be doing our part to ensure Lincoln's 'rebirth of freedom' on a world – and human – scale.

Notes

For comments on earlier versions of this address, I am grateful to Ruth Grant, Stanley Hoffmann, Peter J. Katzenstein, Nannerl O. Keohane, and Joseph S. Nye Jr. For insights into the issue of accountability, I am particularly indebted to Professor Nye.

This chapter reproduces the author's Presidential Address to the American Political Science Association published by the *American Political Science Review* (March 2001) and appears here by kind permission.

1 All references to Aristotle's *Politics* are to Barker's (1948) translation.
2 The budget of the WTO for 2000 is 127,697,010 Swiss francs, or approximately $73.8 million, at September 2000 exchange rates.
3 For a very sophisticated discussion of different forms of accountability, see Scharpf, 1999, esp. ch. 1.

References

Akerlof, George A. (1970) 'The market for lemons', *Journal of Economics*, 84, Aug., pp. 488–500.

Aldrich, John (1993) 'On William Riker's "inheritability" problem: preferences, institutions, and context', paper presented at the Southern Political Science Association, Savannah, Georgia.

Aldrich, John (1995) *Why Parties? The Origin and Transformation of Party Politics in America*, Chicago: University of Chicago Press.

Appadurai, Arjun (1996) *Modernity at Large*, Minneapolis: University of Minnesota Press.

Arendt, Hannah (1958) *The Origins of Totalitarianism* (1951), Cleveland: World Publishing.

Aristotle (1948) *The Politics of Aristotle*, trans. Ernest Barker, Oxford: Clarendon.

Axelrod, Robert M. (1984) *The Evolution of Cooperation*, New York: Basic Books.

Bates, Robert H. (1988) 'Contra contractarianism: some reflections on the new institutionalism', *Politics and Society*, 16, June–Sept., pp. 387–401.

Bates, Robert H. et al. (1998) *Analytic Narratives*, Princeton: Princeton University Press.

Bawn, Kathleen (1993) 'The logic of institutional preferences: German electoral law as a social choice outcome', *American Journal of Political Science*, 37, Nov., pp. 965–89.

Bull, Hedley (1977) *The Anarchical Society: A Study of Order in World Politics*, New York: Columbia University Press.

Coase, Ronald H. (1960) 'The problem of social cost', *Journal of Law and Economics*, 3, Oct., pp. 1–44.

Cohen, G. A. (1978) *Karl Marx's Theory of History: A Defense*, Princeton: Princeton University Press.

Dahl, Robert A. (1976) *Modern Political Analysis*, 3rd edn, Englewood Cliffs, N.J.: Prentice Hall.

Dahl, Robert A. (1989) *Democracy and its Critics*, New Haven: Yale University Press.

Dahl, Robert A. (1999) 'Can international organizations be democratic?', in Ian Shapiro and Casiano Hacker-Cordon (eds), *Democracy's Edges*, Cambridge: Cambridge University Press.

Deutsch, Karl W. (1953) *Nationalism and Social Communication*, Cambridge, Mass.: MIT Press.

Dewey, John ([1927] 1954) *The Public and Its Problems*, Chicago: Swallow Press.

Elster, Jon (1998) 'Deliberation and constitution making', in Jon Elster (ed.), *Deliberative Democracy*, Cambridge: Cambridge University Press.

Fearon, James D. (1995) 'Rationalist explanations for war', *International Organization*, 49, Summer, pp. 379–414.

Fearon, James D. (1998) 'Bargaining, enforcement and international cooperation', *International Organization*, 52, Spring, pp. 269–305.

Firebaugh, Glen (1999) 'Empirics of world income inequality', *American Journal of Sociology*, 104, May, pp. 1597–631.

Frank, Robert H. (1988) *Passions within Reason: The Strategic Role of the Emotions*, New York: W. W. Norton.

Frohlich, Norman and Oppenheimer, Joe A. (1992) *Choosing Justice: An Experimental Approach to Ethical Theory*, Berkeley: University of California Press.

Frohlich, Norman and Oppenheimer, Joe A. (1996) 'Experiencing impartiality to invoke fairness in the n-PD: some experimental results', *Public Choice*, 86, nos 1–2, pp. 117–35.

Geddes, Barbara (1994) *Politician's Dilemma: Building State Capacity in Latin America*, Berkeley: University of California Press.

Goldstein, Judith, Kahler, Miles, Keohane, Robert O. and Slaughter, Anne-Marie (2000) *Legalization and World Politics*, special issue of *International Organization*, 54, no. 3.

Grant, Ruth W. (1997) *Hypocrisy and Integrity: Machiavelli, Rousseau and the Ethics of Politics*, Chicago: University of Chicago Press.

Grewe, Wilhelm G. (2000) *The Epochs of International Law*, trans. Michael Byers, The Hague: De Gruyter.

Habermas, Jürgen (1996) *Between Facts and Norms: Contributions to a Discourse Theory of Law and Democracy*, Cambridge, Mass.: MIT Press.

Held, David, McGrew, Anthony, Goldblatt, David and Perraton, Jonathan (1999) *Global Transformations: Politics, Economics and Culture*, Cambridge: Polity.

Herz, John H. (1959) *International Politics in the Atomic Age*, New York: Columbia University Press.

Hinich, Melvin J. and Munger, Michael (1994) *Ideology and the Theory of Political Choice*, Ann Arbor: University of Michigan Press.

Hirschman, Albert O. (1977) *The Passions and the Interests: Political Arguments for Capitalism before its Triumph*, Princeton: Princeton University Press.

Hobbes, Thomas ([1651] 1967) *Leviathan: or the Matter, Forme and Power of a Commonwealth Ecclesiaticall and Civil*, ed. Michael Oakeshott, Oxford: Blackwell.

Huntington, Samuel P. (1968) *Political Order in Changing Societies*, New Haven: Yale University Press.

Jervis, Robert (1997) *System Effects: Complexity in Political and Social Life*, Princeton: Princeton University Press.

Kahler, Miles (1999) 'Evolution, choice and international change', in David A. Lake and Robert Powell (eds), *Strategic Choice and International Relations*, Princeton: Princeton University Press.

Katzenstein, Peter J. (1993) 'Coping with terrorism: norms and internal security in Germany and Japan', in Judith Goldstein and Robert O. Keohane (eds), *Ideas and Foreign Policy*, Ithaca, N.Y.: Cornell University Press.

Katzenstein, Peter J. (ed.) (1996) *The Culture of National Security: Norms and Identity in World Politics*, New York: Columbia University Press.

Keck, Margaret and Sikkink, Kathryn (1998) *Activists beyond Borders: Advocacy Networks in International Politics*, Ithaca, N.Y.: Cornell University Press.

Keohane, Nannerl O. (1980) *Philosophy and the State in France: The Renaissance to the Enlightenment*, Princeton: Princeton University Press.

Keohane, Robert O. (1984) *After Hegemony: Cooperation and Discord in the World Political Economy*, Princeton: Princeton University Press.

Keohane, Robert O. and Nye, Joseph S. Jr (2001) *Power and Interdependence* (1977), 3rd edn, New York: Addison-Wesley.

Kindleberger, Charles P. (1973) *The World in Depression, 1929–1939*, Berkeley: University of California Press.

Krasner, Stephen D. (1991) 'Global communications and national power: life on the Pareto frontier', *World Politics*, 43, Apr., pp. 336–66.

Levi, Margaret (1997) *Consent, Dissent and Patriotism*, Cambridge: Cambridge University Press.

Lincoln, Abraham (1863) *The Gettysburg Address* (19 Nov.).

Locke, John ([1689] 1967) *Second Treatise of Government*, ed. Peter Laslett, Cambridge: Cambridge University Press.

McGuire, William J. (1985) 'Attitudes and attitude change', in Gardner Lindzey and Elliott Aronson (eds), *Handbook of Social Psychology*, 3rd edn, New York: Random House.

Madison, James ([1787] 1961) *Federalist No. 10*, in *The Federalist Papers*, by Alexander Hamilton, John Jay and James Madison, ed. Jacob E. Cooke, Middletown, Conn.: Wesleyan University Press.

Martin, Lisa M. (1992) 'Interests, power and multilateralism', *International Organization*, 46, Autumn, pp. 765–92.

Martin, Lisa M. (2000) *Democratic Commitments: Legislatures and International Cooperation*, Princeton: Princeton University Press.

Mayhew, David (1974) *Congress: The Electoral Connection*, New Haven: Yale University Press.

Morgenthau, Hans J. (1967) *Politics among Nations: The Struggle for Power and Peace*, New York: Knopf.

Morrow, James D. (1994) *Game Theory for Political Scientists*, Princeton: Princeton University Press.

North, Douglass (1981) *Structure and Change in Economic History*, New York: Norton.

North, Douglass (1990) *Institutions, Institutional Change and Economic Performance*, New York: Cambridge University Press.

Olson, Mancur Jr (1965) *The Logic of Collective Action*, Cambridge, Mass.: Harvard University Press.

Olson, Mancur Jr (1982) *The Rise and Decline of Nations: Economic Growth, Stagflation and Social Rigidities*, New Haven: Yale University Press.

O'Neill, Barry (1999) *Honor, Symbols and War*, Ann Arbor: University of Michigan Press.

Ostrom, Elinor (1990) *Governing the Commons: The Evolution of Institutions for Collective Action*, New York: Cambridge University Press.

Ostrom, Elinor (1998) 'A behavioral approach to the rational choice theory of collective action', *American Political Science Review*, 92, March, pp. 1–22.

Pennock, J. Roland (1966) 'Political development, political systems and political goods', *World Politics*, 18, Apr., pp. 15–34.

Petty, Richard E. and Wegener, Duane T. (1998) 'Attitude change: multiple roles for persuasion variables', in Daniel T. Gilbert, Susan T. Risk and Gardner Lindzey (eds), *Handbook of Social Psychology*, 4th edn, vol. 1, Boston: McGraw-Hill.

Putnam, Robert D. (1993) *Making Democracy Work: Civic Traditions in Modern Italy*, Princeton: Princeton University Press.

Rawls, John (1971) *A Theory of Justice*, Cambridge, Mass.: Harvard University Press.

Remington, Thomas F. and Smith, Steven S. (1996) 'Political goals, institutional context, and the choice of an electoral system: the Russian parliamentary election law', *American Journal of Political Science*, 40, Nov., pp. 1253–79.

Riker, William H. (1980) 'Implications from the disequilibrium of majority rule for the study of institutions', *American Political Science Review*, 74, June, pp. 432–46.

Risse, Thomas (2000) '"Let's argue!" Communicative action in world politics', *International Organization*, 54, Winter, pp. 1–40.

Rousseau, Jean-Jacques ([1762] 1978) *On the Social Contract*, ed. Roger D. Masters, New York: St Martin's.

Scharpf, Fritz (1999) *Governing in Europe*, Oxford: Oxford University Press.

Schelling, Thomas C. (1960) *The Strategy of Conflict*, Cambridge, Mass.: Harvard University Press.

Schumpeter, Joseph A. (1950) *Capitalism, Socialism and Democracy* (1941), 3rd edn, New York: Harper and Row.

Searle, John (1995) *The Construction of Social Reality*, New York: Free Press.

Sen, Amartya K. (1977) 'Rational fools: a critique of the behavioral foundations of economic theory', *Philosophy and Public Affairs*, 6, Summer, pp. 317–44.

Sen, Amartya K. (1999) *Development as Freedom*, New York: Knopf.

Shepsle, Kenneth A. (1986) 'Institutional equilibrium and equilibrium institutions', in Herbert F. Weisberg (ed.), *Political Science: The Science of Politics*, New York: Agathon.

Shepsle, Kenneth A. and Weingast, Barry R. (1995) *Positive Theories of Congressional Institutions*, Ann Arbor: University of Michigan Press.

Shklar, Judith N. (1984) *Ordinary Vices*, Cambridge, Mass.: Harvard University Press.

Simon, Herbert A. (1985) 'Human nature in politics: the dialogue of psychology with political science', *American Political Science Review*, 79, June, pp. 293–304.

Smith, Adam ([1776] 1976) *The Wealth of Nations*, Chicago: University of Chicago Press.

Stein, Arthur A. (1983) 'Coordination and collaboration: regimes in an anarchic world', in Stephen D. Krasner (ed.), *International Regimes*, Ithaca, N.Y.: Cornell University Press.

Tilly, Charles (1975) 'Reflections on the history of European state-making', in *The Formation of National States in Western Europe*, Princeton: Princeton University Press.

Tilly, Charles (1990) *Coercion, Capital and European States AD 990–1990*, Oxford: Blackwell.

Tyler, Tom R. (1990) *Why People Obey the Law*, New Haven: Yale University Press.

Waltz, Kenneth N. (1979) *Theory of International Politics*, Reading, Mass.: Addison-Wesley.

Weber, Max ([1919] 1946) 'Politics as a vocation', in H. H. Gerth and C. Wright Mills (eds), *From Max Weber: Essays in Sociology*, Oxford: Oxford University Press.

Weber, Max ([1920] 1978) *Economy and Society*, ed. Guenther Roth and Claus Wittich, Berkeley: University of California Press.

Wendt, Alexander E. (1999) *Social Theory of International Politics*, Cambridge: Cambridge University Press.

Williamson, Oliver (1975) *Markets and Hierarchies*, New York: Free Press.

Williamson, Oliver (1985) *The Economic Institutions of Capitalism*, New York: Free Press.

Wolfers, Arnold (1962) *Discord and Collaboration*, Baltimore: Johns Hopkins University Press.

World Bank (2000) *Entering the 21st Century: World Development Report 1999–2000*, Oxford: Oxford University Press.

Index